Commentary on Aristotle's *Physics*

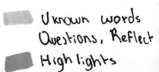

Aristotelian Commentary Series

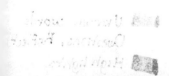

Commentary on Aristotle's *Physics*

St. Thomas Aquinas

Translated by
Richard J. Blackwell, Richard J. Spath, and W. Edmund Thirlkel

Introduction by
Vernon J. Bourke

Foreword by
Ralph McInerny

DUMB OX BOOKS
Notre Dame, Indiana

DUMB OX BOOKS
www.staugustine.net

Contents

BOOK II. THE PRINCIPLES OF NATURAL SCIENCE

BOOK III. MOBILE BEING IN COMMON

BOOK IV. PLACE, VOID AND TIME, THE MEASURES OF MOBILE BEING

BOOK V. THE DIVISION OF MOTION INTO ITS SPECIES

BOOK VIII. THE FIRST MOTION AND THE FIRST MOVER

Foreword to the Dumb Ox Edition

This is the fourth of our reprints of English translations of Thomas Aquinas's commentaries on Aristotle that had gone out of print, thus creating a hardship for students of Aquinas whose Latin is not as reliable as they would like. Finding copies of those translations has been facilitated by the Internet, but for all that they become ever rarer and the prices go up rather than down, according to the law of supply and demand. We should all salute across the years and express our gratitude to those who made the translation we are reprinting here. This is not a commercial enterprise on the part of Dumb Ox Books, since such profits as we make are put into the fund that enables the effort to continue. At omega point, when the project is complete, the logical possibility of profit *tout court* may arise. But by then I will have gone to that bourne from which no traveler returns. This is, to the extent possible for sinful man, a benevolent effort.

Much has been written about the *Physics* of Aristotle since this translation appeared, less about the commentary. A quarter of a century ago and more there were lively discussions as to whether the natural philosophy of Aristotle and Thomas had any other than historical relevance now. The received opinion in the wider scholarly world was that a turn had been taken with Copernicus that set in motion inquiries which can only equivocally be compared with those that went on before. The term "physics" applied to the eight books of Aristotle and to what is done under that name now is taken to have meanings that are *toto coelo* different; indeed the difference is that between the false and the true. For all that, there were students of Thomas who argued that there was a continuing truth value in the natural philosophy of old, and the problem was to find a way to relate it to the science of our time. Indeed, several rival accounts were given, one associated with Louvain, another with Maritain, another with my mentor Charles DeKoninck, and yet another with the Dominicans of River Forest. With the Council and other factors, all that dropped off the radar screen.

Well, not quite. William Wallace, O.P., has been pursuing that spoor through the intervening years and argues unabashedly for a *modus vivendi* between the old physics and the new. Moreover, there is growing interest in the question among younger scholars. They will be particularly happy to have this commentary available once more. Of course its interest is not confined to them. The natural philosophy that enjoyed unrivaled hegemony over so many centuries has an undeniable historical interest and the rising appreciation of Thomas's commentaries should make this edition welcome to medievalists and historians of science. It is reprinted here as is – or as was.

That being said, let me add to the bibliography these two books:

La physique d'Aristotle et les conditions d'une science de la nature, ed. F. De Gandt and P. Souffrin (Paris: J. Vrin, 1991).

The Modeling of Nature: Philosophy of Science and Philosophy of Nature in Synthe-

sis, William A. Wallace (Washington: Catholic University of America Press, 1996).

Ralph McInerny
Notre Dame, May 1999

Translators' Preface

A few introductory remarks on the structure of this volume may facilitate its use. This translation is based on the Leonine edition of St. Thomas, which is the best available text. We have numbered the paragraphs in one consecutive series throughout the entire translation to ease the problem of cross-referencing.

In writing his Commentary St. Thomas obviously used a Latin translation of Aristotle's Physics. This text has not been identified. The Latin version of the Physics which is usually printed together with St. Thomas' Commentary is a later Renaissance translation. We have not deemed it advisable to include in this volume an English translation of this Renaissance Latin version of the Physics since St. Thomas clearly did not use this text. However, all of the Commentary, including the valuable introductory division of the text, has been translated. In translating the Commentary we have collated it with the Oxford English translation of the Physics (by R. P. Hardie and R. K. Gaye), which should be used as a companion to this volume. We have also included the Bekker numbers for all references to Aristotle's text in order to facilitate the references and to permit the use, if desired, of other editions of the Physics.

In any translation, especially of a work which is as technical as this one, textual decisions must be made which are not wholly satisfactory. This becomes most acute when tensions arise between the accurate literal meaning of the original language and the accepted literary style of the second language. We have tried always to give preference to the former over the latter whenever a sacrifice had to be made. There is also the problem of selecting the most acceptable English usages as much as possible and as consistently as possible throughout the entire translation. However, using distinct English expressions for distinct technical expressions in the Latin has at times made this very difficult. Here again our main principle has been to preserve technical meaning as best we could. A special problem is involved in the rendition of the word ratio which bears so many importantly different meanings in St. Thomas' Latin. Wherever we felt that our translation of this word might be open to disagreement, we have added the Latin term in parenthesis for the reader to formulate his own evaluation. This same procedure is used occasionally for other expressions when similar difficulties are involved.

Our special appreciation must be extended to Professor Vernon J. Bourke of Saint Louis University both for his valuable Introduction and for his encouragement and advice since the inception of this translation. We are also indebted to the Very Reverend Hugh E. Dunn, S.J., President of John Carroll University, and to the Reverend Joseph O. Schell, S.J., Director of the Department of Philosophy, John Carroll University, for their support and for making the necessary secretarial assistance available.

We hope that those who do not read Latin will find this volume to be a reliable presentation of what was previously inaccessible to them. And may those who do read Latin be stimulated by this volume to study the original text, for which no translation can be an adequate substitute.

Introduction

Vernon J. Bourke

To offer the twentieth-century reader an English version of a Latin commentary on a treatise written in Greek during the fourth century before Christ is an act which demands some explanation. This Introduction is intended to satisfy, at least in part, that demand.

I. ARISTOTLE'S PHYSICS

The Original Treatise

From B.C. 335 to 323, Aristotle conducted his school of philosophy and science in Athens. One of his regular courses dealt with the nature of the physical world, the *cosmos*. This was the same subject which had engrossed the first philosophers of Greece, from Thales to the *Timaeus* of Plato. Doubtless Aristotle's lecture notes grew through the years, incorporating more and more of his meditations on *phusis* (reality as subject to change), on *kinesis* (motion itself), and on the ultimate origins of motion in the universe.[1] Certain specialized Aristotelian treatises (*On the Heavens, On Generation and Corruption,* and *Meteorology*) are related to this course but the chief record that we now have is the work called the *Physics,* in eight books.[2]

After Aristotle's death (B.C. 323), Theophrastus became head of the Peripatetic school. It is possible that he introduced some changes into the works of Aristotle. There is much debate as to what happened to the master copies during the next two centuries. Some manuscripts which had been in Theophrastus' possession were removed from Athens by Neleus. In the first century before Christ, Andronicus (and possibly other editors) gathered the works of Aristotle and arranged them in the form in which they are now extant. The course on Physics was followed in this classical edition by an assembly of treatises on being-in-general (which latter was then entitled, *ta meta ta phusika,* giving rise to the word, 'metaphysics,' which simply means what follows the *Physics*). Modern Aristotelian scholars (W. Jaeger, J. Owens) have come to the conclusion that the *Metaphysics* is a collection of treatises and notes, arranged by later editors from disparate materials written at different periods by Aristotle. Some (notably J. Zürcher) have suggested that most of the Aristotelian *corpus* was actually written by

---

1   Cf. De Vogel., *Greek Philosophy,* Leiden: E.J Brill, 1953, pp. 68–101; Ross, W. D., *Aristotle,* London: Methuen, 1923, p. 11.

2   Ross, W. D. (ed.), *Aristotle's Physics.* A Revised Text with Introduction and Commentary. Oxford: Clarendon Press, 1936; the same distinguished editor has issued: Aristotle, *Physica,* Oxford (Bibl. Oxon.), 1950. The Greek text in *Aristotelis Opera,* ed. I. Bekker, Berlin, 1831, I, 184–267, is still standard for reference purposes.

Theophrastus—but this view has found little favour. In any case, the eight books of the *Physics* seem to have more unity than the *Metaphysics* and, while the text may have suffered some early editorial modification, present-day experts regard the *Physics* as a rather accurate record of what Aristotle actually taught.[3]

Mediaeval Latin Versions

No Latin translations of Aristotle's *Physics* are known to have been in existence before the twelfth century A.D. With the exception of certain logical treatises, none of the writings of Aristotle were put into Latin in the early Christian centuries. The twelfth and thirteenth centuries witnessed many attempts to remedy this situation.[4]

We can identify five Latin versions or revisions of Aristotle's *Physics* preceding Thomas Aquinas' *Exposition*: (1) an Arabic to Latin translation, attributed to Gerard of Cremona, made at Toledo before 1150 (of which there is now a manuscript in the Library of the Seminary at Aosta); (2) a Greek to Latin version of the first two books, dating from about 1150 (now preserved in *Cod. Vat. Regin.* 1855); (3) another Arabic to Latin version of the complete Physics, mentioned about 1170 by the medical doctors, Ursus di Lodi and Maurus of Salerno; (4) an early thirteenth-century Arabic to Latin text with the *Commentary* by Averroës, translated by Michael Scottus before 1235; and (5) the *Moerbekana*, a revision by William of Moerbeke of the first Greek-Latin version and produced during the lifetime of St. Thomas.[5]

Text used by St. Thomas

When the first Renaissance printers published Aquinas' commentaries on Aristotle, they found that the mediaeval manuscripts lacked a Latin text of Aristotle. The custom was to copy only the first few words (cue-words) of each section of Aristotle as an identification of the entire text under discussion. The usual practice of the manuscripts may be observed in our printed editions of Roger Bacon's commentaries.[6] As a consequence, these printers obtained a Latin version of Aristotle, made by a humanist scholar, and printed it with the commentary by Aquinas. Some modification was made in order to avoid a too apparent discordance from the cue-words in the exposition. In some printings, two texts of Aristotle are given: the *Recens* is the humanist version and the *Antiqua* is a mediaeval translation. Modern printings of Aquinas' commentary on the *Physics* simply reproduce the Renaissance texts of Aristotle; this is true even of the famous *editio Leonina*.[7] This means that our Latin texts of Aristotle, as now printed with the commentaries by St. Thomas, are neither the version of William of Moerbeke nor are they the precise mediaeval translations read by Aquinas.

---

3   See Manison, A., Introduction – la physique aristotélicienne, Louvain: Inst. Sup. de Philosophie, 1946.
4   Van Steenberghen, F., *Aristotle in the West*, Louvain: Nauwelaerts, 1955.
5   Cf. Grabmann, M., *Guglielmo di Moerbeke*, Roma: Pont. Univ. Gregoriana, 1946, pp. 90–91; Mansion, A., 'De jongste Geschiedenis van de middeleeuwsche Aristotelesvertalingen,' *Mededeelingen*, III, 2 (Brussel, 1941).
6   See for instance: Rogeri Baconi, *Quaestiones supra libros IV Physicorum Aristotelis* (Opera hactenus inedita, VIII), ed. F. M. Delorme and R. Steele, Oxford, 1928.

It has been assumed by many scholars (influenced by the account in the early Latin *Lives* of St. Thomas) that Moerbeke supplied Thomas with reliable translations which were used throughout his expositions of Aristotle. There is now some doubt as to the validity of this assumption. In commenting the *Physics*, St. Thomas may not have begun to use the *Moerbekana* until about *Lectio* 2 of Book II. Throughout the exposition of the first Book, Aquinas appears to be reading a pre-Moerbeke version similar to that of *Cod. Urb.* 206, of the Vatican Library. After starting the second Book, he seems to have shifted to the Moerbeke version, a text similar to the *Physica Nova* (*Vat. Lat.* 2083).[8] As a matter of fact, the actual manuscripts used by Thomas probably contained a mixture of various translations (what the German scholars call a *Kontamination*) deriving from the efforts of mediaeval copyists to produce a readable text from the several versions available to them.[9] In the expert judgment of Canon Mansion, the printed text of Aristotle's Physics which most closely approximates the Moerbeke version is one found in an early edition of Giles of Rome.[10]

From the foregoing it becomes apparent that, in the present state of scholarship, one cannot precisely identify the Latin manuscripts of the Physics which Thomas Aquinas used for his commentary. It is, then, not feasible to attempt an English translation of the *Physics, in the text (s) which Aquinas read*. However, it is clear from the *Expositio* that Thomas had a text which was not much different from our present Greek editions. Except for Book VII, Chapters 2–3, one usually has no difficulty in locating the pertinent passages in the Oxford English translation done under the editorship of Sir David Ross.[11] The correspondence between this English version and St. Thomas' commentary is often remarkably clear and always sufficient to justify the translators of the present volume in recommending that its readers consult the Oxford translation of the *Physics*, in the course of their reading.

---

7   The Leonine editors of St. Thomas' commentary on the *Physics* (*Opera Omnia*, ed. Leonina, II, Rome, 1884) used the text of Aristotle printed in the Piana edition (1570) but endeavoured to correct it by collation with three good Vatican MSS. (*Cod. Vat. Urb. Lat.* 206; *Vat. Lat.* 2071, and 2072). They were doomed to failure because the first two MSS. contain a different Latin translation from the third MS. On the see: Mansion, A., 'sur le texte de la version latine médiévale de la Métaphysique et de la Physique d'Aristote dans les Éditions des commentaires de saint Thomas d'Aquin,' *Revue Néoscoloastique de Philosophie*, 34 (1932), 65–69. Father I. T. Eschmann, 'A Catalogue of St. Thomas's Works,' in Gilson, E., *The Christian Philosophy of St. Thomas*, New York: Random House, 1955, p. 402, also speaks of the 'unreliability of the Latin Aristotelian text' in the Leonine printing.

8   This point is vigorously made by Franze Pelster, 'Die Uebersetzungen der aristotelischen Metaphysik in den Werken des hl. Thomas von Aquin,' *Gregorianum*, 17 (1936), 394–97.

9   The *Preface* (pp. 53–54) to *Aristoteles Latinus*, Pars Prior, ed. G. Lacombe *et al.*, Romae, 1939, concludes that Moerbeke's revision is not entirely independent from the earlier Greek-Latin version, though it contains significant corrections.

10   Egidii Romani, *In libros physica auditu Aristotelis commentaria*, Venetiis, 1502, in fol; see Mansion, 'Sur le texte de la version latine. . .,' p. 69; and the discussion by Josef Koch, in his *Introduction* (pp. xli–xliii) to: Giles of Rome, *Errores Philosophorum*, ed. J. Koch and tr. J. Riedl, Milwaukee: Marquette U. Press, 1944.

11   Aristotle, *Physica*, translated by R. P. Hardie and R. K. Gaye, in *The Works of Aristotle*, vol. II, Oxford: Clarendon Press, 1930; reprinted in *The Basic Works of Aristotle*, ed. R. McKeon, New York: Random House, 1941, pp. 218–394.

II. AQUINAS' EXPOSITION

In spite of obvious differences between the thought of an ancient pagan philosopher and a Christian theologian of the late middle ages, it is generally admitted that Thomas Aquinas produced one of the best commentaries on Aristotle's *Physics*. The present work, then, is an excellent explanation of the original work of Aristotle. More than that, it is a clear presentation of the sort of cosmology from which men like Copernicus, Galileo, Kepler, and even Newton took their start in founding modern astronomy and physics.

Occasion and Date of the Commentary

Thomas Aquinas took his degree in theology at the University of Paris in 1256, taught there for three years, and then spent a decade on various assignments in the Dominican houses of study in central Italy. Aristotle's works on natural philosophy had been subject to various ecclesiastical censures at Paris from 1210 to about 1245—in the sense that lecturing on them was forbidden though private study of them was not.[12] Of course, Thomas had encountered some Aristotelian philosophy in his studies of the liberal arts at the University of Naples,[13] in the classes of Albert the Great at Cologne, and through his reading in the works of other philosophers, notably Avicenna. In 1259 (June) a group of Dominican scholars met at Valenciennes and recommended a new programme of studies for the training of members of the Order of Preachers. In this programme, some work in the liberal arts (and so in philosophy) was prescribed for the young men in the Order—apparently with the strong support of both Albert and Thomas.[14] Since Aristotle was by now recognized as the great philosopher, it is obvious that good Latin texts of his major writings had to be obtained and the manner in which a Christian school might use these treatises had to be determined. St. Thomas went on to Italy and in 1262, during the Pontificate of Urban IV (a Pope interested in philosophical learning), was in residence at Orvieto, where the papal court was then situated. Albert the Great was also at Orvieto in that year. Still more significant, a Dominican missionary with a good working knowledge of Greek had been recalled from the East and stationed at Orvieto. He was William of Moerbeke, a man who had already translated in 1260 at Nicea the Greek Commentary by Alexander of Aphrodisias on Aristotle's Meteorologica.[15]

This was quite an assembly of talent at one Dominican house of studies. Though contemporary records are curiously reticent on the matter, it seems that in these years which Thomas spent in Italy (before returning to the University of Paris in 1269) he was the centre of an organized effort to make Aristotle available to the world of western scholarship.[16] In any case, it is historically certain that

---

12   Cf. Grabmann, M., *I divieti ecclesiastici di Aristotele sotto innocenzo III e Gregorio IX*, Roma: Typis Pont. Univ. Gregorianae, 1941.

13   See Crowe, M. B., 'Peter of Ireland, Teacher of St. Thomas,' *Studies* (Dublin) 45 (1956), 443–56.

14   Walz, A., *San Tommaso d'Aquino*, Roma: Edizioni Liturgiche, 1944, pp. 97–98; De Groot, J., *Het Leven van den H. Thomas van Aquino*, Utrecht: Van Rossum, 1907, p. 131. For the text of the programme of studies: *Chartularium Universitatis Parisiensi*, ed. Chatelain-Denifle, I., 385–86.

15   Grabmann, *Guglielmo di Moerbeke*, pp. 39–48.

William of Moerbeke now spent many years (1262 to about 1278) on translations of the works of Aristotle and his Greek commentators.[17] Thomas Aquinas was using the Moerbeke texts, during these same years, for at least some of his commentaries on Aristotle.

It is reasonable to conclude that Aquinas prepared his *Expositio in VIII libros Physicorum Aristotelis* during the 1260's. No dated manuscript of his commentary has been found; nor do the early *Lives* of St. Thomas, or other contemporary documents, provide a precise date for the *Exposition*. The contention that St. Thomas used a pre-Moerbeke text of the *Physics* for the first book of his exposition does not pinpoint the date, for we do not know when William began to translate the work.[18] Canon Mansion made a comparison of Thomas' treatment of time (*In IV Phys.*, Lect. 23) with Albert's paraphrase of the same section of the *Physics* and found that Thomas repeated, 'globally and with close approximation even to details,' the interpretation given by his old teacher, Albert.[19] This means that Thomas' comment post-dates 1257. Indeed, Mansion came to the conclusion that the *terminus post quem* of Thomas' work is 1268. Another study of the chronology of the commentary argues that it precedes the *Summa Theologiae*, I, the *De Potentia* and the *Exposition* of the *Metaphysics*.[20] However, such arguments from doctrinal content are difficult to control and not too reliable for chronological purposes. On the matter of the eternity of the world, for instance, the doctrine of the commentary on the Physics is considered by Grabmann to be different from what we find in the Prima Pars (1, 46, 1) and *De Potentia* (III, 17) and quite like the *Commentary on the Physics* written by Siger of Brabant in 1268.[21] It has been noted recently that Thomas' commentary on the *Posterior Analytics* (I, Lect. 41, n. 16) refers to the second Book of the *Physics*.[22] But the example which Thomas cites is not found in Aristotle's *Physics*; it is in Thomas' own *Exposition*.[23] This citation indicates a priority of the commentary on the Physics but also, possibly, that they are of much the same time. These various data point to the years, 1268–1271, as the period in

---

16   Some years ealier, at the beginning of his paraprase of Aristotle's *Physics*, Albert said precisely this: 'Nostra intentio est omnes dictas partes [he had been speaking of the physics, metaphysics and mathematics of Aristotle] facere Latinis intelligibles' (*in I Physicorum*, Tract. I, cap. 1).

17   In Grabmann's reconstruction of the career of Moerbeke (*G. Di Moerbeke*, pp. 41–48) William is working at Orvieto (1261–1264), at Viterbo (1265–1268). Many documents (Grabmann, *ibid.*, p. 49) attest to the fact that Moerbeke was Papal Penitentiary at the court of Clement IV (1265–1268) and we know that this was a period in which he turned out many translations. See G. Verbeke's *Introduction*, pp. LXIII–LXXXI, to Themistius, *Commentaire sur le Traité de l'âme d'Aristote*, Louvain: Nauwelaerts, 1957, for additional on this period in William's translating activity.

18   See above, note 2, p. xvii. I have checked the cue-words in the first book of Roger Bacon's *Quaestiones* on the *Physics*; they indicate that in Book I Thomas was using a text very similar to that commented by Bacon before 1247.

19   Mansion, 'La théorie arist. Du temps,' *loc cit.*, p. 304.

20   Castagnoli, P., 'I commenti di S. Tommaso ai "Libri Naturales" di Aristotle,' *Divus Thomas* (Piacenza), 34 (1931), pp. 266–72.

21   Grabmann, M., *Die Werke des hl. Thomas von Aquin*, Aufl. 3 (Münster, 1949), p. 275.

22   Pattin, A., 'Bijdrage tot de kronologie van St. Thomas Werken,' *Tijdschrift voor Philosophie*, XIX, 3 (1957), 503.

23   The point is also discussed by Paul Mathews, *A Study of St. Thomas' Commentary on the Posterior Analytics* (St. Louis U. Dissert., 1958), pp. 248–51.

which Thomas commented the *Physics*. Indeed it is unlikely that he worked on the *Physics* during his second Paris professorate (1269–1271). He was then teaching theology; this was one of the busiest periods in his life;[24] he would then be far removed from Moerbeke, whom he seems to have been consulting while doing the commentary. It is probable that the *Exposition* was finished in Italy before Thomas departed for Paris in 1269.

There is still some question as to whether the *Exposition*, as we have it, is the actual report of oral lectures or a written commentary not stemming directly from the classroom. It can hardly be denied that some of Aquinas' commentaries on Aristotle were orally delivered. There is unmistakable evidence that Thomas actually lectured on the first Book *De Anima*. Our present text of this is a *reportatio*, so he must have been giving an oral commentary.[25] Since the general style of these two commentaries is the same, one may conclude with some probability that the *Expositio* on the *Physics* was originally a lecture course for the Dominican students at some house of studies in the Roman province. Quite possibly St. Thomas revised it before having copies made of it. This makes dating still more inexact but for all practical purposes we may put the commentary on the *Physics* in the years 1268–1269.[26]

Style of the Exposition

In general, mediaeval Latin commentators on Aristotle used one of three styles:

(1) *paraphrase*: a loose and sometimes rather personal restatement of the content of a work, without much attention to verbal details of the text (illustrated in the work of Avicenna and Albert); (2) *questions*: a series of problems suggested by the text but not following the original text in all details (exemplified by Roger Bacon's *Quaestiones* on the Physics); and (3) *literal commentaries*: expositions of the original, phrase by phrase (illustrated by some of the commentaries of Averroës). It is in the third genre that St. Thomas' exposition of the *Physics* belongs.

Aquinas presumes that the reader will be able to consult the text of Aristotle's *Physics*. Probably he read aloud a section of this text in class (the *lectio*). Such sections vary in length, do not correspond to chapter divisions, usually approximate what could be put on one page of a modern printed book. The actual comment in each *lectio* usually starts with a sentence making the transition from the preceding *lectio*. Then Thomas proceeds to the *divisio textus*: an analysis of the argument of Aristotle into its main parts, with cue-words used to indicate the divisions. After this comes the *expositio textus*, beginning with the words: 'Dicit ergo primo,' or 'Circa primum sciendum est,' or some such phrase. In this exposition, an explanation is offered for each step or point in the reasoning of Aristotle; the cue-words of the *divisio textus* are repeated so that the reader may follow each

24   Cf. Fabro, C., 'Tommaso d'Aquino,' *Enciclopedia Cattolica*, XII (Firenze, 1954) col. 254: 'periodo piu agitato nella vita del Santo.'

25   Cf. Verbeke, *Introd.*, p. XXXIV, in *Themistius, Commentaire sur le Traité de l'âme*. As Father A. Dondaine suggests (*Secretaires de Saint Thomas*, Roma: Editori di S. Tommaso, 1956, p. 25) most of St. Thomas' works after about 1259 may have been dictated—but not necessarily under classroom conditions.

26   This agrees with Grabmann, *Die Werke*, p. 275; Mansion, 'Theorie arist. Du temps,' pp. 304–5; and the most recent estimate in Pattin, *art. cit.*

part of the argument. Examples may be added or expanded, citations made from other works of Aristotle or his commentators, and on rare occasions Thomas will criticize Aristotle, or more frequently his commentators, for running counter to the Christian faith or for mistakes in reasoning. This usually completes the *lectio*, though in some cases Thomas adds something by way of conclusion or general summary.[27]

Thomas' Attitude toward Aristotle

While St. Thomas devoted his mature life to the teaching of theology, it is clear that he made a profound study of the philosophy of Aristotle and his earlier commentators, Greek, Arabian and Latin. Aristotle's works and theories are cited as frequently in the theological writings of Aquinas as are those of the best known Christian thinker, St. Augustine. In his various expositions of the actual text of Aristotle, Thomas' primary purpose was to present the meaning of the original author and to explain it for his listeners and readers. Thomas does not forget that he is a teacher in a Christian school (so he will, on occasion, point to some discrepancy between an Aristotelian view and Christian belief) but he makes a very objective and faithful effort to interpret what Aristotle wrote. There is little intrusion of religious bias in Thomas' commentaries and there is much evidence of respect for the mind of Aristotle.

Aquinas had well developed philosophical views of his own. Here he owed much to Aristotle but not everything. There are other sources of St. Thomas' personal philosophy: Platonism and Neo-Platonism, Stoicism, Boethianism, Christian Platonism (Augustine and Dionysius), Avicennism, Averroism, and the Jewish scholasticisms of Maimonides and Avicebron. That these influences and his personal predilections may colour the Thomistic commentary, it would be idle to deny. No commentator comes to his text with a blank mind. Aquinas reads Aristotle with the benevolent interest of a well-instructed and thoughtful Christian—which Aristotle was not. Yet, when all this has been admitted, we must recognize Aquinas as an expositor who strove to be objective, scholarly, and as historically accurate as the circumstances permitted.

Lacking the knowledge of Greek to use the original text, Thomas is still critical in his awareness of textual problems. An instance of this attitude is found in *lectio* 10, of the commentary on Book V of the Physics. There is here a passage dealing with 'violent' motion which Thomas suspects as non-authentic. He reports that, according to Averroës, this passage (231a5–20) is lacking in some Arabic MSS., and he adds that it is said to be missing in the Greek copies.[28] He even surmises that it may be an addition from Theophrastus, or some other commentator. Whether Thomas is right or wrong regarding the authenticity of this passage deserves further study; it is a good illustration of his concern for textual authenticity and it shows that he sought information, indirectly, on the Greek text.

---

27 For further information on the style of the Thomistic commentaries on Aristotle see: M. D. Chenu, *Introduction à l'étude de saint Thomas d'Aquin*, Paris: Vrin, 1950, pp. 173–90.

28 The statement, 'in exemplaribus Graecis dicuntur non haberi,' indicates that Thomas has not himself checked the Greek but that he is relying on some Greek scholar, such as William of Moerbeke. Modern editions of the Greek text include this passage without comment.

No doubt Aquinas would be surprised at the critical findings of modern students of Aristotle's text. Unlike Werner Jaeger, Thomas considered that the major works of Aristotle are well-organized, complete and unified works. He assumed that we have them in practically the same condition in which they were written.[29] In fact, we have in the present work[30] an instance of Thomas' express resentment of a suggestion by Averroës that Aristotle had been a bit confused about what he is demonstrating at the beginning of the eighth book. Rather sharply, St. Thomas says that it is ridiculous to claim that Aristotle repeated his whole treatment because he had earlier omitted something. He adds that there must have been plenty of opportunity for Aristotle to correct his book and to supply what might have been lacking in its proper place. That Aristotle would have left the text in disorder, is unthinkable to Aquinas.[31]

On the other hand, St. Thomas never regards Aristotle as an authority on matters of faith. Thus, in the section of the *Physics* that has just been mentioned, Aristotle argued that the world is eternal. Thomas carefully explains the Aristotelian argument and adds this: 'One part of his position, namely, that there was always motion, conflicts with our faith. For according to our faith nothing has always existed except God alone, Who is altogether immobile.'[32] Then Thomas discusses a second way of understanding this text on eternal motion: some Christian interpreters had suggested the possibility of taking immaterial action as motion, and thus arguing that God's action is what is eternal. This would obviate the contradiction between Aristotle and Christian teaching. However, Aquinas does not take this easy way out; he correctly judges that it relies on an equivocal use of motion and he rejects the suggestion.

St. Thomas may have read Aristotle with the mind of a Christian but he never thought that he was required to make Aristotle speak like a Christian. Some of his contemporaries tried to prove such a 'concordism' between Aristotelianism and Catholic beliefs but Aquinas did not consciously share this attitude. His view is bluntly expressed in another short work where there is some question as to Aristotle's teaching on the origin of the rational soul in man. Thomas rather abruptly dismisses the question, saying: 'I don't see what one's interpretation of the text of Aristotle has to do with the teaching of the faith.'[33] Plainly, Aquinas thought that a scholarly commentary on Aristotle was a job by itself, not to be confused with apologetics or theology.

III. MEDIAEVAL PHYSICS AND MODERN SCIENCE

Reality as Subject to Motion

From Aristotle and Eudoxus the middle ages inherited a picture of the structure and workings of the physical universe. The earth was thought to be a sphere (not 'flat' as the legends about the predecessors of Columbus would have us think)

---

29   Cf. Chenu, *Introduction*, p. 187.
30   *In VIII Phys., Lect. 1.*
31   See *infra*, p. 470.
32   *In VIII Phys., Lect. 2.*
33   St. Thomas, *Reponsio ad articulos XLII*, art. 33 (ed. Parma, XVI, 167): 'Nec video quid pertineat ad doctrinam fidei qualiter Philosophi verba exponatur.'

situated at the centre of about fifty concentric and progressively larger spheres. The outermost sphere was pictured as an absolute boundary; beyond it there was no space. These spheres about the earth were thought to be constituted of translucent matter and some of the spheres had smaller opaque bodies imbedded in them. These bodies were the planets. In a static view, one might compare the system to the layers of an onion enclosing the earth as their core, with eight or so pieces of buckshot stuck in different layers. However, the system was not static. The spheres were in motion, rotating in various directions and thus causing the motions of the planets. The earth was considered to be at rest in the centre. This is the astronomy of Aristotle's *De Caelo*; it is pre-supposed in the *Physics* and is part of the contemporary science of Thomas Aquinas' century. Though an incorrect astronomy, the geocentric hypothesis was an important step in man's effort to understand his environment. After Einstein, we know that it is nonsense to ask whether the earth is 'really' in motion or at rest; it is mathematically simpler to postulate that the sun is at rest and that the other celestial bodies are moving in relation to it. Even today, ordinary mortals (and weather bureaux) retain the conviction that the sun rises and sets round a stationary earth.

Another long-lasting and thoroughly erroneous hypothesis in the development of physical science was the four-element theory. Long before Socrates, Greek thinkers assumed that all material things were constituted of earth, air, fire and water. These four were considered simple substances and all other bodies mixtures of these. For more than two thousand years learned men accepted this theory, even when they developed other principles of material analysis. Matter and form, atoms and empty space, substances and accidents—all were accommodated to the four-element theory. It was even extended to the life sciences, giving rise to the physiology of four humours and its consequent applications in medical and nursing practice. Some treatments of colds and fevers, today, are not entirely independent of this old theory. In psychology, the theory suggested the notion of four basic temperaments, of which some vestiges remain in contemporary literature. Indeed the four-element hypothesis (which is very central to the *Physics* and to St. Thomas' comment) has had a most distinguished and successful career. Of course it was wrong but, like many other errors, it had an important influence on the history of man.

Because the geocentric astronomy and the primitive chemistry of Aristotle's *Physics* were erroneous, we should not jump to the conclusion that the whole ancient explanation of nature was therefore wrong. The hylomorphic theory, for instance, is still used in many philosophies of nature.[34] That bodies and their changes are explainable in terms of material and formal components continues to be a basic assumption of much philosophic and scientific thinking. Under other names and with important modifications, this Aristotelian theory partly survives; potency and act, the polarity principle, even particles and structure owe something to it.

Nor can the notion of four kinds of cause be dismissed as completely irrelevant. These Aristotelian principles of explanation provide four different answers

---

34   See Van Melsen, A. G., *The Philosophy of Nature*, Pittsburgh: Duquesne U. Press, 1953; Smith, V., *Philosophical Physics*, New York: Harper, 1950.

to the question: Why is this thing existing, or this event occurring? Thus, to explain an automobile we might describe the stuff of which it has been made (material cause), the structural arrangement and working design (formal cause), the productive sources of the machine (efficient cause), and the purpose for which it may be used (final cause). Such a fourfold causal explanation can provide a very complete answer to many queries about nature. It should be obvious that 'cause' is used in a broad sense in Aristotelico-Thomistic philosophy.[35]

Similarly, the analysis of physical things in terms of substances and their accidental modifications is not entirely archaic. In English, the meaning of substance was changed. With John Locke, it came to mean little more than an inert substratum to which accidents are externally attached.[36] Further ambiguity has developed as a result of the special use of 'substance' as a chemical term. In Aristotle and St. Thomas, substance designates any being which exists by itself, as contrasted to an accident which exists in another being.[37]

Other Aristotelian definitions, concepts and theories will be found in the Physics—notions which have been incorporated into the language and culture of western man. For those who wish a more thorough analysis there is available a book which covers these themes in full detail.[38]

Aquinas' View of Physical Science

The middle ages stressed the substantial and qualitative aspects of the physical universe while modern science is more interested in quantitative and constructural interpretations. For Aristotle and Thomas Aquinas, science is a mental skill in reasoning from premises grounded in sense experience and in intellectual understanding of the universal meanings implicit in that experience. Whatever modern science is, it is not identical with that sort of demonstrative knowledge.[39]

In the century of St. Thomas, there was a growing school of empirical scientists (Witelo, Albert the Great, Roger Bacon and Robert Grosseteste). They anticipated some of the methods of research and interpretation that are still used in modern physics.[40] But Aquinas had little to do with this experimental move-

35   Cf. Klubertanz, G. P., *Introduction to the Philosophy of Being*, New York: Appleton-Century-Crofts, 1955, pp. 119–159.

36   See Collins, J., *A History of Modern European Philosophy*, Milwaukee: Bruce, 1954, pp. 331–32.

37   Cf. Wuellner, B., *Dictionary of Scholastic Philosophy*, Milwaukee: Bruce, 1956, p. 119. This dictionary offers brief and elementary explanations of most of the terms which will be ground in the English translation of the commentary on the *Physics*.

38   McWilliams, J. A., *Physics and Philosophy. A Study of Saint Thomas' Commentary on the Eight Books of Aristotle's Physics*, Washington: Amer. Catholic Philosophical Association, 1946.

39   In his Aquinas Lecture (*Thomas and the Physics of 1958: A Confrontation*, Milwaukee: Marquette U. Press, 1958) Henry Margenau argues that there is much less difference today between Thomism and the latest physics than there was in the nineteenth century. This is true but it is no service to the thought of Aquinas, or of present-day scientists, to ignore but it is no service to the thought of Aquinas, or of present-day scientists, to ignore their obvious differences.

40   Cf. Crombie, A. C., *Robert Grosseteste and the Origins of Experimental Science, 1100–1700*, Oxford: Clarendon Press, 1953; Baeumker, C., *Witelo, ein Philosoph und Naturforscher des XIII Jahrhunderts*, BGPM, III, 2, Münster, 1908.

ment. He did not emphasize the controlled observation of natural phenomena, let alone the making of technical experiments in the modern laboratory sense. Nor did he fully see the use to which mathematics might be put for the interpretation of empirical data.[41] In all this he is less 'modern' than some of his contemporaries, particularly those at Oxford.

Thomas Aquinas' notion of a science of nature owes a good deal to Aristotle's *Posterior Analytics*. He is in full agreement with the view that man has no knowledge, on earth, which does not originate in sense experience. In this, St. Thomas is fundamentally an empiricist, completely rejecting innate knowledge and the sort of thing which will later be called a *priori* forms of understanding. He adopts Aristotle's suggestion that the manifold of sense experience (*empeiria*) suggests certain universal judgments to the human understanding. These first items of intellectual knowledge (principles of understanding, such as that of non-contradiction or some of Euclid's axioms) then function as self-evident premises for further demonstrative reasoning. The origin of these intellectual principles is inductive on the level of sensory presentation but the consequent movement of human reasoning is viewed as deductive. His view of discursive reasoning is akin to the procedures of geometry. However, Thomistic science is not purely deductive: even after the initial induction of premises there is a constant effort to refer to additional information coming through further sense experience. This dependence on the 'phantasms' is especially distinctive of the science of nature.[42]

The last few centuries have witnessed the development of a large number of distinct, natural sciences which treat various limited aspects of physical reality. The techniques of experimental and mathematical physics, of the different types of chemistry, of geology, astronomy, meteorology, and of the many life sciences, have become tremendously diversified. Specialization has pluralized the natural sciences to such an extent that no modern man would pretend to competence in all. Yet there have also been efforts at unification, at a reduction of this plurality to a unified and most general theory of scientific knowledge. Recent developments in nuclear physics seem to make the distinction between physics and chemistry less marked than it was a decade ago. If a unified theory is ever achieved, it will not result from a contraction of knowledge but from a more profound insight into the available data.

Now the emphasis of St. Thomas' philosophy of nature is on a unified science of physical reality. Of course it was easier in the thirteenth century to be optimistic about such a possibility. This does not mean that there was complete ignorance of the diversity of scientific techniques. Encyclopedic writings of the middle ages describe long lists of mechanical arts in which men had acquired some competence.[43] Indeed, to take but one example, it is obvious that the men

41   Cf. Mullahy, B. I., *Thomism and Mathematical Physics*, 2 vols., Quebec: Laval U. Dissert., 1946.
42   For the relations of the various sciences, see: Maurer, A. (ed.), *St. Thomas Aquinas on the Division and Methods of the Sciences*, Toronto: Pont. Inst. of Mediaeval Studies, 1953.
43   See Crombie, A. C., *Augustine to Galileo. The History of Science, A. D. 400–1650*, Cambridge, Mass.: Harvard U. Press, 1953; chapter IV: 'Technics and Science in the Middle Ages,' pp. 143–211.

who built the cathedrals of Europe were not ignorant in mechanics and the architectural arts.[44] Yet these disciplines were then regarded as manual crafts and their practitioners as artisans. Little attention was paid them in academic circles; there were no trade-school courses in the mediaeval university. Today, we must admit that much of what is called physical science is simply technology. Courses in physics and chemistry consist very largely in repeating the same experiments that have become standard textbook procedures. Actually it is difficult to determine how much technological skill a great scientist must have; some of our best have had but little; St. Thomas had none. If modern science has exalted technics, the mediaeval period exalted thinking. This is one of the major differences.

Thomas Aquinas was also a metaphysician: he had a well-developed theory of the general character of reality as a whole. With Aristotle he agreed that there are immaterial substances in existence and he sought the ultimate explanation of the workings of the physical universe in the capacity of immaterial being to originate motion in bodies, without being moved in itself. In this the cosmology of Aquinas is ordered to his metaphysics.[45] Modern physics is not so orientated. Causality today means efficiency. The theme of final causality, so important to Aristotle and Thomas, has almost vanished from physical science. With it has gone the notion of teleological order in the universe. It is noteworthy that the life sciences still use this concept of goal-directed activity but they are the least mathematicized of the natural sciences. Perhaps when we move from quality to quantity we necessarily lose something of the finality of nature.

However, the most precise difference between Thomistic philosophy of nature and present-day physics probably lies in their respective notions of motion and physical activity. Aristotle's famous definition of motion occurs at the beginning of Book III of the *Physics*. He calls motion the 'fulfilment of what exists potentially, in so far as it exists potentially' (201 a 10). The reader will find a lengthy explanation of this definition in the first three lectiones of Aquinas' commentary. The point to be observed here is that the definition rests on a broader theory, that of potency and act, which has dropped out of modern physics.[46] There has been a similar shift in the meaning of action. Since Newton, physics has dropped its Aristotelian correlative, passion. Instead of passion (the condition of something which is being acted on) we have reaction (simply action in a contrary direction). As a result, physical action has come to mean a sort of pure putting-forth of energy. This is the sort of event which, in the view of Aquinas, would take place only in the immaterial world!

Finally, it may seem odd to suggest that Thomistic cosmology is closer to ordinary human experience and convictions than is modern physics. Yet this seems to be so. It is true that we now have a much greater assembly of factual data than either Aristotle or Aquinas possessed concerning the actual behaviour of physical nature. But the movement of our thinking on these data is toward theoretical

44 Daniel-Rops, H., *Cathedral and Crusade*, New York: Dutton, 1957, pp. 339–392.
45 Dreyer, J. L. E., *A History of Planetary Systems from Thales to Kepler*, Cambridge, 1900, p. 109, argues that Aristotle's cosmology is similarly influenced by metaphysics, Cf. Ashley, B. W., 'Aristotle's Sluggish Earth,' *New Scholasticism*, XXXII (1958), 1–31.
46 Einstein, A., and Infeld, L., *The Evolution of Physics*, New York: Simon and Schuster, 1938, pp. 6–7, are completely baffled by the definition, and so they condemn it as 'intuitive.'

construction. Our ultimate terms of analysis (waves, particles, quanta, mass, relations) are not observed facts but highly idealized structures of thought. It is quite impossible to 'picture' the physical universe as the physicist now explains it.[47] The odd result of this constructural effort is that it seems to work. Recent theoretical developments in nuclear physics have had observable consequences of which we are all aware. These consequences appear to offer pragmatic justification for some of the most unrealistic and theoretical speculations that the world has ever known.

St. Thomas Aquinas was a calm man, not easily startled. It is hard to say whether he would be surprised by the thinking of Einstein, Planck, Heisenberg, Born and De Broglie. What would be his attitude toward the more recent adventures of Oppenheimer, Compton, Fermi and Teller? The penetration of the atom and of outer space, the era of atomic fission, fusion, and of Sputnik—these and other achievements of modern physics might ruffle even the equanimity of Aquinas.

IV. BIBLIOGRAPHY

AQUINAS, ST. THOMAS, *In VIII Libros Physicorum Aristotelis* (*Opera Omnia*, ed. Leonina, tome II), Romae: Apud Sedem Commissionis Leoninae, 1884; editio manualis, Turino; Marietti, 1954.

AQUINAS, ST. THOMAS, *Commentary on Book I of the Physics of Aristotle*, translated by R. A. Kocourek, St. Paul, Minn.: College of St. Thomas, 1947.

ARISTOTLE, *Physics: A Revised Text with Introduction and Commentary*, ed. W. D. Ross, Oxford: Clarendon Press, 1936; reprinted by the same editor, without commentary (Bibl. Oxon.), Oxford: Clarendon Press, 1950.

ARISTOTLE, *Physica*, English translation by R. P. Hardie and R. K. Gaye (*Works of Aristotle*, II), Oxford: Clarendon Press, 1930; reprinted in McKeon, R. (ed.), Basic Works of Aristotle, New York: Random House, 1941.

ARISTOTLE, *Physics* (Greek and English), 2 vols.. (Loeb Series), ed. P. H. Wicksteed and M. Cornford, London: Heinemann, 1929–1934.

ASHLEY, B. W., 'Aristotle's Sluggish Earth,' *New Scholasticism*, XXXII (1958), 1B31.

BACON, ROGER, *Quaestiones supra libros IV Physicorum Aristoteles* (Opera hactenus inedita, VIII), F. M. Delorme and R. Steele, Oxford: Clarendon Press, 1928.

BAUR, L., 'Die Form der wissenschaftlichen Kritik bei Thomas von Aquin,' *Aus der Geisteswelt des Mittelalters* (BGPM Suppl. III), Münster, 1935, 688–709.

---

47   Cf. Reichenbach, H., *Atoms and Cosmos, The World of Modern Physics*, New York: Macmillan, 1933, pp. 281–294. For a further discussion of the contrast between the Thomistic theory of knowledge and the explanations given in modern physical science, see: Régis, L. M., *Epistemology*, New York: Macmillan, 1959, pp. 7–31.

CALLUS, D. A., *Introduction of Aristotelian Learning to Oxford*, London: Proc. Aristotelian Society, 1944.

CASTAGNOLI, P., 'I Commenti di S. Tommaso ai Libri Naturales,' *Divus Thomas* (Piacenza), 34 (1931), 261–83.

CHENU, M. D., *Introduction à l'étude de saint Thomas d'Aquin*, Paris-Ottawa: Vrin, 1950.

CROMBIE, A. C., *Augustine to Galileo. The History of Science, A.D. 400-1650*, Cambridge, Mass.: Harvard U. Press, 1953.

CROMBIE, A. C., *Robert Grosseteste and the Origins of Experimental Science, 1100–1700*, Oxford: Clarendon Press, 1952.

CROWE, M. B., 'Peter of Ireland, Teacher of St. Thomas,' *Studies* (Dublin), 45 (1956), 443–456.

DONDAINE, A., *Secrétaires de saint Thomas*, Romae: Commissio Leonina, 1956.

DREYER, J. L. E., *A History of the Planetary Systems from Thales to Kepler*, Cambridge, Eng.: Cambridge U. Press, 1900; reprinted New York: Dover Publ., 1953.

DUCOIN, G., 'Saint Thomas Commentateur d'Aristote,' *Archives de Philosophie*, XX (1957), 240–71, 392–445.

DUHEM, P., *The Aim and Structure of Physical Theory*, translated by P. Wiener, Princeton: Princeton U. Press, 1954.

DUHEM, P., *Le Systéme du Monde. Histoire des doctrines cosmologiques de Platon a Copernic*, 5 vols., Paris, 1913–1917.

DUIN, J. J., 'Nouvelles prJcisions sur la chronologie du Commentum in Metaphysicam de s. Thomas,' *Revue Philos. de Louvain*, 53 (1955), 511–24.

EGIDII ROMANI, *In libros physico auditu Aristotelis Commentaria*, Venetiis, 1502, in fol. (For thirteenth-century Latin text of Aristotle's Physics.)

EINSTEIN, A., and INFELD, L., *The Evolution of Physics*, New York: Simon and Shuster, 1938.

ESCHMANN, I. T., 'Catalogue of the Works of St. Thomas,' in Gilson, E., *The Christian Philosophy of St. Thomas Aquinas*, New York: Random House, 1956, pp. 401–2.

FRANCESCHINI, E., *Aristotele nel Medio Evo latino*, Padova: Atti del IX Congresso Nazionale di Filologia, 1935.

GILSON, E., *History of Christian Philosophy in the Middle Ages*, New York: Random House, 1955.

GRABMANN, M., 'Die Aristoteleskommentare des hl. Thomas v. Aquin,' *Mittelalterliches Geistesleben*, München, 1926, I, 266–13.

GRABMANN, M., *Guglielmo di Moerbeke, O.P., il traduttore delle opere di Aric totle* (Misc. Hist. Pont., XI), Roma: Università Gregoriana, 1945.

GRABMANN, M., *Die Werke des hl. Thomas v. Aquin*, Aufl. 3, Munster i. W.: Aschendorff, 1949.

LACOMBE, G., *et al.*, *Aristoteles Latinus*, Pars Prior (*Corpus Philos. Medii Aevi*), Romae: Union Acad. Internat., 1939.

LAUBENTHAL, R., *Das Verhältnis des hl. Thomas von Aquin zu den Arabern in seinem Physikkommentar*, Wurzburg: U. Dissert., 1933.

MANSION, A., 'Sur le texte de la version latine médiévale de la Métaphysique et de la Physique d'Aristote dans les Éditions des Commentaires de s. Thomas d'Aquin,' *Revue Néoscolastique de Philos.*, 34 (1932), 65–69.

MANSION, A., 'La théorie aristotélicienne du temps,' *Revue Néosc. de Philos.*, 36 (1934), 275–307.

MANSION, A., 'De jongste Geschiedenis van de middeleeuwsche Aristoteles, vertalingen naar eigen Bevindingen getoetst,' *Mededeelingen*, III, 2, Brussels, 1941.

MANSION, A., *Introductionà la physique aristotélicienne*, 2me éd., Louvain: Inst. Sup. de Philos., 1946.

MCWILLIAMS, J. A., *Physics and Philosophy. A Study of St. Thomas' Commentary on the Eight Books of Aristotle's Physics*, Washington: Amer. Cath. Philos. Assoc., 1945.

MARGENAU, H., *Thomas and the Physics of 1958: A Confrontation* (Aquinas Lecture, 1958), Milwaukee: Marquette U. Press, 1958.

MARITAIN, J., *Philosophy of Nature*, New York: Philosophical Library, 1951.

MAURER, A. (ed.), *St. Thomas Aquinas on the Division and Methods of the Sciences*, Toronto: Pont. Inst. of Mediaeval Studies, 1953.

MINIO-PALUELLO, L., 'Note sull' Aristotle medievale,' *Rivista di Filos. Neoscol.*, 42 (1951), 222–30.

MITTERER, A., 'Der Wärmerbegriffe des hl. Thomas nach seinem physikalischen Weltbild,' *Aus der Geisteswelt*, Mhnster, 1935, 720 ff.

MORAUX, P., 'Recherches sur le De Caelo d'Aristote,' *Revue Thomiste*, 51 (1951), 170–96.

MULLAHY, B. I., *Thomism and Mathematical Physics*, 2 vols., Quebec: Laval U. Dissert., 1946.

PATTIN, A., 'Bijdrage tot de kronologie van St. Thomas Werken,' *Tijdschrift voor Philos.*, XIX (1957), 477–504.

PELSTER, F., 'Beiträge zur Aristotelesbenutzung Alberts des Grosse,' *Philos. Jahrbuch*, 47 (1934), 55–64.

PELSTER, F., 'Die Uebersetzungen der aristotelischen Metaphysik in den Werken des hl. Thomas v. Aquin,' *Gregorianum*, 17 (1936), 377–406.

REICHENBACH, H., *Atom and Cosmos*, tr. E. E. Allen, New York: Macmillan, 1933.

SARTON, G., *Introduction to the History of Science*, 3 vols., Baltimore: Williams and Wilkins, 1927–1928.

SMITH, V., *Philosophical Physics*, New York: Harper & Bros., 1950.

THORNDIKE, L., *A History of Magic and Experimental Science*, 4 vols., New York: Macmillan, 1923–1934.

VAN MELSEN, A. G., *The Philosophy of Nature*, Pittsburgh: Duquesne U. Press, 1953.

VAN STEENBERGHEN, F., *Aristotle in the West*, tr. L. Johnston, Louvain: Nauwelaerts, 1955.

VERBEKE, G., *Introduction to*: Themistius, *Commentaire sur le traité de l'âme d'Aristote traduction de Guillaume de Moerbeke*, ed. critique, (Corpus Latinum Comm. in Arist. Graec., I), Louvain: Nauwelaerts, 1957.

St. Louis University
VERNON J. BOURKE

BOOK I
THE PRINCIPLES OF NATURAL THINGS

LECTURE 1 [184a9–b14]
The Matter and the Subject of Natural Science and of This Book. We Must Proceed from the More Universal Principles Which Are Better Know to Us.

The Text of Aristotle
Chapter 1

1. When the objects of an inquiry, in any department, have principles, conditions, or elements, it is through acquaintance with these that knowledge, that is to say scientific knowledge, is attained. For we do not think that we know a thing until we are acquainted with its primary conditions or first principles, and have carried our analysis as far as its simplest elements. Plainly therefore in the science of Nature, as in other branches of study, our first task will be to try to determine what relates to its principles. 184a11–16

2. The natural way of doing this is to start from the things which are more knowable and obvious to us and proceed towards those which are clearer and more knowable by nature; for the same things are not "knowable relatively to us" and "knowable" without qualification. So in the present inquiry we must follow this method and advance from what is more obscure by nature, but clearer to us, towards what is more clear and more knowable by nature. 184a16–21

3. Now what is to us plain and obvious at first is rather confused masses, the elements and principles of which become known to us later by analysis. Thus we must advance from generalities to particulars; for it is a whole that is best known to sense-perception, and a generality is a kind of whole, comprehending many things within it, like parts. 184a21–24

4. Much the same thing happens in the relation of the name to the formula. As name, e.g. "Round," means vaguely a sort of whole: its definition analyses this into its particular senses.
184a26–184b3

5. Similarly a child begins by calling all men "father," and all women "mother," but later on distinguishes each of them. 184b3–5

COMMENTARY OF ST. THOMAS

1. Because this book, The Physics, upon which we intend to comment here, is the first book of natural science, it is necessary in the beginning to decide what is the matter and the subject of natural science.

Since every science is in the intellect, it should be understood that something is rendered intelligible in act insofar as it is in some way abstracted from matter. And inasmuch as things are differently related to matter they pertain to different sciences.

Furthermore, since every science is established through demonstration, and since the definition is the middle term in a demonstration, it is necessary that sciences be distinguished according to the diverse modes of definition.

2. It must be understood, therefore, that there are some things whose existence depends upon matter, and which cannot be defined without matter. Further there are other things which, even though they cannot exist except in sensible matter, have no sensible matter in their definitions. And these differ from each other as the curved differs from the snub. For the snub exists in sensible matter, and it is necessary that sensible matter fall in its definition, for the snub is a curved nose. And the same is true of all natural things, such as man and stone. But sensible matter does not fall

in the definition of the curved, even though the curved cannot exist except in sensible matter. And this is true of all the mathematicals, such as numbers, magnitudes and figures. Then, there are still other things which do not depend upon matter either according to their existence or according to their definitions. And this is either because they never exist in matter, such as God and the other separated substances, or because they do not universally exist in matter, such as substance, potency and act, and being itself.

3. Now metaphysics deals with things of this latter sort. Whereas mathematics deals with those things which depend upon sensible matter for their existence but not for their definitions. And natural science, which is called physics, deals with those things which depend upon matter not only for their existence, but also for their definition.

And because everything which has matter is mobile, it follows that mobile being is the subject of natural philosophy. For natural philosophy is about natural things, and natural things are those whose principle is nature. But nature is a principle of motion and rest in that in which it is. Therefore natural science deals with those things which have in them a principle of motion.

4. Furthermore those things which are consequent upon something common must be treated first and separately. Otherwise it becomes necessary to repeat such things many times while discussing each instance of that which is common. Therefore it was necessary that one book in natural science be set forth in which those things which are consequent upon mobile being in common are treated; just as first philosophy, in which those things which are

common to being insofar as it is being, is set forth for all the sciences.

This, then, is the book, *The Physics*, which is also called *On Physics*, or *Of the Natural to be Heard*, because it was handed down to hearers by way of instruction. And its subject is mobile being simply.

I do not, however, say mobile body, because the fact that every mobile being is a body is proven in this book, and no science proves its own subject. And thus in the very beginning of the *De Caelo*, which follows this book, we begin with the notion of body.

Moreover, after *The Physics* there are other books of natural science in which the species of motion are treated. Thus in the *De Caelo* we treat the mobile according to local motion, which is the first species of motion. In the *De Generatione*, we treat of motion to form and of the first mobile things, i.e., the elements, with respect to the common aspects of their changes. Their special changes are considered in the book *Meteororum*. In the book, *De Mineralibus*, we consider the mobile mixed bodies which are non-living. Living bodies are considered in the book, *De Anima* and the books which follow it.

5. To this book, then, the Philosopher writes a preface in which he shows the order of procedure in natural science.

In this preface he does two things. First he shows that it is necessary to begin with a consideration of principles. Secondly, where he says, **"The natural way of doing this . . ."** [2], he shows that among principles, it is necessary to begin with the more universal principles.

First he gives the following argument. In all sciences of which there are principles or causes or elements, understanding and science proceed from a knowledge of the principles, causes and elements. But the science which is about nature has principles, elements and causes. Therefore it is necessary in it to begin with a determination of principles.

When he says "to understand" he has reference to definitions, and when he says "to have science" he has reference to demonstrations. For as demonstrations are from causes, so also are definitions, since a complete definition is a demonstration differing only by position, as is said in Posterior Analytics, I.

When, however, he speaks of principles or causes or elements, he does not intend to signify the same thing by each. For cause is wider in meaning than element. An element is a first component of a thing and is in it [i.e., in the composed], as is said in Metaphysics, V. Thus the letters, but not the syllables, are the elements of speech. But those things are called causes upon which things depend for their existence or their coming to be. Whence even that which is outside the thing, or that which is in it, though the thing is not first composed of it, can be called a cause. But it cannot be called an element. And thirdly principle implies a certain order in any progression. Whence something can be a principle which is not a cause, as that from which motion begins is a principle of motion, but is not a cause, and a point is a principle of a line but not a cause.

Therefore, by principle he seems to mean moving causes and agents in which, more than in others, there is found an order of some progression. By causes he seems to mean formal and final causes upon which things most of all depend for their existence and their coming to be. By elements he means properly the first material causes.

Moreover he uses these terms disjunctively and not copulatively in order to point out that not every science demonstrates through all the causes. For mathematics demonstrates only through the formal cause. Metaphysics demonstrates through the formal and final causes principally but also through the agent. Natural science, however, demonstrates through all the causes.

He then proves from common opinion the first proposition of his argument. This is also proven in the Posterior Analytics. For a man thinks that he knows something when he knows all its causes from the first to the last. The meaning here of causes, principles, and elements is exactly the same as we have explained above, even though the Commentator disagrees. Furthermore Aristotle says, "... as far as its simplest elements," because that which is last in knowledge is matter. For matter is for the sake of form, and form is from the agent for the sake of the end, unless it itself is the end. For example, we say that a saw has teeth in order to cut, and these teeth ought to be made of iron so they will be apt for cutting.

6. Next where he says, **"The natural way of doing this . . ."** [2], he shows that among principles it is necessary to treat the more universal ones first. And he shows this first by means of an argument, and secondly, by an example, where he says, **"... for it is a whole..."** [3].

First he gives the following argument. It is natural for us to proceed in knowing from those things which are better known to us to those which are better known by nature. But the things which are known to us are confused, such as the universals. Therefore it is necessary for us to proceed from universals to singulars.

7. For purposes of clarifying the first proposition he makes the point that things which are better known to us and things which are better known according to nature are not the same. Rather those things which are better known according to nature are less known to us. And because the natural way or order of learning is that we should come to that which is unknown by us from that which is known by us, it is necessary for us to arrive at the better known in nature from the better known to us.

It must be noted, however, that that which is known by nature and that which is known simply mean the same. Those things are better known simply which are in themselves better known. But those things are better known in themselves which have more being, because each thing is knowable insofar as it is being. However, those beings are greater which are greater in act. Whence these are the most knowable by nature.

For us, however, the converse is true because we proceed in understanding from potency to act. Our knowledge begins from sensible things which are material and intelligible in potency. Whence these things are known by us before the separated substances, which are better known according to nature, as is clear in Metaphysics, II.

He does not, therefore, say known by nature as if nature knew these things, but because they are better known in themselves and according to their proper natures. And he says better known and more certain, because in the sciences not just any kind of knowledge is sought, but a certain knowledge.

Next in order to understand the second proposition, it must be known that those things are here called "confused" which contain in themselves something potential and indistinct. And because to know something indistinctly is a mean between pure potency and perfect act, so it is that while our intellect proceeds from potency to act, it knows the confused before it knows the distinct. But it has complete science in act when it arrives, through resolution, at a distinct knowledge of the principles and elements. And this is the reason why the confused is known by us before the distinct.

That universals are confused is clear. For universals contain in themselves their species in potency. And whoever knows something in the universal knows it indistinctly. The knowledge, however, becomes distinct when each of the things which are contained in potency in the universal is known in act. For he who knows animal does not know the rational except in potency. Thus knowing something in potency is prior to knowing it in act. Therefore, according to this order of learning, in which we proceed from potency to act, we know animal before we know man.

8. It would seem, however, that this is contrary to what the Philosopher says in Posterior Analytics, I, namely, that singulars are better known to us, whereas the universals are better known by nature or simply.

But it must be understood that there he takes as singulars the individual sensible things themselves, which are better known to us because the knowledge of sense, which is of singulars, does precede in us the knowledge of the intellect, which is of universals. And because intellectual knowledge is more perfect, and because the universals are intelligible in act, whereas the singulars are not (since they are material), the universals are better known simply and according to nature.

Here, however, by singulars he means not the individuals themselves, but the species. And these are better known by nature, existing more perfectly, as it were, and being known with a distinct knowledge. But the genera are known by us first, being known, as it were, confusedly and in potency.

It should be known, however, that the Commentator explains this passage in another way. He says that in the passage beginning, **"The natural way of doing this . . ."** [184a16], the Philosopher wishes to explain the method of demonstration of this science, namely, that this science demonstrates through the effect and what is posterior according to nature. Hence what is said here is to be understood of the progression in demonstration and not of the progression in determination. Then in the passage where Aristotle says, **"Now what is plain to us . . ."** [184a22], he intends to make clear (according to the Commentator) what things are better known to us and what is better known by nature, i.e., things which are composed of the simple, understanding "confused" to mean "composed." Finally, then, he concludes, as if to a corollary, that we must proceed from the more universal to the less universal.

It is clear that his explanation is not suitable, because he does not join the whole passage to one intention. Moreover the Philosopher does not intend to set forth the mode of demonstration of this science here, because he will do this in Book II according to his order of treatment. Furthermore, the confused should not be taken to mean composed, but rather to mean indistinct. For nothing could be concluded from such universals because genera are not composed of species.

9. Next, where he says, **". . . for it is a whole . . ."** [3], he clarifies his position with three examples. The first of these is taken from the integral sensible whole. He says that since the sensible whole is better known to the sense, then, the intelligible whole is also better known to the intellect. But the universal is a sort of intelligible whole, because it comprehends many as parts, namely, its inferiors. Therefore the universal is better known to us intellectually.

But it would seem that this proof is not effective, because he uses whole and part and comprehension equivocally.

However it must be said that the integral whole and the universal agree in that each is confused and indistinct. For just as he who apprehends a genus does not apprehend the species distinctly, but in potency only, so also he who apprehends a house does not yet distinguish its parts. Whence it is that a whole is first known to us as confused. This applies to both of these wholes. However, to be composed is not common to each whole. Whence it is clear that Aristotle significantly said "confused" above and not "composed."

10. Next where he says, **"Much the same thing . . ."** [4], he gives another example taken from the integral intelligible whole.

For that which is defined is related to the things defining it as a kind of integral whole, insofar as the things defining it are in act in that which is defined. But he who apprehends a name, for example, man or circle, does not at once distinguish the defining principles. Whence it is that the name is, as it were, a sort of whole and is indistinct, whereas the definition divides into singulars, i.e., distinctly sets forth the principles of that which is defined.

This, however, seems to be contrary to what he said above. For the things which define would seem to be more universal, and these, he said, were first known by us. Furthermore, if that which is defined were better known to us than the things which define, we would not grasp that which is defined through the definition, for we grasp nothing except through that which is better known to us.

But it must be said that the things which define are in themselves known to us before that which is defined, but we know the thing which is defined before we know that these are the things which define it. Thus we know animal and rational before we know man. But man is known confusedly before we know that animal and rational are the things which define man.

11. Next where he says, "Similarly a child . . ." [5], he gives the third example taken from the more universal sensible. For as the more universal intelligible is first known to us intellectually, for example, animal is known before man, so the more common sensible is first known to us according to sense, for example, we know this animal before we know this man.

And I say first according to sense both with reference to place and with reference to time. This is true according to place because, when someone is seen at a distance, we perceive him to be a body before we perceive that he is an animal, and animal before we perceive him to be a man, and finally we perceive that he is Socrates. And in the same way with reference to time, a boy apprehends this individual as some man before he apprehends this man, Plato, who is his father. And this is what he says: children at first call all men fathers and all women mothers, but later they determine, that is, they know each determinately.

From this it is clearly shown that we know a thing confusedly before we know it distinctly.

The Opinions of the Ancient Philosophers about the Principles of Nature and of Beings. It Does Not Pertain to Natural Science to Disprove Some of These Opinions.

The Text of Aristotle
Chapter 2

6. The principles in question must be either (a) one or (b) more than one. If (a) one, it must be either (i) motionless, as Parmenides and Melissus assert, or (ii) in motion, as the physicists hold, some declaring air to be the first principle, others water. If (b) more than one, then either (i) a finite or (ii) an infinite plurality. If (i) finite (but more than one), then either two or three or four or some other number. If (ii) infinite, then either as Democritus believed one in kind, but differing, in shape or form; or different in kind and even contrary.   184b15–22

7. A similar inquiry is made by those who inquire into the number of existents; for they inquire whether the ultimate constituents of existing things are one or many, and if many, whether a finite or an infinite plurality. So they too are inquiring whether the principle or element is one or many.   184b22–25

8. Now to investigate whether Being is one and motionless is not a contribution to the science of Nature. For just as the geometer has nothing more to say to one who denies the principles of his science—this being a question for a different science or for one common to all—so a man investigating principles cannot argue with one who denies their existence. For if Being is just one, and one in the way mentioned, there is a principle no longer, since a principle must be the principle of some thing or things.   184b25–185a5

9. To inquire therefore whether Being, is one in this sense would be like arguing against any other position maintained for the sake of argument   185a5–7

10. (such as the Heraclitean thesis, or such a thesis as that Being is one man) or like refuting a merely contentious argument—a description which applies to the arguments both of Melissus and of Parmenides: their premises are false and their conclusions do not follow. Or rather the argument of Melissus is gross and palpable and offers no difficulty at all: accept one ridiculous proposition and the rest follows—a simple enough proceeding.   185a7–12

11. We physicists, on the other hand, must take for granted that the things that exist by Nature are, either all or some of them, in motion—which is indeed made plain by induction. Moreover, no man of science is bound to solve every kind of difficulty that may be raised, but only as many as are drawn falsely from the principles of the science: it is not our business to refute those that do not arise in this way; just as it is the duty of the geometer to refute the squaring of the circle by means of segments, but it is not his duty to refute Antiphon's proof.
185a12–17

12. At the same time the holders of the theory of which we are speaking do incidentally raise physical questions, though Nature is not their subject; so it will perhaps be as well to spend a few words on them, especially as the inquiry is not without scientific interest.   185a17–20

COMMENTARY OF ST. THOMAS

12. Having completed the preface in which it was shown that natural science ought to begin with the more universal principles, here, according to the order already stated, he begins to pursue those matters which pertain to natural science.

This discussion is divided into two parts. In the first part he treats the universal principles of natural science. In the second part he treats mobile being in common (which is what he intends to treat in this book). This is taken up in Book III, where he says, **"Nature has been defined . . ."** [189].

The first part is divided into two parts. First he treats the principles of the subject of this science, that is, the principles of mobile being as such. Secondly he treats the principles of the doctrine. This he does in Book II, where he says, **"Of things that exist . . ."** [92].

The first part is divided into two parts. First he considers the opinions others have had concerning the common principles of mobile being. Secondly he seeks the truth concerning them, where he says, **"All thinkers, then, agree . . ."** [47].

Concerning the first part he makes three points. First he sets forth the different opinions of the ancient philosophers concerning the common principles of nature. Secondly, where he says, **"Now to investigate . . ."** [8], he shows that it does not pertain to natural science to pursue some of these opinions. Thirdly, where he says, **"The most pertinent question . . ."** [13], he considers these opinions, showing their falsity.

Concerning the first part he makes two points. First he sets forth the different opinions of the philosophers concerning the principles of nature. Secondly, where he says, **"A similar inquiry is made . . ."** [7], he shows that this same diversity exists with reference to the opinions of the philosophers concerning beings.

13. He says, therefore, first of all, [6] that it is necessary that there be one principle of nature or many. And each position has claimed the opinions of the philosophers.

Some of them, indeed, held that there is one principle, others held that there are many. And of those who held that there is one principle, some held that it was immobile, as did Parmenides and Melissus, whose opinion he will examine below. Some, however, held that it was mobile, as did the natural philosophers.

Of these, some held that air was the principle of all natural things, as Diogenes; others that it was water, as Thales; others that it was fire, as Heraclitus; and still others some mean between air and water, such as vapor.

But none of those who held that there was only one principle said that it was earth because of its density. For they held that principles of this sort were mobile, because they said that other things come to be through the rarefication and condensation of certain of these principles.

Of those who held the principles to be many, some held them to be finite, others held that they were infinite.

Of those who held that they were finite (although more than one) some held that there were two, i.e., fire and earth, as Parmenides will say below. Others held that there were three, i.e., fire, air and water (for they thought earth to be in some way composed because of its density). Others, however, held that there were four, as Empedocles did, or even some other number, because even Empedocles himself along with the four elements posited two other principles, namely, friendship and strife.

Those who held that there was an infinite plurality of principles had a diversity of opinions. For Democritus held that indivisible bodies which are called atoms are the principles of all things. And he held that bodies of this sort were all of one genus according to nature, but that they differed according to figure and form, and that they not only differed but even had contrariety among themselves. For he held three contrarieties: one according to figure, which is between the curved and the straight, another according to order, which is the prior and the posterior, and another according to position, namely, before and behind, above and below, to the right and to the left. And so he held that from these bodies existing of one nature different things come to be according to the diversity of the figure, position and order of the atoms. In this opinion, then, he gives us some basis for understanding the opposing opinion, namely that of Anaxagoras who held that the principles were infinite, but not of one genus according to nature. For he held that the principles of nature were the infinite, smallest parts of flesh and bone and other such things, as will be made clear below.

It must be noted, however, that he did not divide these many principles into mobile and immobile. For none of these who held that the first principles were many held that they were immobile. For since all place contrariety in the principles, and since it is natural for contraries to change, immobility could not stand with a plurality of principles.

14. Secondly, at the point where he says, **"A similar inquiry is made . . ."** [7], he shows that there is the same diversity of opinions concerning beings.

He says that in like manner the physicists, when inquiring about those things which are, i.e., about beings, wondered how many there are, i.e., whether there is one or many; and if many, whether finite or infinite.

And the reason for this is that the ancient physicists did not know any cause but the material cause (although

they touched lightly upon the other causes). Rather they held that the natural forms were accidents, as the forms of artificial things are. Since, therefore, the whole substance of artificial things is their matter, so it followed, according to them, that the whole substance of natural things would be their matter.

Hence those who held one principle only, for example, air, thought that other beings were air according to their substance. And the same is true of the other opinions. Hence Aristotle says that the physicists seek what is in that from which things are, i.e., in inquiring about principles they sought the material causes from which beings are said to be. Whence it is clear that when they inquire about beings, whether they are one or many, their inquiry concerns the material principles which are called elements.

15. Next where he says, **"Now to investigate . . ."** [8], he shows that it does not pertain to natural science to disprove some of these opinions.

And concerning this he makes two points. First he shows that it does not pertain to natural science to disprove the opinion of Parmenides and Melissus [8]. Secondly, where he says, **"At the same time the holders of the theory . . ."** [12], he gives a reason why it is useful to the present work to disprove this opinion.

Concerning the first part he makes two points. First he shows that it does not pertain to natural science to disprove the aforesaid opinion. Secondly, where he says, **". . . or like refuting . . ."** [10], he shows that it does not pertain to natural science to resolve the arguments which are brought forth to prove this opinion.

He establishes his first point with two arguments, the second of which begins where he says, **"To inquire therefore . . ."** [9].

He says, therefore, [8] that it does not pertain to natural science to undertake a thorough consideration of the opinion whether being is one and immobile. For it has already been shown that there is no difference, according to the intention of the ancient philosophers, whether we hold one immobile principle or one immobile being.

And that it should not pertain to natural science to disprove this opinion he shows as follows. It does not pertain to geometry to bring forth reasons against an argument which destroys its principles. Rather, this either pertains to some other particular science (if, indeed, geometry is subalternated to some particular science, such as music is subalternated to arithmetic, to which it pertains to dispute against any position denying the principles of music), or it pertains to a common science such as logic or metaphysics. But the aforesaid position destroys the principles of nature. For if there is only one being, and if this being is immobile, such that from it others cannot come to be, then the very nature of a principle is taken away. For every principle is either a principle of some thing or of some things. Therefore, if we posit a principle, a multiplicity follows, because one is the principle and the other is that of which it is the principle. Whoever, therefore, denies multiplicity removes principles. Therefore natural science ought not to argue against this position.

16. Next where he says, **"To inquire therefore . . ."** [9], he shows the same point with another argument. It is not required of any science that it bring forth arguments against manifestly false and improbable opinions. For to worry about one who offers positions contrary to the opinions of the wise is stupid, as is said in Topics, I.

He says, therefore, that to undertake a thorough consideration of the question whether being is one, and hence immobile, is like arguing against any other improbable position. For example, it is like arguing against the position of Heraclitus, who said that all things are always moved and that nothing is true; or against the position of one who would say that the whole of being is one man, which position, indeed, would be altogether improbable. And indeed whoever holds being to be only one immobile thing is forced to hold that the whole of being is some one thing. It is clear, therefore, that it does not belong to natural science to argue against this position.

17. Next when he says, **". . . or like refuting . . ."** [10], he shows that it does not belong to natural science even to resolve the arguments of the aforementioned philosophers. And this for two reasons, the second of which begins where he says, **"We physicists . . ."** [11].

First he proves his position by pointing out that it is not incumbent upon any science to resolve sophistic arguments which have an obvious defect of form or matter. He says that to deal with improbable arguments is like solving a contentious or sophistic argument. But each argument of both Melissus and Parmenides is sophistic, for they err in matter, whence he says that they have accepted what is false, i.e., they assume false propositions, and they err in form, whence he says that they are not syllogizing. But the position of Melissus is much worse, i.e., more vain and foolish and does not cause any difficulty. This will be shown below. Moreover, it is not inconsistent that given one inconsistency another should follow. Therefore it can be concluded that it is not required of the philosopher of nature that he resolve the arguments of this man.

18. He sets forth the second argument for this where he says, **"We physicists . . ."** [11]. The argument is as follows. In natural science it is supposed that natural things are moved, either all or some of them. He says this because there is doubt whether some things are moved and how they are moved, for example, about the soul and the center of the earth, and the pole of heaven, and about natural forms and other such things. But the fact that natural things are moved can be made clear from induction, for it is apparent to the sense that natural things are moved.

It is as necessary that motion be supposed in natural science as it is necessary that nature be supposed. For motion is placed in the definition of nature, for nature is a principle of motion, as will be said below.

Having established this point, that motion is supposed in natural science, he proceeds further to prove his position as follows. Not all arguments must be resolved in any science, but only those which conclude to something false from the principles of that science. Any arguments which do not reach their conclusions from the principles of the science, but from the contraries of these principles, are not resolved in that science. He proves this by an example taken from geometry saying that it pertains to geometry to resolve the problem of squaring, i.e., the squaring of a circle by dissecting the circumference, because this method supposes nothing contrary to the principles of the science of geometry. For somebody wished to find a square equal to a circle by dividing the circumference of the circle into many parts and placing straight lines in each part. And so by finding some figure, which was rectilinear, equal to some of the figures which were contained by the dissections of the circumference and the cords (either many or all), he thought he had found a rectilinear figure equal to the whole circle, to which it was easy to find an equal square through the principles of geometry. And thus he thought that he was able to find a square equal to a circle. But he did not argue well enough, for although these dissections used up the whole circumference of the circle, the figures contained by the dissections of the circumference and the straight lines did not encompass the whole circular surface.

But to resolve the square of Antiphon does not pertain to geometry, because he used principles contrary to those of geometry. For he described in a circle a certain rectilinear figure, for example, a square. And he divided in half the arcs by which the sides of the square were subtended. And from the points of dissection he led straight lines to all the angles of the square. And then there resulted in the circle a figure of eight angles which more closely approached equality with the circle than the square. Then he again divided in half the arcs by which the sides of the octagon were subtended, and thus by leading straight lines from the points of dissection to the angles of this figure there resulted a figure of sixteen angles, which still further approached equality with the circle. Therefore, by always dividing the arcs and leading straight lines to the angles of the figure already existing there will arise a figure very near to equality with the circle. He said, then, that it was impossible to proceed to infinity in the dissection of arcs. Therefore, it was necessary to arrive at some rectilinear figure equal to the circle to which some square could be equal.

But, because he supposed that an arc is not always divisible in half, which is contrary to the principles of geometry, it does not pertain to geometry to resolve an argument of this sort.

Therefore, because the arguments of Parmenides and Melissus suppose being to be immobile (as will be shown below), and since this is contrary to the principles supposed in natural science, it follows that it does not pertain to the natural philosopher to resolve arguments of this sort.

19. Next where he says, **"At the same time . . ."** [12], he states why he will argue against the aforementioned position. He says that because the philosophers mentioned above did speak of natural things, even though they did not create a problem (that is, in the sphere of natural science), it is useful for his present purpose to argue against opinions of this sort. For even though it does not pertain to natural science to argue against such positions, it does pertain to first philosophy.

The Assertion of Parmenides and Melissus That All Things Are One Being Is Refuted

The Text of Aristotle

13. *The most pertinent question with which to begin will be this: In what sense is it asserted that all things are one? For "is" is used in many senses. Do they mean that all things "are" substance or quantities or qualities? And, further, are all things one substance—one man, one horse, or one soul—or quality and that one and the same—white or hot or something of the kind? These are all very different doctrines and all impossible to maintain.*

For if both substance and quantity and quality are, then, whether these exist independently of each other or not, Being will be many.

If on the other hand it is asserted that all things are quality or quantity, then, whether substance exists or not, an absurdity results, if indeed the impossible can properly be called absurd. For none of the others can exist independently: substance alone is independent: for everything is predicated of substance as subject. Now Melissus says that Being is infinite. It is then a quantity. For the infinite is in the category of quantity, whereas substance or quality or affection cannot be infinite except through a concomitant attribute, that is, if at the same time they are also quantities. For to define the infinite you must use quantity in your formula, but not substance or quality. If then Being is both substance and quantity, it is two, not one; if only substance, it is not infinite and has no magnitude; for to have that it will have to be a quantity.

185a20–185b5

14. *Again, "one" itself, no less than "being," is used in many senses, so we must consider in what sense the word is used when it is said that the All is one.*

Now we say that (a) the continuous is one or that (b) the indivisible is one, or (c) things are said to be "one," when their essence is one and the same, as "liquor" and "drink."

If (a) their One is one in the sense of continuous, it is many; for the continuous is divisible ad infinitum.

There is, indeed, a difficulty about part and whole, perhaps not relevant to the present argument, yet deserving consideration on its own account—namely, whether the part and the whole are one or more than one, and how they can be one or many, and, if they are more than one, in what sense they are more than one. (Similarly with the parts of wholes which are not continuous.) Further, if each of the two parts is indivisibly one with the whole, the difficulty arises that they will be indivisibly one with each other also. 185b5–16

15. *But to proceed: If (b) their One is one as indivisible, nothing will have quantity or quality, and so the one will not be infinite, as Melissus says—nor, indeed, limited, as Parmenides says, for though the limit is indivisible, the limited is not.* 185b16–19

16. *But if (c) all things are one in the sense of having the same definition, like "raiment" and "dress," then it turns out that they are maintaining the Heraclitean doctrine, for it will be the same thing,—"to be good" and "to be bad" and "to be good" and "to be not good,"— and so the same thing will be "good" and "not good," and man and horse; in fact, their view will be, not that all things are one, but that they are nothing; and that "to be of such-and-such a quality" is the same as "to be of such-and-such a size."* 185b19–25

COMMENTARY OF ST. THOMAS

20. After he has set forth the opinions of the philosophers concerning principles, here Aristotle argues against them.

First he argues against those who spoke unnaturally about nature. Secondly, where he says, **"The physicists, on the other hand . . ."** [33], he argues against those who spoke of nature in a natural way.

Concerning the first part he makes two points. First he argues against the position of Melissus and Parmenides, and secondly against their arguments, where he says, **"Further the arguments they use . . ."** [18].

Concerning the first part he makes two points. First he argues against the position that "being is one" by using an argument dealing with the "being" which is the subject in this proposition. Secondly, where he says, **"Again, 'one' itself . . ."** [14], he uses an argument dealing with the "one" which is the predicate.

21. He says first [13] that that which should be taken primarily as a principle in arguing against the aforesaid position is the fact that that which is, i.e., being, is said in many ways. For we must ask of those who say that being is one how they are using "being": whether they take it for substance, or for quality, or for one of the other genera. And because substance is divided into the universal and the particular, i.e., into first and second substance, and further into many species, we must ask the following questions. Do they say that being is one as one man or as one horse, or as one soul, or as one quality, such as white or hot or some other such thing? For it makes a great difference which of these is said.

Hence, if being is one, it must either be substance and accident together, or it must be accident alone, or substance alone.

If, however, it is substance and accident together, then being will not be one only, but two. Nor does it differ with reference to this whether substance and accident are together in one thing as one or as different. For even though they are together in one thing, they are not one simply, but one in subject. And so by positing substance with accident it follows that they are not one simply, but many.

If, however, it is said that being is accident only and not substance, this is altogether impossible. For accident can in no way be without substance. For every accident is said of substance as of its subject, and the very definition of accident involves this.

If, however, it is said that being is substance only without accident, then it follows that it would not be a quantity, for quantity is an accident. And this is contrary to the position of Melissus. For he held that being was infinite, whence it follows that it is quantity, because the infinite, properly speaking, does not exist except in quantity. And substance and quality and the like are not said to be infinite except accidentally insofar as they are, for instance, together with quantity. Since, then, Melissus held being to be infinite, he cannot hold that it is substance without quantity. If, therefore, being is substance and quantity together, it follows that being is not one only, but two. If, however, it is substance alone, it is not infinite, because it will not have magnitude or quantity. Hence what Melissus says, namely, that being is one, can in no way be true.

22. Then where he says, **"Again 'one' itself. . ."** [14], he sets forth his second argument which deals with the "one."

Concerning this he makes two points. First he gives the argument. Secondly, where he says, **"Even the** more recent . . ." [17], he shows how some have erred in the solution of this question.

He says first that just as being is said in many ways, so also is one. And so we must consider in what way they say that all things are one.

For "one" is used in three ways: either as the continuous is one, such as a line or a body, or as the indivisible is one, such as a point, or as those things are said to be one whose nature [ratio] or definition is one, as drink and wine are said to be one.

First, therefore, he shows that we cannot say that all are one by continuity, because a continuum is in a certain respect many. For every continuum is divisible to infinity, and so contains many in itself as parts. Hence whoever holds that being is a continuum must hold that it is in a certain respect many.

And this is true, not only because of the number of the parts, but also because of the difference which seems to exist between the whole and the parts.

For there is a question whether the whole and the parts are one or many. And although this question, perhaps, does not pertain to the matter at hand, it is, nevertheless, worthy of consideration for its own sake. And here we consider not only the continuous whole, but also the contiguous whole whose parts are not continuous, such as the parts of a house which are one by contact and composition. It is clear that that which is a whole accidentally is the same as its parts. But this is not true of that which is a whole simply. For if that which is a whole simply were the same as one of the parts, then for the same reason it would be the same as another of the parts. But things which are identical with the same thing are identical with each other. And thus it

would follow that both parts, if they are held simply to be the same as the whole, would be identical with each other. Hence it would follow that the whole would be indivisible having no diversity of parts.

23. Next where he says, "**But to proceed . . .**" [15], he shows that it is impossible for all to be one as the indivisible is one. For that which is indivisible cannot be a quantity, since every quantity is divisible. As a result of this it cannot be a quality, if it is understood that we are speaking of a quality which is founded upon quantity. And if it is not a quantity, it cannot be finite as Parmenides has said, nor can it be infinite as Melissus has said. For an indivisible terminus, such as a point, is an end and is not finite. For the finite and the infinite are found in quantity.

24. Next where he says, "**But if all things . . .**" [16], he shows how it cannot be said that all things are one in definition [ratio]. For if this were true, three absurdities would follow.

The first is that contraries would be one according to definition [ratio], so that the definitions of good and evil would be the same, just as Heraclitus held the definitions of contraries to be the same, as is made clear in Metaphysics, IV.

The second absurdity is that the definitions [ratio] of the good and the non-good would be the same, because non-good follows upon evil. And thus it would follow that the definitions of being and non-being would be the same. And it would also follow that all beings would not only be one being, as they hold, but also they would be non-being or nothing. For things which are one in definition are so related that they may be used interchangeably as predicates. Whence if being and nothing are one according to definition, then it follows, that if all are one being, all are nothing.

The third absurdity is that the different genera, such as quantity and quality, would be the same according to definition [ratio]. He sets forth this absurdity where he says ". . . 'to be of **such-and-such a quality' is the same as 'to be of such-and-such a size'"** [16].

We must note however, that, as the Philosopher says in Metaphysics, IV, against those who deny principles there can be no unqualified demonstration which proceeds from what is more known simply. But we may use a demonstration to contradiction which proceeds from those things which are supposed by our adversary, which things are, for the time being, less known simply. And so the Philosopher, in this argument, uses many things which are less known than the fact that beings are many and not only one—the point about which he argues.

The Later Philosophers Also Were Involved in This Same Error, Namely, That the One and the Many Could Not in Any Way Concur

The Text of Aristotle

17. *Even the more recent of the ancient thinkers were in a pother lest the same thing should turn out in their hands both one and many. So some, like Lycophron, were led to omit "is," others to change the mode of expression and say "the man has been whitened" instead of "is white," and "walks" instead of "is walking," for fear that if they added the word "is" they should be making the one to be many—as if "one" and "being," were always used in one and the same sense. What "is" may be many either in definition (for example "to be white" is one thing, "to be musical" another, yet the same thing may be both, so the one is many) or by division, as the whole and its parts. On this point, indeed, they were already getting into difficulties and admitted that the one was many—as if there was any difficulty about the same thing being both one and many, provided that these are not opposites; for "one" may mean either "potentially one" or "actually one."*   185b25–186a5

COMMENTARY OF ST. THOMAS

25. Having disproven the opinion of Parmenides and Melissus that being is one, the Philosopher here shows that certain later philosophers fell into difficulty on this very same problem.

Parmenides and Melissus erred because they did not know how to distinguish the uses of the term "one." Thus, what is one in a certain respect, they said was one simply. But the later philosophers, also not knowing how to distinguish the uses of the term "one," thought it absurd that one and the same thing should be in some way one and many. Yet, being convinced by the arguments, they were forced to believe it. And so Aristotle says that the later philosophers were "disturbed" (that is, fell into a difficulty similar to that of the ancients, i.e., Parmenides and Melissus) lest they be forced to say that one and the same thing is one and many. Now this seemed absurd to both groups of philosophers. So the earlier philosophers, holding that all is one, rejected all multiplicity. The later philosophers, on the other hand, tried to remove multiplicity from anything they held to be one.

26. Thus some, such as Lycophron, removed the verb is from propositions. They said that we must not say "man is white" but rather "white man." For they thought that man and white were in some way one, otherwise white would not be predicated of man. And it seemed to them that the word "is," since it is a verbal copula, must serve as a copula between two. And so, wishing to remove all multiplicity from that which is one, they said the verb "is" must not be used.

But because such speech seemed to be imperfect, and because an imperfect understanding was produced in the soul of him who heard if names were spoken without the addition of any verb, some, wishing to correct this, changed the mode of speech. They did not say "white man" because of the imperfection of this mode of speech. Nor did they say "man is white" lest they give the impression that there is multiplicity. Rather they said "man whitened," because by this expression "whitened" [albari] a thing is not understood (as it seemed to them), but rather a certain change in the subject.

18

And in like manner they said that we must not say "man is walking" but "man walks," lest by the addition of the verbal copula "is" they make that which they thought to be one (i.e., white man) to be many, as if one and being were used in only one way and not in many.

27. But this is false. For that which is one in one respect can be many in some other respect, as what is one in subject can be many in definition [ratio]. Thus the white and the musical are the same in subject but many in definition [ratio]. Hence it can be concluded that the one may be many.

This may happen also in another way. That which is actually one as a whole may be many according to a division of parts. Whence the whole is one in its totality, but it has multiplicity of parts.

And although those who wished to remove the verb "is" or alter it, as was said above, found some solution to the objection that things could be one in subject and many in definition [ratio], they failed altogether to answer the objection that a thing may be one as a whole but many in its parts. They still believed it to be something of an absurdity that the one should be many.

But it is not absurd if the one and the many are not taken as opposites. For the one in act and the many in act are opposed, but the one in act and the many in potency are not opposed. And because of this he adds that "one" is said in many ways, i.e., one in potency and one in act. And so nothing prohibits the same thing from being one in act and many in potency, as is clear with regard to the whole and the parts.

28. Finally he draws the conclusion which he had uppermost in mind, namely, that it is clear from the foregoing arguments that it is impossible for all beings to be one.

The Argument of Melissus Is Answered

The Text of Aristotle
Chapter 3

18. *If, then, we approach the thesis in this way it seems impossible for all things to be one. Further, the arguments they use to prove their position are not difficult to expose. For both of them reason contentiously—I mean both Melissus and Parmenides. Their premises are false and their conclusions do not follow. Or rather the argument of Melissus is gross and palpable and offers no difficulty at all: admit one ridiculous proposition and the rest follows—a simple enough proceeding.* 186a5–10

19. *The fallacy of Melissus is obvious. For he supposes that the assumption "what has come into being always has a beginning" justifies the assumption "what has not come into being has no beginning."* 186a10–13

20. *Then this also is absurd, that in every case there should be a beginning of the thing—not of the time and not only in the case of coming to be in the full sense but also in the case of coming to have a quality —as if change never took place suddenly. Again, does it follow that Being, if one, is motionless?* 186a13–16

21. *Why should it not move, the whole of it within itself, as parts of it do which are unities, e.g., this water? Again, why is qualitative change impossible?* 186a16–18

22. *But, further, Being cannot be one in form, though it may be in what it is made of. (Even some of the physicists hold it to be one in the latter way, though not in the former.) Man obviously differs from horse in form, and contraries from each other.* 186a19–22

COMMENTARY OF ST. THOMAS

29. Having disproved the position of Parmenides and Melissus, here the Philosopher begins to answer their arguments.

Concerning this he makes three points. First he shows how their arguments are to be answered. Secondly, where he says, **"The fallacy of Melissus . . ."** [19], he answers the argument of Melissus. Thirdly, where he says, **"The same kind of argument..."** [23], he answers the argument of Parmenides.

30. He says [18] that it is not difficult to answer the arguments with which Parmenides and Melissus reasoned. For each syllogized sophistically both in that they assumed false propositions and in that they did not observe the proper form of the syllogism. But the argument of Melissus is the more gross, that is, more vain and foolish, and does not cause any difficulty. For he assumed what is contrary to natural principles and what is manifestly false, namely, that being is not generated. And it is not a serious matter, granting one absurdity, if another should follow.

31. Next when he says, **"The fallacy of Melissus . . ."** [19], he answers the argument of Melissus, which argument is as follows.

What is made has a beginning. Therefore what is not made has no beginning. But being is not made. Therefore it has no beginning, and as a result has no end. But what has neither beginning nor end is infinite. Therefore being is infinite. But what is infinite is immobile, for it would not have outside itself that by which it would be moved. Furthermore what is infinite is one, because if there were many there must necessarily be something outside the infinite. Therefore being is one and infinite and immobile.

Furthermore, in order to show that being is not generated, Melissus used a certain argument which some natural philosophers also used. Aristotle gives this argument below, near the end of Book I.

32. Aristotle disproves this argument of Melissus on four counts.

He argues first against the statement of Melissus that if what is made has a beginning, then what is not made has no beginning. This does not follow. Rather it is a fallacy of consequent. For he argues from the destruction of the antecedent to the destruction of the consequent, whereas the correct form of argumentation would be the converse. Whence it does not follow that if a thing which is made has a beginning, then that which is not made does not have a beginning. The correct conclusion would be that if a thing does not have a beginning, then it is not made.

33. Secondly, where he says, **"Then this also is absurd . . ."** [20], he disproves the argument under discussion with reference to the inference that if something has no beginning, then it is infinite.

For "beginning" may be taken in two ways. In one way we speak of a beginning of time and of generation. And this meaning of beginning is taken when it is said that what is made has a beginning or what is not made has no beginning. In another sense, beginning is the beginning of a thing or a magnitude. And in this sense it would follow that if a thing has no beginning, then it is infinite.

Whence it is clear that Melissus uses the term "beginning" as if it had one

meaning only. Hence Aristotle says that it is absurd to say that every case of beginning is the beginning of a thing, that is, of a magnitude, so that the beginning of time and of generation is not another meaning of the term.

However a simple and instantaneous generation (which is the induction of a form in matter) does not have a beginning. For of a simple generation there is no beginning. But there is a beginning for a whole alteration whose terminus is a generation, since this would not be an instantaneous change. And because of this terminus this is sometimes called a generation.

34. Thirdly, where he says, **"Again does it follow . . ."** [21], he disproves the above position with reference to its third inference, namely, that because being is infinite, it is immobile.

He shows in two ways that this does not follow. First it does not follow in regard to local motion. For a part of water could be moved within water so that it is not moved to any extrinsic place. In this case it would be moved by a joining and separation of the parts. And likewise, if the whole infinite body were water, it would be possible for the parts of it to be moved within the whole and not proceed outside the place of the whole. Again he disproves this with reference to the motion of alteration. For nothing prevents the infinite from being altered either as a whole or in its parts, for it would not be necessary to posit something outside the infinite to account for this.

35. Fourthly, where he says, **"But further . . ."** [22], he disproves the given argument with reference to its fourth inference by which it is concluded that, if being is infinite, it is one. For it does not follow that it is one ac-

cording to species, but rather that it is one according to matter, just as some of the philosophers of nature have held that all things are one according to matter, but not according to species. For it is obvious that man and horse differ in species, and in like manner contraries differ from each other in species.

The Argument of Parmenides Is Answered in A Number of Ways

The Text of Aristotle

23. *The same kind of argument holds good against Parmenides also, besides any that may apply specially to his view: the answer to him being, that "this is not true" and "that does not follow."* **186a22–24**

24. *His assumption that one is used in a single sense only is false, because it is used in several.* **186a24–25**

25. *His conclusion does not follow, because if we take only white things, and if "white" has a single meaning, none the less what is white will be many and not one. For what is white will not be one either in the sense that it is continuous or in the sense that it must be defined in only one way. "Whiteness" will be different from what has whiteness. Nor does this mean that there is anything that can exist separately, over and above what is white. For "whiteness" and "that which is white" differ in definition, not in the sense that they are things which can exist apart from each other. But Parmenides had not come in sight of this distinction.* **186a25–32**

26. *It is necessary for him, then, to assume not only that "being" has the same meaning, of whatever it is predicated, but further that it means (1) what just is and (2) what is just one.*

It must be so, for (1) an attribute is predicated of some subject, so that the subject to which "being" is attributed will not be, as it is something different from "being." Something, therefore, which is not will be. Hence "substance" will not be a predicate of anything else.

For the subject cannot be a being, unless "being" means several things, in such a way that each is something. But ex hypothesi "being" means only one thing. **186a32–186b4**

27. *If, then, "substance" is not attributed to anything, but other things are attributed to it, how does "substance" mean what is rather than what is not? For suppose that "substance" is also "white." Since the definition of the latter is different (for being cannot even be attributed to white, as nothing is which is not "substance," it follows that "white" is not-being—and that not in the sense of a particular not-being, but in the sense that it is not at all. Hence "substance" is not; for it is true to say that it is white, which we found to mean not-being. If to avoid this we say that even "white" means substance, it follows that "being," has more than one meaning.* **186b4–12**

28. *In particular, then, Being will not have magnitude, if it is substance. For each of the two parts must be in a different sense.* **186b12–14**

29. *(2) Substance is plainly divisible into other substances, if we consider the mere nature of a definition. For instance, if "man" is a substance, "animal" and "biped" must also be substances. For if not substances, they must be attributes—and if attributes, attributes either of (a) man or of (b) some other subject. But neither is possible.*

(a) An attribute is either that which may or may not belong to the subject or that in whose definition the subject of which it is an attribute is involved. Thus "sitting" is an example of a separable attribute " while "snubness" contains the definition of "nose," to which we attribute snubness. Further, the definition of the whole is not contained in the definitions of the contents or elements of the definitory formula; that of "man" for instance in "biped," or that of "white man" in "white." If then this is so, a man might possibly not be "biped," or the definition of "man" must come into the definition of "biped"—which is impossible, as the converse is the case. (b) If, on the other hand, we suppose that "biped" and "animal" are attributes not of man but of something else, and are not each of them a substance, then "man" too will be an attribute of something else. But we must assume that substance is not the attribute of anything, and that

the subject of which both "biped" and "animal" and each separately are predicated is the subject also of the complex "biped animal."

Are we then to say that the All is composed of indivisible substances? 186b14–35

COMMENTARY OF ST. THOMAS

36. Having disproved the argument of Melissus, here the Philosopher disproves the argument of Parmenides.

First he disproves the argument. Secondly, where he says, **"Some thinkers did . . ."** [30], he rejects what has been said by some who have argued badly against Parmenides.

Concerning the first part he makes two points. First [23] he sets forth the ways in which the argument of Parmenides is to be refuted. Secondly, where he says, **"His assumption . . ."** [24], he resolves the argument in these ways.

37. Concerning the first part it must be known that the argument of Parmenides was as follows, as is clear from Metaphysics, I. Whatever is other than being is non-being. But what is non-being is nothing. Therefore whatever is other than being is nothing. But being is one, therefore whatever is other than one is nothing. Therefore there is only one being. And from this he concluded that it would be immobile, because it would not have anything by which it would be moved, nor would there be anything outside of it by which it would be moved.

It is clear, moreover, from their very arguments that Parmenides considered being under the aspect [secundum rationem] of being, and so held it to be one and finite; whereas Melissus considered being from the point of view of matter. For Melissus considered being insofar as it is made or not made. And so he held being to be one and infinite.

38. Aristotle says, therefore, [23]

that the same approach must be used against the argument of Parmenides that was used against the argument of Melissus. For as the argument of Melissus was answered on the basis that he assumed false propositions and did not draw his conclusions according to the correct form of the syllogism, so also the argument of Parmenides is answered partly because he assumed false propositions and partly because he did not draw his conclusions correctly.

He says, however, that there are also other appropriate ways of arguing against Parmenides. For it is possible to argue against Parmenides from the propositions which he assumed and which are in a certain respect true and probable. But Melissus proceeded from what was false and improbable, for example, that being is not generated. Because of this, Aristotle did not argue against Melissus from the propositions which he assumed.

39. Next where he says, **"His assumption . . ."** [24], he follows the procedures just mentioned. First according to the first way, and secondly according to the second way, where he says, **"His conclusion does not follow . . ."** [25].

He says, therefore, first that Parmenides assumed false propositions because he held that what is, i.e., being, is used simply, i.e., in one way. Whereas in fact it is used in many ways.

For being is used in one way for substance, in another way for accident; and the latter is used in many ways according to the different genera. Being also can be used commonly for substance and accident.

Hence it is clear that the propositions assumed by Parmenides are true in one sense and false in another. For when it is said that whatever is other than being is non-being, this is true if being is taken, as it were, commonly for substance and accident. If, however, being is taken for accident alone or for substance alone, this is false, as will be shown below.

Likewise when he says that being is one, this is true if being is taken for some one substance or for some one accident. But this will not be true in the sense that whatever is other than that being is non-being.

40. Next where he says, **"His conclusion does not follow . . ."** [25], he follows the second method of answering the argument, i.e., that the argument of Parmenides does not draw its conclusion according to proper form.

He shows this first in an example. And secondly, where he says, **"It is necessary for him . . ."** [26], he adapts this example to the problem at hand.

He says, therefore, first [25] that it can be seen that the argument of Parmenides does not draw its conclusion properly because of the fact that the form of argumentation used is not efficacious in every matter. And this could not be true if a proper form of argumentation were used. For if we take "white" in the place of "being," and if we say that "white" signifies one thing only and is not used equivocally, and if we say that whatever is other than white is non-white, and whatever is non-white is nothing, then it will not follow that white would be one only. For it will not be necessary that all white things are one continuum. Or, to put it differently, white will not neces-

sarily be one by continuity, i.e., from the fact that white is a continuum, it will not be one simply. For a continuum is in a certain respect many, as was said above.

And in like manner white will not be one in definition [ratio], for the white and that which is receptive of the white are different in definition [ratio]. Furthermore there will not be something other than white, as it were, separated from it. For the white is not other than that which is receptive of it because the white is separable from that which is receptive of it, but because the definitions [ratio] of the white and of that which is receptive of it are different. But it was not yet known at the time of Parmenides that something could be one in subject and many in definition [ratio].

41. Next where he says, **"It is necessary for him . . ."** [26], he adapts this example to the matter at hand in order to show how what he has said of the white also applies to being.

Concerning this he makes two points. First he shows that it does not follow that being is one simply. For subject and accident are different according to definition [ratio]. Secondly, where he says, **"In particular then . . ."** [28], he shows that this does not follow because of the multiplicity of parts.

Concerning the first part he makes two points. First he shows that when it is said that "whatever is other than being is non-being," this "being" cannot be taken to mean accident alone. Secondly, where he says, **"If, then, substance . . ."** [27], he shows that this "being" cannot be taken to mean substance alone.

42. He says, therefore, first [26] that when it is said that "whatever is other than being is non-being," if "being" is said to signify one thing, then it will be

necessary that it signify not some one being or what is predicated of some one thing. Rather it will signify what truly is, i.e., substance, and it will signify what is truly one, i.e., the indivisible. For if being were to signify accident, then, since accident would be predicated of a subject, the subject could not be that to which the accident, which is called being, occurs. For if whatever is other than being is non-being (i.e., other than accident), and if the subject is other than the accident, which is here said to be being, then it follows that the subject is nonbeing. And so when accident, which is being, is predicated of the subject which is non-being, it follows that being is predicated of non-being. Hence, Aristotle concludes, "Something, therefore, which is not will be," that is, it will follow that non-being is being. This, however, is impossible. For what is first of all assumed in the sciences is that contradictories are not to be predicated of each other, as is said in Metaphysics, IV. Whence he concludes that if anything is truly being, as is supposed in the proposition "whatever is other than being is non- being," it follows that it is not an accident inhering in something else. For in this case its subject would not be a being. That is, this subject would not have the nature [ratio] of being, unless being should signify many, so that each of the many would be a being. But it was assumed by Parmenides that being signifies one only.

43. Next where he says, **"If, then, substance . . ."** [27], after he has concluded that "being" cannot refer to accident when it is said that "whatever is other than being is non-being," he shows further that "being" cannot refer to substance either. Whence he says that if what truly is does not happen to

something, but other things happen to it, then in the proposition "whatever is other than being is non-being," it is necessary that "what truly is," i.e., substance, be signified by being rather than by non-being.

But this cannot stand. For let it be held that that which truly is, i.e., substance, is white. But white is not that which truly is. For it has already been said that that which truly is cannot happen to something. And this is so because what is not truly, i.e., what is not substance, is not that which is, i.e., is not being. But what is other than being, i.e., other than substance, is non-being. Hence it follows that white is non-being, not only in the sense that it is not this being, as a man is not this being which is an ass, but also in the sense that it is not in any way. For he says that whatever is other than being is non-being, and what is nonbeing is nothing. From this, therefore, it follows that non-being would be predicated of that which truly is, because white is predicated of substance, which truly is. And white does not signify being, as was said. Whence it follows that being is non-being. And this indeed is impossible, because one contradictory is not predicated of another.

Whence, if in order to avoid this inconsistency, we say that true being signifies not only the subject, but also the white itself, it follows that being will signify many. And thus there will not be only one being, for subject and accident are many according to nature [ratio].

44. Next where he says, **"In particular then . . ."** [28], he shows, because of the multiplicity of parts, that it does not follow from the argument of Parmenides that there is only one being. He shows this first with reference to quantitative parts and secondly

with reference to the parts of definition [ratio], where he says, **"Substance is plainly divisible . . ."** [29].

He says, therefore, first that if being signifies only one thing, not only will it not be accident with subject, but neither will it be a magnitude. For every magnitude is divisible into parts. But the natures [ratio] of each of the parts are not the same, but different. Whence it follows that this one being is not a corporeal substance.

45. Secondly, where he says, **"Substance is plainly divisible . . ."** [29], he shows that this being cannot be a definable substance.

For in a definition it is clear that that which truly is, i.e., the substance, is divided into many, each one of which is what truly is, i.e. substance, and each one of which has a different nature [ratio]. Let us suppose that man is one thing which truly is. Since man is a two-footed animal, it is necessary that animal be and that two-footed be. And each of these will be what truly is, i.e., substance. And if they are not substances, they are accidents, either of man or of some other thing. But it is impossible that they be accidents of man.

And to make this clear he assumes two things.

First he assumes that "accident" is used in two ways. One type of accident is separable, and as such can be in something or not in it, for example, to sit. Another type of accident is inseparable and per se. And this latter is the accident in whose definition is placed the subject in which it is. For example, the snub is a per se accident of nose, because nose is placed in the definition of the snub. For the snub is a curved nose.

The second thing which he assumes is that if certain things are placed in the definition of that which is defined, or in the definition of the things on which

the definition depends, then it is impossible that the whole definition of that which is defined be placed in the definition of these certain things. Thus two-footed is placed in the definition of man, and certain other things are placed in the definition of two-footed or animal, from which [i.e., from two-footed and animal] man is defined. Hence it is impossible that man be placed in the definition of two-footed or in the definition of any of the things which fall in the definition of two-footed or of animal. Otherwise we would have a circular definition, and one and the same thing would be both prior and posterior, better known and less known. For every definition is from the prior and the better known, as is said in Topics, VI. And for the same reason, when white is placed in the definition of white man, it is impossible for white man to be placed in the definition of white.

These things having been assumed, the argument is as follows. If two-footed is an accident of man, it must be either a separable accident (and thus it could happen that man is not two-footed, which is impossible) or an inseparable accident (and thus it will be necessary that man be placed in the definition of two-footed). But this also is impossible, because two-footed is placed in the definition of man. It is impossible, therefore, that two-footed be an accident of man. For the same reason animal cannot be an accident. If, however, it is said that both are accidents of something else, it would follow that man also would be an accident of something else. But this is impossible, for it has already been said above that that which truly is is an accident of nothing. But man was assumed to be that which truly is, as is clear from what was said above.

That it would follow that man would be an accident of another if animal and two-footed were accidents of another, he shows as follows. What is said of both animal and two-footed taken separately may be said of them taken together, i.e., two-footed animal. And what is said of two-footed animal may be said of that which is from them, i.e., man, because man is nothing other than a two-footed animal.

Therefore it is clear that if being is held to be one only, we cannot hold that there are quantitative parts, or parts of a magnitude, or parts of a definition. Therefore it follows that every being is numerically indivisible. Otherwise, while holding being to be one, we would be forced to posit a multiplicity because of the parts.

46. The Commentator, however, says that in the passage beginning, **"But we must assume . . ."** [29], Aristotle sets forth the second argument of Parmenides to show that being is one. And this argument is as follows. A being which is one is substance and not accident (and by substance he means body). If, however, that body is divided into two halves, it will follow that being is predicated of each half and of the union of the two. And this either proceeds to infinity, which is impossible in itself, or else the being is divided into points. But this also is impossible. Hence it follows that being is an indivisible one.

But this exposition is fabricated and contrary to the intention of Aristotle, as is sufficiently clear from an examination of the letter of the text according to the first explanation.

He Disproves the Position of Those Who Said That Non-Being Is Something

The Text of Aristotle

30. *Some thinkers did, in point of fact, give way to both arguments. To the argument that all things are one if being means one thing, they conceded that not-being is; to that from bisection, they yielded by positing atomic magnitudes.* 187a1–3

31. *But obviously it is not true that if being means one thing, and cannot at the same time mean the contradictory of this, there will be nothing which is not, for even if what is not cannot be without qualification, there is no reason why it should not be a particular not-being.* 187a3–6

32. *To say that all things will be one, if there is nothing besides Being itself, is absurd. For who understands "being itself" to be anything but a particular substance? But if this is so, there is nothing to prevent there being many beings, as has been said.*

It is, then, clearly impossible for Being to be one in this sense. 187a6–11

COMMENTARY OF ST. THOMAS

47. After the Philosopher has disproved the argument of Parmenides by bringing forth certain inconsistencies found in it, he here disproves the position of those who have conceded these inconsistencies.

Concerning this he makes two points. First he sets forth their position. Secondly, he disproves it where he says, **"But obviously it is not..."** [31].

48. It must be noted first that [in the preceding lesson] the Philosopher used two arguments against the argument of Parmenides. He used one to show that, because of the diversity of subject and accident, it does not follow from the argument of Parmenides that all is one. This argument led to the absurdity that non-being is being, as is clear from what was said above. The other argument proceeded to show that the conclusion that all is one does not follow because, if it were a magnitude, it would follow that this magnitude is indivisible. For if it were divisible, there would be some sort of multiplicity.

49. The Platonists, however, gave in to each argument, conceding the impossibilities to which they led.

They accepted the first argument which led to the conclusion that non-being would be being. Suppose that someone were to say that being signifies one thing, either substance alone or accident alone, and because of this he might also wish to say that all things are one—in regard to this argument, I say, they accepted [the conclusion] that non-being would be being.

For Plato said that accident is non-being. And because of this it is said in Metaphysics, VI that Plato held that sophistry dealt with nonbeing, because it treated most of all those things which are predicated per accidens. Therefore Plato, understanding being to be substance, conceded the first proposition of Parmenides who said that whatever is other than being is non-being. For Plato held that accident, which is other than substance, was non-being.

He did not, however, concede the second proposition, namely, that whatever is non-being is nothing. For although he would say that accident is non-being, he did not say that accident is nothing, but rather that it is something. And because of this, according to Plato, it does not follow that being is one only.

But Plato, when he made magnitudes to be indivisible by dissection, that is, when he said that a magnitude is terminated in indivisibles by division, did assent to the other argument which led to the conclusion that a magnitude would be indivisible. For he held that bodies are resolved into surfaces, and surfaces into lines, and lines into indivisibles, as is clear in De Caelo et Mundo, III.

50. Next where he says, **"But obviously . . ."** [31], he disproves the above position in regard to the point that Plato conceded, namely, that non-being is something. In regard to the other point, namely, that Plato held that there are indivisible magnitudes, this is disproved in its proper place in the following books of natural science.

He disproves the first point in two ways. First he shows that it does not follow from the argument of Plato that non-being is something. Secondly, he disproves Plato's remark that unless we hold this i.e., that the non-being which is accident is something), it will follow that all is one. He does this where he says, **"To say that all things . . ."** [32].

51. He says, therefore, first [31] that the argument by which Plato concluded that being signifies one clearly does not follow. For he held that being is a genus and is predicated univocally of all things by a participation in the first being. And further he held that contradictories cannot be true at the same time. From these two points he thought that it followed that non- being is not nothing, but something. For

if being signifies the one, which is substance, it will be necessary that whatever is not substance is non-being. For if it were being, then since being does not signify anything but substance, it would follow that it would be substance. And so it would at once be substance and non-substance, in which case contradictories would be true at the same time. If, therefore, it is impossible for contradictories to be true at the same time, and if being signifies the one, which is substance, it would follow that whatever is not substance is non-being. But there is something which is not substance, namely, accident. Therefore something is non-being. And so it is not true that non-being is nothing.

But Aristotle shows that this does not follow. For if being signifies principally the one, which is substance, there is nothing to prevent one from saying that accident, which is not substance, is not being simply. But because of this it is not necessary to say that that which is not something, i.e., not substance, is absolute non-being. Hence, although accident is not being simply, it cannot, indeed, be called absolute nonbeing.

52. Next where he says, **"To say that all things . . ."** [32], he shows further that, if the non-being which is accident is not something, it does not follow that all is one. For if being can mean only substance, which truly is, then he says that it is absurd to hold that it would follow that all things are one unless there is something outside of being. For if there is substance, there is nothing to prevent there being a multiplicity of substances, as has already been said, even if magnitude and accident are removed. For the definition of substance is divided into the many things which are in the genus of substance, as man is divided into animal

and two-footed. And further it follows that according to the diverse differentiae of a genus there are many substances in act. And finally he draws the conclusion which he had uppermost in mind, namely, that all things are not one, as Parmenides and Melissus said.

The Opinions of the Physicists Who Spoke of the Principles As Natural Philosophers

The Text of Aristotle
Chapter 4

33. The physicists on the other hand have two modes of explanation.

The first set make the underlying body one—either one of the three or something else which is denser than fire and rarer than air—then generate everything else from this, and obtain multiplicity by condensation and rarefaction. Now these are contraries, which may be generalized into "excess and defect." (Compare Plato's "Great and Small"—except that he makes these his matter, the one his form, while the others treat the one which underlies as matter and the contraries as differentiae, i.e., forms.)

The second set assert that the contrarieties are contained in the one and emerge from it by separation, for example Anaximander and also all those who assert that "what is" is one and many, like Empedocles and Anaxagoras; for they too produce other things from their mixture by segregation. These differ, however, from each other in that the former imagines a cycle of such changes, the latter a single series. Anaxagoras again made both his "homogeneous" substances and his contraries infinite in multitude, whereas Empedocles posits only the so-called elements.

187a12–26

COMMENTARY OF ST. THOMAS

53. After the Philosopher has disproved the opinion concerning principles of those who did not speak of nature as natural philosophers, he here pursues the opinions of those who, not disregarding motion, spoke of the principles of nature as natural philosophers. And he calls these men physicists, i.e., natural philosophers.

Concerning this he makes two points. First he sets forth the diversity of their opinions. Secondly he examines one of these opinions, where he says, **"The theory of Anaxagoras ..."** [34].

54. He says first that according to the opinion of the natural philosophers there are two ways in which things are generated from principles. One of the opinions was advanced by the natural philosophers who held that there is only one material principle. This principle would be either one of three elements, i.e., fire, air, and water (for no one made earth alone the prin-

ciple, as was said above) or else some intermediate between them, for example, that which would be more dense than fire and more subtle than air. They then said that all other things were generated from this one principle by rarity and density. For example, those who made air to be the principle said that fire was generated from air by rarefaction, and water by condensation. However, the dense and the rare are contraries and are reduced to excess and defect as to something more universal. For the dense is what has much matter, whereas the rare has little.

55. And thus they agreed in a certain respect with Plato who held that the great and the small are principles which also pertain to excess and defect. But they differed from Plato as follows. Plato held that the great and the small are on the side of matter, because he posited one formal principle which is a certain idea participated in by dif-

ferent things according to a diversity of matter; the ancient natural philosophers, on the other hand, maintained a contrariety on the part of form, because they held that the first principle is one matter from which many things were constituted in being according to different forms.

56. Other natural philosophers, however, held that things come to be from principles in such a way that contraries themselves and different things are drawn forth from one thing in which they already existed, as it were, mixed and confused.

But they differed as follows. Anaximander held that the principle is one confused state in which there are not many things mixed together. Thus he held one principle only. But Empedocles and Anaxagoras held rather that the principles are the very things which are mixed together in that one confused state. And so they held many principles, although they also held that this one confused state is in some way a principle.

57. But Anaxagoras and Empedocles differed on two points. First, Empedocles held that there is a certain cycle of mixing and separating. For he held that the world has been made and corrupted many times; that is to say, when the world has been corrupted by friendship gathering all into one, the world is then generated again by strife separating and distinguishing. And thus the distinction of things follows upon their being confused, and vice versa. But Anaxagoras held that the world was made only once, such that from the beginning all things were mixed into one. But mind, which began to draw out and to distinguish, will never cease to do this, so that all things never will be mixed into one.

They also differed in another way. Anaxagoras held that the principles are infinite parts which are alike and contrary. Thus there are infinite parts of flesh which are like each other and infinite parts of bone and other things which have similar parts, yet each has a contrariety to the others. Thus the contrariety of the parts of bone to the parts of blood is that of the dry to the moist. But Empedocles held as principles only those four things which are commonly called elements, i.e., fire, air, water, and earth.

LECTURE 9 [187a27–188a18]
The Opinion of Anaxagoras That the Principles Are Infinite Is Refuted

The Text of Aristotle

34. *The theory of Anaxagoras that the principles are infinite in multitude was probably due to his acceptance of the common opinion of the physicists that nothing comes into being from not-being. For this is the reason why they use the phrase "all things were together" and the coming into being of such and such a kind of thing is reduced to change of quality, while some spoke of combination and separation.* **186a26–31**

35. *Moreover, the fact that the contraries proceed from each other led them to the conclusion.* **186a31–32**

36. *The one, they reasoned, must have already existed in the other; for since everything that comes into being must arise either from what is or from what is not, and it is impossible for it to arise from what is not (on this point all the physicists agree) they thought that the truth of the alternative necessarily followed, namely that things come into being out of existent things, i.e., out of things already present, but imperceptible to our senses because of the smallness of their bulk.* **186a32–187b1**

37. *So they assert that everything has been mixed in everything, because they saw everything arising out of everything. But things, as they say, appear different from one another and receive different names according to the nature of the particles which are numerically predominant among the innumerable constituents of the mixture. For nothing, they say, is purely and entirely white or black or sweet, bone or flesh, but the nature of a thing is held to be that of which it contains the most.* **187b1–7**

38. *Now (1) the infinite qua infinite is unknowable, so that what is infinite in multitude or size is unknowable in quantity, and what is infinite in variety of kind is unknowable in quality. But the principles in question are infinite both in multitude and in kind. Therefore it is impossible to know things which are composed of them; for it is when we know the nature and quantity of its components that we suppose we know a complex.* **187b7–13**

39. *Further (2) if the parts of a whole may be of any size in the direction either of greatness or of smallness (by "parts" I mean components into which a whole can be divided and which are actually present in it), it is necessary that the whole thing itself may be of any size. Clearly, therefore, since it is impossible for an animal or plant to be indefinitely big or small, neither can its parts be such, or the whole will be the same. But flesh, bone, and the like are the parts of animals, and the fruits are the parts of plants. Hence it is obvious that neither flesh, bone, nor any such thing can be of indefinite size in the direction either of the greater or of the less.* **187b13–21**

40. *Again (3) according to the theory all such things are already present in one another and do not come into being but are constituents which are separated out, and a thing receives its designation from its chief constituent. Further, anything may come out of anything—water by segregation from flesh and flesh from water. Hence, since every finite body is exhausted by the repeated abstraction of a finite body, it seems obviously to follow that everything cannot subsist in everything else.* **187b21–27**

41. *For let flesh be extracted from water and again more flesh be produced from the remainder by repeating the process of separation; then, even though the quantity separated out will continually decrease, still it will not fall below a certain magnitude. If, therefore, the process comes to an end, everything will not be in everything else (for there will be no flesh in the remaining water); if on the other hand it does not, and further extraction is always possible,*

there will be an infinite multitude of finite equal particles in a finite quantity—which is impossible.   187b27–34

42. *Another proof may be added: since every body must diminish in size when something is taken from it, and flesh is quantitatively definite in respect both of greatness and smallness, it is clear that from the minimum quantity of flesh no body can be separated out; for the flesh left would be less than the minimum of flesh.*   187b35–188a2

43. *Lastly (4) in each of his infinite bodies there would be already present infinite flesh and blood and brain—having a distinct existence, however, from one another, and no less real than the infinite bodies, and each infinite: which is contrary to reason.*   188a2–5

44. *The statement that complete separation never will take place is correct enough, though Anaxagoras is not fully aware of what it means. For affections are indeed inseparable. If then colors and states had entered into the mixture, and if separation took place, there would be a "white" or a "healthy" which was nothing, but white or healthy, i.e. was not the predicate of a subject. So his "Mind" is an absurd person aiming at the impossible, if he is supposed to wish to separate them, and it is impossible to do so, both in respect of quantity and of quality—of quantity, because there is no minimum magnitude, and of quality, because affections are inseparable.*   188a5–13

45. *Nor is Anaxagoras right about the coming to be of homogeneous bodies. It is true there is a sense in which clay is divided into pieces of clay, but there is another in which it is not. Water and air are, and are generated, from each other but not in the way in which bricks come from a house and again a house from bricks.*   188a13–17

46. *And it is better to assume a smaller and finite number of principles, as Empedocles does.*   188a17–18

COMMENTARY OF ST. THOMAS

58. Having set forth the opinions of the natural philosophers concerning the principles, he here pursues one of these opinions, namely, that of Anaxagoras. For this opinion seemed to assign a common cause for all the species of motion.

The discussion is divided into two parts. In the first part he sets forth Anaxagoras' argument; in the second part he raises objections against it, where he says, **"Now the infinite ..."** [38].

Concerning the first part he makes three points. First he sets forth those things which Anaxagoras supposed and from which he argues. Secondly, where he says, **"The one, they reasoned ..."** [36], he sets forth the order of his argument. Thirdly, where he says, **"But things, as they say ..."** [37],

he sets forth Anaxagoras' response to a certain tacit objection.

59. Anaxagoras assumed two things from which he argued. The first of these is a point which is assumed by all of the natural philosophers, namely, that nothing comes to be from nothing. And Aristotle says that, because of this, Anaxagoras seemed to have held the opinion that the principles are infinite. For he accepted as true the common opinion of all philosophers of nature, namely, that what simply is not in no way comes to be. For they assumed this as a principle and then developed their different opinions.

60. Lest they would be forced to hold that something new comes to be which previously was in no way at all, some held that all things from the beginning existed together, either in

some one confused state, as Anaxagoras and Empedocles held, or in some natural principle, such as water, fire, and air, or some intermediate between these.

And in accordance with this they posited two modes of production.

Those who held that all things pre-existed together as in one material principle said that to come to be is nothing other than to be altered. For they said that all things come to be from that one material principle through its condensation and rarefaction.

Others, however, who held that all things pre-existed together in some one confused state and mixture of many, said that the coming to be of things is only a joining together and a separation.

All of these philosophers were deceived because they did not know how to distinguish between potency and act. For being in potency is, as it were, a mean between pure non-being and being in act. Therefore, those things which come to be naturally do not come to be from nonbeing simply, but from being in potency, and not, indeed, from being in act, as they thought. Hence things which come to be did not necessarily pre-exist in act, as they said, but only in potency.

61. Next where he says, **"Moreover the fact that . . ."** [35], he mentions the second thing which Anaxagoras assumed.

Anaxagoras said that contraries come to be from each other. For we see the cold come to be from the hot, and vice versa. And from this he concluded that, since nothing comes to be from nothing, one of the contraries pre-exists in the other.

And this is true, of course, in respect to potency. For the cold is in the hot in potency, but not in act, as Anaxagoras thought. For he was not aware of being in potency, which is a mean between pure non-being and being in act.

62. Next where he says, **"The one, they reasoned . . ."** [36], he sets forth the deductive order of the argument.

Anaxagoras proceeded as follows. If something comes to be, it is necessary that it should come to be either from being or from nonbeing. But he excluded one of these alternatives—namely, that something should come to be from non-being. He does this because of the common opinion of the philosophers mentioned above. Whence he concluded that the remaining member was correct, namely, that a thing comes to be from being. For example, if air comes to be from water, then air pre-existed. For it cannot be said that air comes to be from water unless air pre-existed in water. Hence he wished to say that everything which comes to be from something pre-existed in that from which it comes to be.

But because this seemed to be contrary to what appears to the senses (for it is not apparent to the senses that that which is generated from something pre-exists in it), he forestalled this objection by holding that that which comes to be from something pre-exists in it as certain most minute parts which are not sensible to us because of their smallness. For example, if air comes to be from water, certain minute parts of air are in the water, but not in that quantity in which it is generated. And so he said that by the gathering together of these parts of air by themselves, and by their separation from the parts of water, air comes to be.

Having accepted, therefore, that everything which comes to be from something pre-exists in it, he further assumed that everything comes to be from everything. Whence he concluded that everything would be mixed in everything else as minute, non-sensible parts.

And because an infinite variety of things can come to be from another, he said that infinite minute parts were in each thing.

63. Next where he says, **"But things, as they say . . ."** [37], he excludes a certain tacit objection.

It is possible for someone to object as follows. If infinite parts of everything are in everything, it would follow that things neither differ from each other nor appear to differ from each other.

Therefore, as if he were answering this objection, Anaxagoras says that things appear to differ from each other and are diversely named because of that which is dominant in them, even though there is an infinite number of minute parts contained in any mixture. And so nothing is purely and totally white or black or bone. Rather, that which abounds in each thing seems to be the nature of that thing.

64. Next where he says, **"Now the infinite . . ."** [38], Aristotle refutes the above mentioned position.

Concerning this he makes two points. First he disproves the position absolutely. Secondly, where he says, **" . . . and it is better . . ."** [46], he compares it to the opinion of Empedocles.

Concerning the first part he makes two points. First he sets forth arguments to disprove the opinion of Anaxagoras. Secondly, where he says, **"The statement that . . ."** [44], he disagrees with Anaxagoras' way of understanding his own position.

Concerning the first part he gives five arguments.

The first of these is as follows. Every

infinite thing, in that respect in which it is infinite, is unknown. He explains why he says "in that respect in which it is infinite." If it is infinite in respect to multitude or magnitude, it will be unknown in respect to quantity. If, however, it is infinite in respect to species (for example, if it is composed of an infinite variety of species), then it will be unknown according to quality. And the reason for this is that what is known by the intellect is grasped by the intellect with respect to all that belongs to that thing. But this cannot happen with regard to something infinite. If, therefore, the principles of a thing are infinite, they must be unknown either in respect to quantity or in respect to species.

But if the principles are unknown, those things which are from the principles must be unknown. He proves this as follows. We think that we know any composite when we know from what and from how many [principles] it is composed, i.e., when we know both the species and the quantity of the principles. It follows, therefore, from first to last that, if the principles of natural things are infinite, then natural things are unknown either in respect to quantity or in respect to species.

65. At the point where he says, **"Further if the parts . . ."** [39], he gives the second argument, which is as follows.

If the parts of a whole do not have a determinate quantity, either great or small, but can be any size, either great or small, it is not necessary that the whole have a determinate greatness or smallness. Rather the whole could have any size. This is so because the quantity of the whole comes from the parts. (But this must be understood of the parts existing in act in the whole, as flesh and nerve and bone exist in an animal. Hence he says, ". . . by parts I mean components into which a whole can be divided and which are actually present in it" . And by this he excludes the parts of a continuous whole which are in the whole in potency.)

But it is impossible that an animal or a plant or some such thing be related indeterminately to any size, whether great or small. For there is some quantity so large that no animal exceeds it in size. So also there is some quantity so small that no animal is found to be smaller. And the same must be said of plants. Therefore by denying the consequent it follows that the parts are not of indeterminate quantity. For what is true of the whole is true of the parts. But flesh and bone and things of this sort are parts of an animal, and fruits are parts of plants. Therefore it is impossible that flesh and bone and such things should have an indeterminate quantity, either greater or smaller. Therefore it is not possible that there should be certain parts of flesh or bone which are non-sensible because of smallness.

66. It seems, however, that what is said here is contrary to the statement that a continuum is divisible to infinity. For if the continuous is divisible to infinity, and flesh is, indeed, a kind of continuum, it seems that flesh is divisible to infinity. Therefore, some part of flesh, according to a division to infinity, goes beyond every determinate smallness.

But it must be pointed out that although a body, considered mathematically, is divisible to infinity, the natural body is not divisible to infinity. For in a mathematical body nothing but quantity is considered. And in this there is nothing repugnant to division to infinity. But in a natural body the form also is considered, which form requires a determinate quantity and also other accidents. Whence it is not possible for quantity to be found in the species of flesh except as determined within some termini.

67. He gives the third argument where he says, **"Again according to the theory . . ."** [40].

Concerning this he makes two points. First he sets forth certain things which are the basis of the argument. Secondly, where he says, **"For let flesh . . ."** [41], he sets forth the deductive order of the argument.

Concerning the first part he proposes three things.

The first is that according to the position of Anaxagoras, as was said above, all things are together. And from this Aristotle wishes to reduce Anaxagoras' argument to absurdity. For Anaxagoras said, as was pointed out, that all things which are of a certain kind, i.e., all things which are of like parts, such as flesh and bone and the like, are in each other, and do not come to be from nothing, but are separated from that in which they pre-exist. And each thing is named from that which abounds in it, i.e., from the largest number of parts existing in the thing.

The second point is that everything comes to be from everything, as water comes to be by separation from flesh, and in the same way flesh comes to be from water.

And the third point is that every finite body is reduced by a finite body. That is, if from some finite body, however large, a finite body, however small, is taken away, the smaller can be taken away from the larger until eventually the greater whole is consumed by the smaller through division.

And from these three points Aristotle concludes what he primarily intended, namely, that each thing is not in each thing. And this is contrary to the first of these three points. For in arguments which lead to absurdity the denial of one of the premises is the final conclusion.

68. Next where he says, **"For let flesh . . ."** [41], he develops his argument and assumes what was concluded in the preceding argument.

He says that if flesh is removed from water (since flesh is generated from water), and if again another separation of flesh is made from the remaining water, then although there will always remain a smaller quantity of flesh in the water, still the size of that flesh is not less than a certain smallness, i.e., there happens to be a certain small measure of flesh than which there will not be any smaller flesh, as is clear from the argument given above.

Therefore, having established that there is some small particle of flesh than which there is no smaller, he proceeds as follows.

If from water flesh is separated, and again other flesh, the process of separation will either stop or it will not. If it stops, then there is no flesh in the remaining water, and everything will not be in everything. If it does not stop, then some part of flesh will always remain in the water. Thus in the second separation the remaining flesh is smaller than in the first, and in the third it is smaller than in the second. And since we cannot proceed to infinity in smallness of parts, as was said, then the smallest parts of flesh are equal and infinite in number in some finite body of water. Otherwise separation could not proceed to infinity. It follows, therefore, that if the separation does not stop, but flesh is always removed from water to infinity, then in some finite magnitude, e.g., water, there are certain things which are finite in respect to quantity, and equal to each other, and infinite in respect to number, namely, the infinite smallest parts of flesh. But this is impossible and contrary to what was said above, namely, that every finite body is reduced by some finite body. Therefore the first point, namely, that everything is in everything, as Anaxagoras held, is also impossible.

69. We must note that it is not without reason that the Philosopher used the term "equal" in stating the last absurdity to which this position leads. For if the nature of quantity is considered, it is not absurd that an infinity of unequal parts be in a finite body. For if a continuum is divided according to the same proportion, it will be possible to proceed to infinity, for example, if we take a third of a whole, and then a third of the third, and so on. In this case, however, the parts were not taken as equal in quantity. But if the division is made according to equal parts, we will not be able to proceed to infinity even if we consider only the nature [ratio] of quantity which is found in a mathematical body.

70. He gives his fourth argument where he says, **"Another proof may be added . . ."** [42]. The argument is as follows.

Every body becomes a smaller one when something is taken from it, because every whole is greater than its parts. Since then the quantity of flesh is determinately great or small, as is clear from what was said above, there must be some smallest bit of flesh. Therefore from this nothing can be separated, because the remaining flesh would be smaller than this smallest piece of flesh. Therefore it is impossible that everything comes to be from everything by separation.

71. At the point where he says,

"Lastly in each . . ." [43], he gives his fifth argument, which is as follows. If infinite parts of each thing are in each thing, and everything is in everything, it follows that infinite parts of flesh and infinite parts of blood and brain are in an infinite number of bodies. And regardless of how much is separated, the same amount would always remain. Therefore it would follow that the infinite is in the infinite infinitely. But this is unthinkable.

72. Next where he says, **"The statement that . . ."** [44], he disproves the position of Anaxagoras according to Anaxagoras' own understanding of it.

He does this in two ways. First he shows that Anaxagoras did not understand his own position. Secondly, where he says, **"Nor is Anaxagoras . . ."** [45], he shows that Anaxagoras did not have sufficient evidence for holding this position.

He says, therefore, first that although Anaxagoras has in a certain respect spoken the truth, he himself did not understand what he said when he held that the process of separation would never end. For accidents can never be separated from substance; yet he held that there was a mixture not only of bodies but also of accidents. When something becomes white, he said that this happened by an abstraction of white from the previously existing mixture. If then colors and other accidents of this sort are mixed together, as he said, and if someone on this supposition says all things that are mixed can be separated, it would follow that there would be white and healthy, and yet there would be no subject of which these are predicated and in which they are. But this is impossible. Therefore the truth is that if accidents are in the mixture it is impossible that all mixed things can be separated.

Another absurdity results from the following. Anaxagoras held that all things were mixed from the very beginning, but intellect began to separate them. Now any intellect which attempts to do what cannot be done is not worthy of the name intellect. Hence that intellect will be inconsistent, intending the impossible, if it truly wishes this, i.e., wishes to separate things completely. For this is impossible both from the point of view of quantity, because there is no smallest magnitude, as Anaxagoras said, for from any small quantity something can be subtracted, and from the point of view of quality, because accidents are not separable from their subjects.

73. Next where he says, **"Nor is Anaxagoras . . ."** [45], he disproves this position by reason of the fact that Anaxagoras did not have sufficient evidence.

Since Anaxagoras saw that a thing is made large by the coming together of many small parts which are similar, as a stream is made from many brooks, he believed this to be the case for all things. And thus Aristotle says that Anaxagoras did not correctly understand the generation of things of the same species, i.e., he did not understand that a thing is not always generated by things which are similar in respect to species. For some things are both generated from and are resolved into things like unto themselves, as clay is divided into bricks; in other instances, however, this is not so. For some things are generated from that which is dissimilar. And in these instances there is not merely one mode of production. For some things are made by alteration from that which is unlike, as the sides of a house are made from clay and not from sides; whereas other things are made by composition, as the house is not made of houses, but of sides. It is in this way that air and water come to be from each other, i.e., as from the unlike.

Another reading here is "as the sides are from the house." And thus he sets forth a twofold way in which things come to be from the unlike, i.e., through composition, as the house is made of sides, and by resolution, as the sides come to be from the house.

74. Next where he says, "... and it is better . . ." [46], he disproves the position of Anaxagoras by comparing it with the opinion of Empedocles. He says that it is better to make the principles smaller in number and finite, as Empedocles does, than to make them many and infinite, as does Anaxagoras.

The Opinions of the Ancients Concerning the Contrariety of the First Principles

The Text of Aristotle
Chapter 5

47. *All thinkers then agree in making the contraries principles, both those who describe the All as one and unmoved (for even Parmenides treats hot and cold as principles under the names of fire and earth) and those too who use the rare and the dense. The same is true of Democritus also, with his plenum and void, both of which exist, he says, the one as being, the other as not-being. Again he speaks of differences in position, shape, and order, and these are genera of which the species are contraries, namely, of position, above and below, before and behind; of shape, angular and angle-less, straight and round.* **188a19–27**

48. *It is plain then that they all in one way or another identify the contraries with the principles. And with good reason. For first principles must not be derived from one another nor from anything else, while everything has to be derived from them. But these conditions are fulfilled by the primary contraries, which are not derived from anything else because they are primary, nor from each other because they are contraries.*

But we must see how this can be arrived at as a reasoned result, as well as in the way just indicated.

Our first presupposition must be that in nature nothing acts on, or is acted on by, any other thing at random, nor may anything come from anything else, unless we mean that it does so in virtue of a concomitant attribute. For how could "white" come from "musical," unless "musical" happened to be an attribute of the not-white or of the black? No, "white" comes from "not-white"—and not from any "not-white," but from black or some intermediate color. Similarly, "musical" comes to be from "not-musical," but not from any thing other than musical, but from "unmusical" or any intermediate state there may be.

Nor again do things pass into the first chance thing; "white" does not pass into "musical" (except, it may be, in virtue of a concomitant attribute), but into "not-white"—and not into any chance thing which is not white, but into black or an intermediate color; "musical" passes into "not-musical"—and not into any chance thing other than musical, but into "unmusical" or any intermediate state there may be.

The same holds of other things also: even things which are not simple but complex follow the same principle, but the opposite state has not received a name, so we fail to notice the fact that what is in tune must come from what is not in tune, and vice versa; the tuned passes into untunedness—and not into any untunedness, but into the corresponding opposite. It does not matter whether we take attunement, order, or composition for our illustration; the principle is obviously the same in all, and in fact applies equally to the production of a house, a statue, or any other complex. A house comes from certain things in a certain state of separation instead of conjunction, a statue (or any other thing that has been shaped) from shapelessness—each of these objects being partly order and partly composition.

If then this is true, everything that comes to be or passes away comes from, or passes into, its contrary or an intermediate state. But the intermediates are derived from the contraries—colors, for instance, from black and white. Everything, therefore, that comes to be by a natural process is either a contrary or a product of contraries. **188a27–188b26**

49. *Up to this point we have practically had most of the other writers on the subject with us, as I have said already; for all of them identify their elements, and what they calf their principles,*

with the contraries, giving no reason indeed for the theory, but constrained as it were by the truth itself.   **188b26–30**

50. *They differ, however, from one another in that some assume contraries which are more primary, others contraries which are less so: some those more knowable in the order of explanation, others those more familiar to sense. For some make hot and cold, or again moist and dry, the conditions of becoming; while others make odd and even, or again Love and Strife; and these differ from each other in the way mentioned.*   **188b30–35**

51. *Hence their principles are in one sense the same, in another different; different certainly, as indeed most people think, but the same inasmuch as they are analogous; for all are taken from the same table of columns, some of the pairs being wider, others narrower in extent. In this way then their theories are both the same and different, some better, some worse; some, as I have said, take as their contraries what is more knowable in the order of explanation, others what is more familiar to sense. (The universal is more knowable in the order of explanation, the particular in the order of sense; for explanation has to do with the universal, sense with the particular.) "The great and the small," for example, belong to the former class, "the dense and the rare" to the latter.*

It is clear then that our principles must be contraries.   **188b35–189a10**

COMMENTARY OF ST. THOMAS

75. Having set forth the opinions of the ancient philosophers concerning the principles of nature, Aristotle here begins to seek the truth.

He seeks it first by way of disputation, proceeding from probable opinions. Secondly, where he says, **"We will now give . . ."** [65], he determines the truth demonstratively.

Concerning the first part he makes two points. First he investigates the contrariety of the principles, secondly, where he says, **"The next question is . . ."** [52], he inquires about their number.

Concerning the first part he makes three points. First he sets forth the opinion of the ancients about the contrariety of the principles. Secondly, where he says, **"And with good reason . . ."** [48], he gives an argument in favor of this position. Thirdly he shows how the philosophers are related to each other in saying that the principles are contraries. He does this where he says, **"Up to this point . . ."** [49].

76. He says, therefore, first [47] that all of the ancient philosophers posited contrariety in the principles. And he makes this clear by citing three opinions of the philosophers.

For some philosophers have said that the whole universe is one immobile being. Of these, Parmenides said that all things are one according to reason, but many according to sense. And to the extent that there are many, he posited in them contrary principles, e.g., the hot and the cold. He attributed the hot to fire and the cold to earth.

Secondly there was the opinion of the natural philosophers who posited one material and mobile principle. They said that other things come to be from this principle according to rarity and density. Thus they held that the rare and the dense are principles.

A third opinion was advanced by those who posited many principles. Among them, Democritus held that all things come to be from indivisible bodies which are joined together. And in this contact with each other they left a sort of void. Such voids he called pores, as is clear in De Generatione, I. Therefore he held that all bodies are composed of the fixed and the empty, that is, composed of the plenum and the void. Hence he said that the plenum and the void are principles of nature. But he associated the plenum with being and the void with non-being. And although all of these indivisible bodies are one in nature, he said that different things are composed of them according to a diversity of figure, position, and order. Thus he held that the principles are contraries in the genus of position, i.e., above and below, before and behind, and also contraries in the genus of figure, i.e., the straight, the angular, and the circular. The principles also are contraries in the genus of order, i.e., prior and posterior. (These last contraries are not mentioned in the text because they are obvious.) And thus Aristotle concludes, by a sort of induction, that all of the philosophers held that the principles are contraries in some way. He makes no mention of the opinion of Anaxagoras and Empedocles because he has already explained their position at length above. However, they also placed a certain contrariety in the principles when they said that all things come to be through joining and separating, which agree in genus with the rare and the dense.

77. Next where he says, **"And with good reason"** [48], he gives a probable argument to show that the first principles are contraries. The argument is as follows.

Three things seem to belong to the very nature of principles. First, they are not from other things. Secondly, they are not from each other. Thirdly, all other things are from them. But these three notes are found in the primary contraries. Therefore the primary contraries are principles.

Now in order to understand what he means when he speaks of primary contraries, we must realize that some contraries are caused by other contraries, e.g., the sweet and the bitter are caused by the wet and the dry and the hot and the cold. Since, however, it is impossible to proceed to infinity, but one must come to certain contraries which are not caused by other contraries, he calls these last contraries the primary contraries.

Now the three conditions proper to principles mentioned above are found in these primary contraries. For things which are first are manifestly not from others. Moreover things which are contraries are manifestly not from each other. For even though the cold comes to be from the hot, insofar as that which was previously hot is later cold, nevertheless coldness itself never comes to be from heat, as will be pointed out later. The third point—precisely how all things come to be from the contraries—we must investigate more carefully.

78. Now in order to clarify this latter point he states first that neither action nor passion can occur between things which are contingent in the sense of merely happening to be together, or between things which are contingent in the sense of being indeterminate. Nor does everything come to be from everything, as Anaxagoras said, except perhaps accidentally.

This is first of all seen clearly in simple things. For white does not come to be from musical except accidentally insofar as white or black happen to be in the musical. But white comes to be per se from the non-white, and not from just any non-white, but from that non-white which is black or some mean color. And in like manner, the musical comes to be from the non-musical, and again not from just any non-musical, but from its opposite, which is called the unmusical, i.e., from that which is disposed to be musical but is not, or from some mean between these two. And for the same reason, a thing is not corrupted primarily and per se into just any contingent thing (e.g., the white into the musical) except accidentally. Rather white is corrupted per se into the non-white, and not into just any non-white, but into black or some mean color. And he says the same of the corruption of the musical and of other similar things. The reason for this is as follows. Whatever comes to be or is corrupted does not exist before it comes to be and does not exist after it is corrupted. Whence it is necessary that that which a thing comes to be per se and that into which a thing is corrupted per se be such that it includes in its nature [ratio] the non-being of that which comes to be or is corrupted.

And he shows that the same is true of composite things. He says that the situation is the same with composite things as with simple things, but is more hidden in composite things because the opposites of composite things have no names, as do the opposites of simple things. For the opposite of house has no name, although we give a name to the opposite of white. Hence if the composite is reduced to something with a name, it will be clear. For every composite consists of a certain harmony. Now the harmonious comes to be from the inharmonious, and the inharmonious from the harmonious. And in like manner, the harmonious is corrupted into the inharmonious (not any inharmonious, but the opposite). However, we can speak of the harmonious according to order alone, or according to composition. For some wholes consist of a harmony of order, e.g., an army; and other wholes consist of a harmony of composition, e.g., a house. And the nature [ratio] of each of these is the same. It is also clear that all composites come to be from the non-composed, for example, a house comes to be from non-composed things, and the figured from the non-figured. And in all such things nothing is involved except order and composition.

Thus it is clear by induction, as it were, that everything which comes to be or is corrupted comes to be from contraries or from some intermediate between them, or is corrupted into them. Moreover, intermediates between contraries come to be from the contraries, as the intermediate colors come to be from black and white. Hence he concludes that whatever comes to be according to nature is either a contrary, such as white and black, or comes to be from the contraries, such as the intermediates between the contraries.

This, then, is the principal conclusion which he intended to draw, namely, that all things come to be from contraries, which was the third characteristic of principles.

79. Next where he says, **"Up to this point . . ."** [49], Aristotle shows how the philosophers are related in holding that the principles are contraries. First he shows how they are related with reference to being moved toward this position. Secondly, where he says, **"They differ, however . . ."** [50], he shows how they are related in respect to the position itself.

He says, therefore, [49] as was pointed out above, that many of the philosophers followed the truth to the point where they held that the principles are contraries. Although they indeed held this position, they did not hold it as though moved by reason, but rather as forced to it by the truth itself. For truth is the good of the intellect, toward which the intellect is naturally ordered. Hence as things which lack knowledge are moved to their ends without reason [ratio], so, at times, the intellect of man, by a sort of natural inclination, tends toward the truth, though it does not perceive the reason [ratio] for the truth.

80. Next where he says, **"They differ, however, . . ."** [50], he shows how the aforesaid philosophers are related in respect to the position itself.

Concerning this he makes two points. First he shows how they differ in holding that the principles are contraries. Secondly, where he says, **"Hence their principles . . ."** [51], he shows how they both differ and agree.

He says, therefore, first that the philosophers who held that the principles are contraries differed in two ways. First, those who argued reasonably held that the principles are the primary contraries. Others, however, considering the matter less well, held that the principles are posterior [derived] contraries.

And of those who appealed to the primary contraries, some considered those contraries which were better known to reason, others those contraries which were better known to sense.

Or it could be said that this second difference explains the first. For those things which are better known to reason are prior simply, whereas those things which are better known to sense are posterior simply, and are prior relative to us. However, it is clear that the principles must be prior. Thus, those who judged "prior" according to what

is better known to reason held that the principles are those contraries which are prior simply. On the other hand, those who judged "prior" according to what is better known to sense held that the principles are those contraries which are posterior simply. Hence some held that the hot and the cold are first principles; others, the wet and the dry. And both of these are better known to sense. However the hot and the cold, which are active qualities, are prior to the wet and the dry, which are passive qualities, because the active is naturally prior to the passive.

Others, however, held principles which are better known to reason.

Among these, some held that the equal and the unequal are the principles. For example, the Pythagoreans, thinking that the substance of all things is numbers, held that all things are composed of the equal and the unequal as of form and matter. For they attributed infinity and otherness to the equal because of its divisibility. Whereas to the unequal they attributed finiteness and identity because of its indivisibility.

Others, however, held that the cause of generation and corruption is strife and friendship, that is, the cycles of Empedocles, which are also better known to reason. Whence it is clear that the diversity mentioned above appears in these positions.

81. Next where he says, **"Hence their principles . . ."** [51], he shows how there is also a certain agreement within the differences of the aforementioned positions. He concludes from what he has said above that the ancient philosophers in a way called the same things principles and in a way called different things principles. For they differed insofar as different philosophers assumed different contraries (as

was said above); yet they are the same insofar as their principles were alike according to analogy, i.e., proportion. For the principles taken by all of them have the same proportion.

And this is true in three respects. First, all the principles which they assumed are related as contraries. And thus Aristotle says that they all took their principles from the same columns, i.e., columns of contraries. For they all took contraries as their principles, even though the contraries differed. Nor is it remarkable that they took different principles from the columns of contraries. For among the contraries, some are containers, as the prior and more common; and others are contained, as the posterior and less common. Hence one way in which they spoke alike is that all of them took their principles from the order of contraries.

Another way in which they agree according to analogy is as follows. No matter what principles they accepted, one of these principles is better, and the other is worse. For example, friendship, or the plenum, or the hot, are better; but strife, or the void, or the cold, are worse. And the same thing is true of the other pairs of contraries. This is so because one of the contraries always has privation joined to it. For the source of contrariety is the opposition of privation and habit, as is said in Metaphysics, X.

Thirdly they agree according to analogy by reason of the fact that they all took principles which are better known. But some took principles which are better known to reason, others those which are better known to sense. Since reason treats the universal and sense treats the particular, universals (such as the great and the small) are better known to reason, whereas singulars (such as the rare and the dense, which are less common) are better known to sense.

Then as a final summary, he concludes with that which he had uppermost in mind, namely, the principles are contraries.

LECTURE 11 [189a11–b29]
There are Three Principles of Natural Things, No More, No Less

The Text of Aristotle
Chapter 6

52. The next question is whether the principles are two or three or more in number.

189a11–12

53. One they cannot be; for there cannot be one contrary.

189a12

54. Nor can they be innumerable, because, if so, Being will not be knowable;

189a12–13

55. and in any one genus there is only one contrariety, and substance is one genus;

189a13–14

56. also a finite number is sufficient, and a finite number, such as the principles of Empedocles, is better than an infinite multitude; for Empedocles professes to obtain from his principles all that Anaxagoras obtains from his innumerable principles.

189a14–17

57. Lastly, some contraries are more primary than others, and some arise from others—for example sweet and bitter, white and black—whereas the principles must always remain principles.

189a17–20

58. This will suffice to show that the principles are neither one nor innumerable.

Granted, then, that they are a limited number, it is plausible to suppose them more than two. For it is difficult to see how either density should be of such a nature as to act in any way on rarity or rarity on density. The same is true of any other pair of contraries; for Love does not gather Strife together and make things out of it, nor does Strife make anything out of Love, but both act on a third thing different from both. Some indeed assume more than one such thing from which they construct the world of nature.

189a20–27

59. Other objections to the view that it is not necessary to assume a third principle as a substratum may be added. (1) We do not find that the contraries constitute the substance of any thing. But what is a first principle ought not to be the predicate of any subject. If it were, there would be a principle of the supposed principle: for the subject is a principle, and prior presumably to what is predicated of it.

189a27–32

60. Again (2) we hold that a substance is not contrary to another substance. How then can substance be derived from what are not substances? Or how can non-substance be prior to substance?

189a32–34

61. If then we accept both the former argument and this one, we must, to preserve both, assume a third somewhat as the substratum of the contraries, such as is spoken of by those who describe the All as one nature—water or fire or what is intermediate between them. What is intermediate seems preferable; for fire, earth, air, and water are already involved with pairs of contraries. There is, therefore, much to be said for those who make the underlying substance different from these four; of the rest, the next best choice is air, as presenting sensible differences in a less degree than the others; and after air, water.

189a34–189b8

62. All, however, agree in this, that they differentiate their One by means of the contraries, such as density and rarity and more and less, which may of course be generalized, as has already been said, into excess and defect. Indeed this doctrine too (that the One and excess and defect are the principles of things) would appear to be of old standing, though in different forms; for the early thinkers made the two the active and the one the passive principle, whereas some of the more recent maintain the reverse.

189b8–16

63. To suppose then that the elements are three in number would seem, from these and similar considerations, a plausible view, as I said before. On the other hand, the view that they are more than three in number would seem to be untenable.

For the one substratum is sufficient to be acted on; but if we have four contraries, there will be two contrarieties, and we shall have to suppose an intermediate nature for each pair separately. If, on the other hand, the contrarieties, being two, can generate from each other, the second contrariety will be superfluous.   **189b16–22**

64. *Moreover, it is impossible that there should be more than one primary contrariety. For substance is a single genus of being, so that the principles can differ only as prior and posterior, not in genus; in a single genus there is always a single contrariety, all the other contrarieties in it being held to be reducible to one.*

It is clear then that the number of elements is neither one nor more than two or three; but whether two or three is, as I said, a question of considerable difficulty.   **189b22–29**

COMMENTARY OF ST. THOMAS

82. After the philosopher has investigated the contrariety of the principles, he here begins to inquire about their number.

Concerning this he makes three points. First, he raises the question. Secondly, where he says, **"One they cannot be . . ."** [53], he excludes certain things which are not pertinent to this question. Thirdly, he takes up the question, where he says, **"Granted, then, that . . ."** [58].

He says, therefore, first that after an investigation into the contrariety of the principles, an inquiry about their number should follow, i.e., whether they are two, or three, or more.

83. Next where he says, **"One they cannot be . . ."** [53], he excludes those things which are not pertinent to this question. He shows first that there is not just one principle, and secondly, where he says, **"Nor can they be . . ."** [54], he shows that the principles are not infinite.

He says first that it is impossible for there to be only one principle. For it has been shown that the principles are contraries. But contraries are not just one, for nothing is the contrary of itself; therefore, there is not just one principle.

84. Next where he says, **"Nor can they be . . ."** [54], he gives four arguments to show that the principles are not infinite. The first of these is as follows.

The infinite as such is unknown. If, therefore, the principles are infinite, they must be unknown. But if the principles are unknown, then those things which are from the principles are unknown. It follows, therefore, that nothing in the world could be known.

85. He gives the second argument where he says, **". . . and in any one genus . . ."** [55]. The argument is as follows. The principles must be primary contraries, as was shown above. But the primary contraries belong to the primary genus, which is substance. But substance, since it is one genus, has one primary contrariety. For the first contrariety of any genus is that of the primary differentiae by which the genus is divided. Therefore, the principles are not infinite.

86. He gives the third argument where he says, **". . . also a finite number . . ."** [56]. The argument is as follows. It is better to say that what can come to be from finite principles comes from finite principles rather than from infinite principles. But all things which come to be according to nature are explained by Empedocles through

finite principles, just as they are explained by Anaxagoras through infinite principles. Hence an infinite number of principles should not be posited.

87. He gives the fourth argument where he says, **"Lastly, some contraries . . ."** [57]. The argument is as follows. Principles are contraries. If, therefore, the principles are infinite, it is necessary that all the contraries be principles. But all of the contraries are not principles. This is clear for two reasons. First, the principles must be primary contraries, but not all contraries are primary, since some are prior to others. Secondly, the principles ought not to be from each other, as was said above. But some contraries are from each other, as the sweet and the bitter, and the white and the black. Therefore, the principles are not infinite.

Thus he finally concludes that the principles are neither one nor infinite.

88. However, we must note that the Philosopher proceeds here by way of disputation from probable arguments. Hence he assumes certain things which are seen in many instances, and which cannot be false taken as a whole, but are true in particular instances. Therefore, it is true that in a certain respect contraries do come to be from each other, as was said above, if the subject is taken along with the contraries. For that which is white later becomes black. However, whiteness itself is never changed into blackness. But some of the ancients, without including the subject, held that the primary contraries come to be from each other. Hence, Empedocles denied that the elements come to be from each other. And thus Aristotle significantly does not say in this place that the hot comes to be from the cold, but the

sweet from the bitter and the white from the black.

89. Next where he says, **"Granted then . . ."** [58], he takes up the question under discussion, namely, what is the number of the principles. Concerning this he makes two points. First he shows that there are not just two principles, but three. Secondly, where he says, **"On the other hand . . ."** [63], he shows that there are no more than three principles.

Concerning the first part he makes two points. First, he shows through arguments that there are not just two principles, but that a third must be added. Secondly, where he says, **"If, then, we accept . . ."** [61], he shows that even the ancient philosophers agreed on this point.

90. Concerning the first part [58] he gives three arguments. He says first that since it was shown that the principles are contraries, and so could not be just one, but are at least two, and further since the principles are not infinite, then it remains for us to consider whether there are only two principles or more than two. Since it was shown above that the principles are contraries, it seems that there are only two principles, because contrariety exists between two extremes.

But one might question this. For it is necessary that other things come to be from the principles, as was said above. If, however, there are only two contrary principles, it is not apparent how all things can come to be from these two. For it cannot be said that one of them makes something from the other one. For density is not by nature such that it can convert rarity into something, nor can rarity convert density into something. And the same is true of any other contrariety. For friendship does not move strife and make something out of it, nor does the converse happen. Rather each of the contraries changes some third thing which is the subject of both of the contraries. For heat does not make coldness itself to be hot, but makes the subject of coldness to be hot. And conversely, coldness does not make heat itself to be cold, but makes the subject of heat to be cold. Therefore, in order that other things can come to be from the contraries, it seems that it is necessary to posit some third thing which will be the subject of the contraries.

It does not matter for the present whether that subject is one or many. For some have posited many material principles from which they prepare the nature of beings. For they said that the nature of things is matter, as will be said later in Book II.

91. He gives the second argument where he says, **"Other objections . . ."** [59]. He says that, unless there is something other than the contraries which are given as principles, then there arises an even greater difficulty. For a first principle cannot be an accident which is predicated of a subject. For since a subject is a principle of the accident which is predicated of it and is naturally prior to the accident, then if the first principle were an accident predicated of a subject, it would follow that what is "of" a principle would be a principle, and there would be something prior to the first. But if we hold that only the contraries are principles, it is necessary that the principles be an accident predicated of a subject. For no substance is the contrary of something else. Rather contrariety is found only between accidents. It follows, therefore, that the contraries cannot be the only principles.

Moreover, it must be noted that in

this argument he uses "predicate" for "accident," since a predicate designates a form of the subject. The ancients, however, believed that all forms are accidents. Hence he proceeds here by way of disputation from probable propositions which were well known among the ancients.

92. He gives the third argument where he says, **"Again we hold . . ."** [60]. The argument is as follows. Everything which is not a principle must be from principles. If, therefore, only the contraries are principles, then since substance is not the contrary of substance, it follows that substance would be from non-substance. And thus what is not substance is prior to substance, because what is from certain things is posterior to them. But this is impossible. For substance which is being per se is the first genus of being. Therefore, it cannot be that only the contraries are principles; rather it is necessary to posit some other third thing.

93. Next where he says, **"If, then, we accept . . ."** [61], he shows how the position of the philosophers also agrees with this.

Concerning this he makes two points. First, he shows how they posited one material principle. Secondly, where he says, **"All, however agree . . ."** [62], he shows how they posited two contrary principles besides this one material principle.

However, we must first note that the Philosopher in the preceding arguments seemed to be opposed, in the manner of those who dispute, to both sides of the question. For first he proved that the principles are contraries, and now he brings forth arguments to prove that the contraries are not sufficient for the generation of things. And since disputatious arguments do come to some kind of true conclusion, though it is not the whole |truth|, he concludes one truth from each argument.

He says that if someone thinks that the first argument (which proves that the principles are contraries) is true, and that the argument just given (which proves that contrary principles are not sufficient) is also true, then to maintain both conclusions he must say that some third thing lies beneath the contraries, as was said by those who held that the whole universe is some one nature, understanding nature to mean matter, such as water, or fire or air, or some intermediate state between these, such as vapor, or some other thing of this sort.

This seems especially true in regard to an intermediate. For this third thing is taken as the subject of the contraries, and as distinct from them in some way. Hence, that which has less of the nature of a contrary about it is more conveniently posited as the third principle beyond the contraries. For fire and earth and air and water have contrariety attached to them, e.g., the hot and the cold, the wet and the dry. Hence, it is not unreasonable that they make the subject something other than these and something in which the contraries are less prominent. After these philosophers, however, those who held that air was the principle spoke more wisely, for the contrary qualities found in air are less sensible. After these philosophers are those who held that water was the principle. But those who held that fire was the principle spoke most poorly, because fire has a contrary quality which is most sensible and which is very active. For in fire there is an excellence of heat. If, however, the elements are compared with reference to their subtlety, those who made fire the principle seem to have

spoken better, as is said elsewhere, for what is more subtle seems to be more simple and prior. Hence no one held that earth was the principle because of its density.

94. Next where he says, **"All, however, agree . . ."** [62], he shows how they posited contrary principles with the one material principle.

He says that all who posited one material principle said that it is figured or formed by certain contraries, such as rarity and density, which are reducible to the great and the small and to excess and defect. And thus the position of Plato that the one and the great and the small are the principles of things was also the opinion of the ancient natural philosophers, but in a different way. For the ancient philosophers, thinking that one matter was differentiated by diverse forms, held two principles on the part of form, which is the principle of action, and one on the part of matter, which is the principle of passion. But the Platonists, thinking that many individuals in one species are distinguished by a division of matter, posited one principle on the part of the form, which is the active principle, and two on the part of the matter, which is the passive principle.

And thus he draws the conclusion which he had uppermost in mind, namely, that by considering the above and similar positions, it seems reasonable that there are three principles of nature. And he points out that he has proceeded from probable arguments.

95. Next where he says, **"On the other hand . . ."** [63], he shows that there are no more than three principles. He uses two arguments, the first of which is as follows.

It is superfluous for that which can come to be through fewer principles to come to be through many. But the whole generation of natural things can be achieved by positing one material principle and two formal principles. For one material principle is sufficient to account for passion.

But if there were four contrary principles, and two primary contrarieties, it would be necessary that each contrariety have a different subject. For it seems that there is one primary subject for any one contrariety. And so, if, by positing two contraries and one subject, things can come to be from each other, it seems superfluous to posit another contrariety. Therefore, we must not posit more than three principles.

96. He gives the second argument where he says, **"Moreover it is impossible . . ."** [64]. If there are more than three principles, it is necessary that there be many primary contrarieties. But this is impossible because the first contrariety seems to belong to the first genus, which is one, namely, substance. Hence all contraries which are in the genus of substance do not differ in genus, but are related as prior and posterior. For in one genus there is only one contrariety, namely, the first, because all other contrarieties seem to be reduced to the first one. For there are certain first contrary differentiae by which a genus is divided. Therefore it seems that there are no more than three principles.

It must be noted, however, that each of the following statements is probable: namely, that there is no contrariety in substances, and that in substances there is only one primary contrariety. For if we take substance to mean "that which is," it has no contrary. If, however, we take substance to mean formal differentiae in the genus of substance, then contrariety is found in them.

97. Finally by way of summary he concludes that there is not just one principle, nor are there more than two or three. But deciding which of these is true, that is, whether there are only two principles or three, involves much difficulty, as is clear from the foregoing.

In Every Coming to Be Three Principles Are to Be Found: The Subject, the Terminus of the Production, And its Opposite

The Text of Aristotle
Chapter 7

65. *We will now give our own account, approaching the question first with reference to becoming in its widest sense; for we shall be following the natural order of inquiry if we speak first of common characteristics, and then investigate the characteristics of special cases.*
189b30–32

66. *We say that one thing comes to be from another thing, and one sort of thing from another sort of thing, both in the case of simple and of complex things. I mean the following. We can say (1) the "man becomes musical," (2) what is "not-musical becomes musical," or (3) the "not-musical man becomes a musical man." Now what becomes in (1) and (2)—"man" and "not musical"—I call* simple, *and what each becomes —"musical"—simple also. But when we say the "not-musical man becomes a musical man," both what becomes and what it becomes are complex.*
189b32–190a5

67. *As regards one of these simple "things that become" we say not only "this becomes so-and-so," but also "from being this, it comes to be so-and-so," as "from being not-musical comes to be musical'; as regards the other we do not say this in all cases, as we do not say (1) "from being, a man came to be musical" but only, "the man became musical."*
190a5–8

68. *When a "simple" thing is said to become something, in one case (1) it survives through the process, in the other (2) it does not. For the man remains a man and is such even when he becomes musical, whereas what is not musical or is unmusical does not continue to exist, either simply or combined with the subject.*
190a9–13

69. *These distinctions drawn, one can gather from surveying the various cases of becoming in the way we are describing that, as we say, there must always be an underlying something, namely that which becomes, and that this, though always one numerically, in form at least is not one. (By that I mean that "it can be described in different ways.")*
190a13–17

70. *For "to be man" is not the same as "to be unmusical." One part survives, the other does not: what is not an opposite survives (for "man" survives), but "not-musical" or "unmusical" does not survive, nor does the compound of the two, namely "unmusical man."*
190a17–21

71. *We speak of "becoming that from this" instead of "this becoming, that" more in the case of what does not survive the change—"becoming musical from unmusical," not "from man"—but there are exceptions, as we sometimes use the latter form of expression even of what survives; we speak of "a statue coming to be from bronze," not of the "bronze becoming a statue." The change, however, from an opposite which does not survive is described indifferently in both ways, "becoming that from this" or "this becoming that." We say both that "the unmusical becomes musical," and that "from unmusical he becomes musical." And so both forms are used of the complex, "becoming a musical man from an unmusical man," and "an unmusical man becoming a musical man."*
190a21–31

72. *But there are different senses of "coming to be." In some cases we do not use the expression "come to be," but "come to be so-and-so." Only substances are said to "come to be" in the unqualified sense.*

Now in all cases other than substance it is plain that there must be some subject, namely, that which becomes. For we know that when a thing comes to be of such a quantity or quality or in such a relation, time, or place, a subject is always presupposed, since substance alone is not predicated of another subject, but everything else of substance.

But that substances too, and anything else that can be said "to be" without qualification, come to be from some substratum, will appear on examination. For we find in every case something that underlies from which proceeds that which comes to be; for instance, animals and plants from seed. **190a31–190b5**

73. Generally things which come to be, come to be in different ways: (1) by change of shape, as a statue; (2) by addition, as things which grow; (3) by taking away, as the Hermes from the stone; (4) by putting together, as a house; (5) by alteration, as things which "turn" in respect of their material substance. **190b5–10**

74. It is plain that these are all cases of coming to be from a substratum.

Thus, clearly, from what has been said, whatever comes to be is always complex. There is, on the one hand, (a) something which comes into existence, and again (b) something which becomes that—the latter (b) in two senses, either the subject or the opposite. By the "opposite" I mean the "unmusical," by the "subject," "man," and similarly I call the absence of shape or form or order the "opposite," and the bronze or stone or gold the "subject." **190b10–17**

COMMENTARY OF ST. THOMAS

98. After the Philosopher has investigated the number of principles by means of disputation, he here begins to determine the truth. This section is divided into two parts. First he determines the truth. Secondly, where he says, **"We will not proceed ..."** [81], he excludes from the truth already determined certain difficulties and errors of the ancients.

The first part is divided into two parts. First he shows that in any natural coming-to-be three things are found. Secondly, where he says, **"Plainly, then ..."** [75], he shows from this that these three things are principles.

Concerning the first part he makes two points. First he states his intention, and secondly he pursues his intention, where he says, **"We say that ..."** [66].

99. Because he had said above that the question of whether there are only two principles of nature or three involves much difficulty, he concludes that he must first speak of generation and production as common to all the species of mutation. For in any mutation there is found a certain com-

ing-to-be. For example, when something is altered from white to black, the non-white comes to be from the white, and the black comes to be from the non-black. And the same is true of other mutations. He also points out the reason for this order of procedure. It is necessary to speak first of those things which are common, and afterwards to think of those things which are proper to each thing, as was said in the beginning of the Book.

100. Next where he says, **"We say that one thing ..."** [66], he develops his position. Concerning this he makes two points. First he sets forth certain things which are necessary to prove his position. Secondly, where he says, **"These distinctions drawn ..."** [69], he proves his point.

Concerning the first part he makes two points. First he sets up a certain division, secondly, where he says, **"As regards one ..."** [67], he points out the differences among the parts of the division.

101. He says, therefore, first [66] that in any coming-to-be one thing is said to come to be from another thing with

reference to coming to be in regard to substantial being [esse], or one comes to be from another with reference to coming to be in regard to accidental being [esse]. Hence every change has two termini. The word "termini," however, is used in two ways, for the termini of a production or mutation can be taken as either simple or composite.

He explains this as follows. Sometimes we say man becomes musical, and then the two termini of the production are simple. It is the same when we say that the non-musical becomes musical. But when we say that the non-musical man becomes a musical man, each of the termini is a composite. Yet when coming to be is attributed to man or to the non-musical, each is simple. And thus, that which becomes, i.e., that to which coming to be is attributed, is said to come to be simply. Moreover, that in which the very coming to be is terminated, which is also said to come to be simply, is musical. Thus we say man becomes musical, or the non-musical becomes musical. But when each is signified as coming to be as composed (i.e., both what becomes, i.e., that to which the coming to be is attributed, and what is made, i.e., that in which the coming to be is terminated), then we say that the non-musical man becomes musical. For then there is composition on the part of the subject only and simplicity on the part of the predicate. But when I say that the non-musical man becomes a musical man, then there is composition on the part of each.

102. Next where he says, **"As regards one . . ."** [67], he points out two differences in what was said above.

The first is that in some of the cases mentioned above we use a twofold mode of speech, i.e., we say "this becomes this" and "from this, this comes

to be." For we say "the non-musical becomes musical," and "from the non-musical, the musical comes to be." But we do not speak this way in all cases. For we do not say "the musical comes to be from man," but "man becomes musical."

He points out the second difference where he says, **"When a 'simple' . . ."** [68]. He says that when coming to be is attributed to two simple things, i.e., the subject and the opposite, one of these is permanent, but the other is not. For when someone has already been made musical, "man" remains. But the opposite does not remain, whether it be the negative opposite, as the non-musical, or the privation or contrary, as the unmusical. Nor is the composite of subject and the opposite permanent, for the non-musical man does not remain after man has been made musical. And so coming to be is attributed to these three things: for it was said that man becomes musical, and the non-musical becomes musical, and the non-musical man becomes musical. Of these three, only the first remains complete in a production, the other two do not remain.

103. Next where he says, **"These distinctions drawn . . ."** [69], having assumed the foregoing, he proves his position, namely that three things are found in any natural production.

Concerning this he makes three points. First he enumerates two things which are found in any natural production. Secondly, where he says, **"One part survives . . ."** [70], he proves what he had supposed. Thirdly, where he says, **"Thus, clearly, . . ."** [74], he draws his conclusion.

104. He says, therefore, first [69] that, if anyone, taking for granted what was said above, wishes to consider [coming-to-be] in all the things which

come to be naturally, he will agree that there must always be some subject to which the coming to be is attributed, and that that subject, although one in number and subject, is not the same in species or nature [ratio]. For when it is said of a man that he becomes musical, the man is indeed one in subject, but two in nature [ratio]. For man and the non-musical are not the same according to nature [ratio]. Aristotle does not, however, mention here the third point, namely, that in every generation there must be something generated, for this is obvious.

105. Next where he says, **"One part survives . . ."** [70], he proves the two things which he had assumed. He shows first that the subject to which the coming to be is attributed is two in nature [ratio]. Secondly, where he says, **"But there are different . . ."** [72], he shows that it is necessary to assume a subject in every coming to be.

He shows the first point in two ways. First [70] he points out that in the subject to which the coming to be is attributed there is something which is permanent and something which is not permanent. For that which is not an opposite of the terminus of the production is permanent, for man remains when he becomes musical, but the non-musical does not remain. And from this it is clear that man and the non-musical are not the same in nature [ratio], since the one remains, whereas the other does not.

106. Secondly, where he says, **"We speak of . . ."** [71], he shows the same thing in another way. With reference to the non-permanent things, it is much better to say "this comes to be from this" than to say "this becomes this" (although this latter also may be said, but not as properly). For we say that the musical comes to be from the

non-musical. We also say that the non-musical becomes musical, but this is accidental, insofar as that which happens to be non-musical becomes musical. But in permanent things this is not said. For we do not say that the musical comes to be from man, rather we say that the man becomes musical.

Even in reference to permanent things we sometimes say "this comes to be from this," as we say that a statue comes to be from bronze. But this happens because by the name "bronze" we understand the "unshaped," and so this is said by reason of the privation which is understood.

From this very fact, then, that we use different modes of speech with reference to the subject and the opposite, it is clear that the subject and the opposite, such as man and the non-musical, are two in nature [ratio].

107. Next where he says, **"But there are different . . ."** [72], he proves the other point which he had assumed, namely, that in every natural production there must be a subject.

The proof of this point by argumentation belongs to metaphysics. Hence this is proved in Metaphysics, VII. He proves it here only by induction. He does this first in regard to the things which come to be, secondly in regard to the modes of coming to be, where he says, **"Generally things . . ."** [73].

He says, therefore, first [72] that since "to come to be" is used in many ways, "to come to be simply" is said only of the coming to be of substances, whereas other things are said to come to be accidentally. This is so because "to come to be" implies the beginning of existing. Therefore, in order for something to come to be simply, it is required that it previously will not have been simply, which happens in those things which come to be substantially. For when a man comes to be, he not only previously was not a man, but it is true to say that he simply was not. When, however, a man becomes white, it is not true to say that he previously was not, but that he previously was not such.

Those things, however, which come to be accidentally clearly depend upon a subject. For quantity and quality and the other accidents, whose coming to be is accidental, cannot be without a subject. For only substance does not exist in a subject.

Further, it is clear, if one considers the point, that even substances come to be from a subject. For we see that plants and animals come to be from seed.

108. Next where he says, "**Generally things . . .**" [73], he shows the same thing by induction from the modes of coming to be.

He says that of things which come to be, some come to be by change of figure, as the statue comes to be from the bronze, others come to be by addition, as is clear in all instances of increase, as the river comes to be from many streams, others come to be by subtraction, as the image of Mercury comes to be from stone by sculpture. Still other things come to be by composition, e.g., a house; and other things come to be by alteration, as those things whose matter is changed, either by nature or by art. And in all of these cases it is apparent that they come to be from some subject. Whence it is clear that everything which comes to be comes to be from a subject.

But it must be noted that artificial things are here enumerated along with those things which come to be simply (even though artificial forms are accidents) because artificial things are in some way in the genus of substance by reason of their matter. Or else perhaps he lists them because of the opinion of the ancients, who thought of natural things and artificial things in the same way, as will be said in Book II.

109. Next where he says, "**Thus clearly . . .**" [74], he draws his conclusion. He says that it has been shown from what was said above that that to which coming to be is attributed is always composed. And since in any production there is that at which the coming to be is terminated and that to which the coming to be is attributed, the latter of which is twofold, i.e., the subject and the opposite, it is then clear that there are three things in any coming to be, namely, the subject, the terminus of the production, and the opposite of this terminus. Thus when a man becomes musical, the opposite is the non-musical, the subject is the man, and musical is the terminus of the production. And in like manner, shapelessness and lack of figure and lack of order are opposites, while bronze and gold and stone are subjects in artificial productions.

There Are Two Per Se Principles of the Being and of the Becoming of Natural Things, Namely, Matter and Form, and One Per Accidens Principle, Namely, Privation

The Text of Aristotle

75. Plainly then, if there are conditions and principles which constitute natural objects and from which they primarily are or have come to be—have come to be, I mean, what each is said to be in its essential nature, not what each is in respect of a concomitant attribute—plainly, I say, everything comes to be from both subject and form. For "musical man" is composed (in a way) of "man" and "musical': you can analyze it into the definitions of its elements. It is clear then that what comes to be will come to be from these elements. 190b17–23

76. Now the subject is one numerically, though it is two in form. (For it is the man, the gold—the "matter" generally—that is counted, for it is more of the nature of a "this," and what comes to be does not come from it in virtue of a concomitant attribute; the privation, on the other hand, and the contrary are incidental in the process.) And the positive form is one—the order, the acquired art of music, or any similar predicate. 190b23–29

77. There is a sense, therefore, in which we must declare the principles to be two, and a sense in which they are three; a sense in which the contraries are the principles—say for example the musical and the unmusical, the hot and the cold, the tuned and the untuned—and a sense in which they are not, since it is impossible for the contraries to be acted on by each other. But this difficulty also is solved by the fact that the substratum is different from the contraries, for it is itself not a contrary. The principles therefore are, in a way, not more in number than the contraries, but as it were two; nor yet precisely two, since there is a difference of essential nature, but three. For "to be man" is different from "to be unmusical, and "to be unformed" from "to be bronze." 190b29–191a3

78. We have now stated the number of the principles of natural objects which are subject to Generation, and how the number is reached: and it is clear that there must be a substratum for the contraries and that the contraries must be two. (Yet in another way of putting it this is not necessary, as one of the contraries will serve to effect the change by its successive absence and presence.) 191a3–7

79. The underlying nature is an object of scientific knowledge, by an analogy. For as the bronze is to the statue, the wood to the bed, or the matter and the formless before receiving form to any thing which has form, so is the underlying nature to substance, i.e., the "this" or existent.

This then is one principle (though not one or existent in the same sense as the "this"), and the definition was one as we agreed; then further there is its contrary, the privation. In what sense these are two, and in what sense more, has been stated above. 191a7–15

80. Briefly, we explained first that only the contraries were principles, and later that a substratum was indispensable, and that the principles were three; our last statement has elucidated the difference between the contraries, the mutual relation of the principles, and the nature of the substratum. Whether the form or the substratum is the essential nature of a physical object is not yet clear. But that the principles are three, and in what sense, and the way in which each is a principle, is clear.

So much then for the question of the number and the nature of the principles. 191a15–22

COMMENTARY OF ST. THOMAS

110. After the Philosopher has shown that three things are found in

every natural coming to be, he intends here to show from the foregoing how many principles of nature there are.

Concerning this he makes two points. First he explains his position. Secondly, where he says, **"Briefly, we explained . . ."** [80], in recapitulation he explains what has already been said and what remains to be said.

Concerning the first part he makes two points. First he shows that there are three principles of nature. Secondly he names them, where he says, **"The underlying nature . . ."** [79].

Concerning the first part he makes three points. First he explains the truth about the first principles of nature. Secondly, where he says, **"There is a sense . . ."** [77], from this disclosure of the truth he answers the problems about the principles which were raised above. Thirdly, since the ancients had said that the principles are contraries, he shows whether or not contraries are always required, where he says, **"We have now stated . . ."** [78].

Concerning the first part he makes two points. First he shows that there are two per se principles of nature. Secondly, where he says, **"Now the subject . . ."** [76], he shows that the third principle is a per accidens principle of nature.

111. With reference to the first point he uses the following argument [75]. Those things from which natural things are and come to be per se, and not per accidens, are said to be the principles and causes of natural things. Whatever comes to be exists and comes to be both from subject and from form. Therefore the subject and the form are per se causes and principles of everything which comes to be according to nature.

That that which comes to be according to nature comes to be from subject

and form he proves as follows. Those things into which the definition of a thing is resolved are the components of that thing, because each thing is resolved into the things of which it is composed. But the definition [ratio] of that which comes to be according to nature is resolved into subject and form. For the definition [ratio] of musical man is resolved into the definition [ratio] of man and the definition [ratio] of musical. For if anyone wishes to define musical man, he will have to give the definitions of man and musical. Therefore, that which comes to be according to nature both is and comes to be from subject and form.

And it must be noted that he intends here to inquire not only into the principles of the coming to be but also into the principles of the being. Hence he says significantly that things both are and come to be from these first principles. And by "first principles" he means per se and not per accidens principles. Therefore, the per se principles of everything which comes to be according to nature are subject and form.

112. Next where he says, **"Now the subject . . ."** [76], he adds the third per accidens principle. He says that although the subject is one in number, it is nevertheless two in species and nature [ratio], as was said above. For man and gold and any matter has some sort of number. This is a consideration of the subject itself, such as man or gold, which is something positive, and from which something comes to be per se and not per accidens. It is another thing, however, to consider that which happens to the subject, i.e., contrariety and privation, such as to be unmusical and unshaped. The third principle, then, is a species or form, as order is the form of a house, or musical is the form

of a musical man, or as any of the other things which are predicated in this way.

Therefore the subject and the form are per se principles of that which comes to be according to nature, but privation or the contrary is a per accidens principle, insofar as it happens to the subject. Thus we say that the builder is the per se active cause of the house, but the musician is a per accidens active cause of the house insofar as the builder also happens to be musical. Hence the man is the per se cause as subject of musical man, but the non-musical is a per accidens cause and principle.

113. However someone may object that privation does not belong to a subject while it is under some form, and thus privation is not a per accidens principle of being.

Hence it must be said that matter is never without privation. For when matter has one form, it is in privation of some other form. And so while it is coming to be that which it becomes (e.g., musical man), there is in the subject, which does not yet have the form, the privation of the musical itself. And so the per accidens principle of a musical man, while he is coming to be musical, is the non-musical. For he is a non-musical man while he is coming to be musical. But when this latter form has already come to him, then there is joined to him the privation of the other form. And thus the privation of the opposite form is a per accidens principle of being.

It is clear, therefore, according to the opinion of Aristotle that privation, which is posited as a per accidens principle of nature, is not a capacity for a form, nor an inchoate form, nor some imperfect active principle, as some say. Rather it is the very absence of

form, or the contrary of form, which occurs in the subject.

114. Next where he says, **"There is a sense . . ."** [77], he resolves, in the light of the truth already determined, all the preceding difficulties.

He concludes from the foregoing that in a certain respect it must be said that there are two principles, namely, the per se principles, and in another respect that there are three, if we accept along with the per se principles the per accidens principle. And in a certain respect the principles are contraries, if one takes the musical and the non-musical, the hot and the cold, the harmonious and the inharmonious. Yet in another respect the principles, if they are taken without the subject, are not contraries, for contraries cannot be acted upon by each other, unless it be held that some subject is supposed for the contraries by reason of which they are acted upon by one another.

And thus he concludes that the principles are not more than the contraries, for there are only two per se principles. But there are not just two principles, for one of them according to its being [esse] is other, for the subject according to nature [ratio] is two, as was said. And thus there are three principles, because man and the non-musical, and bronze and the unshaped, differ according to nature [ratio].

Therefore it is clear that the early opinions which argued for a part of the truth were in a certain respect true, but not altogether true.

115. Next where he says, **"We have now stated . . ."** [78], he shows in what way two contraries are necessary, and in what way they are not necessary.

He says that from what has been said it is clear how many principles of the generation of natural things there are, and how it happens that there are this number. For it was shown that it is necessary that two of the principles be contraries, of which one is a per se principle and the other a per accidens principle, and that something be the subject of the contraries, which is also a per se principle. But in a certain respect one of the contraries is not necessary for generation, for at times it is sufficient if one of the contraries bring about the change by its absence and its presence.

116. As evidence of this we must note that, as will be said in Book V, there are three species of mutation, namely, generation and corruption and motion. The difference among these is as follows. Motion is from one positive state to another positive state, as from white to black. Generation, however, is from the negative to the positive, as from the non-white to the white, or from non-man to man. Corruption, on the other hand, is from the positive to the negative, as from the white to the non-white, or from man to non-man. Therefore, it is clear that in motion two contraries and one subject are required. But in generation and corruption there is required the presence of one contrary and its absence, which is privation.

Generation and corruption, however, are found in motion. For when something is moved from white to black, white is corrupted and black comes to be. Therefore in every natural mutation subject and form and privation are required. However, the nature [ratio] of motion is not found in every generation and corruption, as is clear in the generation and corruption of substances. Hence subject and form and privation are found in every mutation, but not a subject and two contraries.

117. This opposition is also found in substances, which are the first genus. This, however, is not the opposition of contrariety. For substantial forms are not contraries, even though differentiae in the genus of substance are contrary insofar as one is received along with the privation of the other, as is clear in the animate and the inanimate.

118. Next where he says, "**The underlying nature . . .**" [79], he clarifies the above-mentioned principles.

He says that the nature which is first subject to mutation, i.e., primary matter, cannot be known of itself, since everything which is known is known through its form. Primary matter is, moreover, considered to be the subject of every form. But it is known by analogy, that is, according to proportion. For we know that wood is other than the form of a bench and a bed, for sometimes it underlies the one form, at other times the other. When, therefore, we see that air at times becomes water, it is necessary to say that there is something which sometimes exists under the form of air, and at other times under the form of water. And thus this something is other than the form of water and other than the form of air, as wood is something other than the form of a bench and other than the form of bed. This "something," then, is related to these natural substances as bronze is related to the statue, and wood to the bed, and anything material and unformed to form. And this is called primary matter.

This, then, is one principle of nature. It is not one as a "this something," that is, as some determinate individual, as though it had form and unity in act, but is rather called being and one insofar as it is in potency to form. The other principle, then, is the nature [ratio] or form, and the third is privation, which is contrary to the form. And how these principles are two and how they are three was explained above.

119. Next where he says, **"Briefly, we explained . . ."** [80], he gives a résumé of what has been said, and points out what remains to be said.

He says, therefore, that it was said first that the contraries are principles, and afterwards that something is subjected to them, and thus there are three principles. And from what was said just now it is clear what the difference is between the contraries: one of them is a per se principle, and the other a per accidens principle. And then it was pointed out how the principles are related to each other, since the subject and the contrary are one in number yet two in nature [ratio]. Then it was pointed out what the subject is insofar as this could be made clear. But it has not yet been decided which is the greater substance, form or matter, for this will be explained at the beginning of Book II. But it has been explained that the principles are three in number, how they are principles, and in what way. And he finally draws the conclusion he had uppermost in mind, namely, that it is clear how many principles there are and what they are.

The Problems and the Errors of the Ancients Which Spring from an Ignorance of Matter Are Resolved by the Truth about the Principles Already Determined

The Text of Aristotle
Chapter 8

81. We will now proceed to show that the difficulty of the early thinkers, as well as our own, is solved in this way alone.

The first of those who studied science were misled in their search for truth and the nature of things by their inexperience, which as it were thrust them into another path. So they say that none of the things that are either comes to be or passes out of existence, because what comes to be must do so either from what is or from what is not, both of which are impossible. For what is cannot come to be (because it is already), and from what is not nothing could have come to be (because something must be present as a substratum). So too they exaggerated the consequence of this, and went so far as to deny even the existence of a plurality of things, maintaining that only Being itself is. Such then was their opinion, and such the reason for its adoption.

191a23–34

82. Our explanation on the other hand is that the phrases "something comes to be from what is or from what is not," "what is not or what is does something or has something done to it or becomes some particular thing," are to be taken (in the first way of putting our explanation) in the same sense as "a doctor does something or has something done to him," "is or becomes something from being a doctor." These expressions may be taken in two senses, and so too, clearly, may "from being," and "being acts or is acted on." A doctor builds a house, not qua doctor, but qua housebuilder, and turns gray, not qua doctor, but qua dark-haired. On the other hand he doctors or fails to doctor qua doctor. But we are using words most appropriately when we say that a doctor does, something or undergoes something, or becomes something from being a doctor if he does undergoes, or becomes qua doctor. Clearly then also "to come to be so-and-so from not-being" means "qua not-being."

It was through failure to make this distinction that those thinkers gave the matter up, and through this error that they went so much farther astray as to suppose that nothing else comes to be or exists apart from Being itself, thus doing away with all becoming.

We ourselves are in agreement with them in holding that nothing can be said without qualification to come from what is not. But nevertheless we maintain that a thing may "come to be from what is not"—that is, in a qualified sense. For a thing comes to be from the privation, which in its own nature is not-being—this not surviving as a constituent of the result. Yet this causes surprise, and it is thought impossible that something should come to be in the way described from what is not.

In the same way we maintain that nothing comes to be from being, and that being does not come to be except in a qualified sense. In that way, however, it does, just as animal might come to be from animal, and an animal of a certain kind from an animal of a certain kind. Thus, suppose a dog to come to be from a dog, or a horse from a horse. The dog would then, it is true, come to be from animal (as well as from an animal of a certain kind) but not as animal; for that is already there. But if anything is to become an animal, not in a qualified sense, it will not be from animal; and if being, not from being nor from not-being either, for it has been explained that by "from not-being" we mean from not-being qua not-being.

Note further that we do not subvert the principle that everything either is or is not.

This then is one way of solving the difficulty. 191a34–191b27

83. Another consists in pointing out that the same things can be explained in terms of potentiality and actuality. But this has been done with greater precision elsewhere. **191b27–29**

84. So, as we said, the difficulties which constrain people to deny the existence of some of the things we mentioned are now solved. For it was this reason which also caused some of the earlier thinkers to turn so far aside from the road which leads to coming to be and passing away and change generally. If they had come in sight of this nature, all their ignorance would have been dispelled. **191b30–34**

COMMENTARY OF ST. THOMAS

120. Having determined the truth about the principles of nature, the Philosopher here excludes certain difficulties of the ancients by means of what has been determined about the principles.

He considers first the problems or errors which stem from an ignorance of matter, and secondly, where he says, "Others indeed . . ." [85], the problems or errors which stem from an ignorance of privation. Thirdly, where he says, "The accurate determination . . ." [91], he reserves for another science the problems which arise with reference to form.

Concerning the first part he makes two points. First he states the problem and the error into which the ancients fell through their ignorance of matter. Secondly, where he says, "Our explanation . . ." [82], he answers their difficulty by means of those things which have already been determined.

121. He says, therefore, first [81] that, after determining the truth about the principles, it must be pointed out that only in this way is every difficulty of the ancients solved. And this is an indication that what has been said about the principles is true. For truth excludes every falsehood and difficulty. But given a position which is in some way false, some difficulty must remain.

Now the problem and error of the ancient philosophers was this. The first ones who philosophically sought the truth and the nature of things were diverted into a path other than the way of truth and the way of nature. This happened to them because of the weakness of their understanding. For they said that nothing is either generated or corrupted. This is contrary to truth and contrary to nature.

The weakness of their understanding forced them to hold this position because they did not know how to resolve the following argument, according to which it seemed to be proven that being is not generated. If being comes to be, it comes to be either from being or from non-being. And each of these seems to be impossible, i.e., that being comes to be from being or that it comes to be from non-being. It is clearly impossible for something to come to be from being, because that which is does not come to be, for nothing is before it comes to be. And being already is, hence it does not come to be. It is also clearly impossible for something to come to be from non-being. For it is always necessary that there be a subject for that which comes to be, as was shown above. From nothing, nothing comes to be. And from this it was concluded that there is neither generation nor corruption of being.

And those who argued in this fashion exaggerated their position to the point where they said that there are not many beings, but only one being. And they said this for the reason already given. Since they held that there is only one material principle, and since they said that nothing is caused from that one principle by way of generation and corruption, but only by way of alteration, then it follows that it would always be one according to substance.

122. Next where he says, **"Our explanation . . ."** [82], he answers the objection just mentioned. Concerning this he makes two points. First, he answers the aforesaid objection in two ways. Secondly, where he says, **"So as we said . . ."** [84], he draws the conclusion which he has uppermost in mind.

The first point is divided into two parts according to the two solutions given, the second of which is found where he says, **"Another consists in . . ."** [83].

123. He says, therefore, first [82] that as far as the mode of speaking is concerned, it makes no difference whether we say that something comes to be from being or from non-being, or that being or non-being does something or is acted upon, or anything else, or whether we say this same sort of thing about a doctor; namely, that the doctor does something or is acted upon, or that something is or comes to be from the doctor.

But to say that the doctor does something or is acted upon, or that something comes to be from the doctor, has two meanings. Therefore, to say that something comes to be from being or from non-being, or that being or non-being makes something, or is acted upon, has two meanings. And the same is true regardless of the terms which are used; e.g., it might be said that something comes to be from white, or that the white does something or is acted upon.

That there is a twofold meaning when we use expressions such as the doctor does something or is acted

upon, or that something comes to be from the doctor, he shows as follows.

We say that a doctor builds. But he does not do this insofar as he is a doctor, but insofar as he is a builder. And in like manner we say that the doctor becomes white, but not insofar as he is a doctor, but insofar as he is black. However in another sense we say that the doctor heals insofar as he is doctor, and in like manner that the doctor becomes a non-doctor insofar as he is a doctor. Thus we say properly and per se that the doctor does something or is acted upon, or that something comes to be from the doctor, when we attribute this to the doctor insofar as he is a doctor. But when something is attributed to him per accidens, it is not insofar as he is a doctor, but insofar as he is something else. Therefore, it is clear that when it is said that the doctor does something or is acted upon, or that something comes to be from doctor, this has two meanings, i.e., per se and per accidens.

Whence it is clear that when it is said that a thing comes to be from non-being, this is to be understood properly and per se if that thing should come to be from non-being insofar as it is non-being. And the same argument applies to being.

But the ancients, failing to perceive this distinction, erred insofar as they thought that nothing comes to be. And they did not think that anything other than their first material principle had substantial existence. For example, those who said that air is the first material principle held that all other things signify a certain accidental existence. Thus they excluded every substantial generation, retaining only alteration. Because of the fact that nothing comes to be per se either from non-being or from being, they thought that it would not be possible for anything to come to be from being or non-being.

124. And we also say that nothing comes to be from non-being simply and per se, but only per accidens. For that which is, i.e., being, is not from privation per se. And this is so because privation does not enter into the essence of the thing made. Rather a thing comes to be per se from that which is in the thing after it has already been made. Thus the shaped comes to be from the unshaped, not per se, but per accidens, because once it already has been shaped, the unshaped is not in it. But this is a remarkable way for a thing to come to be from non-being, and seemed impossible to the ancient philosophers. Therefore, it is clear that a thing comes to be from non-being not per se but per accidens.

125. In like manner, if it is asked whether a thing comes to be from being, we must say that a thing comes to be from being per accidens, but not per se. He shows this by the following example.

Let us suppose that a dog is generated from a horse. Granting this, it is clear that a certain animal comes to be from a certain animal, and thus animal would come to be from animal. However, animal would not come to be from animal per se, but per accidens. For it does not come to be insofar as it is animal, but insofar as it is this animal. For animal already is before the dog comes to be. For the horse already is, but is not a dog. Hence the dog comes to be per se from that which is not a dog. And if animal were to come to be per se, and not per accidens, it would be necessary for it to come to be from non-animal.

And the same is true of being. For a being comes to be from that nonbeing which is not that which the being co-mes to be. Hence a thing does not come to be per se from being or per se from non-being. For this expression per se signifies that a thing comes to be from non-being in the sense that it comes to be from non-being insofar as it is non-being, as was said. And thus when this animal comes to be from this animal, or when this body comes to be from this body, not all animal or non-animal, nor all body or non-body, is removed from that from which the thing comes to be. And likewise not all being [esse] nor all non-being [non-esse] is removed from that from which this being comes to be. For that from which fire comes to be has some being, because it is air, and also has some non-being, because it is not fire.

126. This, then, is one way of resolving the problem raised above. But this approach is not sufficient. For if being comes to be per accidens both from being and from non-being, it is necessary to posit something from which being comes to be per se. For every thing which is per accidens is reduced to that which is per se.

127. In order to designate that from which a thing comes to be per se, he adds a second approach where he says, "Another consists . . ." [83].

He says that the same thing can be explained in terms of potency and act, as is clearly indicated in another place, i.e., in Metaphysics, IX. Thus a thing comes to be per se from being in potency; but a thing comes to be per accidens from being in act or from non-being.

He says this because matter, which is being in potency, is that from which a thing comes to be per se. For matter enters into the substance of the thing which is made. But from privation or from the preceding form, a thing co-mes to be per accidens insofar as the matter, from which the thing comes to be per se, happened to be under such a form or under such a privation. Thus a statue comes to be per se from bronze; but the statue comes to be per accidens both from that which does not have such a shape and from that which has another shape.

128. Finally, where he says, **"So as we said . . ."** [84], he draws the conclusion which he had uppermost in mind. He says that we can truly say that all the difficulties are answered by what has been said above. Driven on by certain difficulties, some of the ancients denied some of the things mentioned above, i.e., generation and corruption, and a plurality of substantially different things. But once matter is understood, all of their ignorance is removed.

Matter is Distinguished from Privation. Matter is Neither Generable Nor Corruptible Per Se

The Text of Aristotle
Chapter 9

85. *Others, indeed, have apprehended the nature in question, but not adequately.*

In the first place they allow that a thing may come to be without qualification from not-being, accepting on this point the statement of Parmenides. Secondly, they think that if the substratum is one numerically, it must have also only a single potentiality—which is a very different thing.   191b35–192a2

86. *Now we distinguish matter and privation, and hold that one of these, namely the matter, is not-being only in virtue of an attribute which it has, while the privation in its own nature is not-being; and that the matter is nearly, in a sense* is, *substance, while the privation in no sense* is.   192a2–6

87. *They, on the other hand, identify their Great and Small alike with not-being, and that whether they are taken together as one or Separately. Their triad is therefore of quite a different kind from ours. For they got so far as to see that there must be some underlying nature, but they make it one—for even if one philosopher makes a dyad of it, which he calls Great and Small, the effect is the same; for he overlooked the other nature. For the one which persists is a Joint cause, with the form, of what comes to be—a mother, as it were. But the negative part of the contrariety may often seem, if you concentrate your attention on it as an evil agent, not to exist at all.*   192a6–12

88. *For admitting with them that there is something divine, good, and desirable, we hold that there are two other principles, the one contrary to it, the other such as of its own nature to desire and yearn for it.*   192a13–18

89. *But the consequence of their view is that the contrary desires its own extinction. Yet the form cannot desire itself, for it is not defective; nor can the Contrary desire it, for contraries are mutually destructive. The truth is that what desires the form is matter, as the female desires the male and the ugly the beautiful—only the ugly or the female not per se but per accidens.*
192a18–25

90. *The matter comes to be and ceases to be in one sense, while in another it does not. As that which contains the privation, it ceases to be in its own nature; for what ceases to be—the privation—is contained within it. But as potentiality it does not cease to be in its own nature, but is necessarily outside the sphere of becoming and ceasing to be. For if it came to be, something must have existed as a primary substratum from which it should come and which should persist in it; but this is its own special nature, so that it will be before coming to be. (For my definition of matter is just this—the primary substratum of each thing, from which it comes to be without qualification, and which persists in the result.) And if it ceases to be it will pass into that at the last, so it will have ceased to be before ceasing to be.*   192a25–34

91. *The accurate determination of the first principle in respect of form, whether it is one or many and what it is or what they are, is the province of the primary type of science; so these questions may stand over till then. But of the natural, i.e. perishable, forms we shall speak in the expositions which follow.*

The above, then, may be taken as sufficient to establish that there are principles and what they are and how many there are. Now let us make a fresh start and proceed.   192a34–192b4

COMMENTARY OF ST. THOMAS

129. Having excluded the problems and errors of the ancient philosophers which stem from their ignorance of matter, the Philosopher here excludes the errors which stem from their ignorance of privation.

Concerning this he makes three points. First, he sets forth the errors of those who wandered from the truth. Secondly, where he says, **"Now we distinguish . . ."** [86], he shows how this position differs from the truth determined by him above. Thirdly, where he says, **"For the one which persists . . ."** [88], he proves that his own opinion is true.

130. He says, therefore, first [85] that some philosophers touched upon matter, but did not understand it sufficiently. For they did not distinguish between matter and privation. Hence, they attributed to matter what belongs to privation. And because privation, considered in itself, is non-being, they said that matter, considered in itself, is non-being. And so just as a thing comes to be simply and per se from matter, so they believed that a thing comes to be simply and per se from non-being.

And they were led to hold this position for two reasons. First they were influenced by the argument of Parmenides, who said that whatever is other than being is non-being. Since, then, matter is other than being, because it is not being in act, they said that it is non-being simply. Secondly, it seemed to them that that which is one in number or subject is also one in nature [ratio]. And Aristotle calls this a state of being one in potency, because things which are one in nature [ratio] are such that each has the same power.

But things which are one in subject but not one in nature [ratio] do not have the same potency or power, as is clear in the white and the musical. But subject and privation are one in number, as for example, the bronze and the unshaped. Hence it seemed to them that they would be the same in nature [ratio] or in power. Hence this position accepts the unity of potency.

131. But lest anyone, because of these words, be in doubt about what the potency of matter is and whether it is one or many, it must be pointed out that act and potency divide every genus of beings, as is clear in *Metaphysics*, IX, and in Book III of this work. Hence, just as the potency for quality is not something outside the genus of quality, so the potency for substantial being is not outside the genus of substance. Therefore, the potency of matter is not some property added to its essence. Rather, matter in its very substance is potency for substantial being. Moreover, the potency of matter is one in subject with respect to many forms. But in its nature [ratio] there are many potencies according to its relation to different forms. Hence in Book III it will be said that to be able to be healed and to be able to be ill differ according to nature [ratio].

132. Next where he says, **"Now we distinguish . . ."** [86], he explains the difference between his own opinion and the opinion just given.

Concerning this he makes two points. First he widens our understanding of his own opinion. Secondly, where he says, **"They, on the other hand..."** [87], he shows what the other opinion holds.

He says, therefore, first that there is

a great difference between a thing's being one in number or subject and its being one in potency or nature [ratio]. For we say, as is clear from the above, that matter and privation although one in subject, are other in nature [ratio]. And this is clear for two reasons. First, matter is non-being accidentally, whereas privation is non-being per se. For "unshaped" signifies non-being, but "bronze" does not signify non-being except insofar as "unshaped" happens to be in it. Secondly, matter is "near to the thing" and exists in some respect, because it is in potency to the thing and is in some respect the substance of the thing, since it enters into the constitution of the substance. But this cannot be said of privation.

133. Next where he says, "They, on the other hand ..." [97], he clarifies his understanding of the opinion of the Platonists.

He says that the Platonists also held a certain duality on the part of matter, namely, the great and the small. But this duality is different from that of Aristotle. For Aristotle held that the duality was matter and privation, which are one in subject but different in nature [ratio]. But the Platonists did not hold that one of these is privation and the other matter, but they joined privation to both, i.e., to the great and the small. They either took both of them together, not distinguishing in their speech between the great and the small, or else they took each separately. Whence it is clear that the Platonists, who posited form and the great and the small, held three completely different principles than Aristotle, who posited matter and privation and form.

The Platonists realized more than

the other ancient philosophers that it is necessary to suppose some one nature for all natural forms, which nature is primary matter. But they made it one both in subject and in nature [ratio], not distinguishing between it and privation. For although they held a duality on the part of matter, namely, the great and the small, they made no distinction at all between matter and privation. Rather they spoke only of matter under which they included the great and the small. And they ignored privation, making no mention of it.

134. Next where he says, "For the one which persists ..." [88], he proves that his opinion is true. Concerning this he makes two points. First he states his position, i.e., that it is necessary to distinguish privation from matter. Secondly, where he says, "The matter comes to be ..." [90], he shows how matter is corrupted or generated.

He treats the first point in two ways, first by explanation, and secondly by reducing [the opposite opinion] to the impossible, where he says, ". . . the other such ..." [98].

135. He says, therefore, first [88] that this nature which is the subject, i.e., matter, together with form is a cause of the things which come to be according to nature after the manner of a mother. For just as a mother is a cause of generation by receiving, so also is matter.

But if one takes the other part of the contrariety, namely, the privation, we can imagine, by stretching our understanding, that it does not pertain to the constitution of the thing, but rather to some sort of evil for the thing. For privation is altogether non-being, since it is nothing other than the negation of a form in a subject, and is outside the whole being. Thus the argument of Parmenides that whatever is other than being is non-being, has a place in regard to privation, but not in regard to matter, as the Platonists said.

He shows that privation would pertain to evil as follows. Form is something divine and very good and desirable. It is divine because every form is a certain participation in the likeness of the divine being, which is pure act. For each thing, insofar as it is in act, has form. Form is very good because act is the perfection of potency and is its good; and it follows as a consequence of this that form is desirable, because every thing desires its own perfection.

Privation, on the other hand, is opposed to form, since it is nothing other than the removal of form. Hence, since that which is opposed to the good and removes it is evil, it is clear that privation pertains to evil. Whence it follows that privation is not the same as matter, which is the cause of a thing as a mother.

136. Next where he says, ". . . the other such . . ." [89], he proves the same thing by an argument which reduces [the opposite position] to the impossible.

Since form is a sort of good and is desirable, matter, which is other than privation and other than form, naturally seeks and desires form according to its nature. But for those who do not distinguish matter from privation, this involves the absurdity that a contrary seeks its own corruption, which is absurd. That this is so he shows as follows.

If matter seeks form, it does not seek a form insofar as it is under this form. For in this latter case the matter does not stand in need of being through this form. (Every appetite exists because of a need, for an appetite is a desire for what is not possessed.) In like manner matter does not seek form insofar as it is under the contrary or privation, for one of the contraries is corruptive of the other, and thus something would seek its own corruption. It is clear, therefore, that matter, which seeks form, is other in nature [ratio] from both form and privation. For if matter seeks form according to its proper nature, as was said, and if it is held that matter and privation are the same in nature [ratio], it follows that privation seeks form, and thus seeks its own corruption, which is impossible. Hence it is also impossible that matter and privation be the same in nature [ratio].

Nevertheless, matter is "a this," i.e., something having privation. Hence, if the feminine seeks the masculine, and if the base seeks the good, this is not because baseness itself seeks the good, which is its contrary; rather it seeks it accidentally, because that in which baseness happens to be seeks to be good. And likewise femininity does not seek masculinity; rather that in which the feminine happens to be seeks the masculine. And in like manner, privation does not seek to be form; rather that in which privation happens to be, namely, matter, seeks to be form.

137. But Avicenna opposes this position of the Philosopher in three ways.

First, matter has neither animal appetite (as is obvious in itself) nor natural appetite, whereby it would seek form. For matter does not have any form or power inclining it to anything, as for example, the heavy naturally seeks the lowest place insofar as it is inclined by its heaviness to such a place.

Secondly, he objects that, if matter seeks form, this is so because it lacks every form, or because it seeks to possess many forms at once, both which are impossible, or because it dislikes the form which it has and seeks to have another form, and this also is meaningless. Hence it seems that we must say that matter in no way seeks form.

His third objection is as follows. To say that matter seeks form as the feminine seeks the masculine is to speak figuratively, i.e., as a poet, not as a philosopher.

138. But it is easy to resolve objections of this sort. For we must note that everything which seeks something either knows that which it seeks and orders itself to it, or else it tends toward it by the ordination and direction of someone who knows, as the arrow tends toward a determinate mark by the direction and ordination of the archer. Therefore, natural appetite is nothing but the ordination of things to their end in accordance with their proper natures. However a being in act is not only ordered to its end by an active power, but also by its matter insofar as it is potency. For form is the end of matter. Therefore for matter to seek form is nothing other than matter being ordered to form as potency to act.

And because matter still remains in potency to another form while it is under some form, there is always in it an appetite for form. This is not because of a dislike for the form which it has, nor because it seeks to be the contrary at the same time, but because it is in potency to other forms while it has some form in act.

Nor does he use a figure of speech here; rather, he uses an example. For it was said above that primary matter is knowable by way of proportion, insofar as it is related to substantial forms as sensible matters are related to accidental forms. And thus in order to explain primary matter, it is necessary to use an example taken from sensible

substances. Therefore, just as he used the example of unshaped bronze and the example of the non-musical man to explain matter, so now to explain matter he uses the example of the appetite of the woman for the man and the example of appetite of the base for the good. For this happens to these things insofar as they have something which is of the nature [ratio] of matter. However, it must be noted that Aristotle is here arguing against Plato, who used such metaphorical expressions, likening matter to a mother and the feminine, and form to the masculine. And so Aristotle uses Plato's own metaphors against him.

139. Next where he says, **"The matter comes to be ..."** [90], he shows how matter is corrupted. He says that in a certain respect matter is corrupted and in a certain respect it is not. For insofar as privation is in it, it is corrupted when the privation ceases to be in it, as if we should say that unshaped bronze is corrupted when it ceases to be unshaped. But in itself, insofar as it is a certain being in potency, it is neither generated nor corruptible. This is clear from the following. If matter should come to be, there would have to be something which is the subject from which it comes to be, as is clear from what was said above. But that which is the first subject in generation is matter. For we say that matter is the first subject from which a thing comes to be per se, and not per accidens, and is in the thing after it has come to be. (And privation differs from matter on both of these points. For privation is that from which a thing comes to be per accidens, and is that which is not in the thing after it has come to be.) It follows, therefore, that matter would be before it would come to be, which is impossible. And in like manner, everything

which is corrupted is resolved into primary matter. Therefore, at the very time when primary matter already is, it would be corrupted; and thus if primary matter is corrupted, it will have been corrupted before it is corrupted, which is impossible. Therefore, it is impossible for primary matter to be generated and corrupted. But by this we do not deny that it comes into existence through creation.

140. Next where he says, **"The accurate determination . . ."** [91], he indicates that since the errors about matter and privation have been eliminated, then the errors and problems about form should also be eliminated. For some have posited separated forms, i.e., ideas, which they reduced to one first idea.

And so he says that first philosophy treats such questions as whether the formal principle is one or many, and how many there are, and what kind there are. Hence these questions will be reserved for first philosophy. For form is a principle of existing, and being as such is the subject of first philosophy. But matter and privation are principles of mutable being, which is considered by the natural philosopher. Nevertheless we shall treat of natural and corruptible forms in the following books on this discipline.

Finally he summarizes what has been said. It has been determined that there are principles, what the principles are, and how many there are. But it is necessary to make a new start in our study of natural science, inquiring, that is, into the principles of the science.

BOOK II
THE PRINCIPLES OF NATURAL SCIENCE

LECTURE 1 [192b8–193a8]
What Is Nature? What Things Have a Nature? What Things Are "According to Nature"?

The Text of Aristotle
Chapter 1

92. *Of things that exist, some exist by nature, some from other causes.*

"By nature" the animals and their parts exist, and the plants and the simple bodies (earth, fire, air, water)—for we say that these and the like exist "by nature."

All the things mentioned present a feature in which they differ from things which are not constituted by nature. Each of them has within itself a principle of motion and of stationariness (in respect of place, or of growth and decrease, or by way of alteration). On the other hand, a bed and a coat and anything else of that sort, qua receiving these designations—i.e., in so far as they are products of art—have no innate impulse to change. But in so far as they happen to be composed of stone or of earth or of a mixture of the two they do have such an impulse, and just to that extent—   **192b8–20**

93. *which seems to indicate that nature is a source or cause of being moved and of being at rest in that to which it belongs primarily, in virtue of itself and not in virtue of a concomitant attribute.*   **192b20–23**

93bis. *I say "not in virtue of a concomitant attribute," because (for instance) a man who is a doctor might cure himself. Nevertheless it is not in so far as he is a patient that he possesses the art of medicine: it merely has happened that the same man is doctor and patient—and that is why these attributes are not always found together. So it is with all other artificial products. None of them has in itself the source of its own production. But while in some cases (for instance houses and the other products of manual labor) that principle is in something else external to the thing, in others—those which may cause a change in themselves in virtue of a concomitant attribute—it lies in the things themselves (but not in virtue of what they are).*

"Nature" then is what has been stated.   **192b23–32**

94. *Things "have a nature" which have a principle of this kind. Each of them is a substance; for it is a subject, and nature always implies a subject in which it inheres.*   **192b32–34**

95. *The term "according to nature" is applied to all these things and also to the attributes which belong to them in virtue of what they are, for instance the property of fire to be carried upwards—which is not a "nature" nor "has a nature" but is "by nature" or "according to nature."*   **192b35–193a2**

96. *What nature is, then, and the meaning of the terms "by nature" and "according to nature," has been stated. That nature exists, it would be absurd to try to prove; for it is obvious that there are many things of this kind, and to prove what is obvious by what is not is the mark of a man who is unable to distinguish what is self-evident from what is not. (This state of mind is clearly possible. A man blind from birth might reason about colors.) Presumably therefore such persons must be talking about words without any thought to correspond.*   **193b3–9**

COMMENTARY OF ST. THOMAS

141. [92] After the Philosopher has treated the principles of natural things in Book I, he here treats the principles of natural science.

Now the things which we ought to know first in any science are its subject and the method by which it demonstrates.

Hence Book II is divided into two parts. First he determines what things belong to the consideration of natural science, and secondly, where he says, **"Now that we have established . . ."** [194b16], he points out the causes from which it demonstrates.

The first part is divided into two parts. First he shows what nature is. Secondly, where he says, **"We have distinguished . . ."** [102], he determines what things natural science considers.

The first part is divided into two parts. First he shows what nature is. Secondly the number of ways [in which the name nature is used] is pointed out, where he says, **"Some identify . . ."** [97].

The first part is divided into two parts. First he shows what nature is. Secondly, where he says, **"That nature exists . . ."** [96], he refutes the position of those who attempt to demonstrate that nature exists.

Concerning the first part he makes two points. First he states what nature is. Secondly, where he says, **"Things 'have a nature' . . ."** [94], he designates those things which are called "nature."

Concerning the first part he makes three points. First he inquires into the definition of nature. Secondly he arrives at the definition, where he says, **". . . nature is . . ."** [93]. Thirdly, he explains this definition, where he says, **"I say . . ."** [93bis]

142. He says, therefore, first that we say that of all beings some are from nature, whereas others are from other causes, for example, from art or from chance.

Now we say that the following things are from nature: every sort of animal, and their parts, such as flesh and blood, and also plants and simple bodies, i.e., the elements, such as earth, fire, air and water, which are not resolved into any prior bodies. For these and all things like them are said to be from nature.

All of these things differ from the things which are not from nature because all things of this sort seem to have in themselves a principle of motion and rest; some according to place, such as the heavy and the light, and also the celestial bodies, some according to increase and decrease, such as the animals and plants, and some according to alteration, such as the simple bodies and everything which is composed of them.

But things which are not from nature, such as a bed and clothing and like things, which are spoken of in this way because they are from art, have in themselves no principle of mutation, except per accidens, insofar as the matter and substance of artificial bodies are natural things. Thus insofar as artificial things happen to be iron or stone, they have a principle of motion in them, but not insofar as they are artifacts. For a knife has in itself a principle of downward motion, not insofar as it is a knife, but insofar as it is iron.

143. But it does not seem to be true that in every change of natural things a principle of motion is in that which is moved. For in the alteration and the generation of simple bodies, the whole principle of motion seems to be from an external agent. For example, when water is heated, or air is converted into fire, the principle of the change is from an external agent.

Therefore, some say that even in

changes of this sort an active principle of motion is in that which is moved, not perfectly, but imperfectly, which principle helps the action of the external agent. For they say that in matter there is a certain inchoateness of form, which they say is privation, the third principle of nature. And the generations and alterations of simple bodies are said to be from this intrinsic principle.

But this cannot be. Since a thing acts only insofar as it is in act, the aforesaid inchoate state of form, since it is not act, but a certain disposition for act, cannot be an active principle. And furthermore, even if it were a complete form, it would not act on its own subject by changing it. For the form does not act, rather the composite acts. And the composite cannot alter itself unless there are two parts in it, one of which alters, the other of which is altered.

144. And so it must be said that a principle of motion is in natural things in the way in which motion belongs to them. Therefore in those things to which it belongs to move, there is an active principle of motion. Whereas in those things to which it belongs to be moved, there is a passive principle, which is matter. And this principle, insofar as it has a natural potency for such a form and motion, makes the motion to be natural. And for this reason the production of artificial things is not natural. For even though the material principle is in that which comes to be, it does not have a natural potency for such a form.

So also the local motion of the celestial bodies is natural, even though it is from a separated mover, inasmuch as there is in the celestial body itself a natural potency for such a motion.

However in heavy and light bodies there is a formal principle of motion. (But a formal principle of this sort cannot be called the active potency to which this motion pertains. Rather it is understood as a passive potency. For heaviness in earth is not a principle for moving, but rather for being moved.) For just as the other accidents are consequent upon substantial form, so also is place, and thus also "to be moved to place." However the natural form is not the mover. Rather the mover is that which generates and gives such and such a form upon which such a motion follows.

145. Next where he says, "... nature is . . ." [93], he concludes from the above the definition of nature in the following manner.

Natural things differ from the non-natural insofar as they have a nature. But they differ from the non-natural only insofar as they have in themselves a principle of motion. Therefore, nature is nothing other than a principle of motion and rest in that in which it is primarily and per se and not per accidens.

Now "principle" is placed in the definition of nature as its genus, and not as something absolute, for the name "nature" involves a relation to a principle. For those things are said to be born which are generated after having been joined to a generator, as is clear in plants and animals, thus the principle of generation or motion is called nature. Hence they are to be laughed at who, wishing to correct the definition of Aristotle, tried to define nature by something absolute, saying that nature is a power seated in things or something of this sort.

Moreover, nature is called a principle and cause in order to point out that in that which is moved nature is not a principle of all motions in the same way, but in different ways, as was said above.

Moreover, he says that nature is a principle "of motion and rest." For those things which are naturally moved to a place, also or even more naturally rest in that place. Because of this, fire is naturally moved upward, since it is natural for it to be there. And for the same reason everything can be said to be moved naturally and to rest naturally in its place. This, however, must not be understood to mean that in everything which is moved natural ly nature is also a principle of coming to rest. For a heavenly body is indeed moved naturally, but it does not naturally come to rest. But on the whole it can be said that nature is not only a principle of motion but also of rest.

Further he says "in which it is" in order to differentiate nature from artificial things in which there is motion only per accidens.

Then he adds "primarily" because even though nature is a principle of the motion of composite things, nevertheless it is not such primarily. Hence that an animal is moved downwards is not because of the nature of animal insofar as it is animal, but because of the nature of the dominant element.

He explains why he says "per se and not per accidens" where he says, **"I say 'not in virtue of . . .' "** [93bis].

It sometimes happens that a doctor is the cause of his own health, and so the principle of his own coming to health is in him, but per accidens. Hence nature is not the principle of his coming to health. For it is not insofar as he is cured that he has the art of medicine, but insofar as he is a doctor. Hence the same being happens to be a doctor and to be cured, and he is cured

insofar as he is sick. And so because these things are joined per accidens, they are also at times separated per accidens. For it is one thing to be a doctor who cures, and another thing to be a sick person who is cured. But the principle of a natural motion is in the natural body which is moved insofar as it is moved. For insofar as fire has lightness, it is carried upward. And these two things are not divided from each other so that the lightness is different than the body which is moved upward. Rather they are always one and the same. And all artificial things are like the doctor who cures. For none of them has in itself the principle of its own making. Rather some of them come to be from something outside, as a house and other things which are carved by hand, while others come to be through an intrinsic principle, but per accidens, as was said. And so it has been stated what nature is.

146. Next where he says, **"Things 'have a nature' . . ."** [94], he defines those things which are given the name "nature."

He says that those things which have in themselves a principle of their motion have a nature. And such are all subjects of nature. For nature is a subject insofar as it is called matter, and nature is in a subject insofar as it is called form.

147. Next where he says, **"The term 'according to nature' . . ."** [95], he explains what is "according to nature."

He says that "to be according to nature" is said both of subjects whose existence is from nature and also of the accidents which are in them and caused by such a principle. Thus to be carried upward is not a nature itself, nor does it have nature, but it is caused by nature.

And thus it has been stated what nature is, and what it is that has nature, and what is "according to nature."

148. Next where he says, **"That nature exists . . ."** [96], he denies the presumptuous position of those who wish to demonstrate that nature exists.

He says that it is ridiculous for anyone to attempt to demonstrate that nature exists. For it is manifest to the senses that many things are from nature, which have in themselves the principle of their own motion. To wish, moreover, to demonstrate the obvious by what is not obvious is the mark of a man who cannot judge what is known in itself and what is not known in itself. For when he wishes to demonstrate that which is known in itself, he uses that which is known in itself as if it were not known in itself. And it is clear that some people do this. A man who is born blind may sometimes reason about colors. But that which he uses as a principle is not known to him per se, because he has no understanding of the thing. Rather he only uses names. For our knowledge has its origin from the senses, and he who lacks one sense, lacks one science. Hence those who are born blind, and who never sense color, cannot understand any thing about color. And so they use the unknown as if it were known. And the converse applies to those who wish to demonstrate that nature exists. For they use the known as if it were not known. The existence of nature is known per se, insofar as natural things are manifest to the senses. But what the nature of each thing is, or what the principle of its motion is, is not manifest.

Hence it is clear from this that Avicenna, who wished that it were possible to prove the existence of nature, unreasonably attempted to disprove what Aristotle has said. However Avicenna did not wish to prove this from natural things, for no science proves its own principles. But ignorance of moving principles does not mean that the existence of nature is not known per se, as was said.

LECTURE 2 [193 a 9–b21]
Nature Is Both Matter and Form, but Primarily Form

The Text of Aristotle

97. *Some identify the nature or substance of a natural object with that immediate constituent of it which taken by itself is without arrangement, e.g. the wood is the "nature" of the bed and the bronze the "nature" of the statue.*

As an indication of this Antiphon points out that if you planted a bed and the rotting wood acquired the power of sending up a shoot, it would not be a bed that would come up, but wood—which shows that the arrangement in accordance with the rules of the art is merely an accidental attribute, whereas the real nature is the other, which, further, persists continuously through the process of making.

But if the material of each of these objects has itself the same relation to something else, say bronze (or gold) to water, bones (or wood) to earth and so on, that (they say) would be their nature and essence. Consequently some assert earth, others fire or air or water or some or all of these, to be the nature of the things that are. For whatever any one of them supposed to have this character—whether one thing, or more than one thing—this or these he declared to be the whole of substance, all else being its affections, states, or dispositions. Every such thing they held to be eternal (for it could not pass into anything else), but other things to come into being and cease to be times without number.

This then is one account of "nature," namely that it is the immediate material substratum of things which have in themselves a principle of motion or change.   **193a9–30**

98. *Another account is that "nature" is the shape or form which is specified in the definition of the thing.*

For the word "nature" is applied to what is according to nature and the natural in the same way as "art" is applied to what is artistic or a work of art. We should not say in the latter case that there is anything artistic about a thing, if it is a bed only potentially, not yet having the form of a bed; nor should we call it a work of art. The same is true of natural compounds. What is potentially flesh or bone has not yet its own "nature," and does not exist "by nature," until it receives the form specified in the definition, which we name in defining what flesh or bone is. Thus in the second sense of "nature" it would be the shape or form (not separable except in statement) of things which have in themselves a source of motion. (The combination of the two, e.g. man, is not "nature" but "by nature" or "natural.")

The form indeed is "nature" rather than the matter; for a thing is more properly said to be what it is when it has attained to fulfilment than when it exists potentially.   **193a30–193b8**

99. *Again man is born from man, but not bed from bed. That is why people say that the figure is not the nature of a bed, but the wood is—if the bed sprouted, not a bed but wood would come up. But even if the figure is art, then on the same principle the shape of man is his nature. For man is born from man.*   **193b8–12**

100. *We also speak of a thing's nature as being exhibited in the process of growth by which its nature is attained. The "nature" in this sense is not like "doctoring," which leads not to the art of doctoring but to health. Doctoring must start from the art, not lead to it. But it is not in this way that nàture (in the one sense) is related to nature (in the other). What grows qua growing grows from something into something. Into what then does it grow? Not into that from which it arose but into that to which it tends. The shape then is nature.*   **193b12–18**

101. *"Shape" and "nature," it should be added, are used in two senses. For the privation too is in a way form. But whether in unqualified coming to be there is privation, i.e. a contrary to what comes to be, we must consider later.*   **193b18–21**

COMMENTARY OF ST. THOMAS

149. Having shown what nature is, the Philosopher here [97] points out the number of ways in which the name "nature" is used. He shows first that nature is predicated of matter, secondly that it is predicated of form, where he says, "Another account . . ." [98]

Concerning the first point we must note that the ancient natural philosophers, being unable to arrive at primary matter, as was said above, held that some sensible body, such as fire or air or water, is the first matter of all things. And so it followed that all forms come to matter as to something existing in act, as happens in artificial things. For the form of knife comes to iron already existing in act. And so they adopted an opinion about natural forms similar to that which is true of artificial forms.

He says, therefore, first that it seems to some that that which is primarily in each thing and which considered in itself is unformed is the substance and nature of natural things, as if we would say that the nature of a bed is wood, and the nature of a statue is bronze. For wood is in the bed and is, when considered in itself, not formed. And Antiphon said that the following is a sign of this: if one should bury a bed in the earth and if the wood by rotting should acquire the potency to germinate something, that which is generated will not be a bed, but wood. Now since the substance is that which remains permanent, and since it belongs to nature to generate what is like itself, he concluded that every disposition in respect to any law of reason [ratio] or art is an accident. And that which remains permanent is substance, which continually undergoes change of dispositions of this sort.

Having supposed, therefore, that the forms of artificial things are accidents, and that matter is substance, Antiphon assumed the other proposition, namely, that just as the bed and statue are related to bronze and wood, so also each natural thing is related to some other thing which is its matter. Thus bronze and gold are related to water (because the matter of all liquifiable things seems to be water), and bone and wood are related to earth, and it is the same with all other natural things. Hence he concluded that the material things which subsist under natural forms are their nature and substance. And because of this some have said that earth is the nature and substance of all things, for example, the first theological poets; whereas the later philosophers chose fire or air or water, or some of these or all of them, as is clear from what was said above. For they said that there are as many substances of things as there are material principles. And they said that all other things are accidents of these material principles, either as passions, or as habits, or as dispositions, or as anything else which is reduced to the genus of accident.

Thus one difference which they posited between material and formal principles is that they said that they differed as substance and accident.

There is, however, another difference, for they also said that these principles differ as the permanent and the corruptible. Since they held that each of the aforementioned simple bodies is a material principle, they said it was permanent, for they did not say that they were changed into each other. But they said that all other things come to be and are corrupted infinitely. For example, if water is the material principle, they said that water is never corrupted, but remains water in all things as their substance. But they said that bronze and gold and other things of this sort are corrupted and generated infinitely.

150. This position is in part true and in part false. With reference to the point that matter is the substance and the nature of natural things, it is true. For matter enters into the constitution of the substance of each natural thing. But insofar as they said that all forms are accidents, this position is false.

Whence from this opinion and from his argument, Aristotle concludes to that which is true, namely, that nature in one way is called matter, which underlies each natural thing which has in itself a principle of motion or of some sort of mutation. For motion is a species of mutation, as will be said in Book V.

151. Next where he says, **"Another account . . ."** [98], he shows that the form is also called nature.

Concerning this he makes two points. First he states his position, i.e., that form is nature. Secondly, where he says, **"Shape and nature . . ."** [193b19], he explains the diversity of forms.

He explains the first point with three arguments. He says, therefore, first that nature is used in another way to refer to the form and species, from which the nature [ratio] of the thing is constituted. He proves this by the following argument.

Just as art belongs to a thing insofar as it is according to art and the artistic, so also nature belongs to a thing insofar as it is according to nature and the natural. But we do not say that that which is only in potency to that which is artistic has anything of art, because it does not yet have the species [e.g.] of a bed. Therefore in natural things that

which is potentially flesh and bone does not have the nature of flesh and bone before it takes on the form in respect to which the definitive nature [ratio] of the thing is established (i.e. that through which we know what flesh and bone are). The nature is not yet in it before it has the form. Therefore the nature of natural things which have in themselves a principle of motion is in another way the form. And this form, although it is not separated from the matter in the thing, still differs from the matter by reason [ratio]. For as bronze and the shapeless, although one in subject, are different in reason [ratio], so also are matter and form.

He says this because unless form were other than matter according to reason [ratio], the ways in which matter is called nature and form is called nature would not be different.

152. Moreover one might believe that since both matter and form are called nature then the composite could also be called nature. For substance is predicated of form and of matter and of the composite.

But he denies this, saying that the composite of matter and form, such as a man, is not the nature itself, but is some thing from nature. For nature [natura] has the nature [ratio] of a principle, but the composite has the nature [ratio] of "being from a principle."

153. From the foregoing argument he proceeds further to show that form is nature more than matter. For a thing is said to be greater insofar as it is in act rather than insofar as it is in potency. Whence form, according to which a thing is natural in act, is nature more than matter, according to which a thing is something natural in potency.

154. He gives the second argument where he says, **"Again man is . . ."** [99].

He says that although a bed does not come to be from a bed, as Antiphon said, man does come to be from man. Whence what they say is true, namely, that the form of bed is not the nature, but the wood is. For if wood should germinate, a bed would not come to be, but wood. Therefore, as this form, which does not arise through germination, is not nature but art, so the form which arises from generation is nature. But the form of a natural thing does arise through generation, for man comes to be from man. Therefore the form of a natural thing is nature.

155. He gives his third argument where he says, **"We also speak . . ."** [100]. Nature can be signified as a generation, for instance, if we should call it birth. Thus nature in the sense of generation, i.e., birth, is the way to nature. For the difference between actions and passions is that actions are named from their principles while passions are named from their terminations. For each thing is named from act, which is the principle of action and the termination of passion. But naming is not the same in passions and actions. For medication is not called the way to medicine, but the way to health. It is necessary for medication to proceed from medicine, not to medicine. But nature in the sense of generation, i.e., birth, is not related to nature as medication is related to medicine. Rather it is related to nature as to a termination, since it is a passion. For that which is born, insofar as it is born, comes from something to something. Hence that which is born is named from that to which it proceeds, and not from that from which it proceeds. That, however, to which birth tends is form. Therefore form is nature.

156. Next where he says, **"Shape and nature . . ."** [101], he shows that the nature which is form is used in two ways, i.e., of the incomplete form and the complete form. This is clear in accidental generation, for example, when something becomes white. For whiteness is a complete form, and the privation of whiteness is in some way a species, insofar as it is joined to blackness, which is an imperfect form. But whether or not in simple generation, which is the generation of substances, there is something which is a privation and also a contrary, so that substantial forms are contraries, must be considered later in Book V and in De Generatione et Corruptione.

How Physics and Mathematics Differ in Their Consideration of the Same Thing

The Text of Aristotle
Chapter 2

102. We have distinguished, then, the different ways in which the term "nature" is used. The next point to consider is how the mathematician differs from the physicist.   193b22–23

103. Obviously physical bodies contain surfaces and volumes, lines and points, and these are the subject-matter of mathematics.   193b23–25

104. Further, is astronomy different from physics or a department of it? It seems absurd that "the physicist should be supposed to know the nature of sun or moon," but not to know any of their essential attributes, particularly as the writers on physics obviously do discuss their shape and whether the earth and the world are spherical or not.   193b25–30

105. Now the mathematician, though he too treats of these things, nevertheless does not treat of them as the limits of a physical body; nor does he consider the attributes indicated as the attributes of such bodies.   193b31–33

106. That is why he separates them; for in thought they are separable from motion, and it makes no difference, nor does any falsity result, if they are separated.   193b33–35

107. The holders of the theory of Forms do the same, though they are not aware of it; for they separate the objects of physics, which are less separable than those of mathematics.

193b35–194a1

108. This becomes plain if one tries to state in each of the two cases the definitions of the things and of their attributes. "Odd" and "even," "straight" and "curved," and likewise "number," "line," and "figure," do not involve motion; not so "flesh" and "bone" and "man"—these are defined like "snub nose," not like "curved."   194a1–7

109. Similar evidence is supplied by the more physical of the branches of mathematics such as optics, harmonics, and astronomy. These are in a way the converse of geometry. While geometry investigates physical lines but not qua physical, optics investigates mathematical lines, but qua physical, not qua mathematical.   194a7–12

COMMENTARY OF ST. THOMAS

157. After the Philosopher has explained what nature is and how many ways the name is used, he here intends to show what it is that natural science considers.

This section is divided into two parts. First he shows how natural science differs from mathematics. Secondly, where he says, **"Since nature has . . ."** [110], he designates that to which the consideration of natural science extends.

Concerning the first part he makes three points. First he states the question. Secondly, where he says, **"Obvi-** ously physical bodies . . ."** [103], he gives his reasons for [raising] the question. Thirdly, he answers the question where he says, **"Now the mathematician . . ."** [105].

He says, therefore, first that after the uses of the name "nature" have been determined, it is necessary to consider how mathematics differs from natural philosophy.

158. Next where he says, **"Obviously physical bodies . . ."** [103], he gives his reasons for [raising] the question. The first of these is as follows.

Whenever sciences consider the

same subjects, they are either the same science, or one is a part of the other. But the mathematical philosopher considers points and lines and surfaces and bodies, and so does the natural philosopher. (For he proves from the fact that natural bodies have planes, i.e., surfaces, and volumes, i.e., solidity, and lengths and points. Moreover the natural philosopher must consider all things that are in natural bodies.) Therefore it seems that natural science and mathematics are either the same or that one is a part of the other.

He gives the second reason where he says, **"Further, is astronomy . . ."** [104]. In connection with this reason he raises the question whether astronomy is altogether other than natural philosophy or a part of it. For it is clear that astronomy is a part of mathematics. Whence, if it is also a part of natural philosophy, it follows that mathematics and physics agree at least in this part.

That astronomy is a part of physics he proves in two ways. First by the following argument. To whomever it belongs to know the substances and natures of certain things, also belongs the consideration of their accidents. But it belongs to the natural philosopher to consider the nature and substance of the sun and the moon, since they are certain natural bodies. Therefore it belongs to the natural philosopher to consider their per se accidents.

He proves this also from the custom of the philosophers. For natural philosophers are found to have treated the shape of the sun and of the moon and of the earth and of the whole world. And these are topics which claim the attention of the astronomers. Therefore astronomy and natural science agree not only in [having] the same subjects but also in the consideration

of the same accidents, and in demonstrating the same conclusions. Whence it seems that astronomy is a part of physics, and as a result physics does not differ totally from mathematics.

159. Next where he says, **"Now the mathematician . . ."** [105], he answers the question raised above. Concerning this he makes two points. First he gives his solution, and secondly he confirms it, where he says, **"This becomes plain . . ."** [108]

Concerning the first part he makes three points. First he answers the question. Secondly, where he says, **"That is why he separates . . ."** [106], he concludes to a sort of corollary from the above. Thirdly, where he says, **"The holders of . . ."** [107], he excludes an error.

160. He says, therefore, first [105] that the mathematician and the natural philosopher treat the same things, i.e., points, and lines, and surfaces, and things of this sort, but not in the same way. For the mathematician does not treat these things insofar as each of them is a boundary of a natural body, nor does he consider those things which belong to them insofar as they are the boundaries of a natural body. But this is the way in which natural science treats them. And, it is not inconsistent that the same thing should fall under the consideration of different sciences according to different points of view.

161. Next where he says, **"That is why he separates . . ."** [106], he concludes to a sort of corollary from what he has just said. Because the mathematician does not consider lines, and points, and surfaces, and things of this sort, and their accidents, insofar as they are the boundaries of a natural body, he is said to abstract from sensible and natural matter. And the reason

why he is able to abstract is this: according to the intellect these things are abstracted from motion.

As evidence for this reason we must note that many things are joined in the thing, but the understanding of one of them is not derived from the understanding of another. Thus white and musical are joined in the same subject, nevertheless the understanding of one of these is not derived from an understanding of the other. And so one can be separately understood without the other. And this one is understood as abstracted from the other. It is clear, however, that the posterior is not derived from the understanding of the prior, but conversely. Hence the prior can be understood without the posterior, but not conversely. Thus it is clear that animal is prior to man, and man is prior to this man (for man is had by addition to animal, and this man by addition to man). And because of this our understanding of man is not derived from our understanding of animal, nor our understanding of Socrates from our understanding of man. Hence animal can be understood without man, and man without Socrates and other individuals. And this is to abstract the universal from the particular.

In like manner, among all the accidents which come to substance, quantity comes first, and then the sensible qualities, and actions and passions, and the motions consequent upon sensible qualities. Therefore quantity does not embrace in its intelligibility the sensible qualities or the passions or the motions. Yet it does include substance in its intelligibility. Therefore quantity can be understood without matter, which is subject to motion, and without sensible qualities, but not without substance. And thus quantities and those things which belong to them are

understood as abstracted from motion and sensible matter, but not from intelligible matter, as is said in Metaphysics, VII.

Since, therefore, the objects of mathematics are abstracted from motion according to the intellect, and since they do not include in their intelligibility sensible matter, which is a subject of motion, the mathematician can abstract them from sensible matter. And it makes no difference as far as the truth is concerned whether they are considered one way or the other. For although the objects of mathematics are not separated according to existence, the mathematicians, in abstracting them according to their understanding, do not lie, because they do not assert that these things exist apart from sensible matter (for this would be a lie). But they consider them without any consideration of sensible matter, which can be done without lying. Thus one can truly consider the white without the musical, even though they exist together in the same subject. But it would not be a true consideration if one were to assert that the white is not musical.

162. Next where he says, **"The holders of the theory . . ."** [107], he excludes from what he has said an error of Plato.

Since Plato was puzzled as to how the intellect could truly separate those things which were not separated in their existence, he held that all things which are separated in the understanding are separated in the thing. Hence he not only held that mathematical entities are separated, because of the fact that the mathematician abstracts from sensible matter, but he even held that natural things themselves are separated, because of the fact that natural science is of universals and not of singulars. Hence he held that man is separated, and horse, and stone, and other such things. And he said these separated things are ideas, although natural things are less abstract than mathematical entities. For mathematical entities are altogether separated from sensible matter in the understanding, because sensible matter is not included in the understanding of the mathematicals, neither in the universal nor in the particular. But sensible matter is included in the understanding of natural things, whereas individual matter is not. For in the understanding of man flesh and bone is included, but not this flesh and this bone.

163. Next where he says, **"This becomes plain . . ."** [108], he clarifies the solution he has given in two ways, first by means of the difference in the definitions which the mathematician and the natural philosopher assign, and secondly by means of the intermediate sciences, where he says, **"Similar evidence . . ."** [109]

He says, therefore, first that what has been said of the different modes of consideration of the mathematician and the natural philosopher will become evident if one attempts to give definitions of the mathematicals and of natural things and of their accidents. For the mathematicals, such as equal and unequal, straight and curved, and number, and line, and figure, are defined without motion and matter, but this is not so with flesh and bone and man. Rather the definition of these latter is like the definition of the snub in which definition a sensible subject is placed, i.e., nose. But this is not the case with the definition of the curved in which definition a sensible subject is not placed.

And thus from the very definitions of natural things and of the math-

ematicals, what was said above about the difference between the mathematician and the natural philosopher is apparent.

164. Next where he says, **"Similar evidence . . ."** [109], he proves the same thing by means of those sciences which are intermediates between mathematics and natural philosophy.

Those sciences are called intermediate sciences which take principles abstracted by the purely mathematical sciences and apply them to sensible matter. For example, perspective applies to the visual line those things which are demonstrated by geometry about the abstracted line; and harmony, that is music, applies to sound those things which arithmetic considers about the proportions of numbers; and astronomy applies the consideration of geometry and arithmetic to the heavens and its parts.

However, although sciences of this sort are intermediates between natural science and mathematics, they are here said by the Philosopher to be more natural than mathematical, because each thing is named and takes its species from its terminus. Hence, since the consideration of these sciences is terminated in natural matter, then even though they proceed by mathematical principles, they are more natural than mathematical sciences.

He says, therefore, that sciences of this sort are established in a way contrary to the sciences which are purely mathematical, such as geometry or arithmetic. For geometry considers the line which has existence in sensible matter, which is the natural line. But it does not consider it insofar as it is in sensible matter, insofar as it is natural, but abstractly, as was said. But perspective conversely takes the abstract line which is in the consideration of mathematics, and applies it to sensible matter, and thus treats it not insofar as it is a mathematical, but insofar as it is a physical thing.

Therefore from this difference between intermediate sciences and the purely mathematical sciences, what was said above is clear. For if intermediate sciences of this sort apply the abstract to sensible matter, it is clear that mathematics conversely separates those things which are in sensible matter.

165. And from this it is clear what his answer is to the objection raised above concerning astronomy. For astronomy is a natural science more than a mathematical science. Hence it is no wonder that astronomy agrees in its conclusions with natural science.

However, since it is not a purely natural science, it demonstrates the same conclusion through another method. Thus, the fact that the earth is spherical is demonstrated by natural science by a natural method, e.g., because its parts everywhere and equally come together at the middle. But this is demonstrated by astronomy from the figure of the lunar eclipse, or from the fact that the same stars are not seen from every part of the earth.

Physics Considers Not Only Matter but Also Every Form Existing in Matter

Text of Aristotle

110. *Since "nature" has two senses, the form and the matter, we must investigate its objects as we would the essence of snubness. That is, such things are neither independent of matter nor can be defined in terms of matter only.* **194a12–15**

111. *Here too indeed one might raise a difficulty. Since there are two natures, with which is the physicist concerned? Or should he investigate the combination of the two? But if the combination of the two, then also each severally. Does it belong then to the same or to different sciences to know each severally?* **194a15–18**

112. *If we look at the ancients, physics would seem to be concerned with the matter. (It was only very slightly that Empedocles and Democritus touched on the forms and the essence.)* **194a18–21**

113. *But if on the other hand art imitates nature, and it is the part of the same discipline to know the form and the matter up to a point (e.g. the doctor has a knowledge of health and also of bile and phlegm, in which health is realized, and the builder both of the form of the house and of the matter, namely that it is bricks and beams, and so forth): if this is so, it would be the part of physics also to know nature in both its senses.* **194a21–27**

114. *Again, "that for the sake of which," or the end, belongs to the same department of knowledge as the means. But the nature is the end or "that for the sake of which." For if a thing undergoes a continuous change and there is a stage which is last, this stage is the end or "that for the sake of which." (That is why the poet was carried away into making an absurd statement when he said "he has the end for the sake of which he was born." For not every stage that is last claims to be an end, but only that which is best.)*

For the arts make their material (some simply "make" it, others make it serviceable), and we use everything as if it was there for our sake. (We also are in a sense an end. "That for the sake of which" has two senses: the distinction is made in our work On Philosophy.) *The arts, therefore, which govern the matter and have knowledge are two, namely the art which uses the product and the art which directs the production of it. That is why the using art also is in a sense directive; but it differs in that it knows the form, whereas the art which is directive as being concerned with production knows the matter. For the helmsman knows and prescribes what sort of form a helm should have, the other from what wood it should be made and by means of what operations. In the products of art, however, we make the material with a view to the function, whereas in the products of nature the matter is there all along.* **194a27–194b8**

115. *Again, matter is a relative term: to each form there corresponds a special matter.* **194b8–9**

116. *How far then must the physicist know the form or essence? Up to a point, perhaps, as the doctor must know sinew or the smith bronze (.e. until he understands the purpose of each); and the physicist is concerned only with things whose forms are separable indeed, but do not exist apart from matter. Man is begotten by man and by the sun as well. The mode of existence and essence of the separable it is the business of the primary type of philosophy to define.* **194b9–15**

COMMENTARY OF ST. THOMAS

166. Having shown the difference between natural science and mathematics, the Philosopher here designates that to which the consideration of natural science extends.

Concerning this he makes two

points. First he shows that it pertains to natural science to consider both form and matter. Secondly, where he says, **"How far then . . ."** [116], he points out the limits of natural science in its consideration of form.

Concerning the first part he makes two points. First he draws his conclusion from what has gone before. Secondly, where he says, **"Here too indeed . . ."** [111], he raises difficulties against his own position.

167. He says, therefore, first [110] that since "nature" is used in two ways, i.e., of the matter and of the form, as was said above, so must it be considered in natural science. Thus when we consider what the snub is, we consider not only its form, i.e., its curvature, but we also consider its matter, i.e., the nose.

Hence in natural science nothing is considered, in respect to matter and also in respect to form, without sensible matter.

And it must be noted that this argument of Aristotle includes two approaches.

In one way we can argue as follows. The natural philosopher ought to consider nature. But nature is both form and matter. Therefore he ought to consider both matter and form.

The other way is as follows. The natural philosopher differs from the mathematician, as was said above, because the consideration of the natural philosopher is like the consideration of the snub, whereas that of the mathematician is like the consideration of the curved. But the consideration of the snub is a consideration of the form and the matter. Therefore the consideration of the natural philosopher is a consideration of both.

168. Next where he says, **"Here too indeed . . ."** [111], he raises a two-fold

problem relative to what he has just said.

The first is as follows. Since "nature" is used for matter and form, is natural science about the matter alone, or the form alone, or about that which is a composite of both?

The second problem is as follows. Supposing that natural science does consider both, is it the same natural science which considers form and matter, or are there different sciences which consider each?

169. Next where he says, **"If we look at the ancients . . ."** [112], he answers the above mentioned problems, and especially the second, showing that it pertains to the consideration of the same natural science to consider both form and matter. For the first question seems to have been adequately answered by what he has said, namely, that the consideration of natural science is the same as the consideration of what the snub is.

Concerning this, therefore, he makes two points. First he states what the ancients seem to have thought. He says that if one wishes to look at the sayings of the ancient natural philosophers, it seems that [for them] natural science is concerned only with matter. For they said either nothing about form, or some small bit, as when Democritus and Empedocles touched upon it insofar as they held that a thing comes to be from many according to a determinate mode of mixing or joining.

170. Secondly, where he says, **"But if on the other hand . . ."** [113], he proves his position with three arguments, the first of which is as follows.

Art imitates nature. Therefore natural science must be related to natural things as the science of the artificial is related to artificial things. But it belongs to the same science of the artificial to know the matter and the form up to a certain point, as the doctor knows health as a form, and bile and phlegm and such things as the matter in which health is. For health consists in a harmony of humors. And in like manner the builder considers the form of the house and also the bricks and the wood which are the matter of the house. And so it is in all the other arts. Therefore it belongs to the same natural science to know both the matter and the form.

171. The reason for saying that art imitates nature is as follows. Knowledge is the principle of operation in art. But all of our knowledge is through the senses and taken from sensible, natural things. Hence in artificial things we work to a likeness of natural things. And so imitable natural things are [i.e., are produced] through art, because all nature is ordered to its end by some intellective principle, so that the work of nature thus seems to be the work of intelligence as it proceeds to certain ends through determinate means. And this order is imitated by art in its operation.

172. He gives the second argument where he says, **"Again 'that for the sake of which' . . ."** [114].

It belongs to the same science to consider the end and those things which are for the end. This is so because the reason [ratio] for those things which are for the end is taken from the end. But nature, which is form, is the end of matter. Therefore it belongs to the same natural science to consider matter and form.

173. That form is the end of matter he proves as follows. In order for something to be the end of a continuous motion two things are required. First it must be the final stage of the

motion, and secondly it must be that for the sake of which the thing comes to be. For something can be last, but not be that for the sake of which something comes to be, and hence not have the nature [ratio] of an end. And because it is of the nature [ratio] of an end that it be that for the sake of which something comes to be, the poet maintained that it would be a jest to say that the end is that for the sake of which something comes to be. This seemed to him to be a trifle, for just as if we were to say "man animal" because animal is in the nature [ratio] of man, so also, that for the sake of which something comes to be is in the nature [ratio] of end. For the poet wished to say that not every last thing is an end, but rather only that which is last and best. This is that for the sake of which something comes to be.

And indeed that the form is last in generation is per se evident. But that it is that for the sake of which something comes to be with respect to matter is made clear by a simile taken from the arts. Certain arts make matter. And of these some make it simply, as the art of the molder makes tiles which are the matter of a house, while others make it operative, i.e., they dispose matter pre-existing in nature for the reception of a form, as the art of the carpenter prepares wood for the form of a ship.

It must further be noted that we use all things which are made by art as though they exist for us. For we are in a sense the end of all artificial things. And he says "in a sense" because, as is said in first philosophy, that for the sake of which something comes to be is used in two ways, i.e., "of which" and "for which." Thus the end of a house as "of which" is the dweller, as "for which" it is a dwelling.

From this, therefore, we can conclude that matter is ordered by two arts, that is, those that direct the arts which make matter, and those that pass judgment on the former. Thus there is one art which uses, and another art which is productive of the artifact, as it were, inducing the form. And this latter art is architectonic with reference to that which disposes matter. Thus the art of the ship builder is architectonic with respect to the art of the carpenter who cuts wood. Hence it is necessary that the art which uses be in a sense architectonic, i.e., the principal art, with respect to the productive art.

Therefore, although each is architectonic, i.e., the art which uses and the productive art, they nevertheless differ. For the art which uses is architectonic insofar as it knows and passes judgment on the form, whereas the other, which is architectonic as productive of the form, knows the matter, i.e., passes judgment on the matter. He makes this clear by an example. The use of a ship pertains to the navigator, and thus the art of the navigator is an art which uses, and hence it is architectonic with respect to the art of the ship builder, and knows and passes judgment on the form. He says that the navigator knows and judges what the shape of the rudder should be. The other art, however, i.e., the art of the ship builder, knows and judges from what wood and from what kind of wood the ship should be made.

It is clear, therefore, that the art which produces the form directs the art which makes or disposes the matter. However the art which uses the completed artifact directs the art which produces the form.

From this, then, we can conclude that matter is related to form as form is related to use. But use is that for the sake of which the artifact comes to be. Therefore, form also is that for the sake of which matter is in artificial things. And so as in those things which are according to art we make matter for the sake of the work of art, which is the artifact itself, likewise matter is in natural things from nature, and not made by us; nevertheless it has the same ordination to form, i.e., it is for the sake of form.

Hence it follows that it belongs to the same natural science to consider the matter and the form.

174. He gives the third argument where he says, **"Again matter is . . ."** [115]. The argument is as follows.

Things which are related belong to one science. But matter is one of the things which are related, because it is spoken of in relation to form. However it is not spoken of as if matter itself were in the genus of relation, but rather because a proper matter is determined for each form. And he adds that there must be a different matter under a different form. Hence it follows that the same natural science considers form and matter.

175. Next where he says, **"How far then . . ."** [116], he shows to what extent natural science considers form.

Concerning this he makes two points. First he raises the question, i.e., to what extent should natural science consider the form and quiddity of a thing. (For to consider the forms and quiddities of things absolutely seems to belong to first philosophy.)

Secondly, he answers the question by saying that as the doctor considers nerves, and the smith considers bronze, up to a certain point, so also the natural philosopher considers forms. For the doctor does not consider nerve insofar as it is nerve, for this belongs to the natural philosopher.

Rather he considers it as a subject of health. So also the smith does not consider bronze insofar as it is bronze, but insofar as it is the subject of a statue or something of the sort. So also the natural philosopher does not consider form insofar as it is form, but insofar as it is in matter. And thus, as the doctor considers nerve only insofar as it pertains to health, for the sake of which he considers nerve, so also the natural philosopher considers form only insofar as it has existence in matter.

And so the last things considered by natural science are forms which are, indeed, in some way separated, but which have existence in matter. And rational souls are forms of this sort. For such souls are, indeed, separated insofar as the intellective power is not the act of a corporeal organ, as the power of seeing is the act of an eye. But they are in matter insofar as they give natural existence to such a body.

That such souls are in matter he proves as follows. The form of anything generated from matter is a form which is in matter. For the generation is terminated when the form is in matter. But man is generated from matter and by man, as by a proper agent, and by the sun, as by a universal agent with respect to the generable. Whence it follows that the soul, which is the human form, is a form in matter. Hence the consideration of natural science about forms extends to the rational soul.

But how forms are totally separated from matter, and what they are, or even how this form, i.e., the rational soul, exists insofar as it is separable and capable of existence without a body, and what it is according to its separable essence, are questions which pertain to first philosophy.

Physics Determines What the Causes Are and How Many Species of Causes There Are

The Text of Aristotle
Chapter 3

117. *Now that we have established these distinctions, we must proceed to consider causes, their character and number. Knowledge is the object of our inquiry, and men do not think they know a thing till they have grasped the "why" of it (which is to grasp its primary cause). So clearly we too must do this as regards both coming to be and passing away and every kind of physical change, in order that, knowing their principles, we may try to refer to these principles each of our problems.* **194b16–23**

118. *In one sense, then, (1) that out of which a thing comes to be and which persists, is called "cause," e. g. the bronze of the statue, the silver of the bowl, and the genera of which the bronze and the silver are species.*

In another sense (2) the form or the archetype, i.e. the statement of the essence, and its genera, are called "causes" (e.g., of the octave the relation of 2:1, and generally number), and the parts in the definition.

Again (3) the primary source of the chance or coming to rest; e.g. the man who gave advice is a cause, the father is cause of the child and generally what makes of what is made and what causes change of what is changed.

Again (4) in the sense of end or "that for the sake of which" a thing is done, e.g., health is the cause of walking about. ("Why is he walking about?" We say: "To be healthy," and, having said that, we think we have assigned the cause.) The same is true also of all the intermediate steps which are brought about through the action of something else as means towards the end, e.g., reduction of flesh, purging, drugs, or surgical instruments are means towards health. All these things are, "for the sake of" the end, though they differ from one another in that some are activities, others instruments.

This then perhaps exhausts the number of ways in which the term "cause" is used.

194b23–195a4

119. *As the word has several senses, it follows that there are several causes of the same thing (not merely in virtue of a concomitant attribute), e.g. both the art of the sculptor and the bronze are causes of the statue. These are causes of the statue* qua *statue, not in virtue of anything else that it may be—only not in the same way, the one being the material cause, the other the cause whence the motion comes. Some things cause each other reciprocally, e.g. hard work causes fitness and vice versa but again not in the same way, but the one as end, the other as the origin of chance. Further the same thing is the cause of contrary results. For that which by its presence brings about one result is sometimes blamed for bringing about the contrary by its absence. Thus we ascribe the wreck of a ship to the absence of the pilot whose presence was the cause of its safety.* **195a4–14**

120. *All the causes now mentioned fall into four familiar divisions. The letters are the causes of syllables, the material of artificial products, fire, etc. of bodies, the parts of the whole, and the premises of the conclusion, in the sense of "that from which." Of these pairs the one set are causes in the sense of substratum e.g., the parts, the other set in the sense of essence—the whole and the combination and the form. But the seed and the doctor and the adviser, and generally the maker, are all sources whence the chance or stationariness originates, while the others are causes in the sense of the end or the good of the rest; for "that for the sake of which"*

means what is best and the end of the things that lead up to it. (Whether we say the "good itself" or the "apparent good" makes no difference.)

Such then is the number and nature of the kinds of cause.   **195a15–27**

COMMENTARY OF ST. THOMAS

176. Having shown what natural science considers, the Philosopher here begins to designate the causes from which it should demonstrate.

This section is divided into two parts. First he treats the causes. Secondly, where he says, **"Now the causes . . ."** [162], he points out the causes from which natural science should demonstrate.

Concerning the first part he makes two points. First he shows the need for treating the causes. Secondly, where he says, **"In one sense . . ."** [118], he begins to treat the causes.

He says, therefore, first [117] that after it has been determined what falls under the consideration of natural science, there remains to be considered the causes—what they are and how many there are.

This is so because the business of studying nature is not ordered to operation, but to science. For we are not able to make natural things, but only to have science of them.

Now we do not think that we know anything unless we grasp the "why," which is to grasp the cause. Hence it is clear that we must observe generation and corruption and every natural change in such a way that we know the causes and that we reduce to its proximate cause each thing concerning which we seek the "why."

He says this because the consideration of causes insofar as they are causes is proper to first philosophy. For a cause insofar as it is a cause does not depend upon matter for its existence, because the nature [ratio] of

cause is found also in those things which are separated from matter. But the consideration of causes because of a certain necessity is taken up by the natural philosopher. However he considers causes only insofar as they are the causes of natural mutations.

177. Next where he says, **"In one sense . . ."** [118], he treats the causes.

Concerning this he makes three points. First he names the clearly diverse species of causes. Secondly, where he says, **"But chance also . . ."** [129], he treats certain less obvious causes. Thirdly, where he says, **"They differ . . ."** [161], he shows that the causes are neither more nor less.

The first part is divided into two parts. First he treats the species of causes. Secondly, where he says, **"Now the modes . . ."** [121], he treats the modes of diverse causes in each species.

Concerning the first part he makes two points. First he sets forth the different species of causes. Secondly, where he says, **"All the causes . . ."** [120], he reduces them to four.

Concerning the first part he makes two points. First he sets forth the different causes. Secondly, where he says, **"As the word . . ."** [119], he points out certain consequences which follow from the above mentioned diversity.

178. He says, therefore, first [118] that in one way a cause is said to be that from which something comes to be when it is in it, as bronze is said to be the cause of a statue and silver the cause of a vase. The genera of these things, i.e., the metallic, or the

liquifiable, and such things, are also called causes of these same things.

He adds "when it is in it" in order to differentiate this cause from the privation and the contrary. For the statue, indeed, comes to be from bronze, which is in the statue when it is made. It also comes to be from the unshaped, which, however, is not in the statue when it is made. Hence bronze is a cause of statue, but the unshaped is not, since it is only a per accidens principle, as was said in Book I.

179. Secondly a cause is said to be the species and exemplar. This is called a cause insofar as it is the quidditative nature [ratio] of the thing, for this is that through which we know of each thing "what it is."

And as was said above that even the genera of matter are called causes, so also the genera of a species are called causes. And he gives as an example that harmony of music which is called the octave. The form of an octave is a proportion of the double, which is a relation of two to one. For musical harmonies are constituted by the application of numerical proportions to sounds as to matter. And since two or the double is the form of that harmony which is the octave, the genus of two, which is number, is also a cause. Thus just as we say that the form of the octave is that proportion of two to one which is the proportion of the double, so also we can say that the form of the octave is that proportion of two to one which is multiplicity. And so all of the parts which are placed in the definition are reduced to this mode of cause. For the parts of the species are placed in the definition, but not the parts of the matter, as is said in Metaphysics, VII. Nor is this contrary to what was said above about matter being placed in the definitions of natural things. For individual matter is not placed in the definition of the species, but common matter is. Thus flesh and bones are placed in the definition of man, but not this flesh and these bones.

The nature of the species, therefore, which is constituted of form and common matter, is related as a formal cause to the individual which participates in such a nature, and to this extent it is said that the parts which are placed in the definition pertain to the formal cause.

It must be noted, however, that he posits two things which pertain to the quiddity of the thing, i.e., the species and the exemplar. For there is a diversity of opinions concerning the essences of things.

Plato held that the natures of species are certain abstracted forms, which he called exemplars and ideas, and because of this he posited the exemplar or paradigm.

However those natural philosophers who said something about form placed the forms in matter, and because of this he named them species.

180. Next he says that that from which there is a beginning of motion or rest is in some way called a cause. Thus one who gives advice is a cause, and the father is a cause of the son, and everything which brings about a change is a cause of that which is changed.

It must be noted with reference to causes of this sort that there are four kinds of efficient cause, namely, the perfecting, the preparing, the assisting, and the advising causes.

The perfecting cause is that which gives fulfilment to motion or mutation, as that which introduces the substantial form in generation.

The preparing or disposing cause is tha

t which renders matter or the subject suitable for its ultimate completion.

The assisting cause is that which does not operate for its own proper end, but for the end of another.

The advising cause, which operates in those things which act because of something proposed to them, is that which gives to the agent the form through which it acts. For the agent acts because of something proposed to him through his knowledge, which the advisor has given to him, just as in natural things the generator is said to move the heavy or the light insofar as he gives the form through which they are moved.

181. Further, he posits a fourth mode of cause. A thing is called a cause as an end. This is that for the sake of which something comes to be, as health is said to be a cause of walking. And this is evident because it answers the proposed question "why." For when we ask, "Why does he walk?," we say, "That he may become healthy"; and we say this thinking that we assign a cause. And thus he gives more proof that the end is a cause than that the other things are causes, because the end is less evident, inasmuch as it is last in generation.

And he adds further that all things which are intermediates between the first mover and the ultimate end are in some way ends. Thus the doctor reduces the body in order to produce health, and so health is the end of thinness. But thinness is produced by purgation, and purgation is produced by a drug, and the drug is prepared by instruments. Hence all of these things are in some way ends, for the thinness is the end of the purging, the purging is the end of the drug, and the drug is the end of the instruments, and the instru-

ents are the ends in the operation or in the seeking for the instruments.

And thus it is clear that these intermediate things differ from each other insofar as some of them are instruments and some of them are operations performed by instruments. And he brings this out lest anyone think that only that which is last is a cause in the sense of "that for the sake of which." For the name "end" seems to refer to something which is last. Thus every end is last, not simply, but in respect to something.

He finally concludes that this is perhaps all the ways in which the name "cause" is used. He adds "perhaps" because of the causes which are per accidens, such as chance and fortune.

182. Next where he says, **"As the word has . . ."** [119], he makes clear three things which follow from what he has said about the different causes.

The first point is that since there are many causes, then one and the same thing has many causes per se, and not per accidens. Thus the art of the sculptor is a cause of a statue as an efficient cause, and bronze is a cause as matter. And so it is that many definitions of one thing are sometimes given in accordance with the different causes. But the perfect definition embraces all of the causes.

The second point is that some things are causes of each other in respect to different species of cause. Thus work is an efficient cause of a good habit, yet a good habit is a final cause of work. For nothing prevents a thing from being prior and posterior to another according to different aspects [ratio]. The end is prior according to reason [ratio], but posterior in existence; the converse is true of the agent. And in like manner, the form is prior to matter in respect to the nature [ratio] of being a complement, but the matter is prior to form in respect to generation and time in everything which is moved from potency to act.

The third point is that the same thing is, at times, the cause of contraries. Thus through his presence the navigator is the cause of the safety of the ship, through his absence, however, he is a cause of its sinking.

183. Next where he says, **"All the causes . . ."** [120], he reduces all the causes mentioned above to four species. He says that all the causes enumerated above are reduced to four modes, which are evident. For the elements, i.e., the letters, are causes of syllables, and in like manner earth is a cause of vases, and silver of a vial, and fire and such things, i.e., the simple bodies, are causes of bodies. And in the same way every part is a cause of the whole, and the propositions in a syllogism are a cause of the conclusion. And all of these things are understood as causes in the same way, namely, as that from which something comes to be is called a cause, for this is common to all the instances mentioned above.

However, of all the things just enumerated some are causes as matter, and some as form, which causes the quiddity of the thing. Thus all parts, such as the elements of syllables, and the four elements of mixed bodies, are causes as matter. But those things which imply a whole or a composition or some species are understood as form. Thus species is referred to the forms of simple things, and the whole and composition are referred to the forms of composites.

184. But there seems to be two difficulties here.

The first is the fact that he says that the parts are material causes of the whole, whereas above he reduced the parts of the definition to the formal cause.

It can be said that he spoke above of the parts of the species which fall in the definition of the whole. But here he speaks of the parts of the matter in whose definition falls the whole. Thus circle falls in the definition of semicircle.

But it would be better to say that, although the parts of the species which are placed in the definition are related to the supposit of nature as a formal cause, they are, nevertheless, related to the very nature of which they are parts as matter. For all parts are related to the whole as the imperfect to the perfect, which is, indeed, the relation of matter to form.

Further a difficulty can be raised with reference to what he says about propositions being the matter of conclusions. For matter is in that of which it is the matter. Hence speaking of the material cause above, he said that it is that from which something comes to be when it is in it. But propositions are apart from the conclusion.

But it must be pointed out that the conclusion is formed from the terms of the propositions. Hence in view of this the propositions are said to be the matter of the conclusion insofar as the terms which are the matter of the propositions are also the matter of the conclusion, although they are not in the same order as they are in the propositions. In this same way flour is called the matter of bread, but not insofar as it stands under the form of flour. And so propositions are better called the matter of the conclusion than conversely. For the terms which are joined in the conclusion are posited separately in the premises. Thus we have two modes of cause.

185. Some things are called causes for another reason, i.e., because they are a principle of motion and rest. And in this way the seed which is active in generation is called a cause. Likewise the doctor is called a cause of health according to this mode; so also the adviser is a cause according to this mode, and everyone who makes something.

Another text has "and propositions." For although propositions, insofar as their terms are concerned, are the matter of the conclusion, as was said above, nevertheless insofar as their inferential power is concerned, they are reduced to this genus of cause. For the principle of the discourse of reason to its conclusion is from propositions.

186. Another meaning of cause is found in other causes, i.e., insofar as the end or the good has the nature [ra-tio] of a cause. And this species of cause is the most powerful of all the causes, for the final cause is the cause of the other causes. It is clear that the agent acts for the sake of the end. And likewise it was shown above in regard to artificial things that the form is ordered to use as to an end, and matter is ordered to form as to an end. And to this extent the end is called the cause of causes.

Now since he has said that this species of cause has the nature of a good, while sometimes in those things which act by choice it happens that the end is evil, he forestalls this difficulty by saying that it makes no difference whether the final cause is a true or an apparent good. For what appears good does not move except under the aspect [ratio] of good.

And thus he finally concludes that the species of cause are as many as were mentioned.

LECTURE 6 [195a 28–b30]
Concerning the Different Modes of Causing and Those Things Which Are Consequent Upon These Different Modes of Causing

The Text of Aristotle

121. *Now the modes of causation are many, though when brought under heads they too can be reduced in number. For "cause" is used in many senses and even within the same kind one may be prior to another (e.g., the doctor and the expert are causes of health, the relation 2:1 and number of the octave), and always what is inclusive to what is particular.*   195a27–32

122. *Another mode of causation is the incidental and its genera, e. g., in one way "Polyclitus," in another "sculptor" is the cause of a statue, because "being Polyclitus" and "sculptor" are incidentally conjoined. Also the classes in which the incidental attribute is included; thus "a man" could be said to be the cause of a statue or, generally, "a living creature." An incidental attribute too may be more or less remote, e.g., suppose that "a pale man" or "a musical man" were said to be the cause of the statue.*   195a32–195b3

123. *All causes, both proper and incidental, may be spoken of either as potential or as actual; e.g., the cause of a house being built is either "house-builder" or "house-builder-building." Similar distinctions can be made in the things which the causes are causes, e.g., of "this statue" or of "statue" or of "image" generally, of "this bronze" or of "bronze" or of "material" generally. So too with the incidental attributes.*   195b3–10

124. *Again we may use a complex expression for either and say, e.g., neither "Polyclitus" nor "sculptor" but "Polyclitus, sculptor."*   195b10–12

125. *All these various uses, however, come to six in number, under each of which again the usage is twofold. Cause means either what is particular or a genus, or an incidental attribute or a genus of that, and these either as a complex or each by itself, and all six either as actual or as potential.*   195b12–16

126. *The difference is this much, that causes which are actually at work and particular exist and cease to exist simultaneously with their effect, e.g., this healing person with this being-healed person and that housebuilding man with that being-built house; but this is not always true of potential causes—the house and the housebuilder do not pass away simultaneously.*   195b16–21

127. *In investigating the cause of each thing, it is always necessary to seek what is most precise (as also in other things): thus man builds because he is a builder, and a builder builds in virtue of his art of building. This last cause then is prior; and so generally.*   195b21–25

128. *Further, generic effects should be assigned to generic causes, particular effects to particular causes, e.g., statue to sculptor, this statue to this sculptor; and powers are relative to possible effects, actually operating causes to things which are actually being effected.*

This must suffice for our account of the number of causes and the modes of causation.

195b25–30

COMMENTARY OF ST. THOMAS

187. After the Philosopher has distinguished the species of causes, he here distinguishes the various modes of causes in respect to the same species of cause.

Concerning this he makes two points. First he distinguishes the different modes of causes. Secondly, where he says, **"The difference is . . ."** [126], he treats certain consequences of this distinction.

Concerning the first part he makes

two points. First he distinguishes the different modes of causes, and secondly, where he says, **"All these various . . ."** [125], he reduces them to a certain number.

Concerning the first part he distinguishes the modes of causes according to four divisions.

He says, therefore, first [121] that the modes of causes are numerous, but if they are reduced to headings, either under some highest, or under some common aspect, they are found to be fewer. Or "headings" may be taken as a combination, for it is obvious that combinations of the modes are fewer than the modes.

188. Therefore the first division or combination of modes is that in the same species of cause one cause is said to be prior to another, as when we understand that the more universal cause is prior. Thus the doctor is the proper and posterior cause of health, whereas the artisan is the more common and prior cause. This is in the species of efficient cause. And the same thing is true in the species of formal cause. For the proper and posterior formal cause of the octave is the proportion of the double, whereas the more common and prior is the numerical proportion which is called multiplicity. And in like manner a cause which contains any cause in the community of its extension is a prior cause.

189. It must be noted, however, that the universal cause and the proper cause, and the prior cause and the posterior cause, can be taken either according to a commonness in predication, as in the example given about the doctor and the artisan, or according to a commonness in causality, as if we say the sun is a universal cause of heating, whereas fire is a proper

cause. And these two divisions correspond to each other.

For it is clear that any power extends to certain things insofar as they share in one nature [ratio], and the farther that that power extends, the more common that nature [ratio] must be. And since a power is proportioned to its object according to its nature [ratio], it follows that a higher cause acts according to a form which is more universal and less contracted. And this can be seen in the order of things. For to the extent that among beings some things are superior, to that extent they have forms which are less contracted and more dominant over matter, which contracts the power of form. And so that which is prior in causing is found to be prior in some way under the aspect [ratio] of a more universal predication. For example, if fire is the first in heating, then the heavens are not only the first in heating but also the first in producing alteration.

190. He gives the second division where he says, **"Another mode of causation . . ."** [122].

He says that just as per se causes are divided into prior and posterior or common and proper, so also are per accidens causes.

For besides per se causes there are per accidens causes and their genera. Thus Polyclitus is a per accidens cause of the statue, while the sculptor is a per se cause. For Polyclitus is a cause of statue insofar as he happens to be a sculptor. And in like manner those things which contain Polyclitus in their commonness, e.g., man and animal, are per accidens causes of statue.

Moreover it must be noted that among per accidens causes some are closer to the per se causes and some are more removed. For everything which is joined to the per se cause but is not of its nature [ratio] is called a per accidens cause. Now a thing can be closer to the nature [ratio] of the [per se] cause or more removed from it, and to this extent the per accidens causes are closer or more removed. Thus, if a sculptor happens to be white and musical, the musical is closer, because it is in the same subject in respect to the same thing, i.e., in respect to the soul in which are both [the art of the] musician and the art of statue making. But the subject itself is still more closely related than the other accidents. Thus Polycletis is closer than white or musical, for these latter are not joined to this sculptor except through the subject.

191. He gives the third division where he says, **"All causes . . ."** [123].

He says that besides the causes properly so called, i.e., the causes per se and the causes per accidens, some things are said to be causes in potency, as being able to operate, while other things are actually operating causes. Thus either the builder in habit or the builder in act can be called the cause of the building of a house.

192. And just as causes are distinguished according to the above mentioned modes, so also the things of which they are the causes are distinguished. For one thing is caused posteriorly and more properly, and another priorly and more commonly. Thus something might be called the cause of this statue, or of statue in general, or still more commonly it might be called the cause of an image. And likewise something might be called the moving cause of this bronze, or of bronze in the universal, or of matter.

So also, in per accidens effects, it can be said that one thing is more common and another less common. An effect is said to be per accidens when it is joined to a per se effect and is outside its nature [ratio]. Thus the per se effect of cooking is delectable food, but the per accidens effect is healthful food. However the converse is true of medicine.

193. He gives the fourth division where he says, **"Again we may use . . ."** [124].

He says that sometimes per se causes are taken as a complex with per accidens causes, as when we say that neither Polyclitus, who is a per accidens cause, nor the sculptor, who is the cause per se, is the cause of the statue, but rather that the sculptor Polyclitus is the cause.

194. Next where he says, **"All these various uses . . ."** [125], he reduces the above mentioned modes to a certain number.

He says that the above mentioned modes are six in number, but each of them is used in two ways. These are the six modes: the singular and the genus, which above he called the prior and the posterior, the accident and the genus of the accident, the simple and the complex. And each of these is divided by potency and act; and so all the modes become twelve. He distinguishes all the modes by potency and act because what is in potency is not simply.

195. Next where he says, **"The difference is . . ."** [126], he treats three things which follow from the distinction of modes just made.

The first point is that causes in act and causes in potency differ as follows. Causes operating in act exist and do not exist simultaneously with those things of which they are the causes in act. For example, if we take singular causes, i.e., proper causes, then this healer exists and does not exist simultaneously with him who becomes healed, and this builder exists simultaneously with that which is built. But this is not true if we take causes in act which are not proper causes. For it is not true that builder exists and does not exist simultaneously with that which is built. For it can happen that the builder is in act but this building is not being built, but some other. But if we take the one who is building this building, and if we take this building insofar as it is being built, then it is necessary that when one is posited, the other must be posited also, and when one is removed the other is removed. But this does not always happen in regard to causes which are in potency. For a home and the man who built it are not corrupted simultaneously.

And thus it follows that just as inferior agents, which are causes of the coming to be of things, must exist simultaneously with the things which come to be as long as they are coming to be, so also the divine agent, which is the cause of existing in act, is simultaneous with the existence of the thing in act. Hence if the divine action were removed from things, things would fall into nothingness, just as when the presence of the sun is removed, light ceases to be in the air.

196. He sets forth the second point where he says, **"In investigating the cause..."** [127]. He says that it is necessary to seek in natural things the first cause of each thing, just as we do in artificial things. So if we should ask why it is that a man builds, we answer "because he is a builder." Likewise, if we ask why he is a builder, we answer, "because he possesses the builder's art." And here the inquiry stops, because this is the first cause in this order. Hence in natural things we should proceed to the first cause. This is so because the effect is not known unless the cause is known. Hence if the cause of an effect is also the effect of some other cause, then it cannot be known unless its cause is known, and so on until we arrive at a first cause.

197. He sets forth the third point where he says, **"Further generic effects . . ."** [128]. Effects should correspond proportionally to causes so that general effects be referred to general causes and singular effects to singular causes. For example, if it is said that the cause of statue is sculptor, then the cause of this statue is this sculptor. In like manner effects in potency should correspond to causes in potency and effects in act to causes in act.

And finally in summary he concludes that this is a sufficient treatment of the species and modes of causes.

Different Opinions About Fortune and Chance, The Hidden Causes

The Text of Aristotle
Chapter 4

129. *But chance and spontaneity also are reckoned among causes: many things are said both to be and to come to be as a result of chance and spontaneity. We must inquire therefore in what manner chance and spontaneity are present among the causes enumerated, and whether they are the same or different, and generally what chance and spontaneity are.*   **195b31–36**

130. *Some people even question whether they are real or not. They say that nothing happens by chance, but that everything which we ascribe to chance or spontaneity has some definite cause, e.g., coming, "by chance" into the market and finding there a man whom one wanted but did not expect to meet is due to one's wish to go and buy in the market. Similarly in other cases of chance it is always possible, they maintain, to find something which is the cause; but not chance,*   **195b36–196a7**

131. *for if chance were real, it would seem strange indeed, and the question might be raised, why on earth none of the wise men of old in speaking of the causes of Generation and decay took account of chance; whence it would seem that they too did not believe that anything is by chance.*   **196a7–11**

132. *But there is a further circumstance that is surprising. Many things both come to be and are by chance and spontaneity and although all know that each of them can be ascribed to some cause (as the old argument said which denied chance), nevertheless they speak of some of these things as happening by chance and others not. For this reason also they ought to have at least referred to the matter in some way or other.*

Certainly the early physicists found no place for chance among the causes which they recognized—love, strife, mind, fire, or the like.   **196a11–19**

133. *This is strange, whether they supposed that there is no such thing as chance or whether they thought there is but omitted to mention it—and that too when they sometimes used it, as Empedocles does when he says that the air is not always separated into the highest region, but "as it may chance." At any rate he says in his cosmogony that "it happened to run that way at that time, but it often ran otherwise." He tells us also that most of the parts of animals came to be by chance.*   **196a19–24**

134. *There are some too who ascribe this heavenly sphere and all the worlds to spontaneity. They say that the vortex arose spontaneously, i.e., the motion that separated and arranged in its present order all that exists.*   **196a24–28**

135. *This statement might well cause surprise. For they are asserting that chance is not responsible for the existence or generation of animals and plants, nature or mind or something of the kind being the cause of them (for it is not any chance thing that comes from a given seed but an olive from one kind and a man from another); and yet at the same time they assert that the heavenly sphere and the divinest of visible things arose spontaneously, having no such cause as is assigned to animals and plants. Yet if this is so, it is a fact which deserves to be dwelt upon, and something might well have been said about it.*   **196a28–196b1**

136. *For besides the other absurdities of the statement, it is the more absurd that people should make it when they see nothing coming to be spontaneously in the heavens, but much happening by chance among the things which as they say are not due to chance; whereas we should have expected exactly the opposite.*   **196b1–5**

137. *Others there are who, indeed, believe that chance is a cause, but that it is inscrutable to human intelligence, as being a divine thing, and full of mystery.*

Thus we must inquire what chance and spontaneity are, whether they are the same or
different, and how they fit into our division of causes.   **196b5–9**

COMMENTARY OF ST. THOMAS

198. Having treated the obvious species and modes of cause, the Philosopher here takes up certain hidden modes, namely, fortune and chance.

Concerning this he makes two points. First he states his intention. Secondly, he pursues his intention, where he says, **"Some people even question..."** [130].

He says, therefore, first that fortune and chance are also reckoned among the causes, since many things are said to come to be or to exist because of fortune and chance.

And so with respect to fortune and chance three things must be considered; namely, how they are reduced to the causes mentioned above, then whether fortune and chance are the same or different, and finally what chance and fortune are.

Next where he says, **"Some people even question..."** [130], he begins his treatment of fortune and chance.

First he sets forth the opinions of others. Secondly, where he says, **"First then we observe..."** [138], he establishes the truth.

Concerning the first part he sets forth three opinions. The second begins where he says, **"There are some..."** [134], and the third, where he says, **"Others there are..."** [137].

Concerning the first part he makes two points. First he sets forth the opinions and arguments of those who deny fortune and chance. Secondly, where he says, **"But there is a further circumstance..."** [132], he argues about some of these reasons.

199. He says, therefore, first [130] that some have questioned whether fortune and chance exist. They deny that they exist for two reasons.

The first argument is that all of those things which are said to come to be by chance or fortune are found to have some determinate cause other than fortune. He gives an example of this sort of thing. If someone coming to the market place should find some man whom he wished to find, but who he did not previously believe would be found, we say that his finding of this man was due to fortune. But the cause of this finding is his will to buy, for the sake of which he went to the market where the man whom he sought was. And the same is true of all other things which are said to be by fortune, for they have some cause other than fortune. And so fortune does not seem to be a cause of anything, and consequently is nothing. For we do not posit fortune except insofar as we hold that some things exist by fortune.

200. He gives the second argument where he says, **"... for if chance were real..."** [131].

He says that if fortune were something, it seems to be inconsistent (and that it is truly inconsistent is shown below) and puzzling why none of the ancient wise men who treated the causes of generation and corruption treated fortune. But, as it seems, those ancients thought that nothing exists by fortune. This second argument is taken from the opinion of the ancient natural philosophers.

201. Next where he says, **"But there is a further circumstance..."** [132], he argues about this second proof, showing what he had assumed above,

namely, that it is inconsistent that the ancient natural philosophers did not treat chance and fortune. He proves this with two arguments.

His first argument is as follows. It seems remarkable, and indeed it is, that the ancient natural philosophers did not treat chance and fortune. For they assumed that they treated the causes of those things which come to be, yet there are many things which come to be by fortune and chance. Hence they should have treated fortune and chance. Nor are they to be excused by the argument given above which denies fortune and chance. For although men know that every effect is reduced to some cause, as the above opinion which denies fortune and chance stated, nevertheless, regardless of this argument, these philosophers held that some things come to be by fortune, and other things do not. Hence these natural philosophers must make mention of fortune and chance at least in order to show that it is false that some things come to be by fortune and chance, and in order to point out the reason why some things are said to be by fortune and some not. Nor can they be excused by reason of the fact that chance and fortune would be reduced to one of the causes which they posited. For they did not think that fortune is one of the things which they thought to be causes, such as friendship or strife or some other such thing.

202. He gives his second argument where he says, **"This is strange . . ."** [133].

He says that whether they thought that fortune existed or not, it is inconsistent that the ancient natural philosophers neglected to treat fortune. For if they thought that there was fortune, it is inconsistent that they did not treat it;

if, however, they thought that there was no fortune, it is inconsistent that they sometimes used it. For example, Empedocles said that air is not always united on high above the earth, as if this were natural to it, but rather this happens by chance. For he says that when the earth was made by strife distinguishing the elements, it happened that air gathered together in this place, and as it came together then, it will hold this course so long as the world remains. But in other worlds, which he held come to be and are corrupted to infinity, as was said above, air would be differently related in many ways to the parts of the universe. And likewise he said that the many parts of animals come to be by fortune, so that in the first production of the world, heads came to be without necks.

203. Next where he says, **"These are some . . ."** [134], he gives the second opinion.

Concerning this he makes two points. First he sets forth the opinion. Secondly, he disproves it where he says, **"This statement might..."** [135].

He says, therefore first, [134] that some have said that chance is the cause of the heavens and all the parts of the world. And they said that the revolution of the world, and the movement of the stars distinguishing and constituting the whole universe below according to this order, is by chance. This seems to be the opinion of Democritus, who says that the heavens and the whole world are constituted by chance through the movement of atoms which are per se mobile.

204. Next where he says, **"This statement might . . ."** [135], he disproves this position with two arguments.

The first argument is that it would seem to be worthy of great wonder that animals and plants are not from fortune but from intellect or nature or some other determinate cause. For it is clear that a thing is not generated from any seed whatsoever, but man from a determinate seed, and the olive from a determinate seed. And since these inferior things do not come to be by fortune, it is worthy of wonder that the heavens and those things which are more divine among the sensible things obvious to us, e.g. the sempiternal parts of the world, are by chance, and should not have any determinate cause, as do animals and plants. And if this is true, it would have been worthwhile to insist and to give a reason why this is so. But the ancients failed to do this.

205. He gives the second argument where he says, **"For besides the other..."** [136]. How can it be true that the celestial bodies are by chance, while inferior bodies are not? This seems to be inconsistent first from the fact that they are the nobler, and secondly it is even more inconsistent in the light of what is seen. For we see that in the heavens nothing comes to be by chance, whereas in inferior bodies, which are not said to be by chance, many things seem to happen by fortune. According to their position it would be more reasonable if the converse were true, so that in those things whose cause is chance or fortune, some things would be found to come to be by chance or by fortune, whereas in those things whose cause is not chance or fortune, these latter would not be found.

206. Next where he says, **"Others there are . . ."** [137], he sets forth the third opinion about fortune.

He says that it seems to some that fortune is a cause, but it is hidden to the human intellect, as if it were something divine and above men. For they wanted to hold the position that all fortuitous events are reduced to some divine ordaining cause, as we hold that all things are ordered by divine providence.

But although this opinion has a radical truth, they did not use the name "fortune" well. For that divine thing which orders cannot be called or named fortune, because to the extent that a thing participates in reason or order, it recedes from the nature [ratio] of fortune. Hence, the inferior cause, which of itself does not have an ordination to the fortuitous event, should much more be called fortune than the superior cause, if such a cause is the one which orders.

He omits an inquiry about this opinion, both because it exceeds the bounds of natural science, and because he shows below that fortune is not a per se cause, but a per accidens cause. Hence how he evaluates these opinions will be made more clear in what follows. And so he concludes that for the clarification of these opinions, we must consider what fortune and chance are, and whether they are the same or different, and how they are reduced to the causes mentioned above.

After Making Certain Divisions Among Effects and Causes, He Concludes To a Definition of Fortune

The Text of Aristotle
Chapter 5

138. First then we observe that some things always come to pass in the same way and others for the most part. It is clearly of neither of these that chance is said to be the cause, nor can the "effect of chance" be identified with any of the things that come to pass by necessity and always, or for the most part. But as there is a third class of events besides these two—events which all say are "by chance"—it is plain that there is such a thing as chance and spontaneity; for we know that things of this kind are due to chance and that things due to chance are of this kind.   196b10–17

139. But, secondly, some events are for the sake of something, others not.   196b17–18

140. Again, some of the former class are in accordance with deliberate intention, others not, but both are in the class of things which are for the sake of something. Hence it is clear that even among the things which are outside the necessary and the normal, there are some in connection with which the phrase "for the sake of something" is applicable. (Events that are for the sake of something include whatever may be done as a result of thought or of nature.)   196b18–22

141. Things of this kind, then, when they come to pass incidentally are said to be "by chance." For just as a thing is something either in virtue of itself or incidentally, so may it be a cause. For instance, the housebuilding faculty is in virtue of itself the cause of a house, whereas the pale or the musical is the incidental cause. That which is per se cause of the effect is determinate, but the incidental cause is indeterminable; for the possible attributes of an individual are innumerable.   196b23–29

142. To resume then; when a thing of this kind comes to pass among events which are for the sake of something, it is said to be spontaneous or by chance. (The distinction between the two must be made later—for the present it is sufficient if it is plain that both are in the sphere of things done for the sake of something.)

Example: A man is engaged in collecting subscriptions for a feast. He would have gone to such and such a place for the purpose of getting the money, if he had known. He actually went there for another purpose, and it was only incidentally that he got his money by going there; and this was not due to the fact that he went there as a rule or necessarily, nor is the end effected (getting the money) a cause present in himself—it belongs to the class of things that are intentional and the result of intelligent deliberation. It is when these conditions are satisfied that the man is said to have gone "by chance." If he had gone of deliberate purpose and for the sake of this—if he always or normally went there when he was collecting payments— he would not be said to have gone "by chance."   196b29–197a5

143. It is clear then that chance is an incidental cause in the sphere of those actions for the sake of something which involve purpose. Intelligent reflection, then, and chance are in the same sphere, for purpose implies intelligent reflection.   197a5–8

COMMENTARY OF ST. THOMAS

207. Having set forth the opinions of others about fortune and chance, the Philosopher here determines the truth.

This section is divided into three parts. First he shows what fortune is. Secondly, where he says, **"They differ . . ."** [152], he shows how fortune and chance differ. Thirdly, where he says, "Both belong to . . ." [159], he points out the genus of cause to which chance and fortune are reduced.

The first part is divided into two parts. First he shows what fortune is. Secondly, where he says, "It is necessary . . ." [144], from the definition of fortune he explains the meaning [ratio] of those things which are said about fortune.

Concerning the first part he makes three points. First he sets forth certain divisions needed for the investigation of the definition of fortune. Secondly, where he says, "To resume then . . ." [142] he shows under which members of these divisions fortune is contained. Thirdly, where he says, "It is clear . . ." [143] he concludes to the definition of fortune.

Now since fortune is posited as a kind of cause, and since it is necessary, in order to understand a cause, to know that of which it is the cause, he first sets forth a division on the part of that of which fortune is the cause. Secondly, where he says, "Things of this kind . . ." [141], he sets forth a division on the part of the cause itself.

208. With reference to the first point he sets forth three divisions.

The first of these [138] is that certain things always come to be, e.g., the rising of the sun; and certain things come to be frequently, e.g., man is born having eyes. But neither of these is said to be by fortune.

But certain other things occur in fewer instances, as when a man is born with six fingers or without eyes. And everyone says that things of this sort come to be by fortune. Hence, it is clear that fortune is something, since to be by fortune and to be in fewer instances are convertible. And he brings this up in opposition to the first opinion which denied fortune.

209. However, it seems that this division of the Philosopher is insufficient, for there are some happenings which are indeterminate. Therefore Avicenna said that in those things which are indeterminate a thing happens to be by fortune, as for example those things which are occasional. And it is no objection that it is not said that it is by fortune that Socrates sits, since this is indeterminate. For although this is indeterminate with respect to the moving potency, it is not indeterminate with respect to the appetitive potency which tends determinately to one thing. And if something should happen outside of this, it would be said to be fortuitous.

Now just as the moving potency, which is indeterminate, does not move to act unless it is determined to one thing by the appetitive potency, so also nothing which is indeterminate moves to act unless it is determined to one thing by something. For that which is indeterminate is, as it were, being in potency. However, potency is not a principle of action, but only act is such. Hence from that which is indeterminate nothing follows unless it is determined to one thing by something, either always or frequently. And because of this, he omitted things which are indeterminate from his discussion of things which come to be.

210. It must also be noted that some define the necessary as that which is never impeded and the contingent as that which occurs frequently but may be impeded in a few instances.

But this is unreasonable. For that is called necessary which has in its nature that which cannot not be, whereas the contingent, as happening frequently, has in its nature that which can not be. But to have or not have some impediment is itself contingent.

For nature does not prepare an impediment for that which cannot not be, since this would be superfluous.

211. He gives the second division where he says, **"But secondly . . ."** [139]. He says that some things come to be for the sake of an end, and other things do not.

This division, however, raises a difficulty, because every agent acts for an end; it acts either by nature or by intellect.

But we must note that he is saying that those things which come to be for themselves do not come to be for the sake of something, insofar as they have in themselves a pleasure or perfection because of which they are pleasing in themselves.

Or else he is speaking of those things which do not occur for the sake of a deliberate end, for example, stroking the beard or some other such thing which takes place at times without deliberation solely from the movement of the imagination. Hence they have an imagined end, but not a deliberated end.

212. He gives the third division where he says, **"Again, some of the former . . ."** [140]. He says that of the things which come to be for the sake of an end, some happen in accordance with will and others do not. Both of these are found among those things which come to be for the sake of something. For not only those things which come to be by will, but also those things which come to be by nature, come to be for the sake of something.

213. Now since those things which come to be either necessarily or frequently come to be from nature or from that which is proposed [by the intellect], it is clear that both in those things which always happen and in those things which happen frequently there are some things which come to be for an end. For both nature and that which is proposed [by the intellect] act for the sake of an end.

And thus it is clear that these three divisions include each other. For those things which come to be from what is proposed [by the intellect] or from nature come to be for the sake of an end, and those things which come to be for the sake of an end come to be always or frequently.

214. Next where he says, **"Things of this kind . . ."** [141], he gives the division which is taken on the part of the cause.

He says that when things of this sort (i.e., things which are from what is proposed [by the intellect] for the sake of something, and which are in few instances) come to be through a per accidens cause, we say that they are by fortune. For as certain aspects of beings are per se and others per accidens, the same is true of causes. Thus the per se cause of a house is the builder's art, while the per accidens cause is the white or the musical.

But it must be noted that per accidens cause is taken in two ways: in one way on the part of the cause, and in another way on the part of the effect.

On the part of the cause, that which is called a per accidens cause is joined to the per se cause. Thus if the white and the musical are called causes of a house, it is because they are accidentally joined to the builder.

On the part of the effect, we sometimes refer to something which is accidentally joined to the effect, as when we say that a builder is the cause of strife because strife arises from the building of a house.

In this sense fortune is said to be a per accidens cause when something is accidentally joined to the effect, for example, if the discovery of a treasure is accidentally joined to the digging of a grave. Thus the per se effect of a natural cause is what follows according to the exigencies of its form, so that the effect of the agent who acts through something proposed [by the intellect] is that which happens because of the intention of the agent. Hence whatever takes place in the effect outside this intention is per accidens.

And I say that this is true if what is outside the intention follows in few cases. For what is always or frequently joined to the effect falls under the intention itself. For it is stupid to say that someone intends something but does not will that which is always or frequently joined to it.

Moreover, he points out a difference between the per se cause and the per accidens cause. The per se cause is limited and determinate, whereas the per accidens cause is unlimited and indeterminate, because an infinity of things can happen to be united.

215. Next where he says, "To resume then . . ." [142], he points out those members of the above divisions under which fortune is contained, and what fortune is.

He says first that fortune and chance, as was said above, pertain to those things which happen for the sake of something. However, the difference between fortune and chance will be determined later.

But now it should be clear that each of them is contained among those things which act for the sake of an end. Thus if one knows that he will receive money in the forum, and if he goes there to take it away, [this does not happen by fortune], but if he did not go there for this purpose, it is per accidens that his arrival should have this effect.

And thus it is clear that fortune is a per accidens cause of things which are for the sake of something.

Further it is clear that fortune is a cause of things which occur in few instances. For carrying money away is said to be by fortune when he who takes money away comes to the house neither necessarily nor frequently.

Moreover, fortune pertains to those things which come to be because of what is proposed [by the intellect]. For taking money away, which is said to be by fortune, is the end of some causes, but not in itself, as in those things which happen by nature. Rather it is the end of those things which come to be as proposed by the intellect. But if someone acting under such a proposal should go in order to take money away, or if he always or frequently takes money away when he comes, this would not be said to be by fortune, just as if anyone frequently or always soaks his feet when he goes to a muddy place, it would not be said that this is due to fortune, even though he did not intend it.

216. Next where he says, "It is clear . . ." [143], he concludes to a definition of fortune which is drawn from what was said above.

He says that it is clear from the foregoing that fortune is a per accidens cause in those things which come to be in a few instances according to what is proposed for the sake of an end. And from this it is clear that fortune and intellect pertain to the same thing. For only those who have an intellect act by fortune, for there is no proposal or will without intellect. And although only those who have an intellect act by fortune, still the more something is subject to the intellect, the less is it subject to fortune.

The Meaning of the Things Which the Ancient Philosophers and the Common Man Say About Fortune

The Text of Aristotle

144. *It is necessary, no doubt, that the causes of what comes to pass by chance be indefinite; and that is why chance is supposed to belong to the class of the indefinite and to be inscrutable to man,*   197a8–10

145. *and why it might be thought that, in a way, nothing, occurs by chance. For all these statements are correct, because they are well grounded. Things do, in a way, occur by chance, for they occur incidentally and chance is an incidental cause. But strictly it is not the cause—without qualification—of anything; for instance, a housebuilder is the cause of a house; incidentally, a flute-player may be so. And the causes of the man's coming, and getting the money (when he did not come for the sake of that) are innumerable. He may have wished to see somebody or been following somebody or avoiding somebody, or may have gone to see a spectacle.*   197a10–18

146. *Thus to say that chance is a thing contrary to rule is correct. For "rule" applies to what is always true or true for the most part, whereas chance belongs to a third type of event. Hence, to conclude, since causes of this kind are indefinite, chance too is indefinite.*   197a18–21

147. *(Yet in some cases one might raise the question whether any incidental fact might be the cause of the chance occurrence, e.g., of health the fresh air or the sun's heat may be the cause, but having had one's hair cut cannot; for some incidental causes are more relevant to the effect than others.)*   197a21–25

148. *Chance or fortune is called "good" when the result is good, "evil" when it is evil.*   197a25–26

149. *The terms "good fortune" and "ill fortune" are used when either result is of considerable magnitude. Thus one who comes within an ace of some great evil or great good is said to be fortunate or unfortunate. The mind affirms the presence of the attribute, ignoring the hair's breadth of difference.*   197a26–30

150. *Further, it is with reason that good fortune is regarded as unstable; for chance is unstable, as none of the things which result from it can be invariable or normal.*   197a30–32

151. *Both are then, as I have said, incidental causes—both chance and spontaneity—in the sphere of things which are capable of coming to pass not necessarily, nor normally, and with reference to such of these as might come to pass for the sake of something.*   197a32–35

COMMENTARY OF ST. THOMAS

217. Having given the definition of fortune, he establishes from this definition the meaning [ratio] of those things which are said about fortune.

First he considers those things which the ancient philosophers said about fortune. Secondly, where he says, **"Thus to say ..."** [146], he considers those things which the common man says about fortune. He has given above three opinions concerning for-tune and chance. And he disproved the second of these opinions as being altogether false, for this position held that fortune is the cause of the heavens and of all worldly things.

Thus, having rejected the second opinion, he here shows that the third opinion, which holds that fortune is hidden to man, is true. Secondly, where he says, **"... and why ..."** [145] he shows how the first opinion, which holds that nothing comes to be by fortune or chance, might be true.

Since it was said above that per accidens or incidental causes are infinite, and since it was also said that fortune is a per accidens cause, he concludes from this that the causes of that which is by fortune are infinite. And since the infinite, insofar as it is infinite, is unknown, it follows that fortune is hidden to man.

218. Next where he says, ". . . and why . . ." [145], he shows how the first opinion might be true. He says that in a way it is true to say that nothing comes to be by fortune. For all of those things which others say about fortune are in a certain respect true, because they have some meaning [ratio]. Since fortune is a per accidens cause, it follows that what is by fortune is something per accidens. But what is per accidens is not simply. Hence it follows that fortune is not the cause of anything simply.

And he clarifies what he has said about each of these opinions through an example. He says that as the builder is the per se cause of a house and is the cause simply, whereas flute player is a per accidens cause of the house; in like manner the fact that someone should come to a place with no intention of taking money away is a per accidens cause of carrying it away. But this per accidens cause is infinite, because it is possible for a man to go to that place because of an infinity of other reasons, e.g., if he came to visit someone, or to pursue an enemy, or to escape from a pursuer, or to see a show of some sort. Now all these things and anything similar are causes of the taking of money which happens by chance.

219. Next where he says, "Thus to say . . ." [146], he explains the meaning

[ratio] of those things which are commonly said about fortune.

First he explains why it is said that that which is by fortune is without reason [ratio]. Secondly, where he says, "Chance, or fortune . . ." [148], he explains why it is said that fortune is good or bad.

Concerning the first part he makes two points. First he proves his position. Secondly he raises a certain difficulty where he says, "Yet in some cases . . ." [147].

220. He says, therefore, first [146] that fortune is rightly said to be without reason [ratio]. For we can reason only about those things which happen always or in most instances. But fortune lies outside of both of these. And so since such causes, which occur in exceptional cases, are per accidens and infinite and without reason [ratio], it follows that causes by fortune are infinite and without reason [ratio]. For every per se cause produces its effect either always or in most cases.

221. Next where he says, "Yet in some cases . . ." [147], he raises a certain difficulty. He says that although it may be said that fortune is a per accidens cause, some will question this.

The problem is whether everything which happens to be a per accidens cause ought to be called a cause of that which comes to be by fortune. Thus it is clear that the per se cause of health can be either nature or the art of the doctor. However, can all those things with which the coming to be of health happens to be connected, such as the wind, and the heat, and shaving of the head, be called causes per accidens? The question, therefore, is whether each of these is a cause per accidens.

Now since we said above that fortune is most properly called a per accidens cause on the part of the effect, since a thing is said to be a cause of that which happens to the effect, it is clear that a fortuitous cause produces something in the fortuitous effect although it does not intend that, but rather something else connected with the effect. According to this wind or heat can be called fortuitous causes of health insofar as they produce some change in the body, upon which change health follows. But removing the hair or some other such thing does not produce anything clearly related to health.

But among the per accidens causes, some are nearer [to the per se cause] and others are more remote. Those which are more remote seem less to be causes.

222. Next where he says, **"Chance or fortune . . ."** [148], he explains why fortune is said to be good or bad.

First he explains why fortune is said to be good or bad simply. He says that fortune is said to be good when something good happens and bad when something bad happens.

223. Secondly, where he says, **"The terms 'good fortune' . . ."** [149], he explains the meaning [ratio] of good fortune and misfortune.

He says that we refer to good fortune and misfortune when [the fortuitous event] has some great good or great evil. For an event is called good fortune when some great good follows; it is called misfortune when some great evil follows.

And since being deprived of a good is included in the notion [ratio] of evil, and being deprived of evil is included in the notion [ratio] of the good, then when one is a little removed from a great good, he is said to be unfortunate if he misses it. On the other hand, if one is close to a great evil and is freed from it, he is said to be fortunate. This is so because the intellect takes that which is only a little removed as if it were not removed at all, but already possessed.

224. Thirdly where he says, **"Further, it is with reason . . ."** [150], he explains why good fortune is uncertain. He says that this is so because good fortune is a kind of fortune. But fortune is uncertain because it pertains to things which are neither always nor frequent, as was said. Hence it follows that good fortune is uncertain.

225. Finally where he says, **"Both are then . . ."** [151], he concludes as a sort of résumé that each, i.e., chance and fortune, is a cause per accidens, and that each pertains to things which do not happen simply, i.e., neither always nor frequently, and that each pertains to things which come to be for the sake of something, as is clear from what was said above.

The Difference Between Chance and Fortune. The Causes Are Neither More Nor Less Than Four

The Text of Aristotle
Chapter 6

152. *They differ in that "spontaneity" is the wider term. Every result of chance is from what is spontaneous, but not everything that is from what is spontaneous is from chance.*

197a36–197b1

153. *Chance and what results from chance are appropriate to agents that are capable of good fortune and of moral action generally. Therefore necessarily chance is in the sphere of moral actions. This is indicated by the fact that good fortune is thought to be the same, or nearly the same, as happiness, and happiness to be a kind of moral action, since it is well-doing. Hence what is not capable of moral action cannot do anything by chance.*   **197b1–6**

154. *Thus an inanimate thing or a lower animal or a child cannot do anything by chance, because it is incapable of deliberate intention; nor can "good fortune" or "ill fortune" be ascribed to them, except metaphorically, as Protarchus, for example, said that the stones of which altars are made are fortunate because they are held in honor, while their fellows are trodden under foot. Even these things, however, can in a way be affected by chance, when one who is dealing with them does something to them by chance, but not otherwise.*   **197b6–13**

155. *The spontaneous on the other hand is found both in the lower animals and in many inanimate objects. We say, for example, that the horse came "spontaneously," because, though his coming saved him, he did not come for the sake of safety. Again, the tripod fell "of itself," because, though when it fell it stood on its feet so as to serve for a seat, it did not fall for the sake of that.*   **197b13–18**

156. *Hence it is clear that events which (1) belong to the general class of things that may come to pass for the sake of something, (2) do not come to pass for the sake of what actually results, and (3) have an external cause, may be described by the phrase "from spontaneity." These spontaneous events are said to be "from chance" if they have the further characteristics of being the objects of deliberate intention and due to agents capable of that mode of action.*

197b18–22

157. *This is indicated by the phrase "in vain," which is used when A, which is for the sake of B; does not result in B. For instance, taking a walk is for the sake of evacuation of the bowels; if this does not follow after walking, we say that we have walked "in vain" and that the walking, was vain. This implies that what is naturally the means to an end is "in vain," when it does not effect the end towards which it was the natural means—for it would be absurd for a man to say that he had bathed in vain because the sun was not eclipsed, since the one was not done with a view to the other. Thus the spontaneous is even according to its derivation the case in which the thing itself happens in vain. The stone that struck the man did not fall for the purpose of striking him; therefore it fell spontaneously, because it might have fallen by the action of an agent and for the purpose of striking.*   **197b22–32**

158. *The difference between spontaneity and what results by chance is greatest in things that come to be by nature; for when anything comes to be contrary to nature, we do not say that it came to be by chance, but by spontaneity. Yet strictly this too is different from the spontaneous proper; for the cause of the latter is external, that of the former internal.*

We have now explained what chance is and what spontaneity is, and in what they differ from each other.   **197b32–198a2**

159. *Both belong to the mode of causation "source of change," for either some natural or some intelligent agent is always the cause; but in this sort of causation the number of possible causes is infinite.*   **198a2–5**

160. *Spontaneity and chance are causes of effects which, though they might result from intelligence or nature, have in fact been caused by something incidentally. Now since nothing which is incidental is prior to what is per se, it is clear that no incidental cause can be prior to a cause per se. Spontaneity and chance, therefore, are posterior to intelligence and nature. Hence, however true it may be that the heavens are due to spontaneity, it will still be true that intelligence and nature will be prior causes of this All and of many things in it besides.*   **198a5–13**

Chapter 7

161. *It is clear then that there are causes, and that the number of them is what we have stated. The number is the same as that of the things comprehended under the question "why." The "why" is referred ultimately either (1), in things which do not involve motion, e.g., in mathematics, to the "what" (to the definition of "straight line" or "commensurable," etc.); or (2) to what initiated a motion, e.g., "why did they go to war?—because there had been a raid"; or (3) we are inquiring "for the sake of what?"—"that they may rule"; or (4), in the case of things that come into being, we are looking for the matter. The causes, therefore, are these and so many in number.*   **198a13–21**

COMMENTARY OF ST. THOMAS

226. Having treated fortune and chance with reference to those aspects in which they are alike, the Philosopher here explains the difference between them.

This section is divided into two parts. First he explains the difference between fortune and chance. Secondly, where he says, "The difference between . . ." [158], he explains that in which this difference primarily consists.

The first part is divided into two parts. First he explains the difference between chance and fortune. Secondly, where he says, "Hence it is clear . . ." [156], he summarizes what he has said about each of them.

227. Concerning the first part he makes two points. First [152] he explains the difference between chance and fortune. He says that they differ by reason of the fact that chance pertains to more things than fortune, because everything which is by fortune is by chance, but not conversely.

228. Secondly, where he says, "Chance and what results . . ." [153], he clarifies the difference mentioned above.

First he designates the things in which fortune is found. Secondly, where he says, "The spontaneous . . ." [155], he shows that chance is found in more things.

Concerning the first part he makes two points. First he designates the things in which fortune is found. Secondly, where he says, "Thus an inanimate thing . . ." [154], he draws a conclusion about those things in which fortune is not found.

229. He says, therefore, first that fortune and that which is by fortune are found in those things in which something is said to happen well. For fortune is found in those things in which there can be good fortune and misfortune.

Now a thing is said to happen well for him to whom action belongs. However, action belongs properly to him who has dominion over his action. For what does not have dominion over its action is that which is acted upon rather than that which acts. And thus action is not in the power of that which is acted upon, but rather in the power of that which acts.

Now since the active or practical life pertains to those who have dominion over their acts (for here is where operation according to virtue or vice is found), it is necessary that fortune pertains to the practical.

A sign of this is the fact that fortune seems to be the same as happiness, or very nearly so. Hence the happy are commonly called the fortunate. For according to those who think that happiness consists in external goods, happiness is the same as fortune; according to those, however, who say that external goods, in which fortune plays a great part, help as instruments in the attainment of happiness, good fortune is close to happiness because it helps one attain it.

Hence, since happiness is a certain operation (for it is good operation, i.e., that of perfected virtue, as is said in Ethics, I, it follows that fortune pertains to the actions in which one happens to act well or is impeded from acting well. And this means that things turn out either well or badly. Hence, since one has dominion over his actions insofar as he acts voluntarily, it follows that in those actions alone where one acts voluntarily should something happen by fortune, but not in others.

230. Next where he says, "Thus an inanimate thing . . ." [154], he draws from the above a conclusion about the things in which fortune is not found.

He says that since fortune is found only in those who act voluntarily, it follows that neither an inanimate thing, nor a child, nor a beast act by fortune, since they do not act voluntarily as having free choice (which is here called "that which is proposed"). Hence, neither good fortune nor misfortune can happen to them except metaphorically. Thus, someone said that the stones from which altars are built are fortunate because honor and reverence are shown them, but the stones next to the altar stones are walked upon. This is said because of a certain likeness to men among whom the honored seemed to be fortunate, whereas those stones which are walked upon are called unfortunate.

But although it follows from the foregoing that such things do not act by fortune, there is nothing to prevent them from being acted upon by fortune. For some voluntary agent may act upon them. Thus, we say that it is good fortune when a man finds a treasure, or it is a misfortune when he is struck by a falling stone.

231. Next where he says, "The spontaneous . . ." [155], he points out that chance is found also in other things.

Concerning this he makes three points. First, he shows that chance is found in other things. Secondly, where he says, "Hence it is clear . . ." [156], he draws a certain conclusion from what was said above. Thirdly, where he says, "This is indicated . . ." [157] he uses an example to clarify the point.

232. He says, therefore, first that chance is found not only in men, who act voluntarily, but also in other animals and even in inanimate things. He gives an example dealing with other animals. It is said that a horse comes by chance when his coming is conducive to his safety, although he did not come for the sake of safety. He gives another example taken from inanimate things.

We say that a tripod falls by chance because, as it stands, it is suitable for sitting, although it did not fall for the sake of this, i.e., so that someone might sit on it.

233. Next where he says, **"Hence it is clear..."** [156], he draws the following conclusion from the above. When things which come to be simply for the sake of something do not come to be for the sake of that which happens, but for the sake of something extrinsic, then we say that these things come to be by chance. But we say that among the things which come to be by chance, only those things which happen in those who have free choice come to be by fortune.

234. Next where he says, **"This is indicated..."** [157], he clarifies what he has stated in this conclusion, i.e., that chance occurs in those things which happen for the sake of something.

A sign of this is the fact that the word "vain" is used, which in the Greek is close to chance. For we use the term "vain" when that which is for the sake of something does not come to be because of that something, i.e., when that for the sake of which something is done does not occur. Thus if one should walk in order to evacuate the bowels, and if this should not occur to the walker, then he is said to have walked in vain, and his walking would be vain. Thus that which is suitable for the coming to be of something is vain and frustrated when it does not accomplish that for whose coming to be it is suitable.

He explains why he says "that for whose coming to be it is suitable." If someone were to say that he bathed in vain because the sun was not eclipsed while he bathed, he would speak ridiculously, because bathing oneself is not apt for producing an eclipse of the sun.

Hence chance, which in the Greek is called "automatum," i.e., per se vain, occurs in those things which are for the sake of something. This is also true of that which is frustrated or vain. For the name per se vain signifies the very thing which is frustrated, just as per se man signifies man himself and per se good signifies good itself.

He gives an example of things which happen by chance. Thus [it is chance] when it is said that a stone, which strikes someone when falling, did not fall for the purpose of striking him. Therefore it fell because of that which is per se vain or per se frustrated, for the stone does not naturally fall for this purpose. However at times a stone does fall as thrown by someone for the purpose of hitting another.

However, although chance and the vain are alike insofar as each is among the things which are for the sake of something, nevertheless they also differ. For a thing is called vain because of the fact that that which was intended does not follow, whereas a thing is called chance because of the fact that something else which was not intended does follow.

Hence sometimes a thing is vain and chance at the same time, for example, when that which was intended does not occur but something else does occur. However, sometimes there is chance but not the vain, as when both that which was intended and something else occur. And there is the vain and no chance when neither that which was intended nor anything else occurs.

235. Next where he says, **"The difference..."** [158], he explains that in which chance most of all differs from fortune.

He says that they differ most of all in the things which happen by nature, because chance has a place here but fortune does not. For when in the operations of nature something happens outside of nature, for example, when a six fingered person is born, we do not say that this happens by fortune, but rather because of that which is per se vain, i.e., by chance.

And so we can take as another difference between chance and fortune the fact that the cause of those things which are by chance is intrinsic, just as the cause of those things which are by nature is intrinsic.

But the cause of those things which are by fortune is extrinsic, just as the cause of those things which are from free choice is extrinsic.

And he finally concludes that he has now explained what the per se vain or chance is, what fortune is, and how they differ from each other.

236. Next where he says, **"Both belong . . ."** [159], he points out the genus of cause to which chance and fortune are reduced.

First he states his position. Secondly, where he says, **"Spontaneity and chance . . ."** [160], he disproves from this a certain opinion mentioned above.

He says, therefore, first that both chance and fortune are reduced to the genus of the moving cause. For chance and fortune are causes either of those things which proceed from nature or of those things which proceed from intelligence, as is clear from what has been said. Hence, since nature and intelligence are causes as things from which motion begins, so fortune and chance also are reduced to the same genus. But since chance and fortune are per accidens causes, their number is indeterminate, as was said above.

237. Next where he says, **"Spontaneity and chance . . ."** [160], he refutes

the opinion of those who maintain that fortune and chance are the causes of the heavens and of all worldly things.

He says that since chance and fortune are per accidens causes of those things of which intellect and nature are the per se causes, and since a per accidens cause is not prior to a per se cause, as nothing per accidens is prior to that which is per se, it follows that chance and fortune are causes which are posterior to intellect and nature. Hence if it should be held that chance is the cause of the heavens, as some maintained, as was said above, it would follow that intellect and nature are first of all causes of some other things and afterwards causes of the whole universe.

Moreover, the cause of the whole universe seems to be prior to the cause of some part of the universe, since any part of the universe is ordered to the perfection of the universe. But it seems to be inconsistent that some other cause is prior to that which is the cause of the heavens. Hence it is inconsistent that chance is the cause of the heavens.

238. Furthermore we must consider that if those things which happen fortuitously or by chance, i.e., outside the intention of inferior causes, are reduced to some superior cause which orders them, then in relation to this latter cause they cannot be said to be fortuitous or by chance. Hence that superior cause cannot be called fortune.

239. Next where he says, **"It is clear then . . ."** [161], he shows that the causes are not more than those mentioned.

This is clarified as follows. The question "why" asks for the cause. But only the above mentioned causes answer the question "why." Therefore, the causes are not more than those which were mentioned. He says that the answers to the question "why" are the same in number as the above mentioned causes.

For sometimes the "why" is reduced finally to what the thing is, i.e., to the definition, as is clear in all immobile things. The mathematicals are of this sort, in which the "why" is reduced to the definition of the straight or of the commensurate, or of some other thing which is demonstrated in mathematics. Since a right angle is defined as that angle which is formed by the falling of one line upon another which makes of both parts two equal angles, then if it should be asked why an angle is a right angle, the reply would be because it is formed by a line making two equal angles from each part. And it is the same in the other instances.

Sometimes the "why" is reduced to the first moving cause. Thus, why does someone fight? Because he has stolen. For this is what brought on the fight.

Sometimes it is reduced to the final cause, as if we should ask for the sake of what does someone fight, and the answer is that he might rule.

Sometimes it is reduced to the material cause, as when it is asked why this body is corruptible, and the answer is because it is composed of contraries.

Thus it is clear that these are the causes and they are just so many.

240. Furthermore there must be four causes.

A cause is that upon which the existence of another follows. Now the existence of that which has a cause can be considered in two ways. First it is considered absolutely, and thus the cause of the existing is the form by which something is in act. Secondly it is considered insofar as a being comes to be in act from being in potency. And since everything which is in potency is reduced to act by that which is a being in act, it is necessary that there be two other causes, namely the matter and the agent which reduces the matter from potency to act. However, the action of the agent tends toward something determinate, and thus it proceeds from some determinate principle. For every agent does that which is suitable to it. But that toward which the action of the agent tends is called the final cause. Therefore, there must be four causes.

But since the form is the cause of existing absolutely, the other three are causes of existence insofar as something receives existence. Hence in immobile things the other three causes are not considered, but only the formal cause is considered.

Natural Philosophy Demonstrates From All of the Four Genera of Causes

The Text of Aristotle

162. *Now, the causes being four, it is the business of the physicist to know about them all, and if he refers his problems back to all of them, he will assign the "why" in the way proper to his science—the matter, the form, the mover, "that for the sake of which."*   198a21–24

163. *The last three often coincide; for the "what" and "that for the sake of which" are one, while the primary source of motion is the same in species as these (for man generates man),*
198a24–27

164. *and so too, in general, are all things which cause movement by being themselves moved; and such as are not of this kind are no longer inside the province of physics, for they cause motion not by possessing motion or a source of motion in themselves, but being themselves incapable of motion. Hence there are three branches of study, one of things which are incapable of motion, the second of things in motion, but indestructible, the third of destructible things.*   198a27–31

165. *The question "why," then, is answered by reference to the matter, to the form and to the primary moving cause.*   198a31–33

166. *For in respect of coming to be it is mostly in this last way that causes are investigated—"what comes to be after what? what was the primary agent or patient?" and so at each step of the series. Now the principles which cause motion in a physical way are two, of which one is not physical, as it has no principle of motion in itself. Of this kind is whatever causes movement, not being itself moved, such as (1) that which is completely unchangeable, the primary reality, and*   198a33–198b3

167. *(2) the essence of that which is coming to be, i.e. the form; for this is the end or "that for the sake of which." Hence since nature is for the sake of something, we must know this cause also.*   198b3–5

168. *We must explain the "why" in all the senses of the term, namely, (1) that from this that will necessarily result ("from this" either without qualification or in most cases);* 198b5–6

169. *(2) that "this must be so if that is to be so" (as the conclusion presupposes the premises) ; (3) that this was the essence of the thing; and*   198b7–8

170. *(4) because it is better thus (not without qualification, but with reference to the essential nature in each case).*   198b8–9

COMMENTARY OF ST. THOMAS

241. Having treated the causes, the Philosopher here shows that the natural philosopher demonstrates from all the causes.

Concerning this he makes two points. First he states his intention. Secondly, where he says, **"The last three . . ."** [163], he explains his position.

He says, therefore, first [162] that inasmuch as there are four causes, as was said above, it pertains to natural science both to know all of them and to demonstrate naturally through all of them by reducing the question "why" to each of the aforementioned causes, i.e., the form, the moving cause, the end and the matter.

Next where he says, **"The last three . . ."** [163], he explains his position. Concerning this he makes two points.

First he sets forth certain things which are necessary to clarify his position. Secondly, where he says, **"The question..."** [165], he proves his position.

Concerning the first point he sets forth two things which are necessary for the proof of what follows. The first of these deals with the relationship of the causes among themselves. The second deals with the consideration of natural philosophy, and is given where he says **"... and so too in general..."** [164].

242. He says, therefore, first [163] that it often happens that three of the causes combine into one, such that the formal cause and the final cause are one in number.

This must be understood to apply to the final cause of generation, not, however, to the final cause of the thing generated. For the end of the generation of man is the human form, but this form is not the end of man. Rather through this form man acts for his end.

But the moving cause is the same as both of these according to species. And this is especially true in univocal agents in which the agent produces something like unto itself according to species, as man generates man. For in these cases the form of the generator, which is the principle of generation, is the same in species as the form of the generated, which is the end of the generation. However in non-univocal agents the species [ratio] is different. For in these cases the things which come to be cannot reach the point where they follow upon the form of the generator according to the same kind [ratio] of species. Rather they participate in some likeness to it, insofar as they are able, as is clear in those things which are generated by the sun. There-

fore, the agent is not always the same in species with the form which is the end of generation, and furthermore, not every end is a form. And because of this it is significant that he said "often."

The matter, however, is neither the same in species nor the same in number as the other causes. For matter as such is being in potency, whereas the agent as such is being in act, and the form or the end is act or perfection.

243. Next where he says, "... and so too ..." [164], he makes his second point which deals with the things which natural philosophy should treat.

He says that it pertains to natural philosophy to consider any movers which move in such a way that they are moved. Things, however, which move, but are not themselves moved, do not belong within the consideration of natural philosophy which properly considers natural things which have in themselves a principle of motion. For movers which are not themselves moved do not have in themselves a principle of motion, since they are not moved but are immobile. Thus, they are not natural things, and as a result do not come under the consideration of natural philosophy.

Hence, it is clear that there are three branches of study, i.e., the study and intention of philosophy is threefold according to the three genera of things which are found.

For some things are immobile, and one philosophical study deals with them. Another philosophical study deals with things which are mobile but incorruptible, such as the celestial bodies. And there is a third philosophical study which deals with things which are mobile and corruptible, such as the inferior bodies.

The first of these studies pertains to metaphysics, while the other two pertain to natural science which treats all mobile things, both corruptible and incorruptible.

Hence some have misunderstood this passage, desiring to reduce these three studies to the three parts of philosophy, namely, mathematics, metaphysics and physics. For astronomy, which seems to consider the incorruptible mobile things, belongs more to natural philosophy than to mathematics, as was said above. For insofar as it applies mathematical principles to natural matter, it considers mobile things. Therefore, this division is taken according to the diversity of things existing outside the mind and not according to the division of the sciences.

244. Next where he says, **"The question 'why' . . ."** [165], he sets forth his position.

Concerning this he makes two points. First he shows that it pertains to natural philosophy to consider all the causes and to demonstrate through them. These are the two points he has proposed above. Secondly, where he says, **"We must explain . . ."** [171], he proves certain things which are assumed in this argument.

Concerning the first part he makes two points. First he shows that natural philosophy considers all the causes. Secondly, where he says, **"We must explain . . ."** [168], he shows that it demonstrates through all of them.

Concerning the first part he makes two points. First he shows that natural philosophy considers the matter and the form and the moving cause. Secondly, where he says, **". . . the essence of that . . ."** [167], he shows that it considers the end.

Concerning the first part he makes two points. First he states his intention, and secondly, he proves it, where he says, **"For in respect of . . ."** [166].

First [165] he concludes from what was said above that the "why" is assigned to natural things by reference to the matter, and to what the thing is, i.e., the form, and to the first mover.

245. Next where he says, **"For in respect of . . ."** [166], he proves his position as follows.

It has been said that natural philosophy considers those things which are moved, both the generable and the corruptible. Therefore, whatever should be considered about generation should be considered by natural philosophy. But with reference to generation one ought to consider the form, the matter, and the moving cause.

Those who wish to consider the causes of generation consider them as follows. First we consider what it is that comes to be after something, as fire come to be after air, since fire is generated from air. And in this way the form, through which the generated is what it is, is considered.

Next we consider what it is that first makes [this], that is, we consider that which first moves to generation. And this is the moving cause.

Next we consider what it is that undergoes this change. And this is the subject and the matter.

With reference to generation we consider not only the first mover and the first subject, but also those things which are consequent upon them. And thus it is clear that it pertains to natural philosophy to consider the form, the mover, and the matter.

However, natural philosophy does not consider every mover. For there are two kinds of moving principles, namely, the moved and the non-moved. Now a mover that is not moved is not natural, because it does not have in itself a principle of motion. And such is the moving principle which is altogether immobile and the first of all movers, as will be shown in Book VIII.

246. Next where he says, "... **the essence of that which . . .**" [167], he shows that natural philosophy also considers the end.

He says that the form and what the thing is also fall under the consideration of natural philosophy, insofar as the end is that for the sake of which the generation occurs. For it was said above that the form and the end coincide in the same thing. And since nature acts for the sake of something, as will be proven below, it must belong to natural philosophy to consider the form not only insofar as it is form but also insofar as it is the end. If, however, nature were not to act for the sake of something, then natural philosophy would consider form insofar as it is form, but not insofar as it is an end.

247. Next where he says, **"We must explain . . ."** [168], he shows how natural philosophy demonstrates through all the causes.

First he shows how it demonstrates through matter and the moving cause, which are the prior causes in generation. Secondly, where he says, "... **that this must be so . . .**" [169], he shows how it demonstrates through the form. Thirdly, where he says, "... **because it is better . . .**" [170], he shows how it demonstrates through the end.

He says, therefore, first [168] that in natural things the "why" must be elaborated fully, i.e., in every genus of cause. Thus if something has gone before, whether it be the matter or the mover, then something necessarily follows. For example, if something is generated from contraries, it is necessary that the latter be corrupted, and if the sun approaches the north pole, the days must become longer, and cold must diminish and heat increase for those who dwell in the northern part.

However, we must realize that it is not always necessary that something follows from a preceding matter or mover. Rather sometimes a thing follows simply or in every case, as in the things mentioned. But sometimes a thing follows in most instances, e.g., from human seed and a mover in generation, it follows in most instances that what is generated has two eyes, but at times this fails to happen. Similarly, because of the fact that matter is so disposed in the human body, it happens that a fever is frequently produced because of festering, but at times this is impeded.

248. Next where he says, "... **that this must be so . . .**" [169], he shows how in natural things demonstration must be made through the formal cause.

In order to understand this, we must know that when something follows from the preceding causes in generation (i.e., from the matter and the mover) by necessity, then a demonstration can be established, as was said above. However, a demonstration cannot be established when something follows in most instances. But then a demonstration should be founded upon that which is posterior in generation in order that something might follow of necessity from another, just as the conclusion follows from the propositions of a demonstration. Thus let us proceed in demonstration as follows: if this should come to be, then this and that are required, for example, if man should be generated, it is necessary that human seed be an agent in the generation.

If, however, we proceed conversely by saying that "human seed is an agent in generation," then the proposition "therefore man will be generated," does not follow as a conclusion follows from propositions. But that which ought to come to be, i.e., that in which the generation is terminated, was (as was said above) "what the thing was to be," i.e., the form.

Hence, it is clear that when we demonstrate according to this mode, i.e., "that 'this must be so if that is to be so'" [198b7], we demonstrate through the formal cause.

249. Next where he says, ". . . because it is better . . ." [170], he shows how natural philosophy demonstrates through the final cause.

He says that natural philosophy sometimes also demonstrates that something is true because it is better that it be so. For example, we might demonstrate that the front teeth are sharp because as such they are better for cutting food, and nature does what is better. Nature does not, however, do what is better simply, but what is better with reference to what belongs to each substance; otherwise nature would give a rational soul, which is better than an irrational soul, to each animal.

The Argument of Those Who Deny That Nature Acts For an End

The Text of Aristotle
Chapter 8

171. *We must explain then (1) that Nature belongs to the class of causes which act for the sake of something; (2) about the necessary and its place in physical problems, for all writers ascribe things to this cause, arguing that since the hot and the cold, etc., are of such and such a kind, therefore certain things necessarily are and come to be—and if they mention any other cause (one his "friendship and strife," another his mind), it is only to touch on it, and then goodbye to it.* **198b10–16**

172. *A difficulty presents itself: why should not nature work, not for the sake of something, nor because it is better so, but just as the sky rains, not in order to make the corn grow, but of necessity? What is drawn up must cool, and what has been cooled must become water and descend, the result of this being that the corn grows. Similarly if a man's crop is spoiled on the threshing-floor, the rain did not fall for the sake of this—in order that the crop might be spoiled—but that result just followed. Why then should it not be the same with the parts in nature, e. g., that our teeth should come up of necessity—the front teeth sharp, fitted for tearing, the molars broad and useful for grinding down the food—since they did not arise for this end, but it was merely a coincident result; and so with all other parts in which we suppose "that there is purpose?" Wherever then all the parts came about just what they would have been if they had come to be for an end, such things survived,being organized spontaneously in a fitting way; whereas those which grew otherwise perished and continue to perish, as Empedocles says his "man-faced ox-progeny" did.*

Such are the arguments (and others of the kind) which may cause difficulty on this point. **198b16–33**

COMMENTARY OF ST. THOMAS

250. Having shown that natural philosophy demonstrates from all the causes, the Philosopher here clarifies certain things which he had assumed, namely, that nature acts for an end and that in some things necessity is not from the causes which are prior in being (which are the matter and the moving cause), but from the posterior causes, which are the form and the end.

Concerning this he makes two points. First he states his intention, and secondly, where he says, **"A difficulty presents itself . . ."** [172], he develops his position.

He says, therefore, first [171] that it must be pointed out that nature is among the number of causes which act for the sake of something. And this is important with reference to the problem of providence. For things which do not know the end do not tend toward the end unless they are directed by one who does know, as the arrow is directed by the archer. Hence if nature acts for an end, it is necessary that it be ordered by someone who is intelligent. This is the work of providence.

After this it must be pointed out how necessity is present in natural things. Is the necessity of natural things always from the matter, or is it sometimes from the matter and the mover, or sometimes from the form and the end.

It is necessary to make this inquiry for the following reason. All of the ancient natural philosophers, when giving the reason [ratio] for natural effects, reduced such effects to this cause, i.e., that it is necessary for these things to happen because of matter. For example, since heat is by nature what it is and naturally produces a certain effect (and in like manner cold and other similar things), then those things which are caused by them must come to be or exist. And if some of the ancient natural philosophers touched upon some cause other than the necessity of matter, they have no reason for taking any glory from the fact. For after such causes were posited by them, e.g., intellect which Anaxagoras posited, and friendship and strife which Empedocles posited, they did not use them except in certain general instances, such as in the constitution of the world. But they omitted such causes when discussing particular effects.

251. Next where he says, **"A difficulty presents itself . . ."** [172], he develops his position.

First he asks whether nature acts for the sake of something, and secondly, where he says, **"As regards what is 'of necessity' . . ."** [184], how necessity is found in natural things.

Concerning the first part he makes two points. First he gives the opinion and argument of those who hold that nature does not act for the sake of something. Secondly, he disproved this position, where he says, **"Yet it is impossible . . ."** [173].

252. Concerning the first point it must be noted that those who held that nature does not act for the sake of something tried to confirm their position by denying that in which nature is most clearly seen to act for the sake of something. That which most strongly demonstrates that nature acts for the

sake of something is the fact that in the operation of nature a thing is always found to come to be as good and as suitable as it can be. Thus, the foot is made in a certain way by nature so that it may be suitable for walking. Hence if it falls short of this natural disposition, it is not fit for this use. And the same is true of other instances.

And since they tried especially to oppose this point, Aristotle says [172] that it can be objected that there is nothing to prevent nature from not acting for the sake of something nor from doing what is always better. For at times we find that from some operation of nature some utility results which nevertheless is not the end of that natural operation, but merely happens to occur. Thus, we might say that Jupiter rains, i.e., God or universal nature, but not for the purpose that grain should grow. Rather rain results from the necessity of matter. For it must be that in the lower regions, because of the closeness of the heat of the sun, vapors are drawn out from the water. Having been carried above because of the heat, when they arrive at the point where heat is lacking because of the distance from the place where the rays of the sun are reflected, it is necessary that the vaporized water which is going up freeze at that very point. When the freezing is completed, the vapors are changed into water. And when water has been generated, it must fall down because of its weight. And when this takes place, it happens that the grain grows. Now it does not rain so that grain might grow. For in the same way grain might be destroyed in some place because of rain, as when grain is gathered on a thrashing floor. Thus, rain does not fall in order to destroy grain, rather this happens by chance when rain falls. And in the same way it seems to happen by chance that grain accidentally grows when rain falls.

Hence it seems that there is nothing to prevent this from being true also in regard to animals, which seem to be disposed for the sake of some end. For example, one might say that because of the necessity of matter some teeth, i.e., the front teeth, happen to be sharp and suitable for cutting food, and the molars happen to be broad and useful for grinding food. Nevertheless, nature did not make the teeth such and so for the sake of these utilities. Rather after teeth have been made by nature in such a way as they develop from the necessity of matter, it is accidental that they acquired such a form. And once this form exists, this utility follows. And the same thing can be said of all other parts which seem to have some determinate form for the sake of some end.

253. But one might say that such utilities follow always or in many cases, and what is always or in most cases suitable exists by nature. In order to forestall this objection they say that from the beginning of the formation of the world the four elements were joined in the constitution of natural things, and thus the many and varied dispositions of natural things were produced. And in all these things only that which happened to be suitable for some utility, as if it were made for that utility, was preserved. For such things had a disposition which made them suitable for being preserved, not because of some agent intending an end, but because of that which is per se vain, i.e., by chance. On the other hand, whatever did not have such a disposition was destroyed, and is destroyed daily. Thus Empedocles said that in the beginning things which were part ox and part man were generated.

254. Therefore, because of this argument, or because of some other similar argument, some will have a difficulty on this point.

But in regard to this argument it must be noted that they use an unsuitable example. For although rain does have a necessary cause in regard to matter, it is nevertheless ordered to some end, namely, the conservation of things generable and corruptible. For in inferior things mutual generation and corruption are for this purpose: that perpetual existence be preserved in them. Hence the growth of grain is poorly taken as an example. For a universal cause is referred to a particular effect.

And it must also be noted that the growth and conservation of growing things on earth occur in most cases because of the rain, whereas their corruption occurs in few instances. Hence although rain is not for their destruction, it does not follow that it is not for their preservation and growth.

LECTURE 13 [198b34–199a33]
It Is Demonstrated That Nature Acts For an End

The Text of Aristotle

173. *Yet it is impossible that this should be the true view. For teeth and all other natural things either invariably or normally come about in a given way; but of not one of the results of chance or spontaneity is this true. We do not ascribe to chance or mere coincidence the frequency of rain in winter, but frequent rain in summer we do; nor heat in the dog-days, but only if we have it in winter. If then, it is agreed that things are either the result of coincidence or for an end, and these cannot be the result of coincidence or spontaneity, it follows that they must be for an end; and that such things are all due to nature even the champions of the theory which is before us would agree. Therefore action for an end is present in things which come to be and are by nature.* **198b34–199a8**

174. *Further, where a series has a completion, all the preceding steps are for the sake of that. Now surely as in intelligent action, so in nature; and as in nature, so it is in each action, if nothing interferes. Now intelligent action is for the sake of an end; therefore the nature of things also is so. Thus if a house, e.g., had been a thing made by nature, it would have been made in the same way as it is now by art; and if things made by nature were made also by art, they would come to be in the same way as by nature.* **199a8–15**

175. *Each step then in the series is for the sake of the next; and generally art partly completes what nature cannot bring to a finish, and partly imitates her. If, therefore, artificial products are for the sake of an end, so clearly also are natural products. The relation of the later to the earlier terms of the series is the same in both.* **199a15–20**

176. *This is most obvious in the animals other than man: they make things neither by art nor after inquiry or deliberation. Wherefore people discuss whether it is by intelligence or by some other faculty that these creatures work,—spiders, ants, and the like. By gradual advance in this direction we come to see clearly that in plants too that is produced which is conducive to the end—leaves, e.g., grow to provide shade for the fruit. If then it is both by nature and for an end that the swallow makes its nest and the spider its web, and plants grow leaves for the sake of the fruit and send their roots down (not up) for the sake of nourishment, it is plain that this kind of cause is operative in things which come to be and are by nature.* **199a20–30**

177. *And since "nature" means two things, the matter and the form, of which the latter is the end, and since all the rest is for the sake of the end, the form must be the cause in the sense of "that for the sake of which."* **199a30–32**

COMMENTARY OF ST. THOMAS

255. Having stated the opinion and argument of those who say that nature does not act for an end, he here disproves this position.

He does this first through appropriate arguments, and secondly, where he says, **"Now mistakes come to pass ..."** [178], through arguments taken from those things from which the opponents tried to prove the contrary position.

256. Concerning the first point he sets forth five arguments. The first [173] is as follows. Everything which happens naturally either happens in every instance or in most instances. But nothing which happens by fortune or by that which is per se vain, i.e., by chance, happens in every instance or in most instances. For we do not say that in the winter it rains frequently by fortune or by chance. But if it rains fre-

quently during the dog days, we would say that this happens by chance. And in like manner, we do not say that it happens by chance that there is heat during the dog days, but only if this should happen during the winter.

From these two points he argues as follows. Everything which happens either happens by chance or for the sake of an end. Now those things which happen outside the intention of an end are said to happen by chance. But it is impossible for those things which happen in every instance or in most instances to happen by chance. Therefore, those things which happen in every instance or in most instances happen for the sake of an end.

Now whatever happens according to nature happens either in every instance or in most instances, as even they admitted. Therefore, whatever happens by nature happens for the sake of something.

257. He gives the second argument where he says, **"Further, where a series . . ."** [174]. He says that there is an end for all things. That which is prior and all of its consequences are done for the sake of the end.

Having assumed this he argues as follows. As something is done naturally, so is it disposed to be done. For "so disposed" [aptum natum] means "naturally." And this proposition is convertible, because as something is disposed to be done, so it is done. However, it is necessary to add this condition: unless it is impeded.

Therefore, let us agree that there is no impediment. Hence as something is done naturally, so is it disposed to be done. But things which happen naturally are done so that they lead to an end. Therefore, they are disposed to be done in such a way that they are for the

sake of an end. And thus nature seeks an end, i.e., nature has a natural disposition for an end. Hence, it is clear that nature acts for the sake of an end.

He clarifies what he has said by an example.

One proceeds from the prior to the posterior in the same way in both art and nature. Thus if artificial things, e.g., houses, were made by nature, they would be made according to the order in which they now are made by art. Thus the foundation would be constructed first, and afterwards the walls would be erected, and finally the roof would be placed on top. For nature proceeds this way in the things which are rooted in the earth, i.e., in plants. Their roots, like a foundation, are fixed in the earth, the trunk, after the manner of a wall, is raised on high, and the branches are on top like a roof.

And in like manner if the things which are produced by nature were made by art, they would be made according to the way they are disposed to be produced by nature. This is clear in regard to health, which happens to be produced by art and by nature. For as nature heals by heating and cooling, so also does art.

Hence it is clear that in nature one thing is for the sake of another, i.e., the prior is for the sake of the posterior. And the same is true of art.

258. He gives the third argument where he says, **". . . and generally art . . ."** [175]. He says that art makes certain things which nature cannot make, such as a house and things of this sort. However, in regard to those things which happen to be produced by art and by nature, art imitates nature, as is clear in regard to health, as was said above. Hence, if things which are made according to art are for the sake of an end, it is clear that things

which are made according to nature also are made for an end, since in each case the prior and the posterior are similarly related.

However, it can be said that this is not a different argument from the one already given, but is complementary to it and a clarification of it.

259. He gives the fourth argument where he says, **"This is most obvious . . ."** [176]. This argument is drawn from those things in nature which more obviously seem to act for the sake of something.

He says that it is most clear that nature acts for the sake of something when we consider animals which act neither through art, nor through inquiry, nor through deliberation. It is manifest in their operations that they act for the sake of something. Because of this some have wondered whether spiders and ants and animals of this sort act through intellect or through some other principle.

But because they always act in the same way, it is clear that they do not act by intellect, but by nature. For every swallow makes a nest in the same way, and every spider a web in the same way, which would not be the case if they acted by intellect and from art.

For not every builder makes a house in the same way, because the artisan judges the form of the thing built and can vary it.

If we proceed beyond animals to plants, it is apparent among them that some things have been made and are useful for an end, as the leaves are useful as a covering for the fruit.

Hence, if these things are due to nature and not to art, i.e., that the swallow makes a nest, and the spider a web, and the plants produce leaves for the sake of the fruit, and the roots of plants are not above, but below, so that they might take nourishment from the earth, it is clear that a final cause is found in things which come to be and are by nature, i.e., by nature acting for the sake of something.

260. He gives the fifth argument where he says, **"And since nature means . . ."** [177].

He says that nature is used in two ways, i.e., for the matter and for the form. The form is the end of generation, as was said above. And the nature [ratio] of an end is that other things come to be for the sake of it. Hence it follows that to be and to come to be for the sake of something should be found in natural things.

LECTURE 14 [199a34–b33]
He Demonstrates That Nature Acts For an End From the Evidence From Which Some Conclude to the Opposite Position

The Text of Aristotle

178. Now mistakes come to pass even in the operations of art: the grammarian makes a mistake in writing and the doctor pours out the wrong dose. Hence clearly mistakes are possible in the operations of nature also. If then in art there are cases in which what is rightly produced serves a purpose, and if where mistakes occur there was a purpose in what was attempted, only it was not attained, so must it be also in natural products, and monstrosities will be failures in the purposive effort. Thus in the original combinations the "ox-progeny" if they failed to reach a determinate end must have arisen through the corruption of some principle corresponding to what is now the seed. 199a33–199b7

179. Further, seed must have come into being first, and not straightway the animals: the words "whole-natured first..." must have meant seed. 199b7–9

180. Again, in plants too we find the relation of means to end, though the degree of organization is less. Were there then in plants also olive-headed vine-progeny, like the "man-headed ox-progeny," or not? An absurd suggestion; yet there must have been, if there were such things among animals. 199b9–13

181. Moreover, among the seeds anything must have come to be at random. 199b13–14

182. But the person who asserts this entirely does away with nature and what exists "by nature." For those things are natural which, by a continuous movement originated from an internal principle, arrive at some completion: the same completion is not reached from every principle; nor any chance completion, but always the tendency in each is towards the same end, if there is no impediment.

The end and the means towards it may come about by chance. We say, for instance, that a stranger has come by chance, paid the ransom, and gone away, when he does so as if he had come for that purpose, though it was not for that that he came. This is incidental, for chance is an incidental cause, as I remarked before. But when an event takes place always or for the most part, it is not incidental or by chance. In natural products the sequence is invariable, if there is no impediment. 199b14–26

183. It is absurd to suppose that purpose is not present because we do not observe the agent deliberating. Art does not deliberate. If the shipbuilding art were in the wood, it would produce the same results by nature. If, therefore, purpose is present in art, it is present also in nature. The best illustration is a doctor doctoring himself: nature is like that.

It is plain then that nature is a cause, a cause that operates for a purpose. 199b26–33

COMMENTARY OF ST. THOMAS

261. After the Philosopher has shown by appropriate arguments that nature acts for the sake of something, he here intends to make this clear by destroying those things through which some embraced the contrary position.

This section is divided into three parts according to the three things by which some seem to be moved to deny that nature acts for an end. The second part begins where he says, "But the person..." [182]. The third part begins where he says, "It is absurd..." [183].

262. The first thing by which some seem to be moved to deny that nature acts for an end is the following. Sometimes we see things happen otherwise

[than is customary], as happens in the case of monsters which are the errors of nature. Whence Empedocles held that at the beginning of the constitution of things certain things were produced which did not have this form and this order which is now commonly found in nature.

263. He brings forth four arguments to overcome this difficulty.

First [178] he shows that although art acts for the sake of something, still in things which are made by art error occurs. For sometimes the grammarian does not write correctly, and the doctor prescribes a drink as a medicinal potion incorrectly.

Hence it is clear that error occurs also in things which are by nature, even though nature acts for the sake of something. Of the things which are made by art for the sake of something, some are made according to art and are made correctly. There are other things, however, in which the artisan fails, not acting according to his art, and in these cases error occurs, even though the art is acting for the sake of something. For if art does not act for a determinate end, then there would be no error no matter how the art was performed. For the operation of the art would be equally related to all things. The very fact, then, that there happens to be error in art is a sign that art acts for the sake of something. The same thing also happens in natural things in which monsters are, as it were, the errors of nature acting for the sake of something insofar as the correct operation of nature is deficient. And this very fact that error occurs in natural things is a sign that nature acts for the sake of something.

The same thing is true of those substances which Empedocles said were produced at the beginning of the world, such as the "ox-progeny," i.e., half ox and half man. For if such things were not able to arrive at some end and final state of nature so that they would be preserved in existence, this was not because nature did not intend this [a final state], but because they were not capable of being preserved. For they were not generated according to nature, but by the corruption of some natural principle, as it now also happens that some monstrous offspring are generated because of the corruption of seed.

264. He gives the second argument where he says, **"Further, seed must have . . ."** [179]. The argument is as follows.

Wherever there are determinate principles and a determinate order of proceeding, there must be a determinate end for the sake of which other things come to be. But in the generation of animals there is a determinate order of proceeding. For it is necessary that seed come to be first, and there is no animal which exists immediately from the beginning. And the seed itself is not immediately hardened, but in the beginning it is soft and tends toward perfection in a certain order. Therefore, there is a determinate end in the generation of animals. Therefore, monsters and errors do not occur in animals because nature does not act for the sake of something.

265. He gives the third argument where he says, **"Again in plants . . ."** [180]. The argument is as follows.

Although nature acts for the sake of something in regard to plants as well as animals, this is less clear. Fewer things can be inferred from the operations of plants.

If, therefore, monsters and errors occur in animals because nature does not act for the sake of something, this should be even more true of plants. As the "man-headed ox-progeny" occurs in animals, does there also occur in plants an "olive-headed vine progeny," i.e., half olive and half vine? It seems absurd to say that these things occur. Nevertheless this must be so if in regard to animals it is true that nature does not act for the sake of something. Therefore, in regard to animals it is not true that nature does not act for the sake of something.

266. He gives the fourth argument where he says, **"Moreover, among the seeds..."** [181]. The argument is as follows.

As animals are generated by nature, so also are the seeds of animals. If, therefore, what occurs in the generation of animals happens in any way whatsoever, and not by nature, as it were, acting for a determinate end, then the same would be true of seeds, i.e., that any sort of seed would be produced by any sort of thing. This is obviously false. Hence, the first [supposition] is also false.

267. Next where he says, **"But the person ..."** [187], he destroys the second point by which some were moved to hold that nature does not act for the sake of something.

This seemed true to some because things which happen naturally seem to proceed from the prior principles, which are the agent and the matter, and not from the intention for an end.

But Aristotle shows the contrary. He says that one who speaks in this manner, i.e., one who says that nature does not act for the sake of something, destroys nature and the things which are according to nature. For those things are said to be according to nature which are moved continuously by some intrinsic principle until they arrive at some end—not to some contingent end, and not from any principle to any end, but from a determinate principle to a determinate end. For progress is always made from the same principle to the same end, unless something impedes it. However, that for the sake of which something is done sometimes happens to occur by fortune, when [that which is done] is not done for the sake of this. For example, if some stranger should come and leave after he has bathed, we say this was by fortune. For he did not bathe himself as if he had come for this purpose, since he did not come for this. Hence his bathing is accidental (for fortune is a per accidens cause, as was said above). But if this should happen always or in most instances to him who comes, it would not be said to be by fortune. But in natural things events occur not per accidens but always, unless something should impede. Hence, it is clear that the determinate end which follows in nature does not follow by chance, but from the intention of nature. And from this it is clear that it is contrary to the meaning [ratio] of nature to say that nature does not act for the sake of something.

268. Next where he says, **"It is absurd . . ."** [183], he destroys the third point by which some hold the opinion that nature does not act for the sake of something. For it seems to some that nature does not act for the sake of something because nature does not deliberate.

But the Philosopher says that it is absurd to hold this opinion. For it is obvious that art acts for the sake of something, yet it is also obvious that art does not deliberate. Nor does the artisan deliberate insofar as he has the art, but insofar as he falls short of the certitude of the art. Hence the most certain arts do not deliberate, as the writer does not deliberate how he should form letters. Moreover, those artisans who do deliberate, after they have discovered the certain principles of the art, do not deliberate in the execution. Thus one who plays the harp would seem most inexperienced if he should deliberate in playing any chord. And from this it is clear that an agent does not deliberate, not because he does not act for an end, but because he has the determinate means by which he acts. Hence since nature has the determinate means by which it acts, it does not deliberate. For nature seems to differ from art only because nature is an intrinsic principle and art is an extrinsic principle. For if the art of ship building were intrinsic to wood, a ship would have been made by nature in the same way as it is made by art. And this is most obvious in the art which is in that which is moved, although per accidens, such as in the doctor who cures himself. For nature is very similar to this art.

Hence, it is clear that nature is nothing but a certain kind of art, i.e., the divine art, impressed upon things, by which these things are moved to a determinate end. It is as if the shipbuilder were able to give to timbers that by which they would move themselves to take the form of a ship.

Finally, he concludes by saying that it is clear that nature is a cause and that it acts for the sake of some thing.

How Necessity Is Found In Natural Things

The Text of Aristotle
Chapter 9

184. As regards what is "of necessity," we must ask whether the necessity is "hypothetical" or "simple" as well.   199b34–35

185. The current view places what is of necessity in the process of production, just as if one were to suppose that the wall of a house necessarily comes to be because what is heavy is naturally carried downwards and what is light to the top, wherefore the stones and foundations take the lowest place, with earth above because it is lighter, and wood at the top of all as being the lightest.   199b35–200a5

186. Whereas, though the wall does not come to be without these, it is not due to these, except as its material cause: it comes to be for the sake of sheltering and guarding certain things. Similarly in all other things which involve production for an end; the product cannot come to be without things which have a necessary nature, but it is not due to these (except as its material); it comes to be for an end. For instance, why is a saw such as it is? To effect so-and-so and for the sake of so-and-so. This end, however, cannot be realized unless the saw is made of iron. It is, therefore, necessary for it to be of iron, if we are to have a saw and perform the operation of sawing. What is necessary then, is necessary on a hypothesis, it is not a result necessarily determined by antecedents. Necessity is in the matter, while "that for the sake of which" is in the definition.   200a5–15

187. Necessity in mathematics is in a way similar to necessity in things which come to be through the operation of nature. Since a straight line is what it is, it is necessary that the angles of a triangle should equal two right angles. But not conversely; though if the angles are not equal to two right angles, then the straight line is not what it is either. But in things which come to be for an end, the reverse is true. If the end is to exist or does exist, that also which precedes it will exist or does exist; otherwise just as there, if the conclusion is not true, the premiss will not be true, so here the end or "that for the sake of which" will not exist. For this too is itself a starting point, but of the reason only, not of the action, while in mathematics the starting-point is the starting point of the reasoning only, as there is no action. If then there is to be a house, such-and-such things must be made or be there already or exist, or generally, the matter relative to the end, bricks and stones if it is a house. But the end is not due to these except as the matter, nor will it come to exist because of them. Yet if they do not exist at all, neither will the house, or the saw—the former in the absence of stones, the latter in the absence of iron—just as in the other case the premises will not be true, if the angles of the triangle are not equal to two right angles.

The necessary in nature, then, is plainly what we call by the name of matter, and the changes in it. Both causes must be stated by the physicist, but especially the end; for that is the cause of the matter, not vice versa;   200a15–34

188. and the end is "that for the sake of which," and the beginning starts from the definition or essence; as in artificial products, since a house is of such-and-such a kind, certain things must necessarily come to be or be there already, or since health is this, these things must necessarily come to be or be there already. Similarly if man is this, then these—if these, then those. Perhaps the necessary is present also in the definition. For if one defines the operation of sawing as being a certain kind of dividing, then this cannot come about unless the saw has teeth of a certain kind; and these cannot be unless it is of iron. For in the definition too there are some parts that are, as it were, its matter.   200a34–200b8

COMMENTARY OF ST. THOMAS

269. Having shown that nature acts for an end, the Philosopher here proceeds to inquire into the second question, i.e., how necessity is found in natural things.

Concerning this he makes three points. First he raises the question. Secondly, where he says, "The current view . . ." [185], he sets forth the opinion of others. Thirdly, where he says, "Whereas, though the wall . . ." [186], he determines the truth.

270. He asks, therefore, [184] whether in natural things there is a simple necessity, i.e., an absolute necessity, or a necessary by condition or by supposition.

In order to understand this, it must be noted that the necessity which depends upon prior causes is an absolute necessity, as is clear from the necessity which depends upon matter. That an animal is corruptible is absolutely necessary. For to be composed of contraries is a consequence of being an animal.

In like manner, that which has necessity from the formal cause is also absolutely necessary. For example, man is rational, or a triangle has three angles equal to two right angles, which is reduced to the definition of triangle.

Similarly, that which has necessity from the efficient cause is absolutely necessary. Thus because of the motion of the sun it is necessary that day and night alternate.

But that which has necessity from that which is posterior in existence is necessary upon condition, or by supposition. For example, it might be said that it is necessary that this be if this should come to be. Necessity of this kind is from the end and from the form insofar as it is the end of generation.

Therefore to ask whether in natural things there is a simple necessity or a necessity by supposition is nothing else than to ask whether necessity is found in natural things from the end or from the matter.

271. Next where he says, "The current view . . ." [185], he gives the opinion of others.

He says that some are of the opinion that the generation of natural things arises from an absolute necessity of matter. For example, one might say that a wall or a house is such as it is by the necessity of matter because heavy things are disposed to move downward and light things to rise above. And because of this the heavy and hard stones remain in the foundation, while earth being lighter rises above the stones, as is clear in walls constructed of tiles which are made of earth. But the timbers which are the lightest are placed at the highest point, i.e., at the roof. Thus they thought that the dispositions of natural things have come to be such as they are from the necessity of matter. For example, it might be said that a man has feet below and hands above because of the heaviness or lightness of humors.

272. Next where he says, "Whereas, though the wall . . ." [186], he determines the truth.

Concerning this he makes two points. First he shows what sort of necessity there is in natural things. Secondly, where he says, "Necessity in mathematics . . ." [187], he compares the necessity of natural things to the necessity which is in the demonstrative sciences.

He says, therefore, first that granting that it seems absurd to say that there is such a disposition in natural things because of the matter, it also appears absurd to say that this is true of artificial things, an example of which has already been given. However, such a disposition is not produced in natural things and in artificial things unless the material principles have an aptitude for such a disposition. For a house would not stand well unless the heavier materials were placed in the foundation and the lighter materials above.

However, it must not be said because of this that the house is so disposed that one part of it is below and another above. [I say] "because of this," i.e., because of the heaviness or lightness of certain parts, (except insofar as the term "because of" refers to the material cause, which is for the sake of the form). Rather the parts of a house are so disposed for the sake of an end, which is to shelter and protect men from the heat and the rain.

And just as it is with a house, so it is with all other things in which something happens to act for the sake of something. For in all things of this sort the dispositions of what is generated or made do not follow without material principles, which have a necessary matter by which they are apt to be so disposed.

However, the things made or generated are not so disposed because the material principles are such, unless the term "because of" refers to the material cause. Rather they are so disposed because of the end. And the material principles seek to be apt for this disposition which the end requires, as is clear in a saw. For a saw has a certain disposition or form. And for this reason it must have such a matter. And it has a certain disposition or form because of some end. However, this end, which is cutting, could not be achieved

unless the saw were of iron. Therefore, it is necessary that a saw be iron, if there must be a saw and if it must be for this end, which is its operation.

Thus it is clear that there is a necessity by supposition in natural things, just as there is such a necessity in artificial things, but not such that that which is necessary is the end. For that which is necessary is posited on the part of the matter, whereas on the part of the end the reason [ratio] for the necessity is posited. For we do not say that there must be such an end because the matter is such. Rather we say conversely that since the end and the future form are such, the matter must be such. And so the necessity is placed in the matter, but the reason [ratio] for the necessity is placed in the end.

273. Next where he says, **"Necessity in mathematics..."** [187], he compares the necessity which is in the generation of natural things to the necessity which is in the demonstrative sciences.

He does this first with reference to the order of necessity, and secondly with reference to that which is the principle of the necessity, where he says, **"... and the end ..."** [188].

He says, therefore, first [187] that in a certain respect necessity is found in the demonstrative sciences in the same way that it is found in things which are generated according to nature.

For an "a priori" necessity is found in the demonstrative sciences, as when we say that since the definition of a right angle is such, it is necessary that a triangle be such and so, i.e., that it have three angles equal to two right angles. Therefore, from that which is first assumed as a principle the conclusion arises by necessity.

But the converse does not follow, i.e., if the conclusion is, then the principle is. For sometimes a true conclusion can be drawn from false propositions. But it does follow that if the conclusion is not true, then neither is the given premise true. For a false conclusion is drawn only from a false premise.

But in things which are made for the sake of something, either according to art or according to nature, this converse does obtain. For if the end either will be or is, then it is necessary that what is prior to the end either will have been or is. If, however, that which is prior to the end is not, then the end will not be, just as in demonstrative sciences, if the conclusion is not true, the premise will not be true.

It is clear, therefore, that in things which come to be for the sake of an end the end holds the same order which the premise holds in demonstrative sciences. This is so because the end also is a principle, not indeed of action, but of reasoning. For from the end we begin to reason about those things which are the means to the end. In demonstrative sciences, however, a principle of action is not considered, but only a principle of reasoning, because there are no actions in demonstrative sciences, but only reasonings. Hence in things which are done for the sake of an end, the end properly holds the place which the premise holds in demonstrative sciences. Hence, there is a similarity on both sides, even though they seem to be related conversely because of the fact that the end is last in action, which does not pertain to demonstration.

Therefore, he concludes that if a house which is the end of a generation, is to come to be, it is necessary that the matter which is for the sake of this end come to be and pre-exist. Thus, tiles and stones must exist first if a house is to come to be. This does not mean that the end is for the sake of the matter, but

rather that the end will not be if the matter does not exist. Thus, there will be no house if there are no stones, and there will be no saw if there were no iron. For just as in demonstrative sciences the premises are not true if the conclusion, which is similar to things which are for an end, is not true, so also is the beginning related to the end, as was said.

Thus it is clear that in natural things that is said to be necessary which is material or is a material motion. And the reason [ratio] for this necessity is taken from the end, for it is necessary for the sake of the end that the matter be such.

And one ought to determine both causes of a natural thing, i.e., both the material and the final cause, but especially the final cause, because the end is the cause of the matter, but not conversely. For the end is not such as it is because the matter is such, but rather the matter is such as it is because the end is such, as was said above.

274. Next where he says, ". . . and the end . . ." [188], he compares the necessity of natural generation to the necessity of the demonstrative sciences with respect to that which is the principle of the necessity.

It is clear that in demonstrative sciences the definition is the principle of the demonstration. And in like manner the end, which is the principle and reason [ratio] for necessity in things which come to be according to nature, is a sort of principle taken by reason and by definition. For the end of generation is the form of the species which the definition signifies.

This also is clear in artificial things. For as the demonstrator in demonstrating takes the definition as a principle, so also does the builder in building, and the physician in curing.

Thus, because the definition of a house is such, this [what is in the definition] must come to be and exist in order that a house might come to be, and because this is the definition of health, this must come to be in order for someone to be cured. And if this and that are to be, then we must accomplish those things which must come to be.

However, in demonstrative sciences definition is threefold.

One of these is a principle of demonstration, for example, thunder is the extinguishing of fire in a cloud. The second is the conclusion of a demonstration, for example, thunder is a continuous sound in the clouds. The third is a combination of these two, for example, thunder is a continuous sound in the clouds caused by the extinguishing of fire in a cloud. This definition embraces within itself the whole demonstration without the order of demonstration. Hence it is said in Posterior Analytics, I, that definition is a demonstration differing by position.

Since, therefore, in things which come to be for the sake of an end the end is like a principle in demonstrative science, and since those things which are for the sake of the end are like the conclusion, there is also found in the definition of natural things that which is necessary because of the end. For if one wishes to define the operation of a saw (which is a division of a certain sort which will not occur unless the saw has teeth, and these teeth are not suitable for cutting unless they are of iron), it will be necessary to place iron in the definition of saw. For nothing prevents us from placing certain parts of matter in the definition, not individual parts, such as this flesh and these bones, but common parts, such as flesh and bones. And this is necessary in the definition of all natural things.

Therefore, the definition which comprises in itself the principle of the demonstration and the conclusion is the whole demonstration. Thus the definition which draws together the end, the form, and the matter comprises the whole process of natural generation.

BOOK III
MOBILE BEING IN COMMON

LECTURE 1 [200b12–201a8]
Natural Science Treats Motion and Those Things Which Are Consequent upon Motion. Certain Divisions Which Are Necessary for the Investigation of the Definition of Motion

The Text of Aristotle
Chapter 1

189. *Nature has been defined as a "principle of motion and change" and it is the subject of our inquiry. We must therefore see that we understand the meaning of "motion"; for if it were unknown, the meaning of "nature" too would be unknown.* **200b12–15**

190. *When we have determined the nature of motion, our next task will be to attack in the same way the terms which are involved in it. Now motion is supposed to belong to the class of things which are continuous; and the infinite presents itself first in the continuous—that is how it comes about that "infinite" is often used in definitions of the continuous ("what is infinitely divisible is continuous"). Besides these, place, void, and time are thought to be necessary conditions of motion. Clearly, then, for these reasons and also because the attributes mentioned are common to, and coextensive with, all the objects of our science, we must first take each of them in hand and discuss it. For the investigation of special attributes comes after that of the common attributes. To begin then, as we said, with motion.* **200b15–25**

191. *We may start by distinguishing (1) what exists in a state of fulfilment only, (2) what exists as potential, (3) what exists as potential and also in fulfilment—one being a "this," another "so much," a third "such," and similarly in each of the other modes of the predication of being. Further, the word "relative" is used with reference to (1) excess and defect, (2) agent and patient, and generally what can move and what can be moved. For "what can cause movement" is relative to "what can be moved," and vice versa.* **200b26–32**

192. *Again, there is no such thing as motion over and above the things. It is always with respect to substance or to quantity or to quality or to place that what changes changes. But it is impossible, as we assert, to find anything common to these which is neither "this" quantum nor quale nor any of the other predicates. Hence neither will motion and change have reference to something over and above the things mentioned; for there is nothing over and above them.* **200b32–201a3**

193. *Now each of these belongs to all its subjects in either of two ways: namely (1) substance—the one is positive form, the other privation; (2) in quality, white and black; (3) in quantity, complete and incomplete; (4) in respect of locomotion, upwards and downwards or light and heavy. Hence there are as many types of motion or change as there are meanings of the word "is."* **201a3–9**

COMMENTARY OF ST. THOMAS

275. Having treated the principles of natural things [Book I] and the principles of this science [Book II], he begins here to pursue his intention by treating the subject of this science, which is mobile being simply.

This discussion is divided into two parts. First he treats motion in itself [Books III–IV–V–VI]. Secondly, where he says, **"Everything that is in motion . . ."** [676], he treats motion in relation to movers and mobile objects [Book VII].

The first part is divided into two

parts. First he treats motion itself [Books III–IV]. Secondly where he says, **"Everything which changes..."** [465], he treats the parts of motion [Book V].

Concerning the first part he makes two points. First he states his intention. Secondly, where he says, **"We may start..."** [191], he develops his position.

Concerning the first part he makes two points. First he states his main intention. Secondly, where he says, **"When we have determined..."** [190], he points out certain related things which he intends to treat as consequences.

276. Concerning the first part [189] he uses the following argument. Nature is a principle of motion and mutation, as is clear from the definition given in Book II. (How motion and mutation differ will be explained in Book V.) Thus it is clear that if one does not know motion, one does not know nature, since motion is placed in the definition of nature. Since, then, we intend to set forth the science of nature, it is necessary to know about motion.

277. Next where he says, **"When we have determined..."** [190], he adds certain things which are concomitant with motion. He uses two arguments, the first of which is as follows.

Whoever treats a certain thing must treat those things which are consequent upon it. For a subject and its accidents are considered in one science.

But the infinite follows upon motion intrinsically. This is clear from the following.

Motion is among the things which are continuous, as will be explained in Book VI. But the infinite falls within the definition of the continuous.

And he adds "first," because the infinite which is found in the addition of

number is caused by the infinite which is found in the division of the continuous. He shows that the infinite falls in the definition of the continuous. For those who define the continuous often use the infinite, inasmuch as they say that the continuous is that which is infinitely divisible.

He says "often" because there is another definition of the continuous which is set forth in the Categories, i.e., a continuum is that whose parts are joined at one common boundary.

These two definitions differ. For since a continuum is a certain whole, it is defined by its parts. But parts have a twofold relation to the whole, one according to composition, insofar as the whole is composed of parts, and secondly, according to resolution, insofar as the whole is divided into parts.

Therefore, this definition of the continuous is given by way of resolution. The definition given in the Categories is by way of composition.

Therefore, it is clear that the infinite follows upon motion intrinsically.

Certain other things, however, follow upon motion extrinsically as external measures, for example, place and the void and time.

For time is the measure of motion itself. Place is a measure of the mobile object according to truth. And the void is a measure according to the opinion of some. Thus he adds that there can be no motion apart from place, the void and time.

Nor does it matter that not all motion is local motion. For nothing is moved unless it exists in place. For every sensible body is in place, and only sensible bodies are moved.

Local motion is also the first motion, and when it is taken away, so also are the others, as will be made clear below in Book VIII.

Therefore, it is clear that the four things mentioned above follow upon motion. Hence they pertain to the consideration of the natural philosopher for the reason [ratio] already given.

278. These things pertain to the consideration of the natural philosopher for another reason which he subsequently adds, namely, the above mentioned things are common to all natural things.

Thus in natural science all natural things must be treated. Now certain of these things must be treated first. For speculation about what is proper is posterior to speculation about what is common, as was said in the beginning. And among these common things motion must be treated first, because the others are consequent upon it, as was said.

279. Next where he says, "We may start..." [191], he pursues what he has proposed.

First he treats motion and the infinite, which follows upon motion intrinsically. Secondly, where he says, "The physicist must have a knowledge..." [277] [Book IV], he treats the other three things, which follow upon motion extrinsically.

The first part is divided into two parts. First he treats motion and secondly, the infinite, where he says, "The science of nature is concerned..." [224].

Concerning the first part he makes two points. First he sets forth certain things which are necessary to investigate the definition of motion. Secondly, where he says, "We have now..." [194], he defines motion.

Concerning the first part he makes two points. First he sets forth certain divisions. For the most convenient way of discovering a definition is by division, as is clear from what the Philosopher says in Posterior Analytics, II, and in Metaphysics, VII. Secondly, where he says, "Again there is no such thing..." [192], he shows that motion falls within the above mentioned divisions.

280. Concerning the first part [191] he sets forth three divisions. The first is that being is divided by potency and act. This division does not distinguish the genera of beings, for potency and act are found in every genus.

The second division is that being is divided into the ten genera, of which one is "a this," i.e., substance, another "quantity," or "quality," or one of the other predicaments.

The third division pertains to one of the genera of beings, namely, relation. For motion seems in some way to belong to this genus, insofar as the mover is referred to the mobile object.

In order to understand this third division, it must be noted that, since relation has the weakest existence because it consists only in being related to another, it is necessary for a relation to be grounded upon some other accident. For the more perfect accidents are closer to substance, and through their mediation the other accidents are in substance.

Now relation is primarily founded upon two things which have an ordination to another, namely, quantity and action. For quantity can be a measure of something external, and an agent pours out its action upon another.

Some relations, therefore, are grounded upon quantity, and especially upon number, to which belongs the first nature [ratio] of measure, as is clear in the double and the half, the multiplied and the divided, and other such things. Moreover the identical and the like and the equal are founded upon unity, which is the principle of number.

Other relations, however, are founded upon action and passion, either according to the act itself, as heating is referred to the heated, or according to that which has acted, as a father is referred to a son because he has begotten him, or according to the power of the agent, as a master is referred to a servant because he can compel him.

The Philosopher explains this division clearly in Metaphysics, V. Here he touches upon it briefly, saying that one type of relation is according to excess and defect, and this is founded upon quantity, such as the double and the half. The other type is according to the active and the passive, and the mover and the mobile object, which are referred to each other, as is clear in itself.

281. Next where he says, "**Again, there is no such thing . . .**" [192], he shows how motion is reduced to the above mentioned divisions.

Concerning this he makes two points. First he shows that there is no motion outside of the genera of things in which motion occurs. Secondly, where he says, "**Now each of these . . .**" [193], he shows that motion is divided as the genera of things are divided.

Concerning the first part it must be noted that since motion, as he will explain below, is an imperfect act, and since whatever is imperfect falls under the same genus as the perfect (not, indeed, according to species, but by reduction, as primary matter is in the genus of substance), there cannot be any motion outside of the genera of things in which motion occurs. This is what he means when he says that motion is not "over and above the things," that is over and above the genera of things in which there is motion, as if it were something extraneous or something common to these genera.

He makes this clear by the fact that everything that is changed is changed according to substance, or according to quantity, or according to quality, or according to place, as will be shown in Book V.

Moreover, in these genera there is no common univocal thing which would be their genus and which would not be contained under some predicament. Rather being is common to them by analogy, as will be shown in Metaphysics, IV. Hence it is clear that there is no motion or mutation outside the above mentioned genera. For there is nothing beyond these genera, since they divide being sufficiently well. He will show below how motion is related to the predicament of action or passion.

282. Next where he says, "**Now each of these . . .**" [193], he shows that motion is divided as the genera of things are divided.

It is clear that in each genus a thing can be in two ways, either as perfect or as imperfect. The reason [ratio] for this is that privation and possession are the first contraries, as is said in Metaphysics, X. Therefore, since all the genera are divided by differentiating contraries, there must be in every genus a perfect and an imperfect. Thus in substance, something is as the form, and something as the privation; in quality, something is as the white which is perfect, another is as the black which is, as it were, imperfect; in quantity, something is a perfect quantity, another imperfect; and in place, something is above which is, as it were, perfect, another below which is, as it were, imperfect, or else something is light and heavy, which are placed in the category "where" by reason [ratio] of their inclination. Hence it is clear that motion is divided in as many ways as being is divided.

For the species of motion differ according to the different genera of beings. Thus growth, which is motion in quantity, differs from generation, which is motion in substance.

And the species of motion differ within the same genus according to the perfect and the imperfect. For generation is motion in substance toward form, whereas corruption is motion toward privation. And in quantity, growth is toward perfect quantity, and decrease is toward imperfect quantity. Why he does not designate the two species in quality and in "where" will be explained in Book V.

LECTURE 2 [201a9–b5]
The Definition of Motion

The Text of Aristotle

194. We have now before us the distinctions in the various classes of being between what is fully real and what is potential. The fulfilment of what exists potentially, in so far as it exists potentially, is motion—   **201a9–11**

195. Namely, of what is alterable qua alterable, alteration: of what can be increased and its opposite what can be decreased (there is no common name), increase and decrease; of what can come to be and can pass away, coming to be and passing away: of what can be carried along, locomotion.   **201a11–15**

196. Examples will elucidate this definition of motion. When the buildable, in so far as it is just that, is fully real, it is being built, and this is building. Similarly, learning, doctoring, rolling, leaping, ripening, aging.   **201a15–19**

197. The same thing, if it is of a certain kind, can be both potential and fully real, not indeed at the same time or not in the same respect, but e.g. potentially hot and actually cold. Hence at once such things will act and be acted on by one another in many ways: each of them will be capable at the same time of causing alteration and of being altered. Hence, too, what effects motion as a physical agent can be moved: when a thing of this kind causes motion, it is itself also moved. This, indeed, has led some people to suppose that every mover is moved. But this question depends on another set of arguments, and the truth will be made clear later. It is possible for a thing to cause motion, though it is itself incapable of being moved. It is the fulfilment of what is potential when it is already fully real and operates not as itself but as movable, that is motion.   **201a19–29**

198. What I mean by "as" is this: bronze is potentially a statue. But it is not the fulfilment of bronze as bronze which is motion. For "to be bronze" and "to be a certain potentiality" are not the same. If they were identical without qualification, i.e. in definition, the fulfilment of bronze as bronze would have been motion. But they are not the same, as has been said.   **201a29–34**

199. (This is obvious in contraries. "To be capable of health" and "to be capable of illness" are not the same; for if they were there would be no difference between being ill and being well. Yet the subject both of health and of sickness—whether it is humor or blood—is one and the same.)   **201a34–201b5**

COMMENTARY OF ST. THOMAS

283. Having set forth certain things which are necessary for investigating the definition of motion, the Philosopher here defines motion.

First he defines it generally, and secondly, specifically, where he says, **"What then motion is . . ."** [223].

Concerning the first part he makes two points. First he shows what motion is. Secondly, where he says, **"The mover, too . . ."** [205], he asks whether motion is the act of the mover or of the mobile object.

Concerning the first part he makes three points. First he sets forth the definition of motion. Secondly, where he says, **"Examples will elucidate . . ."** [196], he explains the parts of the definition. Thirdly, where he says, **"Further it is evident . . ."** [200], he shows that the definition has been well formulated.

Concerning the first part he makes two points. First he sets forth the definition of motion. Secondly, where he says, "... namely, of what..." [195], he gives examples.

284. Concerning the first part it must be noted that some would define motion by saying that motion is a passage from potency to act which is not sudden. These thinkers have erred in formulating the definition because they have placed in the definition of motion certain things which are posterior to motion. For a "passage" is a certain species of motion. Moreover "sudden" has time in its definition, for that is sudden which happens in an indivisible time. But time is defined by motion.

285. And so it is altogether impossible to define motion by what is prior and better known other than as the Philosopher here defines it.

For it has been said that each genus is divided by potency and act. Now since potency and act pertain to the first differences in being, they are naturally prior to motion. And the Philosopher uses these to define motion.

It must be noted, therefore, that to be only in act is one thing, to be only in potency is another thing, and to be a mean between potency and act is a third thing. That, then, which is in potency only is not yet moved. That which is in perfect act is not moved, but has already been moved. That, therefore, is moved which is a mean between pure potency and act, which is, indeed, partly in potency and partly in act, as is clear in alteration. For when water is hot only in potency, it is not yet moved. On the other hand, when it is already heated, the motion of heating is finished. But when it participates in something of heat although imper-

fectly, then it is being moved to heat. For that which is becoming hot gradually participates in heat more and more. Therefore, motion is that imperfect act of heat existing in the heatable, not, indeed, insofar as it is only in act, but insofar as already existing in act it has an ordination to further act. For if this ordination to further act were removed, that act [which it already has], however imperfect, would be the end of the motion and not the motion, as happens when something is partially heated. Furthermore, an ordination to further act belongs to that which exists in potency to it.

Likewise, if the imperfect act were considered only in its ordination to further act, insofar as it has the nature [ratio] of a potency, it would not have the nature [ratio] of motion, but of a principle of motion. For heating can begin from the tepid as well as from the cold.

Hence, motion is neither the potency of that which exists in potency, nor the act of that which exists in act. Rather motion is the act of that which exists in potency, such that its ordination to its prior potency is designated by what is called "act," and its ordination to further act is designated by what is called "existing in potency."

Hence, the Philosopher has defined motion most adequately by saying that motion is the entelechy, i.e., the act, of that which exists in potency insofar as it is such.

286. Next where he says, "... namely, of what..." [195], he exemplifies this in all the species of motion. Thus, alteration is the act of the alterable insofar as it is alterable.

Since motions in quantity and in substance do not have one name, as motion in quality is called alteration, he sets forth two names for motion in quantity. He says that the act of that which can increase and its opposite, i.e., that which can diminish (for which there is no one common name), is increase and decrease. In like manner generation and corruption [is the act] of the generable and the corruptible, and change of place [is the act] of that which can change in place.

Motion is taken here commonly to mean mutation, and not in the strict sense in which motion is distinguished from generation and corruption, as will be said in Book V.

287. Next where he says, **"Examples will elucidate . . ."** [196], he explains the individual parts of the definition. He does this first insofar as motion is called an "act." Secondly, where he says, **"The same thing . . ."** [197], he explains the meaning of "that which exists in potency." Thirdly, where he says, **"What I mean . . ."** [198], he explains the meaning of "insofar as it is such."

With reference to the first part he uses the following argument. That by which something which previously existed in potency comes to be in act is act. But a thing comes to be in act while it is being moved, whereas prior to this, it was existing in potency. Therefore, motion is an act.

Hence he says that from this it is obvious that motion is an act. For he says that the "buildable" is a potency for something. However, when the buildable with respect to this potency which it implies is being reduced to act, then we say it is being built. And this act is passive building.

And it is the same with all other motions, such as learning, healing, rolling, dancing, maturing, i.e., growing, and aging, i.e., decreasing.

For it must be noted that before a thing is moved, it is in potency to two acts, namely, a perfect act which is the end of the motion, and an imperfect act which is motion. Thus, before water begins to be heated, it is in potency to being heated and to being hot. When it is being heated, it is reduced to the imperfect act, which is motion. However it is not yet in perfect act, which is the end of motion. Rather with respect to this, it remains in potency.

288. Next where he says, **"The same thing . . ."** [197], he shows with the following argument that motion is the act of that which exists in potency.

Every act is the proper act of that in which it is always found. Thus, light is found only in the diaphanous, and because of this it is the act of the diaphanous. But motion is always found in that which exists in potency. Therefore, motion is the act of that which exists in potency.

In order to clarify the second proposition, he says that the same thing is in potency and in act, although not at the same time, or in the same respect, as when a thing is hot in potency and cold in act. Hence, it follows from this that many things act upon and are acted upon by each other insofar as each is in potency and in act with reference to the other in different respects. And because every inferior natural body shares in matter, then in each there is a potency for that which is in act in another. And so in all such cases a thing both acts and is acted upon, moves and is moved.

And for this reason it seemed to some that absolutely every mover is moved. But this point will be examined more fully in other places. For it will be shown in Book VIII of this work and in Metaphysics, XII, that there is a certain mover which is immobile, because it is not in potency but is only in act.

But when that which is in potency, while existing in act in some way, acts either upon itself or upon something else insofar as it is mobile (i.e., when the moved is reduced to act, whether it be moved by itself or by another), then the motion is its act. Hence things which are in potency are moved, whether they act or are acted upon. For by acting they are acted upon, and by moving they are moved. Thus, when fire acts upon wood, it is acted upon insofar as it is encompassed by smoke, for flames are nothing but burning smoke.

289. Next where he says, **"What I mean . . ."** [198], he explains the meaning of "insofar as it is such." He does this first with an example, and secondly, with an argument, where he says, **"This is obvious in contraries . . ."** [199].

He says, therefore, first [198] that it was necessary to add "insofar as it is such" because that which is in potency is also something in act. And although the same thing exists both in potency and in act, to be in potency and to be in act are not the same according to nature [ratio]. Thus, bronze is in potency to statue and is bronze in act, yet the nature [ratio] of bronze insofar as it is bronze and insofar as it is a potency for a statue is not the same. Hence motion is not the act of bronze insofar as it is bronze, but insofar as it is in potency to statue. Otherwise, as long as the bronze would exist, it would be moved. And this is clearly false. Hence it is clear that "insofar as it is such" is aptly added.

290. Next where he says, **"This is obvious in contraries . . ."** [199], he explains the same thing with an argument taken from the contraries.

It is clear that the same subject is in potency to contraries, as humor or blood is the same subject which is potentially related to health and sickness. And it is also clear that to be in potency to health and to be in potency to sickness are two different things (I say this according to their ordination to their objects). Otherwise, if to be able to be ill and to be able to be well were the same, it would follow that to be ill and to be healthy would be the same. Therefore, to be able to be ill and to be able to be healthy differ in nature [ratio], but their subject is one and the same.

It is clear, therefore, that the nature [ratio] of the subject insofar as it is a certain being and insofar as it is a potency to another is not the same. Otherwise potency to contraries would be one according to nature [ratio]. So also color and the visible are not the same according to nature [ratio].

Therefore it was necessary to say that motion is the act of the possible insofar as it is possible, lest it be understood to be the act of that which is in potency insofar as it is a certain subject.

LECTURE 3 [201b6–202a2]
The Definition of Motion Has Been Well Formulated

The Text of Aristotle

200. *We can distinguish, then, between the two—just as, to give another example, "color" and "visible" are different—and clearly it is the fulfilment of what is potential as potential that is motion. So this, precisely, is motion. Further it is evident that motion is an attribute of a thing just when it is fully real in this way, and neither before nor after. For each thing of this kind is capable of being at one time actual, at another not. Take for instance the buildable as buildable. The actuality of the buildable as buildable is the process of building. For the actuality of the buildable must be either this or the house. But when there is a house, the buildable is no longer buildable. On the other hand, it is the buildable which is being built. The process then of being built must be the kind of actuality required. But building is a kind of motion, and the same account will apply to the other kinds also.* 201b5–15

Chapter 2

201. *The soundness of this definition is evident both when we consider the accounts of motion that the others have given, and also from the difficulty of defining it otherwise. One could not easily put motion and change in another genus.* 201b16–19

202. *This is plain if we consider where some people put it; they identify motion with "difference" or "inequality" or "not being"; but such things are not necessarily moved, whether they are "different" or "unequal" or "non-existent." Nor is change either to or from these rather than to or from their opposites.* 201b19–24

203. *The reason why they put motion into these genera is that it is thought to be something indefinite, and the principles in the second column are indefinite because they are privative: none of them is either "this" or "such" or comes under any of the other modes of predication.* 201b24–27

204. *The reason in turn why motion is thought to be indefinite is that it cannot be classed simply as a potentiality or as an actuality—a thing that is merely capable of having a certain size is not undergoing change, nor yet a thing that is actually of a certain size, and motion is thought to be a sort of actuality, but incomplete, the reason for this view being that the potential whose actuality it is is incomplete. This is why it is hard to grasp what motion is. It is necessary to class it with privation or with potentiality or with sheer actuality, yet none of these seems possible. There remains then the suggested mode of definition, namely that it is a sort of actuality, or actuality of the kind described, hard to grasp, but not incapable of existing.* 201b27–202a3

COMMENTARY OF ST. THOMAS

291. Having set forth the definition of motion, and having explained the individual parts of the definition, he here shows that the definition is well formulated.

He does this first directly, and secondly, indirectly, where he says, **"The soundness of this . . ."** [201].

292. With reference to the first part [200] he uses the following argument.

Whatever is in potency is at some time in act. But the buildable is in potency. Therefore, there is an act of the buildable insofar as it is buildable. Now this act is either the house or the activity of building. But a house is not the act of the buildable insofar as it is buildable, because the buildable insofar as it is such is reduced to act when it is being built. For when the house already exists, it is not being built. Therefore, it follows that building is the act of the buildable insofar as it is such. Building, however, is a certain motion. Motion, therefore, is the act of that which exists in potency insofar as it is such. And the same argument applies to other motions.

It is clear, therefore, that motion is an act such as was said, and that a thing is moved when it is in such an act, and neither before nor after. For before, when there is only potency, the motion has not yet begun. And after the motion it has already altogether ceased to be in potency because it is in perfect act.

293. Next where he says, **"The soundness of this definition . . ."** [201], he shows indirectly that the definition is well formulated. For motion cannot be defined otherwise.

Concerning this he makes three points. First he states his intention. Secondly, where he says, **"One could not easily . . ."** [202], he sets forth and rejects the definitions of motion given by others. Thirdly, where he says, **"The reason why . . ."** [203], he explains why some have defined motion in this way.

He says, therefore, first that it is clear that motion has been well defined for two reasons: first, because the definitions by which some have defined motion are absurd; secondly, because of the fact that motion cannot be defined otherwise. The reason [ratio] for this is that motion cannot be placed in any genus other than the genus of the act of that which exists in potency.

294. Next where he says, **"One could not easily . . ."** [202], he rejects the definitions of motion given by others.

It must be noted that some have defined motion in three ways.

For they said that motion is otherness, because of the fact that that which is moved is always different.

Next they said that motion is inequality, because that which is moved always approaches nearer and nearer to its terminus.

They also said that motion is that which is not, i.e., non-being. For that which is moved, while it is being moved, does not yet have that to which it is moved. Thus that which is being moved to whiteness is not yet white.

However the Philosopher rejects these definitions in three ways.

He does this first in respect to the subject of motion. For if motion were otherness or inequality or non-being, then that in which these things are would necessarily be moved, because that in which motion is is moved. But it is not necessary that things which are other be moved because of the fact that they are other. And the same is true of things which are unequal and of things which are not. Therefore, it follows that otherness and inequality and non-being are not motion.

Secondly, he shows the same thing in respect to the terminus to which. For motion and mutation are not toward otherness more than toward likeness, nor toward inequality more than toward equality, nor toward non-being more than toward being. For generation is a mutation toward being, and corruption is toward non-being. Therefore, motion is not otherness more than likeness, nor inequality more than equality, nor non-being more than being.

Thirdly, he shows the same thing in respect to the terminus from which. For as some motions are from otherness and from inequality and from non-being, other motions are from the opposites of these. Therefore, motion should not be placed in these genera rather than in their opposites.

295. Next where he says, **"The reason why ..."** [203], he explains why the ancients defined motion in the way mentioned above.

Concerning this he makes two points. First, he explains what he has said. Secondly, where he says, **"The reason in turn ..."** [204], he explains a certain point which he had assumed.

He says, therefore, first [203] that the reason why the ancients held that motion is in the genera mentioned above (i.e., otherness, inequality and non-being) is that motion seems to be something indeterminate, i.e., incomplete and imperfect, not having, as it were, a determinate nature. And because motion is indeterminate it seems that it must be placed in the genus of privatives. For when Pythagoras posited two orders of things, in each of which he placed ten principles, the principles which were in the second order he called indeterminate, because they are privatives. For these things are not determined by a form in the genus of substance, nor by a form of quality, nor by any special form existing in one of these genera, nor even by a form of one of the other predicaments.

Thus in one order the Pythagoreans placed these ten: the finite, the unequal, the one, the right, the masculine, rest, the straight, light, the good, and the equilateral triangle. In the other order they placed the infinite, the equal,

the many, the left, the feminine, motion, the oblique, darkness, evil, and the scalene.

296. Next where he says, **"The reason in turn ..."** [204], he explains why motion is placed among the indeterminate things.

He says that the reason for this is that motion cannot be placed either under potency or under act. For if it were placed under potency, then whatever would be in potency, e.g. to quantity, would be moved according to quantity. And if it were contained under act, then whatever would be a quantity in act would be moved according to quantity. Indeed it is true that motion is an act, but it is an imperfect act, a mean between potency and act. And it is clear that it is an imperfect act because that whose act it is is being in potency, as was said above. Hence it is difficult to grasp what motion is. For it seems at first glance that it is either act simply or potency simply or that it should be contained under privation, as the ancients held that it is contained under non-being or under inequality. But none of these is possible, as was pointed out above. Hence only the above mentioned mode of defining motion remains, namely, motion is an act such as we have said, i.e., the act of that which exists in potency.

However, it is difficult to understand such an act because of the mixture of act and potency. Nevertheless the existence of such an act is not impossible, but may occur.

LECTURE 4 [202a3–21]
Motion Is the Act of the Mobile Object as the Subject in Which and the Act of the Mover as the Cause by Which

The Text of Aristotle

205. *The mover too is moved, as has been said—every mover, that is, which is capable of motion,*   202a3–4

206. *and whose immobility is rest—when a thing is subject to motion its immobility is rest.*   202a4–5

207. *For to act on the movable as such is just to move it. But this it does by contact, so that at the same time it is also acted on.*   202a5–7

208. *Hence we can define motion as the fulfilment of the movable qua movable, the cause of the attribute being contact with what can move, so that the mover is also acted on.*   202a7–8

208bis. *The mover or agent will always be the vehicle of a form, either a "this" or a "such," which, when it acts, will be the source and cause of the change, e.g., the full-formed man begets man from what is potentially man.*   202a8–12

Chapter 3

209. *The solution of the difficulty is plain: motion is in the movable. It is the fulfilment of this potentiality by the action of that which has the power of causing motion;*   202a13–14

210. *and the actuality of that which has the power of causing motion is not other than the actuality of the movable;*   202a15–17

211. *for it must be the fulfilment of both. A thing is capable of causing motion because it can do this, it is a mover because it actually does it.*   202a17–18

212. *But it is on the movable that it is capable of acting. Hence there is a single actuality of both alike,*   202a17–18

213. *just as one to two and two to one are the same interval, and the steep ascent and the steep descent are one—for these are one and the same, although they can be described in different ways. So it is with the mover and the moved.*   202a18–21

COMMENTARY OF ST. THOMAS

297. After the Philosopher has defined motion, he here explains whose act motion is, i.e., whether it is the act of the mobile object or of the mover.

It can be said that he sets forth here another definition of motion which is related to the definition already given as the material is related to the formal and as a conclusion is related to a premise.

The definition is as follows: motion is the act of the mobile object insofar as it is mobile.

This definition is drawn as a conclusion from the one already given. Since motion is the act of that which exists in potency insofar as it is such, and since that which exists in potency insofar as it is such is the mobile object, and not the mover, since the mover insofar as it is such is a being in act, it follows that motion is the act of the mobile object insofar as it is such.

298. Concerning this, therefore, he makes three points. First, he shows that motion is the act of the mobile object. Secondly, where he says, ". . . and the actuality of that . . ." [210], he shows how motion is related to the mover. Thirdly, where he says, "This view has a dialectical difficulty" [214], he raises a difficulty.

Concerning the first part he makes two points. First, he states the definition of motion, namely, motion is the act of the mobile object. Secondly, where he says, **"The solution of the difficulty . . ."** [209], mentions something which, because of what he has said, could be a difficulty.

Concerning the first part he makes three points. First he inquires into the definition of motion. Secondly, where he says, **"Hence we can define . . ."** [208], he concludes to the definition. Thirdly, where he says, **" . . . the cause of the attribute . . ."** [208bis], he explains the definition.

Moreover, in order to inquire into the definition of motion, he states that the mover also is moved. And concerning this he makes two points.

First he proves that every mover is moved. Secondly, where he says, **"For to act . . ."** [207], he shows how the mover is moved.

299. He shows with two arguments that the mover is moved.

First, since everything which is first in potency and later in act is moved in some way, and since the mover is found to be at first a mover in potency and afterwards a mover in act, a mover of this sort is moved. He says that every mover, when it is so constituted that at some time it is mobile in potency, i.e., in potency to motion, is moved, as was said. This is apparent from what he has already said. For he said that motion is the act of that which exists in potency, and this occurs in every natural mover. Hence, it was said above that every physical mover is moved.

300. Secondly, where he says, **" . . . and whose immobility . . ."** [206], he shows the same thing in another way.

Motion is in anything whose immobility is rest. For rest and motion, since they are opposites, come to be with reference to the same thing. But the immobility of a mover, i.e., its cessation from moving, is called rest. For certain things are said to rest when they cease to act. Therefore, every such mover, i.e., one whose immobility is rest, is moved.

301. Next where he says, **"For to act . . ."** [207], he shows how the mover is moved.

This does not happen to the mover because of the fact that it moves, but because of the fact that it moves by contact. For to move is to act in such a way that something is moved. That, moreover, which is thus acted upon by a mover is moved. But this sort of action works by contact, for bodies act by touching. Hence it follows that the mover should also be acted upon, for that which touches is acted upon.

But this must be understood [to be true] when the contact is mutual, i.e., when something touches and is touched, as happens in those things which share in matter, each of which is acted upon by the other while they touch each other. For celestial bodies, which do not share in matter with inferior bodies, act upon inferior bodies in such a way that they are not acted upon by them, and they touch and are not touched, as is said in De Generatione et Corruptione, I.

302. Next where he says, **"Hence we can define . . ."** [208], he sets forth the definition of motion, concluding from the foregoing that, although the mover is moved, nevertheless motion is not the act of the mover but of the mobile object insofar as it is mobile.

He subsequently clarifies this by reason of the fact that being moved is accidental to the mover, and does not belong to it per se. Hence, if a thing is moved insofar as its act is motion, it follows that motion is not the act of the mover, but of the mobile object, not, indeed, insofar as it is a mover, but insofar as it is mobile.

He shows [208bis] from what was said above that being moved is accidental to the mover. For the act of the mobile object, which is motion, occurs because of the contact of the mover. And from this it follows that the mover is acted upon at the same time that it acts, and thus to be moved belongs to the mover per accidens.

He shows as follows that being moved does not belong to the mover per se. Some form always seems to be the mover, such as the form which is in the genus of substance in a change which is according to substance, and a form which is in the genus of quality in alteration, and a form which is in the genus of quantity in increase and decrease. Forms of this sort are causes and principles of motions, because every agent moves according to its form. For every agent acts insofar as it is in act, as man in act produces man in act from man in potency. Hence, since each thing is in act through its form, it follows that form is a moving principle. And thus to move belongs to a thing insofar as it has a form by which it is in act. Hence, since motion is the act of that which exists in potency, as was said above, it follows that motion does not pertain to a thing insofar as it is a mover, but insofar as it is mobile. And so it is stated in the definition of motion that motion is the act of the mobile object insofar as it is mobile.

303. Next where he says, **"The solution of . . ."** [209], he clarifies a certain difficulty which arises from what has been said. For someone might question whether motion is in the mover or in the mobile object.

This difficulty is answered by what has already been said. For it is obvious that the act of anything is in that whose act it is. And thus it is obvious that the act of motion is in the mobile object because it is the act of the mobile object, caused in it, however, by the mover.

304. Next where he says, **". . . and the actuality . . ."** [210], he shows how motion is related to the mover.

First he states his intention, saying that the act of the mover is not other than the act of the mobile object. Hence, although motion is the act of the mobile object, it is also in some way the act of the mover.

305. Secondly, where he says, **". . . for it must be . . ."** [211], he explains his position.

Concerning this he makes three points. First, he shows that the mover has an act, as also does the mobile object. For whatever is named according to potency and act has some act belonging to it. Now that which is moved is called mobile by reason of its potency, insofar as it can be moved, and it is called moved by reason of its act, insofar as it is moved in act. In the same way the mover is called a mover by reason of its potency, insofar as it can move, and it is called a motion in its very action, i.e., insofar as it actually acts. Therefore, it is necessary that act pertain to both the mover and the mobile object.

306. Secondly, where he says, **"But it is on the moveable . . ."** [212], he shows that the act of the mover and of the moved is the same. For a thing is called a mover insofar as it does something, and moved insofar as it is acted upon. But what the mover causes by acting and what the moved receives by being acted upon are the same. He says that the mover acts upon the mobile object, i.e., it causes the act of the mobile object. Hence it is necessary that one act be the act of each, i.e., of the mover and the moved. For what is

from the mover as from an agent cause and what is in the moved as in a patient and a recipient are the same.

307. Thirdly, where he says, "...just as one to two..." [213], he clarifies this with an example.

In respect to things the distance from one to two and from two to one is the same. But these differ according to nature [ratio]. For insofar as we begin the comparison from two and proceed to one, it is called double, whereas if we begin the comparison from the other end, it is called a half. And in like manner the space of rising and of descending is the same, but because of a difference in starting points and finishing points it is called ascent or descent. And the same applies to the mover and the moved. For motion insofar as it proceeds from the mover to the mobile object is the act of the mover, but insofar as it is in the mobile object from the mover, it is the act of the mobile object.

LECTURE 5 [202a22–b29]
Whether Action and Passion Are the Same Motion

The Text of Aristotle

214. *This view has a dialectical difficulty. Perhaps it is necessary that the actuality of the agent and that of the patient should not be the same. The one is "agency" and the other "patiency"; and the outcome and completion of the one is an "action," that of the other a "passion."*   **202a21–24**

215. *Since then they are both motions, we may ask: in what are they, if they are different? Either (a) both are in what is acted on and moved, or (b) the agency is in the agent and the patiency in the patient. (If we ought to call the latter also "agency," the word would be used in two senses.)*   **202a25–28**

216. *Now, in alternative (b) the motion will be in the mover, for the same statement will hold of "mover" and "moved." Hence either every mover will be moved, or, though having motion, it will not be moved.*   **202a28–31**

217. *If on the other hand (a) both are in what is moved and acted on—both the agency and the patiency (e.g., both teaching and learning, though they are two, in the learner), then, first, the actuality of each will not be present in each, and, a second absurdity, a thing will have two motions at the same time. How will there be two alterations of quality in one subject towards one definite quality? The thing is impossible: the actualization will be one.*   **202a31–36**

218. *But (someone will say) it is contrary to reason to suppose that there should be one identical actualization of two things which are different in kind. Yet there will be, if teaching and learning are the same, and agency and patiency. To teach will be the same as to learn, and to act the same as to be acted on—the teacher will necessarily be learning everything that he teaches, and the agent will be acted on.*   **202a36–202b5**

219. *One may reply: (1) It is not absurd that the actualization of one thing should be in another. Teaching is the activity of a person who can teach, yet the operation is performed on some patient—it is not cut adrift from a subject, but is of A on B.*   **202b5–8**

220. *(2) There is nothing to prevent two things having one and the same actualization, provided the actualizations are not described in the same way, but are related as what can act to what is acting. (3) Nor is it necessary that the teacher should learn, even if to act and to be acted on are one and the same, provided they are not the same in definition (as "raiment" and "dress"), but are the same merely in the sense in which the road from Thebes to Athens and the road from Athens to Thebes are the same, as has been explained above. For it is not things which are in a way the same that have all their attributes the same, but only such as have the same definition.*   **202b8–16**

221. *But indeed it by no means follows from the fact that teaching is the same as learning, that to learn is the same as to teach, any more than it follows from the fact that there is one distance between two things which are at a distance from each other, that the two vectors AB and BA are one and the same.*   **202b16–19**

222. *To generalize, teaching is not the same as learning, or agency as patiency, in the full sense, though they belong to the same subject, the motion; for the "actualization of X in Y" and the "actualization of Y through the action of X" differ in definition.*   **202b19–22**

223. *What then Motion is, has been stated both generally and particularly. It is not difficult to see how each of its types will be defined—alteration is the fulfilment of the alterable qua alterable (or, more scientifically, the fulfilment of what can act and what can be acted on, as such)—generally and again in each particular case, building, healing, etc. A similar definition will apply to each of the other kinds of motion.*   **202b23–29**

COMMENTARY OF ST. THOMAS

308. After the Philosopher has shown that motion is the act of the mobile object and of the mover, he now raises a difficulty concerning what has been said.

First he raises the difficulty, and secondly, he answers it, where he says, **"One may reply . . ."** [219].

Concerning the first part he makes two points. First, he sets forth certain things which pertain to the difficulty. Secondly, where he says, **"Since, then, they are both . . ."** [215], he states the difficulty.

309. He says, therefore, first [214] that what has been said raises a difficulty which is dialectical, i.e., logical. For there are probable arguments on both sides.

As an introduction to this difficulty he states that some acts pertain to the active, and some acts pertain to the passive. Thus it was said above that there is an act which pertains to both the mover and the moved. Now the act of the active is called action, while the act of the passive is called passion. And he proves this. For that which is the work and end of each thing is its act and perfection. Hence, since the work and end of an agent is action, and since the work and end of a patient is passion, as is obvious in itself, it follows, as was said, that action is the act of the agent and passion is the act of the patient.

310. Next where he says, **"Since then they are both . . ."** [215], he states the difficulty.

It is clear that both action and passion are motion, for each is the same as motion.

Therefore, action and passion are either the same motion or they are different motions.

If they are different, it is necessary that each of them be in some subject. Therefore, either both of them are in the patient and that which is moved, or else one of them is in the agent, i.e., the action, and the other is in the patient, i.e., the passion. If, moreover, one were to say conversely that that which is in the agent is the passion and that which is in the patient is the action, it is obvious that one speaks equivocally. For that which is a passion will be called an action, and vice versa. However, Aristotle seems to omit a fourth member, i.e., that both would be in the agent. He leaves this out because it has been shown that motion is in the mobile object. Hence, this alternative, that neither would be in the patient but both in the agent, is excluded.

311. Therefore, of the two alternatives which he treats, he deals first with the second one, where he says, **"Now in alternative . . ."** [216]. If one were to say that action is in the agent and passion is in the patient, then since action is a certain motion, as was said, it follows that motion is in the mover. Now the same reasoning [ratio] must apply to both the mover and the moved, i.e., whichever of these has motion is moved. Or one might say that mover and moved have the same nature [ratio] as patient and agent. Thus whatever has motion is moved. Hence it follows either that every mover would be moved, or that something would have motion and would not be moved. Each of these seems to be inconsistent.

312. Next where he says, **"If on the other hand . . ."** [217], he discusses the other alternative. He says that if one were to say that both action and passion, although they are two motions,

are in the patient and the moved, and that teaching which is on the part of the teacher and learning which is on the part of the learner are in the learner, then two absurdities follow.

The first of these arises because he has said that action is the act of the agent. If, therefore, action is not in the agent but in the patient, it would follow that the proper act of each thing is not in that whose act it is.

After this the other absurdity would follow, namely, that some one and the same thing would be moved by two motions. For action and passion are assumed here to be two motions. Now whatever has motion is moved in respect to that motion. If, therefore, action and passion are in the mobile object, it follows that the mobile object would be moved by two motions. And this would be the same as if there were two alterations of one subject which would be terminated in one species. Thus, one subject would be moved by two whitenings, which is impossible. However, it is not absurd for the same subject to be moved simultaneously by two alterations terminating in different species, e.g., whitening and heating. However, it is obvious that action and passion terminate in the same species, for what the agent does and what the patient undergoes are the same.

313. Next where he says, "... the actualization will be one" [218], he examines the other alternative.

One might say that action and passion are not two motions but one. From this he brings out four inconsistencies.

The first is that the acts of things diverse according to species would be the same. For it was said that action is the act of the agent and passion is the act of the patient, which acts are diverse according to species. If, therefore, action and passion are the same

motion, it follows that the acts of things diverse in species are the same.

The second inconsistency is that, if action and passion are one motion, then action is the same as passion. Thus teaching which is on the part of the teacher is the same as learning which belongs to the learner.

The third inconsistency is that to act is the same as to be acted upon, and to teach is the same as to learn.

And the fourth which follows from this is that every teacher learns, and every agent is acted upon.

314. Next where he says, "One may reply . . ." [219], he answers the problem presented above.

It is clear from what was determined above that action and passion are not two motions, but are one and the same motion. For insofar as motion is from the agent it is called action, and insofar as it is in the patient it is called passion.

315. Hence, the inconsistencies which were developed in the first part, in which it was assumed that action and passion are two motions, do not need to be answered. However, one of these difficulties must be answered even if it is supposed that action and passion are one motion. For since action is the act of the agent, as was said above, then if action and passion are one motion, it follows that the act of the agent is in some way in the patient, and thus the act of one thing will be in another. Now four inconsistencies followed from the other part, and thus five inconsistencies remain to be answered.

316. He says, therefore, first that it is not inconsistent for the act of one thing to be in another. For teaching is the act of the teacher, tending, nevertheless, from him to someone else continuously and without interruption. Hence

the same act is his, i.e., the agent's, as "from whom," and is also in the patient as received in him. However, it would be inconsistent if the act of one thing were in another in the way in which it is the act of the former.

317. Next where he says, **"There is nothing . . ."** [220], he answers another inconsistency, namely, that two things would have the same act.

He says that there is nothing to prevent two things from having one act in the sense that the act is not one and the same according to reason [ratio] but is one in things. As was said above, there is the same interval from two to one from one to two, and from that which is in potency to that which is acting and conversely. For the same act in things is the act of two according to different intelligibilities [ratio]. It is the act of the agent insofar as it is "from it" and of the patient insofar as it is "in it."

318. He replies to the other three inconsistencies, one of which is deduced from the other, in reverse order.

He replies first to what was brought out last as more inconsistent. Thus this third point answers the fifth inconsistency.

He says that it is not necessary that the teacher learn, or that the agent be acted upon, even though to act and to be acted upon are the same. This is true as long as we say that these latter are not the same in the sense of things whose natures [ratio] are the same (e.g. raiment and dress). Rather they are the same in the sense of things which are the same in subject and different in respect to reason [ratio], such as the road from Thebes to Athens and the road from Athens to Thebes, as was said before. For it is not necessary for all things which are the same to be the same in every way. Rather they are the same only in subject or in things or ac-

cording to reason [ratio]. And so, even granting that to act and to be acted upon are the same, then since they are not the same according to reason [ratio], as was said, it does not follow that to be acted upon belongs to everything which acts.

319. Next where he says, **"But indeed it . . ."** [221], he replies to the fourth inconsistency. He says that, even if teaching and the learning of the learner are the same, it does not follow that to teach and to learn would be the same. For teaching and learning are said in the abstract, whereas to teach and to learn are said in the concrete. Hence they [teaching and learning] are applied to ends or to termini insofar as the diverse intelligibilities [ratio] of action and passion are taken. Thus although we say that there is the same interval of distance between certain things when they are considered abstractly, if we were to apply [what we say] to the termini of the interval, as when we say this place is distant from that, and that from this, then it is not one and the same.

320. Next where he says, **"To generalize . . ."** [222], he replies to the third inconsistency. He denies the inference by which it was concluded that if action and passion are one motion, then action and passion are the same.

And he says that finally it must be said that it does not follow that action and passion are the same, or that teaching and learning are the same. Rather the motion in which both of these are is the same. And this motion according to one intelligibility [ratio] is action, and according to another is passion. For as far as intelligibility [ratio] is concerned, being the act of this as "in this" is different than being the act of this as "from this." But motion is called action because it is the act of the agent as "from this," while it is called passion because it is the act of the patient as "in this."

And thus it is clear that, although the motion is the same for the mover and the moved because of the fact that it abstracts from both intelligibilities [ratio], nevertheless, action and passion differ because of the fact that they include in their signification these different intelligibilities [ratio].

From this it is apparent that since motion abstracts from the intelligibility [ratio] of action and passion, it is contained neither in the predicament of action nor in the predicament of passion, as some have said.

321. But with reference to this a twofold difficulty remains.

First, if action and passion are one motion and differ only according to reason [ratio], as was said, it seems that there should not be these two predicaments, since the predicaments are the genera of things.

Furthermore, if motion is either action or passion, motion will not be found in substance, in quality, in quantity and in "where," as was said above. Rather motion will be found only in action and passion.

322. For the clarification of these points it must be noted that being is not divided univocally into the ten predicaments as genera are divided into species. Rather it is divided according to the diverse modes of existing. But modes of existing are proportional to the modes of predicating. For when we predicate something of another, we say this is that. Hence the ten genera of being are called the ten predicaments.

Now every predication is made in one of three ways.

One way is when that which pertains to the essence is predicated of some subject, as when I say Socrates is a man, or man is animal. The predicament of substance is taken in this way.

Another mode is that in which that which is not of the essence of a thing, but which inheres in it, is predicated of a thing. This is found either on the part of the matter of the subject, and thus is the predicament of quantity (for quantity properly follows upon matter—thus Plato also held the great to be on the part of matter), or else it follows upon the form, and thus is the predicament of quality (hence also qualities are founded upon quantity as color is in a surface, and figure is in lines or in surfaces), or else it is found in respect to another, and thus is the predicament of relation (for when I say a man is a father, nothing absolute is predicated of man, but a relation which is in him to something extrinsic).

The third mode of predication is had when something extrinsic is predicated of a thing by means of some denomination. For extrinsic accidents are also predicated of substances, nevertheless we do not say that man is whiteness, but that man is white. However, to be denominated by something extrinsic is found in a common way in all things, and in a special way in those things which pertain only to man.

In the common way a thing is found to be denominated by something extrinsic either according to the intelligibility [ratio] of a cause or of a measure. For a thing is denominated as caused and measured by something extrinsic. Now although there are four genera of causes, two of them are parts of the essence, namely matter and form. Hence a predication which can be made in respect to these two pertains to the predicament of substance, e.g., if we say that man is rational and that man is corporeal. But the final cause does not cause anything outside of the agent, for the end has the nature [ratio] of a cause only insofar as it moves the agent. Hence there remains only the agent cause by which a thing can be denominated as by something extrinsic.

Therefore, insofar as a thing is denominated by the agent cause, there is the predicament of passion. For to be acted upon is nothing other than to receive something from an agent. And conversely, insofar as the agent cause is denominated by the effect, there is the predicament of action. For action is an act from the agent to another, as was said above.

Furthermore some measures are extrinsic and some are intrinsic.

Thus the proper length and breadth and depth of each thing is intrinsic. Therefore, a thing is denominated by these as by something inhering intrinsically. Hence this pertains to the predicament of quantity.

However time and place are extrinsic measures. Therefore, insofar as a thing is denominated by time, there is the predicament "when," and insofar as it is denominated by place, there are predicaments "where" and "site," which adds to "where" the order of parts in place.

Now it was not necessary that this latter point be added in respect to time. For the order of parts in time is implied in the very meaning [ratio] of time. For time is the number of motion in respect to before and after. Therefore, a thing is said to be "when" or "where" by a denomination from time or place.

However there is something special in men. For nature has adequately provided other animals with those things which pertain to the preservation of life, as horns for defense, and heavy

and shaggy hides for clothing, and hoofs or something of this sort for walking without injury. And thus when such animals are said to be armed or clothed or shod, in a way they are not denominated by anything extrinsic but by some of their own parts. Hence in these cases this is referred to the predicament of substance, as, for example, if it were said that man is "handed" or "footed."

But things of this sort could not have been given to man by nature, both because they were not suitable for the delicacy of his make up and because of the diversity of the works which belong to man insofar as he has reason. Determinate instruments could not have been provided by nature for such works. But in the place of all of these things there is reason in man, by which he prepares for himself external things in the place of those things which are intrinsic in the other animals. Hence, when a man is said to be armed or clothed or shod, he is denominated by something extrinsic which has the nature [ratio] neither of a cause nor of a measure. Hence there is a special predicament, and it is called "habit."

But it must be noted that this predicament is attributed to other animals also, not insofar as they are considered in their own nature, but insofar as they come under the use of man, as when we say that a horse is decorated or saddled or armed.

323. Therefore, it is clear that, although motion is one, the predicaments which are taken in respect to motion are two insofar as the predicamental denominations are made from different exterior things. For the agent from which, as from something external, the predicament passion is taken

by means of a denomination is one thing. And the patient by which the agent is denominated is another thing. And thus the answer to the first difficulty is clear.

324. The second difficulty is easily answered. For the intelligibility [ratio] of motion is completed not only by that which pertains to motion in the nature of things, but also by that which reason [ratio] apprehends.

For in the nature of things motion is nothing other than an imperfect act which is a certain incipience of perfect act in that which is moved. Thus in that which is being whitened, something of whiteness already has begun to be. But in order for the imperfect act to have the nature [ratio] of motion, it is further required that we understand it as a mean between two extremes. The preceding condition is compared to it as potency to act, and thus motion is called an act. The consequent condition is compared to it as perfect to imperfect or as act to potency. And because of this motion is called the act of that which exists in potency, as was said above.

Hence, if an imperfect thing be taken as not tending toward something perfect, it is called a terminus of motion and will not be a motion in respect to which something is moved. For example, a thing begins to be whitened and the alteration is suddenly interrupted.

With reference to that which pertains to motion in the nature of things, motion is placed by reduction in that genus which terminates the motion, as

the imperfect is reduced to the perfect, as was said above. But with reference to that which reason [ratio] apprehends regarding motion, namely, that it is a mean between two termini, the intelligibility [ratio] of cause and effect is already implied. For a thing is not reduced from potency to act except by some agent cause. And in respect to this motion belongs to the predicament of action and passion. For these two predicaments are taken in respect to the intelligibility [ratio] of agent cause and effect, as was said above.

325. Next where he says, "What then motion is . . ." [223], he defines motion in particular. He says that he has already said what motion is in general and in particular. For from what was said about the definition of motion in general it is clear how motion should be defined in particular. If motion is the act of the mobile insofar as it is such, it follows that alteration is the act of the alterable insofar as it is such. And the same applies to other motions.

He has raised the difficulty of whether motion is the act of the mover or the moved, and he has shown that motion is the act of the active as "from this" and the act of the passive as "in this." Hence, in order to remove all difficulties, we might say somewhat more clearly that motion is the act of the potency of the active and of the passive.

And thus we will also be able to say in a particular instance that building is the act of the builder and of the buildable insofar as it is such. And the same is true of healing and other motions.

LECTURE 6 [202b30–203b14]
Physics Considers the Infinite. The Opinion of the Ancients Concerning the Infinite

The Text of Aristotle
Chapter 4

224. *The science of nature is concerned with spatial magnitudes and motion and time, and each of these at least is necessarily infinite or finite, even if some things dealt with by the science are not,. e.g., a quality or a point—it is not necessary perhaps that such things should be put under either head. Hence it is incumbent on the person who specializes in physics to discuss the infinite and to inquire whether there is such a thing or not, and, if there is, what it is.*

202b30–36

225. *The appropriateness to the science of this problem is clearly indicated. All who have touched on this kind of science in a way worth considering have formulated views about the infinite,*

202b36–203a3

226. *and indeed, to a man, make it a principle of things. (1) Some, as the Pythagoreans and Plato, make the infinite a principle in the sense of a self-subsistent substance, and not as a mere attribute of some other thing.*

203a3–6

227. *Only the Pythagoreans place the infinite among the objects of sense (they do not regard number as separable from these), and assert that what is outside the heaven is infinite. Plato, on the other hand, holds that there is no body outside (the Forms are not outside, because they are nowhere), yet that the infinite is present not only in the objects of sense but in the Forms also.*

203a6–10

228. *Further, the Pythagoreans identify the infinite with the even. For this, they say, when it is cut off and shut in by the odd, provides things with the element of infinity. An indication of this is what happens with numbers. If the gnomons are placed round the one, and without the one, in the one construction the figure that results is always different, in the other it is always the same. But Plato has two infinites, the Great and the Small.*

203a10–16

229. *The physicists, on the other hand, all of them, always regard the infinite as an attribute of a substance which is different from it and belongs to the class of the so-called elements—water or air or what is intermediate between them. Those who make them limited in number never make them infinite in amount. But those who make the elements infinite in number, as Anaxagoras and Democritus do, say that the infinite is continuous by contact—compounded of the homogeneous parts according to the one, of the seed mass of the atomic shapes according to the other.*

Further, Anaxagoras held that any part is a mixture in the same way as the All, on the ground of the observed fact that anything comes out of anything. For it is probably for this reason that he maintains that once upon a time all things were together. (This flesh and this bone were together, and so of any thing: therefore all things—and at the same time too.) For there is a beginning of separation, not only for each thing, but for all. Each thing that comes to be comes to be from a similar body, and there is a coming to be of all things, though not, it is true, at the same time. Hence there must also be an origin of coming to be. One such source there is which he calls Mind, and Mind begins its work of thinking from some starting-point. So necessarily all things must have been together at a certain time, and must have begun to be moved at a certain time. Democritus, for his part, asserts the contrary, namely that no element arises from another element. Nevertheless for him the common body is a source of all things, differing from part to part in size and in shape. It is clear then from these considerations that the inquiry concerns the physicist.

203a16–203b4

230. Nor is it without reason that they all make it a principle or source. We cannot say that the infinite has no effect, and the only effectiveness which we can ascribe to it is that of a principle. Everything is either a source or derived from a source. But there cannot be a source of the infinite or limitless, for that would be a limit of it. Further, as it is a beginning, it is both uncreatable and indestructible. For there must be a point at which what has come to be reaches completion, and also a termination of all passing away. That is why, as we say, there is no principle of this, but it is this which is held to be the principle of other things, and to encompass all and to steer all, as those assert who do not recognize, alongside the infinite, other causes, such as Mind or Friendship. Further they identify it with the Divine, for it is "deathless and imperishable" as Anaximander says, with the majority of the physicists.   **203b4–15**

COMMENTARY OF ST. THOMAS

326. After the Philosopher has treated motion, he begins here to treat the infinite.

First he shows that it pertains to natural science to treat the infinite. Secondly, where he says, **"Belief in the existence . . ."** [231], he begins to treat the infinite.

Concerning the first part he makes two points. First he shows that it pertains to natural science to treat the infinite. Secondly, where he says, **". . . and indeed to a man . . ."** [226], he sets forth the opinions of the ancient philosophers concerning the infinite.

327. He explains the first point both with an argument and with an example.

The argument is as follows. Natural science deals with magnitudes and time and motion. But in these things either the finite or the infinite must be found. For every magnitude or motion or time is contained under one of these, i.e., under the finite or the infinite. Therefore, it pertains to natural science to consider the infinite in terms of whether it is and what it is.

But someone might say that the consideration of the infinite belongs to first philosophy because of its commonness. To overcome this objection he adds that it is not necessary for every being to be finite or infinite. For a point and a passion, i.e., a passive

quality, are contained under neither of these. However, that which pertains to the consideration of first philosophy follows upon being insofar as it is being, and not upon some determinate genus of being.

328. Next where he says, **"The appropriateness . . ."** [225], he explains the same thing with an example taken from the considerations of the natural philosophers.

For all who have reasonably treated philosophy of this sort, i.e., natural philosophy, have made some mention of the infinite. From this there arises a probable argument from the authority of wise men to the effect that natural philosophy should treat the infinite.

329. Next where he says, **". . . and indeed to a man . . ."** [226], he sets forth the opinions of the ancients concerning the infinite. First he shows how they differ. Secondly, where he says, **"Nor is it without reason . . ."** [230], he shows how they agree.

Concerning the first part he makes two points. First he sets forth the opinions about the infinite of those who were not philosophers of nature, i.e., the Pythagoreans and the Platonists. Secondly, where he says, **"The physicists, on the other hand . . ."** [229], he sets forth the opinions of the natural philosophers.

Concerning the first part he makes

two points. First he shows in what respect the Pythagoreans and Platonists agree; and secondly, in what respect they differ, where he says, **"Only the Pythagoreans . . ."** [227].

330. He says, therefore, first [226] that all the philosophers held that the infinite is some sort of a principle of beings. But it was peculiar to the Pythagoreans and the Platonists that they held that the infinite is not an accident of some other nature, but is a certain thing existing in itself. And this was consistent with their opinion because they held that numbers and quantities are the substances of things. But the infinite is in quantity. Hence they held that the infinite is something existing in itself.

331. Next where he says, **"Only the Pythagoreans . . ."** [227], he explains the differences between Plato and the Pythagoreans, first with reference to the position of the infinite, and secondly, with reference to its source, where he says, **"Further the Pythagoreans . . ."** [228].

With reference to the position of the infinite Plato differed from the Pythagoreans in two ways.

The Pythagoreans posited an infinite only in sensible things. For the infinite belongs to quantity, and the first quantity is number. Hence the Pythagoreans did not posit number as separate from sensible things. Rather they said that number is the substance of sensible things. And as a result the infinite exists only in sensible things.

Furthermore, Pythagoras thought that sensible things which are under the heavens are circumscribed by the heavens. Hence there can be no infinite in these things. And because of this he held that the infinite exists in sensible things outside of the heavens.

But Plato, on the contrary, held that nothing is outside the heavens. He did not say that there is any sensible body outside of the heavens, because he said that the heavens contain all sensible things. And he did not even say that the ideas and species of things, which he held to be separated, are outside of the heavens. For "inside" and "outside" signify place. But according to him the ideas are not in any place, because place pertains to corporeal things.

Furthermore, Plato said that the infinite is not only in sensible things but also in the separated ideas. For even in the separated numbers themselves there is something formal, as the one, and something material, as two, from which every number is composed.

332. Next where he says, **"Further the Pythagoreans . . ."** [228], he explains the difference between their opinions with reference to the source of the infinite. He says that the Pythagoreans referred the infinite to one source, namely, to even number. They explained this in two ways.

First, with an argument. That which is encompassed by another and terminated by another, insofar as it is in itself, has the nature [ratio] of the infinite. But what encompasses and terminates has the nature [ratio] of a terminus. Now even number is comprehended and encompassed under the odd. For if some even number is proposed, it clearly is divisible. When, however, by the addition of unity it is reduced to an odd number, a certain indivision follows, as if the even were restricted by the odd. Hence it seems that the even is infinite in itself, and causes infinity in others.

He explains the same thing by means of an example. As evidence of this we must note what happens in geometry. A gnomon is said to be a square erected on the diagonal by the addition of two lines. Thus a gnomon of this sort surrounding a square forms a square. Therefore by comparing this to numbers gnomons can be said to be numbers which are added to other numbers.

Moreover, it must be noted that if one takes odd numbers according to the order of natural progression, and if one adds the first odd number, i.e., three, to unity which is virtually square (insofar as one is a unit), then four is produced, which is a square number, for twice two is four. If, next, to this second square the second odd number, i.e., five, is added, then nine is formed which is the square of three, for three times three is nine. If, further, to this third square the third odd number, i.e., seven, is added, then sixteen is formed which is the square of four. And thus by an ordered addition of odd numbers, the same form of number always results, i.e., a square.

However, a different figure always results from the addition of even numbers. For if the first even number, i.e., two, is added to one, then three is produced, which is a three sided figure. If, next, the second even number, i.e., four, is added, then seven is produced, which is a heptagonal figure. And thus the figure is always varied by the addition of even numbers.

And this seems to be a sign that uniformity pertains to odd numbers, whereas dissimilarity and variety and the infinite pertain to even numbers.

And this is what he says. That which occurs in numbers is an indication that the infinite is consequent upon even number. When gnomons surround the one, i.e., when numbers are added to one, and are outside, i.e., are around other numbers, then sometimes one

species is formed, i.e., one numerical form results from the addition of an even number, and sometimes another species is formed, i.e., by the addition of an odd number. And thus it is clear why Pythagoras attributes infinity to even number.

Plato, however, attributed the infinite to two sources, namely, the great and the small. For according to him these two are on the side of matter, to which the infinite belongs.

333. Next where he says, "The physicists on the other hand ..." [229], he sets forth the opinions of the natural philosophers concerning the infinite.

It must be noted that all the natural philosophers, i.e., those who treated the principles of things naturally, said that the infinite is not subsistent in itself, as was said above. Rather they held that the infinite is an accident of some nature presupposed for it.

Therefore, those who posited only one material principle, whatever it might be, of the things which are called elements, either air or water or some intermediate, said that this principle is infinite.

None of those who made the elements many but finite in number held that the elements are infinite in quantity. For this distinction of elements seems to be contradicted by the infinity of any one of them.

But those who made the elements infinite in number say that some one infinite thing comes to be from all these infinite elements by contact.

334. These latter philosophers were Anaxagoras and Democritus, who differed on two points.

[They differed] first with reference to the quiddity of the infinite principles. For Anaxagoras said that these infinite principles are infinite, similar parts, such as flesh and bone and things of this sort. Democritus, on the other hand, held that such infinite principles are indivisible bodies which differ according to figure. And he said that these bodies are the seeds of all nature.

The other difference is with respect to the relation that these principles have to each other.

Anaxagoras said that each of these infinite parts is mixed with every other part, so that in every part of flesh there would be bone, and vice versa. And the same applies to other things. He held this because he saw that everything comes to be from everything. And since he believed that everything which comes to be from something is in that thing, he concluded that everything is in everything.

And from this he seems to affirm that at one time all things were fused together, and nothing was distinct from anything else. Thus, this flesh and this bone are mixed together, which is demonstrated by the fact that they are generated from each other. And it is the same with any other thing. Therefore, at one time all things were together. This is to posit a beginning of the distinction [of things] not only for some one thing, but for all things together. He proved this as follows.

That which comes to be from another was previously mixed with that thing, and comes to be by reason of the fact that it is separated from it. But all things come to be, although not all at once. Therefore, it is necessary to posit one principle of generation for all things, and not just for each thing. And this one principle he called intellect to which alone it belongs to separate and to gather together, because of the fact that it is unmixed.

Now that which comes to be through intellect seems to have some sort of a beginning. For an intellect works by beginning from a determinate principle. If, therefore, separation occurs because of an intellect, then it is necessary to say that separation would have some sort of a beginning. Hence he concluded that at one time all things were together, and that the motion by which things are separated from each other began at some time, since there was no motion prior to this. Therefore, Anaxagoras held that one principle comes to be from the other.

But Democritus says that one principle does not come to be from another. However, the nature of body, which is common to all indivisible bodies, but differing according to parts and figures, is the principle of all things in respect to magnitude, insofar as he held that all divisible magnitudes are composed of indivisibles.

And thus Aristotle concludes that it pertains to the natural philosopher to consider the infinite.

335. Next where he says, **"Nor is it without reason . . ."** [230], he sets forth four things upon which the ancient philosophers agreed concerning the infinite.

The first of these is that all of them held that the infinite is a principle.

And this was "reasonable," i.e., they had a probable argument. For if the infinite exists, it is not possible that it be in vain, i.e., that it should not have some determinate position in beings. Nor can it have any power other than that of a principle. For everything in the world is either a principle or is from principles. But the infinite cannot have a principle, because that which has a beginning has an end. Hence it follows that the infinite is a principle.

But it must be noted that in this argument they use "principle" and "end" equivocally. For that which is from a principle has a beginning of origin. But a principle and an end of quantity or magnitude is what is repugnant to the infinite.

The second thing which they attributed to the infinite is that it is ungenerated and incorruptible. And this follows from the fact that it is a principle.

For everything which comes to be must have an end as well as have a beginning. Moreover, there is an end to every corruption. However, an end is repugnant to the infinite. Hence to be generable and corruptible is repugnant to the infinite. And thus it is clear that there is no principle of the infinite, but rather the infinite is the principle of other things. And in this argument "principle" and "end" are again used equivocally, as they were above.

The third thing which they attributed to the infinite is that it would contain and govern all things. For this seems to belong to the first principle.

Those who did not posit causes other than matter (which they said is infinite), i.e., agents, such as the intellect which Anaxagoras posited, and love which Empedocles posited, maintained this. For to contain and to govern pertain more to an agent principle than to matter.

The fourth thing which they attributed to the infinite is that it is something divine. For they called everything divine which is immortal or incorruptible. Anaximander and many of the ancient natural philosophers held this.

Arguments Which Persuade Us That the Infinite Exists. The Meanings of "Infinite." An Infinite Separated From Sensible Things Must Be Denied

The Text of Aristotle

231. *Belief in the existence of the infinite comes mainly from five considerations:*

(1) From the nature of time—for it is infinite.

(2) From the division of magnitudes—for the mathematicians also use the notion of the infinite.

(3) If coming to be and passing away do not give out, it is only because that from which things come to be is infinite.

(4) Because the limited always finds its limit in something, so that there must be no limit, if everything is always limited by something different from itself.

(5) Most of all, a reason which is peculiarly appropriate and presents the difficulty that is felt by everybody—not only number but also mathematical magnitudes and what is outside the heaven are supposed to be infinite because they never give out in our thought.

The last fact (that what is outside is infinite) leads people to suppose that body also is infinite, and that there is an infinite number of worlds. Why should there be body in one part of the void rather than in another? Grant only that mass is anywhere and it follows that it must be everywhere. Also, if void and place are infinite, there must be infinite body too; for in the case of eternal things what may be must be. **203b15–30**

232. *But the problem of the infinite is difficult: many contradictions result whether we suppose it to exist or not to exist. If it exists, we have still to ask how it exists; as a substance or as the essential attribute of some entity? Or in neither way, yet none the less is there something which is infinite or some things which are infinitely many? The problem, however, which specially belongs to the physicist is to investigate whether there is a sensible magnitude which is infinite.* **203b30–204a2**

233. *We must begin by distinguishing the various senses in which the term "infinite" is used.*

(1) What is incapable of being gone through, because it is not its nature to be gone through (the sense in which the voice is "invisible").

(2) What admits of being gone through, the process however having no termination, or

(3) What scarcely admits of being gone through.

(4) What naturally admits of being gone through, but is not actually gone through or does not actually reach an end. **204a2–6**

233bis. *Further, everything that is infinite may be so in respect of addition or division or both.* **204a6–7**

Chapter 5

234. *Now it is impossible that the infinite should be a thing which is itself infinite, separable from sensible objects. If the infinite is neither a magnitude nor an aggregate, but is itself a substance and not an attribute, it will be indivisible; for the divisible must be either a magnitude or an aggregate. But if indivisible, then not infinite, except in the sense (1) in which the voice is "invisible." But this is not the sense in which it is used by those who say that the infinite exists, nor that in which we are investigating it, namely as (2), "that which cannot be gone through." But if the infinite exists as an attribute it would not be, qua infinite, an element in substances, any more than the invisible would be an element of speech, though the voice is invisible.* **204a8–17**

235. Further, how can the infinite be itself any thing, unless both number and magnitude, of which it is an essential attribute, exist in that way? If they are not substances, a fortiori the infinite is not.
204a17–20

236. It is plain, too, that the infinite cannot be an actual thing and a substance and principle. For any part of it that is taken will be infinite, if it has parts; for "to be infinite" and "the infinite" are the same, if it is a substance and not predicated of a subject. Hence it will be either indivisible or divisible into infinites. But the same thing cannot be many infinites. (Yet just as part of air is air, so a part of the infinite would be infinite, if it is supposed to be a substance and principle.) Therefore the infinite must be without parts and indivisible. But this cannot be true of what is infinite in full completion; for it must be a definite quantity.

Suppose then that infinity belongs to substance as an attribute. But, if so, it cannot, as we have said, be described as a principle, but rather that of which it is an attribute—the air or the even number.

Thus the view of those who speak after the manner of the Pythagoreans is absurd. With the same breath they treat the infinite as substance, and divide it into parts.

This discussion, however, involves the more general question whether the infinite can be present in mathematical objects and things which are intelligible and do not have extension, as well as among sensible objects. Our inquiry (as physicists) is limited to our special subject-matter, the objects of sense, and we have to ask whether there is or is not among them a body which is infinite in the direction of increase.
204a20–204b4

COMMENTARY OF ST. THOMAS

336. Having set forth the opinions of the ancients concerning the infinite, he begins here to seek the truth.

First he raises objections against each part. Secondly, where he says, **"It is plain from these arguments . . ."** [248], he answers these difficulties.

Concerning the first part he makes two points. First, he sets forth arguments to show that there is an infinite. Secondly, where he says, **"But the problem of the infinite . . ."** [232], he sets forth arguments to show that there is no infinite.

337. With reference to the first part he sets forth five arguments.

The first of these is taken from time, which according to the common opinion of the ancients is infinite. For Plato alone generated time, as will be explained in Book VIII.

He says, therefore, first that there are five arguments to show that there is an infinite.

The first of these is from time, which is infinite according to those who said that time always was and always will be.

338. The second argument is taken from the division of magnitude to infinity. For mathematicians in their demonstrations also use the infinite in magnitude. And this would not be so if the infinite were altogether removed from things. Therefore, it is necessary to posit an infinite.

339. A third argument according to the opinion of many is taken from the perpetuity of generation and corruption. For if the infinite were completely removed, it could not be said that generation and corruption endure to infinity. Hence it would be necessary to say that at some time generation ceases altogether, and this is contrary to the opinion of many. Therefore, it is necessary to posit an infinite.

340. The fourth argument is taken from the apparent nature [ratio] of the finite. For it seems to many that it is of

the very nature [ratio] of the finite that it is always contained by something else. For around us we see that every finite thing is extended as far as some other thing. Therefore, if some designated body is infinite, then the proposition is established [i.e., there is an infinite]. If, however, the designated body is finite, then it must be terminated by another body; and if that body is finite, it must be terminated by still another body. Therefore, this will either proceed to infinity or will end at some infinite body. In either case an infinite is posited. Therefore, it must be that there is no end to bodies if it is always necessary to every finite body to be contained by another.

341. The fifth argument is taken from the apprehension of the intellect or the imagination. He says that that which most of all raises the question leading men to posit the infinite is that the intellect never fails in being able to add something to any given finite thing. Now the ancient philosophers thought that things corresponded to the apprehension of intellect and sense. Hence they said that everything which is seen is true, as is said in Metaphysics, IV. And because of this they believed that there is also an infinite in things. It seems that number is infinite because the intellect by adding unity to any given number forms another species. And for the same reason mathematical magnitudes, which are formed in the imagination, seem to be infinite. For when we are given any magnitude, we can imagine one which is greater. And for the same reason there seems to be a certain infinite space outside the heavens. For we are able to imagine certain dimensions [reaching] to infinity outside the heavens.

If, however, there is an infinite space outside the heavens, it seems to be necessary that there is an infinite body and that there are infinite worlds. This is so for two reasons.

The first reason is as follows. If a whole infinite space is considered, the whole considered in itself is uniform. Therefore, we cannot assign any reason why that space should be void of body in one part more than in another. Therefore, if the corporeal magnitude of this world is found in any part of that space, then it is necessary that in every part of that space be found some corporeal magnitude such as what is of this world. And thus it is necessary that body as well as space be infinite. Or else it is necessary that worlds be infinite, as Democritus held.

The other reason for showing the same thing is as follows. If there is an infinite space, it is either a void or a plenum. If it is a plenum, then our proposition is established: there is an infinite body. If, however, it is a void, then since a void is nothing but a place which is not occupied by a body, though it is possible for it to be occupied, it is necessary, if there is an infinite space, that there also be an infinite place which can be occupied by a body. And thus it will be necessary for there to be an infinite body, because "to be" and "to happen" do not differ in perpetual things. Hence, if an infinite place happens to be occupied by a body, it is necessary to say that it is occupied by an infinite body. Therefore, it seems necessary to say that there is an infinite body.

342. Next where he says, **"But the problem . . ."** [232], he raises objections to the contrary. Concerning this he makes three points.

First he shows that the question has its difficulty, lest the arguments set forth above should seem to conclude to the truth. Secondly, where he says, **"We must begin . . ."** [233], he explains how the word "infinite" is used. Thirdly, where he says, **"Now it is impossible . . ."** [234], he gives arguments to show that there is no infinite.

343. He says, therefore, first that it is difficult to decide whether there is or is not an infinite. For many impossibilities follow from the position of those who hold that the infinite in no way is, as is clear from what has already been said. And many impossibilities also follow from the position of those who hold that there is an infinite, as will be clear from the arguments which follow.

Moreover, there is also the question of what sort of thing the infinite is, i.e., whether it is something existing in itself as some kind of substance, or some accident belonging per se to some nature, or neither of these (i.e., neither existing in itself as substance, nor a per se accident). Nevertheless, if it is an accident, is it an infinite continuum or something infinite in respect to multitude? Now the problem of whether there is an infinite sensible magnitude especially pertains to the consideration of the natural philosopher. For sensible magnitude is natural magnitude.

344. Next where he says, **"We must begin . . ."** [233], he explains the ways in which the term "infinite" is used. He posits two divisions of the infinite.

The first of these is common to the infinite and to all things spoken of as privations.

The term "invisible" is used in three ways, either as that which is not apt to be seen, such as the voice which does not belong to the genus of visible things, or as that which is poorly seen, as what is seen in a dim light or from a distance, or as that which is apt to be seen but is not seen, as what is altogether in the dark.

Thus in one way the infinite is said of that which is not apt to be passed through (for the infinite is the same as the impassable). And this is so because it belongs to the genus of impassable things, such as indivisible things, e.g., a point and a form. It is also in this way that the voice is said to be invisible.

In another way the infinite is said of that which of itself can be passed through, even though this passing through cannot be accomplished by us. For example we might say that the depth of the sea is infinite. Or we might refer to something which can be accomplished but only scarcely and with difficulty, as if we were to say that a journey to India is infinite. Each of these pertains to that which is poorly passable.

In a third way the infinite is said of that which is apt to be passed through as existing in the genus of passable things, but is not passed through to its end, as if there were a line or any other quantity which does not have an end. And this is the infinite properly speaking.

He sets forth the other proper division of the infinite where he says, **"Further, everything that is infinite . . ."** [233bis]. He says that the infinite is called such either by addition, as in numbers, or by division, as in magnitudes, or in both ways, as in time.

345. Next where he says, **"Now it is impossible . . ."** [234], he sets forth arguments for denying the infinite. First he sets forth arguments for denying a separated infinite, which the Platonists posit. Secondly, where he says, **"We may begin . . ."** [237], he sets forth arguments for denying an infinite in sensible things.

Concerning the first part he sets

forth three arguments. In the first argument he says that it is impossible for there to be an infinite separated from sensible things in such a way that this infinite would be something existing in itself, as the Platonists held. For if the infinite is held to be something separated, it either has some quantity (i.e., it is either continuous which is magnitude or discrete which is multitude) or it does not. If it is a substance without the accident of magnitude or multitude, then the infinite must be indivisible. For every divisible thing is either a number or a magnitude. If, however, it is something indivisible, it will not be infinite except in the first way, i.e., as a thing is said to be infinite which is not apt to be passed through, just as the voice is said to be invisible. But this lies outside the meaning of the present question, wherein we inquire about the infinite, and outside the intention of those who posit an infinite. For they do not intend to posit the infinite as something indivisible, but as something impassable, i.e., as something apt to be passed through, though not passed through.

If, on the other hand, it were not only a substance, but would also have the accident of magnitude and multitude to which the infinite pertains (and thus the infinite would be in the substance by reason of that accident), then the infinite as such will not be a principle of the things which are, as the ancients held. Likewise we do not say that the invisible is a principle of speech, even though it is an accident of voice which is a principle of speech.

346. He sets forth the second argument where he says, **"Further, how can the infinite . . ."** [235]. The argument is as follows.

A passion is less separable and existent in itself than its subject. But the infinite is a passion of magnitude and number. But magnitude and number cannot be separated and existing in themselves, as is proved in metaphysics. Therefore neither can the infinite.

347. He sets forth the third argument where he says, **"It is plain . . ."** [236]. He says that it is clear that it cannot be held that the infinite exists in act and that it exists as a substance and as a principle of things.

For the infinite will either be divisible into parts or not divisible into parts. If it will be divisible into parts, it is necessary that every part of it be infinite, if the infinite is a substance. For if the infinite is a substance and is not predicated of a subject as an accident, then it will be necessary that "the infinite" be the same as "to be infinite," i.e., the same as the essence and the nature [ratio] of the infinite. For that which is white and the nature of white are not the same. But that which is man is that which is the nature of man. Hence, if the infinite is a substance, it must be either indivisible or divided into infinite parts, which is impossible. For it is impossible for one and the same thing to be composed of many infinite things, because it would be necessary for the infinite to be terminated by another infinite.

It is clear not only from reason but also from an example that, if the infinite is a substance and is divided, then every part of it is infinite.

For as every part of air is air, so every part of the infinite will be infinite, if the infinite is a substance and a principle. For if it is a principle, the infinite must be a simple substance not composed of diverse parts, just as no part of a man is a man. Since, therefore, it is impossible for any part of the infinite to be infinite, it must be that the infinite is not divisible into parts and is indivisible. But that which is indivisible cannot be infinite in act. For that which is infinite in act is a quantity, and every quantity is divisible. It follows, therefore, that if there is an infinite in act, it is not infinite as a substance, but as under the intelligibility [ratio] of the accident of quantity. And if this is the infinite, it will not be a principle; rather that of which it is an accident [will be a principle]. And this is either some sensible substance, such as air, as the natural philosopher held, or some intelligible substance, such as the even, as the Pythagoreans held.

Hence it is clear that the Pythagoreans inconsistently said that the infinite is a substance, maintaining at the same time that it is divisible. For it follows that every part of the infinite is infinite, which is impossible, as was said above.

348. Lastly he says that the question of whether there is an infinite in mathematical quantities and in intelligible things which have no magnitude is more general than what is being considered at present. For at the present we intend to consider whether in sensible things, concerning which we develop natural science, there is a body infinite in size, as the ancient natural philosophers held.

An Infinite in Act in Sensible Things Cannot Be Granted. This Is Shown First with Logical Arguments, Secondly Natural Arguments, on the Supposition that the Elements of Bodies Are Finite in Number

The Text of Aristotle

237. *We may begin with a dialectical argument and show as follows that there is no such thing. If "bounded by a surface" is the definition of body there cannot be an infinite body either intelligible or sensible. Nor can number taken in abstraction be infinite; for number or that which has number is numerable. If then the numerable can be numbered, it would also be possible to go through the infinite.* **204b4–10**

238. *If, on the other hand, we investigate the question more in accordance with principles appropriate to physics, we are led as follows to the same result. The infinite body must be either (1) compound, or (2) simple; yet neither alternative is possible. (1) Compound the infinite body will not be, if the elements are finite in number. For they must be more than one, and the contraries must always balance, and no one of them can be infinite. If one of the bodies falls in any degree short of the other in potency—suppose fire is finite in amount while air is infinite and a given quantity of fire exceeds in power the same amount of air in any ratio provided it is numerically definite—the infinite body will obviously prevail over and annihilate the finite body. On the other hand, it is impossible that each should be infinite. "Body" is what has extension in all directions and the infinite is what is boundlessly extended, so that the infinite body would be extended in all directions ad infinitum. Nor (2) can the infinite body be one and simple, whether it is, as some hold, a thing over and above the elements (from which they generate the elements) or is not thus qualified. (a) We must consider the former alternative; for there are some people who make this the infinite, and not air or water, in order that the other elements may not be annihilated by the element which is infinite. They have contrariety with each other—air is cold, water moist, fire hot; if one were infinite, the others by now would have ceased to be. As it is, they say, the infinite is different from them and is their source.*

It is impossible, however, that there should be such a body; not because it is infinite—on that point a general proof can be given which applies equally to all, air, water, or anything else—but simply because there is, as a matter of fact, no such sensible body, alongside the so-called elements. Everything can be resolved into the elements of which it is composed. Hence the body in question would have been present in our world here, alongside air and fire and earth and water; but nothing of the kind is observed.

(b) Nor can fire or any other of the elements be infinite. For generally, and apart from the question how any of them could be infinite, the All, even, if it were limited, cannot either be or become one of them, as Heraclitus says that at some time all things become fire. (The same argument applies also to the one which the physicists suppose to exist alongside the elements: for everything changes from contrary to contrary, e.g., from hot to cold). **204b10–205a7**

COMMENTARY OF ST. THOMAS

349. After the Philosopher has refuted the opinion of the ancients who did not speak of the infinite as natural philosophers, inasmuch as they separated it from sensible things, he shows here that there is no infinite, as the natural philosophers held.

He shows this first with logical arguments, and secondly, with natural arguments, where he says, **"If, on the other hand . . ."** [238].

The first arguments are called logical arguments not because they proceed logically from logical terms, but because they proceed according to a logical method, i.e., from the common and the probable, which is proper to the dialectical syllogism.

350. He sets forth [237] two logical arguments. In the first argument it is shown that there is no infinite body.

A body is defined as that which is determined by a surface, just as a line is defined as that whose termini are points. However, no body determined by a surface is infinite. Therefore, no body is infinite—neither a sensible body, which is a natural body, nor an intelligible body, which is a mathematical body.

The word "rationally" must be understood to mean "logically." For logic is called rational philosophy.

351. The second argument shows that there is no infinite in multitude. For everything numerable is numbered, and consequently is passed through by being numbered. But every number and every thing which has a number is numerable. Therefore, everything of this sort is passed through. Therefore, if any number, whether separated or existing in sensible things, is infinite, it would follow that it is possible to pass through the infinite, which is impossible.

352. It must be noted, however, that these arguments are probable and proceed from things which are commonly said. They do not conclude of necessity. For one who holds that some body is infinite would not concede that it is of the nature [ratio] of a body to be terminated by a surface, except perhaps in potency, even though this is probable and generally accepted.

Likewise one who would say that some multitude is infinite would not say that it is a number or that it has number. For number adds to multitude the notion [ratio] of a measure.

For number is a multitude measured by one, as is said in Metaphysics, X. And because of this number is placed in the species of discrete quantity, whereas multitude is not. Rather multitude pertains to the transcendentals.

353. Next where he says, **"If on the other hand . . ."** [238], he sets forth natural arguments to show that there is no infinite body in act.

Concerning these arguments it must be noted that since Aristotle has not yet proven that a celestial body has an essence other than the four elements and since the common opinion of his time was that a celestial body has the nature of the four elements, he proceeds in these arguments, according to his custom, as if there were no sensible body other than the four elements. For before he proves his own opinion, he always proceeds from the supposition of the common opinion of others. Hence after he has proven in De Caelo et Mundo, I, that the heavens have a nature other than the elements, he brings his consideration of the infinite to the certitude of truth by showing universally that no sensible body is infinite.

Here, then, he shows first that there is no infinite sensible body on the supposition that the elements are finite in multitude. Secondly, he shows the same thing universally, where he says, **"The preceding consideration . . ."** [239].

He says, therefore, first that by proceeding naturally, i.e., from the principles of natural science, it can be more certainly understood from what will be said that there is no infinite sensible body. For every sensible body is either simple or composite.

354. First he shows that there is no infinite composite sensible body on the supposition that the elements are finite

in multitude. For it cannot be that one of these elements is infinite and the others finite. For the composition of any mixed body requires that the elements be many and that contraries be in some way balanced. Otherwise the composition could not endure, because that which would be altogether stronger would destroy the others, since the elements are contraries. If, however, one of the elements were infinite and the others were finite, there would be no equality. For the infinite exceeds the finite beyond every proportion. Therefore, it cannot be that only one of the elements which enter into the mixture is infinite.

However, one might say that the infinite element would be weak in the power to act, and so not able to suppress the others, i.e., the finite elements, which are stronger in power. For example, let the infinite be air and the finite fire. And so to preclude this, he says that no matter how much the power of the infinite body falls short of the power of the finite body (as if fire were finite and air infinite), it is necessary to say that air is equal to fire in power according to some multiple of number. For if the power of fire is one hundred times greater than the power of the same quantity of air, then if the air is multiplied one hundred fold in quantity, it will be equal to fire in power. And yet air multiplied one hundred fold is multiplied by some determined number and is exceeded by the power of the whole infinite air. Hence it is clear that the power of fire will be destroyed by the power of infinite air. And so the infinite exceeds and corrupts the finite, however more powerful in nature the latter should seem.

355. In like manner it cannot be that all of the elements of which a mixed body is composed are infinite. For the nature [ratio] of body is to have dimensions in every direction, not in length only, like a line, nor in length and breadth only, like a surface. However, the nature [ratio] of the infinite is to have distances or dimensions which are infinite. Hence the nature [ratio] of an infinite body is to have infinite dimensions in every direction. And thus one thing cannot be composed of many infinite bodies. For each body would occupy the whole world, unless one says that two bodies exist together, which is impossible.

356. Thus, having shown that a composite body cannot be infinite, he shows further that a simple body also cannot be infinite, i.e., neither one of the elements nor some intermediate between them, such as vapor is an intermediate between air and water, is infinite. For some have held that this latter is a principle, saying that other things are generated from it. And they said that this intermediate is infinite, but air, or water, or one of the other elements is not infinite, because it would happen that the other elements would be corrupted by whichever of them was held to be infinite. For the elements have contrariety among themselves, since air is humid, water is cold, fire is hot and earth is dry. Hence, if one of them were infinite, it would corrupt the other, since a contrary is naturally disposed to be corrupted by a contrary. And so they say that something other than an element is infinite, from which the elements are caused as from a principle.

However, he says that this position is impossible insofar as it claims that such an intermediate body is infinite, because with respect to this a certain common argument relative to fire and air and water and also to an intermediate body will be given below. The position stated above is also impossible because it posits some elementary principle other than the four elements.

For there is no sensible body other than those which are called the elements, i.e., air, water and the like. But this would be necessary if something other than the elements were to enter into the composition of bodies. For every composite is resolved into the things of which it is composed. If, therefore, something other than these four elements should enter into the composition of bodies, it would follow that by resolving them into their elements, there should be found here among us some simple body other than these elements. Therefore it is clear that the above position is false insofar as it posits a simple body other than these known elements.

357. Further, he shows with a common argument that none of the elements could be infinite. For if one of the elements were infinite, it would be impossible for the whole universe to be other than that element. And it would be necessary for all the elements to be converted into it, or else they would already have been converted into it because of the excellence of the power of the infinite element over the others. Thus, Heraclitus says that at some time all things will be converted into fire because of the excelling power of fire. The same argument applies both to one of the elements and to the other body which some natural philosophers set up beyond the elements. For that other body must be contrary to the elements, since other things are held to be generated from it. Moreover, change occurs only from contrary to contrary, as from hot to cold, as was pointed out above. Therefore, that intermediate body would destroy the other elements because of its contrariety.

He Proves Without Suppositions that There Is No Actually Infinite Sensible Body

The Text of Aristotle

239. *The preceding consideration of the various cases serves to show us whether it is or is not possible that there should be an infinite sensible body. The following arguments give a general demonstration that it is not possible.* **205a7–9**

240. *It is the nature of every kind of sensible body to be somewhere, and there is a place appropriate to each, the same for the part and for the whole, e.g., for the whole earth and for a single clod, and for fire and for a spark.* **205a9–12**

241. *Suppose (a) that the infinite sensible body is homogeneous. Then each part will be either immovable or always being carried along. Yet neither is possible. For why downwards rather than upwards or in any other direction? I mean, e.g., if you take a clod, where will it be moved or where will it be at rest? For ex hypothesi the place of the body akin to it is infinite. Will it occupy the whole place, then? And how? What then will be the nature of its rest and of its movement, or where will they be? It will either be at home everywhere—then it will not be moved; or it will be moved everywhere—then it will not come to rest. But if (b) the All has dissimilar parts, the proper places of the parts will be dissimilar also, and the body of the All will have no unity except that of contact. Then, further, the parts will be either finite or infinite in variety of kind. (i) Finite they cannot be, for if the All is to be infinite, some of them would have to be infinite, while the others were not, e.g. fire or water will be infinite. But, as we have seen before, such an element would destroy what is contrary to it. But (ii) if the parts are infinite in number and simple, their proper places too will be infinite in number, and the same will be true of the elements themselves. If that is impossible, and the places are finite, the whole too must be finite; for the place and the body cannot but fit each other. Neither is the whole place larger than what can be filled by the body (and then the body would no longer be infinite), nor is the body larger than the place; for either there would be an empty space or a body whose nature it is to be nowhere. (This indeed is the reason why none of the physicists made fire or earth the one infinite body, but either water or air or what is intermediate between them, because the abode of each of the two was plainly determinate, while the others have an ambiguous place between up and down.)* **205a12–39**

242. *Anaxagoras gives an absurd account of why the infinite is at rest. He says that the infinite itself is the cause of its being fixed.* **205b1–4**

243. *This because it is in itself, since nothing else contains it—on the assumption that wherever anything is, it is there by its own nature. But this is not true: a thing could be somewhere by compulsion, and not where it is its nature to be. Even if it is true as true can be that the whole is not moved (for what is fixed by itself and is in itself must be immovable), yet we must explain why it is not its nature to be moved. It is not enough just to make this statement and then decamp. Anything else might be in a state of rest, but there is no reason why it should not be its nature to be moved. The earth is not carried along, and would not be carried along if it were infinite, provided it is held together by the center. But it would not be because there was no other region in which it could be carried along that it would remain at the center, but because this is its nature. Yet in this case also we may say that it fixes itself. If then in the case of the earth, supposed to be infinite, it is at rest, not because it is infinite, but because it has weight and what is heavy rests at the center and the earth is at the center, similarly the infinite also would rest in itself, not because it is infinite and fixes itself, but owing to some other cause.* **205b4–18**

244. *Another difficulty emerges at the same time. Any part of the infinite body ought to remain at rest. Just as the infinite remains at rest in itself because it fixes itself, so too any part of it you may take will remain in itself. The appropriate places of the whole and of the part are alike, e.g., of the whole earth and of a clod the appropriate place is the lower region; of fire as a whole and of a spark, the upper region. If, therefore, to be in itself is the place of the infinite, that also will be appropriate to the part. Therefore it will remain in itself.*   205b18–24

245. *In general, the view that there is an infinite body is plainly incompatible with the doctrine that there is necessarily a proper place for each kind of body, if every sensible body has either weight or lightness, and if a body has a natural locomotion towards the center if it is heavy, and upwards if it is light. This would need to be true of the infinite also. But neither character can belong to it: it cannot be either as a whole, nor can it be half the one and half the other. For how should you divide it? or how can the infinite have the one part up and the other down, or an extremity and a center?*   205b24–31

246. *Further, every sensible body is in place, and the kinds or differences of place are up-down, before-behind, right-left; and these distinctions hold not only in relation to us and by arbitrary agreement, but also in the whole itself. But in the infinite body they cannot exist. In general, if it is impossible that there should be an infinite place, and if every body is in place, there cannot be an infinite body.*   205b31–35

247. *Surely what is in a special place is in place, and what is in place is in a special place. Just, then, as the infinite cannot be quantity—that would imply that it has a particular quantity, e.g., two or three cubits; quantity just means these—so a thing's being in place means that it is somewhere, and that is either up or down or in some other of the six differences of position; but each of these is a limit.*   205b35–206a7

COMMENTARY OF ST. THOMAS

358. After the Philosopher has shown, upon the supposition that the elements are finite, that there is no infinite sensible body, he here shows the same thing without qualification and without any supposition.

First he states his intention. Secondly, he develops his position, where he says, **"It is the nature . . ."** [240].

He says, therefore, first [239] that in the things which follow it is necessary to consider universally with reference to every body, without any presuppositions, whether any natural body happens to be infinite. From the arguments which follow it should become clear that there is no such thing.

Next where he says, **"It is the nature . . ."** [240], he proves his position with four arguments. The second argument begins where he says, **"In general, the view . . ."** [245]. The third

begins where he says, **"Further every sensible body . . ."** [246]. The fourth begins where he says, **"In general, if it is impossible. . ."** [247].

With reference to the first argument he makes three points. First, he assumes certain things which are necessary for the argument. Secondly, he sets forth the argument, where he says, **"Suppose (a) that the infinite . . ."** [241]. Thirdly, he refutes a certain false opinion, where he says, **"Anaxagoras gives . . ."** [242].

359. Therefore, he assumes three things. The first is that every sensible body has a natural aptitude to be in some place.

The second is that some place, among all the places that are, belongs to each natural body.

The third is that the same natural place belongs to both the whole and the part, e.g., to the whole earth and to one clod, to the whole of fire and to one spark. A sign of this is that when a part of a body is put in any part of the place of the whole, it rests there.

360. Next where he says, **"Suppose (a) that the infinite . . ."** [241], he sets forth the argument, which is as follows. If a body is given as infinite, then it is necessary either that the whole be of one species with its parts, such as water or air, or that it have parts of different species, such as a man or a plant.

If all the parts are of one species, it follows from what has been said either that it is altogether immobile and never would be moved, or that it is always moved. Each of these is impossible. For rest is excluded from natural things by one of these alternatives, and motion is excluded by the other. And in either case the intelligibility [ratio] of nature is destroyed, for nature is a principle of motion and rest.

He proves that it would follow that [this body] would be totally mobile or totally at rest by the fact that we could not assign a reason why it would be moved upward rather than downward or in any direction.

He clarifies this with an example. Let us assume that this whole infinite body with like parts is earth. We will not be able to state where some clod of earth would be moved or where it would be at rest, because some body akin to it, i.e., of the same species, will occupy every part of the infinite place. Therefore, can it ever be said that one clod is moved so that it would contain, i.e., would occupy, successively the whole infinite place, as the sun is moved such that it is in every part of the zodiac circle? And how could one clod of earth pass through all the parts of an infinite place? Moreover nothing is moved in an impossible way. If,

therefore, it is impossible for a clod to be moved to occupy a whole infinite place, where will its rest be, and where will its motion be? For it is necessary either that it always be at rest, and so never be moved, or that it always be moved, and so never rest.

361. If, however, the other part of the division is granted, i.e., that the infinite body has parts different in species, it follows that there are different places for the different parts. For the natural place of water is different than the natural place of earth. But from this position it follows first that the body of the infinite whole is not one simply, but accidentally, i.e., by contact. And so there will not be one infinite body, as was supposed.

362. But since someone might not think that this is inconsistent, he adds another argument against this. He says that if the infinite whole is composed of dissimilar parts, then it is necessary for such parts, which are dissimilar in species, to be of species which are either finite in number or infinite in number.

But these parts cannot be of finite species. For if the whole is infinite, then certain parts must be finite in quantity and others infinite. Otherwise the infinite could be composed of things which are finite in number. Granting this, it follows that the parts which are infinite would corrupt the others because of contrariety, as was said above in the preceding argument.

And so none of the ancient natural philosophers who posited one infinite principle said that it was fire or earth, which are extremes. Rather they said that it was water or air or some intermediate between these, because the places of fire and earth are clear and determined, i.e., above and below. However this is not true of water and air. Rather earth is below them and fire above them.

363. And if one should take the other part of the division, i.e., that these partial bodies are infinite in respect to species, it also follows that places are infinite in respect to species, and that the elements are infinite. If, however, it is impossible for the elements to be infinite, as was proved in Book I, and if it is impossible for places to be infinite, since it is impossible to find infinite species of places, then the whole body must be finite.

Since he has argued to the infinity of places from the infinity of bodies, he adds that one must equate body and place. For place cannot be greater than the quantity which body happens to have. Nor can there be an infinite body if place is not infinite. Nor can body be greater than place in any way. For if place is greater than body, it follows that there is a void somewhere. And if body is greater than place, it follows that a part of the body is not in any place.

364. Next where he says, "Anaxagoras gives . . ." [242], he refutes a certain error. First he sets forth the error. He says that Anaxagoras maintained that the infinite is at rest. But Anaxagoras did not suitably assign the reason for its rest. For he said that the infinite supports, i.e., sustains, itself, because it is in itself and not in another, since nothing contains it. And so it cannot be moved outside itself.

365. Secondly, where he says, "... on the assumption..." [243], he refutes this position with two arguments. The first of these is that Anaxagoras has assigned the reason for the rest of the infinite as if it is natural for a thing to be where it is. For he says that the infinite is at rest only because it is in itself. But it is not true that a thing is always where it is naturally disposed to be. For some things are where they are by violence and not by nature.

Therefore, although it is most true that the infinite is not moved since it is sustained by and remains in itself, and thus is immobile, we must still explain why it is not naturally disposed to be moved. For one cannot evade the issue by saying that the infinite is not moved. For there is nothing to prevent us from applying the same argument to anything else which is not moved even though it is naturally disposed to be moved. For if the earth were infinite, then just as it is not moved now when it is at the center, so also it would not be moved then in respect to that part which would be at the center. But this is not because there is no place except the center where it would be sustained. Rather it is because it does not have a natural aptitude to be moved at the center. If, therefore, it is true in respect to the earth that its infinity is not the reason why it is at rest at the center (rather the reason is its heaviness by which it is naturally disposed to remain at the center), so in respect to any other infinite thing there must be a reason to explain why it is at rest. And this reason is not that it is infinite or that it sustains itself.

366. He sets forth the other argument where he says, "Another difficulty emerges..." [244]. He says that if the infinite whole is at rest because it remains in itself, then it follows of necessity that every part is at rest because it remains in itself. For the place of the whole and the place of the part are the same, as was said above, e.g., above for fire and the spark, and below for earth and the clod. If, therefore, the place of

the infinite whole is the whole itself, then it follows that every part of the infinite remains in itself as in its proper place.

367. He sets forth the second argument where he says, **"In general, the view ..."** [246].

He says that it is completely clear that it is impossible to say that there is an infinite body in act and that there is some place for each body, assuming that every sensible body has either heaviness or lightness, as the ancients who posited an infinite said. For if a body is heavy, it must naturally be carried to the center; if it is light, it must be borne upward. If, therefore, there is an infinite sensible body, then in that infinite body there must be an above and a center. But it is impossible for an infinite whole to sustain either of these in itself, i.e., either an above or a center, or even that it sustain each of them in respect to different halves. For how could the infinite be divided so that one part of it is above and the other below? And in the infinite what is the end or the center? Therefore, there is no infinite sensible body.

368. He sets forth the third argument where he says, **"Further, every sensible body ..."** [246]. He says that every sensible body is in place. However, there are six different places: above and below, before and behind, to the right and to the left. And these are determined not only with reference to us, but also in the whole universe itself.

For positions of this sort, in which the beginnings and ends of motion are determined, are determined themselves. Hence in animated things above and below are determined with reference to the motion of growth, before and behind with reference to the

motion of sense, to the right and to the left with reference to progressive motion whose starting point is from the right.

However, in inanimate things in which there are no determinate principles of motions, right and left are named in relation to us. For that column is said to be "on the right" which is to the right of a man, and that is said to be "on the left" which is to the left of a man.

But in the whole universe up and down are determined by the motion of heavy and light things; right is determined by the rising motion of the heavens and left by the falling motion of the heavens; before is the higher hemisphere and behind is the lower hemisphere; up is the meridian and down is the northern region. These, however, cannot be determined in an infinite body. Therefore, it is impossible for the whole universe to be infinite.

369. He sets forth the fourth argument where he says, **"In general, it is impossible ..."** [247]. He says that if it is impossible for there to be an infinite place, since every body is in place, then it follows that it is impossible for there to be an infinite body.

He proves as follows that it is impossible for there to be an infinite place. To be in place and to be in some place are convertible, just as to be man and to be some man, and to be a quantity and to be some quantity, are convertible. Therefore, just as it is impossible for quantity to be infinite because it would then follow that some quantity is infinite, e.g., two cubits or three cubits (which is impossible), so also it is impossible for place to be infinite because it would follow that some place is infinite, either above or below or the like. And this is impossible because each of these signifies some limit, as was said above. Therefore, no sensible body is infinite.

The Infinite Exists, Not As Being in Act, But As Being In Potency. Different Infinites Are Compared with Each Other

The Text of Aristotle

248. *It is plain from these arguments that there is no body which is actually infinite.*

Chapter 6

But on the other hand to suppose that the infinite does not exist in any way leads obviously to many impossible consequences: there will be a beginning and an end of time, a magnitude will not be divisible into magnitudes, number will not be infinite. If, then, in view of the above considerations, neither alternative seems possible, an arbiter must be called in; and clearly there is a sense in which the infinite exists and another in which it does not. 206a6–14

249. *We must keep in mind that the word "is" means either what potentially is or what fully is. Further, a thing is infinite either by addition or by division. Now, as we have seen, magnitude is not actually infinite. But by division it is infinite. (There is no difficulty in refuting the theory of indivisible lines.) The alternative then remains that the infinite has a potential existence.* 206a14–18

250. *But the phrase "potential existence" is ambiguous. When we speak of the potential existence of a statue we mean that there will be an actual statue. It is not so with the infinite. There will not be an actual infinite. The word "is" has many senses, and we say that the infinite "is" in the sense in which we say "it is day" or "it is the games," because one thing after another is always coming into existence. For of these things too the distinction between potential and actual existence holds. We say that there are Olympic games, both in the sense that they may occur and that they are actually occurring.* 206a18–25

251. *The infinite exhibits itself in different ways—in time, in the generations of man, and in the division of magnitudes.* 206a25–27

252. *For generally the infinite has this mode of existence: one thing is always being taken after another, and each thing that is taken is always finite, but always different. Again, "being" has more than one sense, so that we must not regard the infinite as a "this," such as a man or a horse, but must suppose it to exist in the sense in which we speak of the day or the games as existing—things whose being has not come to them like that of a substance, but consists in a process of coming to be or passing away, definite, if you like, at each stage, yet always different.* 206a26–33

253. *But when this takes place in spatial magnitudes, what is taken persists, while in the succession of time and of men it takes place by the passing away of these in such a way that the source of supply never gives out.* 206a33–206b3

254. *In a way the infinite by addition is the same thing as the infinite by division. In a finite magnitude, the infinite by addition comes about in a way inverse to that of the other. For in proportion as we see division going on, in the same proportion we see addition being made to what is already marked off. For if we take a determinate part of a finite magnitude and add another part determined by the same ratio (not taking in the same amount of the original whole), and so on, we shall not traverse the given magnitude. But if we increase the ratio of the part, so as always to take in the same amount, we shall traverse the magnitude, "for every finite magnitude is exhausted by means of any determinate quantity however small. The infinite, then, exists in no other way, but in this way it does exist, potentially and by reduction. It exists fully in the sense in which we say "it is day" or "it is the games"; and potentially as matter exists, not independently as what is finite does. By addition then, also, there is potentially an*

infinite, namely, what we have described as being in a sense the same as the infinite in respect of division. **206b3–18**

255. *For it will always be possible to take something ab extra. Yet the sum of the parts taken will not exceed every determinate magnitude, just as in the direction of division every determinate magnitude is surpassed in smallness and there will always be a smaller part.*

206b18–20

256. *But in respect of addition there cannot be an infinite which even potentially exceeds every assignable magnitude, unless it has the attribute of being actually infinite, as the physicists hold to be true of the body which is outside the world, whose essential nature is air or something of the kind. But if there cannot be in this way a sensible body which is infinite in the full sense, evidently there can no more be a body which is potentially infinite in respect of addition, except as the inverse of the infinite by division, as we have said.* **206b20–27**

257. *It is for this reason that Plato also made the infinites two in number, because it is supposed to be possible to exceed all limits and to proceed ad infinitum in the direction both of increase and of reduction. Yet though he makes the infinites, two he does not use them. For in the numbers the infinite in the direction of reduction is not present, as the monad is the smallest; nor is the infinite in the direction of increase, for the parts number only up to the decad* **206b27-32**

COMMENTARY OF ST. THOMAS

370. After the Philosopher has treated the infinite by means of disputation, he begins here to determine the truth.

First he shows whether there is an infinite, and secondly, what it is, where he says, **"The infinite turns out to be . . ."** [258].

The first part is divided into two parts. First he shows how the infinite exists. Secondly, where he says, **"The infinite exhibits itself . . ."** [251], he compares different infinites with each other.

Concerning the first part he makes three points. First he shows that in one way the infinite exists and in another way it does not. Secondly, where he says, **"We must keep in mind . . ."** [249], he shows that the infinite exists in potency but does not exist as a being in act. Thirdly, where he says, **"But the phrase . . ."** [250], he shows how the infinite exists in potency.

371. He says, therefore, first that it is clear from what has been said above that there is no infinite body in act. It is also clear from what was said above that, if the infinite simply is not, many impossible consequences follow. One of these is that time will have a beginning and an end, which is thought to be absurd by those who hold that the world is eternal.

Furthermore, it would follow that magnitude is not always divisible into magnitudes, but sometimes we would, by the division of magnitudes, arrive at certain things which are not magnitudes. But every magnitude is divisible.

Moreover, it would follow that number may not be increased to infinity.

Therefore, since according to what has already been established neither of these seems to be acceptable, i.e., that there is an infinite in act or that the infinite simply does not exist, it is necessary to say that the infinite exists in one way and in another way does not.

372. Next where he says, **"We must keep in mind . . ."** [249], he shows that the infinite exists as being in potency.

He says that to exist in act is one thing and to exist in potency is another. Now the infinite is said to exist either by addition, as in numbers, or by subtraction, as in magnitudes. For it was shown that a magnitude is not infinite in act. And thus in magnitudes an infinite by addition is not found. However, the infinite is found in magnitudes by division. For it is not difficult to refute the opinion of those who hold that lines are indivisible. Or according to another text, it is not difficult "to divide indivisible lines," i.e., to show that the lines which some say are indivisible are divisible. Hence a thing is said to be infinite by addition or division insofar as it can be added to or divided. It follows, therefore, that the infinite exists as a being in potency.

373. Next where he says, **"But the phrase . . ."** [250], he shows how the infinite exists in potency.

A thing is found to be in potency in two ways. First a thing is in potency in the sense that the whole can be reduced to act. Thus it is possible for this bronze to be a statue because it will at sometime be a statue. However, the infinite is not said to be in potency in the sense that at some later time the whole is in act. Secondly a thing is said to be in potency in the sense that at some later time it comes to be in act, not at once as a whole, but successively.

For a thing is said "to be" in many ways, either because it is a whole all at once, as a man and a house, or because one part of it always comes to be after another. In this latter way a day and the Agonalian games are said to be.

And in this latter way the infinite is said to be both in potency and in act at the same time. For all things of this sort are simultaneously in potency with respect to one part and in act with respect to another. For the Olympic games, i.e., the Agonalian feasts which are celebrated on Mount Olympus, are said to be and to endure insofar as the public games can come to be and do come to be in act. For as long as these feasts continued, part of these games were occurring and another part was, as it were, about to occur.

374. Next where he says, **"The infinite exhibits itself . . ."** [251], he compares different infinites with each other.

First he compares the infinite of time and generation with the infinite which is in magnitudes. Secondly, where he says, **"In a way the infinite . . ."** [254], he compares the infinite in respect to addition with the infinite in respect to division in magnitudes.

Concerning the first part he makes three points. First he states his intention. He says that he will show that the infinite in time and in the generation of men is different than the infinite in the division of magnitudes.

375. Secondly, where he says, **"For generally the infinite . . ."** [252], he explains what is common to all infinites.

He says that in all infinites it is always and universally found that the infinite is always different in respect to some succession, so that whatever is designated in act in the infinite is a finite whole.

Hence, it is not necessary to say that the infinite is a whole existing all at once as a designated "this," like a man or a house. Rather the infinite exists successively, as does a day and the Agonalian games, which do not exist in the way in which a whole, complete substance exists in act.

Moreover, even if generation and corruption go on to infinity, that which is found to be in act is always finite. For in the whole course of generation, even if it goes on to infinity, all the men who are found to be simultaneously in act are finite in number. And this finite group must always be different insofar as certain men succeed others.

376. Thirdly, where he says, **"But when this takes place . . ."** [253], he explains the difference. He says that the finite thing which we take in magnitudes, either by adding or dividing, remains and is not corrupted. But the finite things which are found in the infinite course of time and of human generation are corrupted, so that in this way time and generation do not cease.

377. Next where he says, **"In a way the infinite . . ."** [254], he compares the two infinites which are present in magnitudes, i.e., according to addition and according to division.

Concerning this he makes three points. First, he explains the agreement between these two infinites. Secondly, where he says, **"Yet the sum of the parts . . ."** [255], he explains the difference. Thirdly, where he says, **"But in respect of addition . . ."** [256], he draws a certain conclusion from what he has said.

He says, therefore, first that in a certain way the infinite by addition is the same as the infinite by division. For the infinite by addition comes to be in a manner converse to that of the infinite by division. For insofar as something is divided to infinity, it also seems that a determinate quantity can be added to ad infinitum.

378. He then explains how the infinite by division exists in magnitude. He says that if in a finite magnitude, when a determinate part has been taken by division, one always takes, when dividing, other parts according to the same ratio [ratio], i.e., proportion, but not according to the same quantity in the same proportion, one

will not by dividing pass through that finite thing. For example, if from a line which is a cubit long one takes a half, and from the remainder half again, it is thus possible to proceed to infinity. For the same proportion will be preserved in the subtraction, but not the same quantity of what is subtracted. For in respect to quantity half of a half is less than half of the whole.

But if one would always take the same quantity, the proportion must always grow larger and larger. For example, if from a quantity of ten cubits, one cubit is subtracted, then that which is subtracted is related to the whole in a proportion of one to ten. If, however, one cubit is again subtracted from the remainder, what was subtracted will have a greater proportion, for one cubit is exceeded less by nine than by ten. Therefore, just as by preserving the same proportion the quantity is diminished, so also by taking the same quantity the proportion is increased. If, therefore, in subtracting from a finite magnitude one would always increase the proportion by taking the same quantity, then he will pass through the finite magnitude by dividing. For example, from a line one hundred cubits long one always subtracts one cubit. This is so because any finite thing is consumed if any finite amount is always taken away.

Therefore, the infinite by division exists only in potency. And it is simultaneously in act and in potency, as was said of the day and the public games. And since the infinite is always in potency, it is like matter, which is always in potency. It does not exist in itself as a whole in act, as the finite exists in act. And as the infinite by division is simultaneously in potency and in act, the same must be said of the infinite by addition, which in a way is the same as the infinite by division, as was said. Hence it is clear that the infinite by addition is in potency, because it is always possible to take another by addition.

379. Next where he says, **"Yet the sum of the parts . . ."** [255], he explains the difference between the infinite by addition and the infinite by division.

He says that the infinite by addition is not greater than every given finite magnitude. But the infinite by division is smaller than every determinate smallness.

For let us take some determinate smallness, for example, one inch. If a line one hundred cubits long is divided to infinity by always taking away a half, one will come to something less than one inch.

But in adding to infinity, contrary to what takes place in division, it will be possible to give some finite quantity which will never be surpassed. For let there be given two magnitudes each of which is ten cubits long and a third which is twenty. If, then, that which I subtract to infinity, by always taking one half from one magnitude of ten cubits length, is added to the other which is also ten cubits long, I will never arrive by adding to infinity at that measure of quantity which is twenty cubits long. For to the extent that something will remain in the magnitude from which the subtraction was made, to that extent there will be a deficit of the given measure in the quantity to which the addition is made.

380. Next where he says, **"But in respect of addition . . ."** [256], he draws his conclusion from what has been said.

First he draws the conclusion. Secondly, where he says, **"It is for this reason . . ."** [257], he clarifies it with a remark from Plato.

He says, therefore, first that since addition to infinity does not transcend every determinate quantity, it is not possible, not even in potency, for every determinate quantity to be exceeded by addition. For if there were in nature a potency for an addition transcending every quantity, it would follow that there would be an infinite in act, and this infinite would be an accident of some nature. Thus the natural philosophers said that outside the body of this world which we see there is a certain infinite whose substance is air or some other such thing. If, therefore, it is not possible for there to be an infinite sensible body in act, as has been shown, it follows that there is not in nature a potency for an addition transcending every magnitude, but only a potency for infinite addition as the contrary of division, as was said. Therefore, if there were a potency for an infinite addition transcending every magnitude, it would follow that there would be an infinite body in act. But from an infinite addition in numbers which transcends every number it does not follow that there is an infinite number in act, as will be shown below.

381. Next where he says, **"It is for this reason that Plato . . ."** [257], he clarifies what he has said with a remark from Plato.

He says that since the infinite in the addition of magnitudes is opposed to the infinite by division, Plato posited two infinites, namely, the great, which pertains to addition, and the small, which pertains to division. For the infinite seems to excel, both by addition toward increase, and by division toward decrease, or by tending toward nothing.

But although Plato posited two infinites, he does not use them. For he said that number is the substance of all things. But the infinite by division is not found in numbers, since the smallest number is unity. Nor according to him is there an infinite by addition. For he said that the species of numbers vary only up to ten, and thereafter number is reduced to unity by counting eleven and twelve, etc.

LECTURE 11 [206b33–207a31]
The Definition of the Infinite

The Text of Aristotle

258. *The infinite turns out to be the contrary of what it is said to be. It is not what has nothing outside it that is infinite, but what always has something outside it.*   **206b33–207a2**

259. *This is indicated by the fact that rings also that have no bezel are described as "endless," because it is always possible to take a part which is outside a given part. The description depends on a certain similarity, but it is not true in the full sense of the word. This condition alone is not sufficient: it is necessary also that the next part which is taken should never be the same. In the circle, the latter condition is not satisfied: it is only the adjacent part from which the new part is different.*   **207a2–8**

260. *Our definition then is as follows: A quantity is infinite if it is such that we can always take a part outside what has been already taken. On the other hand, what has nothing outside it is complete and whole. For thus we define the whole—that from which nothing is wanting, as a whole man or a whole box. What is true of each particular is true of the whole as such—the whole is that of which nothing is outside. On the other hand that from which something is absent and outside, however small that may be, is not "all." "Whole" and "complete" are either quite identical or closely akin. Nothing is complete (teleion) which has no end (telos); and the end is a limit.*   **207a8–15**

261. *Hence Parmenides must be thought to have spoken better than Melissus. The latter says that the whole is infinite, but the former describes it as limited, "equally balanced from the middle." For to connect the infinite with the All and the whole is not like joining two pieces of string;*   **207a15–18**

262. *for it is from this they get the dignity they ascribe to the infinite—its containing all things and holding the All in itself—from its having a certain similarity to the whole. It is in fact the matter of the completeness which belongs to size, and what is potentially a whole, though not in the full sense. It is divisible both in the direction of reduction and of the inverse addition. It is a whole and limited; not, however, in virtue of its own nature, but in virtue of what is other than it. It does not contain, but, in so far as it is infinite, is contained.*

Consequently, also, it is unknowable, qua infinite; for the matter has no form. (Hence it is plain that the infinite stands in the relation of part rather than of whole. For the matter is part of the whole, as the bronze is of the bronze statue.)   **207a18–28**

263. *If it contains in the case of sensible things, in the case of intelligible things the great and the small ought to contain them. But it is absurd and impossible to suppose that the unknowable and indeterminate should contain and determine.*   **207a28–32**

COMMENTARY OF ST. THOMAS

382. Having shown how the infinite exists, the Philosopher explains here what the infinite is.

Concerning this he makes three points. First he explains what the infinite is. Secondly, where he says, **"It is reasonable . . ."** [264], he explains the meaning [ratio] of those things which are said of the infinite. Thirdly, where he says, **"It remains to dispose . . ."** [271], he answers the arguments given above.

Concerning the first part he makes two points. First he explains what the infinite is by refuting a false definition. Secondly, where he says, **". . . for it is** from this . . ." [262], he refutes a false opinion which follows from this false definition.

Concerning the first part he makes three points. First he states his intention. Secondly, where he says, **"This is indicated . . ."** [259], he explains his position. Thirdly, where he says, **"Hence, Parmenides . . ."** [261], he draws a conclusion from what he has said.

383. He says, therefore, first [258] that the infinite must be defined contrary to the way in which some have defined it. For some have said that the infinite is "that beyond which there is nothing." But on the contrary, it must be said that the infinite is "that beyond which there is always something."

384. Next where he says, **"This is indicated . . ."** [259], he explains his position.

First he shows that his definition is good. Secondly, where he says, **"On the other hand . . ."** [260], he shows that the definition of the ancients is worthless.

First he shows with an example that the infinite is "that beyond which there is always something."

For some say that rings are infinite because of the fact that they are circular and because it is always possible to take a part in addition to a part already taken.

But this is not said properly but according to a certain similitude. For in order for a thing to be infinite, it is required that beyond any part taken there be some other part, in such a way that the part which was previously taken is never taken again. But this is not so in a circle. For the part which is taken after another part is different only from the part which has just been taken, but not from all the parts previously taken. For one part can be taken

many times, as is clear in circular motion.

If, therefore, rings are said to be infinite because of this similitude, it follows that that which is truly infinite is that beyond which something else can always be taken, if one wishes to take its quantity. For the quantity of the infinite cannot be comprehended. Rather if one wishes to take it, he will take part after part to infinity, as was said above.

385. Next where he says, **"On the other hand . . ."** [260], he proves with the following argument that the definition of the ancients is worthless. "That beyond which there is nothing" is the definition of the perfect and the whole. He proves this as follows.

A whole is defined as that which lacks nothing. Thus we speak of a whole man or a whole arc, in which none of the things which they should possess is missing. And as we say this with respect to a singular whole, such as this or that particular thing, so also this intelligibility [ratio] belongs to that which is truly and properly whole, i.e., the universe, outside of which there simply is nothing. When, however, something is deficient because of the absence of something intrinsic, then it is not a whole.

Therefore, it is clear that this is the definition of a whole: a whole is that outside of which there is nothing. But a whole and the perfect are either altogether the same or else are close according to nature. He says this because a "whole" is not found in simple things which do not have parts. However we do call such things "perfect." From this, then, it is clear that the perfect is that which has nothing outside of itself. But nothing which lacks an end is perfect, for the end is the perfection of each thing. Moreover, the end is the terminus of that which has an end. Hence nothing which is infinite and unterminated is perfect. Therefore, the definition of the perfect, i.e., "that beyond which there is nothing," does not belong to the infinite.

386. Next where he says, **"Hence Parmenides..."** [261], he draws a certain conclusion from what he has said.

Since the definition of the whole does not belong to the infinite, it is clear that Parmenides spoke better than Melissus. For Melissus said that the whole universe is infinite, whereas Parmenides said that the whole is "bounded by exerting itself equally from the middle." In this way he makes the body of the universe to be spherical. For in a spherical figure lines are brought from the center to the boundary, i.e., the circumference, according to equality, fighting as it were, equally among themselves.

And it is rightly said that the whole universe is finite. For the whole and the infinite are not consequent upon each other as if continuous with each other, as thread is joined to thread in weaving. There was a proverb in which things which are consequent upon each other were said to be continuous as thread with thread.

387. Next where he says, **"... for it is from this..."** [262], he refutes a certain false opinion which has arisen from the false definition mentioned above.

He treats this first as it commonly applies to all, and secondly, as it especially applies to Plato, where he says, **"If it contains..."** [263].

He says, therefore, first that since they thought that the infinite is joined to the whole, they took it as a "dignity" of the infinite, i.e., as something per se known, that it contains all and has all

in itself. They did this because the infinite has a certain likeness to the whole, as that which is in potency has a likeness to act. For the infinite insofar as it is in potency is like matter with respect to the perfection of magnitude and is like a whole in potency, but not in act. This is clear from the fact that a thing is called infinite insofar as it can be divided into something smaller and insofar as addition as the opposite of division can occur, as was said above. Therefore, the infinite in itself, i.e., according to its proper nature [ratio], is a whole in potency and is imperfect, such as matter which does not have perfection.

However, it is not a whole and finite in itself, i.e., according to the proper nature [ratio] by which it is infinite. Rather it is such with respect to another, i.e., with respect to an end and a whole, to which it is in potency. For division which can go on to infinity, insofar as it is terminated in something, is said to be perfect, and insofar as it moves toward the infinite, it is imperfect. Now since a whole contains and matter is contained, it is clear that the infinite as such does not contain but is contained. That is, that which pertains to the infinite in act is always contained by something greater, insofar as it is possible to take something beyond it.

388. From the fact that the infinite is, as it were, being in potency, not only does it follow that the infinite is contained and does not contain, but also two other conclusions follow. One of these is that the infinite as such is unknown, because it is, as it were, matter having no species, i.e., form, as was said. And matter is known only through form.

The other conclusion which follows

from the same thing is that the infinite has the nature [ratio] of a part rather than of a whole. For matter is related to the whole as a part. And the infinite is rightly related as a part, insofar as only some part of it can be taken in act.

389. Next where he says, **"If it contains . . ."** [263], he refutes the opinion of Plato, who placed the infinite in both sensible and intelligible things.

He says that from this it is also clear that if the great and the small, to which Plato attributed the infinite, are in both sensible things and intelligible things as containing (because to contain is attributed to the infinite), then it follows that the infinite would contain intelligible things.

But it seems to be absurd and impossible for the infinite, since it is unknown and indeterminate, to contain and determine intelligible things. For the known is not determined by the unknown, but vice versa.

The Meanings of Things Which Are Said about the Infinite

The Text of Aristotle
Chapter 7

264. *It is reasonable that there should not be held to be an infinite in respect of addition such as to surpass every magnitude, but that there should be thought to be such an infinite in the direction of division. For the matter and the infinite are contained inside what contains them, while it is the form which contains.*   207a32–207b1

265. *It is natural too to suppose that in number there is a limit in the direction of the minimum, and that in the other direction every assigned number is surpassed. In magnitude, on the contrary, every assigned magnitude is surpassed in the direction of smallness, while in the other direction there is no infinite magnitude. The reason is that what is one is indivisible whatever it may be, e.g., a man is one man, not many. Number on the other hand is a plurality of "ones" and a certain quantity of them. Hence number must stop at the indivisible; for "two" and "three" are merely derivative terms, and so with each of the other numbers.*   207b1–10

266. *But in the direction of largeness it is always possible to think of a larger number; for the number of times a magnitude can be bisected is infinite. Hence this infinite is potential, never actual: the number of parts that can be taken always surpasses any assigned number. But this number is not separable from the process of bisection, and its infinity is not a permanent actuality but consists in a process of coming to be, like time and the number of time.*
        207b10–15

267. *With magnitudes the contrary holds. What is continuous is divided ad infinitum, but there is no infinite in the direction of increase. For the size which it can potentially be, it can also actually be. Hence since no sensible magnitude is infinite, it is impossible to exceed every assigned magnitude; for if it were possible there would be something bigger than the heavens.*
        207b15–21

268. *The infinite is not the same in magnitude and movement and time, in the sense of a single nature, but its secondary sense depends on its primary sense, i.e., movement is called infinite in virtue of the magnitude covered by the movement (or alteration or growth), and time because of the movement. (I use these terms for the moment. Later I shall explain what each of them means, and also why every magnitude is divisible into magnitudes.)*   207b21–27

269. *Our account does not rob the mathematicians of their science, by disproving the actual existence of the infinite in the direction of increase, in the sense of the untraversable. In point of fact they do not need the infinite and do not use it. They postulate only that the finite straight line may be produced as far as they wish. It is possible to have divided in the same ratio as the largest quantity another magnitude of any size you like. Hence, for the purposes of proof, it will make no difference to them to have such an infinite instead, while its existence will be in the sphere of real magnitudes.*   207b27–34

270. *In the four-fold scheme of causes, it is plain that the infinite is a cause in the sense of matter, and that its essence is privation, the subject as such being what is continuous and sensible. All the other thinkers, too, evidently treat the infinite as matter—that is why it is inconsistent in them to make it what contains, and not what is contained.*   207b34–208a4

COMMENTARY OF ST. THOMAS

390. Having set forth the definition of the infinite, he here explains from this definition the meaning [ratio] of the things which are said about the infinite.

First he explains the meaning of

what is said about the addition and division of the infinite.

Secondly, where he says, **"The infinite is not the same . . ."** [268], he explains why the infinite is found in different things according to an order.

Thirdly, where he says, **"Our account does not . . ."** [269], he explains why mathematicians use the infinite.

Fourthly, where he says, **"In the four-fold scheme . . ."** [270], he explains why the infinite is posited as a principle.

Concerning the first part he makes two points. First he explains the meaning [ratio] of what is said about the infinite with reference to division or addition in magnitudes. Secondly, where he says, **"It is natural too . . ."** [265], he explains the meaning of what is said about numbers by comparing them with magnitudes.

391. Now it was said above that addition to infinity is found in magnitudes in such a way that a determinate magnitude is not exceeded by this addition. But division to infinity is found in magnitude in such a way that any quantity is surpassed in smallness by dividing, as was explained above.

He says, moreover, that it occurs according to reason [ratio]. For since the infinite has the nature [ratio] of matter, it is contained within as matter, whereas that which contains is the species and the form. Furthermore, it is clear from what was said in Book II that the whole has the nature [ratio] of form whereas parts have the nature [ratio] of matter. Since, therefore, in magnitudes we go from the whole to the parts by division, it is reasonable that no terminus is found there which is not surpassed by infinite division. But in addition we go from the parts to the whole, which has the nature [ratio]

of form which contains and terminates. Hence it is reasonable for there to be some determinate quantity which infinite addition does not surpass.

392. Next where he says, **"It is natural too . . ."** [265], he explains the meaning [ratio] of the infinite [as found] in numbers by comparing them with magnitudes.

It is said that in number a limit in smallness is found which is not surpassed by division. But there is not found any limit in greatness. For by addition we find another number which is greater than any given number. Yet the converse is true in magnitudes, as was said.

He explains the reason [ratio] for this. First he explains why in number some limit is found which is not surpassed in smallness by division. The reason [ratio] for this is as follows. Every one thing, insofar as it is one, is indivisible, e.g., an indivisible man is one man, not many. Moreover, it is necessary to reduce every number to one, as is clear from the very nature [ratio] of number. For "number" signifies that there is a plurality of ones. Now every plurality, which surpasses one more or less, is a determinate species of number. Hence, since unity pertains to the nature [ratio] of number, and since indivisibility pertains to the nature [ratio] of unity, it follows that the division of number stops at the indivisible limit.

What he has said about the nature [ratio] of number, namely that numbers are pluralities of ones, he clarifies by means of the species [of number]. For two or three or any other number is denominated by one. Hence it is said in Metaphysics, V, that the substance of six lies in this, that it is six times one, and not in this, that it is twice three or three times two. For otherwise it would follow that there would be many definitions and many substances of one thing, since one number arises in different ways from different parts.

393. Next where he says, **"But in the direction . . ."** [266], he explains the reason why addition in numbers surpasses every determinate multitude.

He says that we can always think of a number which is greater than any given number, because of the fact that magnitude is divided to infinity. For it is clear that division causes multitude. Hence the more a magnitude is divided, the greater is the multitude which arises. And thus the infinite addition of numbers follows upon the infinite division of magnitudes. And so, just as the infinite division of magnitude does not exist in act, but in potency, and exceeds every determinate quantity in smallness, as was said, so also the infinite addition of numbers does not exist in act, but in potency, and exceeds every determinate multitude. But this number which is thus multiplied to infinity is not a number separated from the division of magnitudes.

394. And with reference to this it must be noted that division, as was said, causes multitude. However, division is twofold; one is formal, which is by opposites, and the other is according to quantity.

Now the first division causes multitude, which pertains to the transcendentals insofar as being is divided into the one and the many. But the division of continuous quantity causes number, which is a species of quantity insofar as it has the nature [ratio] of a measure. And this number can be multiplied to infinity just as magnitude is divisible to infinity. But the multitude which follows from the formal division of things is not multiplied to infinity. For the species of things are determinate, just as there is also a determinate quantity in the universe. And thus he says that this number which is multiplied to infinity is not separated from the division of the continuous.

Moreover, this number is not infinite as something permanent, but as always existing in "coming to be," insofar as we successively add to some given number. And the same is true of time and the number of time. For the number of time grows successively by the addition of day to day and not because all days are present at once.

395. Next where he says, **"With magnitudes . . ."** [267], he shows that the contrary is true in magnitudes.

A continuum, as was said, is divided to infinity. But it does not proceed to infinity in greatness, not even in potency. For to the extent that each thing is in potency, to that extent it can be in act. If, therefore, it were in the potency of nature that some magnitude could grow to infinity, it would follow that there would be some infinite sensible magnitude. But this is false, as was said above. It follows, therefore, that there is no potency for the addition of magnitudes to infinity such that every determinate quantity is surpassed. For otherwise it would follow that there would be something greater than the heavens.

396. From this it is clear that what some say is false, namely, that in primary matter there is potency for every quantity. For in primary matter there is potency only for determinate quantity.

From what has been said it is also

clear why it is not necessary for number to be as great in act as it is in potency, as is said here of magnitude. For the addition of number follows from the division of the continuous by which we go from the whole to that which is in potency to number. Hence one cannot arrive at some act which limits the potency. But the addition of magnitude leads to act, as was said.

The Commentator, however, gives another explanation [ratio]. The potency for the addition of magnitude is in one and the same magnitude. But the potency for the addition of numbers is indifferent numbers insofar as something can be added to any number.

But this argument has little value. For just as addition produces different species of number, so also there are different species of measure, insofar as the two-cubit and the three-cubit are said to be species of quantity. Moreover, whatever is added to a greater number is also added to a smaller number. And thus in one and the same number, e.g., two or three, there is potency for infinite addition.

397. Next where he says, **"The infinite is not the same . . ."** [268], he shows how the infinite is found in different ways in different things.

He says that the infinite is not found according to the same nature [ratio] in motion and in magnitude and in time, as if there were one univocal nature predicated of all of these. Rather the infinite is predicated of the latter of these by a reference to the prior. Thus the infinite is predicated of motion because of magnitude in which either local motion or alteration or increase occurs. And it is predicated of time because of motion. This is so because the infinite pertains to quantity, and motion has quantity because of magnitude and

time because of motion, as will be explained below. And so he says that he is using these terms now and will explain later what each of them is and will show that every magnitude is divisible into magnitudes.

398. Next where he says, **"Our account does not rob . . ."** [269], he shows how the mathematicians use the infinite.

He says that the argument set forth above, in which it was stated that there is no infinite magnitude in act, does not destroy the knowledge of mathematicians who use the infinite, e.g., when the geometrician says "let such and such a line be infinite." For they do not need an infinite in act for their demonstrations, nor do they use it. They merely require that there be some line which is as great as is necessary for them, so that from it they are able to subtract what they wish. And for this some greatest magnitude is sufficient. For the greatest magnitude can be divided according to any proportion with respect to some other given magnitude. Hence for purposes of demonstration it does not matter whether it be this way or that, i.e., either infinite or the greatest finite quantity. But with reference to the existence of the thing, it matters greatly whether it is one or the other.

399. Next where he says, **"In the four-fold scheme . . ."** [270], he explains how the infinite is a principle.

He says that since there are four genera of causes, as was said above, it is clear from what has been said that the infinite is a cause as matter. For the infinite has existence in potency, which is proper to matter. But matter is sometimes under form and sometimes under privation. Now the nature [ratio] of matter does not pertain to the infinite insofar as it is under form, but insofar as it is under privation. For the infinite is named in terms of a removal of perfection and limit. And because of this he adds that "the being of the infinite is a privation," i.e., the nature [ratio] of the infinite consists in privation.

And lest anyone think that the infinite is matter as primary matter, he adds that the per se subject of the privation which constitutes the nature [ratio] of the infinite is a sensible continuum.

And this is apparent because the infinite which is in numbers is caused by the infinite division of magnitude. And in like manner the infinite in time and in motion is caused by magnitude. Hence it follows that the first subject of the infinite is a continuum. And since magnitude according to the order of existence is not separated from sensible things, it follows that the subject of the infinite is the sensible.

All the ancients who used the infinite as a material principle also agreed on this. Hence it was inconsistent when they said that the infinite contains. For matter does not contain, but rather is contained.

He Answers the Arguments Which Were Brought Forth in Lecture 7 To Show That the Infinite Exists Not Only in Potency but Also in Act

The Text of Aristotle
Chapter 8

271. *It remains to dispose of the arguments which are supposed to support the view that the infinite exists not only potentially but as a separate thing. Some have no cogency; others can be met by fresh objections that are valid.* 208a5–8

272. *(1) In order that coming to be should not fail, it is not necessary that there should be a sensible body which is actually infinite. The passing away of one thing may be the coming to be of another, the All being limited.* 208a8–11

273. *(2) There is a difference between touching and being limited. The former is relative to something and is the touching of something (for everything that touches touches something), and further is an attribute of some one of the things which are limited. On the other hand, what is limited is not limited in relation to anything. Again, contact is not necessarily possible between any two things taken at random.* 208a11–14

274. *(3) To rely on mere thinking is absurd; for then the excess or defect is not in the thing but in the thought. One might think that one of us is bigger than he is and magnify him ad infinitum. But it does not follow that he is bigger than the size we are, just because some one thinks he is, but only because he is the size he is. The thought is an accident.* 208a14–19

275. *(a) Time indeed and movement are infinite, and also thinking, in the sense that each part that is taken passes in succession out of existence.* 208a20–21

276. *(b) Magnitude is not infinite either in the way of reduction or of magnification in thought. This concludes my account of the way in which the infinite exists, and of the way in which it does not exist, and of what it is.* 208a21–23

COMMENTARY OF ST. THOMAS

400. After the Philosopher has by means of the definition of the infinite explained the meaning [ratio] of things which are said about the infinite, he here answers the arguments which were set forth above to show that the infinite exists.

First he states his intention. Secondly, where he says, **"In order that coming to be..."** [272], he develops his position.

He says, therefore, first [271] that after what has been said about the infinite, it remains to answer the arguments according to which it seemed to be shown that the infinite exists not only in potency, as we have established above, but that it exists in act, as do things which are finite and determinate. For some of these arguments do not conclude of necessity, but are totally false, whereas others partially draw a true conclusion.

401. Next where he says, **"In order that coming to be . . ."** [272], he answers the five arguments which were set forth above to show that the infinite exists.

First he answers the argument which dealt with generation. For it was concluded that, if generation does not cease, then an infinite must exist.

This argument draws a true conclusion with reference to the point that the infinite is in a potency which is successively reduced to act, as was said above. But in order that generation does not cease, it is not necessary for there to be an infinite sensible body in act, as the ancients thought. They held that generation is preserved to infinity as if generation were to occur by extraction from some body. And this could not go on to infinity unless that body were infinite.

But this is not necessary. For in the whole existing finite sensible body generation can endure to infinity by reason of the fact that the corruption of one thing is the generation of another.

402. Next where he says, **"There is a difference . . ."** [273], he answers the argument which dealt with contact. This argument says that it is necessary for every finite body to touch another, and thus it would be necessary to proceed to infinity.

He answers this by saying that "to be touched" and "to be limited" are different. For "to be touched" and "to be included" are predicated in reference to another. For everything which touches touches something. But "limited" is predicated absolutely, and not in reference to another, insofar as a thing is limited in itself by its proper boundaries. Now some finite things touch. But it is not necessary for everything which is touched by one thing to touch another, so that we should proceed in this manner to infinity. Hence it is clear that this argument concludes in no way from necessity.

403. Next where he says, **"To rely on mere thinking . . ."** [274], he answers the argument which dealt with the intellect and the imagination, which the ancients did not distinguish from the intellect.

Through this argument it was shown above that there would be an infinite space outside of the heavens, and consequently an infinite place and an infinite body. But he says that it is absurd to have faith in the understanding in such a way that whatever is apprehended by the intellect or the imagination is true, as some of the ancients thought, whose opinions were disproved in Metaphysics, IV. For if I apprehend that something is larger or smaller than it is, it does not follow that there is some surplus or defect in that thing. Rather this is only in the apprehension of the intellect or the imagination.

For one can think of any man as a multiple of what he is, i.e., twice or triple or increasing in any way to infinity. Yet because of this a quantity of this sort will not be multiplied outside the intellect or beyond a determinate quantity or magnitude. Rather the thing exists in one way, and one understands it in another way.

404. Next where he says, **"Time indeed and movement . . ."** [275], he answers the argument taken from time and motion. He says that time and motion are not infinite in act, because nothing of time is in act except the now. Nor is there anything of motion in act except a certain indivisible. But the intellect apprehends the continuity of time and motion by taking the order of before and after, such that that which was first taken of time or motion does not remain as such. Hence it is not necessary to say that the whole of motion is infinite in act or that the whole of time is infinite in act.

405. Next where he says, **"Magnitude is not infinite . . ."** [276], he answers the argument taken from magnitude. He says that magnitude is not infinite in act either by division or by intelligible increase, as is clear from what was said above.

Lastly, he concludes that he has now treated the infinite.

BOOK IV
PLACE, VOID AND TIME, THE MEASURES OF MOBILE BEING
LECTURE 1 [208a27–209a1]
The Study of Place Pertains to Natural Science. Probable Reasons Are Given to Show That Place Exists

The Text of Aristotle
Chapter 1

277. *The physicist must have a knowledge of Place, too, as well as of the infinite—namely, whether there is such a thing or not, and the manner of its existence and what it is—*

208a27–29

278. *both because all suppose that things which exist are somewhere (the non-existent is nowhere—where is the goat-stag or the sphinx?),*

208a29–31

279. *and because "motion" in its most general and primary sense is change of place, which we call "locomotion."*

208a31–32

280. *The question, what is place? presents many difficulties. An examination of all the relevant facts seems to lead to divergent conclusions. Moreover, we have inherited nothing from previous thinkers, whether in the way of a statement of difficulties or of a solution.*

208a32–208b1

281. *The existence of place is held to be obvious from the fact of mutual replacement. Where water now is, there in turn, when the water has gone out as from a vessel, air is present. When therefore another body occupies this same place, the place is thought to be different from all the bodies which come to be in it and replace one another. What now contains air formerly contained water, so that clearly the place or space into which and out of which they passed was something different from both.*

208b1–8

282. *Further, the typical locomotions of the elementary natural bodies—namely, fire, earth, and the like—show not only that place is something, but also that it exerts a certain influence. Each is carried to its own place, if it is not hindered, the one up, the other down. Now these are regions or kinds of place—up and down and the rest of the six directions. Nor do such distinctions (up and down and right and left, etc.) hold only in relation to us. To us they are not always the same but change with the direction in which we are turned: that is why the same thing may be both right and left, up and down, before and behind. But in nature each is distinct, taken apart by itself. It is not every chance direction which is "up," but where fire and what is light are carried; similarly, too, "down" is not any chance direction but where what has weight and what is made of earth are carried—the implication being that these places do not differ merely in relative position, but also as possessing distinct potencies. This is made plain also by the objects studied by mathematics. Though they have no real place, they nevertheless, in respect of their position relatively to us, have a right and left as attributes ascribed to them only in consequence of their relative position, not having by nature these various characteristics.*

208b8–25

283. *Again, the theory that the void exists involves the existence of place; for one would define void as place bereft of body. These considerations then would lead us to suppose that place is something distinct from bodies, and that every sensible body is in place.*

208b25–29

284. *Hesiod too might be held to have given a correct account of it when he made chaos first. At least he says: "First of all things came chaos to being, then broad-breasted earth," implying that things need to have space first, because he thought, with most people, that everything is somewhere and in place. If this is its nature, the potency of place must be a marvelous thing,*

and take precedence of all other things. For that without which nothing else can exist, while it can exist without the others, must needs be first; for place does not pass out of existence when the things in it are annihilated. 208b29–209a2

COMMENTARY OF ST. THOMAS

406. After the Philosopher in Book III has treated motion and the infinite, which pertains to motion intrinsically insofar as it is of the genus of the continuous, here in Book IV he intends to treat those things which pertain to motion extrinsically. First he treats those things which belong to motion extrinsically as measures of the mobile body. Secondly, where he says, **"Next for discussion . . ."** [390], he treats time which is the measure of the motion itself.

Concerning the first part he makes two points. First he treats place, and secondly the void, where he says, **"The investigation of . . ."** [340].

Concerning the first part he makes two points. First he shows that place must be treated by natural science. Secondly he treats place, where he says, **"The existence of place . . ."** [281].

Concerning the first part he makes two points. First [277] he sets forth his intention. He says that just as it pertains to natural science to determine whether or not the infinite exists, and how it exists, and what it is, in the same way the treatment of place pertains to natural science.

Secondly where he says, **". . . both because all suppose . . ."** [278], he proves what he has said, first from the point of view of place itself, and secondly from our point of view, where he says, **"The question, what is place . . ."** [280].

407. He gives two arguments for the first point. The first [278] is as follows. Things which are common to all natural beings pertain especially to the con-

sideration of natural science. But place is such a thing. For all men have the common opinion that whatever is is in some place.

To prove this they use the sophistical argument of positing the consequent. For they argue as follows.

That which is not is nowhere, that is, it is in no place. For one cannot assign a place to a goat-stag or a sphinx, which are fictions or chimeras.

Therefore they argue that if that which is in no place is not, then whatever is is in place.

But if being in place is proper to all beings, it seems that place pertains to the consideration of the metaphysician rather than physicist.

It must be said that the argument here is drawn from the opinion of those who, because they are unable to transcend the imagination of bodies, hold that all beings are sensible. According to them natural science is first philosophy, which is common to all beings, as is said in Metaphysics, IV.

408. He gives the second argument where he says, **". . . and because 'motion' . . ."** [279]. The argument is as follows.

The consideration of motion pertains to natural philosophy. But motion in regard to place, which we call mutation of place, is the most common of all motions. For certain bodies, i.e., celestial bodies, are moved only by this motion, and nothing is moved by the other motions unless it is moved by this motion. Similarly this motion is more proper because only this motion is truly continuous and perfect, as will be proven in Book VIII. But motion in respect to place cannot be understood unless place is understood. Therefore natural science ought to consider place.

409. Next where he says, "**The question, what is place . . .**" [280], he comes to the same conclusion from our point of view.

Those things about which there are problems must be determined by wise men. Now there are many problems about what place is.

The cause of these problems is twofold. One cause is due to place itself. For not all properties of place lead to the same opinion about place, but from some properties of place it seems that place is one thing, and from other properties it seems that place is something else. The other cause is due to men. For the ancients have not stated the problem of place very well, nor have they sought after the truth very well.

410. Next where he says, "**The existence of place . . .**" [281], he begins to treat place. He does this first by means of disputation, and secondly by determining the truth, where he says, "**The next step . . .**" [299]

Concerning the first part he makes two points. First he inquires by means of disputation whether place is, and secondly what place is, where he says, "**We may distinguish . . .**" [291].

Concerning the first part he makes two points. First he gives arguments to show that place exists, and secondly that place does not exist, where he says, "**True, but even if . . .**" [285].

Concerning the first part he makes two points. First he shows that place exists by arguments taken from the truth of the thing, and secondly from the opinions of others, where he says,

"**Again, the theory that the void . . .**" [283].

411. Concerning the first part [281] he gives two arguments, the first of which is as follows.

He says that it is clear that place is something because of the transmutation of bodies which are moved in respect to place. For just as trans- mutation in respect to forms has led men to a knowledge of matter, because it is necessary that there be some subject in which forms succeed each other, likewise transmutation in respect to place has led men to a knowledge of place. For it is necessary that there be something in which bodies succeed each other. This is what he means when he says that when water flows out from where it now is, as from a vase, then air enters. Therefore since the same place is sometimes occupied by another body, it seems to be clear that place is something other than the things which exist in place and are moved in respect to place. For air is now present where water formerly was, which could not be unless place were something other than both the water and the air. It follows, therefore, that place is something, and that it is a certain receptacle different from both of the things located within it, and that it is the terminus from which and to which of local motion.

412. He gives the second argument where he says, "**Further, the typical locomotions . . .**" [282].

He says that, while the motion of any body shows that place exists, as was said, the local motion of simple natural bodies, such as fire and earth and other light and heavy things of this kind, shows not only that place is something but also that place has a certain potency and power.

For we see that each of these things is carried to its own proper place if not impeded. Heavy things are carried downwards, and light things upwards. From this it is clear that place has a certain power of conserving that which is located in place. And because of this, that which is located in place tends toward its own place by a desire for its own conservation.

From this it is not shown that place has an attracting power except as an end is said to attract.

Moreover upwards and downwards and the rest of the six directions, that is, before and behind, right and left, are parts and species of place.

For such directions are determined in the universe not only by us but also by nature.

And this is clear because upwards or downwards or right or left is not always the same in those things which are denominated by us, but they vary insofar as we turn to the object in different ways. Whence something which remains immobile frequently changes from right to left, and similarly concerning the other directions, insofar as we turn toward objects in different ways.

But in nature upwards and downwards in respect to the motion of light and heavy bodies is something determinate. And the other positions are determined by the motion of the heavens, as is said in Book III. For each part of the world is not upwards or downwards indifferently, but upwards is always where light things are carried, and downwards where heavy things are carried.

But whatever has in itself determinate positions must have potencies by which it is determined. For the potency of right in an animal is other than the potency of left. Whence it follows that place exists and has some potency.

Furthermore he shows by means of mathematical objects that in some things position is denominated only in respect to us. For although mathematical objects do not exist in place, nevertheless position is attributed to them, but only in respect to us. Whence there is no position in them according to nature but only according to understanding, that is, insofar as they are understood by us in some order, either above or below or right or left.

413. Next where he says, "**Again, the theory that the void . . .**" [283], he shows from the opinions of others that place exists.

He does this first from the opinion of those who posit a void. Since each of them affirm that a void exists, they must necessarily say that place exists. For a void is nothing else than place deprived of body. And thus from this and from the previous arguments one can understand that place is something other than bodies and that all sensible bodies exist in place.

414. Secondly, where he says, "**Hesiod too . . .**" [284], he introduces the same opinion of Hesiod, who was one of the ancient theological poets, and who held that chaos was made first.

For Hesiod said that prior to all things chaos was made as a certain disorder and receptacle of bodies, and afterwards broad earth was made in order to receive diverse bodies, as if it were necessary for the receptacle of things to exist first, and then the things themselves. Therefore they held this because they believed, as do many others, that everything which is is in place.

If this is true, it follows that place not only is but that it has a wondrous potency which is the first of all beings. For that which can exist without the others, while the others cannot exist without it, seems to be first. But according to them place can exist without bodies, which they surmised from the fact that we see that place remains when that which is located in place is destroyed. Things, however, cannot exist without place. Hence it follows according to them that place is the first among all beings.

LECTURE 2 [209a2-30]
Six Probable Arguments Are Given to Show That Place Does Not Exist

The Text of Aristotle

285. True, but even if we suppose its existence settled, the question of its nature presents difficulty—whether it is some sort of "bulk" of body or some entity other than that; for we must first determine its genus.

(1) Now it has three dimensions, length, breadth, depth, the dimensions by which all body also is bounded. But the place cannot be body; for if it were there would be two bodies in the same place.   209a2–7

286. (2) Further, if body has a place and space, clearly so too have surface and the other limits of body; for the same statement will apply to them: where the bounding planes of the water were, there in turn will be those of the air. But when we come to a point we cannot make a distinction between it and its place. Hence if the place of a point is not different from the point, no more will that of any of the others be different, and place will not be something different from each of them.   209a7–13

287. (3) What in the world then are we to suppose place to be? If it has the sort of nature described, it cannot be an element or composed of elements, whether these be corporeal or incorporeal; for while it has size, it has not body. But the elements of sensible bodies are bodies, while nothing that has size results from a combination of intelligible elements.   209a13–18

288. (4) Also we may ask: of what in things is space the cause? None of the four modes of causation can be ascribed to it. It is neither cause in the sense of the matter of existents (for nothing is composed of it), nor as the form and definition of things, nor as end, nor does it move existents.   209a18–22

289. (5) Further, too, if it is itself an existent, where will it be? Zeno's difficulty demands an explanation; for if everything that exists has a place, place too will have a place, and so on ad infinitum.   209a23–25

290. (6) Again, just as every body is in place, so, too, every place has a body in it. What then shall we say about growing things? It follows from these premises that their place must grow with them, if their place is neither less nor greater than they are. By asking these questions, then, we must raise the whole problem about place—not only as to what it is, but even whether there is such a thing.   209a26–30

COMMENTARY OF ST. THOMAS

415. After the Philosopher has given arguments to show that place exists, he here gives six arguments to show that place does not exist. In order to begin inquiring whether something is, it is necessary to state what it is, at least to state what is signified by the name. And therefore he says [285] that, although it has been shown that place exists, nevertheless there is still a doubt about what it is if it is. Is it a certain corporeal mass or a nature of some other kind?

416. Regarding this he argues as follows. If place is something, it must be a body, for place has three dimensions—length, breadth, and depth. Moreover, a body is determined by these dimensions, because everything that has three dimensions is a body. But it is impossible for place to be a body. For since place and that which is located in place exist together, it would follow that two bodies exist together, which is impossible. It is, therefore, impossible that place be something.

417. He gives the second argument where he says, "**Further, if body has ...**" [286]. The argument is as follows.

If the place of a body is a certain receptacle of the body other than the body itself, then the place of the surface must be some receptacle other than the surface itself. The same is true of the other terminations of quantity, the line and the point. He proves this condition as follows. Place was shown to be other than bodies from the fact that a body of air now exists where a body of water formerly was. But likewise the surface of air now exists where the surface of water formerly was. Therefore the place of the surface is other than the surface. And similar arguments can be given in regard to the line and the point.

He argues, therefore, by denying the consequent. There cannot be any difference between a point and the place of a point. For since place does not exceed that which is located in place, the place of a point can only be something indivisible. But two indivisible quantities, like two points joined together, are only one. Therefore for the same reason the place of a surface will not be other than the surface, nor will the place of a body be other than the body.

418. He gives the third argument where he says, "**What in the world ...**" [287]. The argument is as follows.

Whatever is is either an element or composed of elements. But place is neither of these. Therefore place does not exist.

He proves the minor as follows. Whatever is an element or composed of elements is included in the number of either corporeal or incorporeal things. But place is not included in the number of incorporeal things because

it has magnitude. And it is not included in the number of corporeal things because it is not a body, as has been proven. Therefore place is neither an element nor composed of elements.

But someone might say that, although place is not a body, nevertheless it is a corporeal element. To refute this he adds that the elements of sensible bodies are corporeal, because elements are not outside of the genus of things composed of the elements. For no magnitude is constituted by intelligible principles which are incorporeal. Hence if place is not a body, it cannot be a corporeal element.

419. He gives the fourth argument where he says, "**Also we may ask ...**" [288]. The argument is as follows.

Whatever is is in some way a cause of something. But place cannot be a cause according to any of the four types of causes. It is not a material cause because things which are are not constituted out of place, which is the meaning of matter. It is not a formal cause because then everything which occupies one place would be of the same species, since the principle of the species is the form. It is not a final cause of things because it seems that place exists for the sake of that which is located in place rather than vice versa. Nor is it an efficient or moving cause because it is the terminus of motion. It seems, therefore, that place is nothing.

420. He gives the fifth argument where he says, "**Further, too, if it is ...**" [289]. This is the argument of Zeno and it is as follows.

Whatever is is in place. Therefore, if place is something, it follows that it is in place, and this latter place is in another place, and so on to infinity, which is impossible. Thus place is not something.

421. He gives the sixth argument

where he says, "**Again, just as every body . . .**" [290]. The argument is as follows.

Every body is in a place, and in every place there is a body, as many probably think. From this it follows that place is neither smaller nor greater than that which is located in place. Since, therefore, that which is located in place increases in size, then place must also increase in size. But this seems impossible because place is immobile. Therefore place is not something.

And finally he concludes that these arguments make us doubt not only what place is but also whether it is.

However these arguments are answered in what follows.

LECTURE 3 [209a31-210a13]
He Argues Whether Place Is Form or Matter

The Text of Aristotle
Chapter 2

291. *We may distinguish generally between predicating B of A because it (A) is itself, and because it is something else; and particularly between place which is common and in which all bodies are, and the special place occupied primarily by each. I mean, for instance, that you are now in the heavens because you are in the air and it is in the heavens; and you are in the air because you are on the earth; and similarly on the earth because you are in this place which contains no more than you. Now if place is what primarily contains each body, it would be a limit, so that the place would be the form or shape of each body by which the magnitude or the matter of the magnitude is defined; for this is the limit of each body. If, then, we look at the question in this way the place of a thing is its form.*   **209a31–109b6**

292. *But, if we regard the place as the extension of the magnitude, it is the matter. For this is different from the magnitude: it is what is contained and defined by the form, as by a bounding plane. Matter or the indeterminate is of this nature; when the boundary and attributes of a sphere are taken away, nothing but the matter is left. This is why Plato in the* Timaeus *says that matter and space are the same; for the "participant" and space are identical. (It is true, indeed, that the account he gives there of the "participant" is different from what he says in his so-called unwritten teaching. Nevertheless, he did identify place and space.) I mention Plato because, while all hold place to be something, he alone tried to say what it is.*   **209b6–17**

293. *In view of these facts we should naturally expect to find difficulty in determining what place is, if indeed it is one of these two things, matter or form. They demand a very close scrutiny, especially as it is not easy to recognize them apart.*   **209b17–21**

294. *But it is at any rate not difficult to see that place cannot be either of them. The form and the matter are not separate from the thing, whereas the place can be separated. As we pointed out, where air was, water in turn comes to be, the one replacing the other; and similarly with other bodies. Hence the place of a thing is neither a part nor a state of it, but is separable from it. For place is supposed to be something like a vessel—the vessel being a transportable place. But the vessel is no part of the thing.*   **209b21–32**

295. *In so far then as it is separable from the thing, it is not the form: qua containing, it is different from the matter.*   **209b32–34**

296. *Also it is held that what is anywhere is both itself something and that there is a different thing outside it. (Plato of course, if we may digress, ought to tell us why the form and the numbers are not in place, if "what participates" is place—whether what participates is the Great and the Small or the matter, as he called it in writing in the* Timaeus.*)*   **209b34–210a2**

297. *Further, how could a body be carried to its own place, if place was the matter or the form? It is impossible that what has no reference to motion or the distinction of up and down can be place. So place must be looked for among things which have these characteristics. If the place is in the thing (it must be if it is either shape or matter) place will have a place; for both the form and the indeterminate undergo change and motion along with the thing, and are not always in the same place, but are where the thing is. Hence the place will have a place.*   **210a2–9**

298. *Further, when water is produced from air, the place has been destroyed, for the resulting body is not in the same place. What sort of destruction then is that? This concludes*

my statement of the reasons why space must be something, and again of the difficulties that may be raised about its essential nature. **210a9–13**

COMMENTARY OF ST. THOMAS

422. After the Philosopher has inquired whether place is by means of disputation, he here inquires what it is.

First he gives disputatious arguments to show that place is either form or matter. Secondly, where he says, **"But it is at any rate . . ."** [294], he gives arguments to the contrary.

Concerning the first part he makes three points. First he gives an argument to show that place is form, and secondly, where he says, **"But, if we regard . . ."** [292], to show that place is matter. Thirdly he introduces a corollary from these arguments, where he says, **"In view of these facts . . ."** [293].

423. He says, therefore, first that just as in beings one thing is being per se and another is called being per accidens, likewise in regard to place a similar distinction must be made. Common place, in which all bodies are, is one thing. Proper place, which is called place primarily and per se, is another thing.

Common place is not called place except per accidens and posteriorly. This is clear from the following.

We can say that you are in the heavens because you are in the air which is in the heavens. And you are in the air and in the heavens because you are on the earth. And you are said to be on the earth because you are in a place which contains nothing more than yourself.

424. Hence that which primarily and per se contains each thing is its place per se. But place in this sense is the terminus at which the thing is terminated. It follows, therefore, that place properly and per se is the terminus of the thing. However form is the terminus of each thing, because through the form the matter of each thing is determined to its proper being, and the magnitude to its determined measure. For the quantities of things are consequent upon their forms. It seems, therefore, according to this view, that place is form.

But it must be realized that in this argument there is a sophism of consequent. For the syllogism is carried out in the second figure from two affirmatives.

425. Next where he says, **"But if we regard . . ."** [292], he gives Plato's argument according to which it seemed to Plato that place is matter.

To understand this it must be known that the ancients thought that place is the space which is between the termini of a container which has the dimensions of length, breadth, and depth. Nevertheless this space does not seem to be identical with any sensible body. For when different sensible bodies come and go, the space remains the same. According to this, therefore, it follows that place is separated dimensions.

426. And from this Plato wished to argue that place is matter. He says that insofar as place seems in some things to be the distance of spatial magnitude separated from any sensible body, it seems that place is matter. For distance itself or the dimension of magnitude is other than the magnitude. For magnitude signifies something terminated by some species, as a line is terminated by points, and a surface by a line, and a

body by a surface, which are the species of magnitude. But the dimension of space is determined and contained under the form, as a body is determined by a plane, that is, by a surface, as a certain terminus. However, that which is contained under the termini seems to be undetermined in itself. But that which is not determined in itself, but is determined by form and the terminated, is matter, which has the nature [ratio] of infinity. For if the sensible passions and the termini by which the dimension of magnitude is formed are removed from a spherical body, nothing remains except matter. Hence it follows that these dimensions, which are indeterminate in themselves and determined by another, are matter.

And this principally followed from the fundamental views of Plato, who held that numbers and quantities are the substances of things.

427. Therefore, since place is dimensions and dimensions are matter, Plato said in the Timaeus that place and matter are the same. For every receptacle of something he called place, not distinguishing between the receptivity of place and of matter. Whence since matter is receptive of forms, it follows that matter is place.

Nevertheless, it must be understood that Plato spoke of the receptacle in different ways. In the Timaeus he said that the receptacle is matter. However, in his unwritten and spoken teachings, that is, when he taught orally in the schools, he said that the receptacle is the great and the small, which he placed on the part of matter, as was said above. Nevertheless to whichever he attributed the receptacle, he always said that the receptacle and place are the same. Thus, therefore, although many have said that

place is something, only Plato tried to establish what it is.

428. Next where he says, **"In view of these facts . . ."** [293], he concludes from what has been said that, if place is either matter or form, it seems reasonable that it be difficult to know what place is. For both matter and form involve the highest speculation and difficulty, and it is not easy to know one of them without the other.

429. Next where he says, **"But it is at any rate . . ."** [294], he gives five arguments to the contrary.

In the first of these arguments he says that it is not difficult to see that place is neither matter nor form. For form and matter are not separated from the thing of which they are. But place does become separated, for water is now present in the place where air formerly was. And also other bodies change places with each other. Whence it is clear that place is neither a material nor formal part of a thing.

Nor is place a habit or any accident. For the parts and accidents are not separable from the thing, but place is separable. He shows this by means of an example. Place seems to be related to that which is located in place as a kind of vase. But there is this difference. Place is immobile but the vase is mobile, as will be explained below.

Thus by the fact that place is separable, it is shown that place is not form. But it is shown that place is not matter not only by the fact that place is separable, but also by the fact that place contains. Matter, however, does not contain, but is contained.

430. He gives the second argument where he says, **"Also it is held . . ."** [295]. He has shown that place is neither matter nor form by the fact that place is separated from that which is located in place. Here he wishes to

show that, even if place were never separated from that which is located in place, from the very fact that we say that something is in place it is apparent that place is neither matter nor form. Everything which is said to be somewhere seems to be something itself and also to be something other than that in which it is. Hence when something is said to be in place, it follows that place is outside of that which is located in place. But matter and form are not outside of the thing. Therefore neither matter nor form is place.

431. He gives the third argument where he says, "**Plato of course . . .**" [296]. Here in a digression he gives a special argument against the position of Plato.

It was said above in Book III that Plato held that the ideas and numbers are not in place. But it follows from his understanding of place that they are in place. For everything which is participated is in the participant. Now he held that species and numbers are participated either by matter or by the great and the small. It follows, therefore, that species and numbers are in matter or in the great and the small. If, therefore, matter or the great and the small is place, it follows that numbers and species are in place.

432. He gives the fourth argument where he says, "**Further, how could a body . . .**" [297].

He says that it will not be possible to explain suitably how something is moved in respect to place if matter and form are place. For it is impossible to ascribe place to those things which are moved neither up nor down nor ac-

cording to any other kind of place. Whence place must be sought in those things which are moved in respect to place. But if place exists in that which is moved as something intrinsic to it (which must be said if place is either matter or form), it follows that place will be in place. For everything which is moved in respect to place is in place. But those things which are in the being as the species and the infinite, that is, the matter, are moved together with the thing. For they are not always in the same place but are where the thing is. Therefore, it must be that matter and form are in place. If, therefore, either of them is place, it follows that place is in place, which is impossible.

433. He gives the fifth argument where he says, "**Further, when water . . .**" [298]. The argument is as follows.

Whenever something is corrupted, the parts of its species are corrupted in some way. But matter and form are parts of the species. Therefore, when the thing is corrupted, the matter and form are corrupted, at least per accidens. If, therefore, place is matter and form, it follows that place is corrupted, if place pertains to the species. For the body which is generated would not be in the same place if the place of air pertained to its species, as when water is generated from air. But this does not explain how place is corrupted. Therefore it cannot be said that place is either matter or form.

Lastly he concludes what has already been said; namely, it seems necessary that there be place and one can have difficulties about its substance.

Various Ways in Which Something Is Said to Be in Something. Whether Something Can Be in Itself. Certain Difficulties about the Existence and Nature of Place Are Answered

The Text of Aristotle
Chapter 3

299. The next step we must take is to see in how many senses one thing is said to be "in" another.

(1) As the finger is "in" the hand and generally the part "in" the whole.

(2) As the whole is "in" the parts; for there is no whole over and above the parts.

(3) As man is "in" animal and generally species "in" genus.

(4) As the genus is "in" the species and generally the part of the specific form "in" the definition of the specific form.

(5) As health is "in" the hot and the cold and generally the form "in" the matter.

(6) As the affairs of Greece center "in" the king, and generally events center "in" their primary motive agent.

(7) As the existence of a thing centers "in" its good and generally "in" its end, i.e. "in that for the sake of which" it exists.

(8) In the strictest sense of all, as a thing is "in" a vessel, and generally "in" place.

210a14–24

300. One might raise the question whether a thing can be in itself, or whether nothing can be in itself—everything being either nowhere or in something else. 210a24–26

301. The question is ambiguous; we may mean the thing qua itself or qua something else. When there are parts of a whole—the one that in which a thing is, the other the thing which is in it—the whole will be described as being in itself. For a thing is described in terms of its parts, as well as in terms of the thing as a whole, e.g., a man is said to be white because the visible surface of him is white, or to be scientific because his thinking faculty has been trained. The jar then will not be in itself and the wine will not be in itself. But the jar of wine will; for the contents and the container are both parts of the same whole. 210a26–33

302. In this sense then, but not primarily, a thing can be in itself, namely, as "white" is in body (for the visible surface is in body), and science is in the mind. It is from these, which are "parts" (in the sense at least of being "in" the man), that the man is called white, etc. But the jar and the wine in separation are not parts of a whole, though together they are. So when there are parts, a thing will be in itself, as "white" is in man because it is in body, and in body because it resides in the visible surface. We cannot go further and say that it is in surface in virtue of something other than itself. (Yet it is not in itself: though these are in a way the same thing,) they differ in essence, each having a special nature and capacity, "surface" and "white." 210a33–210b8

303. Thus if we look at the matter inductively we do not find anything to be "in" itself in any of the senses that have been distinguished; 210b8–9

304. and it can be seen by argument that it is impossible. For each of two things will have to be both, e.g., the jar will have to be both vessel and wine, and the wine both wine and jar, if it is possible for a thing to be in itself; so that, however true it might be that they were in each other, the jar will receive the wine in virtue not of its being wine but of the wine's being wine, and the wine will be in the jar in virtue not of its being a jar but of the jar's being a jar. Now

that they are different in respect of their essence is evident; for "that in which something is" and "that which is in it" would be differently defined. 210b9–17

305. *Nor is it possible for a thing to be in itself even incidentally; for two things would be at the same time in the same thing. The jar would be in itself—if a thing whose nature it is to receive can be in itself; and that which it receives, namely (if wine) wine, will be in it. Obviously then a thing cannot be in itself primarily.* 210b18–22

306. *Zeno's problem—that if Place is something it must be in something—is not difficult to solve. There is nothing to prevent the first place from being "in" something else—not indeed in that as "in" place, but as health is "in" the hot as a positive determination of it or as the hot is "in" body as an affection. So we escape the infinite regress.* 210b22–27

307. *Another thing is plain: since the vessel is no part of what is in it (what contains in the strict sense is different from what is contained), place could not be either the matter or the form of the thing contained, but must be different—for the latter, both the matter and the shape, are parts of what is contained. This then may serve as a critical statement of the difficulties involved.* 210b27–31

COMMENTARY OF ST. THOMAS

434. After the Philosopher has inquired whether place is and what place is by means of disputation, he here begins to determine the truth.

First he sets forth certain things which are necessary for the consideration of the truth. Secondly, where he says, **"What then after all is place?"** [308], he determines the truth.

Concerning the first part he makes three points. First he shows in how many ways something is said to be in something. Secondly, where he says, **"One might raise the question . . ."** [300], he inquires whether something can be in itself. Thirdly, where he says, **"Zeno's problem . . ."** [306], he solves a certain doubt that was previously raised.

435. He posits [299] eight modes in which something is said to be in something.

The first of these is as a finger is said to be in a hand. And universally as any part is said to be in its whole.

The second mode is as a whole is said to be in its parts. Since this mode is not as customary as the first, to clarify

the point he adds that the whole is not outside of the parts and thus must be understood as being in the parts.

The third mode is as man is said to be in animal, or as any species is in its genus.

The fourth mode is as a genus is said to be in the species. And lest this mode seem extraneous, he signifies the reason why he says this. The genus as well as the differentia is part of the definition of the species. Hence in a certain way both the genus and the differentia are said to be in the species as parts in the whole.

The fifth mode is as health is said to be in the hot and the cold, whose interaction constitute health. And universally as any form, accidental or substantial, is said to be in its matter or subject.

The sixth mode is as the affairs of the Greeks are said to be in the king of Greece, and universally as everything which is moved is in a first mover. In this mode I can say that something is in me because it is in my power to make it.

The seventh mode in which something is said to be in something is as in that which is most lovable and desirable, and universally as in an end. In this mode one's heart is said to be in something which one loves and desires.

The eighth mode in which something is said to be in something is as in a vase, and universally as that which is located is in place.

He seems to have omitted the mode in which something is in something as in time. But this is reduced to the eighth mode. For just as place is the measure of the mobile being, so time is the measure of the motion.

436. Moreover he says that something is most properly said to be in something according to the eighth mode.

Hence, according to the rule which he gives in Metaphysics, IV and V, it is necessary that all the other modes are reduced in some way to this mode—that something is in something as in a place. This is made clear as follows.

That which is located is contained in or is included by a place in which it has rest and stability. Therefore, in a way most similar to this, a part is said to be in an integral whole in which it is actually included. Hence it will be said below that that which is located is like a separated part, and a part is like something that has a connected location.

That which is a whole according to reason [ratio] is similar to the integral whole. Consequently it is said that that which is in the definition [ratio] of something is in it, as animal is in man.

However it happens that the part of the integral whole is included actually in the whole, but the part of the universal whole is included potentially in the whole. For the genus extends poten-

tially to more than the species, although the species has more in act. Consequently it is also said that the species is in the genus.

And as the species is contained in the potency of the genus, likewise form is contained in the potency of matter. Hence form is said to be in matter.

And since the whole has the nature of a form in respect to the parts, as was said in Book II, consequently the whole is said to be in the parts. Moreover as the form is included under the passive potency of matter, likewise the effect is included under the active potency of the agent. Hence a thing is said to be in its first mover.

Furthermore it is clear that the appetite rests in the good which is desired and loved, and is made fast in it, as that which is located is in place. Hence the affection of the lover is said to be in that which is loved.

And thus it is clear that all the other modes are derived from the last mode, which is the most proper.

437. Next where he says, "**One might raise the question . . .**" [300], he inquires whether something can be in itself. For Anaxagoras has said above that the infinite is in itself.

Therefore he first raises the question whether one and the same thing can be in itself or whether nothing can be in itself. But everything is either nowhere or in something else.

438. Secondly he answers this question where he says, "**The question is ambiguous**" [301].

First he shows how something can be in itself, and secondly, where he says, "**In this sense then . . .**" [302], how it cannot be in itself.

He says, therefore, first [301] that a thing being in itself can be understood in two ways: first, primarily and per se;

secondly, according to another, that is, according to a part.

In this second way something can be said to be in itself. For when two parts of a whole are so related that one part is that in which something is and the other part is that which is in it, then it follows that the whole is said to be both that in which it is, by reason of one part, and that which is in this, by reason of the other part. Thus a whole is said to be in itself.

For we find that something is said of a thing because of a part. Thus one is called white because his surface is white, and a man is called wise because there is wisdom in the rational part. If, therefore, we take a jar full of wine as a certain whole whose parts are the jar and the wine, neither of the parts, that is, neither the jar nor the wine, will be in itself. But the whole, that is, the jar of wine, will be in itself insofar as each is its part, both the wine which is in the jar and the jar in which the wine is.

In this way, therefore, it happens that something is in itself.

439. Next where he says, "**In this sense then . . .**" [302], he shows that it does not happen that a thing is in itself primarily.

First he states his intention, distinguishing the modes in which something is and is not in itself. Secondly, where he says, "**Thus if we look . . .**" [303], he proves his position.

He says, therefore, that it does not happen that something is in itself primarily.

By stating the opposite view, he shows what it means for a thing to be in itself primarily. White is said to be in a body because the surface is in the body. Hence white is not primarily in the body, but in the surface. And similarly science is said primarily to be in

the soul, but not in the man in whom it is through the soul. Because of these, that is, the soul and the surface, there are statements in which a man is called white or wise. For the soul and the surface are as parts in the man; not that the surface is a part, but because it is related to the nature of a part insofar as it is something of the man, that is, the terminus of the body.

Moreover if we take wine and a jar independently of each other, they are not parts. Hence neither can be in itself. But when they are together, as when the jar is filled with wine, then, because the jar and the wine are then parts, the same thing will be in itself, as was explained, not primarily but through the parts. Likewise white is not in a man primarily, but through the body, and it is in the body through the surface. However it is not in the surface through anything else. Hence it is said to be primarily in the surface.

That in which something is primarily and that which is in it, for example, white and surface, are not the same thing. For surface and white differ according to species, and the nature and potency of each is different.

440. Having shown the difference between being in something primarily and not primarily, he next shows, where he says, "**Thus if we look . . .**" [303], that nothing is in itself primarily.

First he shows that nothing is primarily in itself per se, and secondly that nothing is primarily in itself per accidens, where he says, "**Nor is it possible . . .**" [305].

He establishes the first point in two ways, inductively and by reason.

He says, therefore, first that by considering inductively the individual modes determined above in which a thing is said to be in something, it appears that nothing is in itself primarily and per se. For nothing is a whole or a part or a genus of itself, and likewise in regard to the other modes. He posits this by concluding from what has been set down above. For just as it is clear in regard to white and surface, which are related as form and matter, that they differ in species and power, likewise all the other modes can be considered in the same way.

441. Next where he says, ". . . it can be seen by argument . . ." [304], he proves the same thing by reason.

He says that it is clear through reasoning that it is impossible for a thing to be in itself primarily and per se. For if a thing is primarily and per se in itself, it is necessary that the nature [ratio] of that in which something is and the nature [ratio] of that which is in it belong to the same thing in the same respect. Hence it is necessary that each of them, that is, the container and the contained, be both—for example, the jar would be both the jar and the wine, and the wine would be both the wine and the jar, if it happens that something is in itself primarily and per se. Hence, having granted this, namely, that the wine is both the jar and the wine, and the jar is both the wine and the jar, then if you say that one of them is in the other, for example wine is in the jar, it follows that the wine is received in the jar not insofar as it is wine, but insofar as the wine is the jar. Hence, if being in the jar primarily and per se happens to the jar from the fact that something is primarily and per se in itself, it follows that nothing can be said to be in the jar except insofar as it itself is the jar. And thus, if wine is said to be in the jar, it follows that being in the jar happens to the wine, not because the wine is wine, but because the wine is the jar.

And for the same reason, if the jar receives wine, it receives it not insofar as the jar is a jar, but insofar as the jar is wine. But this is impossible.

Hence it is clear that "that in which" and "that which is in this" differ in nature [ratio]. For the nature [ratio] of that which is in something is other than the nature [ratio] of that in which something is. Therefore it is not possible that a thing be in itself primarily and per se.

442. Next where he says, "Nor is it possible..." [305], he shows that nothing is in itself primarily and per accidens.

A thing is said to be in something per accidens when it is in it because of something else existing in it. For example, we say that a man is on the sea because he is on a ship which is on the sea. He is said to be on the sea primarily because this is not due to a part. Therefore, if it would happen that something is in itself primarily, although not per se but per accidens, it follows that it is in itself because something else is in it. And thus it follows that two bodies are in the same place, that is, the body which is in it and it itself which is in itself. Thus a jar will be in itself per accidens if the jar itself, whose nature is to receive something, is in itself and also that which is received—the wine—is in it. Therefore, if it follows that the jar is in itself because the wine is in the jar, then both the wine and the jar will be in the jar. And thus two bodies would be in the same place. Therefore it is clear that it is impossible for a thing to be in itself primarily.

Nevertheless, it must be understood that sometimes a thing is said to be in itself, not according to an affirmative understanding, which the Philosopher here rejects, but according to a negative understanding. In this sense "to be in itself" does not signify anything except "not being in another."

443. Next where he says, "**Zeno's problem** . . ." [306], he answers a certain difficulty.

First he disposes of Zeno's argument which was brought in to prove that place does not exist. The argument is that if place exists, it must be in another place, and so forth to infinity. But, as he says, this is not difficult to answer now that the modes in which a thing is said to be in something have been distinguished.

There is nothing to prevent one from saying that place is in something. Nevertheless, place is not in something as in a place, but rather according to one of the other modes, as form is in matter, or as an accident is in a subject, insofar as place is the terminus of that which contains.

And he adds this: [Place is in something] "as health is 'in' the hot as a positive determination of it or as the hot is "in" body as an affection" [210b26].

Hence it is not necessary to proceed to infinity.

444. Next where he says, "**Another thing is** . . ." [307], he answers the difficulties raised above as to whether it is the nature of place to be either form or matter. He does this from what has been shown, namely, that nothing is in itself primarily and per se. For from this it is clear that there can be no place or vase, as it were, of that which is contained in itself as a material or formal part. For it is necessary, as was shown, that "that which is in something" and "that in which something is" differ primarily and per se. Hence it follows that neither form nor matter is place. Rather place is something other than that which is located in place. For matter and form are intrinsic parts of that which is located in place.

Finally he concludes that the objections raised above concern place. Some of these objections have already been answered and some will be answered after the nature of place is made clear.

Certain Things Necessary to Investigate the Definition of Place Are Set Forth

The Text of Aristotle
Chapter 4

308. *What then after all is place? The answer to this question may be elucidated as follows. Let us take for granted about it the various characteristics which are supposed correctly to belong to it essentially. We assume then:*

(1) Place is what contains that of which it is the place.

(2) Place is no part of the thing.

(3) The immediate place of a thing is neither less nor greater than the thing.

(4) Place can be left behind by the thing and is separable. In addition:

(5) All place admits of the distinction of up and down, and each the bodies is naturally carried to its appropriate place and rests there, and this makes the place either up or down.

Having laid these foundations, we must complete the theory.   **210b32–211a7**

309. *We ought to try to make our investigation such as will render an account of place, and will not only solve the difficulties connected with it, but will also show that the attributes supposed to belong to it do really belong to it, and further will make clear the cause of the trouble and of the difficulties about it. Such is the most satisfactory kind of exposition.*
                                                                        211a7–12

310. *First then we must understand that place would not have been thought of, if there had not been a special kind of motion, namely that with respect to place. It is chiefly for this reason that we suppose the heaven also to be in place, because it is in constant movement. Of this kind of change there are two species—locomotion on the one hand and, on the other, increase and diminution. For these too involve variation of place: what was then in this place has now in turn changed to what is larger or smaller.*   **211a13–17**

311. *Again, when we say a thing is "moved," the predicate either (1) belongs to it actually, in virtue of its own nature, or (2) in virtue of something conjoined with it. In the latter case it may be either (a) something which by its own nature is capable of being moved, e.g., the parts of the body or the nail in the ship, or (b) something which is not in itself capable of being moved, but is always moved through its conjunction with something else, as "whiteness" or "science." These have changed their place only because the subjects to which they belong do so.*
                                                                        211a17–23

312. *We say that a thing is in the world, in the sense of in place, because it is in the air, and the air is in the world; and when we say it is in the air, we do not mean it is in every part of the air, but that it is in the air because of the outer surface of the air which surrounds it; for if all the air were its place, the place of a thing would not be equal to the thing—which it is supposed to be, and which the primary place in which a thing is actually is.*   **211a23–29**

313. *When what surrounds, then, is not separate from the thing, but is in continuity with it, the thing is said to be in what surrounds it, not in the sense of in place, but as a part in a whole. But when the thing is separate and in contact, it is immediately "in" the inner surface of the surrounding body, and this surface is neither a part of what is in it nor yet greater than its extension, but equal to it; for the extremities of things which touch are coincident.*   **211a29–34**

314. *Further, if one body is in continuity with another, it is not moved in that but with that. On the other hand it is moved in that if it is separate. It makes no difference whether what contains is moved or not.*   **211a34–211b1**

315. *Again, when it is not separate it is described as a part in a whole, as the pupil in the*

eye or the hand in the body: when it is separate, as the water in the cask or the wine in the jar.
For the hand is moved with the body and the water in the cask.   **211b1–5**

COMMENTARY OF ST. THOMAS

445. After the foregoing disputation as to whether place is and what it is, and after certain doubts have been answered, he here begins to determine the truth concerning place.

First he sets forth certain suppositions about place which he will use in treating place. Secondly, where he says, **"We ought to try . . ."** [309], he shows how the definition of place ought to be given. Thirdly, where he says, **"First then we must . . ."** [310], he begins to treat place.

446. He says, therefore, first [308] that what place is will become clear from what follows. It is necessary first to accept certain suppositions, as it were, and principles known per se, that is, those things which seem to belong to place per se.

There are four of these.

All men consider this to be worthwhile: first that place contains that of which it is the place, but nevertheless place is not part of that which is located in place. He says this to exclude the way in which form contains. For the form is part of the thing and contains in a different way than place.

The second supposition is that primary place, that is, that in which a thing is primarily, is equal to that which is located in place, and is neither greater nor smaller.

The third supposition is that place is not absent from anything that is located. Thus everything that is located has place. Nevertheless, this does not mean that one and the same place is never removed from some one thing that is located, because place is separable from that which is located. But when one place is removed from

something that is located, then that which is located comes to be in another place.

The fourth supposition is that upwards and downwards is found in all place as its differentia. Further each body which is outside its proper place is naturally carried to it, and when it is in it, it remains in it. Moreover, upwards and downwards are the proper places of natural bodies to which they are naturally moved and in which they remain. He says this in accordance with the opinion of those who do not posit any body beyond the nature of the four elements. For he has not yet proven that a celestial body is neither light nor heavy. But he will prove this later in De Caelo, I. Now from these suppositions he proceeds to the consideration of other things.

447. Next where he says, **"We ought to try . . ."** [309], he shows how the definition of place ought to be given.

He says that in defining place our attention should be directed to the four things which are required for a perfect definition.

First that it be shown what place is, for a definition is a statement indicating what a thing is.

Secondly that certain objections concerning place be answered, for knowledge of the truth is the solution of difficulties.

Thirdly that from the given definition the properties which are present in place be made clear, for the definition is the middle term in demonstration by which proper accidents are demonstrated of their subjects.

Fourthly that from the definition of place the reason why some have disagreed about place will be made clear, and the reason for all the objections concerning place will be made clear. In this way each thing is defined most perfectly.

448. Next where he says, **"First then we must . . ."** [310], he treats place.

First he shows what place is. Secondly, where he says, **"It is clear, too . . ."** [337], he answers the difficulties that were previously raised. Thirdly, where he says, **"Also it is reasonable . . ."** [338], he establishes the cause of the natural properties of place.

Concerning the first part he makes two points. First he shows what place is, and secondly, how something is in place, where he says, **"If then a body . . ."** [332].

Concerning the first part he makes two points. First he sets forth certain things which are necessary to investigate the definition of place. Secondly, where he says, **"It will now be plain . . ."** [316], he begins to investigate the definition of place.

449. Concerning the first part he sets forth four things. The first of these [310] is that there would have never been any inquiry about place if there were no motion in respect to place. For it was necessary to posit that place is different from that which is located in place, because two bodies are found successively in the same place, and likewise one body is found in two places. In the same way the transmutation of forms in one matter led to a knowledge of matter. And because the heavens are always moved some think that the heavens are in place. But some motions are motions in respect to place per se, that is, local motion, while other motions are motions in respect to place per accidens, that is, increase and diminution. For when quantity is in-

creased or decreased, the body takes on a larger or smaller place.

450. He gives the second point where he says, **"Again, when we say . . ."** [311]. He says that some things are moved per se and actually, for example, any body, while other things are moved per . This happens in two ways.

Some things which can be moved per se are moved per accidens. Thus the parts of a body, while they are in the whole, are moved per accidens, but when they are separated they are moved per se. For example, a nail when fixed in a ship is moved per accidens, but when it is freed from the ship it is moved per se.

Other things cannot be moved per se, but are always moved per accidens. For example, whiteness and science change in place insofar as that in which they are is changed.

He brings this up because in this way something per se or per accidens is constituted as being actually or potentially in place, and thus to be moved.

451. He gives the third point where he says, **"We say that a thing . . ."** [312]. He says that one is said to be in the heavens as in a place because he is in the air which is in the heavens. Nevertheless, we do not say that one is primarily and per se in all air. Rather one is said to be in the air because of the last extremity of the air which contains him. For if all air were the place of something, for example, a man, then the place and that which is located in the place would not be equal, which is contrary to the supposition given above. But that in which something is primarily seems to be the extremity of the containing body, and in this way it is equal.

452. He gives the fourth point where

he says, **"When what surrounds, then . . ."** [313].

First he states the point and secondly he proves it, where he says, **"Further, if one body . . ."** [314].

He says, therefore, first [313] that when the container is not divided from that which is contained, but is continuous with it, then the contained is not said to be in the container as in a place, but as a part is in a whole. For example, let us say that one part of air is contained by all air. He concludes this from the foregoing, for where there is a continuum there is no extremity in act, which he said above was required for place. But when the container is divided from and contiguous to that which is contained, then that which is contained is in place, existing in the extremity of the container primarily and per se. And the container, which is not part of the thing, is neither larger nor smaller in size, but equal. He explains how the container and that which is contained can be equal by the fact that the extremities of things which are contiguous exist together. Hence their extremities must be equal.

453. Next where he says, **"Further, if one body . . ."** [314], he proves this fourth point with two arguments.

The first argument is that, if that which is contained is continuous with the container, then it is not moved in the container but together with it, as a part is moved together with the whole. But when that which is contained is divided from the container, then it can be moved in it, whether the container is moved or not. For a man is moved in a ship whether the ship is at rest or in motion. Therefore, since things are moved in place, it follows that place is a divided container.

454. He gives the second argument where he says, **"Again, when it is not separate . . ."** [315].

He says that when that which is contained is not divided from the container but is continuous with it, then it is said to be in it as a part is in a whole. Thus sight is in the eye as a formal part, and the hand is in the body as an organic part. But when that which is contained is divided from the container, then it is said to be in it as in a vase, like water is in a jar and wine is in a cup. The difference between these is that the hand is moved with the body, but not in the body, while the water is moved in the jar. Therefore, since it was said above that being in place is like being in a vase, and not as a part in a whole, it follows that place is like a divided container.

LECTURE 6 [211b5–212a30]
The Definition of Place

The Text of Aristotle

316. *It will now be plain from these considerations what place is. There are just four things of which place must be one—the shape, or the matter, or some sort of extension between the bounding surfaces of the containing body, or this boundary itself if it contains no extension over and above the bulk of the body which comes to be in it.* **211b5–9**

317. *Three of these it obviously cannot be:* **211b9–10**

318. *(1) The shape is supposed to be place because it surrounds, for the extremities of what contains and of what is contained are coincident.* **211b10–12**

319. *Both the shape and the place, it is true, are boundaries. But not of the same thing: the form is the boundary of the thing, the place is the boundary of the body which contains it.* **211b12–14**

320. *(2) The extension between the extremities is thought to be something, because what is contained and separate may often be changed while the container remains the same (as water may be poured from a vessel)—the assumption being that the extension is something over and above the body displaced.* **211b14–17**

321. *But there is no such extension. One of the bodies which change places and are naturally capable of being in contact with the container falls in—whichever it may chance to be. If there were an extension which were such as to exist independently and be permanent, there would be an infinity of places in the same thing. For when the water and the air change places, all the portions of the two together will play the same part in the whole which was previously played by all the water in the vessel;* **211b18–23**

322. *at the same time the place too will be undergoing change; so that there will be another place which is the place of the place, and many places will be coincident. There is not a different place of the part, in which it is moved, when the whole vessel changes its place: it is always the same; for it is in the (proximate) place where they are that the air and the water (or the parts of the water) succeed each other, not in that place in which they come to be, which is part of the place which is the place of the whole world.* **211b23–29**

323. *(3) The matter, too, might seem to be place, at least if we consider it in what is at rest and is thus separate but in continuity. For just as in change of quality there is something which was formerly black and is now white, or formerly soft and now hard—this is just why we say that the matter exists—so place, because it presents a similar phenomenon, is thought to exist—only in the one case we say so because what was air is now water, in the other because where air formerly was there is now water.* **211b29–36**

324. *But the matter, as we said before, is neither separable from the thing nor contains it, whereas place has both characteristics.* **211b36–212a2**

325. *Well, then, if place is none of the three—neither the form nor the matter nor an extension which is always there, different from, and over and above, the extension of the thing which is displaced—place necessarily is the one of the four which is left, namely, the boundary of the containing body at which it is in contact with the contained body. (By the contained body is meant what can be moved by way of locomotion.)* **212a2–7**

326. *Place is thought to be something important and hard to grasp, both because the matter and the shape present themselves along with it, and because the displacement of the body that is moved takes place in a stationary container, for it seems possible that there should be an interval which is other than the bodies which are moved. The air, too, which is thought to be incorporeal,*

contributes something to the belief: it is not only the boundaries of the vessel which seem to be place, **212a7–14**

327. *but also what is between them, regarded as empty. Just, in fact, as the vessel is transportable place, so place is a non-portable vessel. So when what is within a thing which is moved, is moved and changes its place, as a boat on a river, what contains plays the part of a vessel rather than that of place. Place on the other hand is rather what is motionless: so it is rather the whole river that is place, because as a whole it is motionless.* **212a14–20**

328. *Hence we conclude that the innermost motionless boundary of what contains is place.* **212a20–21**

329. *This explains why the middle of the heaven and the surface which faces us of the rotating system are held to be "up" and "down" in the strict and fullest sense for all men: for the one is always at rest, while the inner side of the rotating body remains always coincident with itself. Hence since the light is what is naturally carried up, and the heavy what is carried down, the boundary which contains in the direction of the middle of the universe, and the middle itself, are down, and that which contains in the direction of the outermost part of the universe, and the outermost part itself, are up.* **212a21–28**

330. *For this reason, too, place is thought to be a kind of surface, and as it were a vessel, i.e. a container of the thing.* **212a28–29**

331. *Further, place is coincident with the thing, for boundaries are coincident with the bounded.* **212a29–30**

COMMENTARY OF ST. THOMAS

455. Having set forth those things which are necessary to investigate the definition of place, he here investigates the definition of place.

Concerning this he makes three points. First he investigates the parts of the definition. Secondly, where he says, **"Hence we conclude . . ."** [328], he concludes to the definition. Thirdly, where he says, **"This explains why . . ."** [329], he shows that the definition has been well established.

Concerning the first part he makes two points. First he investigates the genus of place, and secondly the complementary differentia of its definition, where he says, **"Place is thought to be . . ."** [326].

Furthermore to investigate the genus of place he makes use of a certain division. Concerning this he makes three points. First he proposes the division. Secondly, where he says, **"Three of these . . ."** [317], he rules out three members of this division. Thirdly,

where he says, **"Well, then, if place . . ."** [325], he concludes to the fourth.

456. He says, therefore, first [316] that what place is can now be made clear from what has been set forth.

According to the things that are customarily said about place, it seems that place is one of four things: either the matter, or the form, or the space between the extremities of the container, or if, between the extremities of the container which has dimensions, there is no space outside of the magnitude of the body which is within the containing body, then it will be necessary to mention a fourth possibility, that is, that place is the extremities of the containing body.

457. Next where he says, **"Three of these . . ."** [317], he rules out three members of the given division.

First he states his intention by saying that is clear through what follows that place is not one of the first three.

Secondly, he carries out his intention, first in regard to form, where he says, **"The shape is supposed . . ."** [318], secondly in regard to space, where he says, **"The extension between . . ."** [320], and thirdly in regard to matter, where he says, **"The matter, too . . ."** [323].

458. Concerning the first part he makes two points. First he explains why form would seem to be place. For the form contains, and this seems to be proper to place. The extremities of the containing body and the contained body are together, for the container and that which is contained are contiguous to each other. Thus the containing terminus, which is place, does not seem to be separated from the terminus of the contained body. And thus it seems that place does not differ from form.

459. Secondly, where he says, **"Both the shape and the place . . ."** [319], he shows that form is not place.

Although both place and form agree in that each of them is a certain terminus, nevertheless they are not termini of one and the same thing. Rather form is the terminus of the body of which it is the form, while place is not the terminus of the body of which it is the place, but of the body containing it. And although the termini of the container and of that which is contained are together, nevertheless they are not the same.

460. Next where he says, **"The extension between . . ."** [320], he treats space.

First he explains why space seems to be place. Secondly, where he says, **"But there is no such extension"** [321], he shows that space is not place.

He says, therefore, first that a body contained by place, and divided from

it, is frequently changed from place to place. And bodies reciprocally succeed each other in the same place, such that the container remains immobile, in the way in which water goes out of a vase. Because of this it seems that place is a certain intermediate space between the extremities of the containing body; as if there were something there other than the body which is moved from one place to another. For if there were not something there other than that body, it would follow either that place is not different from that which is located in place or that that which is an intermediate between the extremities of the container could not be place. Moreover just as place must be something other than the contained body, likewise it seems that place would have to be something other than the containing body, because place remains immobile, but the containing body and everything in it is subject to change. However, nothing other than the containing body and the contained body can be understood to be there except the dimensions of space existing in no body. Therefore since place is immobile, it seems that space is place.

461. Next where he says, **"But there is no such extension"** [321], he shows with two arguments that space is not place.

In the first argument he says that it is not true that there is something there within the extremities of the containing body and other than the contained body, which is borne from place to place. Rather within the extremities of the containing body there is a body, whatever it happens to be, which is a mobile body and which is one of those things which are suitably constituted to touch the containing body. But if there could be some intermediate containing space, which is other than the dimensions of the contained body, and which always remains in the same place, then this inconsistency would follow—an infinite number of places would be together. This is so because since water or air or any body or any part of a body would have proper dimensions, then every part will do the same thing in the whole as the water as a whole does in the vase. According to the position of those who believe in space, while the water as a whole is in the vase, there are there other dimensions of space besides the dimensions of the water. However every part is contained by the whole as that which is located is contained by the vase. They differ only in that the part is not divided, while that which is located is divided. Therefore if a part is actually divided, it follows that other dimensions of the whole container are there besides the dimensions of the part.

But it cannot be said that division makes some new dimensions to be there. For division does not cause dimension, rather it divides pre-existing dimension. Therefore before the part would be divided from the whole, there were other proper dimensions of the part besides the dimensions of the whole which pass into the parts. Therefore as many parts as are taken by division in some whole, such that one part contains another, so many dimensions had been distinct there from each other, certain of which passed into others. However, since a continuum is divided to infinity, this means that one takes in some continuous whole an infinity of parts which contain others. It follows, therefore, that there is an infinity of dimensions passing into each other. If, therefore, place is the dimensions of the containing body which

pass into that which is located, then it follows that an infinity of places exist together, which is impossible.

462. Next where he says, "... at the same time ..." [322], he gives the second argument which is as follows.

If the dimensions of the space which is between the extremities of the containing body are place, it follows that place would be changed. For it is clear that when a body, for example, a jar, is changed, the space which is between the extremities of the jar is changed, since the space is only where the jar is. Moreover according to their position everything which is changed to some place is penetrated by the dimensions of the space into which it is changed. It follows, therefore, that some other dimensions enter under the dimensions of the space of the jar. And thus there will be a place of place, and many places are together.

463. Now this difficulty occurs because the place of the contained body, or water, is taken as different from the place of the vase or jar. For according to their opinion the place of the water is the space which is within the extremities of the jar, and the place of the whole jar is the space which is within the extremities of the body which contains the jar. But we do not say that the place of the part, in which the part is moved, is different, since the whole vase is moved in the same way (by "part" here he means the body contained in the vase, as water is contained in the jar). For according to Aristotle, when the vase is moved, the water is moved per accidens, and it does not change its place except insofar as the jar changes its place. Hence it is not necessary that the place into which it goes is the place of the part per se, but only insofar as it is the place of

the jar. But according to those who believe in space, it follows that this place corresponds per se to both the water and the jar. It also follows that space corresponds to them per se, and properly speaking space will be moved and will have place, and not just per accidens.

Now although the containing body is sometimes moved, nevertheless it does not follow according to Aristotle's opinion that place is moved or that there is a place of place. For indeed it does happen that a containing body, in which something is contained, is moved, as air or water or some parts of water. For example, if a ship is on a river, the parts of the water which contain the ship from below are moved, but nevertheless the place is not moved. And he adds, "sed non in quo fiunt loco," [Thomas is quoting the Latin translation of Aristotle] which means, "but that in which things come to be as in a place does not move" [211b28].

He explains how this is true when he adds, "... which is part of the place which is the place of the whole world" [211b29]. For although this container is moved insofar as it is this body, nevertheless, considered according to the order which it has to the whole body of the world, it is not moved. For the other body which succeeds it has the same order and site in comparison to the whole world which the body which previously left had. He, therefore, says that although the water or air is moved, nevertheless the place, considered as a certain part of the place of the whole world having a determined site in the universe, is not moved.

464. Next where he says, "The matter, too ..." [323], he treats matter.

First he explains why matter seems to be place. Secondly, where he says, "But the matter ..." [324], he shows that matter is not place.

He says, therefore, first that matter seems to be place if one considers the transmutation of bodies succeeding each other in the same place, in some one subject which is at rest in respect to place. Attention is not directed here to the fact that place is separated, but rather only to a transmutation in some one continuum. For when a body, which is a continuum and at rest in respect to place, is altered, then that which is one and the same in number is now white, then black, now soft, then hard. Because of this transmutation of forms in a subject, we say that matter is something which remains one when a transmutation of form occurs. And through similar evidence it seems that place is something. For diverse bodies succeed each other in a place which remains permanent.

But we use a different way of speaking in each of these cases. For to designate matter or a subject we say that that which is now water formerly was air. But to designate the unity of place we say that where water now is, there formerly was air.

465. Next where he says, "But the matter ..." [324], he shows that matter is not place. For, as was said above, matter is not divided from that of which it is the matter, nor does it contain it. But both of these characteristics belong to place. Therefore place is not matter.

466. Next where he says, "Well, then, if place ..." [325], having ruled out three members, he concludes to the fourth. He says that, since place is not one of these three, that is, neither the form, nor the matter, nor the space which is other than the dimensions of that which is located, then it is neces-

sary that place is the one member that remains of the four named above, that is, that place is the terminus of the containing body. And lest someone think that that which is contained or located is some intermediate space, he adds that the contained body is called that whose nature it is to be moved in respect to change of place.

467. Next where he says, **"Place is thought to be . . ."** [326], he investigates the differentia of place, that is, that it is immobile.

Concerning this he makes two points. First he shows that a certain error about place arises if this differentia is not properly considered. Secondly, where he says, **"Just, in fact, as the vessel . . ."** [327], he shows how the immobility of place must be understood.

He says, therefore, first that to establish what place is is something important and difficult. One reason for this is that to some it seems that place is matter or form, which require the highest contemplation, as was said above. Another reason is that change in respect to place occurs in something which is at rest and which contains. Since, therefore, nothing seems to contain and to be immobile except space, it seems that place is a certain intermediate space which is different from the magnitudes which are moved in respect to place. The fact that air seems to be incorporeal contributes much to the credibility of this opinion. For where air is, there seems to be no body, but rather a certain spatial vacuum. And thus it seems that place not only is the terminus of the vase but also a certain medium, a vacuum as it were.

468. Next where he says, **"Just, in fact, as the vessel . . ."** [327], in order to exclude the above opinion, he explains how the immobility of place must be understood.

He says that a vase and place seem to differ in that the vase is moved but place is not. Hence, as the vase can be called a movable place, likewise place can be called an immobile vase. Therefore, when something is moved in some body which is moved, as a ship in a river, he refers to that in which it is moved more as a vase than as a containing place. For place "wishes to be immobile," that is, it is appropriate and natural to place for it to be immobile. Because of this it is better to say that the whole river is the place of the ship, for the whole river is immobile. Thus, therefore, the whole river, insofar as it is immobile, is a common place.

However since proper place is part of common place, it is necessary to assign the proper place of the ship in the water of the river, insofar as it has an order to the whole river as immobile. Therefore the place of the ship is determined in the flowing water, not in respect to this water which flows, but in respect to the order or site which this flowing water has to the whole river. And indeed this order or site remains the same in the water which succeeds. Therefore, although the water flows by materially, nevertheless it does not change insofar as it has the nature place, that is, insofar as it is considered in such an order and site in the whole river.

In like manner we ought to say that the extremities of natural mobile bodies are place in respect to the whole spherical body of the heavens, which is fixed and immobile because of the immobility of the center and the poles. Thus, although this part of air contains, or this part of water flows and is moved insofar as it is this water, nevertheless, insofar as this water has the nature of place, that is, a site and order in the whole sphere of the heavens, it always remains permanent.

In a similar way fire is said to remain the same in respect to form, although in respect to matter it changes as different wood is added and consumed.

469. By means of this an objection which can be made against our position that place is the terminus of the container is overcome. Since the container is mobile, the terminus of the container will also be mobile. And thus a thing existing at rest will have diverse places. But this does not follow. For the terminus of the container is not a place insofar as it is these surfaces of this mobile body, but insofar as it has an order or site in an immobile whole. From this it is clear that the whole nature [ratio] of place in everything that contains is from the first container and locator, that is, the heavens.

470. Next where he says, **"Hence we conclude . . ."** [328], he concludes the definition of place from the above; that is, place is the immobile terminus of that which contains primarily. He says "primarily" in order to designate proper place and exclude common place.

471. Next where he says, **"This explains why . . ."** [329], he shows that this definition has been well established because the things which are said of place agree with this definition.

He makes three points. The first is that, since place is an immobile container, the middle of the heavens, that is, the center, and the extremity of circular local motion, that is, the extremity of bodies moved in a circle (the extremity, I say, towards us, that is, the surfaces of the moon), are such that the one—the extremity—seems to be up-ward, and the other—the middle—seems to be downward. And above all things it is most properly said that the center of the sphere always remains permanent. And although the extremity of bodies moved towards us in a circle moves in a circle, nevertheless it remains permanent insofar as it is similarly related, that is, it is the same distance from us. And since natural bodies are moved to their proper places, light bodies are naturally moved upwards and heavy bodies downwards. For both the middle itself and the terminus containing towards the middle are called downwards. And likewise both the extremity and that which is towards the extremity are said to be upwards. Moreover he uses such a way of speaking because the middle is the place of earth, which is heavy simply. But the place of water is towards the middle. And likewise the extremity is the place of fire, which is light simply. But the place of air is towards the extremity.

He gives the second point where he says, **"For this reason, too . . ."** [330]. He says that since place is a terminus, place seems to be like certain surfaces and like a certain containing vase, but not like the space of a containing vase.

He gives the third point where he says, **"Further, place is coincident..."** [331]. He says that since place is a terminus, place and that which is located exist together. For the boundary of that which is located and the terminus of the container, which is place, exist together, because the extremities of things which touch exist together. And according to this it is also understood that place is equal to that which is located, because they are equal in respect to the extremities.

What Things Are in Place Simply. How that Which Is Not in Place Simply Is in Place Accidentally

The Text of Aristotle
Chapter 5

332. *If then a body has another body outside it and containing it, it is in place, and if not, not.*   212a31–32

333. *That is why, even if there were to be water which had not a container, the parts of it, on the one hand, will be moved (for one part is contained in another), while, on the other hand, the whole will be moved in one sense, but not in another. For as a whole it does not simultaneously change its place, though it will be moved in a circle; for this place is the place of its parts. (Some things are moved, not up and down, but in a circle; others up and down, such things namely as admit of condensation and rarefaction.)*   212a32–212b3

334. *As was explained, some things are potentially in place, others actually. So, when you have a homogeneous substance which is continuous, the parts are potentially in place: when the parts are separated, but in contact, like a heap, they are actually in place.*   212b3–6

335. *Again, (1) some things are per se in place, namely every body which is movable either by way of locomotion or by way of increase is per se somewhere, but the heaven, as has been said, is not anywhere as a whole, nor in any place, if, at least, as we must suppose, no body contains it. On the line on which it is moved, its parts have place; for each is contiguous to the next.*

But (2) other things are in place indirectly, through something conjoined with them, as the soul and the heaven. The latter is, in a way, in place, for all its parts are; for on the orb one part contains another.   212b7–13

336. *That is why the upper part is moved in a circle, while the All is not anywhere. For what is somewhere is itself something, and there must be alongside it some other thing wherein it is and which contains it. But alongside the All or the Whole there is nothing outside the All, and for this reason all things are in the heaven; for the heaven, we may say, is the All. Yet their place is not the same as the heaven. It is part of it, the innermost part of it, which is in contact with the movable body; and for this reason the earth is in water, and this in the air, and the air in the aether, and the aether in heaven, but we cannot go on and say that the heaven is in anything else.*   212b13–22

COMMENTARY OF ST. THOMAS

472. After the Philosopher has defined place, he here explains how a thing is in place.

Concerning this he makes two points. First he explains how a thing is in place simply and how not. Secondly, where he says, **"That is why ..."** [333], he explains how that which is not in place simply is in place accidentally.

473. First [332], therefore, he concludes from the foregoing that, since place is the terminus of the container, then any body is in place simply and per se when it is adjacent to another body which contains it from the outside. And a body is least of all in place when it is not adjacent to another body which contains it from the outside. Moreover, there is only one such body in the world, that is, the ultimate sphere, whatever that might be. Hence according to this position it follows that the ultimate sphere is not in place.

474. But this seems impossible. For

the ultimate sphere is moved in place, but nothing which is not in place is moved in place.

This difficulty does not arise for those who hold a belief in space. For it is not necessary for them to say that the ultimate sphere has a containing body in order for it to be in place. Rather, according to them, space, which is understood to penetrate the whole world and all its parts, is the place of the whole world and each of its parts.

But this position is impossible. For it is necessary to say either that place is not something other than that which is located, or that there are dimensions of space which exist per se and nevertheless which enter into the dimensions of sensible bodies. Both of these are impossible.

475. Hence Alexander said that the ultimate sphere in no way is in place. For not every body is necessarily in place, since place does not fall in the definition of body. Because of this he said that the ultimate sphere is not moved in place, either in respect to the whole or in respect to the parts.

But because it is necessary for every motion to be in some genus of motion, Avicenna, following him, said that the motion of the ultimate sphere is not a motion in place, but a motion in site. This is contrary to Aristotle, who says in Book V of this work that there is motion in only three genera, that is, in quantity, quality, and place.

But this position cannot stand. For it is impossible for there to be motion per se speaking in a genus the nature [ratio] of whose species consists in indivisibility. Because of this there is no motion in substance, for the nature [ratio] of each species of substance consists in indivisibility, that is, the species of substance are not said to be greater or less. And also, since motion has succession, substantial form is not produced in existence through motion but through generation, which is the terminus of motion. However, it is quite otherwise with whiteness and other similar things which are participated according to greater or less. Now each species of site has a nature consisting in indivisibility, such that if something is added or subtracted it is not the same species of site. Hence it is impossible that there be motion in the genus of site.

And furthermore the same difficulty remains. For site, insofar as it is a predicament, involves an order of parts in place. Although insofar as site is a differentia of quantity, it does not involve anything except an order of parts in the whole. Therefore it is necessary that whatever is moved in respect to site is moved in respect to place.

476. Moreover others have said, for example, Avempace, that the place of a body which is moved in a circle must be explained differently than the place of a body which is moved in a straight line. For since a straight line is imperfect because it receives addition, a body which is moved in a straight line requires a place which contains it from the outside. But since a circular line is perfect in itself, a body which moves in a circle does not require a place which contains it from the outside, but a place about which it revolves. Hence circular motion is also said to be motion around a middle. Thus they say that the convex surface of the contained sphere is the place of the first sphere. But this is contrary to the common suppositions about place given above, that is, place is a container and place is equal to that which is located.

477. Therefore Averroes said that the ultimate sphere is in place accidentally.

To understand this it must be realized that everything which is held fast by another is said to be in place accidentally due to the fact that that by which it is held fast is in place. This is clear in regard to a nail fixed in a ship, and in regard to a man at rest in the ship. Now it is clear that bodies moved in a circle are held fast by the immobility of the center. Hence the ultimate sphere is said to be in place accidentally insofar as the center about which it revolves exists in place. And it happens that the other inferior spheres have a place per se in which they are contained. But this is not necessarily true of bodies moved in a circle.

But against this one can object that, if the ultimate sphere is in place accidentally, then it follows that it is moved in place accidentally. And thus motion per accidens is prior to motion per se. But to this one can respond that in regard to circular motion it is not required that that which moves per se in a circle is per se in place. However this is required for straight motion.

But this seems to be contrary to Aristotle's definition, given above, of that which is in place accidentally. For he said that things exist or are moved in place accidentally because that in which they are is moved. But a thing is not said to be in place accidentally because something which is altogether extrinsic to it is in place. Since, therefore, the center is altogether extrinsic to the ultimate sphere, it seems ridiculous to say that the ultimate sphere is in place accidentally because the center is in place.

478. Therefore I will rather approve the opinion of Themistius, who said that the ultimate sphere is in place through its parts.

To understand this it must be realized, as Aristotle said above, that place would not be investigated if it were not for motion, which calls attention to place because bodies succeed each other in one place. Hence although a body does not of necessity have place, nevertheless, a body which is moved in respect to place does have place of necessity. Therefore, it is necessary to assign place to a body moved in place insofar as one considers in that motion a succession of diverse bodies in the same place. Thus in things which are moved in a straight line, it is clear that two bodies succeed each other in place in respect to the whole. For the whole of one body leaves the whole place and into that whole place another body enters. Hence it is necessary that a body which is moved in a straight line is in place in respect to its whole self.

But in circular motion, although the whole comes to be in diverse places by reason [ratio], nevertheless the whole does not change place in the subject. For the place always remains the same in the subject, and it is diversified only by reason [ratio], as will be said in Book VI of this work. But the parts change place not only according to reason [ratio] but also in the subject. Therefore, in circular motion attention is directed to succession in the same place, not of whole bodies, but of parts of the same body. Hence for a body moved in a circle a place in respect to the whole is not due of necessity, but only in respect to the parts.

479. But contrary to this it seems that the parts of a continuous body are not in place nor are they moved in respect to place. Rather the whole is moved and the whole is in place. How-

ever it is clear that the ultimate sphere is a continuous body. Therefore its parts are not in place and are not moved in respect to place. And thus it does not seem to be true that place belongs to the ultimate sphere by reason [ratio] of the parts.

But to this it must be said that, although the parts of a continuous whole are not actually in place, nevertheless they are potentially in place insofar as the continuum is divisible. For if a part is divided, it will be in the whole as in a place. Hence in this way the parts of the continuum are moved in place. This is especially apparent in continuous liquids which are easily divided, as in water whose parts are found to be moved within the water as a whole. Therefore, since something is said of a whole by reason [ratio] of the parts, insofar as the parts of the ultimate sphere are potentially in place, the whole ultimate sphere is in place accidentally by reason [ratio] of the parts. And to be thus in place suffices for circular motion.

480. However, one might object that that which is in act is prior to that which is in potency, and thus it seems unsuitable that the first local motion is of a body existing in place through parts, which are potentially in place. To this it must be said that this especially agrees with the first motion. For it is necessary to descend gradually from the one immobile thing to the diversity which is in mobile things. Now the variation according to parts existing potentially in place is less than that according to a whole existing actually in place. Hence the first motion, which is circular and which exists closer to the immobile substances, has less deformity and retains more uniformity. Moreover it is much more suitable to say that the ultimate sphere is in place because of its own intrinsic parts than because of the center which is altogether outside of its substance. And this is more consonant with the opinion of Aristotle, as is clear to one who examines what follows, in which the Philosopher explains how the heavens are in place, where he says, "That is why . . ." [333].

481. Concerning this he makes two points. First he explains how the ultimate sphere is in place. Secondly, where he says, "That is why the upper part . . ." [336], he infers a conclusion from what has been said.

Concerning the first part he makes three points. First he shows that the ultimate sphere is in place through its parts. Secondly, where he says, "As was explained . . ." [334], he explains how its parts are in place. Thirdly, where he says, "Again, some things are . . ." [335], he explains how from the parts it belongs to the whole to be in place.

482. He has said that that which does not have something outside containing it is not in place per se. Therefore, he concludes that if water (concerning which what he is saying is more apparent because of the easy division of its parts) is a body of such a kind that it is not contained by another, as is the ultimate sphere, then its parts will be moved insofar as they are contained under each other, thus existing in some way in place. But the water as a whole in one way will be moved and in another way not. For it will not be moved such that the whole together changes place, as if moved to another place different in subject. But it will be moved in a circle, which motion indeed requires place for the parts but not for the whole. And it will not be moved upwards and downwards, but in a circle. However certain things will

be moved upwards and downwards, changing place in respect to the whole, that is, rare and dense bodies, and heavy and light bodies.

483. Next where he says, **"As was explained . . ."** [334], he explains how the parts of the ultimate sphere are in place. He says, as was said above, that certain things are actually in place and certain things are potentially in place. Hence when a thing is a continuum of similar parts, its parts are potentially in place, as is the case with the ultimate sphere. But when the parts are separated and only contiguous, as happens in a pile of stones, then the parts are actually in place.

484. Next where he says, **"Again, some things are . . ."** [335], he shows how it follows from this that the whole sphere is in place.

He says that certain things are in place per se, as any body which is moved per se in place either by change of place or by increase, as was said above. But the heavens, that is, the ultimate sphere, is not in place in this way, as was said, since no body contains it. But insofar as it is moved in a circle, its parts succeeding each other, place belongs potentially to its parts, as was said, insofar as one of its parts is a "habit," that is, insofar as it is consequently related to another.

Certain things, as the soul and all forms, are in place accidentally. And in this way the heavens, that is, the ultimate sphere, also is in place, insofar as all its parts are in place because each of its parts is contained under the others by the circulation. For in a non-circular body the extreme part remains not contained but only containing. But in a circular body each part is both container and contained, although potentially. Hence by reason [ratio] of all its parts a circular body is in place. And he

takes this to be accidental, that is, through the parts, as above when he said that the parts of a body are moved accidentally in place.

485. Next where he says, **"That is why the upper part . . ."** [336], he induces a certain conclusion from the foregoing.

Since he has said that a body moved in a circle cannot be in place in respect to the whole, but only accidentally by reason [ratio] of the parts, he concludes that the highest body is moved only in a circle because that whole is not anywhere. For that which is somewhere is something and has something outside itself by which it is contained. But outside the whole there is nothing. And because of this all things are said to be in the heavens as in the ultimate container. For the heavens perhaps are the containing whole. He says "perhaps" because it has not yet been proven that there is nothing outside the heavens. However, it must not be thought that place is the body of the heavens, but rather that place is a certain ultimate surface of the heavens toward us, and is like a terminus touching the mobile bodies which are in it. Because of this we say that earth is in water, which is in air, which is in aether, that is, fire, which is in the heavens, which is not further in another.

486. According to Averroes this text must be explained otherwise. The example of the water, which Aristotle brings in first, must not be referred according to Averroes to the ultimate sphere, but to the whole universe, which indeed is moved insofar as its parts are moved. Certain parts, the celestial bodies, are moved in a circle, and others, the inferior bodies, are moved upwards and downwards. That which Aristotle brings in later,

i.e., that certain things are actually in place and others potentially in place, must not be referred to what was previously said, but must be taken as said on its own account. For since Aristotle has said that certain things are in place in respect to the parts and others in respect to the whole, he consequently adds that certain things are actually in place and others potentially in place—and further that certain things are in place per se and others accidentally.

Regarding this it must be noted that according to Averroes the "heavens" is taken here in two ways. First the "heavens" is taken to mean the universe of bodies, especially celestial bodies. Secondly the "heavens" is taken to mean the ultimate sphere. Therefore he says that those things are per se in place which are moved in place, either in respect to the whole or to the parts, as the heavens, that is, the universe. But things like the soul or the heavens, that is, the ultimate sphere, are accidentally in place. For it is necessary to say that all the parts of the universe are in place in some way, the ultimate sphere accidentally, and other bodies per se, insofar as they are contained by an exterior body. And he maintains this constantly to the end.

LECTURE 8 [212b23–213a10]
From the Given Definition of Place the Difficulties Raised in Lecture 2 Are Solved, and the Nature of the Properties of Place is Established

The Text of Aristotle

337. It is clear, too, from these considerations that all the problems which were raised about place will be solved when it is explained in this way: (1) There is no necessity that the place should grow with the body in it, (2) Nor that a point should have a place, (3) Nor that two bodies should be in the same place, (4) Nor that place should be a corporeal interval: for what is between the boundaries of the place is any body which may chance to be there, not an interval in body. Further, (5) place is also somewhere, not in the sense of being in a place, but as the limit is in the limited; for not everything that is in place, but only movable body. **212b22–29**

338. Also (6) it is reasonable that each kind of body should be carried to its own place. For a body which is next in the series and in contact (not by compulsion) is akin, and bodies which are united do not affect each other, while those which are in contact interact on each other. **212b29–33**

339. Nor (7) is it without reason that each should remain naturally in its proper place. For this part has the same relation to its place, as a separable part to its whole, as when one moves a part of water or air: so, too, air is related to water, for the one is like matter, the other form—water is the matter of air, air as it were the actuality of water; for water is potentially air, while air is potentially water, though in another way. These distinctions will be drawn more carefully later. On the present occasion it was necessary to refer to them: what has now been stated obscurely will then be made more clear. If the matter and the fulfilment are the same thing (for water is both, the one potentially, the other completely), water will be related to air in a way as part to whole. That is why these have contact: it is organic union when both become actually one.

This concludes my account of place—both of its existence and of its nature. **212b33–213a11**

COMMENTARY OF ST. THOMAS

487. After the Philosopher has shown what place is, here from the given definition he answers the difficulties about place which were raised above in Lesson Two..

Six arguments were given above to show that place does not exist. He omits two of these; namely, the argument in which it was asked whether place is an element or composed of elements, and the argument in which it was shown that place is not reduced to any genus of cause. For those who posit place do not posit it as an element or cause of things. Hence he makes mention only of the four remaining arguments.

488. The first of these was that, since place is not absent from body nor is body absent from place, then it seems to follow that when a body is increased the place is increased.

But this follows on the supposition that place is a certain space coextensive with the dimensions of the body. Thus when the body grows, that space is understood to grow. But this is not necessary according to the given definition of place, which is the terminus of the container.

489. Another argument was that if the place of a body is other than the body, then also the place of a point is other than the point. Hence it does not

seem possible that place is other than the body, for the place of a point is not other than the point.

But this argument proceeds according to the imagination of those who think that place is a space equal to the dimensions of the body. Hence it would be necessary for a dimension of space to correspond to each dimension of the body, and likewise to each point of the body. But this need not be said if we hold that place is the terminus of the container.

490. Another argument was that if place is something it must be a body because it has three dimensions. And thus it would follow that two bodies are in the same place.

But, according to those who hold that place is the terminus of the containing body, it need not be said that two bodies are in the same place, nor that there is any intermediate corporeal space between the extremities of the containing body. Rather some body is there.

491. Another argument was that if everything that is is in place, it would follow that even place is in place.

This argument is easily solved on the supposition that place is the terminus of the container. For according to this it is clear that place is in something, that is, in the containing body, not as in a place but as the terminus in some finite thing, as a point is in a line and as a surface is in a body. For it is not necessary that everything which is is in something as in a place. This is necessary only for mobile bodies. For motion leads one to distinguish between place and that which is located.

492. Next where he says, "Also it is reasonable . . ." [338], he establishes from the given definition the nature [ratio] of the properties of place. He shows first that a body is naturally car-

ried to its proper place, and secondly, where he says, "Nor is it without reason . . ." [339], that a body naturally remains in its own place.

He says, therefore, first that if place is said to be the terminus of the container, then the cause of each body being carried to its proper place can be reasonably established. For the containing body, to which the contained and located body is consequently related and which is touched by the contained body since their termini exist together, is next to the contained body by nature and not by violence. Now the order of site in the parts of the universe is established according to the order of nature. For that celestial body which is the highest is the most noble. After this according to the nobility of nature among other bodies is fire, and so forth down to earth. Hence it is clear that an inferior body, which is consequently related according to site to a superior body, is next to it in the order of nature. Therefore he adds "not by force" to designate the natural order of site to which the order of natures corresponds. He excludes a violent order of site, as when a terrestrial body is above air or water through violence. And two bodies, which follow each other in the natural order of site and which are established as naturally together in the order of natures, are inactive, i.e., when they are continuous to each other and become one, for which they have an aptitude because of their closeness of nature, then they are inactive. But when distinct existents touch, they are active and passive toward each other because of the opposition of active and passive qualities. Therefore the proximity of nature between the containing and contained body is the reason why a body is naturally moved to its own place. For it is necessary that the gradation of natural places corresponds to the gradation of natures, as was said. But this reason cannot be used if place is space. For in separated dimensions of space no order of nature can be considered.

493. Next where he says, **"Nor is it without reason . . ."** [339], he establishes the cause of bodies being naturally at rest in their own places.

He says that this happens reasonably if we hold that place is the terminus of the containing body. For according to this a located body is related to the containing body as a part to a whole, although it is divided. This appears more clearly in bodies which are easily divided, like air or water, whose parts can be moved by something in the whole, as that which is located is moved in place. And this is true not only as an example of containing one thing under another, but also as a property of nature. For air is related to water as a whole, since water is as matter and air as form. For water is, as it were, the matter of air, and air is as its form. This is apparent because water is in potency to air simply.

But it is true that air also is in a certain way in potency to water, as will be determined later in De Generatione et Corruptione. At the present time it is necessary to accept this in order to explain his position. This is not stated with certitude here, but in De Generatione et Corruptione it will be more certainly stated. For there it will be said that, when air is generated from water, the corruption is accidental and the generation is simple, because a more perfect form is introduced and a more imperfect form

is abandoned. But when water is generated from air, the corruption is simple and the generation is accidental, because a more perfect form is abandoned and a more imperfect form is introduced. Therefore water is simply in potency to air, as imperfect to perfect, but air is in potency to water as perfect to imperfect. Hence air is related as a form and as a whole, which has the nature [ratio] of a form. But water is related as matter and as a part, which pertains to the nature [ratio] of matter. Therefore, although the same thing is both matter and act, since water contains both in itself, nevertheless, the one, that is, the water as imperfect, is in potency properly speaking, and the other, that is, the air, is in act as perfect. Hence water will be related to air in a certain way as a part to a whole. Therefore, when air and water are two distinct things, they touch. But when one thing comes to be from either of them by one changing into the nature of the other, then a union or continuity comes to be. Thus a part is naturally at rest in a whole, as also a body is at rest in its own natural place.

Nevertheless it must be realized that the Philosopher is here speaking of bodies in respect to their substantial forms, which they have from the influence of a celestial body, which is the first place and which gives locating power to all other bodies. But in respect to active and passive qualities, there is opposition among the elements, and one is corruptive of another.

Finally he concludes that the questions of whether place is and what it is have been treated.

The Treatment of the Void Pertains to Natural Philosophy. Opinions and Arguments Affirming and Denying the Existence of the Void

The Text of Aristotle
Chapter 6

340. *The investigation of similar questions about the void, also, must be held to belong to the physicist—namely whether it exists or not, and how it exists or what it is—just as about place. The views taken of it involve arguments both for and against, in much the same sort of way. For those who hold that the void exists regard it as a sort of place or vessel which is supposed to be "full" when it holds the bulk which it is capable of containing, "void" when it is deprived of that—as if "void" and "full" and "place" denoted the same thing, though the essence of the three is different.*   **213a11–19**

341. *We must begin the inquiry by putting down the account given by those who say that it exists, then the account of those who say that it does not exist, and third the current view on these questions.*   **213a19–22**

342. *Those who try to show that the void does not exist do not disprove what people really mean by it, but only their erroneous way of speaking; this is true of Anaxagoras and of those who refute the existence of the void in this way. They merely give an ingenious demonstration that air is something—by straining wine-skins and showing the resistance of the air, and by cutting it off in clepsydras. But people really mean that there is an empty interval in which there is no sensible body. They hold that everything which is is body and say that what has nothing in it at all is void (so what is full of air is void). It is not then the existence of air that needs to be proved, but the non-existence of an interval, different from the bodies, either separable or actual—an interval which divides the whole body so as to break its continuity, as Democritus and Leucippus hold, and many other physicists—or even perhaps as something which is outside the whole body, which remains continuous. These people, then, have not reached even the threshold of the problem, but rather those who say that the void exists.*   **213a22–213b3**

343. *(1) They argue, for one thing, that change in place (.e. locomotion and increase) would not be. For it is maintained that motion would seem not to exist, if there were no void, since what is full cannot contain anything more. If it could, and there were two bodies in the same place, it would also be true that any number of bodies could be together; for it is impossible to draw a line of division beyond which the statement would become untrue. If this were possible, it would follow also that the smallest body would contain the greatest; for "many a little makes a mickle": thus if many equal bodies can be together, so also can many unequal bodies.*   **213b3–12**

344. *Melissus, indeed, infers from these considerations that the All is immovable; for if it were moved there must, he says, be void, but void is not among the things that exist. This argument, then, is one way in which they show that there is a void.*   **213b12–15**

345. *(2) They reason from the fact that some things are observed to contract and be compressed, as people say that a cask will hold the wine which formerly filled it, along with the skins into which the wine has been decanted, which implies that the compressed body contracts into the voids present in it.*   **213b15–18**

346. *Again (3) increase, too, is thought to take place always by means of void; for nutriment is body, and it is impossible for two bodies to be together.*   **213b18–20**

347. *A proof of this they find also in what happens to ashes, which absorb as much water as the empty vessel.*   213b21–22

348. *The Pythagoreans, too, (4) held that void exists and that it enters the heaven itself, which as it were inhales it, from the infinite air. Further it is the void which distinguishes the natures of things, as if it were like what separates and distinguishes the terms of a series. This holds primarily in the numbers; for the void distinguishes their nature. These, then, and so many, are the main grounds on which people have argued for and against the existence of the void.*   213b22–29

COMMENTARY OF ST. THOMAS

494. After the Philosopher has treated place, he here treats the void.

Concerning this he makes two points. First, he explains his intention. Secondly, where he says, **"Those who try to show ..."** [342], he takes up what he has proposed.

Concerning the first part he makes two points. First he shows that the treatment of the void pertains to natural philosophy. Secondly, where he says, **"We must begin ..."** [341], he explains the order in which the void must be treated.

He says, therefore, first [340] that just as the treatment of whether place is and what place is pertains to natural philosophy, so does the treatment of the void. For through similar arguments some have believed and some have disbelieved in the existence of place and the void. Those who say that a void exists posit it as a certain place and a certain vase. For indeed a vase or a place seems to be full when it has in itself the mass of some body; and when it does not, it is said to be void. It is as if place, the void, and the plenum are the same in subject, and differ only according to reason [ratio].

495. Next where he says, **"We must begin ..."** [341], he explains the order in which the void must be treated.

He says that it is necessary to begin by giving the arguments of those who say that a void exists, next the argu-

ments of those who say that a void does not exist, and lastly common opinions about the void, that is, what pertains to the nature [ratio] of a void.

496. Next where he says, **"Those who try to show . . ."** [342], he does what he has said.

First he sets forth those things which are necessary for seeking the truth about the void. Secondly, where he says, **"Let us explain again . . ."** [360], he begins to seek out the truth.

Concerning the first part he makes two points. First he gives the arguments of those who affirm and of those who deny the existence of a void. Secondly, where he says, **"As a step towards . . ."** [349], he gives the common opinion of the void, showing what is the nature [ratio] of the void.

Concerning the first part he makes two points. First he gives the argument of those who deny the existence of a void, and secondly, where he says, **"They argue, for one thing . . ."** [343], the arguments of those who affirm the existence of a void.

497. He says, therefore, first [342] that some of the ancient philosophers, wishing to show that a void does not exist, erred in that they did not argue against the reasoning of those who hold that a void does exist. For they did not show that a void does not exist. Rather they brought in their own arguments to show that that which is full of

air is not a void. This is true of Anaxagoras and others who argue in similar ways. To deny a void they wished to show that air is something, and thus, since a void is that in which nothing is, it follows that that which is full of air is not a void.

They showed that air is something by arguing with their adversaries by means of bags made of animal skin, which, when inflated, can sustain something heavy. This could not be unless air were something. Thus they showed that air is resistant. They also showed this by putting air in clepsydras (that is, in vases which withdraw water) into which water is drawn when the air is withdrawn. Furthermore the entrance of the water is impeded unless the air is removed.

It is clear, therefore, that these men do not object to the position. For everyone who holds that a void exists wishes it to be a void of space in which there is no sensible body. The reason for this is that they think that everything which is is a sensible body, and thus, where there is no sensible body, they believe that there is nothing. Hence, since air is a moderately sensible body, they think that, where there is nothing except air, there is a void.

498. Therefore, to refute their position it is not sufficient to show that air is something. Rather it is necessary to show that there is no space without a sensible body. Further some posit the existence of a void in two ways: first as something separated from bodies, as if we would say that the space which is between the extremities of a house is a void; secondly as actually existing within bodies and distinguishing bodies from each other so that they are not continuous, as Democritus, Leucippus, and many other natural philosophers have said. For they imagine that if the whole of being were continuous, everything would be one. For there would be nothing to determine why bodies should be distinguished here rather than there. Hence between all distinct bodies they held that a spatial void intervenes in which there is no being. And since Democritus held that bodies are composed of many indivisible bodies, in the intervals between these indivisible bodies he posited certain voids, which he called "pores." Thus he said that all bodies are composed of the plenum and the void. And even if the whole body of the world is a continuum and there is no void between the parts of the universe, nevertheless they held that there is a void outside the whole world.

Therefore, it is clear that the above mentioned philosophers who wish to refute the void do not bring in arguments on the question according to the position of the others. For they ought to have shown that there is no void in any of these ways.

499. Next where he says, "They argue, for one thing . . ." [343], he gives the arguments of those who affirm that a void exists. First he gives the arguments of those who have spoken of the void in terms of nature, and secondly, where he says, "The Pythagoreans, too . . ." [348], of those who have not spoken of the void in terms of nature.

Concerning the first part he makes two points. First he gives the argument of those who hold that the void is a certain space separated from bodies, and secondly, where he says, "They reason from the fact . . ." [345]. of those who hold that there is a void in bodies.

Concerning the first part he makes two points. First he gives the argument of those who hold that there is a void. Secondly, where he says, "Melissus, indeed, infers . . ." [344], he explains how Melissus contrariwise used that argument.

500. He says, therefore, first [343] that those who affirm that the void exists bring in better arguments for their position.

One of these is that motion in respect to place, that is, change of place and augmentation, as was said above, could not be if there were no void. They explained this as follows. If something is moved in respect to place, it cannot be moved in a plenum. For a place which is filled by one body cannot receive another. If it could receive another, it would follow that there are two bodies in the same place. And for the same reason, this would be true of everything, for one could not establish any reason why two bodies and not more are in the same place. Now if this happened, namely, that many bodies are in the same place, then it would follow that the smallest place could receive the largest body, because many small things constitute one large thing. Hence if many small equal things are in the same place, so also can many unequal things. Therefore, having proven this conditional statement—that if there is motion, there is a void—they argue by positing the antecedent: motion exists, therefore a void exists.

501. Next where he says, **"Melissus, indeed, infers..."** [344], he shows that Melissus, having assumed the same conditional statement, argued to the contrary by denying the consequent. If there is motion, there is a void; but there is no void; hence there is no motion. Therefore, all being is immobile.

This, then, is one way in which some have proven that there is a void as something separated.

502. Next where he says, **"They reason from the fact..."** [345], he gives

three arguments from those who hold that there is a void in bodies.

The first of these deals with things that are condensed. In things which are condensed, the parts seem to come together or meet each other, and to trample on and compress each other. Thus the example is given that jars receive as much wine with bags as without bags, especially if the bags are thin, because the wine seems to be condensed in the bags. They thought that this condensation happened as if the body became more dense by parts entering into certain voids.

503. He gives the second argument, which deals with increase, where he says, **"Again increase, too..."** [346].

Bodies are increased through nourishment, which is a certain body. But two bodies cannot be in the same place. Therefore in bodies which are increased there must be some voids into which the nourishment is received. Thus, in order for nourishment to be received, there must be a void.

504. He gives the third argument where he says, **"A proof of this..."** [347]. This argument deals with a vase filled with ashes. This vase receives as much water as it would when empty. This could not be unless there are some voids between the parts of the ashes.

505. Next where he says, **"The Pythagoreans, too..."** [348], he gives the opinions of those who do not speak of the void in terms of nature.

He says that the Pythagoreans also affirm the existence of a void, which enters into the parts of the world from the heavens because of the infinite void which they thought exists outside the heavens as a certain air or infinite breath. And as one who breathes divides by his own breathing something that is easily divisible, like water and such things, likewise distinction enters into things as from something that is breathing. They thought that this occurs only by means of a void, as was said of Democritus, as if the void were nothing else than the distinction of things. And since the first distinction and plurality is found in numbers, they placed the void primarily in numbers. Thus through the nature of the void one unity is distinguished from another so that number is not continuous but discrete in nature. But since they have spoken, as it were, equivocally about the void, calling it the distinction of things, this opinion is not examined any further in what follows.

Lastly he concludes that he has now indicated why some say that there is a void and why some do not.

What the Word "Void" Means. The Arguments of Those Who Posit A Void Are Refuted

The Text of Aristotle
Chapter 7

349. *As a step towards settling which view is true, we must determine the meaning of the name.*   213b30–31

350. *The void is thought to be place with nothing in it. The reason for this is that people take what exists to be body, and hold that while every body is in place, void is place in which there is no body, so that where there is no body, there must be void. Every body, again, they suppose to be tangible; and of this nature is whatever has weight or lightness. Hence, by a syllogism, what has nothing heavy or light in it, is void. This result, then, as I have said, is reached by syllogism.*   213b31–214a4

351. *It would be absurd to suppose that the point is void; for the void must be place which has in it an interval in tangible body. But at all events we observe then that in one way the void is described as what is not full of body perceptible to touch; and what has heaviness and lightness is perceptible to touch.*   214a4–9

352. *So we would raise the question: what would they say of an interval that has color or sound—is it void or not? Clearly they would reply that if it could receive what is tangible it was void, and if not, not.*   214a9–11

353. *In another way void is that in which there is no "this" or corporeal substance. So some say that the void is the matter of the body (they identify the place, too, with this), and in this they speak incorrectly; for the matter is not separable from the things, but they are inquiring about the void as about something separable.*   214a11–16

354. *Since we have determined the nature of place, and void must, if it exists, be place deprived of body, and we have stated both in what sense place exists and in what sense it does not, it is plain that on this showing void does not exist, either unseparated or separated; for the void is meant to be, not body but rather an interval in body. This is why the void is thought to be something, viz. because place is,*   214a16–21

355. *and for the same reasons. For the fact of motion in respect of place comes to the aid both of those who maintain that place is something over and above the bodies that come to occupy it, and of those who maintain that the void is something. They state that the void is the condition of movement in the sense of that in which movement takes place; and this would be the kind of thing that some say place is.*   214a21–26

356. *But there is no necessity for there being a void if there is movement. It is not in the least needed as a condition of movement in general, for a reason which, incidentally, escaped Melissus; viz. that the full can suffer qualitative change. But not even movement in respect of place involves a void; for bodies may simultaneously make room for one another, though there is no interval separate and apart from the bodies that are in movement. And this is plain even in the rotation of continuous things, as in that of liquids.*   214a26–32

357. *And things can also be compressed not into a void but because they squeeze out what is contained in them (as, for instance, when water is compressed the air within it is squeezed out);*   214a32–214b1

358. *and things can increase in size not only by the entrance of something but also by qualitative change; e.g., if water were to be transformed into air.*   214b1–3

359. *In general, both the argument about increase of size and that about the water poured on to the ashes get in their own way. For either not any and every part of the body is increased,*

or bodies may be increased otherwise than by the addition of body, or there may be two bodies in the same place (in which case they are claiming to solve a quite general difficulty, but are not proving the existence of void), or the whole body must be void, if it is increased in every part and is increased by means of void. The same argument applies to the ashes. It is evident, then, that it is easy to refute the arguments by which they prove the existence of the void.   **214b3–11**

COMMENATARY OF ST. THOMAS

506. The Philosopher has just said above that we must begin with three things. Therefore, after he has treated two of these, that is, the opinions of those who affirm and of those who deny that a void exists, he here takes up the third point, that is, the common opinions of men concerning the void.

Concerning this he makes three points. First he explains what the word "void" means. Secondly, where he says, **"Since we have determined . . ."** [354], he shows how some have held that there is a void. Thirdly, where he says, **"But there is no necessity . . ."** [356], he refutes the arguments of those who hold that there is a void.

Concerning the first part he makes two points. First he states his intention, and secondly he carries it out, where he says, **"The void is thought . . ."** [350].

507. He says, therefore, first [349] that since some, as was said, have held that a void exists and some have denied it, in order to know the truth it is necessary to establish as a beginning what the word "void" means. For when it is asked whether some passion is present in a subject, it is necessary to establish what the thing is for a beginning. In like manner when it is asked whether something is, it is necessary to establish what the word means for a middle term. For the question of what a thing is is subsequent to the question of whether it is.

508. Next where he says, **"The void is thought . . ."** [350], he explains what the word "void" means. First he gives

the more common meaning. Secondly, where he says, **"In another way . . ."** [353], he gives the meaning used by the Platonists.

Concerning the first part he makes three points. First he explains what the word "void" means. Secondly, where he says, **"It would be absurd . . ."** [351], he explains what must be added to this meaning. Thirdly, where he says, **"So we would raise . . ."** [352], he answers a certain difficulty.

509. He says, therefore, first that according to the opinion of men "void" seems to mean nothing else than a place in which there is nothing. The reason for this is that a void is properly said to be that in which there is no body. For being in place belongs only to a body, and "void" can mean nothing else than a place without something located in it. But since men think that every being is a body, it follows according to their opinion that where there is no body there is nothing.

Further they think that every body is tangible, that is, that it has tangible qualities. A body of this kind is heavy or light. For it was not yet known that a celestial body is beyond the nature of the four elements. Hence since the proper nature [ratio] of a void is that it is a place in which there is no body, it follows that a void is that in which there is no light nor heavy body. This, indeed, is not the nature [ratio] of a void according to the first use of the word, but according to a certain syllogistic deduction from the common opinion of men, who think that every body is light or heavy. Likewise according to the common opinion of men, who think that every being is a body, it follows that a void is that in which there is nothing.

Therefore, the meaning of this word can be taken in three ways. First and properly a void is a place in which there is no body. The other two meanings are according to the opinion of men. The first of these is more common—a void is a place in which there is nothing. The other is more limited—a void is a place in which there is no light or heavy body.

510. Next where he says, **"It would be absurd..."** [351], he explains what must be added to this meaning. He says that it is unsuitable to say that a point is a void since it can be said that there is no tangible body in a point. Therefore, we must add that a void is a place in which there is no tangible body, but there is there a space susceptible of a tangible body; as that which lacks sight but should have it is called blind. Thus he concludes that in one way a void is said to be a space which is not filled by a tangible body, that is, by a body that is light or heavy.

511. Next where he says, **"So we would raise..."** [353], he answers a certain difficulty. The problem is whether or not there is a void in a space in which there is color or sound. This difficulty arises because of the definition given first—that is, a void is that in which there is nothing. He answers this by saying that if a space in which there is only sound or color is susceptive of a tangible body, then it is a void. And if not, it is not a void. This is so because the proper definition of a void is not "that in which there is nothing," except according to the opinion of those who believe that where there is no body there is nothing.

512. Next where he says, **"In another way..."** [353], he gives another meaning of "void" as used by the Platonists.

He says that in another meaning a void is said to be that in which there is not "a this" or any corporeal substance. But "a this" comes to be through the form. Hence some say that the matter of a body, insofar as it is without form, is a void. They also say that matter is place, as was said above. But they do not speak well, for matter is not separable from the things of which it is the matter. Men, however, seek place and the void as something separable from located bodies.

513. Next where he says, **"Since we have determined..."** [354], he shows how some have held that there is a void. First he explains what they say a void is. Secondly, where he says, **"For the fact of motion..."** [355], he explains why they posit a void.

He says, therefore, first that a void is a place deprived of body. Now it has been determined in what way place is and in what way it is not (for it was said that place is not space, but the terminus of the container). Hence it is also clear that a void is not a space either separated from bodies or intrinsic to bodies, as Democritus held. This is so because those who posit a void in either of these ways wish to say that a void is not a body, but the space of a body. Therefore a void seems to be something because place is something. And as place seems to be space, so does a void. Hence if place is not a space beyond bodies, then neither can a void be a space beyond bodies. And since the nature [ratio] of a void is that it is a space of a body beyond bodies, as was said above, it follows that a void does not exist.

514. Next where he says, **"For the**

fact of motion . . ." [355], he explains why they posit a void.

He says that they accept the existence of a void for the same reason that they accept the existence of place, that is, because of motion, as was said above. This is done so that motion in respect to place may be saved, both by those who say that place is something beyond the bodies which are in place and by those who hold that a void exists. But for those who deny place and a void, motion in respect to place does not occur. Thus they think that a void is a cause of motion in the way in which place is; namely, as that in which there is motion.

515. Next where he says, "But there is no necessity . . ." [356], he refutes the arguments of those who hold that a void exists. He does not intend here to give the true solution of the arguments given above, but to give for the present a solution from which it appears that these arguments do not conclude of necessity.

First, therefore, he refutes the arguments of those who hold a separated void, and secondly, where he says, "And things can also be . . ." [357], the arguments of those who hold that there is a void in bodies.

516. He refutes the first position in two ways [356]. First if there is motion, it is not necessary that there is a void. If we speak universally of every species of motion, it is quite apparent that there is no necessity. For nothing prevents a plenum from being changed in quality. Only local motion seems to be excluded if there is no void. Melissus failed to see this when he believed that, if a void is denied, then every species of motion is destroyed.

Secondly he refutes the same position by showing that even local motion is not destroyed if there is no void.

For granting that there is no separable space beyond bodies which are moved, there can be local motion in that bodies enter under each other by way of condensation. And thus a thing is moved in a plenum and not in a void.

This is quite apparent in the generation of continuous bodies, and especially in liquids, as is seen in water. For if a stone is thrown into a large expanse of water, it is clear that certain circles develop around the place of percussion as long as one part of the disturbed water moves another and replaces it. Hence since a smaller part of water enters into a larger part of water by a certain diffusion, the above mentioned circles proceed from small to large until they are totally dissipated.

517. Next where he says, "And things can also be . . ." [357], he refutes the arguments of those who hold that there is a void in bodies.

The first argument deals with condensation. He says that bodies are condensed and parts of a body enter into each other, not because the entering parts enter into a void place, but because there are holes filled with a more subtle body which is squeezed out by the condensation. Thus when water comes together and is compressed, the air which was in it is removed. This is especially clear in sponges and in other such porous bodies. However this answer does not explain the cause of condensation, which he gives below. Rather it shows that in this way the necessity of a void can be clearly refuted.

518. Secondly where he says, ". . . and things can increase . . ." [358], he refutes the argument which deals with increase.

He says that increase occurs not only through the addition of some body entering into the increased body, so that it is thus necessary that there be a void, but also through alteration. Thus when air comes to be from water, the quantity of the air is larger than the quantity of the water. Indeed this is not the true solution of the above argument, but only some remarks for the present, lest it be necessary to posit a void.

However the true solution is given in De Generatione et Corruptione, where it is shown that nourishment is not brought into that which grows as a body distinct from itself, but as converted into its substance, as when wood that is near to fire is converted into fire.

519. Thirdly where he says, **"In general, both the argument . . ."** [359], he refutes both the argument about increase and the argument about water poured into ashes. He says that each of these arguments is self-destructive. This is clear as follows.

There is this difficulty about the argument. It seems either that the whole is not increased, or that the increase does not occur because of the addition of a body, but because of the addition of something incorporeal, or that it happens that two bodies are in the same place. Therefore they wish to answer this difficulty which seems to be contrary both to those who posit a void and to those who do not. But they do not demonstrate that there is a void. For it would be necessary for them to say, if increase is due to a void, that the whole body is a void, because the whole body increases.

The same thing must be said about the ashes. For if a vase filled with ashes receives as much water as a void, then one must say that the whole is a void. Hence this is not due to a void but to the mixture with the water. For water mixed with ashes is condensed and some part of it is emitted. And also the parts of the ashes become more dense by dissolving. A sign of this is that one cannot remove the same amount of water as was formerly there.

Lastly he concludes that it is clear that it is easy to answer the arguments by which they demonstrate that a void exists.

It Is Shown from Motion that There Is No Separated Void

The Text of Aristotle
Chapter 8

360. *Let us explain again that there is no void existing separately, as some maintain. If each of the simple bodies has a natural locomotion, e.g., fire upward and earth downward and towards the middle of the universe, it is clear that it cannot be the void that is the condition of locomotion. What, then, will the void be the condition of? It is thought to be the condition of movement in respect of place, and it is not the condition of this.* 214b12–17

361. *Again, if void is a sort of place deprived of body, when there is a void where will a body placed in it move to? It certainly cannot move into the whole of the void. The same argument applies as against those who think that place is something separate, into which things are carried; viz. how will what is placed in it move, or rest? Much the same argument will apply to the void as to the "up" and "down" in place, as is natural enough since those who maintain the existence of the void make it a place. And in what way will things be present either in place or in the void? For the expected result does not take place when a body is placed as a whole in a place conceived of as separate and permanent; for a part of it, unless it be placed apart, will not be in a place but in the whole. Further, if separate place does not exist, neither will void.* 214b17–28

362. *If people say that the void must exist, as being necessary if there is to be movement, what rather turns out to be the case, if one studies the matter, is the opposite, that not a single thing can be moved if there is a void; for as with those who for a like reason say the earth is at rest, so, too, in the void things must be at rest; for there is no place to which things can move more or less than to another; since the void in so far as it is void admits no difference.* 214b28–215a1

363. *The second reason is this: all movement is either compulsory or according to nature, and if there is compulsory movement there must also be natural (for compulsory movement is contrary to nature, and movement contrary to nature is posterior to that according to nature, so that if each of the natural bodies has not a natural movement, none of the other movements can exist); but how can there be natural movement if there is no difference throughout the void or the infinite? For in so far as it is infinite, there will be no up or down or middle, and in so far as it is a void, up differs no whit from down; for as there is no difference in what is nothing, there is none in the void (for the void seems to be a non-existent and a privation of being); but natural locomotion seems to be differentiated, so that the things that exist by nature must be differentiated. Either, then, nothing has a natural locomotion, or else there is no void.* 215a1–14

364. *Further, in point of fact things that are thrown move though that which gave them their impulse is not touching them, either by reason of mutual replacement, as some maintain, or because the air that has been pushed pushes them with a movement quicker than the natural locomotion of the projectile wherewith it moves to its proper place. But in a void none of these things can take place, nor can anything be moved save as that which is carried is moved.* 215a14–19

365. *Further, no one could say why a thing once set in motion should stop anywhere; for why should it stop here rather than here? So that a thing will either be at rest or must be moved ad infinitum, unless something more powerful get in its way. Further, things are now thought*

to move into the void because it yields; but in a void this quality is present equally everywhere,
so that things should move in all directions. **215a19–24**

COMMENTARY OF ST. THOMAS

520. Having given the opinions of others concerning the void, and having stated the meaning of the word "void," he begins here to seek out the truth.

First he shows that there is no separated void. Secondly, where he says, **"There are some who think . . ."** [378], he shows that a void is not present in bodies.

Concerning the first part he makes two points. First he shows from motion that there is no separated void. Secondly, where he says, **"But even if we consider . . ."** [375], he shows the same thing by considering the void itself.

Concerning the first part he makes two points. First he shows from motion that there is no separated void. Secondly, where he says, **"Further, the truth . . ."** [366], he shows the same thing by means of the speed and slowness in motion.

521. Concerning the first part he gives six arguments. In the first argument he says [360] that it is necessary to say again that there is no separated void, as some hold. He says "again" because this has already been shown in the treatment of place. For if place is not space, it follows that there is no void, as was said.

But now he proves the same thing again from motion. For they posit a void because of motion, as was said. However it is not necessary to posit a void because of motion. The void seems especially to be the cause of local motion. But it is not necessary to posit a void because of local motion, since all simple bodies have natural local motions. Thus the natural motion of fire is upwards, and the motion of earth is downwards and toward the middle. Hence it is clear that the nature of each body, and not a void, is the cause of local motion. Indeed there would be a void if natural bodies were moved because of the necessity of the void. Moreover if there is no cause of local motion, there cannot be a cause of any other motion or of any other thing. Therefore the void would be useless.

522. He gives the second argument where he says, **"Again, if void . . ."** [361]. The argument is as follows.

If there is a void, the cause of natural motion and of natural rest cannot be established. For it is clear that a body is naturally moved to its own natural place and is naturally at rest in it because of the agreeableness which the body has with that place and because it does not agree with the place it left. But a void does not have any nature through which it can agree or disagree with a natural body. If, therefore, there is a void, as a certain place deprived of body, one will not be able to designate the part to which that body is naturally moved. For it cannot be said that it is moved to any part. But this we see is false to the senses, because a body naturally leaves one part and naturally arrives at another.

And this same argument avails against those who hold that place is a certain separated space in which a mobile body is moved. For this will not explain how a body has position in such a place, or how it is moved or is at rest.

For the dimensions of space have no nature by which a similitude or dissimilitude to a natural body can be established. And the argument concerning the void has the same merit as the argument concerning "upwards and downwards," that is, concerning place, whose parts are upwards and downwards. For those who posit a void say that it is place.

Those who posit a void and those who hold that place is space not only cannot explain how something is moved and is at rest in respect to place, but they also cannot explain how something is in place or in a void. For if place is held to be space, it is necessary that the whole body be placed in that space. But according to those who hold that place is the terminus of the containing body, this is not the way in which that which is located is in place as in something separated and as in a containing and sustaining body. It seems to be of the nature [ratio] of place that something is in place as in that which is separated and existing outside. For if a part of a body is not outside of that body, it will not be in it as in a place but as in a whole. Therefore the nature [ratio] of place and of that which is located is such that place is outside of that which is located. But this is not the case if place is a space into which a whole body is immersed. Therefore space is not place. And if space is not place, it is clear that there is no void.

523. He gives the third argument where he says, **"If people say that . . ."** [362].

He says that although the ancient philosophers held that there must be a void if there is motion, the contrary is true. For if there is a void, there is no motion.

He proves this by a comparison. Some have said that the earth is at rest at the center because of the similitude of parts surrounding it on all sides. Thus the earth is at rest because there is no reason why it should be moved toward one part of its surroundings rather than another. And for the same reason it is necessary that that which is in a void is at rest. For it cannot be explained why it should move to one part rather than another. A void, as such, has no differences in its parts, for of nonbeing there are no differences.

524. He gives the fourth argument where he says, **"The second reason is this . . ."** [363].

Natural motion is prior to violent motion, since violent motion is only a certain deviation from natural motion. Therefore, when natural motion is removed, all motion is removed. For when the prior is removed, the posterior is removed. But when a void is posited, natural motion is removed, for the difference of the parts of place to which natural motion is directed is removed. This also happens when an infinite is posited, as was said above.

But there is this difference between the void and the infinite. If there is an infinite, in no way can there be an up or down or middle, as was said in Book III. However, if there is a void, these things can be, but they do not differ from each other. For there is no differentia of nothing and of non-being, and consequently of a void, since a privation is also non-being. But natural change of place requires a difference of places, for diverse bodies are moved to diverse places. Hence it is necessary that natural places differ from each other. Therefore, if there is a void, there will be no natural change of place. And if there is no natural change of place, there will be no change of place. Hence if there is any change of place, there cannot be a void.

525. He gives the fifth argument where he says, **"Further, in point of fact . . ."** [364].

Concerning this argument it must be considered that there is a certain difficulty about things which are thrown. For it is necessary that the mover and the moved be together, as is proven below in Book VII. Nevertheless, that which is thrown is found to be moved even after it is separated from the thrower, as appears in a stone that is thrown and an arrow that is shot by a bow. Therefore, on the supposition that there is no void, this question is solved by means of the air in which the medium is refilled.

This is explained in two ways. Some say that things which are thrown are moved even after they are no longer being touched by the thrower because of "antiparistasim," that is, because of a rebounding or a co-resistance. For the moved air is rebounded to another air, and that to another, and so forth. And by such a rebounding of air to air, the stone is moved.

Others say that the air, which exists as a continuum and is set in motion by the thrower, strikes the thrown body more quickly than the motion by which the thrown body is naturally carried to its proper place. Hence because of the speed of the motion of the air, the thrown body, for example, a stone or something of this kind, is not allowed to fall downward, but is carried on by the impulse of the air. But neither of these causes could be posited if there were a void. Thus a thrown body would be moved only while held, as for example, by the hand of the thrower, and it would immediately fall when it leaves the hand. This is contrary to what we see. Therefore there is no void.

526. He gives the sixth argument where he says, **"Further, no one could say . . ."** [364]. The argument is as follows.

If there is motion in a void, no one can explain why that which is moved stops somewhere. For there is no reason why it should be at rest in one part of the void rather than in another: neither in things which are moved naturally, since there is no difference in the parts of a void, as was said above, nor in things which are moved by violence. For we say that violent motion ceases when the rebounding or impulse of air—according to the two assigned causes—ceases. Therefore it will be necessary either that every body is at rest and nothing moves, or if something is moved, that it be moved ad infinitum, unless some larger body, which impedes its violent motion, gets in its way.

Moreover, to confirm this argument, he adds the reason why some hold that motion occurs in a void, that is, a void gives way and does not resist a mobile body. Hence, since a void gives way equally on all parts, the body is carried ad infinitum in any part.

LECTURE 12 [215a24–216a26]
It Is Shown from the Speed and Slowness in Motion that There Is No Separated Void

The Text of Aristotle

366. *Further, the truth of what we assert is plain from the following considerations. We see the same weight or body moving faster than another for two reasons, either because there is a difference in what it moves through, as between water, air, and earth, or because, other things being equal, the moving body differs from the other owing to excess of weight or of lightness.*

215a24–29

367. *Now the medium causes a difference because it impedes the moving thing, most of all if it is moving in the opposite direction, but in a secondary degree even if it is at rest; and especially a medium that is not easily divided, i.e. a medium that is somewhat dense.*

A, then, will move through B in time C, and through D, which is thinner, in time E (if the length of B is equal to D), in proportion to the density of the hindering body. For let B be water and D air; then by so much as air is thinner and more incorporeal than water, A will move through D faster than through B. Let the speed have the same ratio to the speed, then, that air has to water. Then if air is twice as thin, the body will traverse B in twice the time that it does D, and the time C will be twice the time E. And always, by so much as the medium is more incorporeal and less resistant and more easily divided, the faster will be the movement.

215a29–215b12

368. *Now there is no ratio in which the void is exceeded by body, as there is no ratio of 0 to a number. For if 4 exceeds 3 by 1, and 2 by more than 1, and 1 by still more than it exceeds 2, still there is no ratio by which it exceeds 0; for that which exceeds must be divisible into the excess + that which is exceeded, so that 4 will be what it exceeds 0 by + 0. For this reason 7 too, a line does not exceed a point—unless it is composed of points. Similarly the void can bear no ratio to the full,*

215b12–20

369. *and therefore neither can movement through the one to movement through the other, but if a thing moves through the thinnest medium such and such a distance in such and such a time, it moves through the void with a speed beyond any ratio.*

215b20–22

370. *For let F be void, equal in magnitude to B and to D. Then if A is to traverse and move through it in a certain time, G, a time less than E, however, the void will bear this ratio to the full. But in a time equal to G, A will traverse the part H of D. And it will surely also traverse in that time any substance F which exceeds air in thinness in the ratio which the time E bears to the time G. For if the body F be as much thinner than D as E exceeds G, A, if it moves through F, will traverse it in a time inverse to the speed of the movement, i.e. in a time equal to G. If, then, there is no body in F, A will traverse F still more quickly. But we supposed that its traverse of F when F was void occupied the time G. So that it will traverse F in an equal time, whether F be full or void. But this is impossible.*

215b22–216a4

371. *It is plain, then, that if there is a time in which it will move through any part of the void, this impossible result will follow: it will be found to traverse a certain distance, whether this be full or void, in an equal time; for there will be some body which is in the same ratio to the other body as the time is to the time. To sum the matter up, the cause of this result is obvious, viz. that between any two movements there is a ratio (for they occupy time, and there is a ratio between any two times, so long as both are finite), but there is no ratio of void to full.* **216a4–11**

372. *These are the consequences that result from a difference in the media;* **216a11–12**

373. *the following depend upon an excess of one moving body over another. We see that*

bodies which have a greater impulse either of weight or of lightness, if they are alike in other respects, move faster over an equal space, and in the ratio which their magnitudes bear to each other. Therefore they will also move through the void with this ratio of speed. But that is impossible; for why should one move faster? (In moving through plena *it must be so; for the greater divides them faster by its force. For a moving thing cleaves the medium either by its shape, or by the impulse which the body that is carried along or is projected possesses.) Therefore all will possess equal velocity. But this is impossible.* 216a12–21

374. *It is evident from what has been said, then, that, if there is a void, a result follows which is the very opposite of the reason for which those who believe in a void set it up. They think that if movement in respect of place is to exist, the void must exist, separated all by itself; but this is the same as to say that place is a separate cavity; and this has already been stated to be impossible.* 216a21–26

COMMENTARY OF ST. THOMAS

527. Here he shows from the speed and slowness in motion that there is no void.

Concerning this he makes two points. First he names the causes of the speed and slowness in motion. Secondly, where he says, **"Now the medium causes..."** [367], he argues from these causes to what was proposed.

He says, therefore, first [366] that one and the same heavy body, or anything else, for example, a stone or some such thing, is moved faster because of two reasons—either because of a difference in the medium through which it is moved, for example, through air or earth or water; or because of a difference in the mobile thing itself, in that it is lighter or heavier, other things being equal.

528. Next where he says, **"Now the medium causes . . ."** [367], he argues from these causes to what was proposed. He argues first from the difference in the medium, and secondly, where he says, **". . . the following depend upon . . ."** [373], from the difference in the mobile thing.

Concerning the first part he makes two points. First he gives the argument, and secondly he summarizes by repeating it, where he says, **"To sum the matter up . . ."** [371].

Concerning the first part he makes two points. First he gives the argument, and secondly, where he says, **"For let F be void . . ."** [370], he shows that the conclusion follows from the premises.

529. First [367], therefore, he gives the following argument. The proportion of motion to motion in speed is as the proportion of medium to medium in thinness. But there is no proportion of void space to full space. Therefore motion through a void is not proportioned to motion through a plenum.

He clarifies the first proposition of this argument. He says that the medium through which a thing is moved is the cause of the speed and slowness because it impedes the body which is moved. And the medium especially impedes when it is moved in the opposite direction, as is clear in a ship whose motion is impeded by the wind. However it secondarily impedes even if it is at rest. For if it were moved together with the mobile thing, it would not impede it, but would rather help it, as a river which moves a ship from below. Now among things that impede, that which is not easily divided impedes more. Such a body is more dense. He explains this with an example. A is a body which is moved; B is the space through which it is moved; and C is the time in which A is moved through B. Moreover let us posit a space D which is the same length as B. But D is filled with a thinner body than B, according to some "analogy," that is, according to a proportion with the bodily medium which impedes the motion of the body. For example, let the space B be filled with water and the space D be filled with air. Therefore, as much as air is thinner and less dense than water, so much will the mobile body A move faster through space D than through space B. Hence the proportion of speed to speed is the same as the proportion of air to water in thinness. And as much as the speed is greater, so much is the time smaller. For that motion is called faster which goes through an equal space in less time, as will be said in Book VI. Hence, if air is twice as thin as water, it follows that the time in which A is moved through B, which is filled with water, is twice the time in which it is moved through D, which is filled with air. And thus the time C, in which it crosses the space B, will be twice the time E, in which it crosses the space D. Hence we can say universally that in whatever proportion a medium through which something is moved is thinner and less impeding and easily divisible, in the same proportion the motion will be faster.

530. Next where he says, **"Now there is no ratio . . ."** [368], he clarifies the second proposition. He says that a void is not exceeded by a plenum according to any proportion.

He proves this as follows. A number does not exceed zero by any proportion. A proportion is found only between number to number or to unity. Thus four exceeds three by one, and it

exceeds two by more, and it exceeds one by still more. Thus there is a greater proportion of four to one than to two or to three. But four does not exceed zero by any proportion.

Therefore it is necessary that anything which exceeds be divided into that which it exceeds and the excess, that is, that by which it exceeds. Thus four is divided into three and into one, by which it exceeds. If, therefore, four exceeds zero, it would follow that four is divided into several and zero, which is unsuitable. Hence it also cannot be said that a line exceeds a point, unless it were composed of points and were divided into them. And likewise it cannot be said that a void has any proportion to a plenum. For a void does not enter into the composition of a plenum.

531. Next where he says, ". . . therefore neither can movement . . ." [369], he concludes that there cannot be a proportion between motion through a void and motion through a plenum. Even if a body is moved through something that is very thin in a certain space and time, motion through a void transcends every given proportion.

532. Next where he says, **"For let F be void . . ."** [370], in order to proceed more certainly he proves the same conclusion by deducing to impossibility. He does this because the above conclusion was clearly deduced from posited principles and some questions might arise concerning these principles.

If it be said that motion through a void has some proportion of speed to motion through a plenum, then let there be a void space F which is equal in magnitude to the space B, which is filled with water, and to the space D, which is filled with air.

Now if it be granted that motion

through F has some proportion of speed to motions through B and D, then it is necessary to say that motion through F, which is a void, occurs in some determinate time. For speeds are distinguished in respect to quantities of time, as was said above. Therefore if it be said that the mobile body A crosses a void space F in some time, then let that time be G, which must be less than the time E in which it crosses the space D, which is filled with air. And thus the proportion of the time E to the time G will be the proportion of motion through a void to motion through a plenum. But it will be necessary to admit that in the time G the mobile body A would cross a space filled with a thinner body than is in D. This, indeed, would occur if there could be found some body which differs in thinness from air, which was given as filling the space D, in the same proportion that the time E has to the time G. For example, one might say that this body which fills the space F (formerly given as a void) is fire. If the body which fills the space F is thinner than the body which fills the space D in the same proportion that the time E exceeds the time G, then it would follow that the mobile body A, if it is moved through F (which is a space filled with the thinnest body) and through D (which is a space filled with air), will cross through F on the contrary with a greater speed in the time G. Therefore, if there is no body in F and it is a void space as originally given, the mobile body should be moved faster. But this is contrary to what was granted. For it was granted that the motion would take place through the space F, which is a void, in the time G. And thus, since it would cross the same space in the time G when the space is filled with the

thinnest body, it follows that in the same time the same mobile body will cross one and the same space, whether it be a void or a plenum.

Therefore, it is clear that if there were some time in which a mobile body were moved through any void space, this impossibility would follow: in an equal time it will cross both a plenum and a void. For there will be some body which will have a proportion to another body as one time is proportioned to another.

533. Next where he says, **"To sum the matter up . . ."** [371], he summarizes the points in which the force of the above argument consists.

He says that in recapitulating it is clear why the above inconsistency occurs. Each motion is proportioned to every other motion in respect to speed. For every motion is in time, and any two times, if they are finite, have a proportion to each other. But there is no proportion of a void to a plenum, as was proven. Hence, if it be held that there is motion through a void, an inconsistency necessarily follows.

Finally he concludes that the above inconsistencies occur if the different speeds of motion are taken according to a difference in the media.

534. But many difficulties arise against this position of Aristotle.

The first difficulty is that it does not seem to follow that, if there is motion through a void, then there is no proportion in speed to motion through a plenum. For any motion has a determined speed because of the proportion of the power of the mover to the moved, even if there is no impediment.

This is clear through example and through reason [ratio]. For example, the motion of the celestial bodies is impeded by nothing, nevertheless, they have a determined speed in respect to a determined time. Moreover this is clear through reason [ratio] because, since in the magnitude through which motion occurs there is a prior and a posterior, then there is also a prior and a posterior in the motion. From this it follows that motion occurs in a determined time. And it is true that something can be subtracted from this speed because of an impediment. Therefore, it is not necessary that the proportion of motion to motion in speed be as a proportion of one impediment to another, such that if there is no impediment, then motion occurs in no time. Rather, it is necessary that in respect to the proportion of one impediment to another, there is a proportion of one deceleration to another.

Hence, granting motion through a void, it follows that there is no deceleration from the natural speed. But it does not follow that motion through a void has no proportion to motion through a plenum.

535. However Averroes in his commentary tries to overcome this objection.

First he tries to show that this objection proceeds from a false imagination. He says that those who hold the above objection imagine that an addition occurs in the slowness of motion, just as an addition occurs in the magnitude of a line, because the added part is other than the part to which it is added. The above objection seems to proceed thus: slowness occurs because some motion is added to another motion such that the quantity of natural motion remains the same when the motion which was added by a retarding impediment is subtracted. But he says that this is not the same case. For when motion is retarded, each part of motion becomes

slower; nevertheless, each part of the line does not become greater.

Next he tries to show how Aristotle's argument has necessity. He says that the speed or slowness of motion does arise from a proportion of the mover to the mobile body. But the mobile body must in some way resist the mover, as a patient in some way is contrary to an agent. This resistance can occur because of three things. First it occurs because of the site of the mobile body. For since the mover intends to move the mobile body to some place, the mobile body itself, existing in another place, resists the intention of the mover. Secondly, this resistance arises because of the nature of the mobile body, as occurs in violent motions, as when a heavy body is thrown upward. Thirdly, this resistance arises because of the medium. All three of these must be taken together as one resistance, so that one cause of the slowness of motion results. Therefore, when a mobile body, considered in itself insofar as it differs from the mover, is some being in act, then the resistance of the mobile body to the mover can be found either in the mobile body alone—as happens with the celestial bodies—or in both the mobile body and the medium—as happens with animated bodies which are here. But in regard to heavy and light bodies, when we subtract that which the mobile body has from the mover (that is, the form, which is a principle of motion and which the generator or mover gives), then nothing remains except matter, in regard to which no resistance to the mover can be considered. Hence it follows that in such things the only resistance is from the medium. Therefore, in celestial bodies there is a difference of speed only in respect to the proportion of the mover to the mobile body. In animated bodies there is a difference of speed in respect to the proportion of the mover to both the mobile body and the resisting medium together. And in regard to such things proceeds the above objection, namely, that when we have removed the deceleration which is due to the impeding medium, there remains a determined quantity of time in motion in respect to the proportion of the mover to the mobile body. But in heavy and light things there can be no deceleration of speed except in respect to the resistance of the medium. And Aristotle's argument deals with these latter things.

536. But this seems to be completely worthless. For the quantity of speed is not a mode of continuous quantity, so that motion is added to motion, but a mode of intensive quantity, as when something is whiter than another. Nevertheless, the quantity of time, from which Aristotle argues, is a mode of continuous quantity, and time becomes greater by the addition of time to time. Hence, when the time which is added by the impediment is subtracted, the time of the natural speed remains.

Secondly, when the form which the generator gives is removed from heavy and light things, a quantified body remains only in the understanding. But a body has resistance to a mover because it is quantified and exists in an opposite site. For no other resistance of celestial bodies to their movers can be understood. Hence, not even in regard to heavy and light things does Aristotle's argument follow, as Averroes claims it does.

Therefore it is better and briefer to say that Aristotle's argument is an argument to contradict a position, and is

not a strictly demonstrative argument. For those who posit a void do so in order that motion be not impeded. And thus according to them the cause of motion was due to the medium, which does not impede motion. Therefore against them Aristotle argues as if the whole cause of speed and slowness were due to the medium. He also clearly shows this above when he says that if nature is the cause of the motion of simple bodies, then it is not necessary to posit a void as the cause of their motion. In this way he lets us know that they hold that the whole cause of motion is due to the medium, and not to the nature of the mobile body.

537. Furthermore, a second objection against Aristotle's argument is that, if the medium which is a plenum impedes, as he says, it follows that in this inferior medium there is no pure, unimpeded motion. But this seems unsuitable.

To this the Commentator responds that the natural motion of light and heavy things requires this impediment from the medium, so that there might be a resistance of the mobile body to the mover, at least from the medium.

But it is better to say that all natural motion begins from a nonnatural place and tends to a natural place. Hence, until it reaches the natural place, it is not unsuitable if something unnatural to it be joined to it. For it gradually recedes from that which is against its nature, and tends to that which agrees with its nature. And because of this natural motion is attained in the end.

538. A third objection is that, since in natural bodies there is a definite limit to rarefaction, it does not seem that there is always a rarer and rarer body in respect to every proportion of time to time.

But it must be said that determined rarity in natural things is not due to the nature of the mobile body insofar as it is mobile, but is due to the nature of determined forms which require determined rarities or densities. Furthermore in this book mobile body in general is under discussion. And therefore in his arguments in this book Aristotle frequently uses certain things which are false if the determined natures of bodies are considered. But they are possibilities, if the nature of body in general is considered.

Or it can be said that he proceeds here according to the opinion of the ancient philosophers who posited the rare and the dense as first formal principles. According to them rarity and density can be increased to infinity since they do not follow upon other prior forms by which they are determined as needed.

539. Next where he says, "... the following depend upon . . ." [373], he shows that there is no separated void by means of the speed and slowness of motion insofar as the cause is completely due to the mobile body.

He says that that which is said below follows if we consider the difference of speed or slowness insofar as the mobile bodies which are moved exceed one another. For we see that those things which have a greater inclination either in respect to heaviness or lightness are carried more quickly through an equal, finite space. Such things are either greater in quantity and equally heavy or light, or else they are equal in quantity and are heavier or lighter. I say this on the condition that they are similar in respect to shape. For a broad body, if it is lacking in heaviness or magnitude, is moved more slowly than a body of acute shape. And the proportion of speed is the proportion which the moved magnitudes have to each other either in heaviness or magnitude. Hence, if there is motion through a void, then it will also be necessary that the heavier or lighter or more acute body be moved faster through that void. But this cannot be. For one cannot assign any reason why one body is moved faster than another. For if motion occurs through a space filled with some body, it is possible to assign the cause of a greater or lesser speed according to one of the mentioned causes. This happens because that which is moved is larger and divides the medium more quickly by its own strength; or because of the suitability of the shape, for the acute is more penetrating; or because of a greater inclination, which it has either from its heaviness or lightness; or even because of the violence of that which impedes. But a void cannot be divided more slowly or more quickly. Hence it follows that all things are moved through a void with equal speed. But this is clearly impossible. Therefore he shows from the very velocity of motion that there is no void.

But it must be realized that in the development of this argument there is a difficulty similar to that which appeared in the first argument. For the argument seems to suppose that there is no difference in the speed of motions except the difference of the division of the media. But in the celestial bodies there are diverse speeds for which there is no plenum as a resisting medium which must be divided by the motion of the celestial bodies. This objection must be answered as above.

540. Finally he concludes that it is clear from what has been said that if a void is posited, then there results the contrary of that which those who hold a void suppose. For they proceeded as

if there could be no motion if there were no void. But the contrary has been shown, that is, if there is a void, there is no motion. Therefore the above mentioned philosophers thought that there is a void which is discrete and separated by itself, that is, a certain space having separated dimensions. And they thought that a void of this kind is necessary if there is motion in respect to place. But to posit such a separated void is the same as to say that place is a certain space distinct from bodies. This is impossible, as was shown in the treatment of place.

LECTURE 13 [216a27–216b20]
It Is Shown from the Void Itself That there is no Separated Void

The Text of Aristotle

375. But even if we consider it on its own merits the so-called vacuum will be found to be really vacuous. For as, if one puts a cube in water, an amount of water equal to the cube will be displaced; so too in air; but the effect is imperceptible to sense. And indeed always, in the case of any body that can be displaced, it must, if it is not compressed, be displaced in the direction in which it is its nature to be displaced—always either down, if its locomotion is downwards as in the case of earth, or up, if it is fire, or in both directions—whatever be the nature of the inserted body. Now in the void this is impossible; for it is not body; the void must have penetrated the cube to a distance equal to that which this portion of void formerly occupied in the void, just as if the water or air had not been displaced by the wooden cube, but had penetrated right through it. But the cube also has a magnitude equal to that occupied by the void; a magnitude which, if it is also hot or cold, or heavy or light, is none the less different in essence from all its attributes, even if it is not separable from them;   216a26–216b6

376. I mean the volume of the wooden cube. So that even if it were separated from everything else and were neither heavy nor light, it will occupy an equal amount of void, and fill the same place, as the part of place or of the void equal to itself. How then will the body of the cube differ from the void or place that is equal to it? And if there can be two such things, why cannot there be any number coinciding? This, then, is one absurd and impossible implication of the theory.   216b6–12

377. It is also evident that the cube will have this same volume even if it is displaced, which is an attribute possessed by all other bodies also. Therefore if this differs in no respect from its place, why need we assume a place for bodies over and above the volume of each, if their volume be conceived of as free from attributes? It contributes nothing to the situation if there is an equal interval attached to it as well. Further, it ought to be clear by the study of moving things what sort of thing void is. But in fact it is found nowhere in the world. For air is something, though it does not seem to be so—nor, for that matter, would water, if fishes were made of iron; for the discrimination of the tangible is by touch. It is clear, then, from these considerations that there is no separate void.   216b12–21

COMMENTARY OF ST. THOMAS

541. He shows here that there is no void by means of arguments dealing with the void itself apart from any consideration of motion. He gives three arguments.

He says first [375] that it will be seen by one who considers a void in itself apart from motion that the word "void" is well used by those who say that a void exists. For "void" signifies something which is empty and which is not. And to say that a void exists is to say something which is empty and removed from reason and truth. He shows this as follows. If one places in water a cubic body (that is, a body having six square surfaces), it is necessary that the quantity of water which recedes from its place is equal to the quantity of the cube. And this is true of air as well as water, although it is not as evident, because water is more sensible than air. Therefore, for the same reason, whenever anything is placed in a body, which by nature can be moved in some direction, then it is necessary that that body be moved, unless the parts coalesce either by condensation or by one part entering into another. The body is moved either by yielding (when it has a free exit), for example, a heavy body like earth goes downwards, and a light body like fire goes upwards, and a body that is heavy in respect to one thing and light in respect to another goes in either direction, like air and water; or the body is moved by yielding under the conditions of an imposed body, as when the yielding body is impeded by an imposed body so that it cannot be moved according to its own exigency but according to the exigency of the imposed body. Nevertheless, it is universally true that a body into which another body is placed must yield, lest there be two bodies together.

But it cannot be said that a void yields when a body is placed in it. For a void is not a body. But whatever is moved in any way is a body. Now if there is a void space, and if some body is placed in that space, then it is necessary that the imposed body passes through into that space which formerly was a void, that is, it exists together with it. It is as if water or air would not yield to a wooden cube, but rather these bodies would pass through the very body of the wooden cube, such that the air and water would penetrate into the body of the cube and would exist together with it.

But it is impossible for a cubic, wooden body to exist together with a void space. For the cubic, wooden body has the same magnitude as the void, which is posited as a certain space having dimensions without a sensible body. And although the cubic, wooden body is either hot or cold, or heavy or light, nevertheless according to reason [ratio] that cubic, wooden body is other than all the sensible passions accidental to it—even though in

the thing it is not separable from them. That which according to reason [ratio] is other than the passions is the very body of the wooden cube, that is, it is that which pertains to its corporeity. If, therefore, this body be separated from everything which is other than it according to reason [ratio], it follows that it contains or occupies a part of the void space equal to itself. And thus the body of the wooden cube will be in the same part of both a place and a void equal to itself.

Granting this, it does not seem that there is any difference between the body of the cube and the dimensions of a place or a void. For just as place or void has dimensions without sensible qualities, so also the dimensions of the cubic body are other than passions of this kind, at least according to reason [ratio]. However two magnitudes of equal quantity cannot differ except in respect to site. For it is impossible to imagine that one line is different from another equal line unless we imagine each of them in a different site. Hence if two magnitudes are posited together, it does not seem that they differ. And thus if two equally dimensioned bodies exist together, whether they have sensible passions or not, it follows that the two bodies are one.

Furthermore, if the cubic body and the space, which is a place or a void, would remain two and exist together, one cannot give any reason [ratio] why any other body cannot exist in the same place. And thus, just as the cubic body exists together with the space of a place or a void, likewise some third or even fourth body will be able to exist together with both of them. But this is impossible. For it cannot be said that another sensible body is unable because of matter to exist together with the cubic, wooden body. For place is not due a body by reason [ratio] of matter except insofar as matter is contained under dimensions. Hence the fact that two bodies cannot exist together is not due to the matter or to the sensible passions but only to the dimensions, in which there cannot be diversity, if they are equal, except in respect to site, as was said. Hence if there are dimensions in a void space as there are in a sensible body, then just as two sensible bodies cannot exist together, likewise neither can a sensible body and a void space exist together. This, therefore, is one inconsistency and impossibility that follows from the above position; namely, two bodies exist together.

542. He gives the second argument where he says, "It is also evident . . ." [376]. He says that it is clear that the cube, which is moved and placed in a void space, has dimensions, which all bodies have. Therefore, if the dimensions of the cubic body do not differ according to reason [ratio] from the dimensions of place, and if place is nothing else than body without sensible passions, why is it necessary to assign some place for bodies outside their own bodies? For since such a body has its own dimensions, it seems in no way necessary to posit around it some other dimensions equal in space to its own dimensions. Therefore, if void or place is posited as a certain separated space, it follows that it is not necessary that bodies be in place.

543. He gives the third argument where he says, "Further, it ought to be . . ." [377]. He says that, if a void is something, then this ought to be manifest in mobile things. But a void appears nowhere in the world. For that which is filled with air is not a void, although it seems to be. Air is something, even though it is not perceived by sight. If fish were made of iron and had an appearance similar to water, water could not be distinguished from them by sight. Nevertheless it would not follow that water or even fish do not exist. For not only sight but also touch distinguishes that which is touched. Thus it is clear that air is something. For hot and cold is perceived by touch.

Therefore, from these arguments it appears that a void is not a separated space, neither within the world nor outside the world.

LECTURE 14 [216b21–217b28]
There Is No Void in Bodies

The Text of Aristotle
Chapter 9

378. There are some who think that the existence of rarity and density shows that there is a void. If rarity and density do not exist, they say, neither can things contract and be compressed. But if this were not to take place, either there would be no movement at all, or the universe would bulge, as Xuthus said, or air and water must always change into equal amounts (e.g., if air has been made out of a cupful of water, at the same time out of an equal amount of air a cupful of water must have been made), or void must necessarily exist; for compression and expansion cannot take place otherwise.   216b22–30

379. Now, if they mean by the rare that which has many voids existing separately, it is plain that if void cannot exist separate any more than a place can exist with an extension all to itself, neither can the rare exist in this sense.   216b30–217a1

380. But if they mean that there is void, not separately existent, but still present in the rare, this is less impossible; yet, first, the void turns out not to be a condition of all movement, but only of movement upwards (for the rare is light, which is the reason why they say fire is rare); second, the void turns out to be a condition of movement not as that in which it takes place, but in that the void carries things up as skins by being carried up themselves carry up what is continuous with them. Yet how can void have a local movement or a place? For thus that into which void moves is till then void of a void.   217a1–5

382. Again, how will they explain, in the case of what is heavy, its movement downwards?
                                    217a5–6

383. And it is plain that if the rarer and more void a thing is the quicker it will move upwards, if it were completely void it would move with a maximum speed! But perhaps even this is impossible, that it should move at all; the same reason which showed that in the void all things are incapable of moving shows that the void cannot move, viz., the fact that the speeds are incomparable.   217a6–10

384. Since we deny that a void exists, but for the rest the problem has been truly stated, that either there will be no movement, if there is not to be condensation and rarefaction, or the universe will bulge, or a transformation of water into air will always be balanced by an equal transformation of air into water (for it is clear that the air produced from water is bulkier than the water): it is necessary therefore, if compression does not exist, either that the next portion will be pushed outwards and make the outermost part bulge, or that somewhere else there must be an equal amount of water produced out of air, so that the entire bulk of the whole may be equal, or that nothing moves. For when anything is displaced this will always happen, unless it comes round in a circle; but locomotion is not always circular, but sometimes in a straight line. These then are the reasons for which they might say that there is a void;   217a10–21

385. our statement is based on the assumption that there is a single matter for contraries, hot and cold and the other natural contrarieties, and that what exists actually is produced from a potential existent, and that matter is not separable from the contraries but its being is different, and that a single matter may serve for color and heat and cold.   217a21–26

386. The same matter also serves for both a large and a small body. This is evident; for when air is produced from water, the same matter has become something different, not by acquiring an addition to it, but has become actually what it was potentially, and, again, water is produced from air in the same way, the change being sometimes from smallness to greatness, and sometimes from greatness to smallness.   217a26–31

387. *Similarly, therefore, if air which is large in extent comes to have a smaller volume or becomes greater from being smaller, it is the matter which is potentially both that comes to be each of the two. For as the same matter becomes hot from being cold, and cold from being hot, because it was potentially both, so too from hot it can become more hot, though nothing in the matter has become hot that was not hot when the thing was less hot; just as, if the arc or curve of a greater circle becomes that of a smaller, whether it remains the same or becomes a different curve, convexity has not come to exist in anything that was not convex but straight (for differences of degree do not depend on an intermission of the quality); nor can we get any portion of a flame, in which both heat and whiteness are not present. So too, then, is the earlier heat related to the later. So that the greatness and smallness, also, of the sensible volume are extended, not by the matter's acquiring anything new, but because the matter is potentially matter for both states; so that the same thing is dense and rare, and the two qualities have one matter.*   217a31–217b11

388. *The dense is heavy, and the rare is light. Again, as the arc of a circle when contracted into a smaller space does not acquire a new part which is convex, but what was there had been contracted; and as any part of fire that one takes will be hot; so, too, it is all a question of contraction and expansion of the same matter. There are two types in each case, both in the dense and in the rare; for both the heavy and the hard are thought to be dense, and contrariwise both the light and the soft are rare; and weight and hardness fail to coincide in the case of lead and iron.*   217b11–20

389. *From what has been said it is evident, then, that void does not exist either separate (either absolutely separate or as a separate element in the rare) or potentially, unless one is willing to call the condition of movement void, whatever it may be. At that rate the matter of the heavy and the light, qua matter of them, would be the void; for the dense and the rare are productive of locomotion in virtue of this contrariety, and in virtue of their hardness and softness productive of passivity and impassivity, i.e. not of locomotion but rather of qualitative change. So much, then, for the discussion of the void, and of the sense in which it exists and the sense in which it does not exist.*   217b20–28

COMMENTARY OF ST. THOMAS

544. After the philosopher has shown that there is no separated void, he here shows that there is no void in bodies.

Concerning this he makes three points. First he gives the argument of those who posit such a void. Secondly, where he says, **"Now, if they mean . . ."** [379], he disproves their position. Thirdly, where he says, **"Since we deny . . ."** [384], he answers their argument.

545. He says, therefore, first [378] that there were some philosophers who, by arguing from rarity and density, thought that there is a void in bodies. For it seemed to them that rarefaction and condensation occur because of a void intrinsic to bodies. They said that, if there were no such rarity and density, then it was not possible for the parts of a body to come together with each other and for a body to be compressed by condensation. And if this were not so, then inconsistencies resulted both in regard to local motion and in regard to generation and corruption, or alteration.

This would be true in regard to local motion because it will be necessary to say either that there is no motion at all or that the whole universe is moved by one motion, as the philosopher Xuthus said. This is so because, if a body is moved locally, then, when it takes a place occupied by another body, that body must be expelled and tend to another place, and again the body that is there must go to another place. And unless a condensation of bodies occurs, it will be necessary that all bodies are moved.

In regard to generation or alteration this inconsistency follows. There will always occur an equal change of water to air and of air to water. For example, if air is generated from one measure of water, then it is necessary that somewhere else water be generated equal to the amount of air that was generated. But the quantity of air is greater than the quantity of water from which it is generated. Therefore, the generated air occupies a larger place than the water from which it was generated. Thus it would be necessary either that the whole body of the universe occupies a larger place or that somewhere an equal amount of air is converted into water. Or else one must say that there is a void within bodies so that a condensation of bodies occurs. For they did not think that bodies could be condensed or rarefied unless a void existed in them.

546. Next where he says, **"Now, if they mean . . ."** [379], he refutes the above position. He does this first according to one understanding of it, and secondly according to another, where he says, **"But if they mean . . ."** [380].

He says, therefore, first that those who say that there is a void in bodies can understand this in two ways. The first interpretation is that in each body there are many void holes, as it were, which are separated in site from the other filled parts, as is seen in a sponge, or in a pumice stone, or in other such things. The second interpretation is

that the void is not separated in site from the other parts of the body, as if we would say that the dimensions which they call a void enter into all the parts of the body.

But if they say that a void is in bodies in the first way, then this is clearly disproved from what was said above. For in that argument it was shown that there is no void separated from bodies nor is there any place which has its own space beyond the dimensions of bodies. With the same argument it can be proven there is no rarefied body which has within itself some void spaces distinct from the other parts of the body.

547. Next where he says, **"But if they mean . . ."** [380], he disproves with four arguments the above mentioned position taken according to the second interpretation.

Therefore he says that, if a void is not in bodies as something separable and distinct from the other parts, but nevertheless a void is present in bodies, then this is less impossible. For the inconsistencies given above against a separated void do not follow. Nevertheless certain other inconsistencies do follow.

First, the void will not be the cause of all local motion, as they intended, but only of upward motion. For a void, according to them, is the cause of rarity. But a rare thing is found to be light, as is clear in fire. And a light thing moves upwards. Hence the void will be the cause only of upward motion.

548. He gives the second argument where he says, **". . . second, the void turns out . . ."** [381].

He says that, according to those who posit a void in bodies, the void is the cause of motion, but not as that in which a thing is moved (which is the way in which the void is the cause of motion for those who say that a void is a separated space). Rather they hold that the void is the cause of motion insofar as the intrinsic void itself moves bodies; as if we would say that inflated bags, which are carried upwards because of their lightness, also carry upwards whatever they contain. Thus the void present in bodies carries along with itself the body in which it is.

But this seems to be impossible. For it would then be necessary for the void to be moved and for the void to have some place. And since the void and place would be the same, it would follow that the interior void has an exterior void in which it is moved. This is impossible.

549. He gives the third argument where he says, "**Again, how will they . . .**" [382].

He says that, if the void is the cause of upward motion by carrying a body upwards, then, since there is nothing to explain downward motion, there will be no reason why heavy bodies are moved downwards.

550. He gives the fourth argument where he says, "**And it is plain . . .**" [383].

He says that, if rarity causes upward motion because of its voidness, then it will be necessary for a thing to be moved upwards more quickly in proportion to its being more rare and more void. And if a thing were completely void, it would be moved with the greatest speed.

But this is impossible. That which is completely void cannot be moved for the same reason by which it was shown above that there cannot be motion in a void space. For there would be no comparison of the speeds of the void and of the plenum in any determinate proportion, either in respect to the

space or in respect to the mobile body, because there is no proportion of a plenum to a void. Therefore, the void cannot be the cause of upward motion.

551. Next where he says, "**Since we deny that . . .**" [384], he answers the argument given above.

First he repeats it, explaining it more, and secondly he answers it, where he says, "**. . . our statement is based . . .**" [385].

He says, therefore, first [384] that, since we say that there is no void, either in bodies or outside them, it is necessary to answer the arguments which others bring up, because they present real difficulties.

First he discusses local motion. There will be no local motion at all unless there be rarity and density, which they thought could not be without a void. Or else it will be necessary to say that, when any body is moved, the whole heaven is moved upwards, or a part of it, which they called "the disturbance of the heavens." Moreover in regard to generation and corruption, it will be necessary that water comes to be from air, and elsewhere air comes to be from water, in equal amount. For, since more air is generated than water, then it is necessary (unless there is condensation, which they believed could not occur without a void) either that the body which is held to be ultimate in common opinion (that is, the celestial body) is expanded by the excess of inferior bodies, or else in some place an equal amount of air is converted into water, so that the whole body of the universe is always found to be equal.

Now since it would be possible to object in some way against what Aristotle has said about local motion, he repeats the above argument again in order to refute it. And he says, "**. . . or that nothing moves" [217a18]. For according to the above argument a disturbance of the heavens occurs whenever anything is moved. This is true unless the motion is understood to be circular; for example, A is moved to place B, and B to place C, and C to place D, and D to place A. In the case of circular motion it will not be necessary that the whole universe is disturbed by one motion. But we see that not all of the local motions of natural bodies are circular, for many things are moved in a straight line. Hence a disturbance of the heavens would follow unless there is condensation and a void.

This, therefore, is the reason why some hold that a void exists.

552. Next where he says, ". . . our statement is based . . ." [385], he solves the argument given above. The whole force of the given argument consists in the position that rarefaction and condensation occur by means of a void. Hence Aristotle answers the argument by showing that rarefaction and condensation occur without a void.

First he explains his position, and secondly, where he says, "From what has been said . . ." [389], he induces the conclusion which he primarily intends.

Concerning the first part he makes three points. First he explains his position with an argument, secondly by an example, where he says, "For as the same matter . . ." [387], and thirdly by the effects of rarity and density, where he says, "The dense is heavy . . ." [388].

Concerning the first part he makes two points. First he sets forth certain things which are necessary for his position, and secondly he proves his position, where he says, "The same matter also serves . . ." [386].

553. He sets forth [385] four things

which he takes "from the subjects," that is, from things which are supposed in natural science, and which were explained above in Book I.

The first point is that there is one matter for contraries, such as hot and cold, or any other natural contraries. For the nature of contraries is such that they occur in the same thing.

The second point is that everything which is in act necessarily comes to be from that which is in potency.

The third point is that matter is not separable from contraries so that it exists apart from them. But, nevertheless, matter in its nature [ratio] is other than the contraries.

The fourth point is that matter is not different but the same in number, for it exists now under one contrary and later under another.

554. Next where he says, "The same matter also serves . . ." [386], he explains his position from the above in this way. The matter of contraries is the same in number. But the great and the small are contraries of quantity. Therefore the matter of the great and the small is the same in number.

This is clear in substantial change. For when air is generated from water, the same matter which formerly was under water is made to be under air, not by taking something which it did not formerly have, but rather by a reduction to act of that which was formerly in the potency of matter. The same is true when water is conversely generated from air. But there is this difference. When air is generated from water, a change from small to large occurs. For the quantity of the generated air is greater than the quantity of the water from which it was generated. However, when water is generated from air, a converse change from largeness to smallness occurs. Therefore, when a large amount of air is reduced to a smaller quantity by condensation, or when there is a change from smaller to larger by rarefaction, it is the same matter which comes to be both in act, that is, which comes to be large and small, which prior to this existed in potency.

Therefore, condensation does not occur because some parts come together by entering into other parts, and rarefaction does not occur because connected parts are separated, as those who posit a void in bodies have thought. Rather these things occur because the matter of the same parts takes on now a larger and now a smaller quantity. Hence, to be rarefied is nothing else than for matter to take on larger dimensions by reduction from potency to act. And to be condensed is the opposite. For just as matter is in potency to determinate forms, so also is it in potency to determinate quantity. Hence rarefaction and condensation do not proceed to infinity in natural things.

555. Next where he says, **"For as the same matter . . ."** [387], he explains the same thing by examples. Since rarefaction and condensation pertain to the motion of alteration, he gives an example dealing with other alterations.

He says that the same matter is changed from cold to hot and from hot to cold because each of these was in the potency of matter. Likewise, a thing that is hot comes to be more hot, not because some part of matter becomes hot which formerly was not hot when the body was less hot, but because all the matter is reduced to an act of greater or lesser heat.

He gives another example dealing with the quality in quantity.

He says that if the circumference and convexity of a larger circle is contracted to a smaller circle, it is clear that something more curved results. But this is not because circularity was made in some part which originally was not curved but straight. Rather it is because the same thing, which formerly was less curved, is now more curved.

For in such alterations a thing does not become greater or less either by subtraction or by addition. Rather this is a change of one and the same thing from perfection to imperfection, or vice versa. This is clear because, in a thing which has a simply uniform quality, there is found no part which is without that quality. Thus, in a spark of fire, there is no part in which there is no heat or whiteness, that is, clearness. Thus, therefore, the prior heat comes to the posterior, not because some part which was not hot is made hot, but because that which was less hot becomes more hot.

Hence also the largeness and smallness of a sensible body is not extended or amplified in rarefaction and condensation because matter takes on some addition. Rather this occurs because matter, which formerly was in potency to the great and the small, is changed from one to the other. And, therefore, rarity and density do not occur either by the addition or by the subtraction of parts which enter into each other, but rather because the matter of the rare and the dense is one.

556. Next where he says, **"The dense is heavy . . ."** [388], he explains his position by means of the effects of rarity and density. The difference of other qualities, that is, heavy and light, hard and soft, follow upon the difference of rarity and density. And thus it is clear that rarity and density diversify qualities and not quantities.

He says, therefore, that lightness follows upon rarity, and heaviness follows upon density. And this is reasonable. For rarity results from matter receiving larger dimensions, and density results from matter receiving smaller dimensions. Thus, if we take diverse bodies of equal quantity, the one being rare and the other dense, the dense body has more matter. Moreover, it was said above in the treatment of place that the contained body is compared to the container as matter to form. And thus a heavy body, which tends toward the middle of that which is contained, is understandably more dense since it has more matter. Therefore, the circumference of a greater circle which is reduced to a smaller circle does not receive concavity in one of its parts in which concavity formerly was not, but rather that which formerly was concave is reduced to greater concavity. And also any part of fire that one might take is hot. And likewise a whole body becomes rare and dense by contraction and extension of one and the same matter, insofar as it is moved to a greater or smaller dimension.

This is clear in those qualities which follow upon rarity and density. For heaviness and hardness follow upon density. The nature [ratio] of heaviness has been established. The nature [ratio] of hardness is also clear. For that is called hard which gives more resistance to pushing and division. And that which has more matter is less divisible, because it is less obedient to an agent, since it is more removed from act.

And conversely, lightness and softness follow upon rarity. But in some things, for example, iron and lead, heaviness and hardness do not agree. For lead is heavier but iron is harder. The reason for this is that lead has more earthy things in it, and that which has water in it is less perfectly hardened and assimilated.

557. Next where he says, **"From what has been said . . ."** [389], he concludes to the main point.

He says that it is clear from what has been said that there is no void separated space. Nor is there a void existing simply outside of bodies. Nor is there a void existing in the rare as void holes. Nor does a void exist in potency in a rare body, as say those who do not posit a void in bodies separated from the plenum. Thus in no way is there a void, unless one would inwardly wish to call matter a void. Matter in some way is the cause of heaviness and lightness, and thus is a cause of local motion. For density and rarity are the cause of motion in respect to the contrariety of heavy and light. But in respect to the contrariety of hard and soft they are the cause of passivity and impassivity. For the soft is that which easily undergoes division, but the hard does not, as was said. But this does not pertain to change of place, but rather to alteration.

And thus he concludes that it has been determined how a void exists and how it does not exist.

It Is Argued Whether Time Exists and Whether the Same "Now" Is In All Time

The Text of Aristotle
Chapter 10

390. *Next for discussion after the subjects mentioned is Time. The best plan will be to begin by working out the difficulties connected with it, making use of the current arguments. First, does it belong to the class of things that exist or to that of things that do not exist? Then secondly, what is its nature?*　　　217b29–32

391. *To start, then: the following considerations would make one suspect that it either does not exist at all or barely, and in an obscure way. One part of it has been and is not, while the other is going to be and is not yet. Yet time—both infinite time and any time you like to take—is made up of these. One would naturally suppose that what is made up of things which do not exist could have no share in reality.*　　　217b32–218a3

392. *Further, if a divisible thing is to exist, it is necessary that, when it exists, all or some of its parts must exist. But of time some parts have been, while others have to be, and no part of it is, though it is divisible. For what is "now" is not a part: a part is a measure of the whole, which must be made up of parts. Time, on the other hand, is not held to be made up of ".".*

218a3–8

393. *Again, the "now" which seems to bound the past and the future—does it always remain one and the same or is it always other and other? It is hard to say.*　　　218a8–11

394. *(1) If it is always different and different, and if none of the parts in time which are other and other are simultaneous (unless the one contains and the other is contained, as the shorter time is by the longer), and if the "now" which is not, but formerly was, must have ceased-to-be at some time, the "nows" too cannot be simultaneous with one another, but the prior "now" must always have ceased-to-be. But the prior "now" cannot have ceased-to-be in itself (since it then existed); yet it cannot have ceased-to-be in another "now." For we may lay it down that one "now" cannot be next to another, any more than point to point. If then it did not cease-to-be in the next "now" but in another, it would exist simultaneously with the innumerable "nows" between the two—which is impossible.*　　　218a11–21

395. *Yes, but (2) neither is it possible for the "now" to remain always the same. No determinate divisible thing has a single termination, whether it is continuously extended in one or in more than one dimension; but the "now" is a termination, and it is possible to cut off a determinate time.*　　　218a21–25

396. *Further, if coincidence in time (i.e. being neither prior nor posterior) means to be "in one and the same 'now,'" then, if both what is before and what is after are in this same "now," things which happened ten thousand years ago would be simultaneous with what has happened today, and nothing would be before or after anything else. This may serve as a statement of the difficulties about the attributes of time.*　　　218a25–31

COMMENTARY OF ST. THOMAS

558. After he has treated place and the void, he now treats time.

First he states his intention and the order in which one must proceed. Secondly he follows this out, where he says, **"To start, then ..."** [391].

He says, therefore, first that the treatment of time follows upon what has gone before. By this he points out the problem under consideration. For as with the foregoing, likewise with time, it is first necessary to proceed by proposing extraneous arguments, that is, sophistical arguments, or arguments given by others, as to whether time exists or not, and if it exists, what its nature is.

Next where he says, **"To start, then ..."** [391], he begins to treat time, first by raising objections, and secondly by determining the truth, where he says, **"We must take this..."** [404]

Concerning the first part he makes two points. By raising objections he inquires first whether time is, and secondly, what time is, where he says, **"As to what time is ..."** [397].

Concerning the first part he makes two points. First, he gives two arguments to show that time does not exist. Secondly, where he says, **"Again, the 'now' ..."** [393]. he inquires whether in the whole of time there is one or many "nows."

559. He says, therefore, first [391] that from the following two arguments one can conceive either that time does not exist at all, or that it is something which can be perceived only obscurely and with difficulty.

The first argument is as follows. Anything that is composed of things which do not exist cannot itself exist or have any substance. But time is composed of things which do not exist. For one part of time is the past which does not now exist, and the other part is the future which does not yet exist. And from these two things the whole of time, given as infinite and perpetual, is composed. Therefore it is impossible that time is something.

560. He gives the second argument where he says, **"Further, if a divisible thing..."** [392]. The argument is as follows.

In regard to each divisible thing it is necessary, while it exists, that one or more of its parts exist. But this is not

true of time. For certain parts of time are now past, and other parts are in the future, and no divisible part of time exists in act. The "now," which exists in act, is not a part of time. For a part is either that which measures a whole, as two is a part of six, or at least that from which the whole is composed, as four is a part of six, not as measuring it, but because six is composed of four and two. However, time is not composed of "nows," as will be proven below. Therefore, time is not something.

561. Next where he says, **"Again, the 'now' ..."** [393], he inquires whether the same "now" is in all time.

Concerning this he makes three points. First he raises the question. Secondly, where he says, **"If it is always different ..."** [394], he objects to one part of the question. Thirdly, where he says, **"Yes, but neither is it possible ..."** [395], he objects to the other part of the question.

He says, therefore, first [393] that it is not easy to know whether the "now," which seems to distinguish past from future, always remains the same in the whole of time, or whether it is different.

562. Next where he says, **"If it is always different ..."** [394], he shows with the following argument that the "now" is not different.

Two different parts of time cannot exist simultaneously unless one contains the other. Thus a greater time contains a smaller time. For example, a year contains a month, and a month contains a day. (For a day and a month and a year exist simultaneously.) But one "now," since it is indivisible, does not contain another. Therefore, if we take two "nows" in time, it is necessary that the "now," which formerly was and in a way is not, at some time was corrupted, and that two "nows" never exist simultaneously. But everything that is corrupted must be corrupted in some "now." However, it cannot be said that that former "now" was corrupted in that former "now" itself. For then that "now" was, and nothing is corrupted while it exists. Likewise, it cannot be said that that former "now" was corrupted in a later "now." For it is impossible for two "nows" to be so related to each other that they are immediately consecutive, just as this is also impossible regarding two points. This is assumed here, but will be proven in Book VI. Therefore between any two "nows" there is an infinity of "nows." If, therefore, a former "now" is corrupted in some later "now," then it follows that that "now" which is first exists simultaneously with all the intermediate "nows." This is impossible, as was said. Therefore it is impossible that the "now" be different.

563. Next where he says, **"Yes, but neither is it possible . . ."** [395], he shows with two arguments that the "now" cannot be one and the same.

The first argument is as follows. There cannot be only one terminus of a finite, divisible thing, whether it be a continuum in only one dimension, as a line, or in many dimensions, as a surface and a body. For two points are the termini of one finite line, and many lines of a surface, and many surfaces of a body. But the "now" is the terminus of time. Therefore, when we take some finite time, there must be many "nows."

564. He gives the second argument where he says, **"Further, if coincidence . . ."** [396]. The argument is as follows. Those things are said to be simultaneous, and neither before nor after, which exist in the same "now." Therefore, if the same "now" remains in the whole of time, it follows that things which existed a thousand years ago are simultaneous with things which exist today.

Lastly he concludes that such are the objections concerning the "nows" of time.

By Means of Disputation He Inquires What Time Is and How It Is Related to Motion

The Text of Aristotle

397. As to what time is or what is its nature, the traditional accounts give us as little light as the preliminary problems which we have worked through. 218a31–218b1

398. Some assert that it is (1) the movement of the whole, others that it is (2) the sphere itself. 218b1–3

399. (1) Yet part, too, of the revolution is a time, but it certainly is not a revolution; for what is taken is part of a revolution, not a revolution. Besides, if there were more heavens than one, the movement of any of them equally would be time, so that there would be many times at the same time. 218b3–5

400. (2) Those who said that time is the sphere of the whole thought so, no doubt, on the ground that all things are in time and all things are in the sphere of the whole. The view is too naive for it to be worth while to consider the impossibilities implied in it. 218b5–9

401. But as time is most usually supposed to be (3) motion and a kind of change, we must consider this view. Now (a) the change or movement of each thing is only in the thing which changes or where the thing itself which moves or changes may chance to be. But time is present equally everywhere and with all things. 218b9–13

402. Again, (b) change is always faster or slower, whereas time is not; for "fast" and "slow" are defined by time—"fast" is what moves much in a short time, "slow" what moves little in a long time; but time is not defined by time, by being either a certain amount or a certain kind of it. Clearly then it is not movement. (We need not distinguish at present between "movement" and "change.") 218b13–20

Chapter 11

403. But neither does time exist without change; for when the state of our own minds does not change at all, or we have not noticed its changing, we do not realize that time has elapsed, any more than those who are fabled to sleep among the heroes in Sardinia do when they are awakened; for they connect the earlier "now" with the later and make them one, cutting out the interval because of their failure to notice it. So, just as, if the "now" were not different but one and the same, there would not have been time, so too when its difference escapes our notice the interval does not seem to be time. If, then, the non-realization of the existence of time happens to us when we do not distinguish any change, but the soul seems to stay in one indivisible state, and when we perceive and distinguish we say time has elapsed, evidently time is not independent of movement and change. 218b21–219a1

COMMENTARY OF ST. THOMAS

565. After he has inquired whether time is, here by means of disputation he inquires what time is.

First he disproves the positions of others. Secondly, where he says, "But as time is . . ." [401], he inquires how time is related to motion, which seems to be most closely related to time.

Concerning the first part he makes two points. First he gives the opinions of others concerning time. Secondly, where he says, "Yet part, too, of the revolution . . ." [398], he refutes these opinions.

He says, therefore, first that what time is and what its nature is cannot be settled by means of that which has been handed down from the ancients concerning time. Moreover, the things which they have decided about this matter cannot be reconciled with each other. For some have said that time is the motion of the heavens, and others have said that time is the celestial sphere itself.

566. Next where he says, "Yet part, too, of the revolution . . ." [398], he refutes these opinions. First, he refutes the first opinion, and secondly the other one, where he says, "Those who said . . ." [400].

Concerning the first opinion he gives two arguments, the first of which [398] is as follows.

If time is a revolution, it would be necessary that part of a revolution is a revolution, since a part of time is time. But part of a revolution is not a revolution. Therefore time is not a revolution.

He gives the second argument where he says, "Besides, if there were . . ." [399]. The argument is as follows.

Motion is multiplied according to the multitude of mobile bodies. If, therefore, there were many heavens, there would be many revolutions. And thus, if time is a revolution, it would follow that there would simultaneously be many times. This is impossible. For there cannot simultaneously be two parts of time, unless one contains the other, as was said above.

Nevertheless, these men were motivated to hold that time is a revolution because times seem to be repeated in a circle.

567. Next where he says, "Those who said . . ." [400], he refutes the second opinion.

He says that it seemed to some that time is the sphere of the heavens because all things are in time and are also in the sphere of the whole, because the heavens contain all things. Hence they wished to conclude that time is the sphere of the heavens.

There are two defects in this argument. First, a thing is not said to be in time and in place univocally. Secondly, they argued in the second figure from two affirmatives. Therefore he says that this position is so stupid that it is not necessary to consider the impossibilities which result from it. For it is clear that all the parts of the sphere exist simultaneously, but all the parts of time do not.

568. Next where he says, "But as time is . . ." [401], he inquires how time is related to motion.

First he shows that time is not motion. Secondly, where he says, "But neither does time . . ." [403], he shows that there is no time without motion.

Regarding the first part he gives two arguments to show that time is not motion or mutation, which it very much seems to be. Every motion and mutation is only in that which is changed, or else in the place where that which is changed and that which changes are. The first of these applies to substantial, quantitative, and qualitative motion; the second applies to motion in a "where," which is called local motion. But time is everywhere and among all things. Therefore, time is not motion.

569. He gives the second argument where he says, "Again, change is always . . ." [402]. The argument is as follows.

Every mutation and motion is either fast or slow. But time is neither fast nor slow. Therefore time is neither motion nor mutation. He proves the middle as follows. Fast and slow are determined by time. For that is called fast which is moved through much space in a short time. Conversely, that is called slow which is moved through a short space in much time. But time is not determined by time, either in its quantity or in its quality. For nothing is the measure of itself. Therefore time is neither fast nor slow. And since he had proposed that mutation is either fast or slow, but no mention of motion was made, he adds that for the present, motion does not differ from mutation. In Book V the difference between them will be explained.

570. Next where he says, **"But neither does time ..."** [403], he shows that there is no time without motion. When men are not changed in their apprehensions, or if changed, it escapes them, then it does not seem to them that any time has passed. This is clear in regard to those who are fabled to have slept among the Heroes, or the gods, in Sardos, a city in Asia. The souls of the good and the great are called Heroes, and men revered them as gods, such as Hercules and Bacchus and others. Through certain incantations, some were made insensible, and these, they said, slept among the Heroes. For when they had awakened, they said they had seen wonderful things, and they predicted future events. However, when they returned to themselves, they did not perceive the time that had passed while they were so absorbed. For they joined the first instant in which they began to sleep with the later "now" in which they awoke, as if they were one. They did not perceive the middle time. Therefore, if the "now" were not different, but were one and the same, there would be no middle time. And thus, when the difference between two "nows" goes unnoticed, it would not seem that there is a middle time. Therefore when we do not perceive some mutation, time is not thought of, and it seems to a man that he exists in one indivisible "now." But we perceive that time comes to be when we sense and we number motion or mutation. It clearly follows that there is no time without motion or mutation.

Lastly he concludes that time is not motion, and there is no time without motion.

The Definition of Time Is Given and Explained

The Text of Aristotle

404. *It is evident, then, that time is neither movement nor independent of movement. We must take this as our starting-point and try to discover—since we wish to know what time is—what exactly it has to do with movement. Now we perceive movement and time together; for even when it is dark and we are not being affected through the body, if any movement takes place in the mind we at once suppose that some time also has elapsed; and not only that but also, when some time is thought to have passed, some movement also along with it seems to have taken place. Hence time is either movement or something that belongs to movement. Since then it is not movement, it must be the other.* 219a1–10

405. *But what is moved is moved from something to something, and all magnitude is continuous. Therefore the movement goes with the magnitude. Because the magnitude is continuous, the movement too must be continuous, and if the movement, then the time; for the time that has passed is always thought to be in proportion to the movement.* 219a10–14

406. *The distinction of "before" and "after" holds primarily then, in place; and there in virtue of relative position. Since then "before" and "after" hold in magnitude, they must hold also in movement, these corresponding to those. But also in time the distinction of "before" and "after" must hold; for time and movement always correspond with each other.* 219a14–19

407. *The "before" and "after" in motion identical in substratum with motion yet differs from it in definition, and is not identical with motion.* 219a19–21

408. *But we apprehend time only when we have marked motion, marking it by "before" and "after"; and it is only when we have perceived "before" and "after" in motion that we say that time has elapsed.* 219a22–25

409. *Now we mark them by judging that A and B are different, and that some third thing is intermediate to them. When we think of the extremes as different from the middle and the mind pronounces that the "nows" are two, one before and one after, it is then that we say that there is time, and this that we say is time. For what is bounded by the "now" is thought to be time—we may assume this. When, therefore, we perceive the "now" as one, and neither as before and after in a motion nor as an identity but in relation to a "before" and an "after," no time is thought to have elapsed, because there has been no motion either. On the other hand, when we do perceive a "before" and an "after," then we say that there is time. For time is just this—number of motion in respect of "before" and "after." Hence time is not movement, but only movement in so far as it admits of enumeration.* 219a25–219b2

410. *A proof of this: we discriminate the more or the less by number, but more or less movement by time. Time then is a kind of number.* 219b2–5

411. *(Number, we must note, is used in two senses—both of what is counted or the countable and also of that with which we count. Time obviously is what is counted, not that with which we count: these are different kinds of thing.)* 219b5–9

COMMENTARY OF ST. THOMAS

571. After the Philosopher has investigated time by means of disputation, he begins here to determine the truth.

First he determines the truth about time. Secondly, where he says, **"It is also worth considering . . ."** [451], he raises and answers certain difficulties concerning the truth he has determined.

Concerning the first part he makes two points. First he treats time in itself. Secondly, where he says, **"Time is a measure . . ."** [426] he treats time in comparison with those things which are measured by time.

Concerning the first part he makes three points. First he explains what time is. Secondly, where he says, **"Just as motion is . . ."** [412], he explains what the "now" of time is. Thirdly, where he says, **"It is clear, then . . ."** [420], from the given definition of motion he establishes the meanings [ratio] of those things which are said about time.

Concerning the first part he makes two points. First he gives the definition of time, and secondly he explains it, where he says, **"A proof of this . . ."** [410].

The first part is divided according to the three parts of the definition of time which he examines. The second part begins where he says, **"But what is moved . . ."** [405], and the third part begins where he says, **"Now we mark them . . ."** [409].

572. Therefore, he first examines the point that time pertains to motion.

He says that, since we are asking what time is, we must begin by inquiring how time pertains to motion. It is clear that time does pertain to motion because we sense motion and time together. It happens that sometimes we perceive a passage of time, even if we do not sense any particular, sensible motion, for example, when we are in the dark and do not see the motion of any exterior body. And if we do not suffer any alteration in our bodies from an exterior agent, we will not sense any motion of a sensible body. Nevertheless, if some motion occurs in our soul, for example, a succession of thoughts and images, it immediately

seems to us that some time has passed. Thus by perceiving some sort of motion, we perceive time. And conversely, when we perceive time, we also perceive motion. Hence, since time is not motion itself, as was proven, it follows that time pertains to motion.

573. However, there is a difficulty that arises here concerning the perception of time and motion. If time is consequent upon a sensible motion outside the soul, it follows that he who does not sense that motion will not sense time. However, the contrary of this is held here. But if time is consequent upon a motion of the soul, it would follow that things are not related to time except by the mediation of the soul. And thus time will not be a thing of nature but an intention of the soul, by way of an intention of genus and species. And if time is consequent upon all motion universally, it would follow that there are as many times as there are motions. But this is impossible, because two times are not simultaneous, as was said above.

574. To answer this it must be known that there is one first motion which is the cause of all other motion. Hence, whatever is mutable in existence is such because of that first motion, which is the motion of the first mobile object. Moreover, whoever perceives any motion, either existing in sensible things or in the soul, perceives a mutable existence, and consequently he perceives the first motion from which time follows. Hence, whoever perceives any motion perceives time, although time is consequent upon only the one first motion by which all other motions are caused and measured. And thus there remains only one time.

575. Next where he says, **"But what is moved . . ."** [405], he examines the

second part of the definition of time. It has been stated that time pertains to motion, that is, it is consequent upon motion. We must ask further how time is consequent upon motion—that is, in respect to before and after.

Concerning this he makes three points. First he shows how before and after are found in motion. Secondly, where he says, **"The 'before' and 'after' . . ."** [407]. he shows how before and after are related to motion. Thirdly, where he says, **"But we apprehend time . . ."** [408], he shows that time is consequent upon motion in respect to before and after.

Concerning the first part he makes two points. First he shows that there is continuity in time from motion and magnitude. Secondly, where he says, **"The distinction of . . ."** [406], he shows that there is a before and after in time.

576. He says, therefore, first that everything which is moved is moved from something to something. But the first of all motions is local motion, which is motion from place to place in respect to some magnitude. But time is consequent upon the first motion. Therefore to investigate time it is necessary to consider motion in respect to place. Hence, since motion in respect to place is motion from something to something in respect to magnitude, and since every magnitude is continuous, then it is necessary that motion is consequent upon magnitude in continuity, that is, since magnitude is continuous, motion is continuous. And consequently time is also continuous. For there seems to be the same amount of time as there is of first motion. But time is not measured by the quantity of just any motion. For the slow is moved through a short space in a long time,

and the fast is moved through a long space in a short time. Rather time is consequent upon the quantity of only the first motion.

577. Next where he says, **"The distinction of . . ."** [406], he shows that the same order is found in before and after. He says that before and after are first in place or in magnitude.

This is so because magnitude is quantity which has position. But before and after belong to the nature [ratio] of position. Hence, place has a before and after from its very position. And since there is before and after in magnitude, it is necessary that in motion there is a before and after in proportion to the things which are in magnitude and in place. And consequently there is also a before and after in time. For motion and time are so related that one of them always follows upon the other.

578. Next where he says, **"The 'before' and 'after' . . ."** [407], he shows how before and after are related to motion.

He says that the before and after of time and motion, in respect to that which is, are the motion. But in respect to reason [ratio] they are other than motion and are not motion. For according to reason [ratio] motion is the act of that which exists in potency. But before and after are in motion because of the order of the parts of magnitude. Therefore, before and after are the same as motion in subject, but different in reason [ratio]. Hence, since time is consequent upon motion, as was shown above, it must further be asked whether time is consequent upon motion as motion or upon motion insofar as motion has a before and after.

579. Next where he says, **"But we apprehend time . . ."** [408], he shows

that time is consequent upon motion by reason [ratio] of the before and after.

It was shown that time is consequent upon motion because we know time and motion together. According to this, therefore, time is consequent upon motion according to the knowledge by which time is perceived in motion. But we know time when we distinguish motion by determining a before and after. We say that time passes when we sense a before and after in motion. It follows, therefore, that time is consequent upon motion in respect to before and after.

580. Next where he says, **"Now we mark them . . ."** [409], he shows what time is, namely, the number of motion. He shows this in the same way, that is, by our knowledge of time and motion.

It is clear that we determine that there is time when we take two parts of motion with some medium between them. For when we know the diverse extremes of some medium, the soul also says that there are two "nows," one before, the other after; as if we would say that there is time by numbering the before and after in motion. For time seems to be determined by the "now" itself. This is supposed for the present. It will be clarified later on.

Therefore, when we sense one "now" and do not discern in motion a before and after, or when we discern in motion a before and after but we take the same "now" as the end of the before and the beginning of the after, then it does not seem that time passes, for there is no motion. But when we take a before and after and number them, then we say that time passes. This is so because time is nothing else than the number of motion in respect to before and after. For we perceive

time, as was said, when we number the before and after in motion. Therefore, it is clear that time is not motion, but is consequent upon motion insofar as it is numbered. Hence time is the number of motion.

If someone objects to the above definition by saying that before and after are determined by time and thus the definition is circular, it must be said that before and after are placed in the definition of time insofar as they are caused in motion by magnitude and not insofar as they are measured by time. Thus Aristotle showed above that before and after are first in magnitude rather than in motion, and in motion rather than in time, so that this objection might be excluded.

581. Next where he says, **"A proof of this . . ."** [410], he clarifies the above definition in two ways.

He does this first with an example. We judge something to be more or less by its number. But we judge motion to be more or less by time. Therefore, time is a number.

Secondly where he says, **"Number, we must note . . ."** [411], he clarifies what was said by distinguishing number. He says that number is twofold. First there is that which is number in act or is that which is numerable, as when we say ten men or ten horses. This is called numbered number, because it is a number which is applied to numbered things. Secondly, there is the number by which we number, that is, number taken absolutely; for example, two, three, four. Time is not a number by which we number. For it would then follow that the number of anything would be time. Rather time is numbered number, because the very number of before and after in motion is time, or also because the very things which are before and after are numbered.

Therefore, although number is a discrete quantity, nevertheless time is a continuous quantity because of the numbered thing. Thus, ten measures of cloth is a continuum, even though the number ten is a discrete quantity.

LECTURE 18 [219b9 220a23]
How the Same "Now" Is or Is Not in the Whole of Time. The Meaning of Things Which Are Said of the "Now"

The Text of Aristotle

412. *Just as motion is a perpetual succession, so also is time. But every simultaneous time is self-identical; for the "now" as a subject is an identity, but it accepts different attributes. The "now" measures time, in so far as time involves the "before and after."*   **219b9–12**

413. *The "now" in one sense is the same, in another it is not the same. In so far as it is in succession, it is different (which is just what its being now was supposed to mean), but its substratum is an identity;*   **219b12–15**

414. *for motion, as was said, goes with magnitude, and time, as we maintain, with motion. Similarly, then, there corresponds to the point the body which is carried along, and by which we are aware of the motion and of the "before and after" involved in it. This is an identical substratum (whether a point or a stone or something else of the kind), but it has different attributes —as the sophists assume that Coriscus' being in the Lyceum is a different thing from Coriscus' being in the market-place. And the body which is carried along is different, in so far as it is at one time here and at another there. But the "now" corresponds to the body that is carried along, as time corresponds to the motion. For it is by means of the body that is carried along that we become aware of the "before and after" in the motion, and if we regard these as countable we get the "now." Hence in these also the now as substratum remains the same (for it is what is before and after in movement), but what is predicated of it is different; for it is in so far as the "before and after" is numerable that we get the "now."*   **219b15–28**

415. *This is what is most knowable: for, similarly, motion is known because of that which is moved, locomotion because of that which is carried. For what is carried is a real thing, the movement is not. Thus what is called "now" in one sense is always the same; in another it is not the same: for this is true also of what is carried.*   **219b28–33**

416. *Clearly, too, if there were no time, there would be no "now," and vice versa. Just as the moving body and its locomotion involve each other mutually, so too do the number of the moving body and the number of its locomotion. For the number of the locomotion is time, while the "now" corresponds to the moving body, and is like the unit of number.*   **219b33–220a4**

417. *Time, then, also is both made continuous by the "now" and divided at it. For here too there is a correspondence with the locomotion and the moving body. For the motion or locomotion is made one by the thing which is moved, because it is one—not because it is one in its own nature (for there might be pauses in the movement of such a thing)—but because it is one in definition; for this determines the movement as "before" and "after."*   **220a4–9**

418. *Here, too, there is a correspondence with the point; for the point also both connects and terminates the length—it is the beginning of one and the end of another. But when you take it in this way, using the one point as two, a pause is necessary, if the same point is to be the beginning and the end. The "now" on the other hand, since the body carried is moving, is always different. Hence time is not number in the sense in which there is "number" of the same point because it is beginning and end, but rather as the extremities of a line form a number, and not as the parts of the line do so, both for the reason given (for we can use the middle point as two, so that on that analogy time might stand still),*   **220a9–18**

419. *and further because obviously the "now" is no part of time nor the section any part of the movement, any more than the points are parts of the line—for it is two lines that are parts of one line. In so far then as the "now" is a boundary, it is not time, but an attribute of it; in so far as it numbers, it is number; for boundaries belong only to that which they bound, but number*

COMMENTARY OF ST. THOMAS

582. After the Philosopher has shown what time is, he here treats the "now."

First he shows whether there is the same "now" or different "nows" in the whole of time. This problem was mentioned above. Secondly, where he says, **"Clearly, too, if there were ..."** [416], he establishes from the above the meaning [ratio] of those things which are said of the now.

Concerning the first part he makes three points. First he states that the "now" in a way is the same, and in a way it is not. Secondly, he explains this, where he says, **"The 'now' in one sense ..."** [413]. And thirdly he proves it, where he says, **". . . for motion, as was said ..."** [414].

583. He says, therefore, first [412] that since time is the number of motion, then just as the parts of motion are always different, so are the parts of time. But that which exists together with the whole of time, that is, the "now," is the same. Insofar as it is, it is the same. But in reason [ratio] it is different insofar as it is before and after. And thus the "now" measures time, not insofar as it is the same in subject, but rather insofar as in reason [ratio] it is different and before and after.

584. Next where he says, **"The 'now' in one sense ..."** [413], he explains this. He says that the "now" in a way is always the same, and in a way it is not. For insofar as the "now" is always considered as in another and another according to a succession of time and motion, it is different and is not the same. And this is what we meant when we said above that the "now" is different. For the meaning [ratio] of "now" is taken here as in the onrush of time and

motion. But insofar as the "now" is a certain being, it is the same in subject.

585. Next where he says, **". . . for motion, as was said ..."** [414], he proves what he has said.

First he proves that the "now" is the same in subject but different in reason [ratio]. Secondly, where he says, **"This is what is ..."** [415], he proves that the "now" measures time.

He says, therefore, first that, as was said above, in respect to continuity and before and after, motion is consequent upon magnitude, and time is consequent upon motion. Let us imagine that in geometry a moved point produces a line. In a similar way the same thing must also be true of time, as it is also true of motion. Moreover, if the point by its own motion produces a line, then that very point which is moved is that by which we know the motion and the before and after in the motion. For motion is perceived only because the mobile object is different. That which pertains to a preceding disposition of the mobile object we judge to be prior in the motion, and that which pertains to a following disposition of the mobile object we judge to be posterior in the motion. That which is moved (by which we know motion and by which we discern the before and after in motion) is a point, or a stone, or something else. In regard to that by which it is a certain being, whatever it is, it is the same in subject, but it is different in reason [ratio]. However the sophists use the word "different" in the following way when they say that there is a different Coriscus in the theater and in the market-place. By a sophism of accident they argue as follows: being in the market-place is different than being in the theater. But Coriscus is now in the market-place and later in the theater. Therefore, he is other than himself. Hence it is clear that that which is moved, although it is the same in subject, is different in reason [ratio] in that it is now here and then there.

But just as time is consequent upon motion, likewise the "now" is consequent upon that which is moved. He proves this from the fact that we know the before and after in motion by means of the mobile object. For when we find a mobile object in some part of a magnitude through which it is moved, we judge that motion through one part of the magnitude happened first, and motion through another part of the magnitude follows later. And likewise in the numbering of motion by time, that which distinguishes the before and after of time is the "now," which is the end of the past and the beginning of the future. Therefore, the "now" is related to time as the mobile object is related to motion. Further, by rearranging the proportion, time is related to motion as the "now" is related to the mobile object. Hence, if the mobile object is the same in subject in the whole motion but different in reason [ratio], likewise it will be necessary that the "now" is the same in subject but different in reason [ratio]. For that by which the before and after are distinguished in motion (that is, the mobile object) is the same in subject but different in reason [ratio]. And that according to which the before and after in time are numbered is the "now" itself.

586. Moreover, from these considerations an understanding of eternity can be easily had. For the "now," insofar as it corresponds to a mobile object differently related, distinguishes the before and after in time. And by its flux it produces time, as a point produces a line. Therefore, when different dispositions are removed from a mobile object, there remains a substance which is always the same. Hence the "now" is understood as always stationary, and not as flowing or as having a before and after. Therefore, as the "now" of time is understood as the number of a mobile object, the "now" of eternity is understood as the number, or rather the unity, of a thing which is always the same.

587. Next where he says, **"This is what is . . ."** [415], he shows how the "now" measures time.

He says that that which is best known in time is the "now." And everything is measured by that which is best known in its genus, as is said in Metaphysics, X. He also shows this by means of the relation of motion to the mobile object. Motion is known by that which is moved, and local motion by that which is moved locally, as the less known is known by the more known. This is so because that which is moved is "a this," that is, a certain thing stable in itself, which is not true of motion. Hence the mobile object is more knowable than motion; and motion is known by means of the mobile object. And likewise time is known by means of the "now." Thus he concludes to the main point: that which is called the "now" in a way is always the same, and in a way is not. For it is similar to the mobile object, as was said.

588. Next where he says, **"Clearly, too, if there were . . ."** [416], he establishes the meaning [ratio] of those things which are said of the "now." First he establishes the meaning of the statement, "there is no time except the 'now'." Secondly, where he says, **"Time, then, also is . . ."** [417], he estab-

lishes the meaning of the statement, "the 'now' divides the parts of time and makes them continuous." Thirdly, where he says, *". . . and further because . . ."* [419], he establishes the meaning of the statement, "the 'now' is not a part of time."

589. He says, therefore, first [416] that it is clear that, if there were no time, there would be no "now," and if there were no "now," there would be no time. This is so because of the relation of motion to the mobile object. For just as local motion and that which is moved are together, likewise the number of that which is moved and the number of local motion are together. But time is the number of local motion. Moreover, the "now" is related to that which is moved not as a number (for the "now" is indivisible), but as the unity in number. Therefore, it follows that time and the "now" do not exist without each other. Moreover, it must be noted that time is always related to local motion, which is the first motion. For time is the number of the first motion, as was said.

590. Next where he says, *"Time, then also is . . ."* [417], he establishes the meaning [ratio] of the statement, "time is made continuous and is divided by the 'now'." He does this first by means of motion and the mobile object, and secondly, where he says, *"Here, too, there is . . ."* [418], by means of a line and a point.

He says, therefore, first that it is now clear from the foregoing that time is a continuum because of the "now," and time is divided by the "now." This follows from that which is found in local motion, whose number is time, and from that which is moved in respect to place, to which the "now" corresponds. For it is clear that every motion has unity from that which is

moved, because that which is moved remains one and the same in the whole motion. And when one motion continues, that which is moved is not just any being, but rather the same being which began to be moved in the first place. For if there were another being which was moved later, the first motion would have ended, and there would then be a motion of a different mobile object. Thus it is clear that the mobile object gives unity to motion, and this is its continuity.

However it is true that the mobile object is different according to reason [ratio]. He distinguishes the before and after part of motion as follows. Insofar as motion is considered by one understanding [ratio] or disposition, one realizes that before this there was some other disposition of the mobile object which pertained to a prior part of the motion. Moreover, whatever comes after this will pertain to a later part of the motion. Therefore, the mobile object makes the motion continuous and divides it. And the "now" is related to time in the same way.

591. Next where he says, *"Here, too, there is . . ."* [418], he establishes the same thing by means of a line and a point. He says that that which was said about time and the "now" agrees in a certain way with what is found in a line and a point. For a point makes a line continuous, and divides it insofar as it is the beginning of one part and the end of another.

Nevertheless, there is this difference between a line and a point, and time and the "now." A point and a line are at rest. Hence, one can take the same point twice and use it as two, that is, as a beginning and as an end. And when we so use a point as two, it remains at rest, as is clear in reflex motion in which the end of the first motion is the beginning of the second reflex motion. Because of this it is proven below in Book VIII that reflex motion is not continuous, but a state of rest intervenes.

But the "now" is not at rest, because it corresponds to the mobile object which is always in motion while the motion lasts. Because of this the "now" is always different in respect to reason [ratio], as was said above. Therefore, although time is the number of motion, it does not number motion in that the same time is taken as the beginning of one part and the end of another. Rather time numbers motion when two extremities of time, that is, two "nows" (which, nevertheless, are not parts of time), are taken.

The reason why this kind of numbering pertains to time, rather than the other kind, in which the parts of a line are numbered by a point as a beginning and end, is as follows. When one uses a point twice, an intermediate state of rest results, and this cannot occur in time and in motion. Nevertheless, it must not be understood from what has been said that the same "now" is not the beginning of the future and the end of the past. The point here is that we do not perceive time by numbering motion with one "now," but rather by two "nows," as was said.

For otherwise it would follow that in numbering motion the same "now" would be taken twice.

592. Next where he says, ". . . and further because . . ." [419], he establishes the meaning [ratio] of the statement, "the 'now' is not a part of time."

He says that it is clear that the "now" is not a part of time; just as that by which motion is distinguished, that is, a designated disposition in the mobile object, is not a part of motion. Nor are points parts of a line. Rather two lines are parts of one line.

However, he explains the properties of time by means of motion and a line. For, as was said above, motion is continuous because of magnitude, and time is continuous because of motion.

Finally he concludes that the "now," insofar as it is a terminus, is not time, but is related to time as terminus to terminated. But insofar as time or the "now" numbers things, it numbers things other than time. The reason [ratio] for this is that there is a terminus only of that which is terminated. But numbers are of diverse things; thus, ten is the number of horses and other things. Therefore the "now" is the terminus only of time, but it is the number of all mobile objects which are moved in time.

LECTURE 19 [220a24–b30]
Certain Things Which Are Usually Said about Time Are Clarified

The Text of Aristotle

420. *It is clear, then, that time is "number of movement in respect of the before and after" and is continuous since it is an attribute of what is continuous.*

Chapter 12

The smallest number, in the strict sense of the word "number," is two. But of number as concrete, sometimes there is a minimum, sometimes not: e.g., of a "line," the smallest in respect of is two (or, if you like, one), but in respect of size there is no minimum; for every line is divided ad infinitum. *Hence it is so with time. In respect of number the minimum is one (or two); in point of extent there is no minimum.* **220a24–32**

421. *It is clear, too, that time is not described as fast or slow, but as many or few and as long or short. For as continuous it is long or short and as a number many or few, but it is not fast or slow—any more than any number with which we number is fast or slow.* **220a32–220b5**

422. *Further, there is the same time everywhere at once, but not the same time before and after, for while the present change is one, the change which has happened and that which will happen are different. Time is not number with which we count, but the number of things which are counted, and this according as it occurs before or after is always different, for the "nows" are different. And the number of a hundred horses and a hundred men is the same, but the things numbered are different—the horses from the men.* **220b5–12**

423. *Further, as a movement can be one and the same again and again, so too can time, e.g., a year or a spring or an autumn.* **220b12–14**

424. *Not only do we measure the movement by the time, but also the time by the movement, because they define each other. The time marks the movement, since it is its number, and the movement the time. We describe the time as much or little, measuring it by the movement, just as we know the number by what is numbered, e.g., the number of the horses by one horse as the unit. For we know how many horses there are by the use of the number; and again by using the one horse as unit we know the number of the horses itself. So it is with the time and the movement; for we measure the movement by the time and vice versa.* **220b14–24**

425. *It is natural that this should happen; for the movement goes with the distance and the time with the movement, because they are quanta and continuous and divisible. The movement has these attributes because the distance is of this nature, and the time has them because of the movement. And we measure both the distance by the movement and the movement by the distance; for we say that the road is long, if the journey is long, and that this is long, if the road is long—the time, too, if the movement, and the movement, if the time.* **220b24–32**

COMMENTARY OF ST. THOMAS

593. After the Philosopher has defined time, he here establishes from this definition the meaning [ratio] of things which are said about time.

Concerning this he does four things. First he explains how a minimum is found in time and how not. Secondly, where he says, **"It is clear, too . . ."** [421], he explains why time is called many and few, long and short, but not fast and slow. Thirdly, where he says, **"Further, there is the same . . ."** [422], he explains how time is the same and how not. Fourthly, where he says,

"Not only do we ..." [424], he explains how time is known by motion, and vice versa.

594. He says, therefore, first that it is clear from the definition of motion given above that time is the number of motion in respect to before and after, as was explained above. Furthermore, it is clear from the foregoing that time is continuous. For, although it is not continuous from the fact that it is a number, nevertheless it is continuous because of that of which it is the number. For time is the number of a continuum, that is, motion, as was said above. Time is not a number simply, but a numbered number.

In simple number there is found an altogether minimum number, that is, duality. But if we take the number of a continuous thing, in a way there is a minimum and in a way not. For in respect to multitude there is a minimum, but in respect to magnitude there is not. Thus, in many lines there is a minimum in respect to multitude, either one line or two: one, if that which is simply a minimum in number is taken; but two, if that which is a minimum in the genus of number, having the nature [ratio] of number, is taken. But in lines there is no minimum in respect to magnitude, so that there would be, for example, some smallest line. For any line can always be divided.

Time must be described in like manner. In time there is a minimum in respect to multitude, that is, either one or two; for example, one year or two years, or two days or hours. But in time there is no minimum in respect to magnitude. For in any given time there are parts into which it is divided.

595. Next where he says, "It is clear, too ..." [421], he explains the reason [ratio] why time is not called fast or

slow, but is called many and few, long and short.

It was already shown that time is a number and a continuum. Therefore, insofar as it is a continuum, time is called long and short, as also is a line. And insofar as time is a number, it is called many and few. But fast and slow in no way belong to number. Fast and slow do not belong simply to number, as is clear, nor can they belong to the number of some thing. For fast and slow is said of something insofar as it is numbered. A fast motion is said to be in that which is numbered by a short time, and a slow motion is the opposite. Hence it is clear that in no way can time be called fast or slow.

596. Next where he says, "Further, there is the same ..." [422], he explains how time is the same and how not.

First he explains how it is the same or not simply, and second, accidentally, where he says, "Further, as a movement ..." [423].

He says, therefore, first that time, existing simultaneously, is the same everywhere, that is, in respect to everything which is moved anywhere. For time is not diversified by diverse mobile objects but by diverse parts of the same motion. Therefore, a prior time and later time are not the same. This is so because the present primary motion, whose number is time primarily and principally, is one. But that which is already done and past is a different part of this motion. And the future is another part. Hence, that which was is one time, and that which will be is still another time. This is so because time is not number simply, but the number of some numbered thing, that is, of the before and after in motion. This number is always different and before and after, because the "nows" insofar as they are related to before and after are always different.

But if time were number simply, then the time of a past motion and of a future motion would be the same. For simple number is one and the same for diverse numbered things, as a hundred horses and a hundred men. But numbered number is different for diverse things. A hundred horses are not a hundred men. And since time is the number of the before and after in motion, those things in motion which are related to the before and after as already past are different from those things which are related as future. And because of this past time is different from future time.

597. Next where he says, **"Further, as a movement . . ."** [423], he explains how the same time is repeated accidentally.

He says that as one and the same motion can be repeated, likewise one and the same time can be repeated. For a motion which is one and the same in species, but not in number, is repeated. The sun will be moved at a later time from the same sign of the ram from which it was moved earlier. And the winter or spring or summer or fall was and will be. They are not one in number, but in species.

598. Next where he says, **"Not only do we . . ."** [424], he shows that, just as we know motion by time, we also know time by motion.

He shows this first from the nature [ratio] of number and the numbered. Secondly, where he says, **"It is natural that . . ."** [525], he shows this with a comparison of motion and magnitude.

He says, therefore, first [424] that not only do we measure motion by time, but we also measure time by motion, because they are defined by each other. For it is necessary to take the quantity of one according to the quantity of the other. Time determines motion because it is the number of motion. But conversely motion determines time in respect to us. For occasionally we perceive the quantity of time by motion, as when we say time is many or few according to a measure of motion known to us. Sometimes we know number by numerables, and sometimes vice versa. For we know a multitude of horses by number, and again we know the number of horses by one horse. We do not know how much a thousand is unless we know what a thousand is. It is the same with time and motion. For when the quantity of time is known to us and the quantity of motion is not, then we measure motion by time. And the opposite occurs when motion is known to us and time is unknown.

599. Next where he says, **"It is natural that . . ."** [425], he explains the same thing by comparing motion to magnitude. He says that what was said about time and motion is reasonable. As motion imitates magnitude in quantity, continuity, and , so also time imitates motion. For these things are found in motion because of magnitude, and in time because of motion. Moreover, we measure magnitude by motion and motion by magnitude. For we say that a road is long when we perceive that our motion was long; and conversely, when we consider the magnitude of the road, we say that our motion is long. And this is also true of time and motion, as was said above.

How Motion and Other Things Are in Time. What Things Are and What Things Are Not in Time

The Text of Aristotle

426. *Time is a measure of motion and of being moved, and it measures the motion by determining a motion which will measure exactly the whole motion, as the cubit does the length by determining an amount which will measure out the whole. Further "to be in time" means, for movement that both it and its essence are measured by time (for simultaneously it measures both the movement and its essence, and this is what being in time means for it, that its essence should be measured).* 220b32–221a7

427. *Clearly then "to be in time" has the same meaning for other things also, namely, that their being should be measured by time. "To be in time" is one of two things: (1) to exist when time exists, (2) as we say of some things that they are "in number." The latter means either what is a part or mode of number—in general, something which belongs to number—or that things have a number. Now, since time is number, the "now" and the "before" and the like are in time, just as "unit" and "odd" and "even" are in number, i.e. in the sense that the one set belongs to number, the other to time. But things are in time as they are in number. If this is so, they are contained by time as things in place are contained by place. Plainly, too, to be in time does not mean to coexist with time, any more than to be in motion or in place means to coexist with motion or place. For if "to be in something" is to mean this, then all things will be in anything, and the heaven will be in a grain; for when the grain is, then also is the heaven. But this is a merely incidental conjunction, whereas the other is necessarily involved: that which is in time necessarily involves that there is time when it is, and that which is in motion that there is motion when it is.* 221a7–26

428. *Since what is "in time" is so in the same sense as what is in number is so, a time greater than everything in time can be found. So it is necessary that all the things in time should be contained by time, just like other things also which are "in anything," e.g., the things "in place" by place.* 221a26–30

429. *A thing, then, will be affected by time, just as we are accustomed to say that time wastes things away, and that all things grow old through time, and that there is oblivion owing to the lapse of time, but we do not say the same of getting to know or of becoming young or fair. For time is by its nature the cause rather of decay, since it is the number of change, and change removes what is.* 221a30–221b3

430. *Hence, plainly, things which are always are not, as such, in time; for they are not contained by time, nor is their being measured by time.* 221b3–5

431. *A proof of this is that none of them is affected by time, which indicates that they are not in time.* 221b5–7

432. *Since time is the measure of motion, it will be the measure of rest too—indirectly. For all rest is in time.* 221b7–9

433. *For it does not follow that what is in time is moved, though what is in motion is necessarily moved. For time is not motion; but "number of motion"; and what is at rest, also, can be in the number of motion.* 221b9–12

434. *Not everything that is not in motion can be said to be "at rest"—but only that which can be moved, though it actually is not moved, as was said above. To be in number means that there is a number of the thing, and that its being is measured by the number in which it is. Hence if a thing is "in time" it will be measured by time.* 221b12–16

435. *But time will measure what is moved and what is at rest, the one qua moved, the other*

qua at rest; for it will measure their motion and rest respectively.   **221b16–20**

436. *Hence what is moved will not be measurable by the time simply in so far as it has quantity, but in so far as its motion has quantity. Thus none of the things which are neither moved nor at rest are in time; for "to be in time" is "to be measured by time," while time is the measure of motion and rest.*   **216b20–23**

437. *Plainly, then, neither will everything that does not exist be in time, i.e. those non-existent things that cannot exist, as the diagonal cannot be commensurate with the side. Generally, if time is directly the measure of motion and indirectly of other things, it is clear that a thing whose existence is measured by it will have its existence in rest or motion. Those things therefore which are subject to perishing and becoming—generally, those which at one time exist, at another do not—are necessarily in time; for there is a greater time which will extend both beyond their existence and beyond the time which measures their existence. Of things which do not exist but are contained by time some were, e.g., Homer once was, some will be, e.g., a future event; this depends on the direction in which time contains them; if on both, they have both modes of existence. As to such things as it does not contain in any way, they neither were nor are nor will be. These are those non-existents whose opposites always are, as the incommensurability of the diagonal always is—and this will not be in time. Nor will the commensurability, therefore; hence this eternally is not, because it is contrary to what eternally is. A thing whose contrary is not eternal can be and not be, and it is of such things that there is coming to be and passing away.*   **221b23–222a9**

COMMENTARY OF ST. THOMAS

600. After the Philosopher has treated time in itself, he here treats time in comparison with those things which are in time.

Concerning this he makes two points. First he compares time to those things which are in time. Secondly, where he says, **"The 'now' is the link . . ."** [438], he compares time to those things which are in the "now."

Concerning the first part he makes two points. First he compares time to motion. Secondly, where he says, **"Clearly then 'to be in time' . . ."** [427], he compares time to other things which are in time.

601. Concerning the first part it must be realized that motion is compared to time differently than other things are. For motion is measured by time both in respect to what it is and in respect to its duration or its existence. Other things, like a man or a stone, are measured by time in respect to their existence or their duration, insofar as they have a changeable existence. But in respect to what they are, they are not measured by time but rather the "now" of time corresponds to them, as was said above.

Therefore, he says that [426] time is the measure both of motion itself and of being moved, by which he means the duration of motion.

Moreover, time measures motion in that it determines some part of the motion which measures the whole. And this is necessarily so, for everything is measured by something of the same genus, as is said in Metaphysics, X. This is clear in the measurement of magnitude. For a cubit measures the whole length of a road or a piece of cloth by determining some part of its length, which then measures the whole. Likewise time measures the whole of a motion by means of a part. For by the motion of one hour the motion of a whole day is measured, and by the daily motion the motion of a year is measured. Therefore, for motion to be measured by time is nothing else than for motion to be in a time which is measured by time, both in respect to what it is and in respect to its duration. For motion is measured by time in both respects, as was said.

602. Next where he says, **"Clearly then 'to be in time' . . ."** [427], he explains how time is related to other things. First he explains how other things are in time. Secondly, where he says, **"Since what is 'in time' . . ."** [428], he explains what things can be in time.

He says, therefore, first that motion is in time when it and its existence are measured by time. Hence it is clear that other things are also in time and are measured by time. But only their existence is measured by time, not they themselves. For motion is per se measured by time, but other things are measured by time only insofar as they have motion.

He shows as follows that for a thing to be in time means that its existence is measured by time. To be in time can be understood in two ways. First, a thing is said to be in time when it is together with time. Secondly, things are said to be in time just as things are said to be in number. This latter has two meanings. First, a thing is said to be in number as a part, as two is in four, or as its proper passion, like even and odd, or whatever else belongs to number. Secondly, a thing is said to be in number, not because it itself is a number, but because number belongs to it as a numbered thing, as men are said to be such and such in number.

Now since time is a number, things exist in time in both ways. For the "now," and the before and after, and other such things are in time in the same way that unity, which is a part, and even and odd, which are passions of number, and the perfect and the superfluous, are in number. (A number is perfect when it consists of parts which measure it. For example, the number six, which is measured by one, two, and three, is constituted by these numbers taken together. A number is superfluous when the parts which measure it exceed the whole. For example, the number twelve is measured by one, two, three, four and six, but these numbers taken together total sixteen.) In this way some things are in time because they pertain to time. But things which do not pertain to time are said to be in time as things which are numbered are in number. Hence it is necessary that things which are in time are contained under time as under a number, just as things which are in place are contained under place as under a measure.

Next he examines the first way of existing in time. He says that it is clear that to be in time, and to be when time is, are not the same thing. In the same way to be in motion and in place is not the same as to be when place and motion exist. Otherwise it would follow that all things are in each thing; for example, the heavens would be in a grain of wheat. For when the wheat exists, the heavens also exist.

Moreover, there is the following difference between these two things. When a thing is said to exist when something else exists, it is accidental to the one that it exists simultaneously with the other. But that in which a thing is as in a measure follows with necessity. Thus time necessarily is consequent upon that which exists in time. And motion necessarily is consequent upon that which is in motion, since they exist together.

603. Next where he says, **"Since what is 'in time' . . ."** [428], he shows what things can be in time.

First he shows that not every being is in time. Secondly, where he says, **"Plainly, then, neither . . ."** [437], he shows that not all non-beings are in time.

Concerning the first part he makes two points. First he shows that things which always exist are not in time. Secondly, where he says, **"Since time is the measure . . ."** [432], he shows that even things which are at rest are, as such, in time.

Concerning the first part he makes two points. First he sets forth certain things from which he establishes his position. Secondly, he comes to his conclusion, where he says, **"Hence, plainly, things . . ."** [430].

He sets forth two points. First, when a thing is in time as the numbered is in number, it is necessary that there can be a time which is greater than anything which is in time, just as there can be a number which is greater than anything which is numbered. And because of this it is necessary that all things which are in time are totally contained and included under time, just as things which are in place are included under place.

604. He gives the second point where he says, **"A thing, then, will be . . ."** [429]. Everything which is in time suffers something under time, insofar as passion pertains to the imperfect. He proves this by means of our customary way of speaking. For we are accustomed to say that a long time weakens and corrupts, and that because of time all things in time grow old, and that because of time forgetfulness occurs. For things which we re-

cently knew remain in the memory, but they slip away during the passage of time.

And lest someone should say that perfections should also be attributed to time as are the passions, he next refutes this view. He gives three arguments against the above three points.

Against his point that forgetfulness occurs because of time, he adds that one does not learn because of time. For if one lives for a long time undisturbed by the desire to learn, he does not thereby learn. And thus because of time he forgets.

Against his point that all things grow old in time, he adds that nothing new is done because of time. For from the mere fact that a thing lasts a long time it does not become new, but rather becomes old.

Against his point that time wastes things away, he adds that time does not make a thing good, that is, perfect and whole, but rather weakened and corrupted. The reason for this is that some things are corrupted by time, even if that which corrupts them is not clearly apparent. This is seen in the very nature [ratio] of time. For time is the number of motion. It is the nature [ratio] of motion to separate that which is from a disposition in which it formerly was. Hence, since time is the number of the first motion by which mutability is caused in all things, it follows that because of the passage of time all things in time are removed from their own dispositions.

605. Next where he says, **"Hence, plainly, things . . ."** [430], he draws his conclusion from the premises, and first from the first premise. It was shown that anything which is in time is contained under time. But things which always exist are not contained under time as something which exceeds. Nor

is the duration of these things measured under time. For they endure to infinity, and the infinite cannot be measured. Therefore, things which always exist are not in time. This is true insofar as they exist always. For the celestial bodies always exist according to the existence of their substance, but not according to their place. Therefore, their duration is not measured by time, but their local motion is measured by time.

Secondly, where he says, **"A proof of this . . ."** [431], he proves the same thing from the second premise. He says that a sign of the fact that things which always exist are not in time is that they do not suffer from time, as though they were not existing in time. For they do not waste away or grow old, as was said of things which are in time.

606. Next where he says, **"Since time is the measure . . ."** [432], after he has shown that things which always exist are not in time, he examines in the same way things which are at rest. One might believe that things which are at rest, as such, are not measured by time. Hence, to refute this he shows that time is also the measure of rest.

Concerning this he makes five points. First he states his intention. He says that, since time is the measure of motion per se, it will be the measure of rest per accidens. For all rest is in time, as is all motion.

607. Secondly, where he says, **"For it does not follow . . ."** [433], he denies a certain point from which it would seem that rest is not measured by time. Since time is the measure of motion, one might believe that rest is not in time since it is not in motion. Therefore, to refute this, he says that it is not necessary that everything which is in time be moved, as it is necessary that

everything which is in motion be moved. For time is not motion, but the number of motion. Moreover, there happens to be in the number of motion not only that which is moved but also that which is at rest.

608. Thirdly, where he says, **"Not everything that is . . ."** [434], he proves the proposition that rest is in the number of motion, such that it is measured by time.

To prove this he points out that not everything which is not moved is at rest. Rather rest is a privation of motion in that which can be moved. As was said above in Book III, that whose immobility is rest is moved, for rest is not the negation of motion, but its privation. Thus it is clear that the existence of a being at rest is the existence of a mobile thing. Hence, since the existence of a mobile thing is in time and is measured by time, the existence of a thing at rest is also measured by time. Moreover, we say that a thing is in time as in a number because there is some number of that thing and because its existence is measured by the number of time. Hence it is clear that rest is in time and is measured by time, not insofar as it is rest, but insofar as it is mobile. And because of this he stated above that time is the measure of motion per se and of rest per accidens.

609. Fourthly, where he says, **"But time will measure . . ."** [435], he shows how that which is mobile and that which is at rest are measured by time.

He says that time measures that which is moved and is at rest, not insofar as it is a stone or a man, but insofar as it is moved and is at rest. For measurement properly belongs to quantity. Therefore, that is properly measured by time whose quantity is measured by time. From the measurement of time is known the quantity of motion and the quantity of rest, but not the quantity of that which is moved. Hence, that which is moved is not simply measured by time according to its proper quantity, but according to the quantity of its motion. From this it is clear that time is properly the measure of motion and rest; of motion per se, and of rest per accidens.

610. Fifthly, where he says, **"Thus none of the things . . ."** [436], he points out a corollary of the above. If a thing is measured by time only insofar as it is moved and is at rest, it follows that things which are neither moved nor at rest, as the separated substances, are not in time. For to be in time is to be measured by time. And time is the measure of motion and of rest, as is clear from what has been said.

611. Next where he says, **"Plainly, then, neither . . ."** [437], he shows that not all non-beings are in time.

He says that it is clear from the above that not every non-being is in time, for example, those things which cannot be otherwise, as if the diameter were commensurable with the side of a square. This is impossible because it can never be true. Such things are not measured by time.

He proves this as follows. Time primarily and per se is a measure of motion, and other things are measured by time only per accidens. Therefore, whatever is measured by time happens to be moved or to be at rest. Hence generable and corruptible things, and anything which at one time is and another time is not, are in time because they are moved and are at rest. For there is a certain time greater than they, which excels their duration, and because of this it measures their substances, not according to what they are, but according to their existence or duration.

Among things which are not, but nevertheless are contained by time, certain ones at some time were, as Homer; certain ones at some time will be, as a future event; or if they are contained by past and future time, they were and will be. Those things which in no way are contained by time neither are nor were nor will be. Such things always are not, and their opposites always are. Thus the diameter is always incommensurable with the side. Hence this is not measured by time. And because of this its contrary, that the diameter is commensurable with the side, is not measured by time. Therefore, it always is not because it is contrary to that which always is.

That whose contrary is not always can be and not be, and is generated and corrupted. Such things are measured by time.

He Compares Time to Things Which Are in the "Now." The Meaning of "Now" (Nunc), "Then" (Tunc), "Presently" (Iam), "Lately" (Modo), "Long Ago" (Olim), and "Suddenly" (Repente)

The Text of Aristotle
Chapter 13

438. The "now" is the link of time, as has been said (for it connects past and future time), and it is a limit of time (for it is the beginning of the one and the end of the other). But this is not obvious as it is with the point, which is fixed. 222a10–13

439. It divides potentially, and in so far as it is dividing the "now" is always different, but in so far as it connects it is always the same, as it is with mathematical lines. For the intellect it is not always one and the same point, since it is other and other when one divides the line; but in so far as it is one, it is the same in every respect. So the "now" also is in one way a potential dividing of time, in another the termination of both parts, and their unity. 222a14–19

440. And the dividing and the uniting are the same thing and in the same reference, but in essence they are not the same. So one kind of "now" is described in this way. 222a19–21

441. Another is when the time is near. "He will come now" because he will come to-day; "he has come now" because he came to-day. But the things in the Iliad have not happened "now," nor is the flood "now"—not that the time from now to them is not continuous, but because they are not near. 222a21–24

442. "At some time" means a time determined in relation to the first of the two types of "now," e.g., "at some time" Troy was taken, and "at some time" there will be a flood; for it must be determined with reference to the "now." There will thus be a determinate time from this "now" to that, and there was such in reference to the past event. But if there be no time which is not "sometime," every time will be determined. 222a24–28

443. Will time then fail? Surely not, if motion always exists. Is time then always different or does the same time recur? Clearly time is, in the same way as motion is. For if one and the same motion sometimes recurs, it will be one and the same time, and if not, not. Since the "now" is an end and a beginning of time, not of the same time however, but the end of that which is past and the beginning of that which is to come, it follows that, as the circle has its convexity and its concavity, in a sense, in the same thing, so time is always at a beginning and at an end. And for this reason it seems to be always different; for the "now" is not the beginning and the end of the same thing; if it were, it would be at the same time and in the same respect two opposites. And time will not fail; for it is always at a beginning. 222a28–222b7

444. "Presently" or "just now" refers to the part of future time which is near the indivisible present "now" ("When do you walk?" "Presently," because the time in which he is going to do so is near), and to the part of past time which is not far from the "now" ("When do you walk?" "I have just been walking"). But to say that Troy has just been taken—we do not say that, because it is too far from the "now." 222b7–12

445. "Lately," too, refers to the part of past time which is near the present "now." "When did you go?" "Lately," if the time is near the existing now. "Long ago" refers to the distant past. "Suddenly" refers to what has departed from its former condition in a time imperceptible because of its smallness. 222b12–15

COMMENTARY OF ST. THOMAS

612. After the Philosopher has shown how time is related to things which are in time, he here shows how certain things are named in respect to

time by means of diverse relations to the "now."

Concerning this he makes two points. First he explains the meaning of "now." Secondly, where he says, "'At some time' means . . ." [442], he explains the meaning of certain other things which are determined by the "now."

Concerning the first part he makes two points. First he gives the proper and principal meaning of "now." Secondly, where he says, ". . . another is when the time . . ." [441], he gives a secondary meaning.

613. Concerning the first part [438] he says three things about the "now." The first point is that the "now" continues past time into the future, insofar as it is the terminus of time, that is, the beginning of the future and the end of the past. However, this is not as clear in regard to the "now" as it is in regard to a point. For a point is stationary, and therefore can be taken twice, once as a beginning and once as an end. But this does not happen in regard to the "now," as was said above.

Secondly, where he says, "It divides potentially . . ." [439], he states that time is divided by the "now" as a line is divided by a point. But the "now" divides time insofar as it is considered as many in potency, that is, insofar as it is taken separately as the beginning of one time and the end of another. And in this way it is taken as different "nows." But insofar as it is taken as joining time and continuing it, it is taken as one and the same.

He explains this by means of a comparison with mathematical lines in which it is more manifest. In mathematical lines a point which is designated in the middle of a line is not always understood as the same. For insofar as it divides the line, the point which is the end of one line is understood to be different than the point which is the end of the other line. For insofar as lines are actually divided, they are contiguous. And those things are contiguous whose ends are together. But insofar as a point makes the parts of a line continuous, it is one and the same. For those things are continuous whose end is the same. And such is also the case with the "now" in respect to time. For in one way the "now" can be taken as a division of time according to potency, and in another way as a common terminus of two times, which joins them and makes them continuous.

Thirdly, where he says, "And the dividing . . ." [440], he states that the "now" as dividing and continuing time is one and the same in subject but different according to reason [ratio], as is clear from what has been said. And this is one meaning of the "now."

614. Next where he says, ". . . another is when the time . . ." [441], he gives a secondary meaning of the "now."

He says that there is another meaning of the "now" besides the terminus of time which continues the past into the future. "Now" is that time, either in the past or in the future, which is close to the present "now." Thus we say, "He will come now," because he will come today, and, "He came now," because he came today. But we do not say that the Trojan War happened now, or that the flood happened now. For although all time is continuous, not all time is close to the present "now."

615. Next where he says, "'At some time' means . . ." [442], he explains certain things which are determined by the "now." First he explains the meaning of "then."

Concerning this he makes two

points. First he gives the meaning of "then." Secondly, he raises a problem where he says, **"But if there be . . ."** [443].

He says, therefore, first that the term "then" signifies a time determined by some prior "now," either close to or removed from the present. For we can say, "Then Troy was destroyed," or, "Then the flood occurred." That which is said to have happened "then" must be included by some "now" or preceding instant. For in that "now," which was in the past, there must be some time of a quantity determined by the present time. And thus it is clear that the term "then" differs from the second meaning of "now" in two ways. For "then" always refers to the past, and it refers to the recent and distant past indifferently. But "now" refers to recent times, and it refers to the past and the future indifferently.

616. Next where he says, **"But if there be . . ."** [443], he raises a problem from the above, and answers it.

He said that a time which is said to be "then" is included in the time between a past "now" and the present. Hence any time which is said to be "then" must be finite. But there is no time which cannot be said to be "then." Therefore all time is finite. But every finite time comes to an end. Hence it seems that time ends. But if motion is eternal, and if time is the number of motion, it follows that time does not end. Therefore, if all time is finite, then it will be necessary to say either that there is always a different time or that the same time is repeated over and over again. And this must occur in time as it does in motion. For if there is always one and the same motion, there must be one and the same time. But if there is not one and the same motion,

there will not be one and the same time.

617. Therefore, according to his opinion, motion never began nor will it end, as will be made clear in Book VIII. And thus a motion which is one and the same in species, but not in number, is repeated. For the circular motion which is now is not the same in number as the circular motion which was, but it is the same in species. Nevertheless, the whole of motion is one by continuity, because one circular motion is continued by another, as will be proven in Book VIII. And this must be the same with time as it is with motion.

Consequently he shows that time will never end.

It is clear from the above that the "now" is both a beginning and an end, but not in the same respect. It is an end in respect to the past and a beginning in respect to the future. Thus time is similar to a circle in which concavity and convexity are the same in subject but different in reason [ratio] in respect to diverse things. For the convexity of a circle is found by a comparison to the exterior, and the concavity by a comparison to the interior. Now since there is no time except the "now," as was said above, it follows that time is always at a beginning and at an end. And because of this time seems to be different, for the "now" is not the beginning and the end of the same time but of different times. Otherwise opposites would be in the same thing in the same respect. For beginning and end have opposite natures [ratio]. If, therefore, the same thing is a beginning and an end in the same respect, opposites will be in the same thing in the same respect.

He further concludes from the above that since the "now" is the beginning and the end of time, time will never end. For there can be no time without a "now," as was said above, and the "now" is the beginning of time. Hence time is always in its beginning. But that which is in its beginning is not ending. Therefore time will not end. And for the same reason it can be proven that time did not begin, because the "now" is the end of time.

But this argument proceeds on the supposition that motion is eternal, as he says. On this supposition it is necessary to say that any "now" of time is both a beginning and an end. But if it be said that motion began or will end, then it would follow that there will be a "now" which is a beginning of time and not an end, and there will be a "now" which is an end of time and not a beginning, as happens in a line. For if there is an infinite line, any point designated in it will be both a beginning and an end. But in a finite line there is found a point which is only a beginning or only an end. This will be examined further in Book VIII.

618. Next where he says, "'Presently' or 'just' refers . . ." [444], he shows what "just now" means. This expression has the same meaning as the second meaning of "now." For that is said to be "just now" which is close to the indivisible, present "now," either as part of the future or as part of the past. It is part of the future when one says, "When will he come?" "Just now." For the time in which the future event will occur is near. It is part of the past when it is asked, "When did you come?" "I came just now," is the response. Things which happened long ago we do not describe as "just now." Thus we do not say that Troy was destroyed "just now," for this is removed a great deal from the present "now."

619. Next where he says, "'Lately,' too, refers to . . ." [445], he explains certain other things which pertain to time.

He says that the term "lately" signifies a past which is close to the present "now." Thus if it be asked, "When did he go?" one answers "lately," if that past time is close to the present "now." But we say "long ago" when the past time is far removed from the present "now." Something is said to occur "suddenly" when the time in which it occurs is not sensible because of its shortness.

LECTURE 22 [222b16–223a15]
How Corruption Is Attributed to Time. All Motion and Mutation Is In Time

The Text of Aristotle

446. But it is the nature of all change to alter things from their former condition. In time all things come into being and pass away; for which reason some called it the wisest of all things, but the Pythagorean called it the most stupid, because in it we also forget; and his was the truer view. It is clear then that it must be in itself, as we said before, the condition of destruction rather than of coming into being (for change, in itself, makes things depart from their former condition), and only incidentally of coming into being, and of being.   222b16–22

447. A sufficient evidence of this is that nothing comes into being without itself moving somehow and acting, but a thing can be destroyed even if it does not move at all. And this is what, as a rule, we chiefly mean by a thing's being destroyed by time. Still, time does not work even this change; even this sort of change takes place incidentally in time.   222b22–27

448. We have stated, then, that time exists and what it is, and in how many senses we speak of the "now," and what "at some time," "lately," "presently" or "just," "long ago," and "suddenly" mean.   222b27–29

Chapter 14

449. These distinctions having been drawn, it is evident that every change and everything that moves is in time; for the distinction of faster and slower exists in reference to all change, since it is found in every instance. In the phrase "moving faster" I refer to that which changes before another into the condition in question, when it moves over the same interval and with a regular movement; e.g., in the case of locomotion, if both things move along the circumference of a circle, or both along a straight line; and similarly in all other cases.   222b30–223a4

450. But what is before is in time; for we say "before" and "after" with reference to the distance from the "now," and the "now" is the boundary of the past and the future; so that since "" are in time, the before and the after will be in time too; for in that in which the "now" is, the distance from the "now" will also be. But "before" is used contrariwise with reference to past and to future time; for in the past we call "before" what is farther from the "now," and "after" what is nearer, but in the future we call the nearer "before" and the farther "after." So that since the "before" is in time, and every movement involves a "before," evidently every change and every movement is in time.   223a4–15

COMMENTARY OF ST. THOMAS

620. After the Philosopher has compared time and the "now" to those things which are in time, he here clarifies certain things which were touched on above.

First he shows how corruption is attributed to time. Secondly, where he says, **"These distinctions having been drawn . . ."** [449], he shows how every motion and mutation is in time.

Concerning the first part he makes two points. First he shows his position with an argument, and secondly with an example, where he says, **"A sufficient evidence . . ."** [447].

621. He says, therefore, first [446] that every mutation, by its very nature [ratio], removes the thing which is changed from its natural disposition. But both generation and corruption occur in time. Therefore some have attributed the generation of things, like learning and such things, to time. They say that time is most wise because the generation of science occurs in time. But a certain philosopher named

Paron, of the Pythagorean sect, held the contrary, namely, time is most unlearned since forgetfulness occurs because of the passage of time. And in this matter he spoke more correctly because, as was said above, time itself is the cause of corruption rather than of generation. This is so because time is the number of motion, and mutation in itself is destructive and corruptive. It is the cause of generation and existence only per accidens. For when a thing is moved, it recedes from a disposition which it formerly had. But that it should acquire a disposition is not due to the nature [ratio] of motion insofar as it is motion, but insofar as it is finite and completed. Motion has this perfection from the intention of the agent which moves a thing to a determinate end. Therefore corruption can be attributed rather to mutation and time; but generation and existence is attributed to the agent and the generator.

622. Next where he says, "A sufficient evidence..." [447], he shows the same thing by means of an example. He says that an adequate example of what has been said is that nothing comes to be unless there appears to be an agent moving it. But a thing can be corrupted even when that which moves it to corruption is not clearly apparent. Such corruption we customarily attribute to time, as when someone dies of old age because of a non-apparent, intrinsic, corrupting cause. But when someone is killed with a sword, his corruption is not attributed to time. In generation the generator is always manifest, because nothing is generated by itself. Therefore, generation is not attributed to time, as is corruption. Nevertheless, corruption is not attributed to time in the sense that time causes it, but because it occurs in time and the corrupter is not apparent.

Finally where he says, "We have stated, then . . ." [448], he concludes that he has discussed the following points: that time is; what it is; the meanings of "now"; and the meanings of "then," "lately," "just now," "long ago," and "suddenly."

623. Next where he says, "These distinctions having been drawn . . ." [449], he shows with two arguments that all mutation is in time.

The first argument is as follows. Faster and slower are found in every mutation. But these things are determined by time. For that is said to be moved faster which arrives first at a designated terminus in the same space. Moreover, there must be the same rule for each motion; for example, in local motion each motion must be either circular motion or motion in a straight line. For if one is a circular motion and the other is a motion in a straight line, then one is not moved faster because it arrives first at the terminus. And this must be understood in a similar way for the other genera of mutation. Therefore it follows that all mutation is in time.

624. He gives the second argument where he says, "But what is before..." [450]. In this proof he uses the following proposition: before and after are in time.

This is clear as follows. A thing is said to be before and after because of its distance from the "now," which is the terminus of the past and the future. But these "nows" are in time. Therefore both before and after are in time, for it is necessary that a "now" and a distance from that "now" be in the same thing. Likewise a point and a distance taken in respect to that point are in the same thing, for they are both in a line.

Since he has said that before and after are determined by their distance from the "now," he shows how this is found in the past and in the future conversely. In the past that is said to be before which is more removed from the "now," and the after is closer to it. But in the future it is just the opposite. Therefore, if before and after are in time, and if before and after follow upon all motion, it must be that all motion is in time.

LECTURE 23 [223a16–224a16]
Difficulties Concerning the Existence and Unity of Time Are Answered

The Text of Aristotle

451. It is also worth considering how time can be related to the soul; and why time is thought to be in everything, both in earth and in sea and in heaven. **223a16–18**

452. Is it because it is an attribute, or state, of movement (since it is the number of movement) and all these things are movable (for they are all in place), and time and movement are together, both in respect of potentiality and in respect of actuality? **223a18–21**

453. Whether if soul did not exist time would exist or not, is a question that may fairly be asked; **223a21–22**

454. for if there cannot be some one to count there cannot be anything that can be counted, so that evidently there cannot be number; for number is either what has been, or what can be, counted. **223a22–25**

455. But if nothing but soul, or in soul reason, is qualified to count, there would not be time unless there were soul, but only that of which time is an attribute, i.e. if movement can exist without soul, and the before and after are attributes of movement, and time is these qua numerable. **223a25–29**

456. One might also raise the question what sort of movement time is the number of. Must we not say "of any kind"? **223a29–30**

457. For things both come into being in time and pass away, and grow, and are altered in time, and are moved locally; thus it is of each movement qua movement that time is the number. And so it is simply the number of continuous movement, not of any particular kind of it.

223a30–223b1

458. But other things as well may have been moved now, and there would be a number of each of the two movements. Is there another time, then, and will there be two equal times at once? **223b1–3**

459. Surely not. For a time that is both equal and simultaneous is one and the same time, and even those that are not simultaneous are one in kind; for if there were dogs, and horses, and seven of each, it would be the same number. So, too, movements that have simultaneous limits have the same time, yet the one may in fact be fast and the other not, and one may be locomotion and the other alteration; still the time of the two changes is the same if their number also is equal and simultaneous; and for this reason, while the movements are different and separate, the time is everywhere the same, because the number of equal and simultaneous movements is everywhere one and the same. **223b3–12**

460. Now there is such a thing as locomotion, and in locomotion there is included circular movement, and everything is measured by some one thing homogeneous with it, units by a unit, horses by a horse, and similarly times by some definite time, and, as we said, time is measured by motion as well as motion by time (this being so because by a motion definite in time the quantity both of the motion and of the time is measured): **223b12–18**

461. if, then, what is first is the measure of everything homogeneous with it, regular circular motion is above all else the measure, because the number of this is the best known. Now neither alteration nor increase nor coming into being can be regular, but locomotion can be.

223b18–21

462. This also is why time is thought to be the movement of the sphere, viz. because the other movements are measured by this, and time by this movement. **223b21–23**

463. This also explains the common saying that human affairs form a circle, and that there

is a circle in all other things that have a natural movement and coming into being and passing
away. This is because all other things are discriminated by time, and end and begin as though
conforming to a cycle; for even time itself is thought to be a circle. And this opinion again is
held because time is the measure of this kind of locomotion and is itself measured by such. So
that to say that the things that come into being form a circle is to say that there is a circle of
time; and this is to say that it is measured by the circular movement; for apart from the measure
nothing else to be measured is observed; the whole is just a plurality of measures.

223b23–224a2

464. It is said rightly, too, that the number of the sheep and of the dogs is the same number
if the two numbers are equal, but not the same decad or the same ten; just as the equilateral and
the scalene are not the same triangle, yet they are the same figure, because they are both
triangles. For things are called the same so-and-so if they do not differ by a differentia of that
thing, but not if they do; e.g., triangle differs from triangle by a differentia of triangle, therefore
they are different triangles; but they do not differ by a differentia of figure, but are in one and
the same division of it. For a figure of one kind is a circle and a figure of another kind a triangle
and a triangle of one kind is equilateral and a triangle of another kind scalene. They are the same
figure, then, and that, triangle, but not the same triangle. Therefore the number of two groups
also is the same number (for their number does not differ by a differentia of number), but it is
not the same decad; for the things of which it is asserted differ; one group are dogs, and the other
horses.

We have now discussed time—both time itself and the matters appropriate to the
consideration of it.

224a2–17

COMMENTARY OF ST. THOMAS

625. After the Philosopher has treated time, he here answers certain difficulties concerning time, first in regard to the existence of time, and secondly in regard to the unity of time, where he says, "One might also raise . . ." [456].

Concerning the first part he makes two points. First he raises two difficulties, and secondly he answers them, where he says, "Is it because it is . . ." [452].

He says, therefore, first [451] that the following difficulties are worthy of careful consideration: how is time related to the soul, and why does time seem to be everywhere, that is, on the earth, on the sea, and in the heavens.

626. Next where he says, "Is it because it is . . ." [452] , he answers the above questions. First he answers the second one, which is easier, and then

the first one, where he says, "Whether if soul . . ." [453]

He says, therefore, that time is a certain accident of motion, because it is the number of motion. (An accident is usually called a passion or a state.) Hence, wherever there is motion, there must be time. But all bodies are mobile, at least in respect to local motion, if not the other kinds of motion, for all bodies are in place. Someone might object that, although all bodies are mobile, nevertheless they are not all moved. Rather some are at rest. Thus it does not seem that time is in all things. To refute this he adds that time is together with motion, whether the motion be actual or potential. For everything that can be moved, but is not actually moved, is at rest. And time not only measures motion, but also rest, as was said above. Hence it follows that there is time wherever there is motion, either actual or potential.

627. Next where he says, **"Whether if soul . . ."** [453], he answers the first question.

Concerning this he makes three points. First he asks the question. Secondly, where he says, **". . . for if there cannot be . . ."** [454], he raises an objection regarding the question. Thirdly, where he says, **". . . but only that of which . . ."** [455], he answers the question.

The question, therefore, is whether or not there is time if soul does not exist.

628. Secondly, where he says, **". . . for if there cannot be . . ."** [454], he raises an objection to show that there would be no time. If it is impossible for there to be something which can number, then it is impossible for there to be something numerable, that is, able to be numbered. But if the numerable is not, number is not. For number exists only in that which is actually numbered or in that which is potentially numerable. Therefore it follows that, if something which is able to number does not exist, then number does not exist. But nothing can number except the soul, and among the parts of the soul nothing except the intellect. For to number is to relate numbered things to one first measure, and this is done by reason [ratio]. Therefore, if no intellective soul exists, there is no number. But time is a number, as was said. Therefore, if no intellective soul exists, there is no time.

629. Next where he says, **". . . but only that of which . . ."** [455], he answers the question.

He says that, if there is no soul, one must say either that time does not exist, or, more correctly, that without soul time is some kind of a being—if,

for example, it happens that there is motion but no soul. For if there is motion, it is necessary that there also is time. For before and after are in motion, and the before and after of motion, insofar as they are numerable, are time.

To understand this answer it must be realized that, if there are numbered things, then there must be number. Hence, both numbered things and their number depend on one who numbers. Now the existence of numbered things does not depend on an intellect unless there is some intellect which is the cause of things, as is the divine intellect. However, their existence does not depend on the intellect of the soul. Only numeration itself, which is an act of the soul, depends on the intellect of the soul. Therefore, just as there can be sensible things when no sense power exists, and intelligible things when no intellect exists, likewise there can be number and numerable things when no one who numbers exists.

But perhaps the conditional proposition which he gave first is true; that is, if it is impossible for there to be someone who numbers, then it is impossible for there to be anything numerable. This is similar to the following true proposition: if it is impossible for there to be someone who senses, then it is impossible for there to be something sensible. For if there is something sensible, it can be sensed. And if it can be sensed, then there can be something which senses. Nevertheless, it would not follow that, if there is something which is sensible, then there is something which senses. In the same way it follows that, if there is something numerable, then there can be something which numbers. Hence, if it is impossible for there to be something which numbers, then it is impossible for there to be something numerable. But it does not follow that, if there is no one who numbers, then there is nothing numerable, as the Philosopher's objection proceeds.

If, therefore, motion were to have a fixed existence in things, as a stone or a horse does, then one could say absolutely that, just as there is a number of stones, when soul does not exist, likewise there is a number of motion, which is time, when soul does not exist. But motion does not have a fixed existence in things. Nor is anything concerning motion actually found in things except a certain indivisible part of motion, which is a division of motion. But the totality of motion is established by a consideration of the soul which compares a prior disposition of the mobile object to a later one. Therefore, time also does not have existence outside the soul except in respect to its own indivisible part. For the totality of time is established by the ordering of the soul which numbers the before and after in motion, as was said above. Therefore the Philosopher significantly says that, if soul does not exist, then time is "some kind" of being, that is, an imperfect being. In the same way, if there happens to be motion but no soul, motion is also said to be imperfect.

And because of this the arguments given above to show that time does not exist because it is composed of non-existent parts are answered. For it is clear from the foregoing that time does not have a perfect existence outside the soul, as neither does motion.

630. Next where he says, **"One might also raise . . ."** [456], he raises a difficulty concerning the unity of time, or the relation of time to motion.

Concerning this he makes three points. First he raises the difficulty. Secondly, where he says, **"Must we not say . . ."** [457], he answers it. Thirdly, where he says, **"It is said rightly . . ."** [464], he clarifies a certain point which he had supposed.

He says, therefore, first [456] that, since time is the number of motion, there is the problem of what motion or of what kind of motion it is the number.

Next where he says, **"Must we not say . . ."** [457], he answers the problem. First he refutes a false solution. Secondly, where he says, **"Now there is such . . ."** [460], he gives the true solution.

Concerning the first part he makes three points. First he gives the false solution. Secondly, where he says, **"But other things as well . . ."** [458], he disproves it by reducing it to absurdity. Thirdly, where he says, "Surely not" [459], he shows that this absurdity is an impossibility.

631. The first answer [457], therefore, is that time is the number of any motion.

To prove this he indicates that every motion, that is, generation, increase, alteration, and local motion, is in time. Now that which pertains to every motion pertains to motion as such. Moreover, to be in time is to be numbered by time. Therefore it seems that any motion, as such, has number. Hence, since time is the number of motion, it seems to follow that time is the number of all continuous motion, and not of just some special kind of motion.

632. Next where he says, **"But other things as well . . ."** [458], he disproves the above position. Sometimes it happens that two things are moved simultaneously. If, therefore, time is the number of each motion, it follows that there is a different time for two mo-

tions existing simultaneously. And it would follow further that two equal times exist simultaneously, for example, two days or two hours. However, it is not astonishing if two unequal times, for example, a day and an hour, exist simultaneously.

633. Next where he says, **"Surely not"** [459], he shows that it is impossible for two equal times to exist simultaneously. Every time which is simultaneous and equal is only one time. But time which is not simultaneous is not one in number, but is one in species, as for example, a day with a day, and a year with a year.

He shows this by a comparison with other numbered things. If there are seven horses and seven days, they do not differ in respect to number but in respect to the species of the numbered things. Likewise there is the same time for all motions which are simultaneously terminated in respect to both beginning and end. But motions differ in respect to their proper natures [ratio], insofar as one happens to be fast and the other slow, or the one is local motion and the other is alteration. But the time is the same if the alteration and the local motion, supposing that they are simultaneous, have an equal number. And because of this it is necessary that although motions are different from each other, the time in all of them is the same. For there is one and the same number for things which are equal and simultaneous, wherever they might be.

634. Next where he says, **"Now there is such . . ."** [460], he gives the true answer.

Concerning this he makes three points. First he sets forth certain things which are necessary for his answer. Secondly, where he says, "... if, then,

what is first..." [461], he concludes his answer from these premises. Thirdly, where he says, **"This also is why . . ."** [462], he proves his answer from what has been said by others.

Concerning the first part he sets forth three points.

The first point is that local motion is the first and more simple and regular of all other motions. And circular motion is the first and more simple and regular of all other local motions, as will be proven in Book VIII.

The second point is that each thing is numbered by some one thing of the same genus. Thus unities are numbered by unity and horses by horse, as is clear in Metaphysics, X. Hence it is necessary that time be measured by some determinate time. Thus we see that all times are measured by the day.

The third point which he sets forth is that time is measured by motion and motion by time, as was said above. This is so because the quantity of any motion and time is measured by some determinate motion and by some determinate time.

635. Next where he says, **". . . if, then, what is first . . ."** [461], he concludes from the above that, since that which is first is the measure of all things which are of that genus, then it is necessary that circular motion, which is most regular, is the measure of all motions. Moreover, that motion is called regular which is one and uniform. But this regularity cannot be found in alteration or increase, because they are neither constantly continuous nor of equal speed. However, this regularity can be found in local motion, because some local motions can be continuous and uniform. This is true only of circular motion, as will be proven in Book VIII.

And among all other circular motions, the first motion which revolves the whole firmament in daily motion is the most uniform and regular. Hence that circular motion, as first and more simple and more regular, is the measure of all motions. Moreover, it is necessary that a regular motion be the measure or number of the others. For every measure ought to be most certain, and this is found in things which are uniformly related.

Therefore, from this we can conclude that, if the first circular motion measures all motion, and if motions insofar as they are measured by some motion are measured by time, then it is necessary to say that time is the number of the first circular motion, according to which time is measured, and in regard to which all other motions are measured by time.

636. Next where he says, **"This also is why . . ."** [462], he proves the above position by means of the opinions of others.

He does this first by means of the erroneous opinion of those who were motivated to say that time is the motion of the celestial sphere because all other motions are measured by this motion. For it is clear that we say that a day or a year is completed by looking to the motion of the heavens.

He does this secondly by means of the common use of speech, where he says, **"This also explains . . ."** [463].

He says that, since time is the number of the first circular motion, it is customary to say that there is a certain circle in human affairs and in other things which are naturally moved and generated and corrupted. This is so because all such things are measured by time, and men take the beginning and end of time as if time occurs according

to a certain circularity. For time itself seems to be a kind of circle. Furthermore, this seems to be so because time is the measure of circular motion, and is also measured by circular motion. Therefore to say that there is a certain circle of things which occur in time is nothing other than to say that time is a kind of circle; which is so because time is measured by circular motion. For that which is measured does not seem to be different from the measure. Rather many measures seem to make one whole, thus many unities make one number, and many measures of cloth make one quantity of cloth. This is true when the measure is taken from the same genus.

Therefore, it is clear that time primarily measures and numbers the first circular motion, and through this it measures all other motions. Hence, there is only one time because of the unity of the first motion. Nevertheless whoever senses any motion senses time, because mutability in all mutable things is caused by the first motion, as was said above.

637. Next where he says, **"It is said rightly . . ."** [464], he shows how something which he said above must be understood.

He said that the number of seven dogs and seven horses is the same. He shows how this is true. If the number of some diverse things, for example, sheep and dogs, is equal, then it can be truly said that the number of each of them is the same. For example, both the sheep and the dogs are ten. But it cannot be said that ten itself is the same as the dogs and the sheep. For the ten sheep and the ten dogs are not the same ten. This is so because a genus with the addition of unity or identity can be predicated of many individuals existing in one species. And likewise an ultimate genus can be predicated of many species existing under one proximate genus. Nevertheless one cannot predicate with the addition of unity or identity either the species of the individual or the proximate genus of diverse species.

He next gives an example of this. There are two species of triangle: the equilateral which has three equal sides, and the scalene which has three unequal sides. Now figure is the genus of triangle. Therefore, we cannot say that the equilateral and the scalene are the same triangle. But we can say that they are the same figure, since they are both contained under triangle which is one species of figure. He gives the reason [ratio] for this. Since the same and the diverse are opposed, we can predicate identity where difference is not found, but we cannot predicate identity where difference is found. Moreover, it is clear that the equilateral and the scalene differ from each other by a differentia of triangle, that is, by a proper division of triangle. This is so because they are diverse species of triangle. But the equilateral and the scalene do not differ in respect to a differentia of figure. Rather they are contained under one and the same dividing differentia of figure.

Thus the following is clear. If we divide figure into its species, which are constituted by the differentiae, it will be found that the circle is one thing and the triangle another, and thus they are different species of figure. But if we divide triangle, we will find that one of

its species is the equilateral and the other is the scalene. Thus it is clear that the equilateral and the scalene are one figure, because they are contained under one species of figure, which is triangle. But they are not one triangle, because they are diverse species of triangle.

This is similar to what was proposed above. Number is divided into diverse species, one of which is ten. Therefore, all things which are ten are said to have one number, because they do not differ from each other in respect to the species of number, but are contained under one species of number. But it cannot be said that they are the same ten, for the things to which the number ten is applied differ. For some of them are dogs and some horses.

Aristotle seems to have introduced this lest someone, in upholding the unity of time, be content to say that there is one number of things equal in number, even though they are diverse. For although ten or three is the same because of the unity of the species, nevertheless ten or three is not the same because of the diversity in respect to number from matter. Hence it follows that in respect to its nature [ratio] time is one in species, but not in number. And, therefore, to establish the true unity of time, it is necessary to go back to the unity of the first motion, which is primarily measured by time, and by which time is also measured.

Finally he concludes that time and those things which are proper to the consideration of time have been treated.

BOOK V
THE DIVISION OF MOTION INTO ITS SPECIES
LECTURE 1 [224a21–b34]
Motion Per Se Is Distinguished from Motion Per Accidens. Only Motion Per Se Must Be Treated

The Text of Aristotle
Chapter 1

465. *Everything with changes does so in one of three senses. It may change (1) accidentally, as for instance when we say that something musical walks, that which walks being something in which aptitude for music is an accident. Again (2) a thing is said without qualification to change because something belonging to it changes, i.e. in statements which refer to part of the thing in question: thus the body is restored to health because the eye or the chest, that is to say a part of the whole body, is restored to health. And above all there is the case of a thing which is in motion neither accidentally nor in respect of something else belonging to it, but in virtue of being itself directly in motion. Here we have a thing which is essentially movable: and that which is so is a different thing according to the particular variety of motion: for instance it may be a thing capable of alteration: and within the sphere of alteration it is again a different thing according as it is capable of being restored to health or capable of being heated.*
224a21–30

466. *And there are the same distinctions in the case of the mover: (1) one thing causes motion accidentally, (2) another partially (because something belonging to it causes motion), (3) another of itself directly, as, for instance, the physician heals, the hand strikes.*
224a30–34

467. *We have then the following factors: (a) on the one hand that which directly causes motion, and (b) on the other hand that which is in motion; further we have (c) that in which motion takes place, namely time and (distinct from these three) (d) that from which and (e) that to which it proceeds: for every motion proceeds from something and to something,*
224a34–224b1

468. *that which is directly in motion being distinct from that to which it is in motion and that from which it is in motion: for instance, we may take the three things "wood," "hot," and "cold," of which the first is that which is in motion, the second is that to which the motion proceeds, and the third is that from which it proceeds. This being so, it is clear that the motion is in the wood, not in its form; for the motion is neither caused nor experienced by the form or the place or the quantity. So we are left with a mover, a moved, and a goal of motion.*
224b1–7

469. *I do not include the starting-point of motion: for it is the goal rather than the starting-point of motion that gives its name to a particular process of change. Thus "perishing" is change to not-being, though it is also true that that which perishes changes from being; and "becoming" is change to being, though it is also change from not-being.*
224b7–10

470. *Now a definition of motion has been given above, from which it will be seen that every goal of motion, whether it be a form, an affection, or a place, is immovable, as, for instance, knowledge and heat.*
224b10–13

471. *Here, however, a difficulty may be raised. Affections, it may be said, are motions, and whiteness is an affection:*
224b13–14

472. *thus there may be change to a motion. To this we may reply that it is not whiteness but whitening that is a motion.*
224b14–16

473. *Here also the same distinctions are to be observed: a goal of motion may be so accidentally, or partially and with reference to something other than itself, or directly and with*

no reference to anything else: for instance, a thing which is becoming white changes accidentally to an object of thought, the color being only accidentally the object of thought; it changes to color, because white is a part of color, or to Europe, because Athens is a part of Europe; but it changes essentially to white color. It is now clear in what sense a thing is in motion essentially, accidentally, or in respect of something other than itself, 224b16–22

474. *and in what sense the phrase "itself directly" is used in the case both of the mover and of the moved; and it is also clear that the motion is not in the form but in that which is in motion, that is to say "the movable in activity."* 224b22–26

475. *Now accidental change we may leave out of account; for it is to be found in everything, at any time, and in any respect. Change which is not accidental on the other hand is not to be found in everything, but only in contraries, in things intermediate between contraries and in contradictories, as may be proved by induction.* 224b26–30

476. *An intermediate may be a starting-point of change, since for the purposes of the change it serves as contrary to either of two contraries; for the intermediate is in a sense the extremes. Hence we speak of the intermediate as in a sense a contrary relatively to the extremes and of either extreme as a contrary relatively to the intermediate: for instance, the central note is low relatively to the highest and high relatively to the lowest, and grey is light relatively to black and dark relatively to white.* 224b30–35

COMMENTARY OF ST. THOMAS

638. After the Philosopher has treated motion and those things which follow upon motion in general, he proceeds here to the division of motion.

This discussion is divided into two parts. First he divides motion into its species. Secondly, in Book VI where he says, **"Now if the terms . . ."** [562] he divides motion into its quantitative parts.

The first part is divided into two parts. First he divides motion into its species. Secondly, where he says, **"Let us now proceed . . ."** [505], he treats the unity and opposition of motion.

The first part is divided into two parts. First he distinguishes motion per se from motion per accidens. Secondly, where he says, **"And since every change . . ."** [477], he divides motion per se into its species.

The first part is divided into two parts. First he distinguishes motion per se from motion per accidens. Secondly, where he says, **"Now accidental change . . ."** [475], he teaches that

motion per accidens must be omitted, but motion per se must be treated.

Concerning the first part he makes two points. First he distinguishes motion per se from motion per accidens. Secondly, where he says, **"It is now clear . . ."** [474], he summarizes his conclusions.

In the first part he distinguishes motion per se from motion per accidens in three ways. He does this first in respect to the mobile object; secondly, in respect to the mover, where he says, **"And there are the same . . ."** [466], and thirdly, in respect to the terminus, where he says, **"We have, then, the following . . ."** [467].

639. He says, therefore, first [465] that whatever is changed is said to be changed in three ways.

First, a thing is said to be changed per accidens, as when we say that the musician walks. For it is accidental that this man who walks is a musician.

Secondly, a thing is said to be changed simply because one of its parts is changed, for example, all things which are said to be changed in respect of their parts. He gives an example of alteration. The animal body is said to be healed because the eye or the chest, which are parts of the whole body, is healed.

Thirdly, a thing is said to be moved neither per accidens nor in respect to a part. Rather it itself is moved primarily and per se. He says "primarily" to exclude motion in respect to a part. And he says "per se" to exclude motion per accidens. Furthermore, the per se mobile object varies according to the diverse species of motion. Thus an alterable object is mobile in respect to alteration. And an augmentable object is mobile in respect to increase. And within the species of alteration a curable object, which is moved in respect to health, differs from an object which can be heated. This latter is moved in respect to heating.

640. Next where he says, "**And there are the same ...**" [466], he distinguishes motion per se from motion per accidens in respect to the mover.

He says that the above distinction, which was made in respect to the mobile object, can likewise be applied to the mover.

For a thing is said to move in three ways. First a thing moves per accidens, as when a musician builds. Secondly a thing moves in respect to a part insofar as a part moves, as when a man is said to hit because his hand hits. Thirdly a thing is said to move primarily and per se, as when a doctor cures.

641. Next where he says, "**We have, then, the following ...**" [467], he proceeds to divide motion in the same way in respect to the terminus.

First he sets forth some preambles. Secondly, where he says, "**Here also**

the same distinctions . . ." [473], he gives the division.

Concerning the first part he makes three points. First he states how many things are required for motion. Secondly, where he says, "**. . . that which is directly ...**" [468], he compares these things to each other. Thirdly, where he says, "**Now a definition of motion ...**" [470], he answers a certain difficulty.

He says, therefore, first [467] that five things are required for motion. The first requirement is a first mover from which the motion begins. Secondly, a mobile object which is moved is required. Thirdly there is the time in which the motion occurs. Besides these three things two termini are required: one from which the motion begins, and the other to which the motion proceeds. For all motion is from something to something.

642. Next where he says, "**. . . that which is directly . . .**" [468], he compares these things to each other.

First he compares the mobile object to the two termini of motion. Secondly, where he says, "**I do not include ...**" [469], he compares the two termini of motion to each other.

He says, therefore, first that that which is moved primarily and per se is different from the terminus toward which the motion tends and from the terminus from which the motion began. This is clear in regard to wood, hot, and cold. For in the motion of heating the wood is a mobile object which differs from hot, which is the terminus to which, and from cold, which is the terminus from which.

He says that that which is moved primarily is other than both termini because there is nothing to prevent that which is moved per accidens from being one of the termini. The object, i.e., the wood, becomes hot per se. But the privation and the contrary, i.e., cold, becomes hot per accidens, as was said in Book I.

He next proves that the mobile object is other than both the termini from the fact that the motion is in the object, i.e., in the wood. However, the motion is in neither of the termini, neither in the species of white nor in the species of black. This is clear from the fact that that in which there is motion is moved. But the terminus of motion neither moves nor is moved, whether the terminus of motion be a quality, as in alteration, or a place, as in local motion, or a quantity, as in the motion of increase and decrease. Rather the mover moves the object which is moved toward the terminus to which. Hence, since the motion is in the object which is moved, but not in the terminus, it is clear that the mobile object is other than the terminus of the motion.

643. Next where he says, **"I do not include..."** [469], he compares the two termini to each other.

He says that mutation is denominated by the terminus to which rather than by the terminus from which. Thus, corruption is called a mutation to non-being, although that which is corrupted is changed from being. Conversely, generation is a mutation to being, although it begins from non-being. The name of generation pertains to being; the name of corruption pertains to non-being. The reason [ratio] for this is that in mutation the terminus from which is removed and the terminus to which is acquired. Hence, motion seems to be repugnant to the terminus from which and to be in agreement with the terminus to which. And because of this motion is

denominated by the terminus to which.

644. Next where he says, **"Now a definition of motion..."** [470], he answers a certain difficulty.

Concerning this he makes three points.

First he sets forth two points which are clear from the foregoing. The first of these is that it has been said in Book III what motion is. The second point is that he has just said above that the species, i.e., quality and place and any passive quality, which are the termini of motion, are not moved. For there is no motion in them, as was said. This is clear in knowledge, which is a certain species, and in heat, which is a certain passion or passive quality.

Secondly, where he says, **"Here, however, a difficulty..."** [471], he sets forth a third point concerning which there is a difficulty. He says that one might ask whether passions or passive qualities, like heat and coldness and whiteness and blackness, from which things are not moved, are motions.

Thirdly, where he says, **". . . thus, there may be ..."** [472], he shows that, if this is held, then an inconsistency results. Since whiteness is a terminus toward which there is motion, then if whiteness is a motion, it follows that motion is the terminus of motion, which cannot be, as will be proven below. From this he determines the truth and says that whiteness is not a motion, rather whitening is. However, he adds "perhaps," because he has not yet proven that motion is not terminated in motion.

645. Next where he says, **"Here also the same distinctions ..."** [473], from the fact that the termini of motion are other than the mobile object and the

mover, as was shown, he shows that, besides the division of motion taken in respect to the mover and the mobile object, motion is divided thirdly in respect to the terminus. And since the terminus to which names the motion rather than the terminus from which, as was said, he establishes this division of motion not in respect to the terminus from which but in respect to the terminus to which.

He says that also in respect to the termini one can distinguish that which is moved per accidens, that which is moved in respect to a part and in respect to another, and that which is moved primarily and not in respect to another.

The motion will be per accidens if that which becomes white is said to be changed to that which is understood or known by someone. For to be understood is accidental to the white thing.

The motion will be in respect to a part if that which becomes white is said to be changed in color. For it is said to be changed in color because it is changed in whiteness, which is a part of color. Another example is that I might say that one who comes to Athens comes to Europe, for Athens is a part of Europe.

But the motion will be primary and per se if that which becomes white is said to be changed to a white color.

He does not divide motion in respect to time, which still remains. For time is related to motion as an extrinsic measure.

646. Next where he says, **"It is now clear..."** [474], he summarizes what he has said. He says that it is clear how something is moved per se, per accidens, and in respect to a part. Further it is clear how that which is pri-

mary and per se is found both in the mover and in the mobile object. For he has explained what a primary and per se mover is and what it is to be moved primarily and per se. Further he has shown that there is no motion in a species or quality which is the terminus of motion. Rather motion is in that which is moved, or in the mobile in respect to act, which is the same thing.

647. Next where he says, **"Now accidental change . . ."** [475], he shows what kind of motion must be treated.

First he states his position. Secondly, where he says, **"An intermediate may be . . ."** [476], he clarifies a certain thing which he has said.

He says, therefore, first that mutation which is per accidens, taken in respect to either the mover or the mobile object or the terminus, must be omitted. The reason for this is that motion per accidens is indeterminate. For it is in all things as termini and in all time, and pertains to all objects and to all movers, since an infinity of things can be accidental to one thing. But mutation which is not per accidens is not in all things. Rather it is only in contraries and intermediaries in respect to motion in quantity, quality, and place, and in contradictories, in respect to generation and corruption whose termini are being and non-being. This is clear from induction. Only those things which are determinate fall under art, for there is no art of the infinite.

648. Next where he says, **"An intermediate may be..."** [476], he clarifies a certain thing which he has said; namely, there is motion in intermediaries.

He says that motion occurs from an intermediary to either of the extremes, and vice versa, insofar as we can use

the intermediary as a contrary in rela- might say that an intermediary sound
tion to either extreme. For the interme- between the low and the high is low in
diary, insofar as it agrees with each relation to the high and high in relation
extreme, is in a certain way each of to the low. Again, grey is white in rela-
them. Therefore, one can relate this to tion to black, and vice versa.
that and that to this. For example, one

LECTURE 2 [224b35–225b4]

The Species of Mutation Are Established. It Is Shown Which of These Species Is Motion in the Strict Sense

Text of Aristotle

477. And since every change is from something to something as the word itself metabole indicates, implying, something "after" (meta) something else, that is to say something earlier and something later—that which changes must change in one of four ways: from subject to subject, from subject to non-subject, from non-subject to subject, or from non-subject to non-subject, where by "subject" I mean what is affirmatively expressed.   224b35–225a7

478. So it follows necessarily from what has been said above that there are only three kinds of change, that from subject to subject, that from subject to non-subject, and that from non-subject to subject;   225a7–10

479. for the fourth conceivable kind, that from non-subject to non-subject, is not change, as in that case there is no opposition either of contraries or of contradictories.   225a10–12

480. Now change from non-subject to subject, the relation being that of contradiction, is "coming to be"—"unqualified coming to be" when the change takes place in an unqualified way, "particular coming to be" when the change is change in a particular character: for instance, a change from not-white to white is a coming to be of the particular thing, white, while change from unqualified not-being to being is coming to be in an unqualified way, in respect of which we say that a thing "comes to be" without qualification, not that it "comes to be" some particular thing.   225a12–17

481. Change from subject to non-subject is "perishing"— "unqualified perishing" when the change is from being to not-being, "particular perishing" when the change is to the opposite negation, the distinction being the same as that made in the case of coming to be.   225a17–20

482. Now the expression "not-being" is used in several senses; and there can be motion neither of that which "is not" in respect of the affirmation or negation of a predicate, nor of that which "is hot" in the sense that it only potentially "is," that is to say the opposite of that which actually "is" in an unqualified sense; for although that which is "not-white" or "not-good" may nevertheless be in motion accidentally (for example that which is "not-white" might be a man), yet that which is without qualification "not-so-and-so" cannot in any sense be in motion: therefore it is impossible for that which is not to be in motion. This being so, it follows that "becoming" cannot be a motion; for it is that which "is not" that "becomes." For however true it may be that it accidentally "becomes," it is nevertheless correct to say that it is that which "is not" that in an unqualified sense "becomes." And similarly it is impossible for that which "is not" to be at rest.   225a20–31

483. There are these difficulties, then, in the way of the assumption that that which "is not" can be in motion: and it may be further objected that whereas everything which is in motion is in space, that which "is not" is not in space; for then it would be somewhere.   225a31–32

484. So too, "perishing" is not a motion; for a motion has for its contrary either another motion or rest, whereas "perishing" is the contrary of "becoming."   225a32–34

485. Since, then, every motion is a kind of change, and there are only the three kinds of change mentioned above; and since of these three those which take the form of "becoming" and "perishing," that is to say those which imply a relation of contradiction, are not motions: it necessarily follows that only change from subject to subject is motion. And every such subject is either a contrary or an intermediate (for a privation may be allowed to rank as a contrary) and can be affirmatively expressed, as naked, toothless, or black.   225a34–225b5

COMMENTARY OF ST. THOMAS

649. After the Philosopher has distinguished motion per se from motion per accidens, he here divides mutation and motion per se into their species.

It must be realized here that, when Aristotle defined motion above in Book III, he took the word "motion" as common to all the species of mutation. Here he attributes this meaning to the word "mutation." And he uses "motion" in a more limited sense as a certain species of mutation.

Therefore this part is divided into two parts. In the first part he divides mutation into its species, one of which is motion. In the second part he subdivides motion into its species, where he says, "If, then, the categories . . ." [468].

Concerning the first part he makes two points. First he gives the division of mutation. Secondly, where he says, "Now change from non-subject . . ." [480], he clarifies the parts of this division.

Concerning the first part he makes three points. First he sets forth certain things which are necessary for the division of mutation. Secondly, where he says, "So it follows necessarily . . ." [478], he concludes from this the division of mutation. Thirdly, where he says, ". . . for the fourth . . ." [479], he refutes a certain objection.

650. He says, therefore, first [477] that every mutation is from something to something. This is clear from the very word "mutation" which denotes that something is after another, and that one thing is prior and another posterior. Hence on these suppositions it is necessary that that which is changed be changed in four ways. For either both termini are affirmative, and thus a thing is said to be changed from sub-

ject to subject. Or the terminus from which is affirmative and the terminus to which is negative, and thus a thing is said to be moved from subject to non-subject. Or, conversely, the terminus from which is negative and the terminus to which is affirmative, and thus a thing is said to be moved from non-subject to subject. Or both termini are negative, and thus a thing is said to be changed from non-subject to non-subject. The word "subject" here does not mean that which sustains form, but rather anything which is affirmatively signified.

651. Next where he says, "So it follows necessarily . . ." [478], he concludes from the above division of mutation. He says that it necessarily follows from the above that there are three species of mutation. One species is from subject to subject, as when a thing is changed from white to black. Another is from subject to non-subject, as when a thing is changed from being to non-being. The third species, on the other hand, is from non-subject to subject, as when a thing is changed from non-being to being.

652. Next where he says, ". . . for the fourth . . ." [479], he refutes a certain objection. For one might object that, since he has stated that a thing is changed in four ways, he ought to conclude that there are four species of mutation, and not just three.

But he refutes this objection by saying that there cannot be a species of mutation from non-subject to non-subject. For every mutation is between opposites. But two negations are not opposites, for it cannot be said that they are either contraries or contradictories. A sign of this is that negations are simultaneously true of one and the same thing. Thus a stone is neither healthy nor sick. Hence since mutation per se occurs only between contraries and between contradictories, as was said above, it follows that there is no mutation per se from negation to negation, but only mutation per accidens. For when a thing is changed from white to black, it is changed per accidens from non-black to nonwhite. In this way a thing is said to be changed from non-subject to non-subject. Moreover, that which is in a genus per accidens cannot be a species of that genus. Therefore, there cannot be a species of mutation from non-subject to non-subject.

653. Next where he says, **"Now change from non-subject..."** [480], he clarifies the parts of the given division.

Concerning this he makes three points. First he clarifies two parts of the division. Secondly, where he says, **"Now the expression . . ."** [482], he shows that neither of these is motion. Thirdly, where he says, **"Since, then, every motion . . ."** [485], he concludes that the remaining part of the division is motion.

Concerning the first part he makes two points. First he clarifies one part of the division, and secondly the other, where he says, **"Change from subject..."** [481].

654. He says, therefore, first [480] that mutation from non-subject to subject is between opposites which are contradictories. This is called generation, which is a mutation from non-being to being.

But generation is twofold. For there is simple generation in which a thing is generated simply, and there is another generation in which a thing is generated accidentally. He gives an example of each generation. The first example is of the second type of generation. He says that, when a thing is changed from non-white to white, there is a generation of "this" and not a simple generation. The second example is of the first type of generation. He says that generation from simple non-being to being which is substance is simple generation. According to this we say simply that a thing comes to be and does not come to be. For since generation is mutation from non-being to being, a thing is said to be generated in this way when it is changed from non-being to being.

But when a thing comes to be white from non-white, it is not changed from non-being simply to being simply. For that which is properly changed is the subject, and the subject of white is some being in act. Hence, since the subject remains throughout the whole mutation, at the beginning of the mutation it was also being in act, that is, white. Therefore, this is not called becoming simply, but becoming this, that is, white.

But the subject of substance is not being in act, but being in potency only, that is, primary matter, which at the beginning of generation is under privation and at the end is under form. Therefore a thing becomes simply in respect to the generation of substance.

From this it can be seen that, in respect to a form which presupposes another form in matter, there is no simple generation but only accidental generation. For any form puts a being in act.

655. Next where he says, **"Change from subject..."** [481], he clarifies the other part of the division.

He says that mutation from subject to non-subject is called corruption. But there is simple corruption, which is from substantial being to non-being; and there is another corruption to the opposite negation of any affirmation, as from white to non-white. This latter is a corruption of "this," as was also said in regard to generation.

656. Next where he says, **"Now the expression . . ."** [482], he shows that neither of the foregoing is motion.

First he shows that generation is not motion, and secondly that corruption is not motion, where he says, **"So, too, 'perishing' . . ."** [484].

He proves the first point with two arguments. The first is as follows. That which is simply not a "this" cannot be moved. For that which is not is not moved. But that which is generated simply is not a "this"; for it is simply non-being. Therefore, that which is generated simply is not moved. Therefore simple generation is not motion.

To clarify the first proposition he says that non-being is said in three ways. In regard to two of these ways non-being is not moved. In regard to the third way it is moved per accidens.

In one way being and non-being are said in respect to the composition and division of the proposition, such that they are the same as the true and the false. Such being and non-being are in the mind only, as is said in Metaphysics, VI. Hence motion does not pertain to them.

In another way non-being is said to be that which is in potency, insofar as being in potency is opposed to that which is being in act simply. And such non-being is also not moved.

In a third way non-being is said to be that which is in potency and which does not exclude being in act simply, but only being in this act. Thus non-white and non-good are called non-being. Such non-being can be moved per accidens insofar as such non-being occurs in something existing in act which happens to be moved.

Now since it is impossible for that which is not to be moved, it is clear that that which is simply not a "this" is in no way moved, neither per se nor per accidens. Hence generation cannot be motion. For that which is not becomes or is generated. And although, as was said in Book I, a thing comes to be from non-being per accidens and from being in potency per se, nevertheless it is true to say that that which becomes simply simply is not. Hence it cannot be moved; and for the same reason [ratio] it is not at rest. Thus generation is neither motion nor rest.

Therefore, if one holds that generation is motion, these difficulties follow: non-being is moved and is at rest.

657. He gives the second argument where he says, **". . . and it may be further . . ."** [483]. The argument is as follows.

Whatever is moved is in place. But that which is not is not in place, because it can be said to be anywhere. Therefore that which is not is not moved. This is the same conclusion as the above. The truth of the first proposition arises from the fact that, since local motion is the first motion, it is necessary that whatever is moved be moved with respect to place, and thus is in place. And when that which is prior is removed, things which are consequent are also removed.

658. Next where he says, **"So, too, 'perishing' . . ."** [484], he proves that corruption is not motion. Nothing is contrary to motion except motion or rest. But generation, which is neither motion nor rest, as was shown, is contrary to corruption. Therefore corruption is not motion.

659. Next where he says, **"Since, then, every motion . . ."** [485], he concludes from the above that motion is the remaining part of the division given above.

Motion is a certain species of mutation because in motion there is something after another, which he said above pertains to the nature [ratio] of mutation. But motion is neither generation nor corruption, which are mutations in respect to contradictories. And since there are only three species of mutation, it follows of necessity that motion is mutation from subject to subject.

Moreover by the two "subjects," that is, the two affirmations, we mean contraries or intermediaries. For privation also in a way is a contrary and is sometimes signified affirmatively. Thus naked is a privation, and white and black are contraries.

LECTURE 3 [225b5–226a22]
There Is No Motion Per Se in the Categories Other Than Quantity, Quality, and Where

Text of Aristotle

486. *If, then, the categories are severally distinguished as Being, Quality, Place, Time, Relation, Quantity, and Activity or Passivity, it necessarily follows that there are three kinds of motion—qualitative, quantitative, and local.* **225b5–9**

Chapter 2

487. *In respect of Substance there is no motion, because Substance has no contrary among things that are.* **225b10–11**

488. *Nor is there motion in respect of Relation; for it may happen that when one correlative changes, the other, although this does not itself change, is no longer applicable, so that in these cases the motion is accidental.* **225b11–13**

489. *Nor is there motion in respect of Agent and Patient—in fact there can never be motion of mover and moved, because there cannot be motion of motion or becoming of becoming or in general change of change.* **225b13–16**

490. *For in the first place there are two senses in which motion of motion is conceivable. (1) The motion of which there is motion might be conceived as subject; e.g., a man is in motion because he changes from fair to dark. Can it be that in this sense motion grows hot or cold, or changes place, or increases or decreases? Impossible; for change is not a subject. Or (2) can there be motion of motion in the sense that some other subject changes from a change to another mode of being, as e.g., a man changes from falling ill to getting well? Even this is possible only in an accidental sense. For, whatever the subject may be, movement is change from one form to another. (And the same holds good of becoming and perishing, except that in these processes we have a change to a particular kind of opposite, while the other, motion, is a change to a different kind.) So, if there is to be motion of motion, that which is changing from health to sickness must simultaneously be changing from this very change to another. It is clear, then, that by the time that he has become sick, he must also have changed to whatever may be the other change concerned (for that he should be at rest, though logically possible, is excluded by the theory). Moreover this other can never be any casual change, but must be a change from something definite to some other definite thing. So in this case it must be the opposite change, viz. convalescence. It is only accidentally that there can be change of change, e.g., there is a change from remembering to forgetting only because the subject of this change changes at one time to knowledge, at another to ignorance.* **225b16–33**

491. *In the second place, if there is to be change of change and becoming of becoming, we shall have an infinite regress. Thus if one of a series of changes is to be a change of change, the preceding change must also be so: e.g., if simple becoming was ever in process of becoming, then that which was becoming simple becoming was also in process of becoming, so that we should not yet have arrived at what was in process of simple becoming but only at what was already in process of becoming in process of becoming. And this again was sometime in process of becoming, so that even then we should not have arrived at what was in process of simple becoming. And since in an infinite series there is no first term, here there will be no first stage and therefore no following stage either. On this hypothesis, then, nothing, can become or be moved or change.* **225b33–226a6**

492. *Thirdly, if a thing is capable of any particular motion, it is also capable of the corresponding contrary motion or the corresponding coming to rest, and a thing that is capable*

of becoming is also capable of perishing: consequently, if there be becoming, of becoming, that which is in process of becoming, is in process of perishing at the very moment when it has reached the stage of becoming; since it cannot be in process of perishing when it is just beginning to become or after it has ceased to become; for that which is in process of perishing must be in existence. 226a6–10

493. *Fourthly, there must be a substrate underlying all processes of becoming and changing. What can this be in the present case? It is either the body or the soul that undergoes alteration: what is it that correspondingly becomes motion or becoming? And again what is the goal of their motion? It must be the motion or becoming of something from something to something else.* 226a10–14

494. *But in what sense can this be so? For the becoming of learning cannot be learning: so neither can the becoming, of becoming, be becoming, nor can the becoming, of any process be that process.* 226a14–16

495. *Finally, since there are three kinds of motion the substratum and the goal of motion must be one or other of these, e.g., locomotion will have to be altered or to be locally moved.* 226a16–18

496. *To sum up, then, since everything that is moved is moved in one of three ways, either accidentally, or partially, or essentially, change can change only accidentally, as e.g. when a man who is being restored to health runs or learns: and accidental chance we have long ago decided to leave out of account.* 226a19–23

COMMENTARY OF ST. THOMAS

660. After the Philosopher has divided mutation into generation, corruption, and motion, he here subdivides motion into its parts.

And since opposites are treated by the same science, he first establishes the species of motion, and secondly he shows how many kinds of immobility there are, where he says, **"The term 'immovable' . . ."** [503].

Concerning the first part he makes two points. First he gives a conditional argument through which the division of motion into its parts is established. Secondly, where he says, **"In respect of Substance . . ."** [487], he explains the given conditional argument.

661. He concludes, therefore, from the above that since motion is from subject to subject, and since subjects are in some genus of the categories, then it is necessary that the species of motion be distinguished according to the genera of the categories. For motion takes its denomination and species from its terminus, as was said above. Hence, if the categories are divided into ten genera of things, namely, substance, quality, etc., as is said in the Categories and in Metaphysics, V; and if motion is found in three of them; then there must be three species of motion—namely, motion in the genus of quantity, motion in the genus of quality, and motion in the genus of where, which is called motion in respect to place.

It was explained in Book III how there is motion in these genera and how motion pertains to the categories of action and passion.

Hence it is sufficient here to say briefly that any motion is in the same genus as its terminus, not indeed in the sense that motion to quality is a species of quality, but by reduction. For just as potency is reduced to the genus of act because every genus is divided by potency and act, likewise motion, which is an imperfect act, must be reduced to the genus of perfect act. But insofar as motion is considered as to this from another, or from this to another, it pertains to the category of action and passion.

662. Next where he says, **"In respect of Substance..."** [487], he explains the given conditional argument.

First he shows that there cannot be motion in the genera other than the three mentioned above. Secondly, where he says, **"Since, then, motion can belong ..."** [497], he shows how there is motion in these three genera.

Concerning the first part he makes three points. First he shows that there is no motion in the genus of substance. Secondly, where he says, **"Nor is there motion ..."** [488], he shows that there is no motion in the genus of relation. Thirdly, where he says, **"Nor is there motion ..."** [489], he shows that there is no motion in the genera of action and passion.

He omits three categories; namely, when, site, and state. For "when" signifies being in time. But time is a measure of motion. Hence there is no motion in "when" for the same reason [ratio] that there is no motion in action and passion, which pertain to motion. Site indicates a certain order of parts. But order is a relation. Likewise state refers to a certain relation of a body to that which is joined to it. Hence there cannot be motion in these two categories just as there is no motion in relation.

He proves as follows that there is no motion in the genus of substance. Every motion is between contraries, as was said above. But there is no contrary of substance. Therefore there is no motion in respect to substance.

663. But a difficulty arises here be-cause the Philosopher himself says in De Generatione et Corruptione that fire is contrary to water. And in De Caelo he says that the heavens are neither generable nor corruptible because they do not have a contrary. Hence it seems to follow that things which are corrupted either are contraries or are composed of contraries.

Regarding this some say that one substance can be the contrary of another, as fire is contrary to water, in regard to its form but not in regard to its subject. But according to this Aristotle's proof is not valid, because there would be motion in substance if substantial forms were contraries. There is motion from form to form because in alteration subject is not contrary to subject, but form is contrary to form.

And therefore it must be said that fire is contrary to water in regard to the active and passive qualities, which are hot and cold, wet and dry, and not in regard to substantial forms. For it cannot be said that heat is the substantial form of fire since in other bodies it is an accident of the genus of quality. And that which belongs to the genus of substance cannot be an accident of something.

But even this answer presents a difficulty. It is clear that proper passions are caused by the principles of the subject, which are matter and form. If, therefore, the proper passions of fire and water are contraries, it seems that their substantial forms are contraries, because the causes of contraries are contraries. Moreover in Metaphysics, X, it is proven that every genus is divided by contrary differentiae. But differentiae are taken from forms, as is said in Metaphysics, VIII. It seems, therefore, that there is contrariety in substantial forms.

664. Therefore, it must be said that

the contrariety of differentiae, which is in every genus, is taken according to the common root of contrariety, which is excess and defect. All contraries are reduced to this opposition, as was said in Book I. For all differentiae which divide a genus are related such that one of them is in excess and the other in defect in respect to each other. Because of this Aristotle says in Metaphysics, VIII, that the definitions of things are like numbers, the species of which vary by the addition and subtraction of unity. But nevertheless it is not necessary that in every genus there be contrariety in respect to the nature [ratio] of this and that species, but only in respect to the common nature [ratio] of excess and defect. Since contraries differ to the greatest degree, it is necessary that contrariety be found in any genus when there are found two termini which differ to the greatest degree. And everything else of that genus falls between these two termini.

But there would not be motion in that genus unless there happens to be a continuous passage from one extreme to the other. Therefore, in some genera these two conditions are absent, as is clear in numbers. For although all species of number differ in respect to excess and defect, nevertheless in this genus there are not two extremes which differ to the greatest degree. There is a minimum number—two —but not a maximum. Likewise there is no continuity between species of number, because each species of number is formally completed by unity, which is indivisible, and is not continuous with another unity. The genus of substance is the same. For the forms of diverse species differ from each other in respect to excess and defect insofar as one form is more noble than another. And because of this diverse

forms can cause diverse passions, as was objected. Nevertheless one form of a species is not contrary to another in respect to its own proper nature [ratio].

The first reason for this is that there is no maximum difference between two substantial forms such that there is passage from one form to another in order only through intermediaries. Rather when matter puts off one form, it can indifferently receive diverse forms without order. Hence Aristotle says in De Generatione et Corruptione that when fire is generated from earth, it is not necessary that there be a transition through the intermediate elements.

The second reason is that, since the substantial existence of each thing is in something indivisible, there cannot be a continuity in substantial forms such that there might be a continuous motion from one form to another by the remission of one form and the incoming of another.

Hence Aristotle's proof that there is no motion in substance because there is no contrariety in substance is demonstrative, and not just a probable argument, as the Commentator seems to indicate. Moreover, that there is no motion in substance can also be proven by means of another argument which he gave above; namely, the subject of substantial form is being in potency only.

665. In qualities of the third species there clearly is contrariety in both senses [ratio]. For qualities can be extended and remitted such that there can be continuous motion from quality to quality. Moreover a maximum difference between two determinate extremes is found in the same genus, as in colors between black and white, and in taste between bitter and sweet.

But in quantity and in place one of these, that is, continuity, is clearly found. But the other, that is, a maximum difference of determinate extremes, is not found in them if they are taken according to the common nature [ratio] of quantity and place, but only according as they are taken in some determinate thing. Thus in a species of animal or plant there is some minimum quantity, from which augmentation begins, and a maximum quantity, at which it ends. Likewise in place there are found two termini at a maximum distance in comparison to some motion. The motion begins from one of these and ends at the other, whether it be natural or violent motion.

666. Next where he says, **"Nor is there motion . . ."** [488], he shows that there is no motion in the genus of relation.

For in whatever genus there is per se motion, nothing new of that genus is found in anything unless it changes. Thus a new color is not found in any colored thing, unless it be altered. But something new truly happens to that which is relative to another when that other changes, while it itself does not change. Therefore, in relation there is no motion per se, but only per accidens, insofar as a new relation results from some change. Thus equality or inequality results from change of quantity, and similarity or dissimilarity results from change of quality.

667. In some cases that which is said here does not seem to present a difficulty. But in other cases it does.

For there are certain relations which are not anything real in that of which they are predicated.

This can occur in regard to both extremes of the relation, as when it is said that the self is the same as the self. This relation of identity would be multi-

plied to infinity if anything were the same as itself by means of an added relation. For it is clear that anything is the same as itself. Therefore this is a relation in respect to reason [ratio] only insofar as reason [ratio] takes one and the same thing as the two extremes of a relation. This also occurs in many other cases.

Further there are certain relations of which one is real in the one extreme, and the other is in the other extreme only according to reason [ratio], for example, knowledge and the knowable. For the knowable is relative, not because it itself is referred to by some relation existing in it, but because something else is referred to it, as is made clear by the Philosopher in Metaphysics, V. Another example is when a column is said to be to the right of an animal. Right and left are real relations in the animal because the determinate powers on which these relations are based are found in animals. But in the column these relations are not present in respect to the thing but only in respect to reason [ratio]. For the column does not have those powers which are the foundations of these relations.

Further there are certain relations in which a real relation is found to exist in respect to both extremes: for example, equality and similitude. For quantity and quality, which are the roots of these relations, are found in both extremes. This also occurs in many other relations.

Hence, regarding those relations which posit something in only one extreme, it does not seem difficult to understand how, when that extreme in which the relation really exists is changed, something new is said relative to the other without that other changing. For nothing really happened to it. But in those cases in which a real relation is found in both extremes, it seems difficult to understand how something is said relatively of one, which does not change, because of a change of the other. For nothing new comes to something without a change of that to which it comes.

Hence it must be said that if someone by changing becomes equal to me, and I did not change, then that equality was first in me in some way, as in a root from which it has real being. For since I have a certain quantity, it happens that I am equal to all those who have the same quantity. When, therefore, someone newly takes on this quantity, this common root of equality is determined in regard to him. Therefore nothing new happens to me because of the fact that I begin to be equal to another because of his change.

668. Next where he says, **"Nor is there motion ..."** [489], he proves that there is no motion in the genera of action and passion.

Action and passion do not differ from motion in subject. Rather they add an intelligibility [ratio], as was said in Book III. Hence to say that there is motion in action and passion is the same as to say that there is motion in motion.

Therefore concerning this he makes three points. First he states his intention. Secondly, where he says, **"For in the first place ..."** [490], he proves his position. Thirdly, where he says, **"To sum up, then ..."** [496], he makes a certain distinction in order to clarify his position.

He says, therefore, first [489] that just as there is no motion of that which is relative, likewise there is no motion of agent and patient, nor, to speak absolutely, of mover and moved. For there cannot be motion of motion, or

generation of generation, which are the species of mutation. Nor can there be mutation of mutation, which is their genus. Nor can there be corruption of corruption.

669. Next where he says, **"For in the first place ..."** [490], he proves with six arguments that there cannot be mutation of mutation.

The first is as follows. If there is mutation of mutation, this can be understood in two ways. First there might be a mutation of a mutation as a subject which is moved; just as there is a mutation of a man because the man is changed from white to black. Thus motion of motion as subject or mutation of mutation as subject can be understood as though the motion or mutation were moved; for example, that it becomes warm, or becomes cold, or is moved in place, or increases or decreases. But this is impossible since mutation is not a subject for it is not a per se subsisting substance. Therefore there cannot be a mutation of mutation as subject.

670. Secondly mutation of mutation can be understood as of a terminus, as, for example, when a subject is moved from one species of mutation to another, as from becoming warm to becoming cold or becoming healthy. Thus two mutations are understood as the two termini of one mutation. For example, sickness and health are understood as two termini when a man is changed from sickness to health. But it is impossible for a subject to be moved per se from mutation to mutation. This happens only per accidens.

He proves in two ways that this is not possible per se.

The first proof is as follows. Every motion is a mutation from one determinate species to another determinate species. Likewise generation and corruption, which are divided against motion, have determinate termini. The difference is that generation and corruption occur between termini opposed as contradictories, while motion occurs between termini opposed as contraries.

Therefore, if a subject be changed from mutation to mutation, for example, from becoming sick to becoming white, then at the same time that the subject changes from health to sickness, it will be changed from this mutation to another. For while the subject is still partly at the terminus from which, it is moved toward the terminus to which; just as while someone has some health, he is moved to sickness.

Therefore, if motion from sickness to health be the terminus from which of another motion, then while this very mutation from sickness to health is still going on, the subject will simultaneously be changed from this mutation to another which succeeds it in the subject. But it is clear that when the first mutation has been terminated, that is, when the man is already changed from sickness to health, then any other mutation can thereafter succeed it. This is not surprising. For when the first mutation is terminated, the subject is at rest and is not being changed by any mutation. And for the same reason [ratio] it can be changed by any other mutation.

If, therefore, there is a motion from one mutation to a second which succeeds it in the subject, it follows that this is a motion from the first mutation to some other indeterminate mutation. And this is contrary to the nature [ratio] of per se motion. For every motion is from a determinate terminus to a determinate terminus. For a body is not moved per se from white to just anything, but to black or an intermediate color.

It is clear, therefore, that two mutations are not the per se termini of any mutation.

671. Secondly he proves the same thing with another argument.

If there is mutation per se from a preceding mutation to a subsequent mutation, it is not necessary that the mutation always be to an occurring mutation, that is, to one which occurs simultaneously with the preceding mutation. Thus becoming white can be simultaneous with becoming sick, but becoming healthy cannot be simultaneous with becoming sick, because these are contrary mutations. Nevertheless it happens that becoming white and becoming healthy succeed becoming sick in the same subject. And this is what he means when he says that mutation from one mutation to another will not always be to an occurring mutation, for when it succeeds it is not occurring. Also the non-occurring mutation is between two other termini. For this reason the non-occurring mutation, to which one is changed from becoming sick, will be becoming healthy, which is opposed to becoming sick.

That this is inconsistent is clear from the proposition established above: namely, that while the first mutation is going on, it will be simultaneously changed to a second mutation. Therefore while one is becoming sick, he will simultaneously be becoming healthy. For the terminus of becoming healthy is health—for it is from something to something else, as was said. Hence it follows that while something is being moved to sickness, it is also simultaneously being moved to health. But this is to be moved simultaneously to two contraries, and to tend toward them simultaneously. This is impossible. Thus it is clear that there is no per se mutation from one mutation to another.

But it is clear that this might happen per accidens, as was said above, for he adds that it does happen per accidens, as when a subject is changed now by one mutation and later by another. For example, it might be said that something is changed per accidens from memory to forgetfulness or to any other mutation. For the subject of the mutation at one time is changed to knowledge, and at another time to something else, for example, to health.

672. He gives the second argument where he says, "**In the second place . . .**" [491]. He sets forth two conditional arguments.

The first is that if there be mutation of mutation or generation of generation, then it would somehow be necessary to proceed to infinity. For by the same reason [ratio] the second generation will have another generation, and so forth to infinity.

The second conditional argument is that, if generations and mutations be so ordered that there is a mutation of mutation and a generation of generation, then if there will be a last mutation or generation, there must be a first. He proves this second conditional statement as follows. Let there be something which is generated simply, for example, fire. Now if there is generation of generation, then one must say that at some time this simple generation itself was also generated, and this becoming itself became. But when this generation itself was being generated, that which is generated simply, that is, fire, as yet was not. For a thing does not exist while it becomes. Rather when it is already made, then it exists primarily. Therefore while the generation of fire was being generated, fire was not yet made, and therefore it did not yet

exist. And again the very generation of its generation for the same reason [ratio] at some time was generated. And thus, just as when fire did not yet exist when the generation of fire was being generated, likewise it follows that the generation of fire did not yet exist when the generation of the generation of fire was being generated.

From this it is clear there cannot be a generation of fire if the prior generation is not completed. And for the same reason [ratio] the prior generation cannot occur unless the next prior generation is completed, and so forth back to the first generation. Hence if there were no first generation, there will not be the last, which is the generation of fire. But if one proceeds in generations to infinity, there is no first generation or mutation, because in infinity there is no first. Hence it follows that there is no generation or mutation. And if there is no generation or mutation, then nothing is generated or is moved. Thus if there is generation of generation and mutation of mutation, then nothing is generated or is moved.

But it must be understood that this argument does not deny that mutation can follow mutation per accidens to infinity. It is necessary to say this according to the opinion of Aristotle who held eternal motion. He intends to show, as was said above, that there is no mutation of mutation per se to infinity. For the last would depend on an infinity of predecessors, and would never be completed.

673. He gives the third argument where he says, "**Thirdly, if a thing . . .**" [492]. The argument is as follows.

Both motion and rest are contrary to the same motion. For example, descent and rest in a lower place are contrary to ascent, and likewise generation and corruption are contrary. For contraries naturally occur in regard to the same thing. Therefore whatever is generated can be corrupted. But if there is generation of generation, it is necessary that generation be generated. Therefore generation is corrupted. But that which is corrupted must exist. For just as that which is not is generated, likewise that which is is corrupted. Therefore it is necessary that when something is generated and generation exists, then this same generation is corrupted: not indeed immediately after the generation ends, nor at a later time, but simultaneously. But this seems impossible.

However it must be realized that generation is the terminus of that which is generated as substance. For generation is a transmutation to substance. But the subject of generation is not that which is generated; rather it is its matter. Hence Aristotle does not abandon his own position, by which he intends to show that there is no mutation of mutation as terminus.

674. He gives the fourth argument where he says, **"Fourthly, there must be ..."** [493]. The argument is as follows.

In every generation there must be some matter from which that which is generated comes. Also in every mutation there must be some matter or subject. Thus in alteration the subject in respect to corporeal alterations is the body, and in respect to animal alterations it is the soul. Therefore, if generation is generated, there must be some matter for this generation. This matter is changed to the species of generation, just as the matter of generated fire was changed to the species of fire. But such matter cannot be found.

Under this same argument he gives another approach. In any generation or mutation there must be some termi-

nus to which something is moved. This terminus must be a definite and determinate "this." But neither generation nor motion is such a "this." Therefore it is not possible for there to be a generation of generation or of motion.

675. He gives the fifth argument where he says, **"But in what sense ..."** [494]. The argument is as follows.

Species is related to species in the same way that genus is related to genus. Therefore, if there is generation of generation, then the generation of learning must be learning. But this is clearly false. For learning is the generation of knowledge and not the generation of learning. Therefore there cannot be generation of generation.

676. He gives the sixth argument where he says, **"Finally, since there are ..."** [495]. The argument is as follows.

If there is mutation of mutation either as subject or as terminus, then, since there are three species of motion, as was said, that is, motion in "where," in quantity, and in quality, it follows that one of these species must be the subject and terminus of another as well as of itself. It follows, therefore, that change of place is either altered or is moved in respect to place. This is more evidently impossible in a special case than in general. Therefore, it must not be said that there is mutation of mutation or generation of generation.

677. Next where he says, **"To sum up, then ..."** [496], he shows how there can be mutation of mutation.

He says that since a thing is moved in three ways, as was said above, that is, either per accidens, per se, or in respect to a part, mutation can be changed only per accidens, insofar as the subject of mutation is changed. For example, if someone runs or learns while he becomes healthy, then becoming healthy runs or learns per accidens, like a musician who builds. But we do not intend here to treat that which is moved per accidens. This we have already dismissed above.

He Concludes That There Is Motion Only in Quantity, Quality, and Where. He Explains How There is Motion in These Three Genera and What He Means by "Immobile"

Text of Aristotle

497. *Since, then, motion can belong neither to Being nor to Relation nor to Agent and Patient, it remains that there can be motion only in respect of Quality, Quantity, and Place; for with each of these we have a pair of contraries.*   226a23–26

498. *Motion in respect of Quality let us call alteration, a general designation that is used to include both contraries; and by Quality I do not here mean a property of substance (in that sense that which constitutes a specific distinction is a quality) but a passive quality in virtue of which a thing is said to be acted on or to be incapable of being acted on.*   226a26–29

499. *Motion in respect of Quantity has no name that includes both contraries, but it is called increase or decrease according as one or the other is designated: that is to say motion in the direction of complete magnitude is increase, motion in the contrary direction is decrease.*   226a29–32

500. *Motion in respect of Place has no name either general or particular; but we may designate it by the general name of locomotion, though strictly the term "locomotion" is applicable to things that change their place only when they have not the power to come to a stand, and to things that do not move themselves locally.*   226a32–226b1

501. *Change within the same kind from a lesser to a greater or from a greater to a lesser degree is alteration; for it is motion either from a contrary or to a contrary, whether in an unqualified or in a qualified sense; for change to a lesser degree of a quality will be called change to the contrary of that quality, and change to a greater degree of a quality will be regarded as change from the contrary of that quality to the quality itself. It makes no difference whether the change be qualified or unqualified, except that in the former case the contraries will have to be contrary to one another only in a qualified sense; and a thing's possessing a quality in a greater or in a lesser decree means the presence or absence in it of more or less of the opposite quality.*   226b1–8

502. *It is now clear, then, that there are only these three kinds of motion.*   226b8–10

503. *The term "immovable" we apply in the first place to that which is absolutely incapable of being moved (just as we correspondingly apply the term invisible to sound); in the second place to that which is moved with difficulty after a long time or whose movement is slow at the start—in fact, what we describe as hard to move; and in the third place to that which is naturally designed for and capable of motion, but is not in motion when, where, and as it naturally would be so. This last is the only kind of immovable thing of which I use the term "being at rest"; for rest is contrary to motion, so that rest will be negation of motion in that which is capable of admitting motion.*   226b10–16

504. *The foregoing remarks are sufficient to explain the essential nature of motion and rest, the number of kinds of change, and the different varieties of motion.*   226b16–17

COMMENTARY OF ST. THOMAS

678. Having shown that there is no motion in substance, or in relation, or in action and passion, he indicates in what genera there is motion.

Concerning this he makes three points. First he states his intended conclusion. Secondly, where he says, **"Motion in respect of Quality . . ."**

[498], he explains how there is motion in each of the three genera. Thirdly, where he says, **"Change within the same kind ..."** [501], he answers a difficulty.

He says, therefore, first that since there is no motion in substance, or in relation, or in action or passion, as was shown, it follows that there is motion in only three genera, that is, in quantity, quality, and where. For in each of these genera there is contrariety, which is required by motion.

For this reason he omits three genera, namely, when, site, and state. And it was shown above how there is contrariety in the three genera in which there is motion.

679. Next where he says, **"Motion in respect of Quality ..."** [498], he explains how there is motion in the above mentioned genera.

First he explains how there is motion in quality; secondly, in quantity, where he says, **"Motion in respect of Quantity ..."** [499], and thirdly, in where, where he says, **"Motion in respect of Place ..."** [500].

He says, therefore, first [498] that motion in quality is called alteration.

The common name "alteration" refers to this genus because that which differs in quality is customarily called "other" (alterum). We do not speak of quality here as referring to that which is found in the genus of substance, according to which a substantial difference is said to be predicated as a quality. Rather we speak of passive quality, which is contained in the third species of quality. In this sense quality is said of something done or not done, like hot and cold, white and black, and such things. For in these things there is alteration, as will be proven in Book VII.

680. Next where he says, **"Motion**

in respect of Quantity ..." [499], he explains how there is motion in quantity.

He says that motion in quantity is not named according to its genus, as alteration is. Rather it is named according to its species, which are increase and decrease. Motion from imperfect to perfect magnitude is called increase. And motion from perfect to imperfect magnitude is called decrease.

681. Next where he says, **"Motion in respect of Place ...,"** [500] he shows how there is motion in where.

He says that motion in respect to place does not have a name which is common to the genus, nor a name which is proper to the species. Rather the general name "bringing forth" is applied to it, even though this name is not altogether proper to local motion in general. For only those things which are so moved in respect to place that they do not have the power to stand still are properly said to be "brought forth." Such things are not moved in respect to place by themselves, but by something else.

Therefore, a common name can be applied to motion in quality because qualities are contraries in respect to the proper nature [ratio] of their species. And because of this they are contained under the genus of quality. But in quantity there is no contrariety in respect to the nature [ratio] of its species, but in respect to the perfect and the imperfect, as was said above. And according to this the species are named. And there is contrariety in place only by comparison to a motion in which two termini are at maximum distance. Therefore, since this contrariety refers to something altogether extraneous to this genus, motion in this genus cannot have a name either in general or in respect to its parts.

682. Next where he says, **"Change**

within the same kind . . ." [501], he points out that there could be a difficulty in showing to what species of motion is reduced mutation in respect to more and less. An example would be something becoming less white from more white, and vice versa. One might think that this should be reduced to the motion of increase and decrease. But he shows that this is reduced to the motion of alteration. He says that a mutation of either more or less which is in a species of quality, for example, in whiteness, is an alteration.

He proves this by the fact that alteration is a mutation from contrary to contrary in respect to quality. This happens in two ways: either simply, as when someone is changed from white to black or vice versa; or in a qualified way, as when something is changed from more white to less white or vice versa.

That to be changed in a qualified way is to be changed from contrary to contrary he proves as follows. When a thing is changed from more white to less white, it can be said to be changed from contrary to contrary because it approaches the contrary, that is, black. But when a thing is changed from less white to more white, it is the same as if it were changed from contrary to contrary, that is, from black to white itself. For it becomes more white because it recedes more from black and participates more perfectly in whiteness.

In respect to alteration it makes no difference, except as follows, whether a thing is changed from contrary to contrary either simply or in a qualified way. When a thing is changed simply from contrary to contrary, the termini of the alteration must be two contraries in act, for example, white and black. But mutation of more and less occurs

insofar as there is or is not more or less of one of the contraries.

Lastly, where he says, **"It is now clear . . ."** [502], he concludes that it is clear from the above that there are only three species of motion.

683. Next where he says, **"The term 'immovable' . . ."** [503], he explains the ways in which "immobile" is predicated. He gives three ways.

First, that is said to be immobile which in no way can be moved, for example, God. In a similar way that is said to be invisible which cannot be seen, for example, sound.

Secondly, that is said to be immobile which is moved with difficulty. This occurs in two ways: either because, after a thing begins to be moved, it is moved slowly and with great difficulty, as when one says a lame man is immobile; or because a thing is difficult to begin to be moved, and it is necessary to work at this for a long time, as when we say that a mountain or a large rock is immobile.

Thirdly, that is said to be immobile which can be moved and moved easily, nevertheless it is not being moved when it can, and where it can, and how it can be moved. Only such an object is properly said to be at rest, for rest is the contrary of motion. He takes contrariety here in a wide sense such that it also includes privation. Hence he concludes that rest must be a privation in that which is susceptible of motion. For a contrary and a privation are only in that which is susceptible of an opposite.

Finally, where he says, **"The foregoing remarks . . ."** [504], he concludes his remarks by saying that it is clear from the above what motion is, and what rest is, and how many mutations there are, and which mutations can be called motions.

LECTURE 5 [226b19 227b2]
He Defines "Contact," "Succession," "Continuity," and Other Related Things

Text of Aristotle
Chapter 3

505. Let us now proceed to define the terms "together" and "apart," "in between," "in succession" "contiguous" and "continuous contact" and to show in what circumstances each of these terms is naturally applicable.   **226b18–21**

506. Things are said to be together in place when they are in one place (in the strictest sense of the word "place") and to be apart when they are in different places. Things are said to be in contact when their extremities are together.   **227a7–12**

507. That which a changing thing, if it changes continuously in a natural manner, naturally reaches before it reaches that to which it changes last, is between. Thus "between" implies the presence of at least three things: for in a process of change it is the contrary that is "last": and a thing is moved continuously if it leaves no gap or only the smallest possible gap in the material—not in the time (for a gap in the time does not prevent things having a "between," while, on the other hand, there is nothing to prevent the highest note sounding immediately after the lowest) but in the material in which the motion takes place. This is manifestly true not only in local changes but in every other kind as well.   **226b23–27**

508. A thing is "in succession" when it is after the beginning in position or in form or in some other respect in which it is definitely so regarded, and when further there is nothing of the same kind as itself between it and that to which it is in succession e.g., a line or lines if it is a line, a unit or units if it is a unit, a house if it is a house (there is nothing to prevent something of a different kind being between). For that which is in succession is in succession to a particular thing, and is something posterior; for one is not "in succession" to two, nor is the first day of the month to the second: in each case the latter is "in succession" to the former.   **226b27–34**

509. (Now every change implies a pair of opposites and opposites may be either c gontraries or contradictories; since then contradiction admits of no mean term, it is obvious that "between" must imply a pair of contraries.)

That is locally contrary which is most distant in a straight line; for the shortest line is definitely limited, and that which is definitely limited constitutes a measure. A thing, that is in succession and touches is "contiguous."   **226b34–227a10**

510. The "continuous" is a subdivision of the contiguous: things are called continuous when the touching limits of each become one and the same and are, as the word implies, contained in each other: continuity is impossible if these extremities are two. This definition makes it plain that continuity belongs to things that naturally in virtue of their mutual contact form a unity. And in whatever way that which holds them together is one, so too will the whole be one, e.g. by a rivet or glue or contact or organic union.   **227a10–17**

511. It is obvious that of these terms "in succession" is first in order of analysis; for that which touches is necessarily in succession, but not everything that is in succession touches: and so succession is a property of things prior in definition, e.g. numbers, while contact is not.   **227a17–21**

512. And if there is continuity there is necessarily contact, but if there is contact, that alone does not imply continuity; for the extremities of things may be "together" without necessarily being one; but they cannot be one without being necessarily together. So natural junction is last in coming to be; for the extremities must necessarily come into contact if they are to be naturally joined; but things that are in contact are not all naturally joined, while where there is no contact clearly there is no natural junction either. 227a21–27

513. *Hence, if as some say "point" and "unit" have an independent existence of their own, it is impossible for the two to be identical; for points can touch while units can only be in succession. Moreover, there can always be some hing between points (for all lines are intermediate between points), whereas it is not necessary that there should possibly be anything between units; for there can be nothing between the numbers one and two.* 227a27–32

514. *We have now defined what is meant by "together" and "apart," "contact," "between" and "in succession," "contiguous" and "continuous": and we have shown in what circumstances each of these terms is applicable.* 227a32–227b2

COMMENTARY OF ST. THOMAS

684. After the Philosopher has divided mutation and motion into their species, he proceeds here to determine the unity and contrariety of motion in its species.

Concerning this he makes two points. First he sets forth certain things which are required by what follows. Secondly, where he says, **"There are many senses..."** [515], he takes up the main problem.

Concerning the first part he makes three points. First he states his intention. Secondly, where he says, **"Things are said to be together in place ..."** [506], he works out the problem. Thirdly, where he says, **"We have now defined ..."** [514], he summarizes.

He says, therefore, first that we must next state what is meant by "together," "apart" or "separated," "contact," "middle," "succession," "contiguity," "continuity," and in what way such things are natural.

He sets these definitions down here because he uses them in the demonstrations which follow throughout the whole book; just as in the beginning of Euclid definitions are given which are the principles of the subsequent demonstrations.

685. Next where he says, **"Things**

are said to be together in place ..."** [506], he works out the problem.

First he defines the things which were proposed. Secondly, where he says, **"It is obvious ..."** [511], he compares them to each other.

Concerning the first part he makes three points. First he defines those things which pertain to "contact." Secondly, where he says, **"That which a changing thing ..."** [507], he defines those things which pertain to "succession." Thirdly, where he says, **"The 'continuous' is a subdivision ..."** [510], he defines those things which pertain to "continuity."

Since "together" is included in the definition of "contact," he first defines "together." He says that things are said to be together in place when they are in one primary place. By the primary place of anything he means its proper place. For things are said to be together because they are in one proper place, but not because they are in one common place. Otherwise one could say that all bodies are together because they are all contained under the heavens.

Furthermore he is talking here of things being together in place rather than things being together in time.

This latter point is not presently under discussion.

Contrariwise, things are said to be "separate" or "apart" when they are in different places.

Furthermore, things are said to be in "contact" when their extremities are together. The extremities of bodies are surfaces, the extremities of surfaces are lines, and the extremities of lines are points. Therefore, if there be two lines touching in their extremities, then two points of the two touching lines will be contained under one point of the containing place. But because of this it does not follow that that which is located is greater than its place. For a point added to a point does not produce anything greater. And the same argument holds in the other cases.

686. Next where he says, **"That which a changing thing . . ."** [507], he defines those things which pertain to "succession."

Concerning this he makes three points. First he defines "middle," which is included in the definition of "succession." Secondly, where he says, **"A thing is 'in succession' . . ."** [508], he defines "succession." Thirdly, where he says, **"Now every change implies . . ."** [509], he infers a corollary.

He says, therefore, first that "middle" is that which is naturally arrived at first when something is changed continuously by nature. It is not the ultimate terminus of motion to which something is being moved. For example, if something is changed from A to C through B, then, provided the motion is continuous, it arrives first at B rather than C.

There can be a middle in many ways. For between two extremes there can be many intermediates. Thus between black and white there are many intermediate colors. But there must be at least three things: two extremes and one intermediate. Therefore, the middle is that through which one arrives at the terminus of a mutation; but the terminus of the mutation is a contrary. For it was said above that motion is from contrary to contrary.

687. Since the continuity of motion is included in the definition of "middle," he next explains what it means to be moved continuously.

The continuity of motion can be understood in two ways—either in respect to the time in which a thing is moved or in respect to that through which a thing is moved, for example, magnitude in local motion.

Hence, in order for motion to be continuous, it is necessary that there be no interruption in time. For if the motion be interrupted in time, no matter how briefly, it is not continuous.

But in respect to the magnitude through which a motion occurs, there can be a small interruption without violating the continuity of motion. This is clear in the case of crossing a road in which the stones are placed a small distance from each other. By means of these stones a man crosses from one part of the road to another with a continuous motion.

Therefore, he says that a thing is moved continuously when there is either no interruption or only a very small one. That is, in respect to that through which a thing is moved there is no interruption; or, if there is one, it is very small. But if motion is continuous, there cannot be even the slightest interruption of time.

Furthermore he explains how a thing can lack continuous motion by adding that there is nothing to prevent a thing from being moved continuously if there is a break in the thing—but not in time. Thus when one plays the cithara, one sounds the highest note immediately after the lowest note, leaving out the intermediate notes. This is not a break in time but in the thing in which there is motion.

What has been said about the continuity of motion must be understood of both local motion and the other motions.

688. But it is not clear how the extreme in local motion is a contrary. For place does not seem to be contrary to place. Hence he also clarifies this point.

He says that that which is at a maximum distance in respect to a straight line is a contrary in respect to place. This maximum distance must be understood in relation to the motion, the mobile object, and the mover. Thus, as related to the motion of heavy and light things, the maximum distance in place is the center and extremity of the heavens in respect to us. But in respect to your motion or mine, that place to which we intend to go is at a maximum distance from that place from which we began to be moved.

He explains what he means by "straight line" by adding, "The shortest line is definitely limited, and that which is definitely limited constitutes a measure" [226 b 32-33].

To understand this we must consider that the minimum distance between any two designated points is a straight line. There can be only one such line between two points. But since two curved lines are the arcs of major or minor circles, the curved lines between two points can be multiplied to infinity. Furthermore, every measure must be finite (otherwise it could not designate a quantity, which is the function of a measure). Hence, the maximum distance between two things cannot be measured by a curved line, but only by a straight line, which is finite and determinate.

689. Next where he says, **"A thing is 'in succession' . . ."** [508], he defines "succession" and one of its species, namely, contiguity.

He says that two things are required for a thing to be in succession to another.

The first is that it be after the beginning in some order; either in respect to position, as in things which have an order in place, or in respect to species, as duality is after unity, or in respect to any other kind of determinate order, like power, or dignity, or knowledge, etc.

The second requirement is that, between that which succeeds and that which is succeeded, there be no intermediate of the same genus. Thus one line succeeds another if there is no other line between them. And likewise a unity succeeds a unity, and a house a house. But when something succeeds another, there is nothing to prevent there being an intermediate of another genus between them. Thus an animal might be in the middle between two houses.

Furthermore, he explains why he says, **". . . after the beginning . . ."** [226b34], and **". . . that to which it is in succession . . ."** [227a2]. For he adds that whatever is in succession is in succession in respect to something, not as prior, but as posterior. For we do not say that one succeeds two, nor that the new moon succeeds the second, but vice versa.

Next he defines a species of "succession" which is called "contiguity." He says that not everything which is in succession is contiguous. Rather this occurs only when two things in succession touch, so that there is no intermediate either of the same genus or of any other genus.

690. Next where he says, **"Now every change implies ..."** [509], he concludes from the above that every middle is between contraries in some way. For a middle is that through which something is moved to an extremity. And every mutation is between opposites which are either contraries or contradictories. However there is no middle between contradictories.

691. Next where he says, **"The 'continuous' is a subdivision ..."** [510], he explains what "continuity" is.

He says that "continuity" is a species of "contiguity." For when two things which touch have one and the same terminus, they are said to be continuous. This indeed is what the word "continuous" signifies. For "continuous" is derived from "containing." When, therefore, many parts are contained in one, and are held together as it were, then there is a continuum. This cannot occur when there are two extremities, but only when there is one.

From this he concludes further that there can be continuity only in those things which naturally become one by contact.

For the same reason a whole is in itself one and continuous because one continuum results from many things. This occurs either by being nailed together; or by being brought into each other; or by any kind of touching such that two termini become one; or even by something being born as naturally joined to another, as fruit is born to a tree and in some way is continuous with it.

692. Next where he says, **"It is obvious that ..."** [511], he compares to each

other the three main points discussed above; namely, succession, contact, and continuity.

Concerning this he makes three points. First he compares succession to contact. Secondly, where he says, **"And if there is continuity ..."** [512], he compares contact to continuity. Thirdly, where he says, **"Hence, if as some say ..."** [513], he infers a corollary.

He says, therefore, first [511] that in the order of nature succession is first among these three. It is called prior because it does not follow upon the other two. For everything that is in contact must be in succession, because between things which touch each other there must be some order, at least in position. But it is not necessary that everything which is in succession be touching. For there can be order in things which do not touch, as in things separated from matter. Hence succession is found in things which are prior according to reason [ratio]. For it is found in numbers in which there is no touching. This latter is found only in continuous things. Moreover, according to reason [ratio] numbers are prior to continuous quantities as being more simple and more abstract.

693. Next where he says, **"And if there is continuity ..."** [512], he compares contact to continuity.

He says that for the same reason contact is prior to continuity. For if something is continuous, it is necessary that it is touching. But if something is touching, it is not necessary that it is continuous.

He proves this by the definition [ratio] of each of these things. For it is not necessary that the extremities of two things are one (which is the definition [ratio] of continuity) if they are together (which is the definition [ratio] of contact). But conversely, it is necessary that, if the extremities are one, they are together. The reason [ratio] for this is that that which is one is together with itself.

However, if one uses "together" to mean a relation of distinct things, then such things cannot be one. And accordingly things which are continuous cannot be in contact, but are taken in common. Hence he concludes that a continuity in which one part is included in another in one terminus is the ultimate result in the order of generation. Thus the special is posterior to the common, as animal is generated before man. Hence I call this the "ultimate inclusion" because it is necessary that things touch each other if their extremities are naturally united. But it is not necessary that all things which touch each other be naturally united to each other. And it is clear that in things in which there cannot be contact there cannot be continuity.

694. Next where he says, **"Hence, if as some say ..."** [513], he draws a corollary from the above. If unity and "point" are separated, as some say who hold that mathematicals have a separated existence, it follows that unity and "point" are not the same.

He shows this with two arguments. The first is that points are in things whose nature it is to touch, and these things touch each other in respect to points. However in unities there is not found any contact, but only succession. The second argument is that between two points there is a middle. For every line is a middle between two points. But between two unities it is not necessary that there be any middle. For it is clear that there is no middle between the two unities which constitute duality and the very first unity.

Finally, where he says, **"We have now defined ..."** [514], he summarizes what has been said. The meaning of this text is clear.

Text of Aristotle
Chapter 4

515. *There are many senses in which motion is said to be "one"; for we use the term "one" in many senses. Motion is one generically according to the different categories to which it may be assigned: thus any locomotion is one generically with any other locomotion, whereas alteration is different generically from locomotion.* 227b3–6

516. *Motion is one specifically when besides being one generically it also takes place in a species incapable of subdivision: e.g., color has specific differences; therefore blackening and whitening differ specifically; but at all events every whitening will be specifically the same with every other whitening and every blackening with every other blackening. But whiteness is not further subdivided by specific differences: hence any whitening is specifically one with any other whitening. Where it happens that the genus is at the same time a species, it is clear that the motion will then in a sense be one specifically though not in an unqualified sense: learning is an example of this, knowledge being on the one hand a species of apprehension and on the other hand a genus including the various knowledges.* 227b6–14

517. *A difficulty, however, may be raised as to whether a motion is specifically one when the same thing changes from the same to the same, e.g., when one point changes again and again from a particular place to a particular place: if this motion is specifically one, circular motion will be the same as rectilinear motion, and rolling the same as walking. But is not this difficulty removed by the principle already laid down that if that in which the motion takes place is specifically different (as in the present instance the circular path is specifically different from the straight) the motion itself is also different? We have explained, then, what is meant by saying that motion is one generically or one specifically.* 227b14–21

518. *Motion is one in an unqualified sense when it is one essentially or numerically; and the following distinctions will make clear what this kind of motion is. There are three classes of things in connection with which we speak of motion, the "that which," the "that in which," and the "that during which." I mean that there must be something that is in motion, e.g. a man or gold, and it must be in motion in something, e.g., a place or an affection, and during some time for all motion takes place during a time. Of these three it is the thing in which the motion takes place that makes it one generically or specifically, it is the thing moved that makes the motion one in subject, and it is the time that makes it consecutive; but it is the three together that make it one without qualification: to effect this, that in which the motion takes place (the species) must be one and incapable of subdivision, that during which it takes place (the time) must be one and unintermittent, and that which is in motion must be one—not in an accidental sense (i.e., it must be one as the white that blackens is one or Coriscus who walks is one, not in the accidental sense in which Coriscus and white may be one), nor merely in virtue of community of nature (for there might be a case of two men being restored to health at the same time in the same way, e.g., from inflammation of the eye, yet this motion is not really one, but only specifically one).* 227b21–228a3

519. *Suppose, however, that Socrates undergoes an alteration specifically the same but at one time and again at another: in this case if it is possible for that which ceased to be again to come into being and remain numerically the same, then this motion too will be one: otherwise it will be the same but not one.* 228a3–6

520. *And akin to this difficulty there is another; viz. is health one? and generally are the states and affections in bodies severally one in essence although (as is clear) the things that*

contain them are obviously in motion and in flux? Thus if a person's health at daybreak and at the present moment is one and the same, why should not this health be numerically one with that which he recovers after an interval?   228a6–12

521. *The same argument applies in each case. There is, however, we may answer, this difference: that if the states are two then it follows simply from this fact that the activities must also in point of number be two (for only that which is numerically one can give rise to an activity that is numerically one), but if the state is one, this is not in itself enough to make us regard the activity also as one: for when a man ceases walking, the walking no longer is, but it will again be if he begins to walk again. But, be this as it may, if in the above instance the health is one and the same, then it must be possible for that which is one and the same to come to be and to cease to be many times. However, these difficulties lie outside our present inquiry.*

228a12–20

COMMENTARY OF ST. THOMAS

695. After the Philosopher has given certain definitions which are necessary for what is to follow, he begins to treat the unity and diversity of motion.

First he treats the unity and diversity of motion. Secondly, where he says, **"We have further to determine . . ."** [530], he discusses contrariety, which is a species of diversity.

Concerning the first part he makes two points. First he distinguishes the unity of motion in respect to three common modes. Secondly, where he says, **"Since every motion is continuous . . ."** [522], he subdivides each of these.

Concerning the first part he makes three points. First he explains how motion is said to be one in genus. Secondly, where he says, **"Motion is one specifically . . ."** [516], he explains how it is said to be one in species. Thirdly, where he says, **"Motion is one . . ."** [518], he explains how it is said to be one in number.

696. He says, therefore, first [515] that motion is called "one" in many ways, insofar as "one" itself, taken in common, is also said in many ways; that is, generically, specifically and numerically.

Further he says that motion is one in genus according to the figures of predication. For all motions which are in one order of predication can be called one in genus. Thus, all local motions are one in genus because they are in one category; namely, where. But local motion differs in genus from alteration, which is in the category of quality, as was said above.

697. Next where he says, **"Motion is one specifically . . ."** [516], he explains how motion is one in species.

First he explains his position. Secondly, where he says, **"A difficulty, however . . ."** [517], he raises a difficulty.

He says, therefore, first that motion is called one in species when it is one not only in respect to a genus but also in respect to an individual species; that is, in respect to a last species which is not divided into other species. For there are certain species which are divided into other species. Thus color is a species of quality, but nevertheless it has differentiae by which it is divided into different species. Hence motions in respect to colors can be diverse in species, for example, becoming white and becoming black. But every whitening is the same in respect to species, as is every blackening. For there are no species of whiteness into which it is further divided.

However, if there are certain things which are both genera and species, it is clear that motions which occur in these subalternate species are in a way one in species, but simply speaking they are not one in species. Thus, science is a species of thought and also the genus of the diverse sciences. Hence all teaching, which is motion toward science, is in a way one in species, but not so simply speaking. For the teaching of grammar is a simply different species than the teaching of geometry.

Moreover, it must be realized that in the foregoing he treats the unity and diversity of motion in respect to those genera and species in which there happens to be motion. For motion in some way is reduced to the genus of those things in which there is motion.

698. Next where he says, "**A difficulty, however . . .**" [517], he raises a difficulty concerning the foregoing. The problem is whether motion is necessarily one in species when the same thing is changed many times from the same thing to the same thing. For example, according to geometricians who imagine that a point is moved, let one point be moved many times from this place to that.

It seems to follow from the above that these motions are one in species. For if motions toward the same species, for example, whiteness, are the same in species, much more would two motions toward the same numerical place be the same in species. But if this be granted, a difficulty follows. For then straight motion and circular motion would be one in species. But to be moved from this place to that circularly, i.e., as if through an arc, occurs first. Only secondarily is there straight motion, i.e., as if through a straight line. And likewise it would follow that in the motions of animals walking,

which is through a straight line, would be the same species as rolling, by which an animal is moved through a circular line by revolving itself.

He answers this difficulty by referring to what he has discussed above. It has been established that if that in which motion occurs is different in species, then the motion is different in species. Thus, in order for motion to be the same in species, there must not only be an identity of termini in respect to species, but also an identity of that through which the motion occurs. But it is clear that a straight line and a circular line are different in species. Hence, circular and straight motion, and walking and rolling, are not the same in species, even though they occur between the same termini. For the path is not the same in respect to species.

But if there be the same termini and the same path in respect to species, then the motions are the same in respect to species. And furthermore, if the termini and the path are the same in number, then the motions are clearly repeated in respect to the same species.

699. Next where he says, "**Motion is one . . .**" [518], he gives the third mode according to which motion is called one in number.

Concerning this he makes two points. First he explains what motion is one in number. Secondly, where he says, "**Suppose, however, that Socrates . . .**" [519], he raises a difficulty about this.

He says, therefore, first that according to the foregoing modes motion is not called one simply, but only in a qualified way, that is, generically and specifically. But according to the third mode motion is called one simply, which is oneness in number according to its essence.

He will show what motion is one in this mode by distinguishing those things which are required for motion. The unity of motion consists in three things. These are the object which is moved, the genus or species in which there is motion, and the time when it is moved. He explains each of these individually. He mentions that which is moved because in any motion it is necessary for there to be something which is moved, for example, a man or gold or some body. And likewise it is necessary that any mobile object be moved in some genus or species, for example, in place or in passive quality. And likewise it is necessary to consider when it is moved. For everything that is moved is moved in time. Among these three things the unity of genus or species is found in that in which there is motion, for example, in place or in quality. But in respect to the unity of motion, the unity of genus or species is not due to the time, since there is only one species of time. Rather the continuity of motion without interruption is due to time.

However the unity of motion, according to which it is called one simply, consists in the unity of all three of these. For that in which motion occurs must be one and indivisible in the way in which a last species is called indivisible. Further the time when the motion occurs must be one continuum without interruption. And thirdly that which is moved must be one.

Furthermore he excludes two types of unity in the subject which are not sufficient for motion to be one simply.

The first type is accidental unity. For example, Coriscus and white are one accidentally. Nevertheless, the motion proper to Coriscus and the motion proper to white are not one. For the motion proper to white is to be-

come black. And the motion proper to Coriscus is to walk. These motions, indeed, are different.

The second type is the unity of genus or species. In order for motion to be one in number, it is not sufficient for the subject to be some common genus or species. For it might happen that two men are cured at the same time and in respect to the same species of health, for example, they are cured of ophthalmia, which is a disease of the eyes. In this case there is unity of time, and unity of that in which the motion occurs, and unity of the subject in respect to species. Nevertheless, these two cures are not one in number, but only one in species.

700. Next where he says, **"Suppose, however, that Socrates . . ."** [519], he raises a difficulty.

Concerning this he makes three points. First he gives what at first sight appears to be an example of the numerical unity of motion. Secondly, where he says, **"And akin to this difficulty . . ."** [520], he raises a difficulty about this. Thirdly, where he says, **"The same argument applies . . ."** [521], he determines the truth.

He says, therefore, first that the same mobile object, for example, Socrates, might undergo specifically the same alteration at two different times. For example, he might be cured twice of ophthalmia. At first glance it seems that this repeated alteration will be numerically one motion if the health which is acquired is the same in number. This would be true if that which was corrupted would again come to be as one in number. But this seems to be impossible. For the health which was acquired in the first alteration was later corrupted. And numerically the same health cannot be recovered.

If numerically the same health were

recovered, it would seem that the subsequent alteration would be numerically the same motion as the first. But if numerically the same health were not recovered, the motion will be the same in species, but not in number.

701. Next where he says, **"And akin to this difficulty . . ."** [520], he raises a difficulty about this.

The problem is as follows. If one continuously maintains health, or any other accident, will this health, or any other state or passion in bodies, be one? It seems not, because according to some philosophers all subjects which have qualities or states seem to be in continuous motion and flux.

Suppose that, for one who remains healthy, the health which he had in the morning is one and the same as the health which he has at noon or in the evening. Now if he loses his health and later recovers it, there seems to be no reason [ratio] why the second recovered health is not one in number with the health that he previously had.

Aristotle does not answer this difficulty because it is not pertinent here. It pertains rather to the metaphysician who considers in common the one and the many, and the same and different. Moreover this difficulty is based on a false premise; namely, that all things are in continuous motion and flux. This is what Heraclitus thought, and Aristotle refutes this in Metaphysics, IV. But this is not the same argument. For, while health remains, even though a man's health may vary, that is, he becomes more or less healthy, his being healthy is not interrupted. His being healthy is interrupted when health is totally corrupted.

702. Next where he says, **"The same argument applies . . ."** [521], he determines the truth concerning this problem. He has said above that, if the quality which is recovered is the same, then the second alteration will be numerically the same motion as the first. But if numerically the same quality is not recovered, it follows that there is not numerically one act. After interposing this difficulty, he adds, as though giving a reason [ratio] for the foregoing, that he has said this because it seems at first glance that the nature [ratio] of the unity of quality and of motion is the same.

But they differ as follows. If two motions are the same in such a way that they are one in number, then it necessarily follows that the quality acquired by that motion is one. For the numerically one quality acquired by that act is numerically one act.

But if the quality which is recovered is one, because of this it does not seem that there is one act. For if the terminus of motion is numerically one, it is not necessary for the motion to be numerically one. This is clear in local motion. For when a walking man pauses, that walking ceases. But when he begins to walk again, then there will be walking again. Therefore, if it be said that the walking is one and the same, then one and the same thing both is and is corrupted many times. But this is impossible. Therefore, if it should happen that numerically the same health were restored, it would not follow that the second curing is numerically the same motion as the first. Likewise, the second walking is not numerically the same as the first, even though they are both directed to numerically the same place.

Finally he concludes that these difficulties are outside his main intention, and therefore are dismissed.

More Concerning the Numerical Unity of Motion. Two Secondary Types of Unity in Motion

Text of Aristotle

522. *Since every motion is continuous, a motion that is one in an unqualified sense must (since every motion is divisible) be continuous, and a continuous motion must be one. There will not be continuity between any motion and any other indiscriminately any more than there is between any two things chosen at random in any other sphere: there can be continuity only when the extremities of the two things are one. Now some things have no extremities at all; and the extremities of others differ specifically although we give them the same name of "end": how should e.g. the "end" of a line and the "end" of walking touch or come to be one? Motions that are not the same either specifically or generically may, it is true, be consecutive (e.g., a man may run and then at once fall ill of a fever), and again, in the torch-race we have consecutive but not continuous locomotion; for according to our definition there can be continuity only when the ends of the two things are one. Hence motions may be consecutive or successive in virtue of the time being continuous, but there can be continuity only in virtue of the motions themselves being continuous, that is when the end of each is one with the end of the other. Motion, therefore, that is in an unqualified sense continuous and one must be specifically the same, of one thing, and in one time. Unity is required in respect of time in order that there may be no interval of immobility, for where there is intermission of motion there must be rest, and a motion that includes intervals of rest will be not one but many, so that a motion that is interrupted by stationariness is not one or continuous, and it is so interrupted if there is an interval of time. And though of a motion that is not specifically one (even if the time is unintermittent) the time is one, the motion is specifically different, and so cannot really be one, for motion that is one must be specifically one, though motion that is specifically one is not necessarily one in an unqualified sense. We have now explained what we mean when we call a motion one without qualification.*　　　　　**228a20–228b11**

523. *Further, a motion is also said to be one generically, specifically, or essentially when it is complete, just as in other cases completeness and wholeness are characteristics of what is one; and sometimes a motion even if incomplete is said to be one, provided only that it is continuous.*
　　　　　228b11–15

524. *And besides the cases already mentioned there is another in which a motion is said to be one, viz. when it is regular; for in a sense a motion that is irregular is not regarded as one, that title belonging rather to that which is regular, as a straight line is regular, the irregular being as such divisible. But the difference would seem to be one of degree.*　　　　　**228b15–19**

525. *In every kind of motion we may have regularity or irregularity: thus there may be regular alteration, and locomotion in a regular path, e.g., in a circle or on a straight line, and it is the same with regard to increase and decrease.*　　　　　**228b19–21**

526. *The difference that makes a motion irregular is sometimes to be found in its path: thus a motion cannot be regular if its path is an irregular magnitude, e.g., a broken line, a spiral, or any other magnitude that is not such that any part of it taken at random fits on to any other that may be chosen. Sometimes it is found neither in the place nor in the time nor in the goal but in the manner of the motion; for in some cases the motion is differentiated by quickness and slowness: thus if its velocity is uniform a motion is regular, if not it is irregular.*　　　　　**228b21–28**

527. *So quickness and slowness are not species of motion nor do they constitute specific differences of motion, because this distinction occurs in connection with all the distinct species of motion. The same is true of heaviness and lightness when they refer to the same thing: e.g.,*

they do not specifically distinguish earth from itself or fire from itself.

228b28–229a1

528. *Irregular motion, therefore, while in virtue of being continuous it is one, is so in a lesser degree, as is the case with locomotion in a broken line; and a lesser degree of something always means an admixture of its contrary.* 229a1–3

529. *And since every motion that is one can be both regular and irregular, motions that are consecutive but not specifically the same cannot be one and continuous; for how should a motion composed of alteration and locomotion be regular? If a motion is to be regular its parts ought to fit one another.* 229a3–6

COMMENTARY OF ST. THOMAS

703. The Philosopher has stated that three things are required for motion to be one simply; namely, unity of time, unity of that in which there is motion, and unity of subject. Here he intends to prove this.

"To be one simply" has many meanings [522]. One meaning is to be one as indivisible. Another is to be one as continuous. Motion cannot be called simply one as something indivisible, because no motion is indivisible. Hence it follows that motion is called one as something continuous. For motion to be simply one, it must be continuous. And this continuity of motion is sufficient for its unity. Hence motion is one if it is continuous. Therefore, whatever is required for the continuity of motion is also required for the unity of motion.

704. Three things are required for motion to be continuous. The first requirement is unity of the species. Every motion cannot be continuous with every other motion. The same applies to other cases of continuity. For not just anything can be continuous with anything else, whatever this other happens to be. Rather those things can be continuous whose extremities are one. This is the definition [ratio] of continuity, as was said above.

But certain things have no extremities; for example, forms and all indivisible things. Hence there cannot be continuity in such things. There are other things which have extremities and which are divisible and quantified, but they are not the same in name or in nature [ratio]. These things also cannot be continuous. For there can be no contact between any of them. One cannot say that a line and walking touch each other, or that they have one extremity, which is required for them to be continuous.

From this it is clear that things which belong to different genera and species cannot be continuous with each other.

Hence, motions which differ in genus or species can be consecutive to each other; thus, someone after running can immediately develop a fever. But the running and the development of the fever are in different genera. And even in the same genus, for example, local motion, one local motion can be consecutive to another but not continuous with it. This occurs in the "diffusion of the torch"—when the torch is transferred from one hand to another. These diverse motions are not continuous. Or one might understand this as follows. The local motion of the liquid which sustains the flame (which is called "diffusion") is followed by the local motion of the flame (which is called "light").

The above mentioned mutations, which differ in genus or species, are not continuous. For they do not have one extremity, which belongs to the nature [ratio] of continuity. Hence, motions which differ in genus or species can be consecutive to each other, that is, can in some way touch each other, without any interruption of time, insofar as time is continuous. Time is continuous for the same reason [ratio] that motion is continuous, that is, insofar as there is one extremity. For in one instant of time whose parts are continuous, there is nothing to prevent one motion from ending and another motion of a different genus or species from beginning. Such motions will be consecutive, but not continuous. Hence it follows from the foregoing that, for motion to be continuous, it must be one in species. This unity of species is in the motion from the thing in which the motion occurs, insofar as it is indivisible in species.

705. The second requirement for the continuity of motion is that there be one object. For the motions of different objects can be consecutive, but not continuous, as was said of the torch which is moved by different hands.

706. The third requirement for the unity and continuity of motion is the unity of time. There can be no intervening state of immobility or rest. If there is an interruption of the time of a motion such that the object is not moved, then it follows that at that time there is rest. For if rest intervenes, there are many motions and not one. Rather than one motion there are many motions between which is rest. Hence, if there is a motion which is interrupted by rest, it is neither one nor continuous. Motion is interrupted by rest if there is time in between, as was shown. Hence, for motion to be continuous, there must be one continuous time.

Nevertheless this is not enough. Motion which is not one in species is not continuous, even if the time is not interrupted. Although it is one in respect to time, it will be different in respect to species. For motion to be one continuum, it must be one in species. But it does not follow that motion which is one in respect to species is one simply.

Hence it is clear that all three of the above are required for motion to be one simply. He concludes that he has now explained which motion is one simply.

707. Next where he says, **"Further, a motion is also . . ."** [523], after having given the three principal modes of unity in motion, he gives two other secondary modes, which pertain to a certain form of unity rather than to unity itself.

He gives the second secondary mode where he says, **"And besides the cases . . ."** [523].

He says, therefore, first that motion is said to be one in genus or in species or in substance in the same way that motion is said to be numerically one, that is, because it is completed. Likewise in other cases completeness and wholeness pertain to the nature [ratio] of unity. For we do not speak of one man or one shoe unless it be a whole.

Sometimes the incomplete, as long as it is continuous, is called one. The reason for this is that oneness can pertain to quantity (and thus only continuity is sufficient for unity) or to substantial form, which is the perfection of the whole (and thus that which is complete and whole is called one).

708. Next where he says, **"And besides the cases . . ."** [524], he gives the other secondary mode of unity. Motion which is regular or uniform is said

to be one, just as in other cases that which is the same in all of its parts is said to be one.

Concerning this he makes three points. First he states this mode of unity, namely, regular motion is said to be one. Secondly, where he says, **"In every kind of motion . . ."** [525], he shows where regularity and irregularity are found. Thirdly, where he says, **"The difference that makes . . ."** [526], he explains the types of irregularity.

He says, therefore, first that besides the above mentioned modes of unity, regular or uniform motion is said to be one. For it seems that regular or uniform motion is one rather than irregular or uneven motion. For example, motion which is wholly straight is uniform.

Irregular motion does not seem to be one because it is divisible into dissimilar parts. But indivisibility belongs to the nature [ratio] of unity, because the one is undivided being. But, nevertheless, irregular motion is in some way one.

The unity of regular and irregular motion seems to differ in respect to more or less. For regular motion is more one than irregular motion, just as a body of similar parts is more one than a body of dissimilar parts.

709. Next where he says, **"In every kind of motion . . ."** [525], he shows in what motions regularity and irregularity are found.

He says that regular and irregular motions are found in every genus and species of motion. Thus, it is possible for a thing to be altered regularly, as when a whole alteration is regular. Also, it is possible for a thing to be moved locally through a regular or uniform magnitude, as when a thing is moved through a circle or a straight line. Likewise there is regular motion in increase and decrease.

710. Next where he says, **"The difference that makes . . ."** [526], he begins his treatment of irregular motion.

First he establishes the modes of irregularity. Secondly, where he says, **"Irregular motion, therefore . . ."** [528], he shows how irregular motion is one, as he had said above.

Concerning the first part he makes two points. First he establishes two modes of irregularity in motion. Secondly, where he says, **"So quickness and slowness . . ."** [527], he draws certain conclusions from this.

He says, therefore, first [526] that the differentia which causes the irregularity of motion sometimes is due to the thing in which the motion occurs. This is especially clear in local motion. For it is impossible for motion which does not cross through a regular or uniform magnitude to be regular or uniform.

By a regular or uniform magnitude he means one in which each part uniformly follows another part, and thus any part could be replaced by any other part. This is clearly the case in a circular line and also in a straight line. And an irregular magnitude is one in which some part does not uniformly follow upon another part. A clear case of this is two lines which form an angle. The one line is not joined to the other in a straight line, although the parts of the line are added to each other in a straight line.

Therefore, both circular and straight motions are regular. But reflex or oblique motions, which make an angle, are not regular and do not occur in a regular magnitude. And there might be some other motion through some other magnitude, some part of which is not uniformly added to some other part. Or one part of the magnitude may not properly touch another part. For if that part which contains the angle is replaced by a part which does not contain an angle, there will be no proper contact.

711. The second differentia which causes irregularity is not due to the place, nor to the time, nor to that in which the motion occurs (for there is motion not only in place, but also in quality and quantity). This latter can be referred to the object in which there is motion.

Rather this second mode of irregularity is due to diversity in the manner of the motion. This second mode of irregularity is called speed or slowness. A motion whose speed is the same throughout the whole is called regular. And it is called irregular when one part is faster than the others.

712. Next where he says, **"So quickness and slowness ..."** [527], he draws two corollaries from the above.

The first is that speed and slowness are neither species nor specific differences of motion, because they are found in all species of motion. For speed and slowness are determinations of regularity and irregularity, which are found in every species of motion, as was said above. And no species or differentia is found in every species of its own genus.

The second corollary is that speed and slowness are not the same as heaviness and lightness. For each of these latter always moves to the same place. Thus, the motion of earth, which is heavy, is always toward its place, which is downward. And the motion of fire is toward its proper place, which

is upward. But speed and slowness are found in diverse motions, as was said.

713. Next where he says, **"Irregular motion, therefore . . ."** [528], he explains how irregular motion is one. Secondly, where he says, **"And since every motion ..."** [529], he infers a corollary from this.

He says, therefore, first that irregular motion can be called one insofar as it is continuous. But it is less one than regular motion is, just as a line which has an angle is said to be less one than a straight line. This is especially clear in reflex motion, for it seems that there are, as it were, two motions.

That which is less one seems to have some kind of multitude. For a thing is less when it has a mixture of its contrary. Thus, that which is less white is mixed in some way with black, at least as approaching it in some way.

Thus it is clear that irregular motion is both one, insofar as it is continuous, and is also in some way many, insofar as it is less one.

714. Next where he says, **"And since every motion . . ."** [529], he concludes from the immediate foregoing a point which he had stated above; namely, motions which are diverse in species cannot be continuous. Every motion that is one can be regular or irregular. But a motion which is composed of motions diverse in species cannot be regular. For how could a regular motion be composed of alteration and local motion? For a motion to be regular it is necessary that its parts agree with each other. Therefore, it follows that diverse motions which do not follow each other in the same species are not one continuous motion. This was stated above and was explained with an example.

The Contrariety of Motions

The Text of Aristotle
Chapter 5

530. We have further to determine what motions are contrary to each other, and to determine similarly how it is with rest. And we have first to decide whether contrary motions are motions respectively from and to the same thing, e.g., a motion from health and a motion to health (where the opposition, it would seem, is of the same kind as that between coming to be and ceasing to be); or motions respectively from contraries, e.g., a motion from health and a motion from disease; or motions respectively to contraries, e.g., a motion to health and a motion to disease; or motions respectively from a contrary and to the opposite contrary, e.g., a motion from health and a motion to disease; or motions respectively from a contrary to the opposite contrary and from the latter to the former, e.g., a motion from health to disease and a motion from disease to health; for motions must be contrary to one another in one or more of these ways, as there is no other way in which they can be opposed. 229a7–16

531. Now motions respectively from a contrary and to the opposite contrary, e.g., a motion from health and a motion to disease, are not contrary motions; for they are one and the same. (Yet their essence is not the same, just as changing from health is different from changing to disease.) 229a16–20

532. Nor are motions respectively from a contrary and from the opposite contrary contrary motions, for a motion from a contrary is at the same time a motion to a contrary or to an intermediate (of this, however, we shall speak later), 229a20–22

533. but changing to a contrary rather than changing from a contrary would seem to be the cause of the contrariety of motions, the latter being the loss, the former the gain, of contrariness. 229a22–25

534. Moreover, each several motion takes its name rather from the goal than from the starting-point of change, e.g., motion to health we call convalescence, motion to disease sickening. 229a25–27

535. Thus we are left with motions respectively to contraries, and motions respectively to contraries from the opposite contraries. Now it would seem that motions to contraries are at the same time motions from contraries (though their essence may not be the same; "to health" is distinct, I mean, from "from disease," and "from health" from "to disease"). 229a27–30

536. Since then change differs from motion (motion being change from a particular subject to a particular subject), it follows that contrary motions are motions respectively from a contrary to the opposite contrary and from the latter to the former, e.g., a motion from health to disease and a motion from 229a30–229b2

537. disease to health. Moreover, the consideration of particular examples will also show what kinds of processes are generally recognized as contrary: thus falling ill is regarded as contrary to recovering one's health, and being taught as contrary to being led into error by another, for their goals are contrary. (It being possible to acquire error, like knowledge, either by one's own agency or by that of another.) Similarly we have upward locomotion and downward locomotion, which are contrary lengthwise, locomotion to the right and locomotion to the left, which are contrary breadthwise, and forward locomotion and backward locomotion, which too are contraries. 229b2–10

538. On the other hand, a process simply to a contrary, e.g., that denoted by the expression "becoming white," where no starting-point is specified, is a change but not a motion. 229b10–11

539. And in all cases of a thing that has no contrary we have as contraries change from and change to the same thing. Thus coming to be is contrary to ceasing to be, and losing to gaining. But these are changes and not motions. **229b11–14**

540. And wherever a pair of contraries admits of an intermediate, motions to that intermediate must be held to be in a sense motions to one or other of the contraries; for the intermediate serves as a contrary for the purposes of the motion, in whichever direction the change may be, e.g., grey in a motion from grey to white takes the place of black as starting-point, in a motion from white to grey it takes the place of black as goal; and in a motion from black to grey it takes the place of white as goal: for the middle is opposed in a sense to either of the extremes, as has been said above. Thus we see that two motions are contrary to each other only when one is a motion from a contrary to the opposite contrary and the other is a motion from the latter to the former. **229b14–22**

COMMENTARY OF ST. THOMAS

715. After the Philosopher has treated the unity and diversity of motion, he here treats the contrariety of motions. This latter is a species of diversity, as is clear in Metaphysics, X.

This discussion is divided into two parts. First he explains how one must understand contrariety in both motion and rest. Secondly, where he says, **"Again, a further difficulty . . ."** [554], he raises certain difficulties about this contrariety.

Concerning the first part he makes two points. First he treats the contrariety of motion, and secondly, the contrariety of rest, where he says, **"But since a motion appears . . ."** [541].

Concerning the first part he makes three points. First he distinguishes the different modes in which there would seem to be contrariety in motion. Secondly, where he says, **"Now motions respectively . . ."** [531], he eliminates certain of these modes. Thirdly, where he says, **"Since then change differs . . ."** [536], he establishes the true mode of contrariety in motion and mutation.

716. He says, therefore, first that we must next determine which motions are contraries. Likewise, the contrariety of rest to motion, and of rest to rest, must be determined.

But in order to treat this problem,

we ought first to distinguish the modes in which the nature [ratio] of contrariety in motions can be universally understood. He distinguishes five modes.

The first is that the nature [ratio] of contrariety in motions be understood as the arrival at and the removal from the same terminus. He expresses this as follows: **". . . contrary motions are motions respectively from and to the same thing, e.g., a motion from health and a motion to health . . ."** [229a9–10]. According to this definition [ratio] generation and corruption would seem to be contraries. For generation is motion to being, and corruption is motion from being.

In the second mode the nature [ratio] of the contrariety of motions is understood as the contrariety of the termini from which motion begins. He expresses this as follows: **". . . or motions respectively from contraries, e.g., a motion from health and a motion from disease . . ."** [229a11–12].

In the third mode the contrariety of motions is understood as the contrariety of the termini at which motion ends. He expresses this as follows: **". . . or motions respectively to contraries, e.g., a motion to health and a motion to disease . . ."** [229a12]

In the fourth mode the contrariety

of motions is understood as the contrariety of the terminus from which to the terminus to which. He expresses this as follows: "... or motions respectively from a contrary and to the opposite contrary, e.g., a motion from health and a motion to disease ..." [229a13].

In the fifth mode the contrariety is understood in respect to both of the termini. He expresses this as follows: "... or motions respectively from a contrary to the opposite contrary and from the latter to the former, e.g., a motion from health to disease and a motion from disease to health ..." [229a13–14].

The contrariety of motions must be understood according to one or more of these modes. For motion is not opposed to motion in any other way [ratio].

717. Next where he says, "Now motions respectively ..." [531], he eliminates two of these modes. First he eliminates the fourth mode, which was the contrariety of the terminus from which to the terminus to which. Secondly, where he says, "Nor are motions respectively ..." [532], he eliminates the second mode, which was the contrariety of the termini from which motion begins. Thirdly, where he says, "Thus we are left with ..." [535], he explains how two of the remaining modes are related to each other.

He says, therefore, first [531] that motion from one contrary cannot be said to be contrary to motion to the other contrary. Thus, one would be saying that motion from health is contrary to motion to sickness. One and the same thing is not contrary to itself. Motion from health is one and the same in subject as motion to sickness. But these motions differ in reason [ratio], in this sense, that to be moved from health is not the same in reason [ratio] as to be moved to sickness. For the one implies the relation of the motion to the terminus from which, and the other the relation of the same motion to the terminus to which. Therefore, the contrariety of motion must not be understood as the contrariety of one terminus to the other.

718. Next where he says, "Nor are motions respectively ..." [532], he shows that the contrariety of motions must not be understood as the contrariety of the termini from which motion begins.

He shows this with three arguments. The first is as follows.

Two motions which tend toward the same thing are not contraries. But two motions which recede from contraries can tend toward one and the same thing. There is equal motion from contrary to contrary or to a middle (which will be discussed later). Thus from either contrary there can be motion to one middle. Therefore, motions are not contraries because of the fact that they begin to be moved from contraries.

719. He gives the second argument where he says, "... but changing to a contrary ..." [533].

The definition [ratio] of contrariety in motion must be taken from precisely that which makes motion contrary. But the contrariety of the termini at which motion ends seems to be more of a cause of the contrariety of motions than the contrariety of the termini from which motion begins. For when one speaks of motions beginning at contrary termini, one speaks of the removal of contrariety. But when one speaks of motions arriving at contraries, one speaks of the establishment of contrariety. Therefore, the contrariety of motions is not to be understood only in respect to the terminus from which.

720. He gives the third argument where he says, **"Moreover, each several motion . . ."** [534]. The argument is as follows.

A thing receives contrariety from the same thing from which it receives its name and species. For contrariety is a difference in respect to form, as is clear in Metaphysics, X. But each motion is named and receives its species from the terminus to which rather than from the terminus from which. Thus, motion to health is called "curing," and motion to sickness is called "becoming sick." This was explained above. Hence, the contrariety of motions must be taken in respect to the terminus to which rather than in respect to the terminus from which. This is the same conclusion as above.

721. Next where he says, **"Thus we are left with . . ."** [535], he concludes that, since the two modes dealing with the contrariety of the termini have been eliminated, there remain two other modes—the third and the fifth. One of these deals only with the contrariety of the termini to which, which he indicates where he says, **". . . motions respectively to contraries . . ."** [229a27]. The other deals with the contrariety of both of the termini, which he indicates where he says, **". . . motions respectively to contraries from the opposite contraries . . ."** [229a27–28]. Furthermore, the first mode did not deal with any contrariety of termini, but with the arrival at and removal from the same terminus. He concludes, finally, that perhaps these two remaining modes are the same in subject, for motions to contraries are also from contraries. But perhaps in respect to reason [ratio] they are not the same,

because motion has different relations to its termini, as was said above. His example is that motion to health and motion from sickness are the same in subject, but not in reason [ratio]. It is the same with motion from health and motion to sickness.

722. Next where he says, **"Since then change differs . . ."** [536], he shows how contrariety is found in motion. He shows this first in regard to motion to a contrary. Secondly where he says, **"And wherever a pair of contraries . . ."** [540], he shows this in regard to motion to a middle.

Concerning the first part he makes two points. First he shows what causes contrariety in motions, and secondly in mutations, where he says, **"On the other hand . . ."** [538].

Concerning the first part he makes two points. First he establishes his position with a syllogism, and secondly by induction, where he says, **"Moreover, the consideration of . . ."** [537].

He first [536] gives the following argument. The contrariety of things is established by their proper species and nature [ratio]. The proper specific nature [ratio] of motion is that it has two termini and it is a mutation from a certain affirmative subject to a certain affirmative subject. (In this way motion differs from mutation which does not always have two affirmative termini.) Hence it follows that the contrariety of motion requires contrariety in respect to both of the termini. Thus, properly speaking, motion from contrary to contrary is contrary to motion from contrary to contrary. For example, motion from health to sickness is contrary to motion from sickness to health.

723. Next where he says, **"Moreover, the consideration of . . ."** [537], he shows the same thing by induction.

First he mentions bodily alteration. Becoming sick is contrary to becoming healthy. The former is motion from health to sickness, and the latter is motion from sickness to health. This is also clear in alterations of the soul. To be deceived, not by one's self but by another, is contrary to learning. These motions are to contraries from contraries. For learning is a motion from ignorance to knowledge, and being deceived is a motion from knowledge to ignorance.

He explains why he adds "not by one's self." It sometimes happens that one acquires knowledge by one's self. This is called discovery. And sometimes one acquires knowledge, not by one's self, but from another. This is called learning. In the same way it sometimes happens that one is deceived by one's self, and sometimes by another. This latter is properly opposed to learning.

Such contrariety is also apparent in local motion. Upward motion is contrary to downward motion. These are contraries in respect to length. Motion to the right is contrary to motion to the left. These are contraries in respect to width. Forward motion is contrary to backward motion. These are contraries in respect to depth.

But it must be realized that he is speaking here of these differences of position, that is, length, width, and depth, insofar as they are in man. For upward and downward are considered in respect to the length of man; right and left in respect to his width, and forward and backward in respect to his thickness, which is called depth.

It must also be realized that contrariety in respect to upward and downward is also found in natural motions. But contrariety in motions in respect to right and left, and forward and backward, is not found in nature but in motion from the soul, which moves to these contrary parts.

724. Next where he says, **"On the other hand . . ."** [538], he shows how there is contrariety in mutations.

First he shows how contrariety of mutation is found in things in which there is contrariety. Secondly, where he says, **"And in all cases . . ."** [539], he shows how this is found in things in which there is no contrariety.

He says, therefore, first that if there is contrariety only in respect to the terminus to which (as when that which is to a contrary is called contrary), this does not produce contrariety of motion, but of mutation, which is generation and corruption. Thus, to become white and to become black are contraries. And it is not necessary that the contrariety of these generations include a contrariety of the terminus from which. For in generation the terminus from which is not affirmative but negative. White comes to be from non-white, but not from something affirmative. For change from subject to subject is not mutation, but motion.

725. Next where he says, **"And in all cases . . ."** [539], he shows that in things in which there is no contrariety, such as substances and such things, the contrariety of mutation is due to the arrival at and removal from the same terminus. He says that in things in which there is no contrary, the contrariety of mutation is due to a removal from and an arrival at the same thing. For example, the arrival at the form of fire, which pertains to the generation of fire, and the removal from this same form, which pertains to the corruption of fire, are contraries. Hence, generation is contrary to corruption, and each

removal is contrary to each arrival. However, such things are not motions, but mutations.

It is clear, therefore, that of the five modes given above, two of them, the second and the fourth, have no application. But one of them applies to the contrariety of motions, and two apply to the contrariety of mutations.

726. Next where he says, "**And wherever a pair of contraries . . .**" [540], he treats the contrariety of motion in respect to a middle.

He says that, whenever a middle is found between contraries, motions which terminate at this middle must be said to be contraries in the same way that motions which terminate at contraries are contraries. For a motion uses a middle as a contrary, so that from this middle there can be motion to either contrary. For example, from grey, which is a middle between black and white, a thing is changed to white as if it were changed from black to white. And conversely, a thing is changed from white to grey as if it were changed to black. And a thing is changed from black to grey as if it were changed to white. For since grey is a middle between both of these extremes, it is said to be either of them. In comparison to white it is black, and in comparison to black it is white, as was said above.

Finally he draws his main conclusion. Motion is contrary to motion in respect to the contrariety of both of the extremes.

The Contrariety of Rest to Motion and Rest to Rest

Text of Aristotle
Chapter 6

541. *But since a motion appears to have contrary to it not only another motion but also a state of rest, we must determine how this is so. A motion has for its contrary in the strict sense of the term another motion, but it also has for an opposite a state of rest (for rest is the privation of motion and the privation of anything may be called its contrary),* **229b23–26**

542. *and motion of one kind has for its opposite rest of that kind, e.g., local motion has local rest. This statement, however, needs further qualification: there remains the question, is the opposite of remaining at a particular place motion from or motion to that place?* **229b26–29**

543. *It is surely clear that since there are two subjects between which motion takes place, motion from one of these (A) to its contrary (B) has for its opposite remaining in A, while the reverse motion has for its opposite remaining in B.* **229b29–31**

544. *At the same time these two are also contrary to each other; for it would be absurd to suppose that there are contrary motions and not opposite states of rest. States of rest in contraries are opposed. To take an example, a state of rest in health is (1) contrary to a state of rest in disease,* **229b31–230a2**

545. *and (2) the motion to which it is contrary is that from health to disease. For it would be absurd that its contrary motion should be that from disease to health, since motion to that in which a thing is at rest is rather a coming to rest, the coming to rest being found to come into being simultaneously with the motion; and one of these two motions it must be. And rest in whiteness is of course not contrary to rest in health.* **230a2–7**

546. *Of all things that have no contraries there are opposite changes (viz. change from the thing and change to the thing, e.g., change from being and change to being), but no motion.* **230a7–9**

547. *So, too, of such things there is no remaining, though there is absence of change.* **230a9–10**

548. *Should there be a particular subject, absence of change in its being will be contrary to absence of change in its not-being. And here a difficulty may be raised: if not-being is not a particular something, what is it, it may be asked, that is contrary to absence of change in a thing's being? and is this absence of change a state of rest?* **230a10–12**

549. *If it is, then either it is not true that every state of rest is contrary to a motion or else coming to be and ceasing to be are motion. It is clear then that, since we exclude these from among motions, we must not say that this absence of change is a state of rest:* **230a12–16**

550. *we must say that it is similar to a state of rest and call it absence of change. And it will have for its contrary either nothing or absence of change in the thing's not-being, or the ceasing to be of the thing; for such ceasing to be is change from it and the thing's coming to be is change to it.* **230a16–18**

COMMENTARY OF ST. THOMAS

727. After the Philosopher has treated the contrariety of motions, he here treats the contrariety of states of rest. First he explains the contrariety of rest to motions, and secondly to muta-tions, where he says, "Of all things that have . . ." [546].

Concerning the first part he makes two points. First he shows that rest is contrary to motion. Secondly, where he says, ". . . and motion of one kind . . ." [542], he shows what states of rest are contrary to what motions.

He says, therefore, first [541] that not only motion, but also rest, seems to be contrary to motion. Hence it must be determined how rest is contrary to motion. In the simple and proper and strict sense motion is contrary to motion. But rest is also opposed to motion, since it is a privation of motion, and a privation is in some way a contrary. For act and privation is the first contrariety, as is said in Metaphysics, X. In all contraries the relation [ratio] of act and privation is found. For one of the contraries is always, as it were, a privation in respect to the other, for example, white in respect to black, and bitter in respect to sweet.

728. Next where he says, ". . . and motion of one kind . . ." [542], he shows what rest is contrary to what motion.

Concerning this he makes three points. First he raises the problem. Secondly, where he says, "It is surely clear . . ." [543], he determines the truth in this matter. Thirdly, where he says, ". . . and (2) the motion to which . . ." [545], he proves his position.

In the problem which he raises, one thing is presupposed, namely, not every state of rest is opposed to every motion. Rather some states of rest are opposed to some motions. For example, rest in place is opposed to motion in place. But since this is stated universally, a further question must be asked. Is motion to white (i.e. becoming white) or motion from white (i.e. becoming black) opposed to rest in the terminus white?

729. Next where he says, "It is surely clear . . ." [543], he determines the truth. He does this first in regard to the contrariety of motion to rest, and

secondly in regard to the contrariety of rest to rest, where he says, "At the same time . . ." [544].

He says, therefore, first that since motion occurs between two subjects, that is, between two affirmative termini, then rest in the terminus is contrary to motion from that terminus to its contrary. For example, rest in whiteness is contrary to motion from white to black. Furthermore, rest in the other contrary is contrary to motion from that contrary to the first one. For example, rest in blackness is contrary to motion from black to white.

730. Next where he says, "At the same time . . ." [544], he treats the contrariety of rest to rest.

He says that states of rest in contrary termini are contrary to each other. For if the motions are contrary to each other, it is impossible for the states of rest not to be opposed to each other. He gives an example of how states of rest in opposite termini are opposed. Rest in health is opposed to rest in sickness.

731. Next where he says, ". . . and (2) the motion to which . . ." [545], he proves what he has said about the contrariety of rest to motion.

He says that rest in health is opposed to motion from health to sickness. For it would be irrational for rest in health to be opposed to motion from sickness to health.

He proves this as follows. When there is motion to a terminus, its arrival at that terminus is not opposed to the motion, but rather is its completion and perfection. He shows as follows that rest in the terminus to which is the perfection of motion. Rest occurs together with motion, for to be moved to a terminus is the same thing as becoming a state of rest. Hence, since motion is the cause of that state of rest, it cannot be opposed to it, because nothing causes its opposite. But it is necessary that either rest in the terminus to which or rest in the terminus from which be contrary to motion. For it cannot be said that rest in some other species is contrary to motion or rest; for example, that rest in whiteness is contrary to rest in health or to motion to health. Therefore, since rest in the terminus to which is not contrary to motion, it follows that rest in the terminus from which is contrary to motion.

732. Next where he says, **"Of all things that have . . ."** [546], he determines the contrariety of rest to mutations.

Concerning this he makes three points. First he summarizes what he has already said about the contrariety of mutations. Secondly, where he says, **"So, too, of such things . . ."** [547], he shows that non-mutation, but not rest, is opposed to mutation. Thirdly, where he says, **". . . we must say that it is . . ."** [550], he shows how non- mutation is contrary to mutation.

Hence he first summarizes what was said above. In mutations in which there is no contrariety in the termini, for example, in the generation and corruption of substance, the opposition arises from the arrival at and removal from the same terminus. For mutation from some terminus is opposed to mutation to that same terminus. Thus mutation from being, or corruption, is opposed to mutation to being, or generation. Nevertheless, neither of these is a motion.

733. Next where he says, **"So, too, of such things . . ."** [547], he shows that rest is not opposed to these mutations.

Concerning this he makes three points. First he states his position. Secondly, where he says, **"Should there be a particular . . ."** [548], he inserts a

difficulty. Thirdly, where he says, **"If it is, then either . . ."** [549], he proves his position.

He says, therefore, first that in mutations which do not occur between contraries, there is no opposed state of rest. Rather that which is opposed to mutation, as rest is opposed to motion, can be called an immutation, or a non-mutation.

734. Next where he says, **"Should there be a particular . . ."** [548], he inserts a difficulty concerning this. It was said that mutation to being is contrary to mutation from being. This latter is mutation to non-being.

That which is called non-being can be understood in two ways. First, non-being might have a subject. This subject is either being in act, as non-white is in a body, or only being in potency, as privation of substantial form is in primary matter. Or non-being might be understood as having no subject. This is absolute non-being.

If non-being is taken in the first way, that is, as having a subject, then it can be discovered how one non-mutation is contrary to another. For it could then be said that non-mutation to being is opposed to non-mutation to non-being. For when non-being has a subject, there is nothing to prevent us from saying that that subject remains in that non-being. In other words it is not changed.

But if non-being be taken as not having any subject, then a difficulty arises. To what non-mutation is the non-mutation or rest in being contrary? That which in no way is cannot be said to be at rest or to remain immutably permanent. And since it is necessary for some non-mutation to be contrary to non-mutation or rest in being, it becomes clear that that non- being from which generation occurs and to which corruption tends is a non-being which has a subject.

735. Next where he says, **"If it is, then either . . ."** [549], he proves what he has stated above, namely, that rest is not opposed to generation and corruption.

If it be granted that there is rest, then one of two things follows. Either not every rest is contrary to motion, or else generation and corruption are motions. Hence it is clear that that which is opposed to generation and corruption is not called rest unless generation and corruption are motions, which was disproved above.

736. Next where he says, **". . . we must say that it is . . ."** [550], he shows how non-mutation is contrary to mutation.

He says that the contrariety of immutation to mutation is similar to the contrariety of rest to motion. Immutation in being is contrary either to no immutation (which would be the case if non-being were to have no subject) or to non-mutation in non-being, if non-being has a subject. This is a contrariety in the way in which rest is opposed to rest. And non-mutation in being is also opposed to corruption in the way in which rest is opposed to motion.

But non-mutation in being is not opposed to generation. For corruption recedes from the immutation or rest in being, but generation tends toward it. And rest in the terminus from which, but not rest in the terminus to which, is opposed to motion and mutation.

LECTURE 10 [230a19–231a18]
Certain Difficulties Are Answered

The Text of Aristotle

551. Again, a further difficulty may be raised. How is it, it may be asked, that whereas in local change both remaining and moving may be natural or unnatural, in the other changes this is not so? e.g., alteration is not now natural and now unnatural, for convalescence is no more natural or unnatural than falling ill, whitening no more natural or unnatural than blackening; so, too, with increase and decrease: these are not contrary to each other in the sense that either of them is natural while the other is unnatural, nor is one increase contrary to another in this sense, and the same account may be given of becoming and perishing: it is not true that becoming is natural and perishing unnatural (for growing old is natural), nor do we observe one becoming to be natural and another unnatural. We answer that if what happens under violence is unnatural, then violent perishing is unnatural and as such contrary to natural perishing.   **230a18–29**

552. Are there then also some becomings that are violent and not the result of natural necessity, and are therefore contrary to natural becomings, and violent increases and decreases, e. g,. the rapid growth to maturity of profligates and the rapid ripening of seeds even when not packed close in the earth? And how is it with alterations? Surely just the same: we may say that some alterations are violent while others are natural, e.g., patients alter naturally or unnaturally according as they throw off fevers on the critical days or not.   **230a29–230b6**

553. But, it may be objected, then we shall have perishings contrary to one another, not to becoming. Certainly: and why should not this in a sense be so? Thus it is so if one perishing is pleasant and another painful: and so one perishing will be contrary to another not in an unqualified sense, but in so far as one has this quality and the other that.   **230b6–10**

554. Now motions and states of rest universally exhibit contrariety in the manner described above, e.g., upward motion and rest above are respectively contrary to downward motion and rest below, these being instances of local contrariety; and upward locomotion belongs naturally to fire and downward to earth, i.e. the locomotions of the two are contrary to each other. And again, fire moves up naturally and down unnaturally; and its natural motion is certainly contrary to its unnatural motion. Similarly with remaining: remaining above is contrary to motion from above downwards, and to earth this remaining comes unnaturally, this motion naturally. So the unnatural remaining of a thing is contrary to its natural motion, just as we find a similar contrariety in the motion of the same thing: one of its motions, the upward or the downward, will be natural, the other unnatural.   **230b10–21**

555. Here, however, the question arises, has every state of rest that is not permanent a becoming, and is this becoming a coming to a standstill? If so, there must be a becoming of that which is at rest unnaturally, e.g., of earth at rest above: and therefore this earth during the time that it was being carried violently upward was coming to a standstill. But whereas the velocity of that which comes to a standstill seems always to increase, the velocity of that which is carried violently seems always to decrease: so it will be in a state of rest without having become so.   **230b21–26**

556. Moreover "coming to a standstill" is generally recognized to be identical or at least concomitant with the locomotion of a thing to its proper place.   **230b26–28**

557. There is also another difficulty involved in the view that remaining in a particular place is contrary to motion from that place. For when a thing is moving from or discarding something, it still appears to have that which is being discarded, so that if a state of rest is itself contrary to the motion from the state of rest to its contrary, the contraries rest and motion will be simultaneously predicable of the same thing.   **230b28–31**

558. *May we not say, however, that in so far as the thing is still stationary it is in a state of rest in a qualified sense? For, in fact, whenever a thing is in motion, part of it is at the starting-point while part is at the goal to which it is changing: and consequently a motion finds its true contrary rather in another motion than in a state of rest. With regard to motion and rest, then, we have now explained in what sense each of them is one and under what conditions they exhibit contrariety.*   **230b32–231a4**

559. *With regard to coming to a standstill the question may be raised whether there is an opposite state of rest to unnatural as well as to natural motions. It would be absurd if this were not the case; for a thing may remain still merely under violence: thus we shall have a thing being in a non-permanent state of rest without having become so. But it is clear that it must be the case; for just as there is unnatural motion, so, a thing may be in an unnatural state of rest.*

231a5–9

560. *Further, some things have a natural and an unnatural motion, e. g., fire has a natural upward motion and an unnatural downward motion: is it, then, this unnatural downward motion or is it the natural downward motion of earth that is contrary to the natural upward motion? Surely it is clear that both are contrary to it though not in the same sense: the natural motion of earth is contrary inasmuch as the motion of fire is also natural, whereas the upward motion of fire as being natural is contrary to the downward motion of fire as being unnatural. The same is true of the corresponding cases of remaining.*   **231a9–17**

561. *But there would seem to be a sense in which a state of rest and a motion are opposites.* [*The text Thomas comments on continues: For when it moves from this and leaves it behind, it seems still to have what it leaves behind. Wherefore, if rest itself is contrary to that whence motion toward the contrary arises, contraries will simultaneously exist, if it comes to rest or still remains to a degree. Completely to that which which is moved, this indeed there, this in that into which it is changed. For which reason motion would be more contrary to motion than to rest. We have spoken of what a motion absolutely one is, of motion and rest, how each is one and which contrary to which.*]

COMMENTARY OF ST. THOMAS

737. After the Philosopher has treated the contrariety of motions and of states of rest, he here raises certain difficulties concerning the foregoing.

Concerning this he makes two points. First he states the difficulties and answers them. Secondly, where he says, **"With regard to coming . . ."** [559], he mentions certain clarifications, which clarifications are open to question.

The first part is divided according to the three difficulties which he raises. These divisions are clear in the text.

Concerning the first difficulty he makes two points. First he states the difficulty. Secondly, where he says,

"We answer that if . . ." [552], he answers it.

738. First [551] he states the difficulty. Why is it that in the genus of local motion some motions and some states of rest are found to be natural and some unnatural, while this is not found in the other genera of motion? For example, why is not one alteration natural and another unnatural? Becoming healthy does not seem to be more natural or unnatural than becoming sick, for each of these proceeds from a natural, intrinsic principle.

The same problem arises with becoming white and becoming black and with increase and decrease. Neither of the former motions is contrary to the other in such a way that one is natural and the other unnatural. For each of them occurs naturally. And one increase is not contrary to another in such a way that one is natural and the other unnatural.

The same argument applies to generation and corruption. It cannot be said that generation is natural and corruption unnatural. For growing old, which is the road to corruption, occurs naturally. Furthermore, we do not observe that one generation is natural and another unnatural.

739. It seems that what he says here is contrary to what he says in De Caelo, II; namely, that old age and every defect and corruption is contrary to nature.

But it must be said that old age and corruption and decrease in a way are contrary to nature and in a way are in accord with nature.

For if one considers a thing's proper nature, which is called its particular nature, it is clear that every corruption and defect and decrease is contrary to nature. For the nature of each thing tends toward the conservation of its proper subject. And the contrary results from the defect and weakness of the nature.

But if one considers the nature universally, then all such things arise from some natural, intrinsic principle. For example, the corruption of an animal arises from the contrariety of hot and cold. And the same explanation applies to the other cases.

740. Next where he says, "We answer that if . . ." [552], he answers this difficulty by destroying it.

Concerning this he makes two points. First he shows that natural and unnatural motion is found in every genus. Secondly, where he says, "Now

motions and states . . ." [554], he shows how the natural and the unnatural in motions and in states of rest are contrary.

Concerning the first part he makes two points. First he establishes the truth. Secondly, where he says, "But, it may be objected . . ." [553], he answers an objection.

He says, therefore, that that which occurs by violence is unnatural. (For the violent is that whose principle is extrinsic, and that which is changed contributes none of the force. But the natural is that whose principle is intrinsic.) Hence it follows that violent corruption is contrary to natural corruption as unnatural corruption is contrary to natural corruption.

And for the same reason he concludes that certain generations are violent and not according to fate; that is, they do not proceed according to the order of natural causes. (The order of natural causes can be called fate.) This clearly occurs when one produces roses or some kind of fruit by artificial means at an unusual time. Another example is when frogs or some other natural beings are generated by artificial means. Since these generations are violent, they are consequently unnatural and contrary to natural generations.

Next he shows the same thing in regard to increase and decrease. Some increases are violent and unnatural. For example, some people mature more quickly than usual because of their softness and their food; that is, because they are nourished by wholesome and abundant food. The same thing occurs in the growth of wheat. For grain grows unnaturally when there is an abundance of ground and when by proper distribution it is not closely and densely packed down.

The same thing occurs in alterations. Some alterations are violent and some natural. This is especially clear in becoming cured. Some people lose their fever during the non-critical days. These people are altered unnaturally. Others lose their fever during the critical days. These are altered naturally.

741. Next where he says, **"But it may be objected . . ."** [553], he objects to the above.

That which is unnatural is contrary to that which is natural. Hence, if there be natural and unnatural generation, and likewise corruption, it follows that corruptions are contrary to each other and not to generation. For one thing cannot be contrary to two things.

He answers this by saying that there is nothing to prevent generation from being contrary to generation, and corruption to corruption. This is true even if there would be no contrariety of natural and unnatural. For if one generation or corruption is pleasant and another harsh, then generation must be contrary to generation and corruption to corruption.

Generation and corruption are called pleasant when the more noble is generated from the corruption of the less noble. For example, fire is generated from the corruption of air. Generation and corruption are called harsh when the less noble is generated from the corruption of the more noble. For example, air is generated from fire.

But if corruption is opposed to corruption, it does not follow that it is not opposed to generation. For corruption is opposed to generation according to the nature [ratio] of its own genus. But corruption is opposed to corruption according to the nature [ratio] of a proper species. Thus, avarice is opposed to liberality according to the

contrariety of vice to virtue. But it is opposed to prodigality according to the nature [ratio] of a proper species. He concludes that corruption is not contrary to corruption simply, that is, universally. Rather, one corruption is of one type, and the other of another type; that is, violent and unnatural, or pleasant and harsh.

742. Next where he says, **"Now motions and states . . ."** [554], he shows how there is contrariety in motion and in rest in respect to that which is natural and unnatural.

He says that not only is generation contrary to generation and to corruption in respect to what is natural and unnatural, but all motions and states of rest are contrary in this way. For example, upward motion is contrary to downward motion (for up and down are contraries of place). And each of these motions is natural to some body. For fire is naturally borne upwards and earth downwards. Further, for each of these motions there are different contraries in respect to what is natural and unnatural. This is what he means where he says, ". . . the **locomotions of the two are contrary to each other**" [230b13].

Or this could mean that the bodies themselves which are moved have different contraries of motion in respect to what is natural and unnatural. For upward motion is natural to fire, but to be moved downwards is unnatural to fire. Thus it is clear that natural motion is contrary to unnatural motion.

The same applies to states of rest. For rest in an upward state is contrary to motion from up to down. But such a state of rest is unnatural to earth, and downward motion is natural. Hence, according to the foregoing it is clear that an unnatural state of rest of a body is contrary to its natural motion. In regard to the same body motions are also contrary to each other in such a way that the natural motion of the body is contrary to its unnatural motion. And it is the same with states of rest. For one of the contrary states of rest will be natural; for example, up for fire and down for earth. And the other will be unnatural, for example, down for fire and up for earth.

743. Next where he says, **"Here, however, the question arises . . ."** [555], he raises the second difficulty. Is there a generation for every state of rest which has not always existed? This generation of a state of rest is called a "coming to a standstill" [stare]. This is done so that we will not understand "coming to a standstill" and "being at rest" [quiescere] to mean the same thing. Rather "coming to a standstill" means "to arrive at a state of rest." This perhaps sounds better in the Greek.

He seems to answer this question in the negative with two arguments.

The first is that, if there is a generation for every state of rest which has not always existed, then it follows that there is generation of an unnatural state of rest (as when earth is in an upward state of rest). But rest can be generated only by a preceding motion. And the motion which precedes an unnatural state of rest is a violent motion. Thus it would follow that when earth was violently borne upwards, its state of rest was generated. But this cannot be. For when a state of rest is being generated by motion, the motion always becomes faster in proportion as it approaches the state of rest. For the generated thing is the perfection of the generation. And insofar as anything is closer to its perfection, it is proportion-

ately more powerful and more intense. Hence it follows that the motion by which rest is generated becomes proportionately faster as it approaches nearer to the state of rest. This is quite clear in natural motions.

But in things that are moved by violence the opposite occurs. For they are always found to be proportionately more remiss as they approach nearer to the state of rest. Therefore, a violent state of rest has no generation. And thus he says that a thing will be violently in a state of rest without this state of rest having been generated.

744. He gives the second argument where he says, **"Moreover, 'coming to a standstill' . . ."** [556]. The argument is as follows. "Coming to a standstill," or the generation of rest, is either altogether the same as the natural motion by which a thing is borne to its proper place, or else occurs together with this motion.

It is clear that these are the same in subject but different according to reason [ratio]. For the terminus of natural motion is to be in the natural place. And to be in the natural place and to be at rest there are the same in subject. Hence natural motion and the generation of rest are the same in subject, and they differ only in reason [ratio]. Moreover, it is clear that a violent state of rest is not generated by natural motion. Therefore, a violent state of rest has no "coming to a standstill" or generation.

745. Next where he says, **"There is also another . . ."** [557], he raises the third difficulty concerning what was said above; namely, that rest in a terminus is contrary to the motion which recedes from that terminus.

This seems to be false. For when someone is moved from a terminus in place, or when a terminus of quantity or quality is being abandoned, then, while one is being moved, one seems to have that which is being abandoned or deserted. For the total place is not left behind suddenly, but successively. And likewise one loses whiteness successively. Hence, while one is being moved, one still remains in the terminus from which. Therefore, if the rest by which something remains in the terminus from which is contrary to the receding motion, then it would follow that two contraries exist together. This is impossible.

746. He answers this difficulty where he says, "May we not say . . ." [558].

He says that that which is moved by receding from a terminus rests in that terminus from which it recedes, not simply, but in a qualified sense. That is, it remains in that terminus partially but not totally. For it is universally true that one part of that which is moved is in the terminus from which and another part is in the terminus to which. And it is not impossible for one contrary to be mixed with the other contrary in a qualified way. But the more unmixable they are, the more contrary they are. Therefore, motion is more contrary to motion, with which it is never mixed, than is rest, which is mixed with motion in a certain way.

Lastly he concludes that he has now stated how unity and contrariety are found in motion and in rest.

747. Next where he says, "With regard to coming . . ." [559], he gives some clarifications of the foregoing. However these points are said to be not included in the Greek texts. And the Commentator says that they are not found in some of the Arabic texts. It seems rather that these remarks are taken from the writings of Theo-

phrastus or some other commentator on Aristotle.

Nevertheless three things are stated here to clarify the foregoing.

The first of these pertains to the difficulty raised above concerning the generation of an unnatural state of rest. He says that one might raise a problem about "coming to a standstill'; that is, the generation of rest. If all motions which are unnatural have an unnatural state of rest, is that state of rest generated? If it be said that there is no "coming to a standstill" for a violent state of rest, then an impossibility follows. For it is clear that that which is moved by violence will remain at rest by violence. From this it would follow that a thing could be not always at rest, without its state of rest having come into being. This seems to be impossible. But it is clear that at times there are violent states of rest. For just as things are moved unnaturally, also things are at rest unnaturally.

Moreover it must be noted that what is said here seems to be contrary to what was said above. Hence Averroes says that the difficulty raised above is answered here.

But it is better to say that that which was stated above is more true, even though that which is said here is true in a certain way. For a violent state of rest does not properly have a generation which proceeds from a cause which per se produces the state of rest. This is how a natural state of rest is generated. Rather it has a per accidens generation by means of a defect in the producing power. For a violent state of rest occurs when the violence of the mover ceases or is impeded. Therefore, violent motion is decreased at the end, while natural motion is increased at the end.

Furthermore, it must be realized that there is another version of the text here which has a different meaning. This version is the following: one might ask whether there is an unnatural state of rest which is contrary to unnatural motion.

The meaning here is not that unnatural rest is properly opposed to unnatural motion, as Aristotle teaches above. Rather he is speaking here generally and improperly about the common opposition of rest to motion.

He says that it seems irrational if there be no unnatural rest. For it is clear that the violence of the mover will cease at some time. And unless some state of rest consequently results, the motion will not arrive at any "standstill." Thus it is clear that a violent state of rest is opposed to violent motions. For that which is moved unnaturally also has an unnatural state of rest.

748. Next where he says, **"Further, some things have . . ."** [560], he gives the second clarification. This is an explanation of what was said about the contrariety of natural and violent motion.

He says that in some things there is both natural and unnatural motion. For example, fire is moved upward naturally and downward unnaturally. The question is whether the violent downward motion of fire or natural downward motion of earth is contrary to the natural upward motion of fire.

He answers that both are contrary, but not in the same way. The downward motion of earth is contrary to the upward motion of fire as natural to natural. But the downward motion of fire is contrary to the upward motion of fire as violent to natural. And the same explanation [ratio] applies to the contrariety of states of rest.

749. Next where he says, **"But there would seem . . ."** [561], he gives the third clarification. This is an explanation of what was said about the contrariety of rest to motion.

He says that perhaps motion is opposed to rest, not simply, but to a certain degree. For when one is being moved from that in which he was at rest, and when he is abandoning that state, it seems that he still has that which is being abandoned. Hence, if rest here is contrary to motion from here to a contrary, it would follow that the contraries are together. But to some degree it is still at rest while it remains in the terminus from which. And it is universally true of that which is moved that something is in the terminus from which and something is in the terminus to which. Hence, rest is opposed to motion less than the contrary motion is opposed, as was explained above.

And finally he summarizes for the sake of clarity.

The very same words which were used above are repeated here. From this it is clear that these are not the words of Aristotle, but of some commentator.

BOOK VI
THE DIVISION OF MOTION INTO ITS QUANTITATIVE PARTS
LECTURE 1 [231a21–b18]
No Continuum Is Composed of Indivisible Parts

The Text of Aristotle
Chapter 1

562. Now if the terms "continuous," "in contact," and "in succession" are understood as defined above—things being "continuous" if their extremities are one, "in contact" if their extremities are together, and "in succession" if there is nothing of their own kind intermediate between them—nothing that is continuous can be composed of indivisibles: e.g., a line cannot be composed of points, the line being continuous and the point indivisible. 231a21–26

563. For the extremities of two points can neither be one (since of an indivisible there can be no extremity as distinct from some other part) nor together (since that which has no parts can have no extremity, the extremity and the thing of which it is the extremity being distinct). 231a26–29

564. Moreover, if that which is continuous is composed of points, these points must be either continuous or in contact with one another: and the same reasoning applies in the case of all indivisibles. Now for the reason given above they cannot be continuous; and one thing can be in contact with another only if whole is in contact with whole or part with part or part with whole. But since indivisibles have no parts, they must be in contact with one another as whole with whole. And if they are in contact with one another as whole with whole, they will not be continuous: for that which is continuous has distinct parts: and these parts into which it is divisible are different in this way, i.e., spatially separate. 231a29–231b6

565. Nor, again, can a point be in succession to a point or a moment to a moment in such a way that length can be composed of points or time of moments: for things are in succession if there is nothing of their own kind intermediate between them, whereas that which is intermediate between points is always a line and that which is intermediate between moments is always a period of time. 231b6–10

566. Again, if length and time could thus be composed of indivisibles, they could be divided into indivisibles, since each is divisible into the parts of which it is composed. But, as we saw, no continuous thing is divisible into things without parts. 231b10–11

567. Nor can there be anything of any other kind intermediate between the parts or between the moments: for if there could be any such thing it is clear that it must be either indivisible or divisible, and if it is divisible, it must be divisible either into indivisibles or into divisibles that are infinitely divisible, in which case it is continuous. 231b11–15

568. Moreover, it is plain that everything continuous is divisible into divisibles that are infinitely divisible; for if it were divisible into indivisibles, we should have an indivisible in contact with an indivisible, since the extremities of things that are continuous with one another are one and are in contact. 231b15–18

COMMENTARY OF ST. THOMAS

750. The Philosopher has already treated the division of motion into its species and the unity and contrariety of motions and states of rest. Here in Book VI he intends to treat those things which pertain to the division of motion in respect to its quantitative parts.

This discussion is divided into two

parts. First he shows that motion, like all other continua, is divisible. Secondly, where he says, **"The present also is ..."** [599], he explains how motion is divided.

The first part is divided into two parts. First he shows that no continuum is composed of indivisible parts. Secondly, where he says, **"It is evident, then ..."** [597], he shows that no continuum is indivisible.

The first part is divided into two parts. First he shows that no continuum is composed of indivisible parts. Secondly (since these proofs seem to pertain more to magnitude) he shows that the same argument [ratio] applies to magnitude, motion, and time, where he says, **"The same reasoning applies ..."** [569].

Concerning the first part he makes two points. First he summarizes certain definitions given above which he uses here to demonstrate his position. Secondly, where he says, **"For the extremities of ..."** [563], he proves his position.

751. He says, therefore, first [562] that if the definitions given above of continuity, contiguity, and succession are correct (namely, the continuous is that whose extremities are one; the contiguous is that whose extremities are together; and succession is in things between which there is no middle of the same genus), from these definitions it follows that it is impossible for a continuum to be composed of indivisible parts; for example, that a line be composed of points, the line being a continuum and the point indivisible. He adds these latter remarks lest anyone use the words "point" and "line" differently.

752. Next where he says, **"For the extremities of ..."** [563], he proves his position.

First he introduces two arguments to prove his position. Secondly, where he says, **"Nor can there be ..."** [567], he brings out certain things which can be questioned in these arguments.

Concerning the first argument he makes two points. First he shows that a continuum is not composed of indivisible parts either by means of continuity or by contiguity. Secondly, where he says, **"Nor, again, can a point ..."** [565], he shows that a continuum is not composed of indivisible parts in succession.

Concerning the first part he gives two arguments. The first is as follows.

The parts which compose one thing, either by continuity or by contiguity, must have extremities which either are one or are together.

But the extremities of points cannot be one. For an extremity is determined in respect to some other part. But in an indivisible thing there is not something which is an extremity and something else which is some other part.

Likewise it cannot be said that the extremities of points are together. For there cannot be an extremity of an indivisible thing. An extremity is always other than that of which it is an extremity. But there cannot be two different things in that which is indivisible.

Therefore it follows that a line cannot be composed of points, either by continuity or by contiguity.

753. He gives the second argument where he says, **"Moreover if that which ..."** [564]. The argument is as follows.

If a continuum is composed of points, the points must be either continuous or contiguous to each other. And this same argument, namely, that a continuum is not composed of indivisible parts, also applies to all other indivisible things.

The first argument is sufficient to prove that indivisible things cannot be continuous with each other.

But he brings in another argument to prove that they cannot be contiguous. The argument is as follows. Whenever anything touches another, either the whole of one touches the whole of the other, or part of one touches part of the other, or part of one touches the whole of the other. But since that which is indivisible has no parts, it cannot be said that part of one touches part of the other, or that part of one touches the whole of the other. And thus, if two points touch, it is necessary that the whole touches the whole. But a continuum cannot be composed of two parts of which the whole of one touches the whole of the other. For every continuum has distinct parts, one of which is here and the other there. And in those things that have position, the continuum is divided into diverse and distinct positions. But things which touch in respect to the whole are not distinct in place or position. Therefore it follows that a line cannot be composed of points in contact.

754. Next where he says, **"Nor, again, can a point..."** [565], he proves that a continuum is not composed of indivisible parts in succession.

A point is not successively related to another point in such a way that they can constitute a line. Nor is one "now" successively related to another "now" in such a way that they can constitute time. For one thing is in succession to another when there is no middle of the same genus between them, as was explained above. But the middle between two points is always a line. And if a line were composed of points, as was assumed, it would follow that the middle between two points is always

another point. And likewise the middle between two "nows" is time. Therefore, a line is not composed of points in succession, nor is time composed of "nows" in succession.

755. He gives his second main argument where he says, **"Again, if length . . ."** [566]. This argument is based on the other definition of continuity, which was given above at the beginning of Book III; namely, the continuous is that which is infinitely divisible. The argument is as follows.

A line or a time is divided into that from which it is composed. Therefore, if each of these is composed of indivisible parts, it follows that they are divided into indivisible parts. But this is false. For no continuum is divisible into indivisible parts, for then it would not be infinitely divisible. Therefore, no continuum is composed of indivisible parts.

756. Next where he says, **"Now can there be . . ."** [567], he clarifies two things which were said above.

The first point is that the middle between two points is a line, and that the middle between two "nows" is time. He clarifies this as follows.

If there are two points, they must differ in site [situs], otherwise they would not be two, but one. Moreover, they cannot touch each other, as was shown above. Hence it follows that they are at a distance and that there is some middle between them. But no other middle is possible except a line between points and a time between "nows."

He proves this as follows. If between points there be some middle other than a line, it is clear that that middle is either divisible or indivisible. If it is indivisible, it must be distinct in site [situs] from each of the points. And since it does not touch, there must again be some other middle between that indivisible middle and the extremities. This goes on to infinity unless there be a divisible middle. On the other hand, if the middle between the two points is divisible, then it will be divisible into either indivisible or infinitely divisible parts. But it cannot be said that it is divided into indivisible parts. For then the same difficulty of how the divisible can be composed of indivisible parts will be repeated. Therefore it follows that the middle is divisible into infinitely divisible parts. But this is the definition [ratio] of continuity. Hence, that middle is a continuum. Moreover, there can be no other middle between two points except a line. Thus the middle between any two points is a line.

For the same reason time is the middle between any two "nows." And it is the same in other cases of continuity.

757. Next where he says, **"Moreover, it is plain . . ."** [568], he clarifies the second point given above; namely, that every continuum is divisible into divisible parts.

If it be granted that a continuum is divisible into indivisible parts, it would follow that two indivisible things touch each other so that they can constitute the continuum. For continuous things must have one extremity, as is clear from the definition of continuity. And the parts of a continuum must touch each other. For if the extremities are one, it follows that they are together, as was said in Book V. Therefore, since it is impossible for two indivisible things to touch each other, it is impossible for a continuum to be divided into indivisible parts.

If Magnitude Is Composed of Indivisible Parts, Then So Is Motion. But This Is Impossible

The Text of Aristotle

569. The same reasoning applies equally to magnitude, to time, and to motion: either all of these are composed of indivisibles and are divisible into indivisibles or none. **231b18–20**

570. This may be made clear as follows. If a magnitude is composed of indivisibles, the motion over that magnitude must be composed of corresponding indivisible motions: **231b20–22**

571. e.g., if the magnitude ABC is composed of the indivisibles A, B, C, each corresponding part of the motion DEF of Z over ABC is indivisible. **231b22–25**

572. Therefore, since where there is motion there must be something that is in motion, and where there is something in motion there must be motion, therefore the being-moved will also be composed of indivisibles. So Z traversed A when its motion was D, B when its motion was E, and C similarly when its motion was F. **231b25–28**

573. Now a thing that is in motion from one place to another cannot at the moment when it was in motion both be in motion and at the same time have completed its motion at the place to which it was in motion: e.g. if a man is walking to Thebes, he cannot be walking to Thebes and at the same time have completed his walk to Thebes; **231b28–232a1**

574. and, as we saw, Z traverses the partless section A in virtue of the presence of the motion D. Consequently, if Z actually passed through A after being in process of passing through, the motion must be divisible: for at the time when Z was passing through, it neither was at rest nor had completed its passage but was in an intermediate state; while if it is passing through and has completed its passage at the same moment, then that which is walking will at the moment when it is walking have completed its walk and will be in the place to which it is walking; that is to say, it will have completed its motion at the place to which it is in motion. And if a thing is in motion over the whole ABC and its motion is the three D, E, and F, and if it is not in motion at all over the partless section A but has completed its motion over it, then the motion will consist not of motions but of starts, **232a1–8**

575. and will take place by a thing's having completed a motion without being in motion: for on this assumption it has completed its passage through A without passing through it. So it will be possible for a thing to have completed a walk without ever walking; for on this assumption it has completed a walk over a particular distance without walking over that distance. **232a8–11**

576. Since, then, everything must be either at rest or in motion, and Z is therefore at rest in each of the sections A, B, and C, it follows that a thing can be continuously at rest and at the same time in motion; for, as we saw, Z is in motion over the whole ABC and at rest in any part (and consequently in the whole) of it. **232a11–15**

577. Moreover, if the indivisibles composing DEF are motions, it would be possible for a thing in spite of the presence in it of motion to be not in motion but at rest; while if they are not motions, it would be possible for motion to be composed of something other than motions. **232a15–17**

COMMENTARY OF ST. THOMAS

758. The arguments given above are rather clear in regard to lines and other continuous quantities which have position and in which contact is properly found. He wishes here to show that the same reasoning [ratio] applies to magnitude, time, and motion.

This discussion is divided into two

parts. First he states his intention. Secondly, where he says, **"This may be made..."** [570], he proves his position.

He says, therefore, first that for the same reasons [ratio] magnitude and time and motion are either all composed of indivisible parts and divided into indivisible parts, or else none of them are. For whatever is granted for one of these necessarily applies also to the others.

759. Next where he says, **"This may be made ..."** [570], he proves his position. He does this first in regard to magnitude and motion, and secondly in regard to time and magnitude, where he says, **"And if length and motion ..."** [578].

Concerning the first part he makes three points. First he states his position. Secondly, where he says, **"... e.g. if the magnitude..."** [571], he gives an example. Thirdly, where he says, **"Therefore, since where ..."** [572], he proves his position.

His position is as follows. If magnitude is composed of indivisible parts, then the motion which crosses a magnitude will be composed of indivisible motions equal in number to the indivisible parts from which the magnitude is composed.

760. He gives the following example. Let there be a line A B C which is composed of three indivisible parts, A, B, and C. Let Z be a mobile object which is moved in the space of the line A B C; and let the motion of Z be D E F. If the parts of the space or line are indivisible, then the designated parts of the motion must also be indivisible.

Next where he says, **"Therefore, since where ..."** [572], he proves his position.

Concerning this he makes three points. First he sets forth certain things which are necessary to prove his position. Secondly, where he says, "... and, as we saw ..." [574], he proves that if magnitude is composed of points, then motion is not composed of motions but of minute impulses [momenta]. Thirdly, where he says, "... and will take place..." [575], he shows that motion cannot be composed of minute impulses.

761. He makes two preliminary points. The first is that in respect to every part of a given motion there must be something which is moved. And conversely, if something is moved, it is necessary that some motion be present to it. And if this is true, then the mobile object Z must be moved through A, which is part of the whole magnitude, by that part of the motion which is D. And in regard to B, another part of the magnitude, it is moved by another part of the motion which is E. And in regard to C, the third part of the magnitude, it is moved by the third part of the motion which is F. Thus the individual parts of the motion correspond to the individual parts of the magnitude.

He gives the second point where he says, **"Now a thing that is ..."** [573]. He says that that which is being moved from one terminus to another cannot simultaneously be "being moved" and "having been moved." For it is being moved when it is being moved. For example, if someone is walking to Thebes, it is impossible for him simultaneously to be walking to Thebes and to have walked to Thebes.

These two points are stated as though they are per se evident. The fact that something must be moved in order for motion to be present is also clear in all accidents and forms. For in order that a thing be white, it must have whiteness. And conversely, if whiteness be present, it is necessary that something be white. Furthermore, it is apparent from the succession in motion that a thing cannot simultaneously be "being moved" and "having been moved." For it is impossible for two parts of time to exist simultaneously, as was said in Book IV. Thus is it impossible for "being moved" to be simultaneous with "having been moved," which is the terminus of the motion.

762. Next where he says, "... and, as we saw ..." [574], he proves his position from the foregoing.

When some part of motion is present, it is necessary that something is moved. And when something is moved, motion must be present. Therefore, if the mobile object Z is moved in respect to A, an indivisible part of the magnitude, it is necessary that some motion, D, be present to Z. Hence, Z either is simultaneously "being moved" and "has been moved" through A, or it is not. If these are not simultaneous, that is, the object is "being moved" before it "has been moved," then it follows that A is divisible. For while Z was being moved, it was not at rest in A, because the state of rest precedes the motion. Nor had it traversed the whole of A, for it was not yet moved through A. (Nothing is ever being moved through a space through which it has already gone.) Rather the object must be in an intermediate state. Therefore, when the object is being moved through A, it has already crossed part of A and another part still remains. And thus it follows that A is divisible, which is contrary to what was assumed.

If the object is being moved through A and has been moved through A simultaneously, then it follows that while it is coming it has already arrived. It will have come and will have been moved to where it is being moved. This is contrary to the second preliminary point.

Thus it is clear that nothing can be moved in respect to an indivisible magnitude. For otherwise it must be that either "being moved" and "having been moved" are simultaneous, or else the magnitude is divided.

Let us grant that nothing can be moved through the indivisible magnitude A. Then, if one says that the mobile object is moved through the whole magnitude A B C, and if the whole motion by which it is moved is D E F, and if nothing is being moved in the indivisible magnitude A, but already has been moved, then it follows that motion is not composed of motions but of minute impulses. This is true because of the following. That part of the motion which is D corresponds to that part of the magnitude which is A. Now if D were a motion, it would be necessary for it to be a motion through A, because the mobile object is moved by the motion which is present to it. But it has been proven that, in respect to the indivisible magnitude A, the object is not being moved, but only has been moved when it has crossed this indivisible magnitude. Therefore it follows that D is not a motion but a minute impulse, by which it is called a motion, just as "to be moved" is called a motion. And a minute impulse is related to motion in the same way that an indivisible point is related to a line. The same argument applies to the other parts of the motion and the magnitude. Therefore it necessarily follows that if magnitude is composed of indivisible parts, then motion is composed of indivisible minute impulses. This is what he intended to prove.

763. But it is impossible for motion to be composed of minute impulses, just as it is impossible for a line to be

composed of points. Hence where he next says, "... **and will take place ...**" [575], he shows that this is impossible in three ways.

The first is as follows. If motion is composed of minute impulses, and if magnitude is composed of indivisible parts, so that the object is not being moved but has been moved through an indivisible part of the magnitude, then it follows that the object has been moved even though it was not previously moved. It was granted that in respect to an indivisible magnitude the object has been moved, but is not being moved. For the object cannot be moved in an indivisible magnitude. Hence it follows that the object has crossed a magnitude without at some time being in a state of crossing it. This is impossible, just as it is impossible for something to be past without having ever been present.

764. But since this impossibility can be admitted by one who says that motion is composed of minute impulses, he brings out a second impossibility where he says, "**Since, then, every-thing ...**" [576]. The argument is as follows.

Everything which is naturally in motion or at rest must be either in motion or at rest. But while the mobile object is in A, it is not being moved. And likewise while it is in B and in C, it is not being moved. Hence, while it is in A and in B and in C it is at rest. Therefore it follows the object is simulta-neously and continuously in motion and at rest.

That this follows he proves in this way. It was granted that the object is moved through the whole magnitude A B C. Further, it was granted that in respect to each part of the magnitude the object is at rest. But that which is at rest through each part is at rest through the whole. Therefore, it follows that the object is at rest through the whole magnitude. And thus it follows that the object is continuously at rest and in motion through the whole magnitude. This is altogether impossible.

765. He gives the third impossibility where he says, "**Moreover, if the indivisibles ...**" [577]. The argument is as follows.

It was shown that if magnitude is composed of indivisible parts, then so is motion. Hence, these indivisible parts of motion, D, E, and F, are either so constituted that each of them is a motion, or they are not. Now if each of these is a motion, then since each of them corresponds to an indivisible part of the magnitude in which the object is not being moved but has been moved, it follows that the mobile object is not moved by the present motion, but is at rest. This is contrary to the first supposition. And if they are not motions, it follows that motion is composed of non-motions. This seems impossible, just as it is impossible for a line to be composed of non-lines.

The Divisibility of Time Follows from the Divisibility of Magnitude, and Vice Versa

The Text of Aristotle

578. *And if length and motion are thus indivisible, it is neither more nor less necessary that time also be similarly indivisible, that is to say be composed of indivisible moments;* **232a18–19**

579. *for if the whole distance is divisible and an equal velocity will cause a thing to pass through less of it in less time, the time must also be divisible, and conversely, if the time in which a thing is carried over the section A is divisible, this section A must also be divisible.*

232a19–22

Chapter 2

580. *And since every magnitude is divisible into magnitudes—for we have shown that it is impossible for anything continuous to be composed of indivisible parts, and every magnitude is continuous—it necessarily follows that the quicker of two things traverses a greater magnitude in an equal time, an equal magnitude in less time, and a greater magnitude in less time, in conformity with the definition sometimes given of "the quicker."* **232a23–27**

581. *Suppose that A is quicker than B. Now since of two things that which changes sooner is quicker, in the time FG, in which A has changed from C to D, B will not yet have arrived at D but will be short of it: so that in an equal time the quicker will pass over a greater magnitude.*

232a27–31

582. *More than this, it will pass over a greater magnitude in less time; for in the time in which A has arrived at D, B being the slower has arrived, let us say, at E. Then since A has occupied the whole time FG in arriving at D, it will have arrived at H in less time than this, say FJ. Now the magnitude CH that A has passed over is greater than the magnitude CE, and the time FJ is less than the whole time FG; so that the quicker will pass over a greater magnitude in less time.* **232a31–232b5**

583. *And from this it is also clear that the quicker will pass over an equal magnitude in less time than the slower.* **232b5–6**

584. *For since it passes over the greater magnitude in less time than the slower, and (regarded by itself) passes over KL the greater in more time than KN the lesser, the time PQ in which it passes over KL will be more than the time PR in which it passes over KN: so that, the time PQ being less than the time PV in which the slower passes over KN, the time PR will also be less than the time PV: for it is less than the time PQ, and that which is less than something else that is less than a thing is also itself less than that thing. Hence it follows that the quicker will traverse an equal magnitude in less time than the slower. Again, since the motion of anything must always occupy either an equal time or less or more time in comparison with that of another thing, and since, whereas a thing is slower if its motion occupies more time and of equal velocity if its motion occupies an equal time, the quicker is neither of equal velocity nor slower, it follows that the motion of the quicker can occupy neither an equal time nor more time. It can only be, then, that it occupies less time, and thus we get the necessary consequence that the quicker will pass over an equal magnitude (as well as a greater) in less time than the slower.*

232b6–14

586. *And since every motion is in time and a motion may occupy any time, and the motion of everything that is in motion may be either quicker or slower, both quicker motion and slower motion may occupy any time:* **232b20–23**

587. *and this being so, it necessarily follows that time also is continuous. By continuous I*

mean that which is divisible into divisibles that are infinitely divisible: and if we take this as the definition of continuous, it follows necessarily that time is continuous. 232b23–26

588. *For since it has been shown that the quicker will pass over an equal magnitude in less time than the slower, suppose that A is quicker and B slower, and that the slower has traversed the magnitude CD in the time FG. Now it is clear that the quicker will traverse the same magnitude in less time than this: let us say in the time FH. Again, since the quicker has passed over the whole CD in the time FH, the slower will in the same time pass over CJ, say, which is less than CD. And since B, the slower, has passed over CJ in the time FH, the quicker will pass over it in less time: so that the time FH will again be divided. And if this is divided the magnitude CJ will also be divided just as CD was; and again, if the magnitude is divided, the time will also be divided. And we can carry on this process for ever, taking the slower after the quicker and the quicker after the slower alternately, and using what has been demonstrated at each stage as a new point of departure: for the quicker will divide the time and the slower will divide the length. If, then, this alternation always holds good, and at every turn involves a division, it is evident that all time must be continuous. And at the same time it is clear that all magnitude is also continuous; for the divisions of which time and magnitude respectively are susceptible are the same and equal.* 232b26–233a12

589. *Moreover, the current popular arguments make it plain that, if time is continuous, magnitude is continuous also, inasmuch as a thing passes over half a given magnitude in half the time taken to cover the whole: in fact without qualification it passes over a less magnitude in less time; for the divisions of time and of magnitude will be the same.* 233a12–17

COMMENTARY OF ST. THOMAS

766. After the Philosopher has shown that both magnitude and the motion which crosses it are, for the same reasons [ratio], not composed of indivisible parts, he shows here that the same is true of time and magnitude.

This discussion is divided into two parts. First he shows that the division of time follows from the division of magnitude, and vice versa. Secondly, where he says, "**And if either is infinite . . .**" [590], he shows that the infinity of one of these follows from the infinity of the other.

Concerning the first part he makes two points. First he states his position, and secondly he demonstrates it, where he says, "**. . . for if the whole . . .**" [579].

He says, therefore, first [579] that time also must be divisible or indivisible and composed of indivisible parts,

as was the case with magnitude and motion.

767. Next where he says, "**. . . for if the whole . . .**" [579], he proves his position with three arguments. The first is taken from equal velocities. The second is taken from faster and slower velocities, where he says, "**And since every magnitude . . .**" [580]. The third is taken from the mobile object itself, where he says, "**Moreover, the current popular . . .**" [589].

He says, therefore, first that the nature [ratio] of an equal velocity is such that an object will cross a smaller magnitude in less time. Hence, let there be given a divisible magnitude which a mobile object crosses in some given time. It follows that the mobile object, having equal velocity, crosses part of the magnitude in less time. And thus it is necessary for the given time to be divisible. Conversely, let there be given a divisible time in which a given mobile object is moved through some given magnitude. It follows that the mobile object, having equal velocity, is moved through less of the magnitude in a smaller part of the total time. And thus it follows that the magnitude A is divisible.

768. Next where he says, "And since every magnitude . . ." [580], he shows the same thing by means of two mobile objects, one of which is faster than the other.

First he sets forth certain things which are necessary to prove his point. Secondly, where he says, "And since every motion . . ." [586] he proves his point.

Concerning the first part he makes two points. First he shows how the faster is related to the slower in regard to being moved through a greater magnitude. Secondly, where he says, "And from this . . ." [583], he shows how the faster is related to the slower in regard to being moved through an equal magnitude.

Concerning the first part he makes two points. First he states his position by repeating a certain thing said above which is necessary for the proofs which follow. Secondly, where he says, "Suppose that A . . ." [581], he proves his position.

769. Hence he states again that every magnitude is divisible into magnitudes. This is clear from what was shown above; namely, it is impossible for a continuum to be composed of indivisible parts. It is clear that every magnitude belongs to the genus of continuous things. From this it follows that in an equal time a faster body must be moved through a greater magnitude. It even happens that in a smaller time a faster body is moved through a greater magnitude. And this is how

some people define "faster'; namely, that which is moved farther in an equal time and even in a smaller time.

770. Next where he says, "Suppose that A . . ." [581], he proves the two points made above.

First he proves that in an equal time a faster body is moved through a greater space. Secondly, where he says, "More than this . . ." [582], he proves that even in a smaller time a faster body is moved through a greater space.

Let there be two mobile objects, A and B, and let A be faster than B. And let there be a magnitude C D which A crosses in the time F G. Moreover both A, which is faster, and B, which is slower, are moved through the same magnitude, and begin to be moved simultaneously.

Granting these suppositions, he argues as follows. In an equal time a faster body is moved farther. But A is faster than B. Hence when A arrives at D, B has not yet arrived at D, which is the terminus of the magnitude. Rather B will be at some distance from D. Nevertheless in this time B will have been moved through some part of the magnitude. Hence, since any part is less than the whole, it follows that, in the time F G, A is moved through a greater magnitude than B, which in the same time is moved through part of the magnitude. Thus it follows that in an equal time the faster body crosses through more space.

771. Next where he says, "More than this . . ." [582], he shows that in a smaller time the faster body crosses through more space.

It was said that at the time when A has already arrived at D, B which is slower is still at some distance from D. Let it be granted then that at the same time B has arrived at E. Now since every magnitude is divisible, as was said above, the remainder of the magnitude—E D—which is the distance that the faster body exceeded the slower one, is divided into two parts at the point H. It is clear that the magnitude C H is less than the magnitude C D. But the same mobile body is moved through a smaller magnitude in less time. Hence, since A arrived at D in the total time F G, it arrives at the point H in less time. Let this time be F J.

The argument continues as follows. The magnitude C H, which A crosses, is greater than the magnitude C E, which B crosses. But the time F J in which A crosses the magnitude C H is less than the total time F G, in which the slower B crosses the magnitude C E. Hence it follows that the faster body crosses through a greater space in less time.

772. Next where he says, **"And from this . . ."** [583], he shows how the faster is related to the slower in regard to being moved through an equal magnitude.

First he states his position, and secondly he proves it, where he says, **"For since it passes . . ."** [584].

He says, therefore, first [583] that from the foregoing it can be made clear that a faster body crosses an equal space in less time.

Secondly, where he says, **"For since it passes . . ."** [584], he proves this with two arguments.

The first argument has two suppositions. The first of these has already been proven; namely, a faster body crosses a greater magnitude in less time than a slower body. The second supposition is per se evident; namely, a mobile body, considered in itself, in a greater time crosses a greater magnitude than in a smaller time.

For the mobile body A, which is

faster, crosses the magnitude K L in the time P Q. And it will cross part of the magnitude, K N, in a smaller time, P R. This latter time is less than the time P Q in which it crosses K L, just as K N is also smaller than K L.

From the first supposition it follows that the total time P Q, in which A crosses the whole magnitude K L, is less than the time V in which B, which is slower, crosses the smaller magnitude K N. For it was said that a faster body crosses a greater magnitude in less time.

From these suppositions he proceeds as follows. The time P Q is less than the time V in which B, which is slower, crosses the magnitude K N. And the time P R is less than the time P Q. Therefore it follows that the time P R is less than the time V. For if something is less than that which is smaller, it will also be less than that which is greater. Hence, since it was granted that in the time P R the faster body was moved through the magnitude K N, and since the slower body was moved through the same magnitude in the time V, it follows that the faster body was moved through an equal space in less time.

773. He gives the second argument where he says, **"Again, since the motion . . ."** [585]. The argument is as follows.

Anything which is moved through an equal magnitude with some other mobile body is moved through that magnitude in either an equal time or less time or more time. Moreover, that which is moved through an equal magnitude in the greater time is the slower body, as was proven above. And that which is moved through an equal magnitude in an equal time is equal in velocity, as is per se evident. Now since that which is faster has neither an equal nor a slower velocity, it follows that it is not moved through an equal magnitude in either a greater or an equal time. Hence it follows that it is moved in less time.

Thus it has been proven that a faster body must cross an equal magnitude in less time.

774. Next where he says, **"And since every motion . . ."** [586], he proves his position; namely, for the same reasons [ratio] both time and magnitude are either divided into infinitely divisible parts or else they are composed of indivisible parts.

Concerning this he makes three points. First he sets forth certain things which are necessary for the following proof. Secondly, where he says, **". . . and this being so . . ."** [587], he states his position. Thirdly, where he says, **"For since it has been . . ."** [588], he proves his position.

Therefore, he states first that every motion is in time. This was proven in Book IV. Further he states that in any time there can be motion. This is clear from the definition of time given in Book IV.

A second point is that whatever is moved can happen to move faster or slower. This means that any mobile object can be found to be moved sometimes faster and sometimes slower.

But this statement seems to be false because the velocities of motions in nature are determined. For there is a motion which is so fast that nothing can be faster; namely, the motion of the first mobile object.

To this it must be answered that we can speak of the nature [natura] of things in two ways, either according to their common nature [ratio] or according to their connection with proper matter. Nothing prevents that which is not impeded by its common nature

[ratio] from being impeded in regard to its connection with some determinate matter. For example, the existence of many suns is not impeded by the nature [ratio] of the form of the sun. Rather this occurs because the whole matter of the species is contained under one sun. And likewise the common nature [natura] of motion does not prevent the possibility of finding a velocity greater than any given velocity. Rather this is prevented by the determinate powers of movers and mobile bodies. Aristotle is here treating motion according to its common nature [ratio], and is not yet applying motion to determinate movers and mobile bodies. Hence here in Book VI he frequently uses propositions which are true in respect to the common consideration of motion, but are not true in respect to the application of motion to determinate mobile bodies.

And likewise it is not contrary to the nature [ratio] of magnitude that every magnitude is divided into smaller ones. Therefore in this book he uses the proposition that for any given magnitude there is another smaller magnitude. But in applying magnitude to a determinate nature [natura], there is some minimum magnitude. For every nature [natura] requires a determinate magnitude and smallness, as was said in Book I.

From the two points above he concludes to a third. In any given time there is a faster and slower motion than the motion given in that time.

775. Next where he says, **". . . and this being so . . ."** [587], he draws his conclusion from the foregoing.

He says that, since the foregoing is true, time must be a continuum; that is, it must be divisible into infinitely divisible parts.

Granting that this is the definition of

a continuum, then time must be continuous if magnitude is continuous. For the division of time follows from the division of magnitude, and vice versa.

Next where he says, **"For since it has been . . ."** [588], he proves this point; namely, that time and magnitude are divided in the same way.

It was shown that a faster body crosses an equal space in less time. Let A be the faster body and B the slower body. The slower body B is moved through the magnitude C D in the time F G.

It is clear that A, which is faster, is moved through the same magnitude in less time. Let this time be F H.

Further, since A, which is faster, crosses the whole magnitude C D in the time F H, then B, which is slower, in the same time crosses a smaller magnitude C J. And since B, which is slower, crosses the magnitude C J in the time F H, then A, which is faster, will cross this same magnitude in a still shorter time. And thus the time F H will be divided again. And when the time is divided, the magnitude C J will be divided for the same reason [ratio]. For in part of that time the slower body is moved through a smaller magnitude. And if the magnitude is divided, the time will also be divided again. For the faster body will cross that part of the magnitude in a shorter time. This goes on to infinity by taking a slower mobile body after the motion of the faster body, and then a faster after the

slower, etc., and by using what has been demonstrated; namely, a faster body crosses an equal magnitude in less time, and a slower body crosses a smaller magnitude in an equal time.

Thus we divide the time in terms of the faster body and the magnitude in terms of the slower body.

Hence, if it is true that this alternation from faster to slower and from slower to faster can occur to infinity, and if a division of time and of magnitude always results from such an alternation, then it is clear that every time, and likewise every magnitude, is a continuum; that is, is divisible into infinitely divisible parts. For time and magnitude are divided by the same equal divisions, as was shown.

776. Next where he says, **"Moreover, the current . . ."** [589], he gives the third argument to show that time and magnitude are divided in the same way. This argument considers only one mobile body.

It is also clear from arguments that are customarily used that if time is a continuum, that is, is divisible into infinitely divisible parts, then magnitude is also a continuum in the same way. For when one and the same mobile body is moved regularly, then just as it crosses a whole magnitude in a whole time, it crosses half the magnitude in half the time. And universally it crosses a smaller magnitude in a smaller time. This occurs because both time and magnitude are divided in the same way.

The Finite and the Infinite Are Found in Both Magnitude and Time in the Same Way. It Is Proven That No Continuum Is Indivisible

The Text of Aristotle

590. And if either is infinite, so is the other, and the one is so in the same way as the other; i.e. if time is infinite in respect of its extremities, length is also infinite in respect of its extremities; if time is infinite in respect of divisibility, length is also infinite in respect of divisibility; and if time is infinite in both respects, magnitude is also infinite in both respects.

233a17–21

591. Hence Zeno's argument makes a false assumption in asserting that it is impossible for a thing to pass over or severally to come in contact with infinite things in a finite time. For there are two senses in which length and time and generally anything continuous are called "infinite": they are called so either in respect of divisibility or in respect of their extremities. So while a thing in a finite time cannot come in contact with things quantitatively infinite, it can come in contact with things infinite in respect of divisibility; for in this sense the time itself is also infinite: and so we find that the time occupied by the passage over the infinite is not a finite but an infinite time, and the contact with the infinites is made by means of moments not finite but infinite in number.

233a21–31

592. The passage over the infinite, then, cannot occupy a finite time, and the passage over the finite cannot occupy an infinite time: if the time is infinite the magnitude must be infinite also, and if the magnitude is infinite, so also is the time.

233a31–34

593. This may be shown as follows. Let AB be a finite magnitude, and let us suppose that it is traversed in infinite time C, and let a finite period CD of the time be taken. Now in this period the thing in motion will pass over a certain segment of the magnitude: let BE be the segment that it has thus passed over. (This will be either an exact measure of AB or less or greater than an exact measure: it makes no difference which it is.) Then, since a magnitude equal to BE will always be passed over in an equal time, and BE measures the whole magnitude, the whole time occupied in passing over AB will be finite; for it will be divisible into periods equal in number to the segments into which the magnitude is divisible.

233a34–233b7

594. Moreover, if it is the case that infinite time is not occupied in passing over every magnitude, but it is possible to pass over some magnitude, say BE, in a finite time, and if this BE measures the whole of which it is a part, and if an equal magnitude is passed over in an equal time, then it follows that the time, like the magnitude, is finite.

233b7–11

595. That infinite time will not be occupied in passing over BE is evident if the time be taken as limited in one direction; for as the part will be passed over in less time than the whole, the time occupied in traversing this part must be finite, the limit in one direction being given.

233b11–14

596. The same reasoning will also show the falsity of the assumption that infinite length can be traversed in a finite time.

233b14–15

597. It is evident, then, from what has been said that neither a line nor a surface nor in fact anything continuous can be indivisible.

This conclusion follows not only from the present argument but from the consideration that the opposite assumption implies the divisibility of the indivisible.

233b15–19

598. For since the distinction of quicker and slower may apply to motions occupying any period of time and in an equal time the quicker passes over a greater length, it may happen that it will pass over a length twice, or one and a half times, as great as that passed over by the slower; for their respective velocities may stand to one another in this proportion. Suppose, then, that the quicker has in the same time been carried over a length one and a half times as great as that traversed by the slower, and that the respective magnitudes are divided, that of the quicker, the magnitude ABCD, into three indivisibles and that of the slower into the two indivisibles EF, FG. Then the time may also be divided into three indivisibles; for an equal magnitude will be passed over in an equal time. Suppose then that it is thus divided into JK, KL, LM. Again, since in the same time the slower has been carried over EF, FG, the time may also be similarly divided into two. Thus the indivisible will be divisible, and that which has no parts will be passed over not in an indivisible but in a greater time. It is evident, therefore, that nothing continuous is without parts. 233b19–32

COMMENTARY OF ST. THOMAS

777. After he has shown that magnitude and time are divided in the same way, he shows here that both the finite and the infinite are found in magnitude and in time in the same way.

Concerning this he makes three points. First he states his position. Secondly, where he says, **"Hence Zeno's argument . . ."**[591], he answers a difficulty. Thirdly, where he says, **"The passage over . . ."** [592], he proves his position.

778. He says, therefore, first that if either of these, that is, time and magnitude, is infinite, then so is the other. And they are each infinite in the same way.

He explains this by distinguishing two types of infinity. If time is infinite in its extremities, then magnitude is also infinite in its extremities. Time and magnitude are said to be infinite in their extremities in the sense that they have no extremities. For example, imagine a line which is not terminated at any points, or a time which is not terminated at any first or last moment.

Further, if time is infinite by division, then length will be infinite by division. This is the second type of infinity. A thing is said to be infinite by division when it can be divided to infinity. This pertains to the nature [ratio] of continuity, as was said. And if

time were infinite in both of these ways, then length would also be infinite in both of these ways.

These two types of infinity are appropriately contrasted. For the first type of infinity is due to the lack of indivisible extremities. The second type is due to the designation of indivisible points in the middle. For a line is divided by points which are designated within the line.

779. Next where he says, **"Hence Zeno's argument . . ."** [591], he answers from the foregoing a difficulty of Zeno the Eleatic. Zeno wished to prove that nothing is moved from one place to another, for example from A to B.

It is clear that between A and B there is an infinity of intermediate points, because a continuum is divisible to infinity. Hence, if something is moved from A to B, it must cross an infinity and touch each one of an infinity of parts. This cannot happen in a finite time. Therefore in no time, however great, as long as it is finite, can anything be moved through any space, however small.

The Philosopher says that this argument is based on a false judgment. For length and time and any continuum can be said to be infinite in two ways, as was said; that is, infinite by division and infinite in the extremities. Now if there were a mobile body and a space, which are infinite in quantity, that is, infinite in the extremities, they would not touch each other in a finite time. But if they are infinite by division, this could happen. For a time which is finite in quantity is infinite by division. Hence it follows that the infinite is crossed, not indeed in a finite time, but in an infinite time. The infinity of points in the magnitude are crossed in the infinity of "nows" in time, but not in a finitude of "nows."

It must be realized that this answer is ad hominem, and not to the truth. Aristotle will make this clear below in Book VIII.

780. Next where he says, **"The passage over ..."** [592], he proves what he has stated above.

First he restates his position, and secondly he proves it, where he says, **"This may be shown ..."** [593].

He says, therefore, first [592] that no mobile body can cross an infinite space in a finite time, nor can it cross a finite space in an infinite time. Rather, if the time is infinite, the magnitude must be infinite, and vice versa.

Next where he says, **"This may be shown ..."** [593], he proves his position.

First he proves that the time cannot be infinite if the magnitude is finite. Secondly, where he says, **"The same reasoning..."** [596], he proves the converse; namely, the time cannot be finite if the length is infinite.

781. He proves the first point with two arguments. The first is as follows.

Let there be a finite magnitude A B and an infinite time C. C D is some finite part of this infinite time. Now since the mobile body crosses the finite magnitude A B in the whole time C, then in that part of the time which is C

D it crosses some part (B E) of the magnitude. Since the magnitude A B is finite and larger, and B E is finite and smaller, then, if B E is taken many times, it must either measure the whole of A B or fall short of or excel it in measurement. For every finite smaller quantity is related to a finite larger quantity in this way, as is clear in numbers. Three, which is smaller than six, measures six when taken twice. But twice three does not measure five, which is also larger than three, but excels five. For twice three is more than five. Likewise, twice three does not measure seven, but falls short of it. For twice three is less than seven. Nevertheless three times three excels seven. Now B E is related to A B in one of these three ways. For the same mobile body will always cross a magnitude equal to B E in a time equal to C D. But if B E is taken many times, it will either measure the whole of A B or excel it. Therefore, if C D is taken many times, it also will either measure the whole time C or will excel it. And thus the total time C, in which the body crosses the whole finite magnitude, must be finite. For the time must be divided into numerically equal parts, just as the magnitude is.

782. He gives the second argument where he says, **"Moreover, if it is ..."** [594]. The argument is as follows.

Although it has been granted that the mobile body crosses the finite magnitude A B in an infinite time, nevertheless it cannot be granted that it crosses every magnitude in an infinite time. For we see that many finite magnitudes are crossed in finite times.

Hence, let there be a finite magnitude B E which is crossed in a finite time. But since B E is finite, it measures A B, which is also finite. And the same mobile body crosses a magnitude equal to B E in a finite time equal to the time in which it crosses B E. And thus the total of the finite equal times, which are taken to measure or constitute the whole time, will be the same as the total of the equal magnitudes B E, which constitute the whole of A B. Thus it follows that the total time is finite.

783. This argument is different from the first one. In the first argument B E was given as a part of the magnitude A B. In the second argument B E is given as some other separated magnitude.

When he adds, **"That infinite time . . ."** [595], he points out the necessity of the second argument given above.

One might jokingly object to the first argument by saying that, just as the mobile body crosses the whole magnitude A B in an infinite time, it also crosses any part of A B in the same way. And thus it will not cross the part B E in a finite time. But since it cannot be granted that a mobile body crosses every magnitude in an infinite time, it is necessary to bring in the second argument to the effect that B E is some other magnitude which the body crosses in a finite time. And he adds that it is clear that the mobile body does not cross the magnitude B E in an infinite time, **"if the time be taken as limited in one direction"** [233b13]; that is, if we take some magnitude other than the first one. This other magnitude is called B E and is crossed in a finite time. For if the body crosses part of the magnitude in less time than the whole, then this magnitude B E must be finite, **"the limit in one direction being given"** [233b14]; that is, A B. He says, as it were, the following. If the time in which the body crosses B E

is finite and is less than the infinite time in which it crosses A B, then B E must be less than A B. And since A B is finite, B E is finite.

784. Next where he says, **"The same reasoning . . ."** [596], he states that the same proof shows that it is impossible for the length to be infinite and the time finite. For just as a part of an infinite time is finite, likewise a part of an infinite length is finite.

785. Next where he says, **"It is evident . . ."** [597], he proves that no continuum is indivisible.

He says, first, that if a continuum is indivisible, an impossibility follows. Secondly, where he says, **"For since the distinction . . ."** [598], he gives a proof which points out this impossibility.

He says, therefore, first that it is clear from what has been said that neither a line, nor a surface, nor any other continuum is indivisible. From the foregoing it is clearly impossible for a continuum to be composed of indivisible parts, although it can be composed of continuous parts. Another reason is that the indivisible would be divided.

786. Next where he says, **"For since the distinction . . ."** [598], he gives a proof which brings out this impossibility. He first sets forth certain things which were established above. The first is that in any time there can be faster and slower motion. The second is that a faster body crosses more magnitude in an equal time. The third is that there are diverse proportions between various velocities and between various crossed magnitudes. For example, they can be double, which is a proportion of two to one. Or they can be one and a half [hemioliam]. Another name for this is sexquialtera, a

proportion of three to two. Or there can be any other proportion.

From these suppositions he proceeds as follows. Let one velocity be one and a half times faster than another. This is a proportion of three to two. And let the faster body cross a magnitude A B C D which is composed of three indivisible magnitudes A B, B C, and C D. In the same time the slower body, according to the granted proportion, must cross a magnitude composed of two indivisible magnitudes. This is the magnitude E F G. Now since time and magnitudes are divided in the same way, the time in which the faster body crosses the three indivisible magnitudes must be divided into three indivisible parts. For the body must cross an equal magnitude in an equal time. Therefore, let there be a time J K L M which is divided into three indivisible parts. But since the slower body in the same time is moved through E F G, which are two indivisible magnitudes, the time must be divided in two. And thus it follows that the indivisible is divided. For it will be necessary for the slower body to cross one indivisible magnitude in one and a half indivisible units of time. It cannot be said that it crosses one indivisible unit of magnitude in one indivisible unit of time. For then the first body is not being moved faster than the slower body. Therefore it follows that the slower body crosses an indivisible magnitude in more than one indivisible unit of time and less than two. Thus one indivisible unit of time must be divided.

And if it be granted that the slower body is moved through three indivisible magnitudes in three indivisible units of time, it follows in the same way that an indivisible magnitude is divided. For in one indivisible unit of time, the faster body will be moved through more than one indivisible magnitude but through less than two.

Hence it is clear that no continuum can be indivisible.

The "Now" of Time Is Indivisible. In the "Now" of Time Nothing Is Either Moved or At Rest. Whatever Is Moved Is Divisible. Certain Difficulties Are Answered

The Text of Aristotle
Chapter 3

599. *The present also is necessarily indivisible—the present, that is, not in the sense in which the word is applied to one thing in virtue of another, but in its proper and primary sense; in which sense it is inherent in all time.* **233b33–35**

600. *For the present is something that is an extremity of the past (no part of the future being on this side of it) and also of the future (no part of the past being on the other side of it): it is, as we have said, a limit of both. And if it is once shown that it is essentially of this character and one and the same, it will at once be evident also that it is indivisible.* **233b35–234a5**

601. *Now the present that is the extremity of both times must be one and the same;* **234a5–6**

602. *for if each extremity were different, the one could not be in succession to the other, because nothing continuous can be composed of things having no parts; and if the one is apart from the other, there will be time intermediate between them, because everything continuous is such that there is something intermediate between its limits and described by the same name as itself. But if the intermediate thing is time, it will be divisible; for all time has been shown to be divisible. Thus on this assumption the present is divisible.* **234a6–11**

603. *But if the present is divisible, there will be part of the past in the future and part of the future in the past; for past time will be marked off from future time at the actual point of division.* **234a11–14**

604. *Also the present will be a present not in the proper sense but in virtue of something else; for the division which yields it will not be a division proper.* **234a14–16**

605. *Furthermore, there will be a part of the present that is past and a part that is future, and it will not always be the same part that is past or future: in fact one and the same present will not be simultaneous: for the time may be divided at many points. If, therefore, the present cannot possibly have these characteristics, it follows that it must be the same present that belongs to each of the two times.* **234a16–20**

606. *But if this is so it is evident that the present is also indivisible; for if it is divisible it will be involved in the same implications as before. It is clear, then, from what has been said that time contains something indivisible, and this is what we call a present.* **234a20–24**

607. *We will now show that nothing can be in motion in a present. For if this is possible, there can be both quicker and slower motion in the present. Suppose, then, that in the present M the quicker has traversed the distance AB. That being so, the slower will in the same present traverse a distance less than AB, say AC. But since the slower will have occupied the whole present in traversing AC, the quicker will occupy less than this in traversing it. Thus we shall have a division of the present, whereas we found it to be indivisible. It is impossible, therefore, for anything to be in motion in a present.* **234a24–31**

608. *Nor can anything be at rest in a present; for, as we were saying, that only can be at rest which is naturally designed to be in motion but is not in motion when, where, or as it would naturally be so; since, therefore, nothing is naturally designed to be in motion in a present, it is clear that nothing can be at rest in a present either.* **234a31–34**

609. *Moreover, inasmuch as it is the same present that belongs to both times and it is possible for a thing to be in motion throughout one time and to be at rest throughout the other,*

and that which is in motion or at rest for the whole of a time will be in motion or at rest, as the case may be, in any part of it in which it is naturally designed to be in motion or at rest: this being so, the assumption that there can be motion or rest in a present will carry with it the implication that the same thing can at the same time be at rest and in motion: for both the times have the same extremity, viz. the present.   234a34–234b5

610. *Again, when we say that a thing is at rest, we imply that its condition in whole and in part is, at the time of speaking, uniform with what it was previously; but the present contains no "previously"; consequently, there can be no rest in it.*

It follows then that the motion of that which is in motion and the rest of that which is at rest must occupy time.   234b5–9

Chapter 4

611. *Further, everything that changes must be divisible. For since every change is from something to something, and when a thing is at the goal of its change it is no longer changing and when both it itself and all its parts are at the starting-point of its change it is not changing, (for that which is in whole and in part in an unvarying condition is not in a state of change); it follows, therefore, that part of that which is changing must be at the starting-point and part at the goal; for as a whole it cannot be in both or in neither.*   234b10–17

611bis. *(Here by "goal of change" I mean that which comes first in the process of change: e.g., in a process of change from white the goal in question will be grey, not black; for it is not necessary that that which is changing should be at either of the extremes.) It is evident, therefore that everything that changes must be divisible.*   234b17–20

COMMENTARY OF ST. THOMAS

787. The Philosopher has shown that no continuum is indivisible or composed of indivisible parts. From this it is clear that motion is divisible. Hence he here treats the division of motion.

First he sets forth certain things which are necessary for the division of motion. Secondly, where he says, **"Now motion is divisible..."** [612], he determines the division of motion.

Concerning the first part he makes two points. First he shows that there is neither motion nor rest in an indivisible point of time. Secondly, where he says, **"Further, everything that changes..."** [611], he shows that that which is indivisible cannot be moved.

Concerning the first part he makes two points. First he shows that the indivisible point of time is the "now." Secondly, where he says, **"We will now show..."** [607], he shows that in

the "now" nothing is moved or is at rest.

Concerning the first part he makes three points. First he states his intention. Secondly, where he says, **"For the present..."** [600], he gives certain things from which his position can be proven. Thirdly, where he says, **"Now the present..."** [601], he brings out the consequence of these points.

788. It must first be realized that "now" is sometimes used, not in its proper meaning, but in an extended meaning. For example, we say that something which is done in the whole of the present day is done now. Now the whole present day is not called present in the proper sense, but in an extended sense. For it is clear that part of the present day has passed, and another part is yet to come. That which is past or future is not now. Thus it is clear that the whole present day is not

a "now" primarily and per se, but only in regard to part of itself. And the same is true of an hour and of any other time.

Hence he says that that which is called a "now" primarily and per se, and not in the extended sense, is necessarily indivisible. And further this "now" is necessarily in every time.

789. Next where he says, **"For the present . . ."** [600], he proves his position.

It is clear that for every finite continuum there is some extremity outside of which there is nothing of that of which it is the extremity. For example, there is no line outside of the point which terminates the line. And past time is a continuum which is terminated at the present.

Therefore, there is an extremity of the past outside of which there is no past and within which there is no future. And likewise, there is an extremity of the future, within which there is no past. This extremity is the terminus of both the past and the future. For since the whole of time is a continuum, the past and the future must be joined at one terminus. Hence, if it be demonstrated that there is something which is a "now" in itself and not just in regard to a part of itself, it will simultaneously be clear that this "now" is indivisible.

790. Next where he says, **"Now the present . . ."** [601], he brings out a certain consequence of the foregoing.

Concerning this he makes two points. First he shows that on the supposition that the "now" is indivisible the same "now" must be both the terminus of the past and the terminus of the future. Secondly, where he says, **"But if this is so . . ."** [606], he shows conversely that the "now" is indivisible if the same "now" is the terminus of both past and future.

Concerning the first part he makes two points. First he concludes from what has been said that the same "now" must be the terminus of both the past and the future.

791. Secondly, where he says, **"For if each extremity . . ."** [602], he proves this with the following argument. If the "now" which is the beginning of the future is different than the "now" which is the end of the past, then these two "nows" must be either in succession to each other such that they immediately succeed each other, or else one of them must be separated from and at some distance from the other. But it cannot be said that one succeeds the other. For thus it would follow that time is composed of an aggregate of "nows," which is impossible because no continuum is composed of indivisible parts, as was shown above. Nor can it be said that the one is separated from and at some distance from the other. For then it would be necessary for there to be an intermediate time between these two "nows." It is the nature of every continuum that there is an intermediate continuum between any two of its indivisible points. For example, there is a line between any two points.

He shows in two ways that this is impossible. First, if there is some intermediate time between the two above-mentioned "nows," it would follow that there is something of the same genus between the two termini. This is impossible. For there cannot be an intermediate line between the extremes of two lines which are touching or are in succession. This would be contrary to the nature [ratio] of succession. For, as was said above, things are in succession when there is no intermediary of the proximate genus. And thus, since future time succeeds past time, there cannot be any intermediate time between the terminus of the past and the terminus of the future.

He proves the same thing in another way as follows. Whatever is intermediate between past and future is called the "now." Hence, if there be an intermediate time between the extremities of the past and the future, it would follow that this whole time is called a "now." But every time is divisible, as was shown. Thus it would follow that the "now" is divisible.

792. He has stated above the principles by which it can be proven that the "now" is indivisible. However, since he has not yet deduced this conclusion from the principles, he next shows that the "now" is indivisible. He does this where he says, **"But if the present..."** [603].

He proves this with three arguments.

The first is that, if the "now" is divisible, then it would follow that part of the past is in the future and part of the future is in the past. For the "now" is the extremity of both the past and the future. And every extremity is in that of which it is the extremity, as the point is in the line. Thus it is necessary that the whole "now" is both in the past as its end and also in the future as its beginning. But if the "now" is divided, this division must determine a past and a future. For every division in time distinguishes a past from a future, because of all the parts of time one is related to another as past to future. Hence it would follow that part of the "now" is past and part is future. And thus, since the "now" is in both the past and the future, it would follow that part of the future is in the past and part of the past is in the future.

He gives the second argument where he says, **"Also the present..."**

[604]. If the "now" is divisible, it will not be a "now" in the proper sense, but in an extended sense. For nothing which is divisible is the very division by which it is divided. And the division of time is the "now." For the division of a continuum is nothing other than the terminus which is common to the two parts. And this is what we mean by the "now': the common terminus of past and future. Thus it is clear that that which is divisible cannot be a "now" in the proper sense.

He gives the third argument where he says, **"Furthermore, there will be ..."** [605]. The argument is as follows.

When time is divided, there is always one part which is past and another which is future. Hence, if the "now" is divided, part of it must be past and part future. But the past and the future are not the same. Therefore it would follow that the "now" is not the same as itself, as a whole existing all at once. (This is contrary to the nature [ratio] of what is called a "now." For when we say "now," we mean "all at once in present existence.") Rather there would have to be much diversity and succession in the "now," just as there is in time, which is divided in many ways.

793. He has shown that the "now" would be divisible if the extremity of the past and the extremity of the future were not the same "now." Now, after having denied the consequent, he concludes by denying the antecedent.

He says that since it is impossible for the "now" to be divisible, it must be said that the same "now" is the extremity of both times.

Next where he says, **"But if this is so..."** [606], he shows conversely that, if the "now" of the past and the future is the same, then the "now" must be indivisible. For if it were divisible, all of the above-mentioned impossibilities would follow. It cannot be said that the "now" is divisible as though there exists one "now" for the past and another "now" for the future. Nor can it be said that the "now" is divisible if there is the same "now" for past and future. From this he concludes that there clearly must be in time something which is indivisible. This is called the "now."

794. Next where he says, **"We will now show . . ."** [607], he shows that there can be neither motion nor rest in the "now." He does this first in regard to motion, and secondly in regard to rest, where he says, **"Nor can anything . . ."** [608].

He says, therefore, first that it is clear from what follows that nothing can be moved in the "now." If there could be motion in the "now," then in that "now" two mobile beings, one of which is faster than the other, could be moved. Thus, let the "now" be M, and let the faster body be moved through the magnitude A B in M. But in an equal time a slower body is moved through a smaller magnitude. Hence, in this time the slower body is moved through the smaller magnitude A C. But the faster body crosses this same space in a shorter time. Therefore, since the slower body was moved through the magnitude A C in the whole "now," it follows that the faster body is moved through this same magnitude in a time smaller than the now." Hence the "now" is divided. But it was shown that the "now" is indivisible. Therefore nothing can be moved in the "now."

795. Next where he says, **"Nor can anything . . ."** [608], he shows with three arguments that the same is true of rest.

The first argument is as follows. It was said in Book V that a thing is at rest when it can by nature be moved, but is not being moved when, and how, and in what respect it is natural for it to be moved. For example, it cannot be said that there is a privation of sight in the following cases: when a being which does not naturally have sight, like a stone, lacks it; or when a thing lacks the time in which it would naturally have sight, like a dog before the ninth day; or when a thing lacks a part, like a foot or hand, in which it does not naturally have sight; or when a thing lacks a manner of sight which it does not have naturally, like a man who does not see as acutely as an eagle. Now rest is a privation of motion. Hence only that which by nature can be moved when and how it is natural for it to be moved is at rest. But it was shown that nothing is naturally moved in the "now." Thus it is clear that nothing is at rest in the "now."

He gives the second argument where he says, **"Moreover, inasmuch as . . ."** [609]. The argument is as follows.

That which is moved in some whole time is moved in each part of that time in which it is natural for it to be moved. And likewise that which is at rest in some whole time is at rest in each part of that time in which it is natural for it to be at rest. But when there are two times, in one of which there is rest and in the other of which there is motion, the same "now" is in both of these times. An example of this is the case of something which is moved after a state of rest, or is at rest after being moved. Hence, if something is naturally in motion and is at rest in the "now," it would follow that something could be simultaneously at rest and in motion. This is impossible.

He gives the third argument where he says, **"Again, when we say . . ."** [610]. The argument is as follows.

We say that a thing is at rest when, in respect to both its whole and its parts, it is the same now as it was previously. And thus a thing is said to be moved when it is not the same now as it was previously, either in respect to place, or quantity, or quality. But in the "now" there is no "previous." For the "now" would otherwise be divisible since the "previous" pertains to the past. Hence nothing is at rest in the "now." From this he further concludes that whatever is moved and whatever is at rest is moved and is at rest in time.

796. Next where he says, **"Further, everything that changes . . ."** [611], he shows with the following argument that whatever is moved is divisible.

Every mutation is from something to something. But when a thing is in the terminus to which it is being changed, it is not being changed any more, but has been changed. For nothing is simultaneously being changed and already changed, as was said above. When a thing in respect to its whole and all of its parts is still in the terminus from which it might change, it is not then being changed. For it was said above that that which is the same in itself and in all of its parts is not being moved, but rather is at rest. He adds "all of its parts" because when a thing begins to be changed it leaves the place which it previously occupied, not totally, but part by part.

Nor can it be said that, while a thing is being moved, it is in both of the termini in respect to both its whole and its parts. For then it would be in two places simultaneously.

Nor can it be said that it is in neither of the termini. We are speaking here of the proximate terminus to which it is

changed, and not of the ultimate terminus. For example, if a thing is being changed from white to black, black is the ultimate extreme, and grey is the proximate extreme. And likewise, if a line, A B C D, is divided into three equal parts, it is clear that the mobile body, which at the beginning of the motion is in the part A B as in a place equal to itself, at another part of its motion is in neither A B nor C D. This is when it is wholly in B C.

Hence, when it is said that that which is moved, while it is being moved, must be in both termini, we are speaking of the proximate terminus, not the ultimate terminus.

It follows, therefore, that whatever is changed, while it is changing, is in one of the termini in respect to part of itself and is in the other terminus in respect to part of itself. For example, when a thing is changed from A B to B C, then in this motion the part which is leaving the place A B is entering the place B C. And when a thing is moved from white to black, the part which ceases to be white becomes grey or pale.

Thus it is clear that whatever is changed is divisible, because it is partly in one terminus and partly in the other.

797. However it should be realized that the Commentator raises a difficulty concerning this. If Aristotle intends here to prove that only mobile bodies which are moved by motions in the genera of quantity, quality and "where" are divisible, then his proof is not universal but particular. But that which is changed in respect to substance is also found to be divisible. Hence it seems that, when he speaks of that which is changed by any transmutation, he includes generation and corruption in substance. This is also

apparent from the words he uses. He does not speak of "that which is moved" but of "that which is changed" [234b10].

But then it seems that his proof is not valid. For some transmutations are indivisible; for example, substantial generations and corruptions, which do not occur in time. In such transmutations it is not true that that which is changed is partly in one terminus and partly in the other. For when fire is generated, it is not partly fire and partly not fire.

798. He brings forth many solutions of this difficulty. One is the solution of Alexander, who says that no transmutation is indivisible or not in time.

But he refutes this. For otherwise one denies a certain probable position for which Aristotle and all the Peripatetics are well known; namely, certain transmutations are not in time, for example, illumination and such things.

He also mentions the solution of Themistius who says that, although some transmutations are not in time, this is overlooked here. And Aristotle uses that which is clear; namely, transmutation occurs in time.

But he refutes this. The division of mutation is the same as the division of mutable objects. And at the present the divisibility of mobile objects is more obscure than the divisibility of mutation. Hence Aristotle's demonstration would not be effective. For one might say that, although things which are changed by clearly divisible mutations are divisible, nevertheless there are other, overlooked mutable objects which are indivisible.

He also gives the solution of Avempace who says that he is not here dealing with the division of mutable bodies in respect to quantity but in respect to the subject being divided by

contrary accidents, from one of which it is changed to the other.

799. He later adds his own solution that those mutations which are said to occur not in time are the termini of certain divisible motions. Thus it can happen that a thing is changed in no time insofar as any motion is terminated in an instant. And since that which is per accidens is omitted in demonstrations, Aristotle in this demonstration uses the proposition that every mutation is divisible and in time.

800. But if one considers the matter rightly, this objection is not to the point. For in his demonstration Aristotle does not use as a principle the proposition that every mutation is divisible. Rather he proceeds on the contrary from the division of the mobile body to the division of mutation, as will be clear below. And he says later that divisibility is in the mobile body before it is in motion or mutation. He uses per se known principles which must be conceded in regard to any mutation; namely, that there is not yet any mutation when that which is to change is wholly and in all its parts still in the terminus from which it changes; that it is not being changed, but already has been changed, when it is in the terminus to which; and that the whole cannot be in both the termini nor in neither of them. This was explained above. Hence it necessarily follows that in any mutation that which is changed, while it is being changed, is partly in one terminus and partly in the other.

But this is found in different ways in different mutations. In mutations in which there is a middle between the extremes, that which is changed, while it is being changed, is partly in one extreme and partly in the other, in respect to the extremes themselves. In mutations in which there is no middle between the termini, that which is being changed is not according to its diverse parts in the diverse extremes in respect to the extremes themselves, but in respect to something which is joined to them. Thus, when matter is changed from the privation to the form of fire, while it is being changed it is indeed under a privation in respect to itself. But it is partly under the form of fire, not in respect to itself, but in respect to something joined to it; namely, in respect to the proper disposition for fire which it partially receives before it has the form of fire. Hence Aristotle will prove below that even generation and corruption are divisible. For that which is generated was generated previously. And that which is corrupted was corrupted previously.

And perhaps this is what Alexander means when he says that every transmutation is divisible; namely, either in respect to itself or in respect to a motion joined to it.

Also Themistius thinks that Aristotle has assumed what was clear and omits what was not clear. For this is not yet the place for treating of the divisibility or indivisibility of mutations. This is reserved for later treatment.

What Aristotle says here holds good for all mutations, divisible or indivisible. For indivisible mutations are also in a way divisible, not in respect to their own proper extremes, but in respect to things which are joined to them. And this is what Averroes wishes to convey when he says that it is per accidens that some mutations are not in time.

801. There is also another difficulty here. In alterations it does not seem to be true that that which is altered, while it is being altered, is partly in one terminus and partly in the other. For the motion of alteration does not proceed in such a way that first one part is altered and then another. Rather the whole is first less warm and afterwards is more warm. Further, in De Sensu et Sensato Aristotle says, "And in general, even in qualitative change the case is different from what it is in local movement [both being different species of kinesis]. Local movements, of course, arrive first at a point midway before reaching their goal (and sound, it is currently believed, is a movement of something locally moved), but we cannot go on to assert this [arrival at a point midway] in like manner of things which undergo qualitative change. For this kind of change may conceivably take place in a thing all at once, without one half of it being changed before the other; e.g., it is conceivable that water should be frozen simultaneously in every part.

802. In answer to this it must be said that here in Book VI Aristotle is treating motion insofar as it is continuous. Now continuity primarily and per se and properly is found only in local motion. For only local motion can be continuous and regular, as will be shown in Book VIII. Hence the demonstrations given in this book pertain to local motion perfectly and to other motions not totally, but insofar as they participate in continuity and regularity.

Thus it must be said that a locally moved body always partially enters the place to which it is tending before it enters this place wholly. But in regard to alteration this is true in a certain way and in another way it is not. For it is clear that every alteration occurs by means of the power of the agent who alters. Now the greater this power is, the more it can alter the body. Therefore, since the altering agent has a finite power, the alterable body is subjected to the determinate quantity of its power and receives the impression of the agent all at once. Thus the whole is altered simultaneously and not part by part. But that which is altered further alters something else which is joined to it, although it is less effective as an agent. Thus the power of altering becomes progressively less potent. For example, fire immediately warms one part of the air, and the air which is warmed warms another part. In this way one part is altered after another. Hence, after the text of De Sensu et Sensato quoted above, Aristotle adds, "But still, for all that, if the body which is heated or frozen is extensive, each part of it successively is affected by the part contiguous, while the part first changed in quality is so changed by the cause itself which originates the change, and thus the change throughout the whole need not take place co-instantaneously and all at once."

Nevertheless we must realize that there is a certain succession even in that which is altered all at once. Since alteration occurs by means of the contact of the altering agent, then the parts of the altered body which are closer to the altering agent receive the impression of the altering agent more perfectly at the beginning. And the body arrives at perfect alteration successively according to the order of its parts. This is especially true when there is in the alterable body something which resists the altering agent.

Hence his conclusion, namely, that that which is changed, while it is changing, is partly in the terminus from which and partly in the terminus

to which, as though one part arrives at the terminus to which before the others, is true simply and absolutely for local motion. But in the motion of alteration this is true in a qualified way, as was said.

803. But some have said conversely that that which is said here applies more to the motion of alteration than to local motion.

They say that the proposition—"that which is being changed is partly in the terminus from which and partly in the terminus to which" —does not mean that one part of that which is being moved is in one terminus and another part in the other terminus. Rather this proposition refers to the parts of the termini. For that which is being moved has part of the terminus from which and part of the terminus to which. For example, that which is being moved from whiteness to blackness does not primarily have whiteness perfectly nor blackness perfectly. Rather it participates imperfectly in both. But in local motion this is true only insofar as that which is being moved, while it is in between the two extremes, participates in both extremes in a qualified way. For example, if earth is being moved to the place of fire, then while it is being moved through the proper place of air, it has part of each terminus insofar as the place of air is both up in respect to the place of earth and down in respect to the place of fire.

804. But this explanation is forced and contrary to the opinion of Aristotle.

This is clear first from Aristotle's own words. For he concludes ". . . it **follows, therefore, that part of that which is changing must be at the starting-point and part at the goal"**

[234b15–16]. Hence, he is speaking of the parts of the mobile body and not the parts of the termini.

Secondly, this is clear from his intention. For he is trying to prove that that which is changed is divisible. This could not be concluded from the foregoing explanation. Hence Avempace says that he does not intend here to prove that the mobile body is divisible into quantitative parts, but rather is divisible in respect to its forms. In other words, that which is changed from contrary to contrary, while it is being changed, has part of each contrary. But Aristotle's expressed intention is to show that the mobile body is divisible into its quantitative parts, as is the case with other continua. Furthermore, he uses this point in the following demonstrations.

Moreover, it does not seem to be true that he proves the divisibility of the mobile body in respect to continuity by means of the divisibility of motion, as some say. For from the fact that the mobile body, while it is being moved, participates in both termini and does not immediately have the terminus to which perfectly, it is clear that mutation is divisible in respect to continuity. And thus, since the divisible cannot be divided into indivisible parts, it also follows that the mobile body is a continuum. In what follows Aristotle clearly establishes the division of motion by means of the division of the mobile body. Hence, if he intends here to conclude to the division of the mobile body from the division of motion, his proof would be circular.

Thirdly, this explanation seems to be inconsistent with Aristotle's own explanation where he says, **"Here by 'goal of change' I mean that which co-**mes **"first in the process of change ..."** [234b17]. From this it is clear that he does not mean to say that the mobile body is partly in the terminus from which and partly in the terminus to which because it is in the middle and, as it were, participates in both extremes. Rather he means that in respect to one of its parts the mobile body is in one extreme and in respect to another part it is in the middle.

805. But when Aristotle in this explanation speaks of **"that which comes first"** [234b17], there seems to be a difficulty. Because of the infinite divisibility of magnitude, it seems that there cannot be a "that which comes first."

Hence it must be said that "that which comes first" in local motion is the place which is contiguous to the place from which the body is changed. This place is not part of the first place. If this second place were part of the first place, then it would not be the first place to which the body is moved. This can be made clear as follows. Let A B be the place from which some mobile body is moved. And let B C be an equal place in contact with A B. Since A B is divisible, let it be divided at the point D. Further, let there be marked off in B C, beginning at C, a distance equal to B D. Let this distance be G C. Now it is clear that the mobile body is moved to the place D G before it is moved to the place B C. And further, since A D is divisible, there will be another prior place and so on to infinity.

And likewise in the motion of alteration there must be a "that which comes first." This is an intermediate of another species. For example, when something is changed from white to black, grey, and not less-white, should be taken as the intermediate.

LECTURE 6 [234b21–235b5]
Two Ways in Which Motion Is Divided

The Text of Aristotle

612. *Now motion is divisible in two senses. In the first place it is divisible in virtue of the time that it occupies. In the second place it is divisible according to the motions of the several parts of that which is in motion: e.g., if the whole AC is in motion, there will be a motion of AB and a motion of BC.* 234b21–24

613. *That being so, let DE be the motion of the part AB and EF the motion of the part BC. Then the whole DF must be the motion of AC; for DF must constitute the motion of AC inasmuch as DE and EF severally constitute the motions of each of its parts. But the motion of a thing can never be constituted by the motion of something else; consequently the whole motion is the motion of the whole magnitude.* 234b24–29

614. *Again, since every motion is a motion of something, and the whole motion DF is not the motion of either of the parts (for each of the parts DE, EF is the motion of one of the parts AB, BC) or of anything else (for, the whole motion being the motion of a whole, the parts of the motion are the motions of the parts of that whole; and the parts of DF are the motions of AB, BC and of nothing else; for, as we saw, a motion that is one cannot be the motion of more things than one): since this is so, the whole motion will be the motion of the magnitude ABC.* 234b29–34

615. *Again, if there is a motion of the whole other than DF, say HI, the motion of each of the parts may be subtracted from it; and these motions will be equal to DE, EF respectively; for the motion of that which is one must be one. So if the whole motion HI may be divided into the motions of the parts, HI will be equal to DF; if on the other hand there is any remainder, say JI, this will be a motion of nothing; for it can be the motion neither of the whole nor of the parts (as the motion of that which is one must be one) nor of anything else: for a motion that is continuous must be the motion of things that are continuous. And the same result follows if the division of HI reveals a surplus on the side of the motions of the parts. Consequently, if this is impossible, the whole motion must be the same as and equal to DF. This then is what is meant by the division of motion according to the motions of the parts; and it must be applicable to everything that is divisible into parts.* 234b34–235a10

616. *Motion is also susceptible of another kind of division, that according to time. For since all motion is in time and all time is divisible, and in less time the motion is less, it follows that every motion must be divisible according to time.* 235a10–13

617. *And since everything that is in motion is in motion in a certain sphere and for a certain time and has a motion belonging to it, it follows that the time, the motion, the being-in-motion, the thing that is in motion, and the sphere of the motion must all be susceptible of the same divisions (though spheres of motion are not all divisible in a like manner: thus quantity is essentially, quality accidentally divisible).* 235a13–18

618. *For suppose that A is the time occupied by the motion B. Then if all the time has been occupied by the whole motion, it will take less of the motion to occupy half the time, less again to occupy a further subdivision of the time, and so on to infinity.* 235a18–22

619. *Again, the time will be divisible similarly to the motion; for if the whole motion occupies all the time half the motion will occupy half the time, and less of the motion again will occupy less of the time.* 235a22–24

620. *In the same way the being-in-motion will also be divisible. For let C be the whole being-in-motion. Then the being-in-motion that corresponds to half the motion will be less than*

the whole being-in-motion, that which corresponds to a quarter of the motion will be less again, and so on to infinity.   **235a25–28**

621. *Moreover by setting out successively the being-in-motion corresponding to each of the two motions DC (say) and CE, we may argue that the whole being-in-motion will correspond to the whole motion (for if it were some other being-in-motion that corresponded to the whole motion, there would be more than one being-in-motion corresponding to the same motion), the argument being the same as that whereby we showed that the motion of a thing is divisible into the motions of the parts of the thing; for if we take separately the being-in-motion corresponding to each of the two motions, we shall see that the whole being-in-motion is continuous.*

235a28–34

622. *The same reasoning will show the divisibility of the length, and in fact of everything that forms a sphere of change (though some of these are only accidentally divisible because that which changes is so); for the division of one term will involve the division of all.*   **235a34–37**

623. *So, too, in the matter of their being finite or infinite, they will all alike be either the one or the other.*   **235a37–235b1**

624. *And we now see that in most cases the fact that all the terms are divisible or infinite is a direct consequence of the fact that the thing that changes is divisible or infinite; for the attributes "divisible" and "infinite" belong in the first instance to the thing that changes. That divisibility does so we have already shown; that infinity does so will be made clear in what follows.*   **235b1–5**

COMMENTARY OF ST. THOMAS

806. Having set forth certain things which are necessary for the division of motion, he begins here to treat the division of motion.

This discussion is divided into two parts. First he treats the division of motion. Secondly, where he says, **"Zeno's reasoning . . ."** [660], he refutes from what has been determined certain errors about motion.

The first part is divided into two parts. First he treats the division of motion, and secondly the division of rest, where he says, **"Since everything to which . . ."** [653].

The first part is divided into two parts. First he treats the division of motion. Secondly, where he says, **"Now since the motion . . ."** [644], he treats the finite and the infinite in motion. For both the divisible and the infinite seem to pertain to the nature [ratio] of a continuum.

The first part is divided into two parts. First he explains how motion is divided. Secondly, where he says, **"Since everything that changes . . ."** [625], he treats the order of the parts of motion.

Concerning the first part he makes two points. First he states two ways in which motion is divided. Secondly, where he says, **"And since everything . . ."** [617], he shows what things are divided together with motion.

Concerning the first part he makes two points. First he states the ways in which motion is divided. Secondly, where he says, **"That being so . . ."** [613], he explains these ways.

807. He says, therefore, first that motion is divided in two ways. First, motion is divided in respect to time. For it was shown that motion is not in the "now," but in time. Secondly, motion is divided in respect to the motions of the parts of the mobile body. Let A C be a mobile body which is divided. It was shown that whatever is moved is divisible. Hence, if the whole

of A C is moved, then both of its parts, A B and B C, must also be moved.

However, it must be realized that the division of motion in respect to the parts of the mobile body can be understood in two ways. First this can mean that the body is moved part after part. This cannot occur when the whole in itself is moved. For in this case all the parts are moved together, not separately from the whole, but within the whole itself. The second way in which the division of motion in respect to the parts of the mobile body can be understood is as follows. The division of an accident, whose subject is divisible, occurs by a division of its subject. For example, if this whole body is white, then whiteness is accidentally divided by a division of the body. The division of motion in respect to the parts of the mobile body is here taken in this second way. Thus, each part of the mobile body is moved together with the whole so that the motions of all the parts are simultaneous. In this way the division of motion in respect to the parts of the mobile body differs from the division of motion in respect to time. For in the latter the two parts of the motion are not simultaneous. However, if the motion of one part is related to the motion of another part, not simply, but in respect to some determinate sign, then the motion of the one part precedes the motion of the other part in time. For if the mobile body A B C is moved through the magnitude E F G such that E F is equal to the whole of A C, then it is clear that B C will cross through this sign F before A B will. In this way the divisions of motion in respect to the parts of time and in respect to the parts of the mobile body run together.

808. Next where he says, **"That being so . . ."** [613], he explains the two ways in which motion is divided. First he shows that motion is divided in respect to the parts of the mobile body. Secondly, where he says, **"Motion is also susceptible . . ."** [616], he shows that motion is divided in respect to the parts of time.

He establishes the first point with three arguments. The first is as follows.

Of the parts which are moved by the whole motion, let D E be the motion of the part A B. And let E F be the motion of the other part B C. Just as the whole mobile body A C is composed of A B and B C, in the same way the whole motion D F is composed of D E and E F. Hence, each part of the mobile body is moved by the corresponding part of the motion, such that no part of the mobile body is moved by the motion of another part (for otherwise the whole motion would pertain to one part which would be moved by its own motion and by the motion of the other part). Therefore it must be said that the whole motion D F pertains to the whole mobile body A C. And thus the motion of the whole is divided by motion of the parts.

809. He gives the second argument where he says, **"Again, since every motion . . ."** [614]. The argument is as follows.

Every motion is a motion of some mobile body. But the whole motion D F is not the motion of either of the parts. For neither is moved by the whole motion, rather each is moved by a part of the motion, as was said. Nor can it be said that D F is the motion of some other mobile body separated from A C. For if this whole motion were the motion of some other whole body, then it would follow that the parts of this motion would be the motions of the parts of that other mobile body. But the parts of this motion D F are the motions of the parts of the mobile body, A B and B C, and of nothing else. For if they were the motions of both these and other parts, it would follow that one motion would be many, which is impossible. Hence it follows that the whole motion is the motion of the whole magnitude, just as the parts of the motion are the motions of the parts. And thus the motion of the whole is divided by the parts of the mobile body.

810. He gives the third argument where he says, **"Again, if there is . . ."** [615]. The argument is as follows.

Whatever is moved has some motion. Hence, if the whole motion D F is not the motion of the whole mobile body A C, then there must be some other motion of A C. Let this motion be H I. The motions of each of the parts is subtracted from the motion H I. The motions of the parts must be equal to D E F because for one mobile body there is only one motion. Hence, it cannot be said that the motions of the parts, which were subtracted from H I (given as the motion of the whole), are greater or less than D E and E F (given as the motions of these very parts). Hence, the motions of the parts either exhaust the whole of H I when subtracted, or they fall short of it, or else they exceed it. If they exhaust the whole of H I and neither fall short nor exceed it, then it follows that the motion H I is equal to the motion D F, which is the motion of the parts, and does not differ from D F. If the motions of the parts falls short of H I, such that H I exceeds D F by J I, then this motion J I is the motion of no mobile body. For it is not the motion of the whole of A C nor of its parts. For of one mobile body there is only one motion, and another motion has already been assigned to both the whole and the parts. Nor can it be said that J I is the motion of some other mobile body.

For the whole motion H I is a continuous motion, and a continuous motion must be a motion of a continuous body, as was shown in Book V. Hence, the part J I of this continuous motion cannot be the motion of a mobile body which is not continuous with A B C.

An inconsistency also follows if it be said that the motions of the parts exceed H I by division. For it would then follow that the parts exceed the whole, which is impossible. Hence, if it is impossible for the motion of the parts to either fall short of or to exceed the motion of the whole, then the motion of the parts must be equal to and the same as the motion of the whole.

This is a division in respect to the motions of the parts. Such a division must also be found in the motion, because whatever is moved is divisible.

811. Next where he says, **"Motion is also susceptible . . ."** [616], he shows with the following argument that motion is divided according to the division of time.

Every motion is in time. And every time is divisible, as was proven. Therefore, since there is less motion in a smaller time, every motion must be divided in respect to time.

812. Next where he says, **"And since everything . . ."** [617], he shows what things are divided together with motion.

Concerning this he makes three points. First he points out five things which are divided together. Secondly, where he says, **"So, too, in the matter . . ."** [623], he shows that the finite and the infinite are found together in all five of these. Thirdly, where he says, **"And we now see . . ."** [624], he shows in which one of these five is primarily found division and the infinite.

Concerning the first part he makes two points. First he states his intention.

Secondly, where he says, **"For sup-pose that A ..."** [618], he explains his position.

He says, therefore, first that whatever is moved is moved in "something," that is, in respect to some genus or species. And it is moved in some time. And there is some motion for every mobile body. Therefore, the following five things must be divided together: the time, the motion, the "being moved," the mobile body which is moved, and that in which there is motion, either place or quality or quantity.

Nevertheless, there is not the same kind of division for all the things in which there is motion. Rather in some of these cases there is division per se and in some per accidens. There is division per se of all things which pertain to the genus of quantity, that is, local motion and increase and decrease. But there is division per accidens in things which pertain to quality, that is, alteration.

813. Next where he says, **"For sup-pose that A ..."** [618], he explains what he has said.

First he shows that time and motion are divided together. Secondly, where he says, **"In the same way ..."** [620], he shows that motion and "being moved" are divided together. Thirdly, where he says, **"The same reasoning ..."** [622], he shows that the same is true of motion and of that in which there is motion.

Concerning the first part he makes two points. First he shows that motion is divided by the division of time. Secondly, where he says, **"Again, the time will be ..."** [619], he shows conversely that time is divided by the division of motion.

He proceeds as follows. Let A be the time in which something is moved. And let B be the motion which occurs

in this time. Now if something is moved through a whole magnitude in a whole time, it is clear that in half the time it will be moved through less of the magnitude. Moreover to be moved by the whole motion is the same as being moved through the whole magnitude. And to be moved by part of the motion is the same as being moved through part of the magnitude. Hence it is clear that if a body is moved in the whole time by the whole motion, then in part of the time it will be moved by a smaller motion. And if the time is divided again, there will be found a still smaller motion, and so on to infinity. From this it is clear that motion is divided by the division of time.

Next where he says, **"Again, the time will be ..."** [619], he shows conversely that if motion is divided, time is also divided. For if a body is moved through a whole motion in a whole time, then it will be moved through half the motion in half the time. And there will always be a lesser motion in a smaller time, if the mobile body has the same or equal velocity.

814. Next where he says, **"In the same way ..."** [620], he shows that motion and "being moved" are divided together.

Concerning this he makes two points. First he shows that "being moved" is divided by the division of motion. Secondly, where he says, **"Moreover by setting out ..."** [621], he shows that motion is divided by the division of "being moved."

He says, therefore, first that in the same way it is proven that "being moved" is divided by the division of time and motion. Let C be the "being moved." It is clear that the body is moved not only in respect to part of the motion but also in respect to the whole motion. Hence it is clear that, in respect to half of the motion, part of the "being moved" is less than the whole "being moved." And it will be still less in respect to half of this half, and so on to infinity. Hence just as the time and the motion are infinitely divided, so is the "being moved."

Next where he says, **"Moreover by setting out . . ."** [621], he proves conversely that motion is divided by the division of "being moved."Let there be two parts of a motion, D C and C E, in respect to both of which a body is moved. And thus, if the parts of the motion correspond to the parts of "being moved," then the whole motion must correspond to the whole "being moved." For if there were more of one than the other, we would argue here about motion and "being moved" as we argued above when we showed that the motion of the whole is divisible into the motion of parts which neither fall short of nor exceed the whole. In the same way the parts of the "being moved" cannot fall short of nor exceed the parts of the motion. For since there must be a "being moved" which corresponds to each part of the motion, it must be that the whole "being moved" is a continuum corresponding to the whole motion. And thus the parts of the "being moved" will always correspond to the parts of the motion, and the whole will correspond to the whole. And hence the one is divided by the other.

815. Next where he says, **"The same reasoning . . ."** [622], he shows that the same is true of that in which there is motion.

He says that it can be demonstrated in the same way that the length in which a body is moved in place is divisible in respect to the division of the time, and of the motion, and of the "being moved."

What we say about length in local motion must be understood to apply also to everything in which there is motion, except that certain things are divisible per accidens, for example, qualities in alteration, as was said.

Further, all these things are so divided because that which is changed is divisible, as was shown above. Hence, when one of these is divided, all of them must be divided.

816. Next where he says, **"So, too, in the matter . . ."** [623], he shows that, just as the foregoing are so related in regard to divisibility, they are also so related in regard to being either finite or infinite. Thus, if one of these is finite, they are all finite. And if one is infinite, so are the others.

817. Next where he says, **"And we now see . . ."** [624], he shows in which of the foregoing are primarily found divisibility and the finite or the infinite.

He says that the fact that all the others are divided and are finite or infinite follows primarily from that which is changed. For that which is naturally first in motion is the mobile body itself; and divisibility and being finite or infinite are immediately present in it from its very nature. And thus from the mobile body is derived the divisibility or the finitude of the others.

It was shown above how the mobile body is divisible and how the others are divided by it. But it will be shown below in this Book how the mobile body is related to the infinite.

The Part of Time in Which a Thing Has First Been Moved Is Indivisible.
How There Can Be a First Motion

The Text of Aristotle
Chapter 5

625. *Since everything that changes changes from something to something, that which has changed must at the moment when it has first changed be in that to which it has changed.*

235b6–8

626. *For that which changes retires from or leaves that from which it changes; and leaving, if not identical with changing, is at any rate a consequence of it. And if leaving is a consequence of changing, having left is a consequence of having changed; for there is a like relation between the two in each case. One kind of change, then, being change in a relation of contradiction, where a thing has changed from not-being to being it has left not-being. Therefore it will be in being; for everything must either be or not be. It is evident, then, that in contradictory change that which has changed must be in that to which it has changed. And if this is true in this kind of change, it will be true in all other kinds as well; for in this matter what holds good in the case of one will hold good likewise in the case of the rest.* 235b8–18

627. *Moreover, if we take each kind of change separately, the truth of our conclusion will be equally evident, on the ground that that which has changed must be somewhere or in something. For, since it has left that from which it has changed and must be somewhere, it must be either in that to which it has changed or in something else. If, then, that which has changed to B is in something other than B, say C, it must again be changing from C to B; for it cannot be assumed that there is no interval between C and B, since change is continuous. Thus we have the result that the thing that has changed, at the moment when it has changed, is changing, to that to which it has changed, which is impossible: that which has changed, therefore, must be in that to which it has changed. So it is evident likewise that that which has come to be, at the moment when it has come to be, will be, and that which has ceased to be will not-be; for what we have said applies universally to every kind of change, and its truth is most obvious in the case of contradictory change. It is clear, then, that that which has changed, at the moment when it has first changed, is in that to which it has changed.* 235b18–30

628. *We will now show that the "primary when" in which that which has changed effected the completion of its change must be indivisible, where by "primary" I mean possessing the characteristics in question of itself and not in virtue of the possession of them by something else belonging to it. For let AC be divisible, and let it be divided at B. If then the completion of change has been effected in AB or again in BC, AC cannot be the primary thing in which the completion of change has been effected. If, on the other hand, it has been changing in both AB and BC (for it must either have changed or be changing in each of them), it must have been changing in the whole AC; but our assumption was that AC contains only the completion of the change. It is equally impossible to suppose that one part of AC contains the process and the other the completion of the change; for then we shall have something prior to what is primary. So that in which the completion of change has been effected must be indivisible. It is also evident, therefore, that that in which that which has ceased to be has ceased to be and that in which that which has come to be has come to be are indivisible.* 235b30–236a7

629. *But there are two senses of the expression "the primary when in which something has changed." On the one hand it may mean the primary when containing the completion of the process of change—the moment when it is correct to say "it has changed"; on the other hand it may mean the primary when containing the beginning of the process of change. Now the*

primary when that has reference to the end of the change is something really existent; for a change may really be completed, and there is such a thing as an end of change, which we have in fact shown to be indivisible because it is a limit. But that which has reference to the beginning is not existent at all; for there is no such thing as a beginning of a process of change, and the time occupied by the change does not contain any primary when in which the change began.

236a7–17

630. *For suppose that AD is such a primary when. Then it cannot be indivisible; for, if it were, the moment immediately preceding the change and the moment in which the change begins would be consecutive (and moments cannot be consecutive). Again, if the changing thing is at rest in the whole preceding time CA (for we may suppose that it is at rest), it is at rest in A also: so if AD is without parts, it will simultaneously be at rest and have changed; for it is at rest in A and has changed in D. Since then AD is not without parts, it must be divisible, and the changing thing must have changed in every part of it (for if it has changed in neither of the two parts into which AD is divided, it has not changed in the whole either; if, on the other hand, it is in process of change in both parts it is likewise in process of change in the whole; and if again it has changed in one of the two parts, the whole is not the primary when in which it has changed: it must therefore have changed in every part). It is evident, then, that with reference to the beginning of change there is no primary when in which change has been effected; for the divisions are infinite.*

236a17–27

631. *So, too, of that which has changed there is no primary part that has changed. For suppose that of DE the primary part that has changed is DF (everything that changes having been shown to be divisible); and let HI be the time in which DF has changed. If, then, in the whole time DF has changed, in half the time there will be a part that has changed, less than and therefore prior to DF; and again there will be another part prior to this, and yet another, and so on to infinity. Thus of that which changes there cannot be any primary part that has changed. It is evident, then, from what has been said, that neither of that which changes nor of the time in which it changes is there any primary part.*

236a27–35

632. *With regard, however, to the actual subject of change—that is to say that in respect of which a thing changes—there is a difference to be observed. For in a process of change we may distinguish three terms—that which changes, that in which it changes, and the actual subject of change, e.g., the man, the time, and the fair complexion. Of these the man and the time are divisible; but with the fair complexion it is otherwise (though they are all divisible accidentally; for that in which the fair complexion or any other quality is an accident is divisible). For of actual subjects of change it will be seen that those which are classed as essentially, not accidentally, divisible have no primary part. Take the case of magnitudes: let AB be a magnitude, and suppose that it has moved from B to a primary "where" C. Then if BC is taken to be indivisible, two things without parts will have to be contiguous (which is impossible); if on the other hand it is taken to be divisible, there will be something prior to C to which the magnitude has changed, and something else again prior to that, and so on to infinity, because the process of division may be continued without end. Thus there can be no primary "where" to which a thing has changed. And if we take the case of quantitative change, we shall get a like result; for here too the change is in something continuous. It is evident, then, that only in qualitative motion can there be anything essentially indivisible.*

236a35–236b18

COMMENTARY OF ST. THOMAS

818. After the Philosopher has shown how motion is divided, he here treats the order of the parts of motion.

First he inquires whether there is a first in motion. Secondly, where he says, **"Now everything that** changes..." [633], he explains how the things that are in motion precede each other.

Concerning the first part he makes two points. First he shows that that in which something has first been changed is indivisible. Secondly, where he says, **"But there are two..."** [629], he explains how there can be a first in motion and how not.

Concerning the first part he makes two points. First he sets forth a certain thing which is necessary to prove his position. Secondly, where he says, **"We will now show..."** [628], he establishes his position.

Concerning the first part he makes two points. First he states his intention. Secondly, where he says, **"For that which changes..."** [626], he proves his position.

819. He says, therefore, first [625] that, since whatever is changed is changed from one terminus to another, then whatever is changed, when it has already been changed, must be in the terminus to which.

Next where he says, **"For that which changes..."** [626], he proves this with two arguments. The first argument is particular, the second universal.

The first argument is as follows. Whatever is changed must either leave the terminus from which it is changed (as is clear in local motion in which the place from which it is changed remains, and the mobile body is moved to some distance from it), or else the terminus from which must be removed (as in alteration, for when something becomes black from white, the whiteness leaves). To clarify this statement he adds that to be changed is either identical with "leaving" or else is consequent upon "leaving." And thus to have been changed is conse-

quent upon "having left" the terminus from which. Moreover, it is clear that these are the same in subject but different in reason [ratio]. For "to leave" refers to the terminus from which, but change is denominated by the terminus to which. And to clarify what he has said he adds, "... for there is a like relation between the two in each case" [235b12]; that is, "to have left" is related to "to have been changed" in the same way that "to leave" is related to "to be changed."

From the foregoing he argues to prove his position in regard to one species of change. This is the change between contradictory opposites, that is, between being and non-being, as is clear in generation and corruption. It is clear from the foregoing that whatever is being changed leaves the terminus from which. It is also clear that whatever has been changed has already left the terminus from which. Hence, when something has been changed from non-being to being, it has already left non-being. But it can be truly said of anything that it is either being or non-being. Therefore, that which has been changed from non-being to being is in being when it has been changed. And likewise, that which has been changed from being to non-being must be in non-being. Hence it is clear that, in change in respect to contradictories, that which has been changed is in that to which it has been changed. And if this is true of this type of change, then it is also true for the same reason of the other types of change. And hence that which was first stated is clear.

820. He gives the second, general argument where he says, **"Moreover if we take..."** [627]. He says that this same thing can be made clear by considering each type of change. In local change this point is manifest.

For whatever has been changed must be somewhere, either in the terminus from which or somewhere else. But since that which has been changed has already left that from which it has been changed, it must be somewhere else. Therefore it must either be in the terminus to which, which we intend to show, or in some other place. If it is in the terminus to which the point is proven. But if it is somewhere else, we are saying that something is being moved to B, but when it has been changed, it is not in B but in C. Then it must be said that it is also changed from C to B, for C and B are not consecutively related. For all mutations of this kind are continuous. And in a continuum one sign is not consecutively related to another, for there must be between them something else of the same genus, as was proven above. Hence, if that which has been changed, when it has been changed, is in C, and if it is being changed from C to B, which is the terminus to which, then it follows that, when it has been changed, it is being changed to that to which it has been changed. This is impossible. For "being changed" and "having been changed" are not simultaneous, as was said above. It makes no difference whether these termini C and B are taken to refer to local motion or to any other kind of mutation. Hence it is universally and necessarily true that that which has been changed, when it has been changed, is in that to which it has been changed, that is, the terminus to which.

And from this he concludes further that that which has been made, when it has been made, has being; and that which has been corrupted, when it has been corrupted, is non-being. For this was universally shown of all mutation. And this is especially clear in mutation

in respect to contradictories, as is clear from what has been said.

Thus it is clear that that which has been changed, when it has first been changed, is in that to which it has been changed.

He adds the word "first." For after it has been changed to something, it can be changed again, and thus would not be there. But when it has first been changed, it must be there.

821. Next where he says, **"We will now show . . ."** [628], he shows that that which has been changed primarily and per se is in an indivisible. He says that the time in which that which has been changed was primarily changed must be indivisible.

He explains why he adds the word "primarily." A thing is said to have been changed in something primarily when it has not been changed in that something by reason [ratio] of any of the parts of the latter—as when a mobile body is said to be changed in a day because it was changed in some part of that day. It is not changed primarily in that day. He proves as follows that the time in which something is primarily changed is indivisible.

Let A C be divisible and divided at B. Now it must be said that the mobile body either has been changed in each part, or is being changed in each part, or else is being changed in one part and has been changed in the other part. But if it has been changed in each part, then it was not primarily changed in the whole, but in the part. If it be granted that the body is being changed in each part, then it must be said that it is being changed in the whole. For a thing is said to be changed in a whole time when it is changed in each part of that time. But this is contrary to our supposition. For it was assumed that the body has been changed in the whole A

C. Moreover, if it be granted that the body is being changed in one part and has been changed in the other part, the same inconsistency follows. For it would not then have been primarily changed in the whole, because, since the part is prior to the whole and since a body is being changed in a part of time prior to the whole, it would follow that there is something prior to what is primary. This is impossible. Hence it must be said that the time in which something has primarily been changed is indivisible.

From this he concludes further that whatever has been corrupted and whatever has been made was corrupted and made in an indivisible time. For generation and corruption are the termini of alteration. Hence, if any motion is terminated in an instant (to have been changed primarily is the same thing as motion being terminated), it follows that generation and corruption occur in an instant.

822. Next where he says, **"But there are two . . ."** [629], he explains how there can be a first in motion.

Concerning this he does two things. First he proposes the truth, and secondly he proves it, where he says, **"For suppose that A D . . ."** [630].

He says, therefore, first that the expression "that in which something is primarily changed" can be taken in two ways. First, this may mean that in which the mutation is primarily perfected or terminated. For it can truly be said that something has been changed when the mutation has already been completed. Secondly, this expression may be understood to mean that in which something first begins to be changed. In this sense it is not primarily true to say that it has already been changed.

Speaking of motion in the first sense

which refers to the termination of the mutation, there is a "that in which something is primarily changed." For it sometimes happens that a mutation is primarily terminated, because there is a terminus for any mutation. It is in this sense that we meant that that which primarily has been changed is indivisible. And this is clear for this reason: there is an end or terminus of motion. And the terminus of every continuum is indivisible.

But if we take this expression in the second sense which refers to the beginning of change, that is, the first part of motion, then there is no "that in which something is primarily changed." For there is no first part of mutation which is not preceded by some other part. And likewise there is no first part of time in which something is primarily being changed.

823. Next where he says, **"For suppose that A D . . ."** [630], he proves that, in regard to the beginning, there is no first in which something is changed.

First he proves this with an argument taken from time. Secondly, where he says, **"So, too, of that which . . ."** [631], he proves this with an argument taken from the mobile body. And thirdly, where he says, **"With regard, however . . ."** [632], he proves this with an argument taken from that in which the motion occurs.

The first argument is as follows. Let A D be a time in which something is primarily changed. This time is either divisible or indivisible. If it is indivisible, two inconsistencies follow. The first is that the "nows" in time would be consecutive. This inconsistency follows because time is divided in the same way as motion, as was shown above. If some part of the motion were in A D, then it must be said that A D is a part of the time. And thus time would be composed of indivisibles. But the indivisible unit of time is the "now." Hence it would follow that the "nows" are consecutive to each other in time.

The second inconsistency is as follows. Let us grant that in the time C A, which precedes the time A D, the mobile body, which was given as being moved in A D, is totally at rest. If it is at rest in the whole of C A, it follows that it is at rest in A, which is a part of C A. Hence if A D is indivisible, as was granted, it would follow that the body is simultaneously at rest and in motion. For it was concluded that it is at rest in A, and it was granted that it is being moved in A D. And if A D is indivisible, then A and A D are the same. Hence it would follow that the body is at rest and in motion at the same time.

But it must be noted that, if something is at rest in a whole time, it does not follow that it is at rest in the ultimate indivisible part of that time. For it was shown above that in the "now" nothing is in motion or at rest. But Aristotle concludes here from the point which was granted by his adversary; namely, that the time in which something is primarily moved is indivisible. And if it could happen that something is moved in the indivisible "now" of time, it could happen for the same reason that something is at rest in the indivisible "now" of time.

Having denied that A D, in which something is primarily moved, is indivisible, it necessarily follows that it is divisible. And from the fact that something is primarily being moved in A D, it follows that it is being moved in every part of A D. He proves this as follows. Let A D be divided into two parts. Then the mobile body is being changed either in neither part, or in both parts, or in only one part. If it is

being changed in neither part, it follows that it is not being changed in the whole. If it is being changed in both parts, then it can be held that it is being changed in the whole. But if it is being moved in only one part, then it would follow that it is being moved in the whole, not primarily, but by reason of the part. Therefore, since it was granted that the body is being moved primarily in the whole, it must be granted that it is being moved in each part of A D. But time is divided to infinity, as is true of any continuum. And thus there is always a smaller part prior to a greater part, for example, the day is smaller than the month, and the hour is smaller than the day. Hence it is clear that there is no time in which something is primarily being moved, that is, there is no part of time in which something is primarily being moved. Thus it cannot be held that a day is that in which something is primarily moved. For it is being moved in the first hour of that day before it is moved in the whole day.

824. Next where he says, **"So, too, of that which . . ."** [631], he proves the same thing by considering the mobile body. He concludes from the foregoing that in that which is being changed there is nothing which is being changed first. If this be understood in respect to the motion of the whole or a part, some determinate sign is crossed. For it is clear that the first part of the mobile body crosses a determinate sign first, and secondly a second part, and so forth. Further, he is not speaking here of absolute motion. For it is clear that the whole and all of its parts are moved simultaneously. But the mobile body does not cross a determinate sign all at once. Rather this always occurs part by part. Hence, just as there

is no first part of the mobile body before which there is no other smaller part, likewise there is no part of the mobile body which is moved first. Since time and the mobile body are divided in the same way, as was shown above, he concludes in regard to the mobile body the same thing that was properly demonstrated of time. He proves this as follows.

Let D E be a mobile body. Now since every mobile body is divisible, as was proven above, let D F be the part which is moved first. And D F is moved by crossing some determinate sign in the time H I. Hence, if D F has been changed in this whole time, then it follows that that which was changed in half this time was moved less than and prior to D F. And for the same reason there will be something else prior to this part, and again another prior to that, and so on to infinity. For time is divided to infinity. Hence it is clear that in the mobile body there is nothing which was changed first.

And thus it is clear that there cannot be a first in motion either in respect to the time or in respect to the mobile body.

825. Next where he says, **"With regard, however..."** [632], he proves the same thing in regard to that in which the motion occurs.

He says that "that which is changed," or better, "that in respect to which something is changed," is different than the time and the mobile body. For in a mutation there are three things: the mobile body which is changed, for example, a man; that in which it is changed, the time; and that to which it is changed, for example, white. Two of these, the time and the mobile body, are infinitely divisible. But in regard to "white" there is a different nature [ratio]. For "white" is not divisible per se. Rather "white" and all other such things are divisible per accidens, insofar as that of which "white" or any other quality is an accident is divisible.

The per accidens division of "white" can occur in two ways. First, in respect to quantitative parts. For example, when a white surface is divided into two parts, the "white" will be divided per accidens. Secondly, in respect to intention and remission. For the fact that one and the same part is more or less white is not due to the very nature [ratio] of whiteness. (If whiteness were separated, it would not be called more or less white, just as no substance is susceptible to more or less.) Rather this is due to the diverse modes of participating whiteness by a divisible subject. Hence, omitting that which is divided per accidens, if we take things in respect to which there is motion and which are divided per se and not per accidens, then also in these things there is no first.

He makes this clear first in regard to the magnitude in which local motion occurs. Let there be a spatial magnitude which includes A B. And let this magnitude be divided at C. And let it be granted that something is moved first from B to C. Now B C is either divisible or indivisible. If it is indivisible, it follows that an indivisible will be joined to an indivisible, because for the same reason the second part of the motion will be in an indivisible. For, as was said above about time, it is necessary to divide magnitude and motion in the same way. But if B C is divisible, there will be some sign closer to B than C is. And thus the body will be changed to that sign before it is changed to C. And again there will be something prior to that sign, and so on to infinity. For the division of magnitude is endless. Therefore it is clear that there is no first to which the body has been changed by local motion.

This is likewise clear in the mutation of quantity, which is increase and decrease. For this is also a mutation in respect to a continuum, that is, in respect to a quantity which is growing or decreasing. Since such a quantity is divisible to infinity, there is in it no first.

And thus it is clear that only in qualitative mutation can there be some-

thing which is indivisible per se. Nevertheless, insofar as a quality is divisible per accidens, there is likewise no first in such a mutation. For there is either a succession of mutation insofar as a part is altered after another part (for it is clear that there is no first part of "white" just as there is no first part of magnitude), or else there is a succession of alteration insofar as the same thing is either more white or less white. For a subject can variously be more white and less white in an infinity of ways. And thus alteration can be continuous and not have a first.

Before Every "Being Moved" There Is a "Has Been Moved." And Before Every "Has Been Moved" There Is a "Being Moved"

The Text of Aristotle
Chapter 6

633. *Now everything that changes changes in time, and that in two senses: for the time in which a thing is said to change may be the primary time, or on the other hand it may have an extended reference, as e.g., when we say that a thing changes in a particular year because it changes in a particular day. That being so, that which changes must be changing in any part of the primary time in which it changes. This is clear from our definition of "primary," in which the word is said to express just this; it may also, however, be made evident by the following argument. Let VQ be the primary time in which that which is in motion is in motion; and (as all time is divisible) let it be divided at J. Now in the time VJ it either is in motion or is not in motion, and the same is likewise true of the time JQ. Then if it is in motion in neither of the two parts, it will be at rest in the whole; for it is impossible that it should be in motion in a time no part of which is in motion. If on the other hand it is in motion in only one of its parts of the time, VQ cannot be the primary time in which it is in motion; for its motion will have reference to a time other than VQ. It must, then, have been in motion in any part of VQ.*   **236b19–32**

634. *And now that this has been proved, it is evident that everything that is in motion must have been in motion before. For if that which is in motion has traversed the distance JK in the primary time VQ, in half the time a thing that is in motion with equal velocity and began its motion at the same time will have traversed half the distance. But if this second thing whose velocity is equal has traversed a certain distance in a certain time, the original thing that is in motion must have traversed the same distance in the same time. Hence that which is in motion must have been in motion before.*   **236b32–237a3**

635. *Again, if by taking the extreme moment of the time—for it is the moment that defines the time, and time is that which is intermediate between moments—we are enabled to say that motion has taken place in the whole time VQ or in fact in any period of it. Motion may likewise be said to have taken place in every other such period. But half the time finds an extreme in the point of division. Therefore motion will have taken place in half the time and in fact in any part of it; for as soon as any division is made there is always a time defined by moments. If, then, all time is divisible, and that is intermediate between moments is time, everything that is changing must have completed an infinite number of changes.*   **237a3–11**

636. *Again, since a thing that changes continuously and has not perished or ceased from its change must either be changing or have changed in any part of the time of its change, and since it cannot be changing in a moment, it follows that it must have changed at every moment in the time: consequently, since the moments are infinite in number, everything that is changing must have completed an infinite number of changes.*   **237a11–17**

637. *And not only must that which is changing have changed, but that which has changed must also previously have been changing,*   **237a17–19**

638. *since everything that has changed from something to something has changed in a period of time. For suppose that a thing has changed from A to B in a moment. Now the moment in which it has changed cannot be the same as that in which it is at A (since in that case it would be in A and B at once); for we have shown above that that which has changed, when it has changed, is not in that from which it has changed. If, on the other hand, it is a different moment, there will be a period of time intermediate between the two; for as we saw, moments are not consecutive.*   **237a19–25**

639. *Since, then, it has changed in a period of time, and all time is divisible, in half the time it will have completed another change, in a quarter another, and so on to infinity: consequently when it has changed, it must have previously been changing.*   **237a25–28**

640. *Moreover, the truth of what has been said is more evident in the case of magnitude, because the magnitude over which what is changing is continuous. For suppose that a thing has changed from C to D. Then if CD is indivisible, two things without parts will be consecutive. But since this is impossible, that which is intermediate between them must be a magnitude and divisible into an infinite number of segments: consequently, before the change is completed, the thing changes to those segments. Everything that has changed, therefore, must previously have been changing;*   **237a28–35**

641. *for the same proof also holds good of change with respect to what is not continuous, changes, that is to say, between contraries and between contradictories. In such cases we have only to take the time in which a thing has changed and again apply the same reasoning.*

237a35–237b3

642. *So that which has changed must have been changing, and that which is changing must have changed, and a process of change is preceded by a completion of change and a completion by a process; and we can never take any stage and say that it is absolutely the first. The reason of this is that no two things without parts can be contiguous; and therefore in change the process of division is infinite, just as lines may be infinitely divided so that one part is continually increasing and the other continually decreasing.*   **237b3–9**

643. *So it is evident also that that which has become must previously have been in process of becoming, and that which is in process of becoming must previously have become, everything (that is) that is divisible and continuous; though it is not always the actual thing that is in process of becoming of which this is true: sometimes it is something else, that is to say, some part of the thing in question, e.g., the foundation-stone of a house. So, too, in the case of that which is perishing and that which has perished; for that which becomes and that which perishes must contain an element of infiniteness as an immediate consequence of the fact that they are continuous things; and so a thing cannot be in process of becoming without having become or have become without having been in process of becoming. So, too, in the case of perishing and having perished: perishing must be preceded by having perished, and having perished must be preceded by perishing. It is evident, then, that that which has become must previously have been in process of becoming, and that which is in process of becoming; must previously have become: for all magnitudes and all periods of time are infinitely divisible.*

Consequently no absolutely first stage of change can be represented by any particular part of space or time which the changing thing may occupy.   **237b9–22**

COMMENTARY OF ST. THOMAS

826. After the Philosopher has shown in what sense there is a first in motion and in what sense not, he here explains the mutual order of things found in motion.

First he sets forth a certain point which is necessary for the proof of his position. Secondly, where he says, **"And now that this . . ."** [634], he proves his position.

827. He says, therefore, first that whatever is changed is changed in time, as was shown above. But a thing is said to be changed in time in two ways: first, primarily and per se; and secondly, in respect to another, that is, by reason of a part, as when a thing is said to be changed in a year because it was changed in a day.

Having made this distinction, he

states what he intends to prove; namely, if a thing is changed primarily in some time, it must be changed in every part of that time. He proves this in two ways.

He proves this first from the definition of "primary." For something is said to happen to a thing primarily when it happens to it in respect to each of its parts, as was said at the beginning of Book V.

Secondly he proves this same thing with the following argument. Let V Q be a time in which something is primarily moved. And since every time is divisible, let V Q be divided at J. It must be said that in that part of the time which is V J the body is either moved or not moved. The same is true of the part J Q. If it be granted that the body is moved in neither of these parts, it follows that it is not moved in the whole V Q, but is at rest in V Q. For it is impossible for a thing to be moved in a time in no part of which it is moved. Moreover, if it be granted that the body is moved in one part of the time, but not in the other, then it would follow that it is not moved primarily in the time V Q. For the body must be moved in respect to each part, and not in respect to just one part. Therefore, it must be said that it is moved in every part of the time V Q. And this is what we wished to demonstrate; namely, when a thing is moved primarily in some time, it is moved in every part of that time.

828. Next where he says, **"And now that this . . ."** [634], he proceeds to the proof of his main point. Concerning this he does two things. First he brings in demonstrations to prove his position. Secondly, where he says, **"So that which has . . ."** [642], he concludes to the truth which has been determined.

Concerning the first part he makes

two points. First he shows that, before every "being moved," there is a "has been moved." Secondly, where he says, **"And not only must . . ."** [637], he shows conversely that before any "has been moved," there is a "being moved."

829. He proves the first point with three arguments. The first is as follows. Let it be granted that a mobile body is moved through the magnitude J K in the primary time V Q. Now it is clear that another mobile body, which is of equal velocity and which began to be moved simultaneously with the first body, will be moved through half this magnitude in half the time. And since the first mobile body, which was given as being moved through the whole magnitude, has the same velocity, it follows that in half the time V Q it also was moved through the same magnitude, that is, through part of the whole magnitude J K. Hence it follows that that which is being moved previously was moved.

In order that that which is said here be understood more clearly, it should be realized that "having been moved" is said to be the terminus of a motion in the same way that a point is said to be the terminus of a line. For whatever line or part of a line you might take, it can always be said that, before the whole line ends, there is some point in respect to which the line is divided. And likewise before any motion, or any part of a motion, there is something which has been changed. For while the mobile body is in the state of being moved to some terminus, it has already crossed some sign in respect to which it is said to be already changed. Further, a point within a line is in potency before the line is divided, but it is in act when the line has been divided. For a point is the division of the line.

Likewise, that which I call a "has been changed" within a motion is in potency when the motion is not terminated there. But it is in act if the motion is terminated there. And since that which is in act is better known than that which is in potency, Aristotle proved that that which is continuously being moved has already been moved by means of another mobile body of equal velocity whose motion was already terminated. It would be the same situation if one were to prove that in some line there is a point in potency by means of another line of the same nature [ratio] which is actually divided.

830. He gives the second argument where he says, **"Again, if by taking . . ."** [635]. The argument is as follows.

In the total time V Q, or in any other time, a thing is said to have been moved because there is an ultimate "now" of that time. This does not mean that the body is moved in that "now," but that the motion is terminated in that "now." Hence, by "having been moved" he here means the termination of the motion and not the state of "being moved at some time." Therefore, the motion must be terminated in the ultimate "now" of the time which measures the motion. For this "now" determines the time; that is, it is the terminus of the time, just as a point is the terminus of a line. And every time must be an intermediate between two "nows," just as a line is an intermediate between two points. Hence, since "being moved" is in time, it follows that "having been moved" is in the "now," which is the terminus of the time. And if this is true of the motion which occurs in the total time, it must likewise be true of the parts of the motion which occur in part of the time. For it was al-

ready shown that that which is moved primarily in a total time is moved in each part of that time. Further, any given part of time is terminated at some "now." For the extremity of half of a time must be a division, that is, a "now," which divides the two parts of the time. For this reason it follows that that which is moved through a whole was previously moved in the middle, because the "now" determines the middle. And the same argument applies to any other part of the time. For no matter how time is divided, it is always found that every part of time is determined by two "nows." And no matter what "now" is taken after the first "now" of the time which measures the motion, the body has already been moved in that "now." For any "now" that is taken is the terminus of the time which measures the motion.

Every time is divisible into other times. Every time is an intermediate between two "nows." And, as has been proven, the body has been changed in every "now" which is an extremity of the time which measures the motion. Because of this it follows that whatever is being changed has been changed an infinite number of times. For "having been changed" is the terminus of a motion, just as a point is the terminus of a line, and as a "now" is the terminus of a time.

In any line an infinite number of points can be designated before the last point. And in any time an infinite number of "nows" can be designated before the last "now." For both of these are divisible to infinity. In the same way in any "being moved" an infinite number of "having been moved" can be designated. For a motion is divisible to infinity, just as is a line or a time, as was proven above.

831. He gives the third argument

where he says, "**Again, since a thing…**" [636]. The argument is as follows.

Whatever is being changed continuously, as long as it is not corrupted or does not cease to be moved, must either be "being moved" or "having been moved" in every "now" of the time in which it is moved. But it is not being moved in the "now," as was shown above. Therefore it is necessary that it has been moved in every "now" of the time which measures this continuous motion. But in any time there is an infinity of "nows." For the "now" is the division of time, and time is infinitely divisible. Therefore, whatever is being changed has been changed an infinite number of times. And thus it follows that before every "being moved" there is a "has been moved," not as if it existed outside of the "being moved," but in it as terminating one of its parts.

832. Next where he says, "**And not only must …**" [637], he proves conversely that before every "has been moved" there is a "being moved."

He proves this first in respect to the time, and secondly in respect to the thing according to which the motion occurs, where he says, "**Moreover, the truth …**" [640].

Concerning the first part he makes three points. First he states his position. Secondly, where he says, "**. . . Since everything that has changed …**" [638], he demonstrates a certain thing which is necessary to prove his position. Thirdly, where he says, "**Since, then, it has changed …**" [639], he brings forth the proof of his main position.

He says, therefore, first that not only is it necessary that whatever is being changed already has been changed, but it is also necessary that whatever has been changed was previously be-

ing changed. For "having been changed" is the terminus of "being moved." Hence, before a thing has been changed, there must be a preceding "being moved."

833. Next where he says, "**. . . since everything that has changed . . .**" [638], he gives a certain point which is necessary for the proof of his position. This point is that whatever is changed from something to something has been changed in time.

It must be noted that "having been changed" does not here mean the same thing as "motion being terminated." For it was shown above that that part of time in which a thing is said primarily to have been changed is indivisible. Rather, "having been changed" here means that the thing was previously being moved: as if one were to say that whatever was being moved was being moved in time.

He proves this as follows. If this were not true, then the thing would have been changed in a "now" from A to B, that is, from one terminus to another. Granting this, it follows that when it is in A, the terminus from which, it has not yet been changed in that "now." For it was shown above that that which is changed, when it has been changed, is not in the terminus from which but in the terminus to which. Hence it would follow that the mobile body would be in A and in B simultaneously. Hence it must be said it is in A in one "now" and has been changed in another "now." But between any two "nows" there is an intermediate time. For two "nows" cannot be immediately joined to each other, as was shown above. Thus it follows that whatever is changed is changed in time.

834. However it seems that this conclusion indicates that generation and

corruption occur in an instant and that there is no intermediary between the termini of generation and corruption. For if between the "now" when the body is in the terminus from which and the "now" when the body is in the terminus to which there is an intermediate time, it would then follow that there is an intermediary between being and non-being. For in that intermediate time that which is changed is neither being nor non-being.

But since the argument given here is demonstrative, it must be said that in a way it applies even to generation and corruption. For even these mutations in a way occur in a short period of time [momentaneae], although there cannot be any intermediary between their extremes.

Therefore it must be said that that which is changed from non-being to being, or vice versa, is not simultaneously in both non-being and being. But, as will be said in Book VIII, this does not mean that there is an ultimate instant in which that which is being generated is non-being. Rather this means that there is a first instant in which it is being, such that in the whole time which precedes that instant it is non-being. And between the time and the instant that terminates the motion there is no intermediary. Thus it is not necessary that there be an intermdiary between being and non-being. Rather, since the time which precedes the instant in which the body was first generated measures some motion, it follows that just as that instant in which the body was first generated is the terminus of the preceding time which measures the motion, likewise "to begin to be" is the terminus of the preceding motion.

Therefore, if this beginning of being be called generation, it is the terminus

of a motion, and it occurs in an instant. For the termination of motion, which is the state of "having been changed," occurs in an indivisible part of time, as was shown above.

But if generation be taken to mean this beginning of being together with the whole preceding motion of which it is the terminus, then it does not occur in an instant, but in time. In the whole preceding time that which is generated is non-being, and in the ultimate instant it is being. And the same must be said of corruption.

835. Next where he says, **"Since, then, it has changed . . ."** [639], he proves his main point with the following argument.

Whatever has been changed was changed in time, as has been proven. But all time is divisible. And that which is changed in some time is changed in every part of that time. Hence it must be said that that which has been changed in some whole time was previously being changed in half the time, and again in half of that half, and so on to infinity, for time is infinitely divisible. Hence it follows that whatever has been changed was previously being changed; and thus before every "having been changed" there is a preceding "being changed."

836. Next where he says, **"Moreover, the truth . . ."** [640], he proves the same thing by means of an argument dealing with that in respect to which the change occurs.

He does this first in respect to motions in quantity, and secondly in respect to the other mutations, where he says, **". . . for the same proof . . ."** [641].

He says, therefore, first that that which was said in common about all mutations from the point of view of time, can be more clearly understood from the point of view of magnitude.

For magnitude is more evident than time. And magnitude is continuous, just as time is. And there is change in magnitude, both in respect to place and in respect to increase and decrease.

Hence, let there be something which has changed from C to D. It cannot be said that the whole of C D is indivisible. For C D must be a part of some magnitude, just as the motion from C to D is a part of a whole motion. For magnitude and motion are divided in the same way, as was shown above. But if something which is indivisible is a part of a magnitude, it follows that two indivisibles would be immediately joined. This is impossible, as was shown above. Hence it cannot be said that the whole of C D is indivisible. Thus it must be that there is a certain magnitude between C and D, which consequently can be divided to infinity. But "being changed" in part of a magnitude is always prior to "having been changed" through the whole magnitude. Hence it must be that whatever has been changed previously was being changed, just as before any whole magnitude there must be a part of that magnitude.

837. Next where he says, "... for the same proof . . ." [641], he shows that the same thing must be true of the other mutations. These latter do not occur in respect to something continuous. He is speaking of alteration, which occurs between contrary qualities, and of generation and corruption, which occur between contradictory opposites. For although in these cases his point cannot be demonstrated from the point of view of the thing in respect to which the motion occurs, nevertheless one can consider the time in which such mutations occur, and proceed in the same way.

Hence in these three mutations, that is, alteration, corruption, and generation, only the first argument has value. But in the other three mutations, that is increase, decrease, and local motion, both arguments have value.

838. Next where he says, "So that which has . . ." [641], he concludes to his main point. He does this first in general, and secondly in a special way in respect to generation and corruption, where he says, "So it is evident. . ." [643].

He concludes, therefore, from the foregoing that whatever has been changed must previously have been "being changed," and whatever is being changed must previously have been changed. And thus it is true to say that in the state of "being changed" there is a previous "having been changed," and in the state of "having been changed" there is a previous "being changed." And hence it becomes clear that in no way is there a first.

The reason for this is that in motion an indivisible is not joined to an indivisible such that the whole motion is composed of indivisibles. For if this were the case, there would be a first. But this is not true, because motion is divisible to infinity, just as a line is. Lines are infinitely diminished by division, and infinitely increased by the addition which is opposed to diminishing; that is, that which is subtracted from one line is added to another, as was shown in Book III. For in a line it is clear that before any part of that line there is a point in the middle of that part. And before that middle point there is another part of the line, and so on to infinity. Nevertheless the line is not infinite, because before the first point of the line there is no part of the line.

Motion must be understood in the same way. For since any part of motion is divisible, then before any part of motion there is an indivisible in the middle of that part. This indivisible is a "has been changed." And before that indivisible there is a part of the motion, and so on to infinity. Nevertheless it does not follow that motion is infinite. For before the first indivisible of motion there is no part of the motion. However, that first indivisible is not called a "having been changed," just as the first point of a line is not called a division.

839. Next where he says, **"So it is evident . . ."** [643], he concludes the same thing in a special way in regard to generation and corruption.

He does this because in generation and corruption "having been changed" is related to "being changed" differently than in the other kinds of mutation.

For in the other cases "having been changed" and "being changed" occur in respect to the same thing. Thus "having been altered" and "being altered" both occur in respect to white. For "being altered" is "being changed" in respect to whiteness. And "having been altered" is "having been changed" in respect to whiteness. And the same must be said of local motion and of increase and decrease.

But in generation "having been changed" occurs in respect to one thing, and "being changed" occurs in respect to something else. For "having been changed" occurs in respect to the form. But "being changed" does not occur in respect to the negation of the form, which in itself is not susceptible to more and less. Rather "being changed" occurs in respect to something joined to the negation which is susceptible of more and less. This is a

quality. Therefore "having been generated," and also "having been corrupted," is the terminus of "being altered." And since a motion is named by the terminus to which, as was said at the beginning of Book V, this "being altered," which has two termini—a substantial form and a quality—is named in two ways. For it can be called a "being altered," and a "becoming" and "being corrupted."

And by "becoming" and "being corrupted" he here means that "being altered" which is terminated at being or non-being. Hence he says, ". . . that which has become must previously have been in process of becoming, and that which is in process of becoming must previously have become, everything (that is) that is divisible and continuous" [237b10–12]. This is added, as the Commentator says, to exclude certain things, that is, understanding and sensation, which occur indivisibly without a continuous motion. These things are called motions only equivocally, as is said in De Anima, III. Or else it can be said that the Philosopher adds this in order that generation be understood to include the whole preceding continuous motion.

840. But that which becomes, having previously been made, is found in different things in different ways.

For simple things, like air or fire, have a simple generation. In such things part is not generated before part. Rather the whole and the parts are generated and altered simultaneously. And in such things that which has been made was previously becoming itself and that which becomes previously has been made itself because of the continuity of the preceding alteration.

However, certain things are composed of dissimilar parts, one part of which is generated after another. For example, in an animal the heart is generated first, and in a house the foundation is generated first. In such things that which becomes was previously made, not itself, but something else. He adds that that which becomes has not always been previously made itself. Rather sometimes part of it has been made, for example, the foundation of the house. But since it is necessary to arrive at some part which becomes a whole at once, it must be that in some part that which becomes has been made in respect to some terminus taken in the preceding alteration. For example, while the animal is being generated, the heart has already been made. And while the heart is being generated, something else has already been made. This latter is not a part of the heart. Rather some alteration, ordained to the generation of the heart, has been completed.

And what is said of generation must also be said of corruption. For in that which becomes and is corrupted there is immediately present a certain infinity, because it is continuous. Becoming and being corrupted are themselves continua. And hence there is no becoming unless something has previously been made. And a thing has not been made unless it was previously becoming. And the same thing must be said of "being corrupted" and "having been corrupted." For "having been corrupted" is always prior to "being corrupted." And "being corrupted" is prior to "having been corrupted."

Hence it is clear that whatever has been made must previously have been becoming. And whatever becomes must previously have been made in some way. This is so because every magnitude and every time is divisible to infinity. And therefore in whatever time something becomes, this will not be the first time because there is a prior part. And that which was said of generation and corruption must also be understood to be true of illumination. For illumination is the terminus of the local motion of an illuminating body, just as generation and corruption are the termini of alterations.

The Finite and the Infinite Are Found Together in Magnitude, Time, Motion, and the Mobile Body

The Text of Aristotle
Chapter 7

644. *Now since the motion of everything that is in motion occupies a period of time, and a greater magnitude is traversed in a longer time, it is impossible that a thing should undergo a finite motion in an infinite time, if this is understood to mean not that the same motion or a part of it is continually repeated, but that the whole infinite time is occupied by the whole finite motion.*　　　　　　　　　　　　　　　　　　　　　　　　　　　　　**237b23–26**

645. *In all cases where a thing is in motion with uniform velocity it is clear that the finite magnitude is traversed in a finite time. For if we take a part of the motion which shall be a measure of the whole, the whole motion is completed in as many equal periods of the time as there are parts of the motion. Consequently, since these parts are finite, both in size individually and in number collectively, the whole time must also be finite; for it will be a multiple of the portion, equal to the time occupied in completing the aforesaid part multiplied by the number of the parts.*　　　　　　　　　　　　　　　　　　　　　　　　　　　**237b26–33**

646. *But it makes no difference even if the velocity is not uniform. For let us suppose that the line AB represents a finite stretch over which a thing has been moved in the infinite time, and let CD be the infinite time. Now if one part of the stretch must have been traversed before another part (this is clear, that in the earlier and in the later part of the time a different part of the stretch has been traversed; for as the time lengthens a different part of the motion will always be completed in it, whether the thing in motion changes with uniform velocity or not; and whether the rate of motion increases or diminishes or remains stationary this is none the less so), let us then take AE a part of the whole stretch of motion AB which shall be a measure of AB. Now this part of the motion occupies a certain period of the infinite time: it cannot itself occupy an infinite time, for we are assuming that that is occupied by the whole AB. And if again I take another part equal to AE, that also must occupy a finite time in consequence of the same assumption. And if I go on taking parts in this way, on the one hand there is no part which will be a measure of the infinite time (for the infinite cannot be composed of finite parts whether equal or unequal, because there must be some unity which will be a measure of things finite in multitude or in magnitude, which, whether they are equal or unequal, are none the less limited in magnitude); while on the other hand the finite stretch of motion AB is a certain multiple of AE: consequently the motion AB must be accomplished in a finite time. Moreover it is the same with coming to rest as with motion. And so it is impossible for one and the same thing to be infinitely in process of becoming or of perishing.*　　　　　　　　　　**237b34–238a19**

647. *The same reasoning will prove that in a finite time there cannot be an infinite extent of motion or of coming to rest, whether the motion is regular or irregular. For if we take a part which shall be a measure of the whole time, in this part a certain fraction, not the whole, of the magnitude will be traversed, because we assume that the traversing of the whole occupies all the time. Again, in another equal part of the time another part of the magnitude will be traversed; and similarly in each part of the time that we take, whether equal or unequal to that part originally taken. It makes no difference whether the parts are equal or not, if only each is finite; for it is clear that while the time is exhausted by the subtraction of its parts, the infinite magnitude will not be thus exhausted, since the process of subtraction is finite both in respect of the quantity subtracted and of the number of times a subtraction is made. Consequently the*

infinite magnitude will not be traversed in a finite time; and it makes no difference whether the magnitude is infinite in only one direction or in both; for the same reasoning will hold good.
238a20–31

648. *This having been proved, it is evident that neither can a finite magnitude traverse an infinite magnitude in a finite time, the reason being the same as that given above: in part of the time it will traverse a finite magnitude and in each several part likewise, so that in the whole time it will traverse a finite magnitude.*
238a32–36

649. *And since a finite magnitude will not traverse an infinite in a finite time, it is clear that neither will an infinite traverse a finite in a finite time. For if the infinite could traverse the finite, the finite could traverse the infinite; for it makes no difference which of the two is the thing in motion: either case involves the traversing of the infinite by the finite. For when the infinite magnitude A is in motion a part of it, say CD, will occupy the finite B, and then another, and then another, and so on to infinity. Thus the two results will coincide: the infinite will have completed a motion over the finite and the finite will have traversed the infinite; for it would seem to be impossible for the motion of the infinite over the finite to occur in any way other than by the finite traversing the infinite either by locomotion over it or by measuring it. Therefore, since this is impossible, the infinite cannot traverse the finite.*
238a36–238b14

650. *Nor again will the infinite traverse the infinite in a finite time. Otherwise it would also traverse the finite, for the infinite includes the finite.*
238b14–15

651. *We can further prove this in the same way by taking the time as our starting-point.*
238b16

652. *Since, then, it is established that in a finite time neither will the finite traverse the infinite, nor the infinite the finite, nor the infinite the infinite, it is evident also that in a finite time there cannot be infinite motion; for what difference does it make whether we take the motion or the magnitude to be infinite? If either of the two is infinite, the other must be so likewise; for all locomotion is in space.*
238b17–22

COMMENTARY OF ST. THOMAS

841. After the Philosopher has treated the division of motion, he here treats the finite and the infinite in motion. For since division pertains to the nature [ratio] of a continuum, so do the finite and the infinite. Moreover, he has shown above that division is found simultaneously in motion, magnitude, time, and the mobile body. He now shows that the same is true of the infinite.

Concerning this he makes three points. First he shows that the infinite is found in the same way in magnitude and in time. Secondly, where he says, **"This having been proved . . ."** [648], he shows that the infinite is also found in the mobile body in the same way. Thirdly, where he says, **"Since, then, it**

is . . ." [652], he shows that the infinite is found in motion in the same way.

Concerning the first part he makes two points. First he shows that if magnitude is finite, then time cannot be infinite. Secondly, where he says, **"The same reasoning . . ."** [647], he shows conversely that if time is finite, then magnitude cannot be infinite.

Concerning the first part he makes two points. First he states his intention. Secondly, where he says, **"In all cases where . . ."** [645], he proves his position.

842. He first repeats two things which are necessary to prove his position. One of these is that whatever is moved is moved in time. The second is that in a longer time a greater magni-

tude will be crossed by the same mobile body. From these two suppositions he intends to prove a third proposition; namely, it is impossible to cross a finite magnitude in an infinite time. This is not to be understood as meaning that the mobile body re-crosses the same magnitude or some part thereof many times. Rather he means that in the whole time the body is moved through the whole magnitude. He adds this in order to exclude circular motion, which always occurs in a finite magnitude but which can occur in an infinite time, as he will say in Book VIII.

843. Next where he says, **"In all cases where . . ."** [645], he proves his position. He does this first on the assumption that the mobile body is moved through the whole magnitude with equal velocity. Secondly, where he says, **"But it makes no . . ."** [646], he proves his point on the assumption that the body is not moved uniformly and regularly.

He says, therefore, first that if there be a mobile body which is moved through a whole magnitude with equal velocity, then, if it crosses a finite magnitude, this must occur in a finite time. For let there be one part of the magnitude which measures the whole; for example, a third or a fourth of the magnitude. Hence, if the mobile body is moved through the whole magnitude with equal velocity, and if "equal velocity" means that an equal space is crossed in an equal time, it follows that the mobile body crosses the whole magnitude in as many equal times as there are parts of the magnitude. For example, if we take a fourth part of the magnitude, the body will cross it in a certain time. And it will cross another fourth in another equal time. And

hence it will cross the whole magnitude in four equal times.

Therefore, since the parts of the magnitude are finite in number, and since each part is finite in quantity, and since the body crosses all the parts in as many equal times, it follows that the whole time in which the body crosses the whole magnitude is finite. For it will be measured by a finite time, because there are as many times in which the body crosses a part of the magnitude as there are parts of the magnitude. And thus the total time will have been multiplied in respect to the multiplication of the parts. And every multiple is measured by that which is under the multiple. For example, a double is measured by a half, and a triple by a third, and so forth. Furthermore, the time in which the body crosses part of the magnitude is finite. For if it were infinite, it would follow that the body would cross both the whole and the part in an equal time. This is contrary to what was supposed. Hence the total time must be finite, because no infinity is measured by something which is finite.

844. But someone might say that, although the parts of the magnitude are equal and measure the whole magnitude, nevertheless it can happen that the parts of the time are not equal; for example, when there is not an equal velocity in a whole motion. And thus the time in which the body is moved through part of the magnitude will not measure the time in which it is moved through the whole magnitude. Consequently, where he says, **"But it makes no . . ."** [646], he shows that this does not affect his position.

Let there be a finite space A B which is crossed in an infinite time C D. In this whole motion one part must be crossed prior to another. And it is also clear that different parts of the magnitude are crossed in different parts of the time. Thus it is necessary that two parts of the magnitude are not crossed in one and the same part of the time, and in two parts of the time one and the same part of the magnitude is not crossed. And thus, if some part of the magnitude is crossed in some time, then in a longer time not only that part but also other parts of the magnitude must be crossed. And this is true whether the mobile body is moved with equal velocity or not. The latter occurs either when the velocity is increased more and more, as in natural motions, or when it is decreased more and more, as in violent motions.

On these suppositions let A E be a part of the space A B, and let it measure the whole of A B such that it is some part of A B, either a third or a fourth. Hence this part of the space is crossed in some finite time. It cannot be held that A E is crossed in an infinite time. For the whole space is crossed in an infinite time, and a part is crossed in less time than the whole.

If we take another part of the space equal to A E, this part must be crossed in a finite time for the same reason, for the whole space is crossed in an infinite time.

By continuing this process one will take as many finite times as there are parts of the space. The total time in which the body is moved through the whole space will be constituted by these times.

But it is impossible for any part of an infinite to measure a whole, either in respect to magnitude or in respect to multitude. For it is impossible for an infinite to consist of parts which are finite in number, each one of which is fi-

nite in quantity, either equal or unequal. For whatever is measured by some one thing, in respect to either multitude or magnitude, must be finite.

I say "multitude and magnitude" because something is measured because it has a finite magnitude, whether the measuring parts are equal or unequal. When they are equal, the part measures the whole in both multitude and magnitude. But when the measuring parts are unequal, the part measures the whole in multitude but not in magnitude. Thus it is clear that any time which has parts which are finite in number and in quantity, either equal or unequal, is finite. But the finite space A B is measured by as many finite things as happen to compose A B. And the parts of the time and the parts of the magnitude must be equal in number. And each part must be finite in quantity. Therefore it follows that the body is moved through the whole space as in a finite time.

845. Next where he says, **"The same reasoning . . ."** [647], he shows conversely that if time is finite, then magnitude is also finite.

He says that it can be shown with the same argument that an infinite space cannot be crossed in a finite time. Nor indeed can rest be infinite in a finite time. It makes no difference whether the body is moved regularly, that is, with equal velocity, or irregularly. Since the time is given as finite, let us take a part in this time which measures the whole time. In this part of the time the mobile body crosses part of the magnitude (but not the whole magnitude, for it crosses the whole magnitude in the whole time). Further in another equal time it crosses another part of the magnitude. And in the same way there is a part of the magnitude for each part of the time. It makes no difference whether the second part of the magnitude is equal to the first part (which happens when the body is moved with equal velocity) or is not equal to the first part (which happens when the body is not moved with equal velocity). This makes no difference as long as each part taken in the magnitude is finite. This must be said, for otherwise the body would be moved in part of the time as much as it is moved in the whole. Thus it is clear that by a division of the time the whole infinite space is exhausted by a finite subtraction. For since the time is divided into equal finite parts, and since there must be as many parts of the magnitude as there are of the time, it would follow that an infinite space would be consumed by a finite subtraction. For the magnitude must be divided in as many ways as the time. But this is impossible. Therefore it is clear that an infinite space is not crossed in a finite time. And it makes no difference whether the magnitude of the space is infinite in one direction or in both. For the same argument applies to both cases.

846. Next where he says, **"This having been proved . . ."** [648], he shows that the finite and the infinite are found in the mobile body in the same way that they are found in magnitude and in time.

Concerning this he makes three points. First he shows that, if time and magnitude are finite, then the mobile body is not infinite. Secondly, where he says **"Nor again will . . ."** [650], he shows that if magnitude is infinite and time finite, then the mobile body is not infinite. Thirdly, where he says, **"We can further prove . . ."** [651]. he shows that, if magnitude is finite and time in-

finite, then the mobile body cannot be infinite.

He proves the first point with two arguments. In the first argument he says that since it has been demonstrated that a finite magnitude is not crossed in an infinite time, nor is an infinite magnitude crossed in a finite time, for the same reason it is clear that an infinite mobile body cannot cross a finite magnitude in a finite time. Let us take some part of the finite time. In that part of the time the finite space will be crossed by a part, but not the whole, of the mobile body. And in another part of the time the same thing will happen, and so forth. And thus there must be as many parts of the mobile body as there are parts of the time. But the infinite is not composed of finite parts, as was shown. Therefore it follows that a mobile body which is moved in a total finite time is finite.

847. He gives the second argument where he says, **"And since a finite . . ."** [649].

This second argument differs from the first one because in the first argument he assumed as a principle the middle proposition which he used in a proof above. But here he uses as a principle the conclusion which he demonstrated above. It was shown above that a finite mobile body cannot cross an infinite space in a finite time. Hence for the same reason it is clear that an infinite mobile body cannot cross a finite space in a finite time.

If an infinite mobile body crosses a finite space, it follows that a finite mobile body also crosses a finite space. For since both the mobile body and the space are quantified, when these two quantities are given, it makes no difference which one is moved and which one is at rest. In this case the space is at rest, and the mobile body is moved.

It is clear that, whichever is given as being moved, the finite crosses the infinite. Let the infinite body A be in motion. And let C D be some finite part of A. When the whole is being moved, the finite part C D will be in the space signified by B. And when the motion is continued, another part of the infinite mobile body will become located in that space, and so forth to infinity. Hence, just as the mobile body crosses the space, the space also in a way crosses the mobile body insofar as the diverse parts of the mobile body are successively alternated with the corresponding space. Hence it is clear that an infinite mobile body is moved through a finite space, and simultaneously the finite crosses the infinite. For the infinite cannot be moved through a finite space unless the finite crosses the infinite, either in such a way that the finite is carried through the infinite (as when the mobile body is finite and the space is infinite) or at least in such a way that the finite measures the infinite (as when the space is finite and the mobile body infinite). For in the latter case, although the finite is not carried through the infinite, nevertheless the finite measures the infinite insofar as the finite space becomes joined to the individual parts of the infinite mobile body. Now since this is impossible, it follows that the infinite mobile body does not cross a finite space in a finite time.

848. Next where he says, **"Nor again will . . ."** [650], he shows that the mobile body cannot be infinite when the space is infinite and the time finite. He says that an infinite mobile body does not cross an infinite space in a finite time. For in every infinite there is a finite. If, therefore, an infinite mobile body crosses an infinite space in a finite time, it follows that it crosses a finite space in a finite time. This is contrary to what was shown above.

849. Next where he says, **"We can further prove . . ."** [651], he says that the same demonstration applies if the time is infinite and the space finite. For if an infinite mobile body crosses a finite space in an infinite time, it follows that in a finite part of that time it crosses a part of the space. And thus the infinite will cross the finite in a finite time, which is contrary to what was shown above.

850. Next where he says, **"Since, then, it is . . ."** [652], he shows that the finite and the infinite are found in motion in the same way as in the foregoing.

He says that a finite mobile body does not cross an infinite space, and an infinite mobile body does not cross a finite space, and an infinite mobile body does not cross an infinite space in a finite time. From these points it follows that there cannot be an infinite motion in a finite time. For the quantity of motion is taken according to the quantity of space. Hence it makes no difference whether the motion or the magnitude is said to be infinite. If one of these is infinite, the other must be infinite, for there cannot be a part of local motion outside of place.

The Division of Rest and of Coming to Rest

The Text of Aristotle
Chapter 8

653. *Since everything to which motion or rest is natural is in motion or at rest in the natural time, place, and manner, that which is coming to a stand, when it is coming to a stand, must be in motion; for if it is not in motion it must be at rest; but that which is at rest cannot be coming to rest.*　　　　　　　238b23–26

654. *From this it evidently follows that coming to a stand must occupy a period of time; for the motion of that which is in motion occupies a period of time, and that which is coming to a stand has been shown to be in motion: consequently coming to a stand must occupy a period of time.*

Again, since the terms "quicker" and "slower" are used only of that which occupies a period of time, and the process of coming to a stand may be quicker or slower, the same conclusion follows.　　　　　　　238b26–30

655. *And that which is coming to a stand must be coming to a stand in any part of the primary time in which it is coming to a stand. For if it is coming to a stand in neither of two parts into which the time may be divided, it cannot be coming to a stand in the whole time, with the result that that which is coming to a stand will not be coming to a stand. If on the other hand it is coming to a stand in only one of the two parts of the time, the whole cannot be the primary time in which it is coming to a stand; for it is coming to a stand in the whole time not primarily but in virtue of something distinct from itself, the argument being the same as that which we used above about things in motion.*　　　　　　　238b31–36

656. *And just as there is no primary time in which that which is in motion is in motion, so too there is no primary time in which that which is coming to a stand is coming to a stand, there being no primary stage either of being in motion or of coming to a stand. For let AB be the primary time in which a thing is coming to a stand. Now AB cannot be without parts; for there cannot be motion in that which is without parts, because the moving thing would necessarily have been already moved for part of the time of its movement: and that which is coming to a stand has been shown to be in motion. But since AB is therefore divisible, the thing is coming to a stand in every one of the parts of AB; for we have shown above that it is coming to a stand in every one of the parts in which it is primarily coming to a stand. Since, then, that in which primarily a thing is coming to a stand must be a period of time and not something indivisible, and since all time is infinitely divisible, there cannot be anything in which primarily it is coming to a stand.*　　　　　　　238b36–239a10

657. *Nor again can there be a primary time at which the being at rest of that which is at rest occurred; for it cannot have occurred in that which has no parts, because there cannot be motion in that which is indivisible, and that in which rest takes place is the same as that in which motion takes place: for we defined a state of rest to be the state of a thing to which motion is natural but which is not in motion when (that is to say in that in which) motion would be natural to it. Again, our use of the phrase "being at rest" also implies that the previous state of a thing is still unaltered, not one point only but two at least being thus needed to determine its presence: consequently that in which a thing is at rest cannot be without parts. Since, then, it is divisible, it must be a period of time, and the thing must be at rest in every one of its parts, as may be shown by the same method as that used above in similar demonstrations.*

So there can be no primary part of the time; and the reason is that rest and motion are always in a period of time, and a period of time has no primary part any more than a magnitude or in fact anything continuous; for everything continuous is divisible into an infinite number of parts.   **239a10–22**

658. *And since everything that is in motion is in motion in a period of time and changes from something to something, when its motion is comprised within a particular period of time essentially—that is to say when it fills the whole and not merely a part of the time in question—it is impossible that in that time that which is in motion should be over against some particular thing primarily.*   **239a23–26**

659. *For if a thing—itself and each of its parts—occupies the same space for a definite period of time, it is at rest; for it is in just these circumstances that we use the term "being at rest"—when at one moment after another it can be said with truth that a thing, itself and its parts, occupies the same space. So if this is being at rest it is impossible for that which is changing to be as a whole, at the time when it is primarily changing, over against any particular thing (for the whole period of time is divisible), so that in one part of it after another it will be true to say that the thing, itself and its parts, occupies the same space. If this is not so and the aforesaid proposition is true only at a single moment, then the thing will be over against a particular thing not for any period of time but only at a moment that limits the time. It is true that at any moment it is always over against something stationary; but it is not at rest; for at a moment it is not possible for anything to be either in motion or at rest. So while it is true to say that that which is in motion is at a moment not in motion and is opposite some particular thing, it cannot in a period of time be over against that which is at rest; for that would involve the conclusion that that which is in locomotion is at rest.*   **239a26–239b4**

COMMENTARY OF ST. THOMAS

851. After the Philosopher has treated those things which pertain to the division of motion, he here treats those things which pertain to the division of rest. And since "coming to rest" is the generation of rest, as was said in Book V, he first treats those things which pertain to "coming to rest." Secondly, where he says, **"Nor again can there . . ."** [657], he treats those things which pertain to rest.

Concerning the first part he makes three points. First he shows that whatever is "coming to rest" is being moved. Secondly, where he says, **"From this it evidently . . ."** [654], he shows that whatever is "coming to rest" is "coming to rest" in time. Thirdly, where he says, **"And that which is . . ."** [655], he explains how there is a first in "coming to rest."

852. He shows the first point [653] as follows. Whatever is naturally subject to motion must be either in motion or

at rest at the time and in the respect and in the manner in which it is naturally subject to motion. But that which is "coming to rest," that is, that which tends toward rest, is not yet at rest. For otherwise a thing would simultaneously be tending toward rest and be at rest. Therefore, whatever is "coming to rest," that is, whatever is tending toward rest, is being moved while it is "coming to rest."

853. Next where he says, **"From this it evidently . . ."** [654], he proves with two arguments that whatever is "coming to rest" is "coming to rest" in time. The first argument is as follows. Whatever is moved is moved in time, as was proven above. But whatever is "coming to rest" is being moved, as we have just now proven. Therefore, whatever is "coming to rest" is "coming to rest" in time.

The second argument is as follows. Fastness and slowness are determined according to time. But "coming to rest," that is, tending toward rest, occurs faster and slower. Therefore whatever is "coming to rest" is "coming to rest" in time.

854. Next where he says, **"And that which is . . ."** [655], he explains how there is a first in "coming to rest."

Concerning this he makes two points. First he explains how a thing is said to come to rest in a primary time, insofar as the primary is opposed to that which is called partial. Secondly, where he says, **"And just as there . . ."** [656], he shows that there is no primary part in "coming to rest."

He says, therefore, first [655] that if in some time a thing is said to be "coming to rest" primarily and per se, it must be "coming to rest" in every part of that time. Let the time be divided into two parts. If it be said that it is not "coming to rest" in either part, it follows that it is not "coming to rest" in the whole time in which it was given as "coming to rest." Therefore, that which is "coming to rest" is not "coming to rest."

Nor can it be said that it is "coming to rest" in only one part of the time. For then it would not be primarily "coming to rest" in the whole time, but only by reason [ratio] of a part. Hence it follows that it is "coming to rest" in both parts of the time. Thus it is said to be "coming to rest" primarily in the whole time because it is "coming to rest" in both parts of the time, as was said above of that which is being moved.

855. Next where he says, **"And just as there . . ."** [656], he shows that there is no first part in "coming to rest."

He says that just as there is no primary part of time in which a mobile body is being moved, likewise there is no primary part in "coming to rest."

For neither in "being moved" nor in "coming to rest" can there be a primary part.

If this is not conceded, let A B be a primary part of time in which something is "coming to rest." A B cannot be indivisible. For it was shown above that there is no motion in an indivisible time, because that which is being moved has always already been moved through something, as was shown above. Further, it has just now been demonstrated that whatever is "coming to rest" is being moved. Hence it follows that A B is divisible. Therefore the body is "coming to rest" in every part of A B. For it was just shown that when in some time a thing is said to be "coming to rest" primarily and per se, and not by reason [ratio] of a part, then it is "coming to rest" in every part of that time. Therefore, since the part is prior to the whole, A B is not the first thing in which the body was "coming to rest." But everything in which something is "coming to rest" is a time. And no time is indivisible, rather every time is infinitely divisible. Therefore, it follows that there will be no first in which a thing is "coming to rest."

856. Next where he says, **"Nor again can there . . ."** [657], he shows that the same is true of rest.

Concerning this he makes two points. First he shows that there is no first in rest. Secondly, where he says, **"And since everything . . ."** [658], he considers a point which distinguishes motion from rest.

Since the same argument explains why there is no first in motion, "coming to rest," and rest, therefore from the things which he has said above about motion and "coming to rest" he concludes that the same is true of rest. He says that there is no first in which that which is at rest is at rest. To prove this he repeats a certain point which was proven above; namely, nothing is at rest in the indivisible of time. He also repeats two arguments by which this was proven above.

The first is that there is no motion in the indivisible of time. But "being moved" and "being at rest" occur in the same thing. For we speak of "being at rest" only when that which is naturally subject to motion is not being moved at the time and in the respect (for example, in respect to a quality or place or some such thing) in which it is naturally subject to motion. Therefore it follows that nothing is at rest in the indivisible of time.

The second argument is as follows. We say that a thing is at rest when it is the same now as it was before. Thus we do not judge a state of rest by only one instance, but by a comparison of two instances to each other such that there is the same state in the two instances. But in the indivisible of time there is no now and before; there are not two instances. Therefore that part of time in which a thing is at rest is not indivisible.

Having proven this he proceeds to the proof of his main point. If that in which a thing is at rest is divisible, having in itself a prior and a posterior, it follows that this is a time. For this is the nature [ratio] of time. And if this is a time, then the body must be at rest in every part of that time. He will demonstrate this in the same way that he argued above in regard to motion and "coming to rest." If the body is not at rest in every part, then it is at rest either in no part or in only one part. If it is at rest in no part, then it is not at rest in the whole. If it is at rest in only one part, then it is at rest primarily in that part and not in the whole. If the body is

at rest in every part of the time, then there will be no first in rest, just as there is no first in motion.

The reason for this is that everything is at rest or in motion in time. But in time there is no first, just as there is no first in magnitude or in any continuum. For every continuum is infinitely divisible, and thus before any part there is always a smaller part. And thus there is no first in motion or in "coming to rest" or in rest.

857. Next where he says, **"And since everything . . ."** [658], he considers a certain point which distinguishes that which is being moved from that which is at rest.

First he states his point, and secondly he proves it, where he says, **"For if a thing . . ."** [659].

In regard to the first part he sets forth two suppositions. The first is that whatever is moved is moved in time. The second is that whatever is changed is changed from one terminus to another. From these two propositions he intends to draw this conclusion: if a mobile body is moved primarily and per se, and not just by reason [ratio] of a part, it cannot exist in respect to some one and the same state of that in which the motion occurs (for example, in one and the same place or in one and the same disposition of whiteness) in some time (taking the time in itself and not in respect to some part of time).

It is necessary to take "mobile body" here as meaning "that which is moved primarily." For nothing prevents a body being moved in respect to a part while the body itself remains through the whole time in one and the same place. For example, a man who is sitting moves his foot.

Further in respect to the time he says, **". . . when its motion is comprised within a particular period of** time essentially—that is to say when it fills the whole and not merely a part of the time in question . . ." [239a24–25]. For while a thing is being moved, it can be said to be in some one and the same place on a certain day. But this is said because it was in that place, not during the whole day, but in some "now" of that day.

858. Next where he says, "For if a thing..." [659], he proves his position.

He says that if that which is changed is through some whole time in some one and the same state, for example, in one place, it follows that it is at rest. For in a certain time both the body itself and each of its parts are in one and the same place. And it was said above that a body is at rest when it can be truly said that it and its parts are in one and the same state in different "nows." Hence, if this is the definition of "being at rest," and if a body is not simultaneously in motion and at rest, then it follows that that which is being moved is not totally in something, for example, in one and the same place, in respect to some whole time, and not just some part of time.

He explains why this follows. All time is divisible into diverse parts, one of which is prior to another. Hence, if through a whole time a body is in some one thing, it will be true to say that in the different parts of time the mobile body and its parts are in one and the same thing, for example, place. But this is "being at rest." For if it is said that in the diverse parts of time the body is not in one and the same state, but is in one and the same state only through one "now," it does not follow that there is a time in which it is in one and the same thing. Rather it follows that it is in one and the same thing in respect to the "now."

Moreover, although it follows that a thing is at rest if it is in one and the same state in time, nevertheless this does not follow if it is there in only one "now." For in each "now" of a time in which there is motion that which is being moved remains or exists in respect to that in which the motion occurs, for example, in respect to place or quality or quantity. However, it is not at rest, for it has already been shown that there is no rest or motion in the "now." Rather it is true to say that nothing is being moved in the "now." And in this "now" even that which is being moved is somewhere accidentally.

But that which is being moved is not at rest accidentally in time. For otherwise, while a thing is being moved, it would be at rest. This is impossible. It follows, therefore, that that which is being moved, while it is being moved, is never in one and the same state through two "nows," but only through one.

859. This is clear in local motion. Let there be a magnitude A C which is divided in half at B. And let there be a body O which is equal to each of these, that is, A B and B C. And let O be moved from A B to B C. If these places are taken as totally distinct from each other, then there are only two places here. But it is clear that the mobile body leaves the first place and enters the second place successively and not all at once. Hence, insofar as place is divisible to infinity, the number of places is multiplied to infinity. For if A B is divided in half at D, and if B C is divided in half at E, it is clear that D E will be a place different from both A B and B C. And if this division is carried on infinitely in the same way, there will always be another place.

The same thing is also clear in alteration. For that which changes from white to black crosses through infinite grades of whiteness, blackness, and intermediate colors.

However, although there are an infinity of intermediaries, it does not follow that the body will not arrive at the extremity. For these middle places are not infinite in act, but only in potency, just as magnitude is not actually divided to infinity, but is divisible in potency.

The Arguments of Zeno, Who Tried to Deny All Motion, Are Answered

The Text of Aristotle
Chapter 9

660. *Zeno's reasoning, however, is fallacious, when he says that if everything when it occupies an equal space is at rest, and if that which is in locomotion is always occupying such a space at any moment, the flying arrow is therefore motionless. This is false; for time is not composed of indivisible moments any more than any other magnitude is composed of indivisibles.* **239b5–9**

661. *Zeno's arguments about motion, which cause so much disquietude to those who try to solve the problems that they present, are four in number. The first asserts the non-existence of motion on the ground that that which is in locomotion must arrive at the halfway stage before it arrives at the goal. This we have discussed above.* **239b9–14**

662. *The second is the so-called "Achilles," and it amounts to this, that in a race the quickest runner can never overtake the slowest, since the pursuer must first reach the point whence the pursued started, so that the slower must always hold a lead. This argument is the same in principle as that which depends on bisection, though it differs from it in that the spaces with which we successively have to deal are not divided into halves. The result of the argument is that the slower is not overtaken; but it proceeds along the same lines as the bisection-argument (for in both a division of the space in a certain way leads to the result that the goal is not reached, though the "Achilles" goes further in that it affirms that even the quickest runner in legendary tradition must fail in his pursuit of the slowest), so that the solution must be the same. And the axiom that that which holds a lead is never overtaken is false: it is not overtaken, it is true, while it holds a lead: but it is overtaken nevertheless if it is granted that it traverses the finite distance prescribed. These then are two of his arguments.*
239b14–30

663. *The third is that already given above, to the effect that the flying arrow is at rest, which result follows from the assumption that time is composed of moments: if this assumption is not granted, the conclusion will not follow.* **239b30–33**

664. *The fourth argument is that concerning the two rows of bodies, each row being composed of an equal number of bodies of equal size, passing each other on a race-course as they proceed with equal velocity in opposite directions, the one row originally occupying the space between the goal and the middle point of the course and the other that between the middle point and the starting-post. This, he thinks, involves the conclusion that half a given time is equal to double that time.* **239b33–240a1**

665. *The fallacy of the reasoning lies in the assumption that a body occupies an equal time in passing with equal velocity a body that is in motion and a body of equal size that is at rest; which is false.* **240a1–4**

666. *For instance (so runs the argument), let AA be the stationary bodies of equal size, BB the bodies, equal in number and in size to AA, originally occupying the half of the course from the starting-post to the middle of the A's, and CC those originally occupying the other half from the goal to the middle of the A's, equal in number, size, and velocity to BB. Then three consequences follow:*

First, as the B's and the C's pass one another, the first B reaches the last C at the same moment as the first C reaches the last B. Secondly, at this moment the first C has passed all the A's, whereas the first B has passed only half the A's, and has consequently occupied only half the time occupied by the first C, since each of the two occupies an equal time in passing each A.

Thirdly, at the same moment all the B's have passed all the C's: for the first C and the first B will simultaneously reach the opposite ends of the course , since (so says Zeno) the time occupied by the first C in passing each of the B's is equal to that occupied by it in passing each of the A's, because an equal time is occupied by both the first B and the first C in passing all the A's. This is the argument, but it presupposed the aforesaid fallacious assumption. **240a4–18**

667. *Nor in reference to contradictory change shall we find anything unanswerable in the argument that if a thing is changing from not-white, say, to white, and is in neither condition, then it will be neither white nor not-white; for the fact that it is not wholly in either condition will not preclude us from calling it white or not-white. We call a thing white or not-white not necessarily because it is wholly either one or the other, but because most of its parts or the most essential parts of it are so: not being in a certain condition is different from not being wholly in that condition. So, too, in the case of being and not-being and all other conditions which stand in a contradictory relation: while the changing thing must of necessity be in one of the two opposites, it is never wholly in either.* **240a119–29**

668. *Again, in the case of circles and spheres and everything whose motion is confined within the space that it occupies, it is not true to say that the motion can be nothing but rest, on the ground that such things in motion, themselves and their parts will occupy the same position for a period of time, and that therefore they will be at once at rest and in motion. For in the first place the parts do not occupy the same position for any period of time: and in the second place the whole also is always changing to a different position; for if we take the orbit as described from a point A on a circumference, it will not be the same as the orbit as described from B or C or any other point on the same circumference except in an accidental sense, the sense that is to say in which a musical man is the same as a man. Thus one orbit is always changing into another, and the thing will never be at rest. And it is the same with the sphere and everything else whose motion is confined within the space that it occupies.* **240a29–240b7**

COMMENTARY OF ST. THOMAS

860. After the Philosopher has treated the division of motion and rest, he here refutes certain things which have caused some to fall into error concerning motion.

Concerning this he makes three points. First he answers the arguments of Zeno, who denied all motion. Secondly, where he says, **"Our next point is . . ."** [669], he shows that the indivisible is not moved. This is contrary to Democritus, who held that indivisibles are always in motion. Thirdly, where he says, **"Our next point is . . ."** [673], he shows that every mutation is finite. This is contrary to Heraclitus, who held that everything is always in motion.

Concerning the first part he makes two points. First he gives and answers

a certain argument of Zeno which pertains to what he has just set forth in regard to motion. Secondly, where he says, **"Zeno's arguments . . ."** [661], he explains all of Zeno's arguments in order.

861. He says, therefore, first that Zeno reasons fallaciously and uses an apparent syllogism to show that nothing is moved, not even that which seems to be moved with the greatest speed, like a flying arrow. His argument is as follows. Whatever is in a place equal to itself is either in motion or at rest. But in each "now" whatever is being moved is in a place equal to itself. Therefore in each "now" it is either moved or at rest. But it is not moved. Therefore it is at rest. Moreover, if it is not moved in any "now,"

but rather seems to be at rest, then it follows that in the total time it is not moved, but rather is at rest.

This argument could be answered by means of that which was shown above; namely, in the "now" there is neither motion nor rest. But this answer does not refute Zeno's intention. For it is sufficient for Zeno's purpose if it can be shown that there is no motion in a whole time. And this seems to follow from the fact that there is no motion in the "now" of time. Therefore Aristotle answers in another way, saying that the conclusion of the argument is false and does not follow from the premises.

In order that a thing be moved in some time, it must be moved in each part of that time. But the "now" is not a part of time. For time is not composed of indivisible "nows," just as magnitude is not composed of indivisibles, as was proven above. Hence from the fact that there is no motion in the "now," it does not follow that there is no motion in time.

862. Next where he says, **"Zeno's arguments . . ."** [661], he gives in order all the arguments which Zeno used to deny motion.

Concerning this he makes three points. First he shows how Zeno denied local motion with his arguments. Secondly, where he says, **"Nor in reference to . . ."** [667], he shows how Zeno denied the other species of mutation. Thirdly, where he says, **"Again, in the case . . ."** [668], he shows how Zeno denied circular motion in a special way.

863. Concerning the first part he gives four arguments. He says that Zeno used four arguments against motion which have caused difficulty for many who wished to answer them.

The first argument is as follows. If a thing is being moved through a whole space, it must first cross half that space before it comes to the end. But since that half is divisible, it must first cross half of that half, and so forth to infinity, since magnitude is infinitely divisible. But the infinite cannot be crossed in a finite time. Therefore nothing can be moved.

Aristotle says that he has answered this argument above at the beginning of Book VI where he said that time is divided to infinity in the same way that magnitude is divided to infinity. But this answer applies to one who asks if the infinite can be crossed in a finite time rather than to the question itself, as he will say in Book VIII. In this latter place he answers this argument by saying that a mobile body does not use the infinities in magnitude as if they existed in act, but rather in potency. If the mobile body uses a point in space as a beginning and as an end, then it would use that point as existing in act. It would then be necessary for the body to be at rest there, as he will show. And thus, if the body must cross an infinity existing in act, then it would never arrive at the end.

864. He gives the second argument where he says, **"The second is . . ."** [662]. He says that this is called the "Achilles" argument, as though it is invincible and insoluble.

The argument is as follows. If a thing is being moved, it follows that that which runs slower, if it began to be moved first, is never joined or touched by that which is very fast.

He proves this as follows. If a slow body begins to be moved in some time before a very fast body, then in that time the slow body has crossed some space. And before a very fast body which pursues can touch the very slow body which flees, the very fast body must go from the place from which the fleeing body began up to the place which the fleeing body reached in the time that the pursuing body was not being moved. But the very fast body must cross that space in some time. In this time the slower body has crossed another space, and so forth to infinity. Therefore the slower body will always have some space by which it precedes the very fast body which pursues it. And thus the faster body will never touch the slower body. But this is impossible. Therefore, it should rather be said that nothing is moved.

865. In answering this argument Aristotle says that this argument is the same as the first, which proceeded by a division of space into two halves insofar as there is a middle. But this second argument differs from the first as follows. The magnitude of space in the second argument is not divided into two halves but is divided according to the proportion of excess of the faster body to the slower in motion. For in the first time in which only the slower body was moved there is a greater magnitude. Since the second time in which the faster body crosses this space is shorter, the magnitude crossed by the slower body is smaller, and so forth to infinity. Hence, since the time and the magnitude are infinitely divided, it seems from this argument that the slower body is never joined by the faster body.

But this comes to the same thing as was said in the first argument about the division of magnitude into two halves. For in each argument it seems that the mobile body cannot arrive at a terminus because of the division of magnitude to infinity, in whatever

way it is divided. That is, the magnitude is either divided into two halves, as in the first argument, or it is divided according to the excess of the faster to the slower, as in the second argument. But the second argument adds that the fastest body cannot catch up with a slower body while it is pursuing it. This is said with a certain grandeur of words in order to cause wonderment, but does not contribute to the force of the argument.

Hence it is clear that the same answer must be given to both the first and the second arguments. In the first argument it was falsely concluded that the mobile body would never arrive at a terminus of the magnitude because of the infinite division of the magnitude. Likewise, the conclusion of the second argument to the effect that a preceding slower body is not joined by a pursuing faster body is false. For this is nothing else than that the mobile body does not arrive at some terminus.

It is true that, while the slower body precedes, the faster body is not joined with it. Nevertheless, at some time it will be joined with it, if it is granted that a mobile body can cross a finite magnitude in a finite time. For the faster pursuing body will cross the whole magnitude by which the slower fleeing body precedes it. And it will cross a greater magnitude in less time than the time in which the slower body is moved through some determinate quantity. Thus the faster body will not only catch up with the slower body, but will also pass it. Therefore these two arguments of Zeno are answered.

866. He gives the third argument where he says, **"The third is..."** [663]. He says that Zeno's third argument; namely, that the flying arrow is at rest, was given above before he began to

enumerate the arguments. As he said above, this seems to follow because Zeno supposed that time is composed of "nows." If this is not granted, one cannot argue to this conclusion.

867. He gives the fourth argument where he says, "**The fourth argument . . .**" [664].

Concerning this he makes three points. First he gives the argument. Secondly, where he says, "**The fallacy of . . .**" [665], he answers the argument. Thirdly, where he says, "**For instance . . .**" [666], he clarifies the argument with an example.

He says, therefore, first that Zeno's fourth argument deals with things which are moved on a race-course. Two equal magnitudes are moved through a part of the space of the race-course which is equal to each magnitude in quantity. The motions are contrary, that is, one of the equal magnitudes is moved through this space of the race-course in one direction, and the other in the other direction. Also one of these mobile magnitudes begins to be moved from the end of the race-course equal to it. The other begins to be moved from the middle of the race-course, or from the middle of the space in the given race-course. Further, each body is moved with equal velocity. Having constructed this situation, Zeno thought that half of the time would be equal to double the time. And since this is impossible, he wished to infer further from this that motion is impossible.

868. Next where he says, "**The fallacy of . . .**" [665], he answers the argument.

He says that Zeno was deceived because he has on the one hand a mobile body being moved next to a moved magnitude, and on the other hand he

has a body being moved next to a magnitude at rest which is equal to the moved magnitude. And since he supposed that the velocities of the mobile bodies are equal, he held that in an equal time there is motion of equal velocity for the equal magnitudes, of which one is in motion and the other is at rest. This is clearly false. For when a thing is moved next to a magnitude which is at rest, there is only one motion. But when a thing is moved next to a moved magnitude, there are two motions. And if these motions are in the same direction, the time should be added. But if these motions are in opposite directions the time should be decreased according to the quantity of the other motion. For if a magnitude is moved with equal or greater velocity in the same direction as an adjacent mobile body, the mobile body will never be able to cross it. But if the magnitude is moved with a smaller velocity, the mobile body will cross it at some time. However, the time would be shorter if the magnitude were at rest. However, the contrary is the case if the magnitude is moved in the opposite direction than the mobile body. For the faster the magnitude is moved, the shorter the time in which the mobile body crosses it. For the motions operate in such a way that they cross each other.

869. Next when he says, "**For instance . . .**" [666], he clarifies what he has said with an example. Let A refer to three magnitudes equal to each other. These magnitudes are at rest. This is to be understood as though A refers to a space of three cubits. And let B refer to three other magnitudes equal to each other, for example, a mobile body of three cubits. These magnitudes begin to be moved from the middle of the space. And also let C refer to

three other magnitudes which are equal in number, magnitude, and velocity to B. These magnitudes begin to be moved from the end of the space, that is, from the last A.

On these assumptions the first B by its motion will come together with the last A, and the first C by its motion will come together with the first A at the opposite extremity. And the first C will also be together with the last B, having crossed all the B's which are moved in the opposite direction from C. When this has been done, the first C has crossed all the A's, but B has crossed only half the A's. Hence, since B and C have equal velocity, and since an equal velocity crosses a smaller magnitude in a shorter time, it follows that the time in which B has arrived at the last A is half the time in which C has arrived at the first A at the opposite end. For both B and C cross each A in an equal time.

Therefore, supposing that the time in which B arrives at the last A is half the time in which C arrives at the first A at the opposite end, we must also consider how Zeno wished to conclude that this half time is equal to this double time. Granting that the time of the motion of C is twice the time of the motion of B, then in the first half of the time B was at rest and C was in motion. Thus in that half of the time C arrived at the middle of the space where B is. And then B began to be moved in one direction and C in the other direction. Moreover when B arrives at the last A it must have crossed all of the C's. For the first B and the first C are simultaneously in the opposite extremes; that is, C is in the first A, and B is in the last A. And as Zeno said, C comes next to each B in the same time that it crosses each of the A's. This is true because both the B and the C cross one A in an

equal time. And thus, if B and C cross the same space in an equal time, it seems that C crosses both a B and an A in an equal time. Therefore the time in which C crosses all the B's is equal to the time in which it crosses all the A's. But the time in which C crosses all the B's is equal to the time in which C or B crosses half of the A's, as was said. Moreover it was proven that the time in which B crosses half of the A's is half the time in which C crosses all of the A's. Therefore it follows that a half is equal to a double, which is impossible.

This, therefore, is Zeno's argument. But it falls into the error mentioned above; namely, that C crosses B, which is moved in the opposite direction, and A, which is at rest, in the same time. This is false, as was said above.

870. Next where he says, "Nor in reference to . . ." [667], he gives the argument by which Zeno denied mutation between contradictories.

The argument is as follows. Whatever is changed, while it is being changed, is in neither of the termini. For while it is in the terminus from which, it is not yet being changed. And while it is in the terminus to which, it already has been changed. Therefore, if a thing is being changed from one contradictory to another, for example, from nonwhite to white, it follows that while it is being changed, it is neither white nor non-white. This is impossible.

Now although this impossibility follows for those who hold that the indivisible is moved, nevertheless for us who hold that whatever is moved is divisible no impossible results here. For if the moving body is not wholly in one of the extremes, it is not necessary that it cannot be called either white or non-white. For one part of it is white, and another part is not white. Moreover, a body is not called white because the whole is white, but because many of the main parts are white. These are the parts which are more properly and naturally white. For not being white or non-white is not the same as not being totally white or non-white.

What has been said of white or non-white must also be understood of unqualified being or non-being and of all things which are opposed as contradictories, like hot and non-hot, and such things. For that which is being changed must always be in one of the contrary opposites, and it will be named by that in which it is principally present. But it does not follow that the whole is always in neither of the extremities, as Zeno thought.

However it must be realized that this answer is sufficient to refute the argument which Zeno primarily intends here. But the truth in regard to this matter will be made clearer in Book VIII. For it is not true that in every case a part is altered or generated before another part. Rather sometimes the whole is changed all at once, as was said above. The answer given here does not apply to this case. Rather the answer which is given in Book VIII applies.

871. Next where he says, **"Again, in the case . . ."** [668], he answers the argument by which Zeno denied spherical motion.

Zeno said that it is impossible for a thing to be moved in a circle or in a sphere or in any other way in which a body does not progress from the place in which it is, but rather is moved in the same place. He proved this with the following argument. Whatever is through some time in one and the same place in respect to its whole and its parts is at rest. But things which are given as being moved in a circle are through some time in the same place in respect to the whole and its parts. Therefore it follows that they are simultaneously in motion and at rest, which is impossible.

The Philosopher objects to this argument in two ways.

First, Zeno said that the parts of a moved sphere are in the same place through some time. Against this Aristotle says that the parts of a moved sphere are at no time in the same place. For Zeno was dealing with the place of the whole. And it is true that, while the sphere is being moved, no part of it is outside the place of the whole sphere. But Aristotle is speaking of the proper place of a part insofar as a part can have a place. It was said in Book IV that the parts of a continuum are in place potentially. Moreover, it is clear that in spherical motion a part changes its proper place, but not the place of the whole. For where one part was, another part follows.

Secondly, he objects to the above argument insofar as Zeno said that the whole remains in the same place through some time. Against this Aristotle says that even the whole is always being changed to another place. This is clear as follows. In order for there to be two diverse places, it is not necessary that one of these places be totally outside of the other. Rather sometimes the second place is partially joined to the first place and partially divided from the first place. This can be seen in things which are moved in a straight line. Let a body of one cubit be moved from the place A B, which is one cubit, to the place B C, which is one cubit. While this body is being moved from the one place to the other, it must partly leave the one place and enter the other. Thus, if it leaves the place A B as far as A D, it will enter the place B C as far as B E. Hence it is clear that the place D E is different from the place A B. But it is not totally separated from A B, but only partially.

If it be granted that the part of the mobile body which enters the second place is returned to the part of the place which the body left, then there would be two places which are separated from each other in no way. These places differ only according to reason [ratio] insofar as the beginning of the place is taken at diverse signs where the body is; that is, some sign is taken in the mobile body as a beginning. Thus there are two places according to reason [ratio], but one place in respect to the subject.

Thus what he says here must be understood to mean that there are different circles here insofar as the circle begins at A, or B, or C, or at any other sign. On the other hand, it might be said that the circles are the same in subject, as a man and a musical man are the same in subject, for the one is accidental to the other. Hence it is clear that the body is always moved from one circular place to another, and it is not at rest, as Zeno tried to prove. And the same thing applies to the sphere and to all other things like wheels, pillars, and such things, which are moved within a proper place.

That Which Is Without Quantitative Parts Can Be Moved Only Accidentally

The Text of Aristotle
Chapter 10

669. *Our next point is that that which is without parts cannot be in motion except accidentally: i.e. it can be in motion only in so far as the body or the magnitude is in motion and the partless is in motion by inclusion therein, just as that which is in a boat may be in motion in consequence of the locomotion of the boat, or a "part may be in motion in virtue of the motion of the whole" (It must be remembered, however, that by "that which is without parts" I mean that which is quantitatively indivisible (and that the case of the motion of a part is not exactly parallel): for parts have motions belonging essentially and severally to themselves distinct from the motion of the whole. The distinction may be seen most clearly in the case of a revolving sphere, in which the velocities of the parts near the center and of those on the surface are different from one another and from that of the whole; this implies that there is not one motion but many.) As we have said, then, that which is without parts can be in motion in the sense in which a man sitting in a boat is in motion when the boat is traveling, but it cannot be in motion of itself.* 240b8–20

670. *For suppose that it is changing from AB to BC—either from one magnitude to another, or from one form to another, or from some state to its contradictory—and let D be the primary time in which it undergoes the change. Then in the time in which it is changing it must be either in AB or in BC or partly in one and partly in the other; for this, as we saw, is true of everything that is changing. Now it cannot be partly in each of the two: for then it would be divisible into parts. Nor again can it be in BC; for then it will have completed the change, whereas the assumption is that the change is in process. It remains, then, that in the time in which it is changing, it is in AB. That being so, it will be at rest; for, as we saw, to be in the same condition for a period of time is to be at rest. So it is not possible for that which has no parts to be in motion or to change in any way; for only one condition could have made it possible for it to have motion, viz. that time should be composed of moments, in which case at any moment it would have completed a motion or a change, so that it would never be in motion, but would always have been in motion. But this we have already shown above to be impossible: time is not composed of moments, just as a line is not composed of points, and motion is not composed of starts; for this theory simply makes motion consist of indivisibles in exactly the same way as time is made to consist of moments or a length of points.* 240b20–241a6

671. *Again, it may be shown in the following way that there can be no motion of a point or of any other indivisible. That which is in motion can never traverse a space greater than itself without first traversing a space equal to or less than itself. That being so, it is evident that the point also must first traverse a space equal to or less than itself. But since it is indivisible there can be no space less than itself for it to traverse first: so it will have to traverse a distance equal to itself. Thus the line will be composed of points; for the point, as it continually traverses a distance equal to itself, will be a measure of the whole line. But since this is impossible, it is likewise impossible for the indivisible to be in motion.* 241a6–14

672. *Again, since motion is always in a period of time and never in a moment, and all time is divisible, for everything that is in motion there must be a time less than that in which it traverses a distance as great as itself. For that in which it is in motion will be a time, because all motion is in a period of time; and all time has been shown above to be divisible. Therefore, if a point is in motion, there must be a time less than that in which it has itself traversed any distance. But this is impossible; for in less time it must traverse less distance, and thus the*

indivisible will be divisible into something less than itself, just as the time is so divisible; the fact being that the only condition under which that which is without parts and indivisible could be in motion would have been the possibility of the infinitely small being in motion in a moment: for in the two questions—that of motion in a moment and that of motion of something indivisible—the same principle is involved.   **241a15–26**

COMMENTARY OF ST. THOMAS

872. After the Philosopher has answered the arguments of Zeno, who denied motion, he here intends to show that that which is without parts is not moved. In doing this he refutes the opinion of Democritus, who held that atoms are in themselves mobile.

Concerning this he makes two points. First he sets forth his intention, and secondly he proves his position, where he says, **"For suppose that . . ."** [670]; He says, therefore, first that, granting what was proven above, we must say that that which is without parts cannot be moved, except perhaps per accidens. For example, a point is moved per accidens in a whole body or in any other magnitude, like a line or a surface, in which there is a point.

873. To be moved by the motion of another happens in two ways. The first is when that which is moved by the motion of another is not a part of that other. For example, that which is in a boat is moved by the motion of the boat, or whiteness is moved by the motion of a body of which it is not a part. The second is when a part is moved by the motion of the whole.

Since "being without parts" has many meanings, as also does "being with parts," he explains what he means by "being without parts." He says, ". . . by 'that which is without parts' I mean that which is quantitatively indivisible . . ." [240b13]. "Being without parts" can also refer to "being without parts in respect to species," as when we say that fire or water is without parts because it cannot be resolved

into many bodies of diverse species. But nothing prevents that which is without parts in this sense from being moved. Therefore he intends to deny motion of that which is quantitatively without parts.

874. He has said that a part is moved by the motion of the whole. But someone might say that a part is not moved in any way. Therefore he adds that some motions of the parts, insofar as there are parts, are diverse from the motion of the whole, insofar as there is a motion of the whole.

This difference can best be understood in spherical motion. For the velocity of the parts which are moved near the center is not the same as the velocity of the parts which are near the exterior surface of the sphere. Nor is it the same as the velocity of the whole. It is as though there is not one but diverse motions. For it is clear that that which crosses a greater magnitude in an equal time is faster. And while the sphere is being moved, it is clear that an exterior part of the sphere crosses a greater circle than an interior part. Hence the velocity of the exterior part is greater than the velocity of the interior part. However, the velocity of the whole is the same as the velocity of the interior and the exterior part.

However, this diversity of motions must be understood according to the way in which motion pertains to the parts of a continuum, that is, potentially. The motion of the whole and of the parts is one motion in act. But the motions of the parts are potentially diverse from each other and from the motion of the whole. And thus, when it is said that a part is moved per accidens by the motion of the whole, this means that that which is per se in potency is so moved per accidens. This is not motion per accidens in the sense in which accidents or forms are said to be moved per accidens.

875. Having made this distinction in regard to that which is moved, he explains his intention. He says that that which is quantitatively without parts can be moved per accidens by the motion of a body. However, it is not moved as a part, because no magnitude is composed of indivisibles, as was shown. Rather it is moved in the way that something is moved by the motion of another of which it is not a part, as a man sitting in a boat is moved by the motion of the boat. But that which is without parts is not moved per se.

He has already proven this above, not as his main point, but incidentally. Hence he here explains the truth more fully beyond the argument given above. He adds arguments which effectively prove his position.

876. Next where he says, **"For suppose that . . ."** [670], he proves his position with three arguments. The first is as follows. Let that which is without parts be moved from A B to B C. In this argument it makes no difference whether A B and B C are two magnitudes or two places, as in local motion and increase and decrease, or two qualities, as in alteration, or two contradictory opposites, as in generation and corruption. And let E D be the time in which the thing is changed from the one terminus to the other primarily, that is, not by reason [ratio] of a part. In this time that which is changed must be either in A B, the terminus from

which, or in B C, the terminus to which, or partly in the one terminus and partly in the other. For whatever is changed must be in one of these three states, as was said above. One cannot grant the third member; namely, that it is in both termini according to its diverse parts. For then it would be composed of parts, and it was granted that it is without parts. And likewise one cannot grant the second member; namely, that it is in B C or the terminus to which. For when it is in the terminus to which, it has already been changed, as is clear from the above. And it was granted that in this time the body is being changed. It follows, therefore, that during the whole time in which the indivisible is being changed, it is in A B or the terminus from which. And from this it follows that it is at rest. For being at rest is nothing else than being in one and the same condition through some whole time. Since in every time there is a prior and a posterior because time is divisible, then whatever is in one and the same condition through some time is the same now as it was before. And this is being at rest. But it is impossible for a thing to be at rest while it is being changed. Therefore, it follows that that which is without parts is not moved or changed in any way.

There could be a motion of an indivisible thing only if time were composed of "nows." For in the "now" there is always a "has been moved" or "has been changed." And since the "has been moved" as such is not being moved, it follows that in the "now" nothing is being moved, but rather has been moved. Hence, if time were composed of "nows," it could be granted that the indivisible is moved in time. For it could be granted that in each of the "nows" from which time is composed, the indivisible is in one condition. And in the whole time, that is, in all the "nows," it is in many conditions. And thus it would be moved in the whole time, but not in any one "now."

But it is impossible for time to be composed of "nows," as was shown above. For it was shown that time is not composed of "nows," and that a line is not composed of points, and that motion is not composed of impulses [momenta]. By impulses we mean states of "having been changed." And he who says that the indivisible is moved, or that motion is composed of indivisibles, is saying that time is composed of "nows," or that magnitude is composed of points, which is impossible. Therefore that which is without parts cannot be moved.

877. He gives the second argument where he says, **"Again, it may be shown . . ."** [671]. He says that from what follows it can be shown that neither a point nor any other indivisible can be moved. This is a special argument dealing with local motion: Whatever is moved in respect to place cannot cross a magnitude greater than itself before it crosses a magnitude equal to or less than itself. Rather the mobile body always crosses a magnitude equal to or less than itself before it crosses a magnitude greater than itself. Hence, if this is so, then a point, if it is moved, will clearly cross a magnitude less than or equal to itself before it crosses a magnitude greater than itself. But it is impossible for a point to cross something less than itself, because it is indivisible. Hence it follows that it will cross something equal to itself. And thus it is necessary that this point number all the points in the line. For since the point is moved by a motion equal to the line because it is moved through

the whole line, it follows that the point measures the whole line. And this is done by numbering all the points. Therefore, it follows that the line is composed of points. And since this is impossible, the indivisible cannot be moved.

878. He gives the third argument where he says, **"Again, since motion . . ."** [672]. The argument is as follows.

Whatever is moved is moved in time. And nothing is moved in the "now," as was proven above. Moreover, it was shown above that all time is divisible. Therefore, in whatever time something is moved, there will be a smaller time in which some smaller mobile body is moved. For, given the same velocity, it is clear that a smaller mobile body crosses some designated distance in less time than a larger body. For example, a part is moved in less time than the whole, as is clear from the above. Therefore, if a point is moved, there will be some time which is less than the time in which the point is moved. But this is impossible, for it would follow that in that smaller time something smaller than a point is moved. And thus the indivisible would be divisible into something smaller, just as time is divided into time. The indivisible could be moved only if it were possible for something to be moved in the indivisible "now." For just as there could be nothing smaller than the "now" in which a body is moved, likewise there could not be some smaller mobile body.

And thus it is clear that motion occurring in the "now" and the indivisible being moved are the same thing. But it is impossible for motion to occur in the "now." Therefore the indivisible cannot be moved.

No Mutation Is Infinite In Its Proper Species. How Motion Can Be Infinite In Time

The Text of Aristotle

673. *Our next point is that no process of change is infinite; for every change, whether between contradictories or between contraries, is a change from something to something. Thus in contradictory changes the positive or the negative, as the case may be, is the limit, e.g., being is the limit of coming to be and not-being is the limit of ceasing to be; and in contrary changes the particular contraries are the limits, since these are the extreme points of any such process of change, and consequently of every process of alteration; for alteration is always dependent upon some contraries. Similarly contraries are the extreme points of processes of increase and decrease: the limit of increase is to be found in the complete magnitude proper to the peculiar nature of the thing that is increasing, while the limit of decrease is the complete loss of such magnitude.*
241a26–241b2

674. *Locomotion, it is true, we cannot show to be finite in this way, since it is not always between contraries. But since that which cannot be cut (in the sense that it is inconceivable that it should be cut, the term "cannot" being used in several senses)—since it is inconceivable that that which in this sense cannot be cut should be in process of being cut, and generally that that which cannot come to be should be in process of coming to be, it follows that it is inconceivable that that which cannot complete a change should be in process of changing to that to which it cannot complete a change. If, then, it is to be assumed that that which is in locomotion is in process of changing, it must be capable of completing the change. Consequently its motion is not infinite, and it will not be in locomotion over an infinite distance; for it cannot traverse such a distance. It is evident, then, that a process of change cannot be infinite in the sense that it is not defined by limits.*
241b2–12

675. *But it remains to be considered whether it is possible in the sense that one and the same process of change may be infinite in respect of the time which it occupies. If it is not one process, it would seem that there is nothing to prevent its being infinite in this sense; e.g., if a process of locomotion be succeeded by a process of alteration and that by a process of increase and that again by a process of coming to be: in this way there may be motion for ever so far as the time is concerned; but it will not be one motion, because all these motions do not compose one. If it is to be one process, no motion can be infinite in respect of the time that it occupies, with the single exception of rotatory locomotion.*
241b12–20

COMENTARY OF ST. THOMAS

879. After the Philosopher has shown that that which is without parts is not moved, he intends here to show that no mutation is infinite. This is contrary to Heraclitus, who held that everything is always being moved.

Concerning this he makes two points. First he shows that no mutation is infinite in its proper species. Secondly, where he says, **"But it remains . . ."** [675], he shows how mutation can be infinite in time.

Concerning the first part he makes two points. First he shows that the mutations other than local motion are not infinite in species. Secondly, where he says, **"Locomotion, it is true . . ."** [674], he shows that the same is true of local motion.

880. The first argument is as follows. It was said above that every mutation is from something to something. And it is clear that there are predetermined termini for mutations between contra-

dictory opposites, that is, in generation and corruption, and for mutations between contraries, that is, in alteration and in increase and decrease. In mutations between contradictory opposites, the terminus is either an affirmation or a negation. For example, the terminus of generation is being, and the terminus of corruption is non-being.

And likewise in mutations between contraries, the contraries themselves are the termini or extremes at which such mutations are terminated. Hence, since every alteration is from a contrary to a contrary, it follows that every alteration has a terminus.

And the same must be said of increase and decrease. For the terminus of increase is completed magnitude. (By this I mean a completion in accordance with the condition of the proper nature. For the completion of magnitude that belongs to a man is different than that which belongs to a horse.) And the terminus of decrease is the total removal of such a nature from completed magnitude.

Thus it is clear that each of the above-mentioned mutations has an extreme at which it is terminated. But nothing which is terminated is infinite. Therefore none of these mutations can be infinite.

881. Next where he says, **"Locomotion, it is true . . ."** [674], he begins to treat local motion.

First he shows that the argument applied to the other mutations does not apply to local motion. It was proven above that the other mutations are finite because they are terminated at a contrary or a contradictory opposite. But we cannot prove in the same way that local motion is finite. For not every local motion is between contraries in an unqualified way. For contrar-

ies are at a maximum distance from each other.

Unqualified maximum distance is found in the natural motions of the heavy and the light. For the place of fire is at a maximum distance from the centre of the earth. This is determined for such bodies in nature. Hence these mutations are between contraries in an unqualified sense. Hence in regard to these mutations it could be shown, as it was shown in regard to the other mutations, that they are not infinite.

But in violent or voluntary motions a maximum distance is not determined in an unqualified sense by definite termini. Rather the distance is determined by the purpose or by the violence of the mover, who either does not wish or is not able to move the body to a greater distance. Hence in this case there is a maximum distance only in a qualified sense, and consequently there is contrariety only in a qualified sense. Therefore it cannot be shown by means of the termini that no local motion is infinite.

882. Consequently he proves this with another argument as follows. That which cannot be cut is not cut. Now a thing is said to be impossible in many ways; that is, this could mean that something does not exist in any way, or that something can exist only with difficulty. Therefore, he indicates what he means by "impossible" here. By "impossible" he means that something cannot exist in any way. And that which cannot be made cannot be "becoming" for the same reason. For example, if it is impossible for contradictories to exist simultaneously, then this cannot be "becoming." And for the same reason that which cannot be "having been changed" into something cannot be "being changed" to that. For nothing

tends toward the impossible. But whatever is changed in respect to place is being changed to something. Hence it is possible for it to arrive there through motion. But the infinite cannot be crossed. Therefore nothing is moved locally through an infinity. Hence no local motion is infinite.

Thus it is universally clear that no mutation can be infinite in the sense that it is not limited by definite termini from which it has its species.

883. Next where he says, **"But it remains..."** [675], he shows how motion can be infinite in time.

He says that it must be considered whether a motion which always remains one and the same in number can be infinite in time. There is nothing to prevent a motion which is not one in it-self from enduring through an infinite time. He says this with some reservation, for he adds, **". . . it would seem that there is nothing to prevent . . ."** [241b14]. Later on he will inquire into this. He then gives an example. Let us say that after a local motion there is an alteration, and after this an increase, and after this a generation, and so forth to infinity. Such a motion might endure always for an infinite time. But this motion could not be one in number. For from such motions a numerical unity does not result, as was shown in Book V. But a motion which always remains one in number does not endure through an infinite time except in one case. For one continuous circular motion can endure through an infinite time, as will be shown in Book VIII.

BOOK VII
THE COMPARISON OF MOVERS AND MOBILE OBJECTS

LECTURE 1 [241b24–242a15]
Whatever Is Moved Must Be Moved by Another

The Text of Aristotle
Chapter 1

676. *Everything that is in motion must be moved by something. For if it has not the source of its motion in itself it is evident that it is moved by something other than itself, for there must be something else that moves it.* **241b34–36**

676bis. *If on the other hand it has the source of its motion in itself, let AB be taken to represent that which is in motion essentially of itself and not in virtue of the fact that something belonging to it is in motion. Now in the first place to assume that AB, because it is in motion as a whole and is not moved by anything external to itself, is therefore moved by itself—this is just as if, supposing that JK is moving KL and is also itself in motion, we were to deny that JL is moved by anything on the ground that it is not evident which is the part that is moving it and which the part that is moved.* **241b37–44**

677. *In the second place that which is in motion without being moved by anything does not necessarily cease from its motion because something else is at rest; but a thing must be moved by something if the fact of something else having ceased from its motion causes it to be at rest. Thus, if this is accepted, everything that is in motion must be moved by something. For AB, which has been taken to represent that which is in motion, must be divisible, since everything that is in motion is divisible. Let it be divided, then, at C. Now if CB is not in motion, then AB will not be in motion; for if it is, it is clear that AC would be in motion while BC is at rest, and thus AB cannot be in motion essentially and primarily. But ex hypothesi AB is in motion essentially and primarily. Therefore if CB is not in motion AB will be at rest. But we have agreed that that which is at rest if something else is not in motion must be moved by something. Consequently, everything that is in motion must be moved by something; for that which is in motion will always be divisible, and if a part of it is not in motion the whole must be at rest.* **241b44–242a49**

COMMENTARY OF ST. THOMAS

884. After the Philosopher in the preceding books has treated motion in itself and its consequences and its parts, he begins here to treat motion in comparison to movers and mobile objects. This discussion is divided into two parts.

First he proves the existence of a first motion and a first mover. Secondly, in Book VIII where he says, **"It remains to consider . . ."** [748], he investigates the nature of the first motion and the first mover.

The first part is divided into two parts. First he proves the existence of a first motion and a first mover. And secondly, since things which are of one order are related to each other, he treats the comparison of motions to each other, where he says, **"A difficulty may be raised . . ."** [709].

Concerning the first part he makes three points. First he sets forth what is needed to prove his position. Secondly, where he says, **"Since everything . . ."** [678], he proves his position. Thirdly, where he says, **"That which is the first movement . . ."** [682], he explains a certain thing which he had assumed.

885. He states, therefore, first that whatever is moved must be moved by another. In some things this is obvious. For there are certain things which do not have within themselves the principle of their own motion. Rather the principle of their motion is extrinsic, as in things which are moved through force. If, therefore, there is something which does not have within itself the principle of its own motion, but the principle of its motion is extrinsic, it is clear that it is moved by another. But if there is some mobile object which would have within itself the principle of its own motion, about this there can be some question as to whether it is moved by another. And therefore concerning this he tries to show that it is moved by another. Let A B be a mobile object which is not moved by another. A B is moved in itself and primarily and not because some part of it is moved. For otherwise it would not be moved in itself but in respect to a part. Furthermore, if something moves itself and is not moved by another, it must be moved primarily and per se. For example, if something is not hot from another, it must be hot primarily and per se.

Granting this, he proceeds to prove his position in two ways. First he eliminates that from which it especially seems that a thing is not moved by another. Secondly, where he says, "In the second place . . ." [677], he shows directly that nothing can be moved by itself.

A thing especially seems not to be moved by another when it is not moved by something exterior but by an interior principle.

He says, therefore, first [676] that A B is thought to be moved by itself because the whole is moved, and it is not moved by something exterior. It is as if one were to say that a mobile thing, of which one part is moved and another part moves, would move itself because one cannot distinguish which part may be moving and which part may be moved. For example, let J K L be such a mobile object. The part J K moves the part K L, but it is not known which of these parts moves and which is moved. He wishes, moreover, that the first mobile object, A B, the whole of which is moved by an interior principle, be understood as a living body the whole of which is moved by a soul. However, he wishes that the mobile object J K L be understood as some body which is not wholly moved. Rather one bodily part is moving, and the others are moved. In this mobile object it is clear that that which is moved is moved by another. And from this he wishes to show the same thing of a living body which seems to move itself. For this is proper to it insofar as one part moves another, that is, the soul moves the body, as will be explained more fully in Book VIII.

886. Next where he says, "In the second place . . ." [677], he shows directly with the following argument that everything which is moved is moved by another.

Whatever is moved by itself does not rest from its own motion because of the rest of any other mobile object. He accepts this as though known per se. From this he concludes further that if a mobile object comes to rest because of the rest of another object, then it is moved by that other object. Furthermore, granting this, he concludes that whatever is moved must be moved by another. That this follows from these premises he proves as follows.

The mobile object which we have supposed to be moved by itself, namely A B, must be divisible. For whatever is moved is divisible, as was proven above. Therefore, since it is divisible, no difficulty arises if it should be divided. Let it be divided, therefore, at the point C so that one part of it is B C and the other part A C. If, therefore, B C is part of A B, then when the part B C is at rest, the whole of A B must be at rest. If, therefore, the whole is not at rest, but a part is at rest, then the whole is moved and one part is at rest. But since one part is given as being at rest, then it cannot be granted that the whole is moved, except by reason of the other part. Thus when B C, which is one part, is at rest, then A C, which is the other part, is being moved. But no whole of which only one part is moved is moved primarily and per se. Therefore, A B is not moved primarily and per se, which was supposed. Hence, when B C is at rest, the whole of A B must be at rest. And so that which is being moved will stop, that is, will cease to be moved, because of the rest of another. But it has been stated above that if a thing comes to rest and ceases to be moved because of the rest of another, then it is moved by that other. Therefore A B is moved by another.

And the same reasoning applies to any other mobile object, because everything which is moved is divisible. And for the same reason, when a part is at rest, the whole must be at rest. It is clear, therefore, that whatever is moved is moved by another.

887. There has been much objection to this proof of Aristotle.

Galenus objects to Aristotle's statement that if only one part of a mobile object is moved and the others are at rest, then the whole is not moved per se. He says that this is false because things which are moved with respect to a part are moved per se.

But Galenus was deceived by the equivocation of "per se." For "per se" sometimes is used insofar as it is opposed only to that which is per accidens. And thus that which is moved with respect to a part is moved per se, as Galenus thought. Sometimes, however, it is used insofar as it is opposed both to that which is per accidens and to that which exists in respect to a part. And this is called not only "per se" but also "primarily." And it is thus that Aristotle understands per se here. This is clear because when he concluded that A B is not moved per se, he added that it was agreed that it is moved by itself primarily.

888. But of greater urgency is the objection of Avicenna. He says that this argument proceeds from an impossible supposition, from which an impossible conclusion follows, and not from that which was given; namely, that a thing is moved by itself. For if we grant that a mobile object is moved primarily and per se, it is natural for it to be moved with respect to both the whole and the parts. If, therefore, it is granted that some part of it is at rest, there will be an impossible position. And from this position there follows the impossibility which Aristotle brings out; namely, that the whole would not be moved primarily and per se, as was given.

One might answer this objection, however, by saying that although it is impossible for a part to be at rest with respect to a determinate nature, insofar as it is a body of a certain species, for example, the heavens or fire, nevertheless, this is not impossible if the common nature [ratio] of body is considered. For a body, insofar as it is a body, is not prevented from being at rest or in motion.

But Avicenna rejects this answer in

two ways. First because with equal reason it can be said that a whole body is not prevented from being at rest because it is a body, just as was said of a part. And so for the proof of the proposition it was superfluous to assume the division of the mobile object and the rest of the part. The second reason is that a proposition is simply reduced to impossibility if the predicate is repugnant to the subject by reason of the specific difference, even though it is not repugnant to it by reason of its genus. For it is impossible for a man to be irrational even though he is not prevented from being irrational because he is an animal. So, therefore, it is simply impossible for a part of a moving body to be itself at rest. For this is contrary to the nature [ratio] of such a body, although this is not contrary to the common nature [ratio] of body.

889. Therefore, rejecting this answer, Averroes answers otherwise. He says that a condition can be true when the antecedent is impossible and the consequent is impossible. For example, if man is an ass, he is an irrational animal. It must be granted, therefore, that if a mobile object moves itself, it is impossible for either the whole or a part to be at rest, just as it is impossible that fire is not hot because it is the cause of its own heat. Hence this condition is true: if a part of a mobile object which moves itself is at rest, then the whole is at rest. Moreover, if Aristotle's words are weighed carefully, he never uses the rest of a part except in an expression having the force of a conditional proposition. For he does not say, "B C is at rest." Rather he says, "If B C is at rest, then A B must be at rest"; and again, "When a part is at rest, the whole is at rest." And from this true condition Aristotle demonstrates the proposition.

But Averroes says that this demonstration is not a simple demonstration. Rather it is a demonstration signi or demonstration quia in which such conditions are used.

However, this answer is reliable insofar as Averroes speaks about the truth of the condition. But it seems that it must be said that it is not a demonstration quia, but propter quid. For it contains the reason why it is impossible for a mobile object to move itself.

To see this it must be understood that a thing's moving of itself is nothing other than its being the cause of its own motion. That which is itself the cause of something must primarily agree with it. For that which is first in any genus is the cause of the things which come afterward. Thus fire, which is the cause of heat for itself and for others, is the first hot thing. However, Aristotle has shown in Book VI that there is no first in motion or in time or in magnitude or in the mobile object because of their divisibility. Therefore, there cannot be discovered a first whose motion does not depend on something prior. For the motion of a whole depends on the motion of its parts and is divided into them, as was proven in Book VI. Therefore, Aristotle thus shows the reason why no mobile object moves itself. For there cannot be a first mobile object whose motion does not depend on its parts; just as if I were to show that a divisible thing cannot be the first being because the being of whatever is divisible depends on its parts. And thus this condition is true: "if a part is not moved, the whole is not moved," just as this condition is true: "if a part is not, the whole is not."

890. Hence even the Platonists, who held that things move themselves, said that nothing corporeal or divisible moves itself. Rather, to move itself is

limited to spiritual substance which knows itself and loves itself. Without exception all operations are called motions. Even Aristotle in De Anima, III, says that sensation and understanding are motions insofar as motion is the act of the perfect. But here he is speaking of motion as the act of the imperfect, that is, the act of that which exists in potency. In respect to this motion the indivisible is not moved, as was proven in Book VI and as is here assumed. And thus it is clear that Aristotle, who holds that whatever is moved is moved by another, does not differ in meaning but only in words from Plato, who holds that some things move themselves.

Mobile Objects and Motions Cannot Proceed to Infinity. There Must Be an Immobile First Mover

The Text of Aristotle

678. *Since everything that is in motion must be moved by something, let us take the case in which a thing is in locomotion and is moved by something that is itself in motion, and that again is moved by something else that is in motion, and that by something else, and so on continually:*   **242a49–54**

679. *then the series cannot go on to infinity, but there must be some first mover. For let us suppose that this is not so and take the series to be infinite. Let A then be moved by B, B by C, C by D, and so on, each member of the series being moved by that which comes next to it. Then· since* ex hypothesi *the mover while causing motion is also itself in motion, and the motion of the moved and the motion of the mover must proceed simultaneously (for the mover is causing motion and the moved is being moved simultaneously); it is evident that the respective motions of A, B, C, and each of the other moved movers are simultaneous. Let us take the motion of each separately and let E be the motion of A, F of B, and G and H respectively the motions of C and D; for though they are all moved severally one by another, yet we may still take the motion of each as numerically one, since every motion is from something to something and is not infinite in respect of its extreme points. By a motion that is numerically one I mean a motion that proceeds from something numerically one and the same to something numerically one and the same in a period of time numerically one and the same; for a motion may be the same generically, specifically, or numerically: it is generically the same if it belongs to the same category, e.g., substance or quality; it is specifically the same if it proceeds from something specifically the same to something specifically the same, e.g., from white to black or from good to bad, which is not of a kind specifically distinct; it is numerically the same if it proceeds from something numerically one to something numerically one in the same period of time, e.g., from a particular white to a particular black, or from a particular place to a particular place, in a particular period of time; for if the period of time were not one and the same, the motion would no longer be numerically one though it would still be specifically one. We have dealt with this question above. Now let us further take the time in which A has completed its motion, and let it be represented by J. Then since the motion of A is finite the time will also be finite. But since the movers and the things moved are infinite, the motion EFGH, i.e., the motion that is composed of all the individual motions, must be infinite. For the motions of A, B, and the others may be equal, or the motions of the others may be greater; but assuming what is conceivable, we find that whether they are equal or some are greater, in both cases the whole motion is infinite. And since the motion of A and that of each of the others are simultaneous, the whole motion must occupy the same time as the motion of A; but the time occupied by the motion of A is finite: consequently the motion will be infinite in a finite time, which is impossible.*   **242a54–242b53**

680. *It might be thought that what we set out to prove has thus been shown, but our argument so far does not prove it, because it does not yet prove that anything impossible results from the contrary supposition; for in a finite time there may be an infinite motion, though not of one thing, but of many: and in the case that we are considering this is so: for each thing accomplishes its own motion, and there is no impossibility in many things being in motion simultaneously.*   **242b53–59**

681. *But if (as we see to be universally the case) that which primarily is moved locally and corporeally must be either in contact with it or continuous with that which moves it, the things*

moved and the movers must be continuous or in contact with one another, so that together they
all form a single unity: 242b59–63

681bis. *whether this unity is finite or infinite makes no difference to our present argument;*
for in any case since the things in motion are infinite in number the whole motion will be
infinite, if, as is theoretically possible, each motion is either equal to or greater than that which
follows it in the series; for we shall take as actual that which is theoretically possible. If, then, A,
B, C, D form, an infinite magnitude that passes through the motion EFGH in the finite time J,
this involves the conclusion that an infinite motion is passed through in a finite time: and
whether the magnitude in question is finite or infinite this is in either case impossible. Therefore
the series must come to an end, and there must be a first mover and a first moved; for the fact
that this impossibility results only from the assumption of a particular case is immaterial, since
the case assumed is theoretically possible, and the assumption of a theoretically possible case
ought not to give rise to any impossible result. 242b63–243a31

COMMENTARY OF ST. THOMAS

891. After the Philosopher has shown that whatever is moved is moved by another, here he proceeds to prove the principle proposition; namely, that there is a first motion and a first mover.

Concerning this he makes two points. First he states his intention. Secondly, where he says, **"For let us suppose . . ."** [679], he proves his position.

He says, therefore, first that since it has been shown universally that whatever is moved is moved by another, then this must also be true of local motion. Hence, whatever is moved in place is moved by another. He applies what was demonstrated universally above to local motion because local motion is the first of motions, as will be shown in Book VIII. And so with respect to this motion he proceeds here to the proof of a first mover.

Let there be something which is moved with respect to place. This is moved by another. This other is either moved or is not moved. If it is not moved, the proposition is established, namely, that there is a mover which is immobile. This immobility is a property of the first mover. If, however, the

mover is itself moved, then it must be moved by another mover; and again, this mover, if it is also moved, is moved by another. Now this cannot continue to infinity, but must stop with something. There will be, therefore, some first mover which will be the first cause of motion, such that it is not moved itself but moves others.

892. Next where he says, **"For let us suppose . . ."** [679], he proves what he has supposed.

Concerning this he makes three points. First he states the proof. Secondly, where he says, **"It might be thought . . ."** [680], he shows that this proof is not sufficient. Thirdly, where he says, **"But if (as we see . . ."** [681], he adds a certain thing which strengthens the argument.

He says, therefore, first that if it is not granted that there is some first cause of motion because whatever is moved is moved by another, then it follows that movers and motions proceed to infinity. And he shows that this is impossible. Let A be something which is moved in respect to place by B. And B is moved by C; C is moved by D; and this continues by ascending to infinity. It is clear that when a thing moves because it is moved, the mover and the mobile object are moved simultaneously. For example, if the hand by its own motion moves a staff, the hand and the staff are moved simultaneously. Hence B is moved simultaneously when A is moved; and for the same reason when B is moved, C is moved simultaneously; and when C is moved, D is moved simultaneously. Therefore the motions of A and of all the others are simultaneous and in the same time. And the motion of each one of these infinites can be considered separately. Now each one of these mobile objects is moved by each one of the movers, but not in such a way that one of them is moved by all. Rather, individual objects are moved by individual movers. Nevertheless, although the movers and mobile objects are infinite, the motion of each mobile object is one in number. And although all the motions are infinite in number, they are not infinite in the extremes, that is, they are not infinite by a privation of extremes. Rather the motion of each one is finite, having a determinate extreme.

He proves as follows that the motion of each of the infinite mobile objects is finite and one in number. Since everything which is moved is moved between two termini, i.e., from something to something, then in respect to the different modes of identity of the termini the motion itself must be one in different ways, that is, either in number, or in species, or in genus.

Motion is one in number when it is from the numerically same terminus from which and to the numerically same terminus to which. Moreover the motion must occur in numerically the same time and the mobile object must be numerically the same. In order to explain what he has said, he adds that

a motion is one in number when it is from the same thing and to the same thing, for example, from "this white," which indicates a thing which is one in number, to "this black," which also indicates something which is one in number. And the motion must occur with respect to "this time," which also is one in number. For if the motion occurs with respect to another time, although it be equal, the motion would not be one in number but only in species.

A motion is one in genus when it is in the same category, either substance or any other genus. For example, every generation of substance is the same in genus, and likewise every alteration is the same in genus.

And motion is one in species when it is from the same thing with respect to species and to the same thing with respect to species. For example, every blackening, which is from white to black, is the same in species. And likewise every perversion from good to evil is the same in species. These points were discussed in Book V.

Let us grant these two suppositions; namely, the mover and the moved are moved simultaneously, and the motion of any mobile object can be taken as finite and one. Let E be the motion of the mobile object A. Let F be the motion of B. And let G H be the motion of C D and of all the following mobile objects. Let the time in which A is moved be J. Since the motion of A is determinate and finite, then the time J of this motion is also determinate and not infinite. For it was shown in Book VI that the finite and the infinite are found together in time and in motion. From what has been said it is clear that in the same time in which A is moved, B also is moved, and so are all the others. Therefore, the motion of all, which is E

F G H, is in a finite time. But this motion is infinite because it is the motion of infinite things. Therefore, it follows that there is an infinite motion in a finite time, which is impossible. This follows because in the time in which A is moved all of the others, which are infinite in number, are moved. And as far as this proposition is concerned it makes no difference whether the motion of every mobile object is of equal velocity or whether the inferior mobile objects are moved more slowly and in a longer time. For it follows absolutely that there is an infinite motion in a finite time because each one of the mobile objects necessarily has a velocity and a finite slowness. But there cannot be an infinite motion in a finite time. Therefore, mobile objects and movers cannot proceed to infinity.

893. Next where he says, **"It might be thought..."** [680], he shows that the preceding argument does not come to a proper conclusion. He says that in the above discussion there seems to be a demonstration of the principal proposition, namely, that movers and mobile objects do not proceed to infinity. However, it is not adequately demonstrated that no inconsistency follows from the premises. For it is possible and it happens that there is infinite motion in a finite time. However, this is not one and the same motion, but different motions insofar as the things which are moved are infinite. For nothing prevents infinite things from moving simultaneously in a finite time. And this was the conclusion of the foregoing argument. For there were infinite, diverse mobile objects, and so their motions were diverse. But the unity of motion requires not only a unity of time and of termini, but also a unity of the mobile object, as was said in Book V.

894. Next where he says, **"But if (as we see . . ."** [681], he shows how the above argument can be made effective.

First he shows how it can be effective after a supposition has been made. Secondly, where he says, **"Whether this unity . . ."** [681bis], he shows how it is effective simply.

He says, therefore, first that what is primarily moved locally and bodily and immediately by some moving mobile object must be touched by it, as a staff is touched by a hand, or it must be continuous with it, as one part of air is continuous with another, and as one part of an animal is continuous with another part. In all cases it seems to happen that the mover is always joined to the mobile object in one of these ways.

Let one of these ways be assumed, namely, that from all the infinite mobile objects and movers there is effected a unity, namely, the whole universe, through a certain continuation. Since this actually occurs, let it be granted. And let that whole, which is a certain magnitude and continuum, be called A B C D, and let its motion be called E F G H. Now someone might say that E F G H is the motion of finite mobile objects, and thus it cannot be the motion of the whole infinite. Hence he adds that it makes no difference to the proposition whether the magnitude which is moved is assumed to be finite or infinite. For as when A is moved in the finite time J, all of the finite mobile objects, which are infinite in number, are simultaneously moved. And thus in the same time the whole infinite magnitude is moved simultaneously. Hence an impossibility follows, whichever of these is assumed. It makes no difference whether there is a finite magnitude consisting of magnitudes infinite in number, or whether there is an infinite magnitude whose motion takes place in finite time. For it was shown above that an infinite mobile object cannot be moved in a finite time. Therefore, that which follows, namely, that movers and mobile objects proceed to infinity, is impossible. It is clear, therefore, that one thing being moved by another does not proceed to infinity. Rather this will come to an end somewhere, and there will be some first mobile object which is moved by another immobile thing.

895. The foregoing proof proceeds from a certain supposition, namely, that all the infinite movers and mobile objects are mutually continuous and constitute one magnitude. And so it might seem to someone that this argument does not conclude without qualifications. Therefore he adds that it makes no difference that this proof has proceeded from a certain supposition. For an impossibility cannot follow from a contingent supposition, even if it is false. Since, therefore, the foregoing argument leads to an impossibility, this impossibility does not follow from the contingent supposition. Rather, it follows from something else which must be impossible, because an impossibility follows from it. And so it is clear that in demonstrations which lead to an impossibility, it makes no difference whether a false or a true contingency is joined to the impossible. For when a false contingency is added, that from which an impossibility follows is shown to be impossible, just as when a true contingency is added. For just as the impossible cannot follow from the true, neither can it follow from the contingent.

896. But someone might say that it is not contingent that all mobile objects are continuous. Rather it is impossible for the elements to be continuous with each other and with the celestial bodies. But it must be said that the contingent and the impossible are taken in different ways when something is demonstrated of a genus and when something is demonstrated of a species. For when a species is treated, that must be taken as impossible which is repugnant to either the genus or the specific difference from which the nature [ratio] of the species is constituted. But when a genus is treated, everything which is not repugnant to the nature [ratio] of the genus is taken as contingent, even though it may be repugnant to the differentia which constitutes the species. For example, if I am speaking of animal, I can say that every animal being winged is contingent. But if I descend to the consideration of man, it would be impossible for this animal to be winged. Now Aristotle is speaking here about movers and mobile objects in general and is not yet applying his remarks to determinate mobile objects. To be contiguous or continuous is indifferently related to the nature [ratio] of the mover and the mobile object. Therefore, he states as a contingency that all mobile objects are continuous with each other. This, however, is impossible if mobile objects are considered according to their determinate natures.

LECTURE 3 [243b31–244b2]
In Local Motion the Mover and the Moved Must Be Together

The Text of Aristotle[1]
Chapter 2

682. *That which is the first mover of a thing—in the sense that it supplies not "that for the sake of which" but the source of the motion—is always together with that which is moved by it (by "together" I mean that there is nothing intermediate between them). This is universally true wherever one thing is moved by another.*   243a32–35

683. *And since there are three kinds of motion, local, qualitative, and quantitative, there must also be three kinds of mover, that which causes locomotion, that which causes alteration, and that which causes increase or decrease.*

Let us begin with locomotion, for this is the primary motion. Everything that is in locomotion is moved either by itself or by something else.   243a35–40

684. *In the case of things that are moved by themselves it is evident that the moved and the mover are together; for they contain within themselves their first mover, so that there is nothing in between.*   243a11–15

685. *The motion of things that are moved by something else must proceed in one of four ways; for there are four kinds of locomotion caused by something other than that which is in motion, viz. pulling, pushing, carrying, and twirling. All forms of locomotion are reducible to these.*   243a15–18

686. *Thus pushing on is a form of pushing in which that which is causing motion away from itself follows up that which it pushes and continues to push; pushing off occurs when the mover does not follow up the thing that it has moved; throwing when the mover causes a motion away from itself more violent than the natural locomotion of the thing moved, which continues its course so long as it is controlled by the motion imparted to it.*   243a18–243b2

687. *Again, pushing apart and pushing together are forms respectively of pushing off and pulling: pushing apart is pushing off, which may be a motion either away from the pusher or away from something else, while pushing together is pulling, which may be a motion towards something else as well as towards the puller. We may similarly classify all the varieties of these last two, e.g., packing and combing: the former is a form of pushing together, the latter a form of pushing apart. The same is true of the other processes of combination and separation (they will all be found to be forms of pushing apart or of pushing together), except such as are involved in the processes of becoming and perishing. (At the same time it is evident that there is no other kind of motion; but combination and separation: for they may all be apportioned to one or other of those already mentioned.)*   243b3–12

688. *Again, inhaling is a form of pulling, exhaling a form of pushing; and the same is true of spitting and of all other motions that proceed through the body, whether excretive or assimilative, the assimilative being forms of pulling, the excretive of pushing off. All other kinds of locomotion must be similarly reduced; for they all fall under one or other of our four heads. And again, of these four, carrying and twirling are reducible to pulling and pushing. For*

---

1   NB, lines 243a3–248a9 (Book VII, Chapters 2 and 3) of the Oxford English translation of the *Physics* vary considerably from the corresponding section of the Latin translation of the *Physics* printed with St. Thomas's commentary. To avoid confusion we have included in Appendix A a literal English rendition of this section of the Latin *Physics*. In Lectures 3, 4, 5, and 6 of Book VII all references to Aristotle's *Physics* are made to the English text in Appendix A.

carrying always follows one of the other three methods; for that which is carried is in motion accidentally, because it is in or upon something that is in motion, and that which carries it is in doing so being either pulled or pushed or twirled; thus carrying belongs to all the other three kinds of motion in common. And twirling is a compound of pulling and pushing; for that which is twirling a thing must be pulling one part of the thing and pushing another part, since it impels one part away from itself and another part towards itself.   243b12–244a4

689. *If, therefore, it can be shown that that which is pushing and that which is pulling are adjacent respectively to that which is being pushed and that which is being pulled,*   244a4–5

690. *it will be evident that in all locomotion there is nothing intermediate between moved and mover.*   244a5–6

691. *But the former fact is clear even from the definitions of pushing and pulling; for pushing is motion to something else from oneself or from something else, and pulling is motion from something else to oneself or to something else, when the motion of that which is pulling is quicker than the motion that would separate from one another the two things that are continuous; for it is this that causes one thing to be pulled on along with the other.*   244a7–11

692. *(It might indeed be thought that there is a form of pulling that arises in another way: that wood, e.g., pulls fire in a manner different from that described above. But it makes no difference whether that which pulls is in motion or is stationary when it is pulling: in the latter case it pulls to the place where it is, while in the former it pulls to the place where it was.)*

244a11–244b2

COMMENTARY OF ST. THOMAS

897. Since in the preceding demonstration the Philosopher assumed that the mover is either contiguous or continuous with the mobile object, he intends here to prove this.

First he proves the proposition. Secondly, where he says, **"All things which are . . ."** [Appendix A, 697], he proves a certain thing which he assumes in this proof.

Concerning the first part he makes two points. First he states his intention. Secondly, where he says, **"Since there are three . . ."** [Appendix A, 683], he proves the proposition.

He says, therefore, first [682] that the mover and the thing moved are together. But a thing is said to move in two ways. First a thing can move as an end moves an agent. A mover of this kind is sometimes at a distance from the agent which it moves. Secondly, a thing can move as that which is the principle of motion moves. It is this kind of mover which he discusses

here. And because of this he adds, ". . . not as the cause for the sake of which but as the principle of motion . . ."

Further, the mover as the principle of motion is sometimes proximate and sometimes remote. He is speaking here of the proximate mover, and therefore he calls it the first mover. By "first" he means that which is proximate to the mobile object and not that which is first in the order of movers.

And since he has said in Book V that those things are together which are in the same place, then when he says that the mover and the moved are together, one might think that, when one body is moved by another, they are both in the same place. Therefore, in order to reject this, he adds that by "together" he here means not that they are in the same place but that there is no intermediary between the mover and the moved. Thus they are either touching or are continuous since their termini are together or are one.

And since in the preceding demonstration he has discussed only local motion, one might think that he holds this to be true only of this kind of motion. Therefore in order to reject this, he adds that it is said universally that the mover and the moved are together and not just specifically in regard to local motion. For it is common to every species of motion for the mover and the moved to be together in the manner indicated.

898. Next where he says, "**Since there are three . . .**" [Appendix A, 683], he proves the proposition.

Concerning this he makes two points. First he enumerates the species of motion. Secondly, where he says, "**Whatever is moved . . .**" [Appendix 684], he proves the proposition in respect to each type of motion.

He says, therefore, first that there are three motions: one with respect to place, which is called change of place; another with respect to quality, which is called alteration; another with respect to quantity, which is called increase or decrease. He makes no mention of generation and corruption because these are not motions, as was proven in Book V. But since there are termini of motion, i.e., of alteration, as was considered in Book VI, then when the proposition has been proven in regard to alteration, the same conclusion follows in regard to generation and corruption.

Therefore, just as there are three species of motion, so there are three species of mobile objects and movers. And in all of these cases it is true to say that the mover and the moved are together, as will be shown for each one of them. But this must first be shown in respect to local motion, which is the first of motions, as will be proven in Book VIII.

899. Next where he says, "**Whatever is moved . . .**" [Appendix A, 684], he proves the proposition in regard to each of the three kinds of motion mentioned above.

First he treats local motion. Secondly, where he says, "**Neither is there . . .**" [Appendix A, 693], he treats alteration. Thirdly, where he says, "**And that which is increased . . .**" [Appendix A, 696], he treats increase and decrease.

Concerning the first part he makes two points. First he proves the proposition in things in which it is more obvious. Secondly, where he says, "**That which is moved . . .**" [Appendix A, 685], he proves the proposition in things in which it is more obscure.

He says, therefore, first that it is necessary to say that everything which is moved in respect to place is moved either by itself or by another. The statement that a thing is moved by itself can be understood in two ways. This can be understood in one way by reason of the parts. Thus he will show in Book VIII that in regard to things which move themselves one part moves and another part is moved. Secondly, a thing can be understood to move itself primarily and per se. For example, the whole itself moves the whole itself. He has proven above that nothing moves itself in this way. If, however, it is conceded that a thing is moved by itself in either way, it is clear that the mover will be in the very thing which is moved, either as the same thing is in its own self, or as a part is in a whole as a soul is in an animal. And so it will follow that the mover and that which is moved are together so that there is nothing intermediate between them.

900. Next where he says, "**That which is moved . . .**" [Appendix A, 685], he shows the same thing with re-

spect to things which are moved in place by another, concerning which it is less obvious.

Concerning this he makes three points. First he distinguishes the modes in which a thing happens to be moved by another. Secondly, where he says, "**Therefore it is clear . . .**" [Appendix A, 690], he reduces these modes to two. Thirdly, where he says, "**This is clear from . . .**" [Appendix A, 691], he proves the proposition in regard to these two modes.

Concerning the first part he makes two points. First he divides the modes in which a thing is moved by another. He says that there are four modes, namely, pushing, pulling, carrying and twirling. For all motions which are from another are reduced to these.

901. Secondly, where he says, "**Pushing is either . . .**" [Appendix A, 686], he explains the four modes mentioned above.

First he explains pushing, which occurs when the mover by its moving makes a mobile object to be at a distance from the mover. He divides pushing in two, namely pushing on and pushing off. Pushing on is said to occur when the mover so strikes a mobile object that it does not break free of it when driving it on, but tends together with it toward the place to which it leads. Pushing off occurs when the mover so moves the mobile object that it breaks loose from it and does not accompany it up to the end of the motion.

902. Secondly, where he says, "**Carrying will be . . .**" [Appendix A, 687], he explains "carrying." He says that carrying is based on the three other motions, namely, pushing, pulling, and twirling, just as that which is per accidens is based on that which is per se. For that which is carried is not

moved per se but per accidens insofar as some other thing is moved in which it itself is (as when someone is carried by a boat in which he is), or on which it is (as when one is carried by a horse). However, that which carries is moved per se, because things which are moved per accidens cannot go on to infinity. And so the first carrier must be moved per se by some motion, either by a pushing, or a pulling, or a twirling. From this it is clear that carrying is contained in the three other motions.

903. Thirdly, where he says, "**Pulling occurs when . . .**" [Appendix A, 688], he explains the third mode, namely pulling.

It should be understood that pulling differs from pushing because in pushing the mover is related to the mobile object as the terminus from which of its motion. But in pulling the mover is related to the mobile object as the terminus to which. That, therefore, is said to pull which moves another toward itself.

To move something toward one's self with respect to place occurs in three ways.

This happens first in the way in which an end moves. Hence an end is also said to pull. Thus the poets say, "Pleasure attracts each man." In this way it can be said that place pulls that which is naturally moved to a place.

In another way it can be said that a thing pulls because it moves something toward itself by altering it in some manner, from which alteration it happens that the thing altered is moved with respect to place. In this way a magnet is said to pull iron. For just as a generator moves heavy and light things insofar as he gives them a form through which they are moved to a place, so also a magnet imparts some quality to iron through which the iron is moved toward the magnet.

And that this is true is evident from three things.

First a magnet does not pull iron from any distance, but only from nearby. But if iron were moved to a magnet only as to an end, as a heavy thing is moved to its own place, it would tend toward it from any distance.

Secondly, if a magnet is greased with other things, it cannot attract iron. It is as if these other things either impede the alterative force of the iron or else change it to its contrary.

Thirdly, in order for a magnet to attract iron, the iron must first be rubbed with the magnet, especially if the magnet is small. It is as if the iron receives some power from the magnet in order to be moved to it. Thus a magnet attracts iron not only as an end, but also as a mover and an alterer.

In a third way a thing is said to attract something because it moves it toward itself by local motion only. And thus pulling is defined here as one body pulling another such that that which is pulling is moved together with that which is pulled.

904. He says that pulling occurs when the motion of that which pulls something toward itself or toward another is faster and is not separated from that which is pulled. He says, moreover, "toward itself or toward another" because a voluntary mover can use another as itself. Hence it can push from another as from itself, and pull toward another as toward itself. But this does not happen in natural motion. For natural pushing is always from the pusher, and natural pulling is toward the puller.

He adds, moreover, "when the motion is faster." For it sometimes happens that that which is pulled is also moved per se to the place to which it is pulled, but it is forced to move by the faster pulling motion. And since the puller moves by its own motion, the motion of the puller must be faster than the natural motion of that which is pulled.

He also adds, "... it is not separated from that which is pulled" in order to distinguish it from pushing. For in pushing, the pusher is sometimes separated from that which it pushes and sometimes it is not. But the puller is never separated from that which it pulls. Rather the puller is moved together with that which is pulled.

He also explains why he said "toward itself or toward another." For in voluntary motions pulling occurs both toward one's self and toward another, as was said.

905. And since there are certain motions in which the nature [ratio] of pulling is not so manifestly seen, he next shows that these are reduced to the modes of pulling which he has proposed, namely, toward itself and toward another. He says that all other pullings, which are not named pullings, are reduced to these two modes of pulling. For they are the same in species with them to the extent that motions receive their species from their termini. Even these pullings are toward themselves or toward another, as is evident in inhaling and exhaling. For "inhaling" is a pulling in of air; "exhaling" is a pushing out of air; and similarly, "spitting" is an expulsion of spit. And the same can be said of all other motions in which some bodies are taken in or expelled. For an emission is reduced to a pushing, and a receiving to a pulling.

And similarly "striking" [spathesis] is a pushing, and "combing" [kerkisis] is a pulling. For "spathe" in Greek means either a sword or a spatula. Hence "spathesis" is the same as "spathatio," that is, striking with a sword, which occurs by pushing. And therefore the other text which says "speculation" seems to be corrupt through the fault of the transcriber, because for "spathatio" he has written "speculatio." "Combing," moreover, is an attraction. In Greek "kerkis" is a certain instrument which the weavers use. In weaving they draw this instrument toward themselves. In Latin this instrument is called a "radius." Hence the other text has "radiatio."

Among these two and other motions of ejecting or receiving, "combination," which pertains to attraction because a combiner moves something toward another, is different than separation, which pertains to pushing, because pushing is the motion of one thing from another. Therefore it is clear that every local motion is a combination or a separation. For every local motion is either from something or to something. Consequently, it is clear that every local motion is either a pushing or a pulling.

906. Next where he says, **"Twirling is composed . . ."** [Appendix A, 689], he explains what twirling is. He says that twirling is a motion composed of pulling and pushing. For when something is twirled, it is pushed from one side and pulled from another.

Next where he says, **"Therefore it is clear . . ."** [Appendix A, 690], he shows that all of the four motions mentioned above are reduced to pushing and pulling. And the same thing must be said of all of these and of these two. For since carrying consists of the three others, and since twirling is composed of pushing and pulling, it follows that all local motion which is from another is

reduced to pushing and pulling. Hence it is clear that if in pushing and pulling the mover and the moved are together, such that the pusher is together with that which is pushed and the puller with that which is pulled, consequently it is universally true that there is nothing intermediate between a mover in respect to place and the moved.

907. Next where he says, **"This is clear from . . ."** [Appendix A, 691], he proves the proposition in regard to these two motions.

First he gives two arguments to prove the proposition. Secondly, where he says, **"There is throwing . . ."** [Appendix A, 692], he refutes an objection.

The first argument is taken from the definition of each motion. Pushing is a motion from the mover itself or from something else to something else. And so at least at the beginning of the motion the pusher must be together with that which is pushed, until the pusher moves that which is pushed from itself or from another. But pulling is a motion toward one's self or toward another, as was said; and the puller is not separated from that which is pulled. From this it is clear that in these two motions the mover and the moved are together.

The second argument is taken from combination and separation. It was said that pushing is a separation and pulling is a combination. And he says that **"thus far there is coming together, i.e., combination, and going apart, i.e., division"** [Appendix A, 691]. Now it is not possible for something to combine or separate unless it is present in those things which are being combined or separated. And so it is clear that in pushing and pulling the mover and the moved are together.

908. Next where he says, **"There is throwing . . ."** [Appendix A, 692], he refutes a certain objection which can be raised concerning pushing. In regard to pulling it was said that the motion of the puller is not separated from that which is pulled. But in regard to pushing it was said that sometimes the pusher withdraws from that which is pushed. And this type of pushing is called pushing away, a species of which is "throwing," which occurs when a thing is thrown to a distance through violence. And so in throwing it seems that the mover and the moved are not together. Therefore, in order to refute this, he says that throwing occurs when the motion of that which is moved is swifter than its natural motion, and this occurs because some strong pushing has been done. For when something is thrown by a strong impulse, the air is moved by a swifter motion than its natural motion; and the thrown body is carried toward the motion of the air. And as long as the impulse of the air remains, the thrown object is moved. He says that, when such an impulse has been made, a thrown object is carried along as long as there is in the air a motion which is stronger than its natural motion.

Having removed this difficulty, he concludes that the mover and the moved are together and there is no intermediate between them.

In Alteration and in Increase and Decrease the Mover and the Moved Are Together

The Text of Aristotle

693. Now it is impossible to move anything either from oneself to something else or from something else to oneself without being in contact with it: it is evident, therefore, that in all locomotion there is nothing intermediate between moved and mover. Nor again is there anything intermediate between that which undergoes and that which causes alteration:

244b2–5

694. this can be proved by induction; for in every case we find that the respective extremities of that which causes and that which undergoes alteration are adjacent. For our assumption is that things that are undergoing alteration are altered in virtue of their being affected in respect of their so-called affective qualities, since that which is of a certain quality is altered in so far as it is sensible, and the characteristics in which bodies differ from one another are sensible characteristics; for every body differs from another in possessing a greater or lesser number of sensible characteristics or in possessing the same sensible characteristics in a greater or lesser degree. But the alteration of that which undergoes alteration is also caused by the above-mentioned characteristics, which are affections of some particular underlying quality. Thus we say that a thing is altered by becoming hot or sweet or thick or dry or white; and we make these assertions alike of what is inanimate and of what is animate, and further, where animate things are in question, we make them both of the parts that have no power of sense-perception and of the senses themselves. For in a way even the senses undergo alteration, since the active sense is a motion through the body in the course of which the sense is affected in a certain way. We see, then, that the animate is capable of every kind of alteration of which the inanimate is capable; but the inanimate is not capable of every kind of alteration of which the animate is capable, since it is not capable of alteration in respect of the senses: moreover the inanimate is unconscious of being affected by alteration, whereas the animate is conscious of it, though there is nothing to prevent the animate also being unconscious of it when the process of the alteration does not concern the senses. Since, then, the alteration of that which undergoes alteration is caused by sensible things, in every case of such alteration it is evident that the respective extremities of that which causes and that which undergoes alteration are adjacent.

244b5–245a5

695. Thus the air is continuous with that which causes the alteration, and the body that undergoes alteration is continuous with the air. Again, the color is continuous with the light and the light with the sight. And the same is true of hearing and smelling; for the primary mover in respect to the moved is the air. Similarly, in the case of tasting, the flavor is adjacent to the sense of taste. And it is just the same in the case of things that are inanimate and incapable of sense-perception.

245a5–10

696. Thus there can be nothing intermediate between that which undergoes and that which causes alteration. Nor, again, can there be anything intermediate between that which suffers and that which causes increase; for the part of the latter that starts the increase does so by becoming attached in such a way to the former that the whole becomes one. Again, the decrease of that which suffers decrease is caused by a part of the thing becoming detached. So that which causes increase and that which causes decrease must be continuous with that which suffers increase and that which suffers decrease respectively; and if two things are continuous with one another there can be nothing intermediate between them.

It is evident, therefore, that between the extremities of the moved and the mover that are
respectively first and last in reference to the moved there is nothing intermediate.

245a10–245b2

COMMENTARY OF ST. THOMAS

909. After he has shown in regard to local motion that the mover and the moved are together, he shows that the same thing is true of alteration; namely, that there is nothing intermediate between that which alters and that which is altered. He proves this first by induction. In all things which are altered it is clear that the ultimate thing which alters and the first thing which is altered are together.

It seems, however, that this is difficult to see in certain alterations, as when the sun warms the air without warming the intermediate orbs of the planets; and as when a fish, caught in a net, benumbs the hands dragging the net without having the same effect on the net.

But it must be said that things which are passive receive the action of things which are active according to their proper mode. Therefore, the intermediates which are between the first thing which alters and the ultimate thing which is altered undergo something from the first thing which alters, but perhaps not in the same manner as the ultimate thing which is altered. The net, therefore, suffers something from the benumbing fish, but not numbness, because it has no capacity for it. And the intermediate orbs of the planets receive something from the sun, namely light, but not heat.

910. Secondly, where he says, **"Quality is altered . . ."** [Appendix A, 694], he proves the same thing with an argument. The argument is as follows.

Every alteration is similar to the alteration which occurs in respect to the senses. But in an alteration of the senses, the alterer and the thing altered are together. Therefore, this is true of every alteration. He proves the first point as follows. Every alteration occurs with respect to a sensible quality, which is the third species of quality. For bodies are altered with respect to these things in which bodies are primarily different from one another. These are the sensible qualities, as heaviness and lightness; hardness and softness, which are perceived by touch; sound and silence, which are perceived by hearing (but, nevertheless, if sound is taken in act, it is a quality in the air, and consequently a local motion; hence it does not seem with respect to a quality of this kind that there is alteration primarily and per se; but if sound is taken appropriately, then a thing becomes audible or not audible through an alteration); whiteness and blackness, which pertain to sight; sweet and bitter, which pertain to taste; wet and dry, density and rarity, which pertain to touch. And the same argument applies to their opposites and intermediates. And likewise there are other things which fall under the senses, like warmth and cold, and smoothness and roughness, which are also grasped by touch.

Such things are passions contained under the genus of quality. They are called passions because they force a passion on the senses or because they are caused by passions, as is said in the Categories. They are called, moreover, "passions of sensible bodies" because sensible bodies differ in respect to them insofar as one is warm and another cold, one is heavy and another light, and so forth, or insofar as one of the foregoing is in two things to a greater or lesser degree. For fire differs from water in respect to the difference of hot and cold, and from air in respect to greater and lesser heat. Furthermore, differences in sensible bodies occur insofar as they undergo one of these, though it may not be in them naturally. For example, we say that things which are heated differ from things which are cooled, and things which become sweet differ from things which become bitter, through some passion and not from nature.

To be altered with respect to qualities of this kind happens to every sensible body, both animate and inanimate. In animate bodies certain parts are "animated," that is, sensitive, as the eye and the hand, and other parts are "not animated," that is, not sensitive, as hair and bones. Both types of parts are altered with respect to qualities of this kind, because the senses suffer in the act of sensing. For the actions of the senses, like hearing and vision, are motions through the body with some passion of the senses. For the senses do not have any action except through a bodily organ. And it is proper for a body to be moved and altered. Hence passion and alteration are more appropriately predicated of the senses rather than intellect, whose operation is not through a bodily organ.

Thus it is clear that animate bodies are altered in respect to all the qualities and all the motions by which inanimate bodies are altered. But this statement cannot be converted. For in animate bodies there is found alteration in respect to the senses, which is not found in inanimate bodies. For inanimate bodies do not have knowledge of their alteration. Rather this is concealed from them. This would not be the case if they were altered in respect to sensation.

And lest anyone think that it is impossible for a thing to be altered with respect to a sensible quality without sensing the alteration, he adds that not only is this true of inanimate things but it happens even to animate things. For nothing prevents even animate bodies from being unaware when they are altered. This happens when alteration occurs in such beings without an alteration of the senses, as when they are altered with respect to their non-sensitive parts.

From this it is clear that if the passions of the senses are such that there is no intermediary between the agent and the patient, and if every alteration is through passions of this type by which the senses are altered, then it follows that the alterer introducing the passions and the thing altered undergoing them are together, and there is nothing intermediate between them.

911. Next where he says, **"Moreover air is . . ."** [Appendix A, 695], he proves the second point, namely, that in the alteration of the senses the alterer and the thing altered are together. For air is continuous with the sense, for example, sight, and is joined to it without an intermediary. And the visible body is continuous with the air. And the surface of a visible body, which is the subject of color, is terminated at light, that is, at the illuminated air, which is terminated at sight. And so it is clear that the air which is altered and that which alters it are together, and similarly sight which is altered is together with the air which alters. And the same is true of hearing and smelling, if they are compared to that which moves primarily, that is, to the sensible

body. For these sensations occur through an extrinsic medium. Taste and flavor are together for they are not joined through some extrinsic medium, and the same is true of touch. And in this way he maintains that in inanimate and insensible things the alterer and the thing altered are together.

912. Next where he says, **"And that which is increased . . ."** [Appendix A, 696], he proves the same thing in regard to the motion of increase and decrease. First he treats the motion of increase. That which is increased and the increaser must be together because increase is a kind of addition. Through the addition of some quantity a thing is increased. And the same is true of decrease, for the cause of decrease is the subtraction of some quantity.

This proof may be understood in two ways. First one could say that the quantity which is added or subtracted is the proximate mover in these motions. For Aristotle says in De Anima, II, that flesh increases insofar as it is a quantity. And so it is clear that the moved is together with the mover. For a thing cannot be added to or subtracted from another if it is not together with it. This argument also deals with the principal agent. For every addition is a type of gathering, and subtraction is a type of separation. Moreover, it was shown above that in the motion of gathering and separating the mover and the moved are together. Hence it follows that this is also true of increase and decrease.

And thus he finally concludes universally that there is no intermediary between the ultimate mover and the first thing moved.

There Is No Alteration in the Fourth Species of Quality (Form and Figure) in the First Species of Quality (Habit and Disposition) in Regard to the Body

The Text of Aristotle
Chapter 3

697. *Everything, we say, that undergoes alteration is altered by sensible causes, and there is alteration only in things that are said to be essentially affected by sensible things. The truth of this is to be seen from the following considerations.* **245b3–6**

698. *Of all other things it would be most natural to suppose that there is alteration in figures and shapes, and in acquired states and in the processes of acquiring and losing these; but as a matter of fact in neither of these two classes of things is there alteration.* **245b6–9**

699. *In the first place, when a particular formation of a thing is completed, we do not call it by the name of its material: e.g., we do not call the statue "bronze" or the pyramid "wax" or the bed "wood," but we use a derived expression and call them "of bronze," "waxen," and "wooden" respectively. But when a thing has been affected and altered in any way we still call it by the original name: thus we speak of the bronze or the wax being dry or fluid or hard or hot. And not only so: we also speak of the particular fluid or hot substance as being bronze, giving the material the same name as that which we use to describe the affection.*

Since, therefore, having regard to the figure or shape of a thing we no longer call that which has become of a certain figure by the name of the material that exhibits the figure, whereas having regard to a thing's affections or alterations we still call it by the name of its material, it is evident that becomings of the former kind cannot be alterations. **245b9–246a4**

700. *Moreover it would seem absurd even to speak in this way, to speak, that is to say, of a man or house or anything else that has come into existence as having been altered. Though it may be true that every such becoming is necessarily the result of something's being altered, the result, e.g., of the material's being condensed or rarefied or heated or cooled, nevertheless it is not the things that are coming into existence that are altered, and their becoming is not an alteration.* **246a4–9**

701. *Again, acquired states, whether of the body or of the soul, are not alterations. For some are excellences and others are defects, and neither excellence nor defect is an alteration: excellence is a perfection (for when anything acquires its proper excellence we call it perfect, since it is then if ever that we have a thing in its natural state: e.g., we have a perfect circle when we have one as good as possible), while defect is a perishing of or departure from this condition. So just as when speaking of a house we do not call its arrival at perfection an alteration (for it would be absurd to suppose that the coping or the thing is an alteration or that in receiving its coping or its tiling a house is altered and not perfected), the same also holds good in the case of excellences and defects and of the persons or things that possess or acquire them; for excellences are perfections of a thing's nature and defects are departures from it: consequently they are not alterations.* **246a9–246b3**

COMMENTARY OF ST. THOMAS

913. Since in the preceding argument the Philosopher has assumed that every alteration occurs with respect to sensible things, he intends here to prove this.

First he states his intention. Secondly, where he says, **"Of the other things . . ."** [Appendix A, 698], he proves the proposition.

He says, therefore, first [Appendix

A, 697] that from the following it must be realized that all things which are altered are altered with respect to sensible qualities, and consequently only those things are capable of being altered which per se are affected by qualities of this kind.

914. Next where he says, "Of the other things..." [Appendix A, 698], he proves the proposition by arguing from the major.

First he states the major. Secondly, where he says, "That from which the form . . ." [Appendix A, 699], he proves a certain thing which he has assumed.

He says, therefore, first that over and above sensible qualities, alteration especially seems to occur in the fourth species of quality, which is quality with respect to quantity, namely form and figure, and in the first species of quality, which contains habit and disposition. For it seems that there is alteration in these cases because qualities of this kind are removed with respect to something new or are acquired with respect to something new. And it does not seem that this can occur without a mutation. But alteration is mutation in respect to quality, as was shown above.

But in the above mentioned qualities of the first and fourth species, alteration does not occur primarily and principally, but secondarily. For qualities of this kind are consequent upon certain alterations of the primary qualities. For example, it is clear that when a material subject becomes dense or rarefied, there follows a mutation with respect to figure, and similarly when it becomes warm or grows cold, there follows a mutation with respect to sickness and health, which pertains to the first species of quality. Rarity and density, and warmth and cold, are sensible qualities, thus it is clear that there is no alteration primarily and per se in the first and fourth species of quality. Rather the removal and reception of qualities of this kind are consequent upon an alteration which occurs with respect to sensible qualities.

From this it is also clear why he makes no mention of the second species of quality, which is natural power or lack of power. For it is clear that natural power or the lack of it is received or removed only through a natural change of alteration. Therefore, he omits this as if it were obvious.

915. Next where he says, "That from which the form . . ." [Appendix A, 699], he proves what he has assumed.

First he proves that there is no alteration in the fourth species of quality. Secondly, where he says, "Nor is there alteration . . ." [Appendix A, 701], he proves that there is no alteration in the first species of quality.

Concerning the first point he gives two arguments. The first is taken from a mode of speaking. It must be realized that form and figure differ from each other in that figure signifies the termination of quantity. For a figure is that which is contained by a terminus or termini. And a form is said to be that which gives specific being to an artifact. For the forms of artifacts are accidents.

He says, therefore, that that which becomes the form of a statue we do not call "form," that is, the matter of the statue is not predicated of the statue principally and directly. The same is true of the figure of a pyramid or a bed. Rather in such cases the matter is predicated denominatively, for we say a triangle is "of bronze" or "waxen" or "wooden." And the same is true of other things. But in things which are altered we predicate the passion of the subject, for we say that bronze is damp or strong or warm. And conversely we say that the damp or the warm is bronze, equally predicating the matter of the passion, and vice versa. We also say that man is white, and the white is man. Since, therefore, in forms and figures the matter is not predicated equally with figure, such that the one is predicated of the other principally and directly, but matter is predicated of figure and form only denominatively, while in things which are altered the subject and the passion are predicated equally of each other, it follows that in forms and figures there is no alteration. Rather this occurs only in sensible qualities.

916. He gives the second argument where he says, **"Further there is another . . ."** [Appendix A, 700]. This argument is taken from a property of the thing.

It is ridiculous to say that a man or a house or any other thing is altered because it receives the end of its own perfection. For example, if a house is completed because it is covered, or because it is faced with brick, or because it is roofed, it is ridiculous to say that the house is altered when it is roofed or faced with brick. For it is clear that there is no alteration of things which come to be insofar as they come to be. Rather each thing is completed and comes to be insofar as it receives its proper form and figure. Therefore, there is no alteration in the reception of form and figure.

917. To understand these arguments one must realize that among all qualities figures are especially consequent upon and reveal the species of things. This is particularly clear with respect to plants and animals, in which no more certain judgment of the diver-

sity of species can be had than the judgment of the diversity of their figures. This is so because, just as quantity is more closely related to substance than the other accidents, likewise figure, which is a quality of quantity, is most closely related to the form of the substance. Hence, just as some say that dimensions are the substance of things, others say that figures are substantial forms. And because of this an image, which is an expressed representation of a thing, is noticed by its figure more than by its color or something else. And since art is the imitator of nature, and since an artifact is an image of a natural thing, the forms of artifacts are figures or something very similar.

And, therefore, because of the similarity of such forms and figures to substantial forms, the Philosopher says that with respect to the reception of form and figure there is no alteration but perfection. This is also true because the matter of such things is predicated only denominatively, as is also true of natural substances. For we do not say that man is earth but that man is "earthen."

918. Next where he says, **"Nor is there alteration . . ."** [Appendix A, 701], he shows that there is no alteration in the first species of quality.

He shows this first in regard to the habits and dispositions of the body. Secondly, where he says, **"Nor is there alteration . . ."** [Appendix A, 702], he shows this in regard to the habits and dispositions of the soul.

Concerning the first point he gives the following argument. Even corporeal habits, which belong to the first species of quality, are virtues and vices. For universally virtue is that which makes the one who has it good, and its operation results in good.

Hence, that is called a virtue of the body in respect to which the body is well constituted and acting well, for example, health. And the contrary is true of vice, for example, sickness. Moreover, every virtue and vice is predicated in relation to something. He explains this with examples. Health, which is a virtue of the body, is a certain proportion of hot and cold things. This proportion arises from the proper proportion of the "things which are within," i.e., the humors, from which the body is composed, to each other and to the "container," i.e., the whole body. For that harmony of the humors which is health for a lion is not health for a man, but his death, because human nature cannot endure it.

However the Commentator says that "container" means the containing air. But the first interpretation is better. For the health of an animal is not determined in relation to the air. Rather, conversely, the disposition of air is called healthy in relation to the animal.

Likewise, beauty and barrenness are predicated in relation to something. (Barrenness is understood as a disposition by which one is led to motion and action.) Such things are certain dispositions of that which is complete in its own nature in comparison to an "optimum," that is, to an end, which is operation. For it was said that dispositions of this kind are called virtues because they make the one who has them good and their operation produces good. Therefore, such dispositions are predicated in relation to a proper operation, which is the "optimum" of the thing.

It is not necessary to say that "optimum" means something extrinsic, as that which is most beautiful or most healthy, as the Commentator says. For a relation to an extrinsic, optimum disposition pertains to beauty and health, but a relation to good operation belongs to them per se.

And lest anyone should understand "perfect" as meaning "already having attained an end," he says that "perfect" here means that which is disposed to health according to nature. Nor is it to be understood here that such habits and dispositions in themselves are relations. For then they would not be in the genus of quality but in the genus of relation. Rather their nature [ratio] depends on some relation.

Therefore, since such habits are in relation to something, and since in relation there is neither motion nor generation nor alteration, as was proven in Book V, it is clear that in such habits there is no alteration primarily and per se. Rather their transmutation follows from some prior transmutation of hot and cold, or some such things, just as relations also begin to be as the result of some motion.

There is No Alteration in the First Species of Quality in Regard to Habits of the Soul

The Text of Aristotle

702. *Further, we say that all excellences depend upon particular relations. Thus bodily excellences such as health and a good state of body we regard as consisting in a blending of hot and cold elements within the body in due proportion, in relation either to one another or to the surrounding atmosphere; and in like manner we regard beauty, strength, and all the other bodily excellences and defects. Each of them exists in virtue of a particular relation and puts that which possesses it in a good or bad condition with regard to its proper affections, where by "proper" affections I mean those influences that from the natural constitution of a thing tend to promote or destroy its existence.* 246b3–10

703. *Since, then, relatives are neither themselves alterations nor the subjects of alteration or of becoming or in fact of any change whatever,* 246b10–12

704. *it is evident that neither states nor the processes of losing and acquiring states are alterations, though it may be true that their becoming or perishing is necessarily, like the becoming or perishing of a specific character or form, the result of the alteration of certain other things, e.g., hot and cold or dry and wet elements or the elements, whatever they may be, on which the states primarily depend. For each several bodily defect or excellence involves a relation with those things from which the possessor of the defect or excellence is naturally subject to alteration: thus excellence disposes its possessor to be unaffected by these influences or to be affected by those of them that ought to be admitted, while defect disposes its possessor to be affected by them or to be unaffected by those of them that ought to be admitted.* 246b12–20

705. *And the case is similar in regard to the states of the soul, all of which (like those of body) exist in virtue of particular relations, the excellences being perfections of nature and the defects departures from it: moreover, excellence puts its possessor in good condition, while defect puts its possessor in a bad condition, to meet his proper affections. Consequently these cannot any more than the bodily states be alterations, nor can the processes of losing and acquiring them be so, though their becoming is necessarily the result of an alteration of the sensitive part of the soul, and this is altered by sensible objects; for all moral excellence is concerned with bodily pleasures and pains, which again depend either upon acting or upon remembering or upon anticipating. Now those that depend upon action are determined by sense-perception, i.e., they are stimulated by something sensible; and those that depend upon memory or anticipation are likewise to be traced to sense-perception; for in these cases pleasure is felt either in remembering what one has experienced or in anticipating what one is going to experience. Thus all pleasure of this kind must be produced by sensible things; and since the presence in any one of moral defect or excellence involves the presence in him of pleasure or pain (with which moral excellence and defect are always concerned), and these pleasures and pains are alterations of the sensitive part, it is evident that the loss and acquisition of these states no less than the loss and acquisition of the states of the body must be the result of the alteration of something else. Consequently, though their becoming is accompanied by an alteration, they are not themselves alterations.* 246b20–247a19

706. *Again, the states of the intellectual part of the soul are not alterations, nor is there any becoming of them. In the first place it is much more true of the possession of knowledge that it depends upon a particular relation. And further, it is evident that there is no becoming of these states. For that which is potentially possessed of knowledge becomes actually possessed of it not by being set in motion at all itself but by reason of the presence of something else: i.e., it is when*

it meets with the particular object that it knows in a manner the particular through its
knowledge of the universal. 247b1–7

707. *(Again, there is no becoming of the actual use and activity of these states, unless it is*
thought that there is a becoming of vision and touching and that the activity in question is
similar to these.) 247b7–9

708. *And the original acquisition of knowledge is not a becoming or an alteration; for the*
terms "knowing" and "understanding" imply that the intellect has reached a state of rest and
come to a standstill, and there is no becoming that leads to a state of rest, since, as we have said
above, no change at all can have a becoming. Moreover, just as to say, when anyone has passed
from a state of intoxication or sleep or disease to the contrary state, that he has become possessed
of knowledge again is incorrect in spite of the fact that he was previously incapable of using his
knowledge, so, too, when anyone originally acquires the state, it is incorrect to say that he
becomes possessed of knowledge; for the possession of understanding and knowledge is produced
by the soul's settling down out of the restlessness natural to it. Hence, too, in learning and in
forming judgments on matters relating to their sense-perceptions children are inferior to adults
owing to the great amount of restlessness and motion in their souls. Nature itself causes the
soul to settle down and come to a state of rest for the performance of some of its functions, while
for the performance of others other things do so; but in either case the result is brought about
through the alteration of something in the body, as we see in the case of the use and activity of
the intellect arising from a man's becoming sober or being awakened. It is evident, then, from
the preceding argument that alteration and being altered occur in sensible things and in the
sensitive part of the soul and, except accidentally, in nothing else. 247b9–248a9

COMMENTARY OF ST. THOMAS

919. After the Philosopher has shown that there is no alteration in the first species of quality with respect to dispositions of the body, he here shows the same thing with respect to habits of the soul.

First he treats the appetitive part. Secondly, where he says, **"Nor is there alteration . . ."** [Appendix A, 706], he treats the intellective part.

Concerning the first part he makes two points. First he shows that there is no alteration primarily and per se in the transmutation of virtue and vice. Secondly, where he says, **"Both the reception of . . ."** [Appendix A, 703], he shows that the transmutation of virtue and vice follows from an alteration.

920. He concludes, therefore, first from the above that in regard to the virtues and vices of the soul which pertain to the appetitive part there is no alteration primarily and per se. In

drawing this conclusion he indicates that in proving the following points he will use the same arguments with which he proved the foregoing points.

For this proof he assumes a certain proposition, namely, that virtue is a type of perfection. He proves this as follows. Each thing is perfect when it is able to attain its proper virtue, just as a natural body is perfect when it is able to produce something like itself, which is the virtue of nature.

He proves this as follows. A thing is most perfect in respect to nature when it possesses the virtue of nature, for the virtue of nature is an indication of the completion of nature. Moreover, when a thing possesses its nature completely, then it is called perfect. This is true not only of natural things but also of mathematicals, whose forms are taken as their natures. For a thing is most circular, that is, it is a perfect circle, when it is most perfect in respect to nature, that is, when it has the perfection of its form.

It is, therefore, clear that since the virtue of each thing follows from the perfection of its form, then each thing is perfect when it has its own virtue. And thus it follows that virtue is a perfection.

When this proposition has been thusly proven, the Commentator says that one must argue as follows. Every perfection is simple and indivisible. But in no case is either motion or alteration simple and indivisible, as was proven above. Therefore in respect to virtue there is no alteration.

But this process does not apply to what is added in respect to vice, namely, that vice is the corruption and removal of perfection. For although perfection is simple and indivisible, nevertheless, to withdraw from perfection is not simple and indivisible. Rather this occurs in many ways. Nor is it the custom of Aristotle to omit that on which a conclusion chiefly depends, unless it can be understood from things posited nearby.

Therefore it is better to say that he argues here about virtue just as he did above about form and figure. For nothing is said to be altered when it is perfected, nor for the same reason, when it is corrupted. If, therefore, virtue is a perfection, and vice a corruption, then there is no alteration in respect to virtue and vice, just as there is no alteration in respect to forms and figures.

921. Next where he says, "Both the reception of . . ." [Appendix A, 703], he shows that the transmutation of virtue and vice follows from an alteration.

First he states his intention. He says that the reception of virtue and the removal of vice, or vice versa, occurs when something is altered. The recep-

tion and removal of virtue and vice follow from this alteration. However, neither of them is an alteration primarily and per se.

Next where he says, "It is clear that something . . ." [Appendix A, 704], he proves his position. He says that it is clear from the following that something must be altered in order that virtue or vice be received and removed.

He seems to prove this in two ways. He does this first with respect to two opinions of men concerning virtue and vice.

The Stoics said that virtues are certain impassive things, and there cannot be virtue in the soul unless all passions like fear, hope, and such things are removed from the soul. They said that such passions are certain disturbances and sicknesses of the soul. And they said that virtue is a certain tranquillity, as it were, and health of the soul. On the other hand they said that every passivity of the soul is a vice.

The opinion of the Peripatetics, derived from Aristotle, is that virtue consists in a determinate moderation of the passions. For moral virtue is a mean between passions, as is said in Ethics, II. And according to this, vice, as opposed to virtue, is not any kind of passivity but a certain tendency toward the passions which are contrary to virtue either by way of excess or defect.

Whichever view may be true, in order that virtue be received there must be a transmutation of the passions, i.e., the passions are either totally removed or are modified. For since passions are in the sensitive appetite, alteration occurs with respect to them. It follows, therefore, that the reception or removal of virtue and vice occurs with respect to some alteration.

922. Secondly, where he says, **"All moral virtue occurs . . ."** [Appendix A, 705], he proves the same thing as follows. Every moral virtue consists of some pleasure or sadness. For he is not just who does not rejoice in just acts and who is not saddened by their opposites. And the same applies to the other moral virtues. This is so because the operation of every appetitive power in which there is moral virtue is terminated at pleasure and sadness. Pleasure results from the attainment of that toward which the appetite is moved, and sadness from the triumph of that which the appetite flees. And thus one who desires or hopes is delighted when he attains what he desires or hopes for; and similarly he is angered whenever he takes vengeance; and one who fears and hates is saddened when the evil which he flees triumphs. Every sadness or pleasure occurs either in respect to the act of a present thing or through memory of a past thing, or through hope for something future. Therefore, if there is pleasure in respect to act, the cause of this pleasure is sensation. For an object does not properly cause pleasure if it is not sensed. Likewise, if pleasure occurs through memory or hope, this proceeds from the senses as long as we either recall whatever pleasures we have undergone with respect to the senses in the past, or as long as we hope to undergo such things in the future. From this it is clear that pleasure and sadness belong to the sensitive part, in which alteration occurs, as was said above. If, therefore, moral virtue and the opposite vice exist in pleasure and sadness, and if there is alteration in respect to pleasure and sadness, then it follows that the reception or removal of virtue and vice follow from an alteration.

But it is to be noted that he distinctly says that the whole of moral virtue exists in pleasures and sadnesses, in distinction from intellectual virtue, which has its own pleasure. But this latter pleasure does not pertain to the senses. Hence it has no contrary, nor is it altered, except metaphorically.

923. Next where he says, **"Nor is there alteration . . ."** [Appendix A, 706], he shows that there is no alteration in the intellective part of the soul.

He proves first this in general; and secondly, in particular, where he says, **"Neither, therefore, is there . . ."** [Appendix A, 707].

Concerning the first part he introduces the following argument. Knowing is primarily called a relation, namely, to the knowable, the assimilation of which in the knower is knowledge.

This he proves as follows. In no genus other than relation does it happen that something new comes to a thing without it changing. For one thing becomes equal to another, not by its own mutation, but by that of the other. We see, moreover, that knowledge occurs without any mutation in intellective potency but only through something existing in the sensitive part. For from experiences of particulars, which pertain to the sensitive part, we achieve a knowledge of the universal in the intellect, as was proven in Metaphysics, I, and in Posterior Analytics, II. Since, therefore, there is no motion in relation, as was proven above, it follows that there is no alteration in the acquisition of knowledge.

924. Next where he says, **"Neither, therefore, is there . . ."** [Appendix A, 707], he shows in particular that there is no alteration in the intellective part.

He does this first by considering the one who has knowledge. This refers to the use of knowledge. Secondly, where he says, **"Since the reception of . . ."** [Appendix A, 708], he considers the first acquisition of knowledge.

He says, therefore, first that since there is no alteration in the intellective part, it cannot be said that the very act of knowledge, which is consideration, is a generation, unless one would say that the eye's exterior act of looking, and the act of touching something, are generations. For just as sight is the act of the visual power and touching is the act of the tactile power, so consideration is the act of the intellective power. Act is not said to be the generation of a principle, but rather a process from an active principle. And so understanding is neither generation nor alteration. Nevertheless, nothing prevents an act from following from generation or alteration, as making hot follows from the generation of fire. And likewise seeing or touching follows from the immutation of the sense by a sensible object.

925. Next where he says, **"Since the reception of . . ."** [Appendix A, 708], he shows that in the acquisition of knowledge there is neither generation or alteration.

Whatever happens to a thing only through the rest and abating of disturbances or motions does not happen through generation or alteration. But understanding, which is speculative thought, and prudence, which is practical reason, come to the soul through the rest and abating of corporeal motions and sensible affections. Understanding and prudence, therefore, do not come to the soul through generation or alteration.

For the clarification of this argument, he adds examples. Let it be proposed that someone who has knowledge is sleeping, or is not sober,

or is ill. It is clear that he is unable to use his knowledge and to act in accordance with it. And it is clear that when this disturbance becomes quiet, and the mind returns to its own state, then he is able to use his knowledge and act in accordance with it. Nevertheless we do not say that when the sleeping man is aroused, or when the drunken man becomes sober, or when the mind of the sick man is returned to its proper state through health, that then he is made to be one who knows as if knowledge were newly generated in him. For there was in him an habitual potency "for the suitability of knowledge," i.e., to be restored to the appropriate state in which he could use his knowledge.

He says, moreover, that something of this kind occurs when one acquires knowledge originally. For this seems to take place because of a certain rest and abating of disturbance, i.e., of disordered motions, such as are in boys both with respect to the body, since the whole nature is changing because of growth, and also with respect to the sensitive part, since the passions are dominant in them.

Hence that which he calls "rest" can be applied to the disturbance of bodily motion, which becomes quiet when nature achieves its state. That which he calls "abating" can be applied to the passions of the sensitive parts, which are not wholly at rest, but which are inactive. That is, they are subdued by reason and do not ascend to disturb reason, just as we speak of a settling in liquids, when the lees sink to the bottom and that which is above remains pure.

This is the reason why young men cannot learn by taking what is said by others. With their internal senses they are unable to pass judgment on what they have heard or on anything which presents itself to their thought as well as their seniors or elders (which mean the same, for "presbyter" in Greek is the same as "senior" in Latin). This is because there are many disturbances and motions around these young men, as was said. But a disturbance of this kind may be removed completely, or at least mitigated, sometimes by nature as when one has reached advanced old age in which motions of this kind cease and sometimes by other causes such as practice and habit. Then they are able to learn well and judge well. Thereafter exercise of the moral virtues, through which such passions are curbed, is especially effective for acquiring knowledge.

Whether the disturbance of the passions ceases through nature or through the exercise of virtue, some alteration is involved because passions of this kind are in the sensitive part. In the same way there is also a bodily alteration when one who is sleeping arises and awakens and proceeds to act. From this it is clear that the acquisition of knowledge is not an alteration, but follows from an alteration.

From this he further concludes universally that alteration occurs in the external senses, and in the sensibles, and in the whole sensitive part of the soul (which he says because of the internal passions). But in no other part of the soul is there alteration, except per accidens.

926. What Aristotle says here about the acquisition of knowledge seems to follow the Platonic opinion. For Plato held that, just as separated forms are the causes of the generation and existence of natural things because corporeal matter in some way participates in these separated forms, likewise they are also the cause of knowledge in us because our soul in some way partici-

pates in them. This participation of separated forms in our soul is knowledge. So it will be true that knowledge is received from a principle, not through the generation of knowledge in the soul, but only through the rest of the bodily and sensible passions by which the soul is impeded from using knowledge. Thus it will also be true that, with no mutation in the intellect, a man becomes a knower only because of the presence of the sensible things which we experience, as is also true of relations. For according to this sensible things are not necessary for knowledge, except that the soul is aroused in some way by them.

Aristotle's opinion, however, is that knowledge occurs in the soul because intelligible species, abstracted by the agent intellect, are received into the possible intellect, as is said in De Anima, III. Hence, in the same place, it is said that to know is to suffer something, although the passivity of sense and intellect is different.

Nor is it inconsistent that Aristotle uses this opinion from Plato. For before he proves his own opinion, he customarily uses the opinion of others. For example, in Book III he used Plato's opinion that every sensible body has heaviness and lightness, the contrary of which he himself shows in De Caelo, I.

927. Nevertheless, these arguments are also valid according to the opinion of Aristotle.

To see this it must be realized that that which is receptive can be related to the form which it receives in three ways.

Sometimes the receiver is in the ultimate disposition for the reception of a form, with no hindrance existing either in itself or in another. In this case the receiver immediately receives the form, without any alteration, because of the presence of the agent, as is clear in air which is illuminated by the presence of the sun.

Sometimes, however, the receiver is not in the ultimate disposition for the reception of a form. In this case there is required a per se alteration according to which matter acquires a disposition in order to be suited to this form, as when fire comes to be from the air.

Sometimes the receiver is in the ultimate disposition for form, but there is some hindrance, as when air is hindered from receiving light, either because of closed windows or because of clouds. In this case an alteration or a mutation per accidens is required to remove the hindrance.

Now the possible intellect, considered in itself, is always in the ultimate disposition to receive the intelligible species. Therefore, if there is no hindrance, then immediately upon presentation of the objects taken through experience the intelligible species comes to it, just as a form is in a mirror as a result of the presence of a body. And his first argument, in which he says that knowledge is a relation, deals with this. But if there is a hindrance, as happens in youths, such hindrances must be banished so that the intelligible species may be received in the intellect. And thus an alteration is necessary per accidens.

LECTURE 7 [248a10–249a7]
The Comparison of Motions. He Shows in General What Is Required for Things to Be Comparable

The Text of Aristotle
Chapter 4

709. *A difficulty may be raised as to whether every motion is commensurable with every other or not. Now if they are all commensurable and if two things to have the same velocity must accomplish an equal motion in an equal time, then we may have a circumference equal to a straight line, or, of course, the one may be greater or less than the other. Further, if one thing alters and another accomplishes a locomotion in an equal time, we may have an alteration and a locomotion equal to one another: thus an affection will be equal to a length, which is impossible.*
248a10–15

710. *But is it not only when an equal motion is accomplished by two things in an equal time that the velocities of the two are equal? Now an affection cannot be equal to a length. Therefore there cannot be an alteration equal to or less than a locomotion; and consequently it is not the case that every motion is commensurable with every other.*
248a15–18

711. *But how will our conclusion work out in the case of the circle and the straight line? It would be absurd to suppose that the motion of one thing in a circle and of another in a straight line cannot be similar, but that the one must inevitably move more quickly or more slowly than the other, just as if the course of one were downhill and of the other uphill.*
248a18–22

712. *Moreover it does not as a matter of fact make any difference to the argument to say that the one motion must inevitably be quicker or slower than the other; for then the circumference can be greater or less than the straight line; and if so it is possible for the two to be equal. For if in the time A the quicker passes over the distance B and the slower (C) passes over the distance C, B will be greater than C; for this is what we took "quicker" to mean; and so quicker motion also implies that one thing traverses an equal distance in less time than another; consequently there will be a part of A in which B will pass over a part of the circle equal to C, while C will occupy the whole of A in passing over C.*
248a22–248b4

713. *None the less, if the two motions are commensurable, we are confronted with the consequence stated above, viz. that there may be a straight line equal to a circle. But these are not commensurable; and so the corresponding motions are not commensurable either.* **248b4–6**

714. *But may we say that things are always commensurable if the same terms are applied to them without equivocation? E.g., a pen, a wine, and the highest note in a scale are not commensurable: we cannot say whether any one of them is sharper than any other; and why is this? they are incommensurable because it is only equivocally that the same term "sharp" is applied to them: whereas the highest note in a scale is commensurable with the leading-note, because the term "sharp" has the same meaning as applied to both. Can it be, then, that the term "quick" has not the same meaning as applied to straight motion and to circular motion respectively? If so, far less will it have the same meaning as applied to alteration and to locomotion.*
248b6–12

715. *Or shall we in the first place deny that things are always commensurable if the same terms are applied to them without equivocation? For the term "much" has the same meaning whether applied to water or to air, yet water and air are not commensurable in respect of it; or, if this illustration is not considered satisfactory, "double" at any rate would seem to have the same meaning, as applied to each (denoting in each case the proportion of two to one), yet water and air are not commensurable in respect of it.*
248b12–15

716. *But here again may we not take up the same position and say that the term "much" is*

equivocal? In fact there are some terms of which even the definitions are equivocal; e.g., if "much" were defined as "so much and more," "so much" would mean something different in different cases; "equal" is similarly equivocal; and "one" again is perhaps inevitably an equivocal term; and if "one" is equivocal, so is "two."   **248b15–20**

717. *Otherwise why is it that some things are commensurable while others are not, if the nature of the attribute in the two cases is really one and the same?*   **248b20–21**

718. *Can it be that the incommensurability of two things in respect of any attribute is due to a difference in that which is primarily capable of carrying the attribute? Thus horse and dog are so commensurable that we may say which is the whiter, since that which primarily contains the whiteness is the same in both, viz. the surface; and similarly they are commensurable in respect of size. But water and speech are not commensurable in respect of clearness, since that which primarily contains the attribute is different in the two cases.*   **248b21–25**

719. *It would seem, however, that we must reject this solution, since clearly we could thus make all equivocal attributes univocal and say merely that that which contains each of them is different in different cases; thus "equality," "sweetness," and "whiteness" will severally always be the same, though that which contains them is different in different cases.*   **248b25–249a2**

720. *Moreover, it is not any casual thing that is capable of carrying any attribute: each single attribute can be carried primarily only by one single thing.*   **249a2–3**

721. *Must we then say that, if two things are to be commensurable in respect of any attribute, not only must the attribute in question be applicable to both without equivocation, but there must also be no specific differences either in the attribute itself or in that which contains the attribute—that these, I mean, must not be divisible in the way in which color is divided into kinds? Thus in this respect one thing will not be commensurable with another, i.e., we cannot say that one is more colored than the other where only color in general and not any particular color is meant; but they are commensurable in respect of whiteness.*   **249a3–8**

COMMENTARY OF ST. THOMAS

928. The Philosopher has shown that there must be a first in mobile objects and movers. Now since things which are of one order seem to be comparable, and since the state of being prior and posterior implies a comparison, he wishes next to inquire into the comparison of motions.

Concerning this he makes two points. First he shows what motions are comparable to each other. Secondly, where he says, **"Now since wherever..."** [738], he shows how motions are compared to each other.

Concerning the first part he makes three points. First he raises a difficulty. Secondly, where he says, **"But is it not only..."** [710], he objects to the parts of this difficulty. Thirdly, where he says,

"But may we say that..." [714], he answers the difficulty.

He raises the difficulty first in general, asking whether or not every motion is comparable to every other motion, and secondly, in particular, raising the difficulty in regard to motions of one genus. Now if every motion is comparable to every other motion with respect to its speed or slowness (it was shown in Book VI that a thing is equally fast when it is moved in equal time and through equal space), it follows that circular motion is equal to straight motion and is greater and less in velocity. Further it follows that a circular line is equal to a straight line in quantity, or greater and less. From this it follows that an equal velocity is that which is moved through an equal space in an equal time.

Next he raises the difficulty in respect to motions of different genera. If all motions are comparable in velocity, it will follow that if in an equal time one thing is altered and another thing is moved with respect to place, then the alteration is equal in velocity to the change of place. And further, from the definition of equal velocity it will follow that a passion, that is, a passive quality, with respect to which there is alteration, is equal to the length of space which is crossed by the local motion. This is obviously impossible because they do not agree in having the same nature [ratio] of quantity.

929. Next where he says, **"But is it not only . . ."** [710], he objects to the proposed difficulty. He does this first in respect to the comparison of alteration and change of place, and secondly, where he says, **"But how will our..."** [711], in respect to the comparison of circular and straight motion. From the preceding argument which leads to an impossibility, he first concludes to the contrary of that which was assumed. It is as if he were to say: it is granted that it is impossible for a passion to be equal to a length. But a thing is equally fast when it is moved in an equal time through an equal space. Therefore, since no passion is equal to a length, it follows that change of place is not equal in velocity to alteration, nor is it greater or less. From this it can be concluded further that not all motions are comparable.

930. Next where he says, **"But how will our . . ."** [711], he deals with the other part of the difficulty, namely, straight and circular motion.

First he objects to the point that cir-cular motion is equal in velocity to straight motion. Secondly, where he says, **"None the less, if the two motions . . ."** [713], he objects to the contrary.

Concerning the first part he makes two points. First he objects to the proposition. Secondly, where he says, **"Moreover it does not..."** [712], he rejects a trivial answer.

He objects first [709] as follows. Circular motion and motion in a straight line are different local motions, just as are upward and downward motions. But it is at once necessary that a thing is moved faster or slower if one thing is moved up and another down, or even if the same thing is sometimes moved up and sometimes down. It seems, therefore, that it must be said likewise that motion in a straight line is faster or slower than circular motion, whether the same thing is moved in a circle and in a straight line, or whether there be two different things.

It should be noticed that in this argument he makes no mention of equal velocity, but only of faster and slower velocity. For this argument is taken from the comparison of upward motion, whose principle is lightness, and downward motion, whose principle is heaviness. Some have thought that heaviness and lightness are the same as fastness and slowness (which he has rejected in Book V.

931. Next where he says, **"Moreover it does not . . ."** [712], he rejects a certain trivial explanation. On the basis of the previous argument one could concede that circular motion is faster or slower than straight motion, but not equally fast.

He rejects this by saying that it makes no difference to the present argument if one were to say that that

COMMENTARY ON ARISTOTLE'S PHYSICS

which is moved in a circle must be moved faster or slower than that which is moved in a straight line. For according to this circular motion will be either greater or less in velocity than straight motion. From this it follows that it may also be equal.

And that this follows, he shows in this way. Let A be the time in which a faster motion passes through B, which is a circle; and let another slower motion pass in the same time through C, which is a straight line. Since, therefore, in the same time a faster motion crosses a greater distance, it will follow that the circle B will be greater than the straight line C, for thus we defined "faster" above in Book VI [lesson 3]. But in the same place we said that the faster crosses an equal distance in less time. Therefore, in part of the time A the body which is moved in a circle will cross part of the circle B, and in the same time it will cross C. For in the whole time A the slower body will cross the whole of C. It follows, therefore, that that part of the circle will be equal to the whole of C, because the same thing crosses an equal distance in an equal time. And thus a circular line will be equal to a straight line, and the circular motion consequently will be equally as fast as the straight motion.

932. Next where he says, **"None the less if the two motions . . ."** [713], he objects to the contrary. If circular motion and straight motion are comparable in velocity, there follows what was just said, namely, that a straight line is equal to a circle. For that which is equally fast is moved through an equal space. But a circular line and a straight line are not comparable such that they can be called equal. Therefore, circular and straight motion cannot be said to be equally fast.

933. Next where he says, **"But may we say that . . ."** [714], he answers the above difficulty.

First he inquires in general as to what may be comparable to what. Secondly, where he says, **"Similarly in the case of . . ."** [722], he adapts this to the problem.

Concerning the first part he makes three points. First he treats one thing which is required for comparison. Secondly, where he says, **"Can it be that the . . ."** [718], he treats the second requirement. Thirdly, where he says, **"Must we then say . . ."** [721], he concludes with the third requirement.

Concerning the first part he makes three points. First he states what is required for comparison. Secondly, where he says, **"Or shall we in the first place . . ."** [715], he objects to the contrary. Thirdly, where he says, **"But here again may we not . . ."** [716], he answers the objection.

934. He says, therefore, first that whatever things are not equivocal seem to be comparable. Or in other words, the subjects of things which are not predicated equivocally may be com-parable to each other. For example, "sharp" is used equivocally: in one sense it is applied to magnitudes, according to which an angle is said to be sharp and a pen is said to be sharp; in another sense it is applied to flavors, according to which wine is said to be sharp; in a third sense it is applied to tones, according to which the ultimate tone, that is, the highest, in melodies, or the string of a harp, is said to be sharp.

Therefore, a comparison cannot be made so as to designate which may be sharper; the pen, the wine, or the highest tone. For "sharp" is predicated equivocally of them. But the highest tone may be compared in regard to sharpness to the one next to it in the order of melody. For "sharp" is predicated of both not equivocally, but according to the same nature [ratio].

Therefore, in regard to the proposed question it can be said that a straight motion and a circular motion are not comparable with respect to velocity. For velocity is used equivocally in these two cases. And much less is there the same definition [ratio] of velocity in alteration and change of place. Hence these are much less comparable.

935. Next where he says, **"Or shall we in the first place . . ."** [715], he objects to what has been said. He says that at first sight it does not seem to be true that if things are not equivocal, then they are comparable. For there are some non-equivocal things which are not comparable. For example, the word "much" is applied in the same sense [ratio] to air and water, but nevertheless air and water are not comparable with respect to multitude.

Moreover, if someone is unwilling to concede that "much" signifies the same thing because of its commonness, at least he will agree that "double," which is a species of the multiple, signifies the same thing in air and water. In each case it signifies a proportion of two to one. Nevertheless air and water are not comparable with respect to double and half, so that it may be said that water is the double of air, or vice versa.

936. Next where he says, **"But here again may we not . . ."** [716], he answers this objection.

Concerning this he makes two points. First he gives his answer. Secondly, where he says, **"Otherwise why is it that . . ."** [717], he strengthens his answer by raising a question.

He says, therefore, first that "much" and "double" are not comparable when predicated of air and water for the same reason mentioned above in respect to "sharp" which is predicated of a pen, wine, and a tone. For the term "much" is also equivocal.

And since one might object that "much" has the same meaning [ratio] when it is predicated of both, to reject this he adds that even the definitions of certain things are equivocal. For example, if one were to say that the definition of "much" is "so much and more," then "just so much" and "equal," which are the same, are equivocal. For the "equal" is that which has one quantity. However "one quantity" does not have the same meaning [ratio] in all things. Moreover, it was granted that the meaning [ratio] of "much" implies a comparison, such that it is opposed to "few," and it is not taken absolutely, such that it is opposed to "one."

What he had said about "much" he says also about "double." For although the meaning [ratio] of "double" is a proportion of two to one, nevertheless this meaning [ratio] also contains an equivocation. For perhaps it can be said that "one" is equivocal. And if one is predicated equivocally, the same is true of two, because two is nothing other than twice one.

Moreover, it must be realized that, although many things are not equivocal according to the abstract consideration of logic or mathematics, nevertheless they are sometimes predicated equivocally according to the consideration of one who applies the concrete nature [ratio] of natural things to matter. For they are not received in every matter according to the same nature [ratio]. For example, quantity and unity, which is the principle of number, are not found according to the same nature [ratio] in celestial bodies and fire and air and water.

937. Next where he says, **"Otherwise why is it that . . ."** [717], he confirms what has been said by raising a question. For if it is said that there is one nature of "much" and "double" and other such things which are not comparable, just as there is for things which are predicated univocally, then there remains the question of why some things which have one nature are comparable, and others are not. For it seems that the same judgment should be made for similar things.

Next where he says, **"Can it be that the . . ."** [718], he answers this question by establishing the second requirement for comparison.

Concerning this he makes two points. First he establishes the second requirement for comparison. Secondly, where he says, **"It would seem, however . . ."** [719], he shows that this is not yet sufficient.

He says, therefore, first that this may be the reason why some things which are of one nature are comparable and others are not: if one nature is received in different things according to one primary subject, then these things will be mutually comparable. For example, horse and dog can be compared in respect to whiteness, such that one of them may be called whiter. For not only is the same nature of whiteness in each, but there is also one primary subject in which whiteness is received, namely, the surfaces. And similarly, magnitude is comparable in each, so that one may be called larger. For there is the same subject of magnitude in each, namely, the substance of the mixed body. But water and tone are not comparable with respect to magnitude, so that it may be said that a tone is greater than water, or vice versa. For although magnitude with respect to itself is the same, the

thing receiving it is not the same. Insofar as it is predicated of water, its subject is a substance, but insofar as it is predicated of a tone, its subject is sound, which is a quality.

938. Next where he says, **"It would seem, however . . ."** [719], he shows with two arguments that this is not sufficient.

The first is as follows. If things are comparable only because their subject is not different, it would follow that all things have one nature. For it can be said of any diverse things that they did differ only because they are in different primary subjects. And accordingly it would follow that what is equal and what is sweet and what is white have one and the same nature, and they differ only because they are in different receivers. And it seems impossible for all things to have one nature.

Moreover it must be realized that the Platonic opinion attributes the diversity of things only to the diversity of the receiver. This opinion attributes unity to form and duality to matter such that the whole nature [ratio] of diversity proceeds from the material principle. And so he held that both unity and being are predicated univocally and signify one nature. And the species of things are diversified according to the diversity of receivers.

The second argument, which he gives where he says, **"Moreover, it is not . . ."** [720], is that not everything is a receiver for everything. Rather one thing is primarily the receiver for one thing. Thus form and the receiver are predicated of each other. If, therefore, there are many primary receivers, there must be many received natures. Or if there is one received nature, there must be one primary receiver.

939. Next where he says, **"Must we**

then say . . ." [721], he concludes to the third thing which is required for things to be comparable.

He says that things which are comparable not only must not be equivocal, which was the first requirement, but also they must have no difference, either in respect to the primary subject in which a thing is received, which was the second requirement, or in respect to that which is received, which is form or nature, and this is the third requirement.

He gives an example of this third point. Since color is divided into different species of color, it is not comparable in respect to what is predicated of them. Nevertheless, it is not predicated equivocally, and it has one primary subject, namely, surface, which is the primary subject of the genus, but not of any species of color. For we cannot say that a thing which is black or white is more colored. For this comparison is not according to some determined species of color but according to common color itself. In regard to white, however, which is not divided into different species, a comparison can be made of all white things such that it may be said which is whiter.

From the Principles Established in the Preceding Lecture He Shows Which Motions Are Comparable to Each Other

The Text of Aristotle

722. *Similarly in the case of motion: two things are of the same velocity if they occupy an equal time in accomplishing a certain equal amount of motion.* **249a8–12**

723. *Suppose, then, that in a certain time an alteration is undergone by one half of a body's length and a locomotion is accomplished by the other half: can we say that in this case the alteration is equal to the locomotion and of the same velocity? That would be absurd, and the reason is that there are different species of motion.* **249a12–13**

724. *And if in consequence of this we must say that two things are of equal velocity if they accomplish locomotion over an equal distance in an equal time, we have to admit the equality of a straight line and a circumference.* **249a13–14**

725. *What, then, is the reason for this? Is it that locomotion is a genus or that line is a genus? (We may leave the time out of account, since that is one and the same.) If the lines are specifically different, the locomotions also differ specifically from one another; for locomotion is specifically differentiated according to the specific differentiation of that over which it takes place.* **249a13–16**

726. *(It is also similarly differentiated, it would seem, accordingly as the instrument of the locomotion is different: thus if feet are the instrument, it is walking, if wings it is flying; but perhaps we should rather say that this is not so and that in this case the differences in the locomotion are merely differences of posture in that which is in motion.)* **249a16–19**

727. *We may say, therefore, that things are of equal velocity if in an equal time they traverse the same magnitude; and when I call it "the same" I mean that it contains no specific difference and therefore no difference in the motion that takes place over it. So we have now to consider how motion is differentiated;* **249a19–21**

728. *and this discussion serves to show that the genus is not a unity but contains a plurality latent in it and distinct from it, and that in the case of equivocal terms sometimes the different senses in which they are used are far removed from one another, while sometimes there is a certain likeness between them, and sometimes again they are nearly related either generically or analogically, with the result that they seem not to be equivocal though they really are.* **249a21–25**

729. *When, then, is there a difference of species? Is an attribute specifically different if the subject is different while the attribute is the same, or must the attribute itself be different as well? And how are we to define the limits of a species? What will enable us to decide that particular instances of whiteness or sweetness are the same or different? Is it enough that it appears different in one subject from what it appears in another? Or must there be no sameness at all?* **249a25–29**

730. *And further, where alteration is in question, how is one alteration to be of equal velocity with another? One person may be cured quickly and another slowly, and cures may also be simultaneous: so that, recovery of health being an alteration, we have here alterations of equal velocity, since each alteration occupies an equal time.* **249a29–249b1**

731. *But what alteration? We cannot here speak of an "equal" alteration: what corresponds in the category of quality to equality in the category of quantity is "likeness."* **249b2–3**

732. *However, let us say that there is equal velocity where the same change is accomplished in an equal time.* **249b4**

733. *Are we, then, to find the commensurability in the subject of the affection or in the affection itself?* **249b5**

734. *In the case that we have just been considering it is the fact that health is one and the same that enables us to arrive at the conclusion that the one alteration is neither more nor less than the other, but that both are alike. If on the other hand the affection is different in the two cases, e.g., when the alterations take the form of becoming white and becoming healthy respectively, here there is no sameness or equality or likeness inasmuch as the difference in the affections at once makes the alterations specifically different, and there is no unity of alteration any more than there would be unity of locomotion under like conditions. So we must find out how many species there are of alteration and of locomotion respectively. Now if the things that are in motion—that is to say, the things to which the motions belong essentially and not accidentally—differ specifically, then their respective motions will also differ specifically; if on the other hand they differ generically or numerically, the motions also will differ generically or numerically as the case may be.* **249b5–14**

735. *But there still remains the question whether, supposing that two alterations are of equal velocity, we ought to look for this equality in the sameness (or likeness) of the affections, or in the things altered, to see e.g. whether a certain quantity of each has become white. Or ought we not rather to look for it in both? That is to say, the alterations are the same or different according as the affections are the same or different, while they are equal or unequal according as the things altered are equal or unequal.* **249b14–19**

736. *And now we must consider the same question in the case of becoming and perishing: how is one becoming of equal velocity with another? They are of equal velocity if in an equal time there are produced two things that are the same and specifically inseparable, e.g., two men (not merely generically inseparable as e.g., two animals). Similarly one is quicker than the other if in an equal time the product is different in the two cases. I state it thus because we have no pair of terms that will convey this "difference" in the way in which unlikeness is conveyed.* **249b19–23**

737. *If we adopt the theory that it is number that constitutes being, we may indeed speak of a "greater number" and a "lesser number" within the same species, but there is no common term that will include both relations, nor are there terms to express each of them separately in the same way as we indicate a higher degree or preponderance of an affection by "more," of a quantity by "greater."* **249b23–26**

COMMENTARY OF ST. THOMAS

940. After the Philosopher has shown in general what is required for things to be comparable, he here applies this discovered truth to the comparison of motions.

He does this first in general, and secondly by comparing the motions of diverse genera, where he says, **"Suppose, then, that in a certain time . . ."** [723], and thirdly by comparing the motions of one genus to each other, where he says, **"And if in consequence . . ."** [724].

He says, therefore, first that just as it is required in order for other things to be comparable that they be not equivocal and that there be the same primary receiver and the same species, likewise equal velocity of motion is said of that which is moved in an equal time through as much of another equal distance by a mutation of the same species.

941. Next where he says, **"Suppose, then, that in a certain time . . ."** [723], he treats the comparison of motions of diverse genera.

He says according to the foregoing

that if one mobile object is altered and another is moved with respect to place, can it not be said that the velocity of the alteration and the change of place is equal? But to say this is inconsistent. The reason for this is that motion has diverse species, and it was said before that things which are not of one species are not comparable. Since, therefore, change of place is not the same species as alteration, the velocities of local motion and alteration are not comparable.

942. Next where he says, **"And if in consequence . . ."** [724], he treats the comparison of motions of one genus in one genus.

He does this first in respect to local motion, secondly in respect to alteration, where he says, **"And further, where alteration . . ."** [730], and thirdly in respect to generation and corruption, where he says, **"And now we must consider . . ."** [736].

He does not mention increase and decrease because the same reasoning [ratio] applies here as in local motion since they occur in respect to some magnitude.

Concerning the first part he makes three points. First he shows what is required for two local motions to be comparable to each other. Secondly, where he says, **"It is also similarly . . ."** [726], he rejects a certain thing which seems to be required here. Thirdly, where he says, **"We may say, therefore . . ."** [727], he concludes to his main point.

Concerning the first part he makes two points. First he concludes that an inconsistency follows if it is said that all local motions are comparable. Secondly, where he says, **"What, then, is the reason . . ."** [725], he explains why they are not all comparable.

943. He says, therefore, first [724] that if all things which are moved locally through an equal magnitude in an equal time have equal velocity, and if every local motion has equal velocity, it follows that the straight and the circular are equal. This may be understood in two ways: first in regard to straight and circular motion; secondly in regard to a straight and a circular line. The latter is better, for this follows from what he has stated. For if every straight and circular motion have equal velocity, and if motions are equally fast when they cross equal magnitudes in an equal time, then it follows that a straight and a circular magnitude are equal. And this latter is absurd.

944. Next where he says, **"What, then, is the reason . . ."** [725], he inquires into the cause of the non-comparability of straight and circular motions.

He has concluded that if motions have equal velocity, then it follows that the magnitudes are equal, which seems absurd. Therefore, one might ask whether the cause of this non-comparability is due to the motion or the magnitudes. He asks whether the reason why a straight motion and a circular motion do not have equal velocity is that local motion is a genus containing beneath it diverse species (it was said just above that things of diverse species are not comparable), or whether the reason is that a line is a genus containing beneath it the straight and the circular as diverse species. The time cannot be the cause of this incomparability, for all time is indivisible with respect to species.

To this question, therefore, he answers that both are joined together. For in both cases there is found a difference of species, such that the difference of species in local motion is caused by the difference of species in the magnitude over which there is motion. He says that if that over which a thing is moved has species, it follows that local motion has species.

945. Next where he says, **"It is also similarly . . ."** [726], he rejects something which may seem to be required for the identity of species and the comparability of local motions.

He says that sometimes local motions are differentiated in respect to that through which the local motion occurs as through an instrument. For example, if feet are that by which a thing is moved, the motion is called walking, and if wings are used, the motion is called flying.

But this does not cause a difference of species in local motions but a difference in the figures of local motion, that is, this difference of mutations is not according to species but only according to some figure of motion, as the Commentator explains.

But it may be better to say that he intends here to say that local motion is not differentiated in species through the instruments of motion but through the figures of the magnitude over which the motion passes. For thus the straight and the circular differ. The reason for this is that motions do not receive their species from mobile objects but rather from the things in regard to which mobile objects are moved. And the instruments are due to the mobile objects while the figures are due to that in which the motion occurs.

946. Next where he says, **"We may say, therefore . . ."** [727], he concludes to his position.

Concerning this he makes three points. First he concludes to his main point. Secondly, where he says, **". . . and this discussion serves . . ."** [728], he develops from the above conclusion a point which is worthy of consideration. Thirdly, where he says, **"When, then, is there a difference . . ."** [729], he investigates the diversity of species.

He concludes, therefore, first [727] that since motions are not comparable unless they are of one species, and since local motions are not of one species unless there is the same magnitude in respect to species, it follows that those things are of equal velocity which are moved in an equal time with respect to the same magnitude. "Same" is understood here to mean "not different in species." For in the same way motion also is not different in species. Therefore, in the comparison of motions one must consider what difference of motion there may be. If there is a difference in genus or species, they are not comparable. But if there is an accidental difference, they are comparable.

947. Next where he says, **". . . and this discussion serves . . ."** [728], he develops from the foregoing something which is worthy of consideration, namely a genus is not simply one, but a species is simply one. This is indicated in the preceding argument in which it was shown that things which are of one genus are not comparable, while things which are of one species are comparable. Since it was said above that the nature of comparables is the same, it seems that a genus is not one nature, but a species is one nature.

The reason for this is that species is taken from the ultimate form, which in the nature of things is simply one. Genus, however, is not taken from a form which is one in the nature of things, but only from reason [ratio]. For man is not an animal through a form other than that by which man is man. Therefore all men, who are of one species, agree in the form which constitutes the species, because each of them has a rational soul. But there is not in man, or a horse, or an ass some common soul which constitutes animal beyond that soul which constitutes man, or horse, or ass (for if there were, then genus would be one and comparable, as is species). Rather the form of a genus is received only in the understanding by the abstraction of the intellect from differences.

Therefore, a species is a unity which derives from one form existing in the nature of things. But a genus is not a unity because the diverse species of a genus receive predication according to the diverse forms existing in the nature of things. Thus a genus is one logically, but not physically.

Therefore, a genus is in some way one, but not simply. Rather genera hide many joined things, that is, because of the similarity and nearness to unity of a genus, the equivocation of many things is latent in it.

There are some equivocal terms so disparate that only the name is common. For example, a dog is said to be a celestial constellation and a barking animal.

There are others which have some similarity. For example, the name "man" is said of a real man and a picture of a man insofar as the latter has some similarity to a real man.

Other equivocal terms are very close because of a conformity in genus. (For example, when "body" is said of a celestial body and a corruptible body, the term is used equivocally, speaking naturally, because their matter is not one. Nevertheless, they agree in logical genus, and because of this agreement in genus they seem to be not completely equivocal.) Or else they are very close in respect to some similarity, for example, he who teaches school

is called a master, and likewise he who heads a house is called the master of the house, but equivocally. But this is a very close equivocation because of the similarity. For each is a director, one of learning, the other of a house. Because of this closeness either of genus or of similarity, they do not seem to be equivocal, but they are.

948. Next where he says, **"When, then, is there a difference . . ."** [729], since he has said that consideration must be given to the difference of motions to determine whether motions differ in species, he here asks how difference of species may be understood in regard both to motions and to other things. And since a definition signifies the essence of a species, he asks two questions: one about the species and the other about the definition.

In regard to species he asks first whether we must judge that there is a different species only because the same nature is in different receivers, as the Platonists held. According to the above this is impossible. It was said that a genus is not simply one. Therefore, the diversity of species is not the result of the same thing being in different things, except according to the Platonists, who held that a genus is simply one. And because of this, as if answering the question, he adds, **". . . or must the attribute itself be different as well?"** [729], as if he were to say that there is not a different species because the same thing is in another but because a different nature is in a different receiver.

He asks a second question about definition. The question is, "What is its terminus?" In other words, what is the definition which defines a species. Since things which are the same in definition are the same simply, he adds, as if answering, that the proper definition of a thing is that by which we are able to discern whether it is the same or different, for example, white or sweet. The term "different" can be understood in two ways, even as before. First white is said to be different than sweet because in whiteness there is found a different natural subject than in sweetness. Secondly they are different because they differ not only with respect to the natural subject, but because they are totally not the same. These two are the same as those proposed above: namely, "if the same is in another or if another is in another." For it is clear that there is the same meaning [ratio] of identity and diversity in both species and definition.

949. Next where he says, **"And further, where alteration . . ."** [730], he treats the comparison of alterations.

Concerning this he makes two points. First he shows that one alteration has a velocity equal to another. Secondly, where he says, **"But what alteration?"** [731], he inquires how equality of velocity is present in alteration.

He asks, therefore, first how one alteration is equal in velocity to another. And he proves that two alterations are equal in velocity. To be cured is to be altered. And it happens that one cure is quick and another slow, and some cures are simultaneous. Therefore, one alteration is equal in velocity to another. For that is said to be moved with equal velocity which is moved in an equal time.

950. Next where he says, **"But what alteration?"** [731], he points out that for local motion to be equal in velocity, there is required not only equality of time but also equality of the magnitude which is crossed. Granting that in alteration equality of time is required for equal velocity, he asks what else is

required. This is what he means when he says, "But what alteration?," that is, what can be said to be of equal velocity when an alteration occurs in equal time?

The reason for this difficulty is that equality is not found in quality, in respect to which alteration occurs, such that we could say that an alteration has equal velocity when it arrives at an equal quantity in an equal time, which was said of local motion and which can be said of increase and decrease. Rather just as equality is found in quantity, so similarity is found in quality.

He answers this difficulty where he adds, **"However, let us say . . ."** [732].

First he gives his answer to the difficulty. He says that an alteration ought to be said to have equal velocity if the same thing, that is, the thing which is altered, is changed in an equal time.

951. Secondly, where he says, **"Are we, then, to find . . ."** [733], he raises a question in regard to this answer. The question which he asks first is as follows. It was said that an alteration has equal velocity if the same thing is altered in an equal time. But that which is altered can be understood in two ways, namely, the passion with respect to which the alteration occurs and the subject of the passion. Therefore, the question is whether this comparison should be taken with respect to the identity of the passion or with respect to the identity of the subject of the passion.

952. Secondly, where he says, **"In the case that . . ."** [734], he answers one part of the question. He says that in alteration a double identity should be present in respect to the passion so that the alteration may have equal velocity. First, there should be the same quality in respect to species. For example, the

same health is present in the eyes or some such thing. Secondly, the same received quality should be present in the same way, and neither more nor less. But if the passion, that is, the passive quality, is different in respect to species, for example, if one thing becomes white and another healthy, then in these two passions nothing is the same, or equal, or similar. And so because of the diversity of these passions there are diverse species of alteration and not one alteration just as it was said above that straight and circular motion are not one local motion. Therefore in comparing both local motions and alterations, one must consider whether the species of alteration or of local motion are the same or many. And this can be understood from the things in which there is motion. For if the things which are moved, that is, if the things in respect to which there is motion per se and not per accidens, differ in species or genus, then the motions also differ in species or genus. And if they differ in number, the motions also differ in number, as was said in Book V.

953. Thirdly, where he says, **"But there still remains . . ."** [735], having answered one part of the question which he asked, he seeks an answer for the other part. The question is whether the judgment that alterations are similar or have equal velocity ought to relate only to the passion, as to whether it is the same, or whether it should relate to the subject which is altered. For example, if a certain part of this body became white in this time, and if another equal part of the body became white in the same or an equal time, may the alteration be said to have equal velocity?

His answer is that one should consider both, namely, the passion and the subject, but in different ways. For we judge that an alteration is the same or different because the passion is either the same or different. But we judge that an alteration is equal or unequal insofar as part of the altered subject is equal or unequal. For if a large part of this body becomes white and if another small part becomes white, the alteration will be the same in species but not equal.

954. Next where he says, **"And now we must consider . . ."** [736], he shows how comparison should be made with respect to generation and corruption.

He does this first in respect to the proper opinion, and secondly in respect to Plato's opinion, where he says, **"If we adopt the theory . . ."** [737].

He says, therefore, first in regard to generation and corruption that in order that generation have equal velocity, we must consider if in an equal time the very thing which is generated is also indivisible in respect to species. For example, if in each generation a man is generated in an equal time, the generation has equal velocity. But generation does not have equal velocity only because an animal is generated in an equal time. For certain animals, because of their own perfection, require a longer time for generation. But a generation is said to be faster if the other is generated in an equal time. For example, if a horse is generated in the same amount of time in which a dog is generated, then the generation of the horse is faster.

In regard to alteration he said that two things must be considered relative to the passion, namely, if there is the same health, and if it exists in the same way, neither more nor less. But in regard to generation, he says that only one thing must be considered, namely, if there is the same thing which is generated. He gives the reason for this by saying, ". . . because we have no pair of terms that will convey this 'difference' in the way in which unlikeness is conveyed." It is as if he were to say that in generation the only consideration is whether there is the same thing which is generated because in generation we do not have something which can be varied in two ways so that some difference arises, as in alteration there occurs a difference in that one and the same quality is varied in respect to more and less. For the substance of that which is generated does not receive more and less.

955. Next where he says, **"If we adopt the theory . . ."** [737], he treats the comparison of generation according to Plato's opinion. Plato held that number is the substance of a thing because he thought that the one which is the principle of number is the same as the one which is convertible with being and which signifies the substance of a thing. Moreover, oneness is totally of one nature and species. Therefore, if number, which is nothing other than an aggregation of units, is the substance of things according to the

Platonists, it will follow that greater and smaller number will be predicated with respect to the diverse species of quantity, however, with respect to substance it will be similar in species. Thus Plato posited the species of oneness. But the contraries, the great and the small, by which things are diversified, are due to matter. And so it follows that just as one and the same health is two insofar as it receives more and less, so also substance, which is number, although it is of one species in respect to unity, will have duality insofar as it is a larger or smaller number. But in substance there is no common name which signifies either one, that is, the diversity which arises from the largeness or smallness of number. When a passion is present to a greater extent or excels in any way whatsoever, it is called "more," for example, more white or more healthy. And when a quantity excels, it is called "greater," as a greater body or greater surface. But we do not have a name which signifies in common the excelling of substance, which arises from the largeness of number according to the Platonists.

Rules for the Comparison of Motions

The Text of Aristotle
Chapter 5

738. *Now since wherever there is a mover, its motion always acts upon something, is always in something, and always extends to something (by "is always in something" I mean that it occupies a time; and by "extends to something" I mean that it involves the traversing of a certain amount of distance; for at any moment when a thing is causing motion, it also has caused motion, so that there must always be a certain amount of distance that has been traversed and a certain amount of time that has been occupied).* **249b27–30**

739. *If, then, A the mover has moved B a distance C in a time D, then in the same time the same force A will move 1/2B twice the distance C, and in 1/2D it will move 1/2B the whole distance C; for thus the rules of proportion will be observed.* **249b30–250a4**

740. *Again if a given force moves a given weight a certain distance in a certain time and half the distance in half the time, half the motive power will move half the weight the same distance in the same time. Let E represent half the motive power A and F half the weight B: then the ratio between the motive power and the weight in the one case is similar and proportionate to the ratio in the other, so that each force will cause the same distance to be traversed in the same time.* **250a4–9**

741. *But if E move s F a distance C in a time D, it does not necessarily follow that E can move twice F half the distance C in the same time.* **250a9–12**

742. *If, then, A moves B a distance C in a time D, it does not follow that E, being half of A, will in the time D or in any fraction of it cause B to traverse a part of C the ratio between which and the whole of C is proportionate to that between A and E (whatever fraction of A E may be): in fact it might well be that it will cause no motion at all; for it does not follow that, if a given motive power causes a certain amount of motion, half that power will cause motion either of any particular amount or in any length of time: otherwise one man might move a ship, since both the motive power of the ship-haulers and the distance that they all cause the ship to traverse are divisible into as many parts as there are men.* **250a12–19**

743. *Hence Zeno's reasoning is false when he argues that there is no part of the millet that does not make a sound; for there is no reason why any such part should not in any length of time fail to move the air that the whole bushel moves in falling. In fact it does not of itself move even such a quantity of the air as it would move if this part were by itself; for no part even exists otherwise than potentially.* **250a19–25**

744. *If on the other hand we have two forces each of which separately moves one of two weights a given distance in a given time, then the forces in combination will move the combined weights an equal distance in an equal time; for in this case the rules of proportion apply.* **250a25–28**

745. *Then does this hold good of alteration and of increase also? Surely it does; for in any given case we have a definite thing that causes increase and a definite thing that suffers increase, and the one causes and the other suffers a certain amount of increase in a certain amount of time. Similarly we have a definite thing that causes alteration and a definite thing that undergoes alteration, and a certain amount, or rather degree, of alteration is completed in a certain amount of time: thus in twice as much time twice as much alteration will be completed and conversely twice as much alteration will occupy twice as much time;* **250a28–250b2**

746. *and the alteration of half of its object will occupy half as much time and in half as much*

time half of the object will be altered: or again, in the same amount of time it will be altered
twice as much. 250b2–4

747. *On the other hand if that which causes alteration or increase causes a certain amount*
of increase or alteration respectively in a certain amount of time, it does not necessarily follow
that half the force will occupy twice the time in altering or increasing the object, or that in twice
the time the alteration or increase will be completed by it: it may happen that there will be no
alteration or increase at all, the case being the same as with the weight. 250b4–7

COMMENTARY OF ST. THOMAS

956. After the Philosopher has shown what motions are mutually comparable, he here explains how they are compared.

He does this first with respect to local motion, and secondly with respect to the other motions, where he says, "Then does this hold . . ." [745].

Concerning the first part he makes two points. First he states the things which must govern the mutual comparison of local motions. Secondly, where he says, "If, then, A the mover . . ." [739], he establishes from the above the rules for comparison.

He says, therefore, first that that which moves locally always moves some mobile object in some time and through some quantity of space. This must be so, because as was proven in Book VI to move something and to have moved something are always together. For it was proven there that whatever is being moved has already been moved through some part of space and through some part of time. From this it follows that that which is moved is quantified and divisible, as is that through which it is moved and also the time in which it is moved. However, not every mover is quantified, as will be proven in Book VIII. Nevertheless, it is clear that some movers are quantified. And he here gives the rules of comparison in regard to this type of mover.

957. Next where he says, "If, then, A

the mover . . ." [739], he gives the rules of comparison. He does this first in regard to the division of the mobile object, and secondly in regard to the division of the mover, where he says, "Again if a given force . . ." [740].

He says, therefore, first that A is given as a mover. And let B be the mobile object, let C be the length of space which is crossed, and let D be the time in which A moves B through C. If, therefore, there is assumed some other moving power which is equal to the power of A, it follows that that power will move half of the mobile object B in the same time through a length which is twice that of C. And it will move half of the mobile object through the whole length C in half the time D.

From these words of the Philosopher two general rules can be established.

The first is that if some power moves some mobile object through some space in some time, then half of that mobile object will be moved through twice the space either by an equal power in the same time or by the same power in another equal time.

The other rule is that an equal power will move half of the mobile object through the same space in half the time. The reason for this is that the same analogy, that is, the same proportion, is thus preserved. For it is clear that the velocity of motion arises from the victory of the power of the mover

over the mobile object. To the extent that the mobile object is less, so much will the power of the mover exceed it more and thus move it faster. Moreover, the velocity of motion lessens the time and increases the length of space. For that is faster which in the same time crosses a greater magnitude, or an equal magnitude in less time, as was proven in Book VI. Therefore, one must subtract from the time or add to the length of space in the same proportion in which one subtracts from the mobile object, provided that the mover is the same or equal.

958. Next where he says, **"Again if a given force . . ."** [740], he treats the comparison of motions in regard to the mover. He does this first in regard to the division of the mover, and secondly in regard to the opposite unification, where he says, **"If on the other hand . . ."** [744].

Concerning the first part he makes three points. First he gives the true comparison. Secondly, where he says, **"But if E moves F . . ."** [741], he rejects a false comparison. Thirdly, where he says, **"Hence Zeno's . . ."** [743], he answers Zeno's argument.

He says, therefore, first that if a power moves the same mobile object in the same time through so much space, then this same power moves half of the mobile object in half the time through the same space, or in the same time it moves half of the mobile object through twice the space, as was said of an equal power. And further, if the power is divided, half of the power will move half of the mobile object through the same space in an equal time. But it must be understood that the power is of such a kind that it is not corrupted by division. For he is speaking in terms of a common consideration and is not yet applying his

remarks to some special nature, just as he has done in all that precedes. And he gives an example. Let E be half of the power A. And let F be half of the mobile object B. Now just as A moved B through C in time D, so E will move F through the same space in an equal time, for here also is preserved the same proportion of the motive power to the heavy body which is moved. From this it follows that in an equal time there will be motion through an equal space, as was said.

959. Next where he says, **"But if E moves F . . ."** [741], he rejects two false comparisons. The first is that there may be an addition to a mobile object but not an addition to the moving power. Hence he says that if E, which is half of the motive power, moves F, which is half of the mobile object, in the time D through the space C, then it is not necessary that this halved power, which is E, move a mobile object twice as large as F in an equal time through half of the space C. For it could be that it is not possible for a halved power to move a doubled mobile object. But if it could move, this comparison would hold.

The second false comparison arises when the mover is divided and the mobile object is not. He rejects this where he says, **"If, then, A moves B . . ."** [742]. He says that if the moving power A moves the mobile object B in the time D through the space C, then it is not necessary that half of the mover move the whole mobile object B in the time D, not even through some part of the space C, which part is proportioned to the whole space C as we conversely compared A to F, that is, as we compared the whole motive power to part of the mobile object. For that was an appropriate comparison, but this is not. For it can happen that half of a mover will not move a whole mobile object through any space. If a whole power moves a whole mobile object, it does not follow that half of that power will move the whole mobile object either through some space or in some time. Otherwise it would follow that one single man could move a ship through some space if the power of those who pull is divided with respect to the number of those who pull and with respect to the length of space through which all together pull the ship.

960. Next where he says, "**Hence, Zeno's . . .**" [743], he answers according to the foregoing the argument of Zeno, who wished to prove that any grain of millet makes a sound when thrown to the ground because a whole measure of millet makes a sound when thrown to the ground. Aristotle says that this argument of Zeno is not true, that is, it is not true that any grain of millet will make a sound when it falls to the ground. For there is nothing to prevent one from saying that a grain of millet at no time moves enough air to make a sound, which air a whole falling measure does move to make a sound.

And from this we can conclude that, if some small part which exists in a whole moves, it is not necessary that that part can move when it exists separately and per se. For a part is in a whole not in act, but in potency, especially in continuous things. For as a thing is a being, it is also one. And a one is that which is undivided in itself and divided from others. But a part existing in a whole is not divided in act but only in potency. Hence it is neither a being nor a one in act but only in potency. And for this reason it is not the part which acts but the whole.

961. Next where he says, "**If on the other hand . . .**" [744], he gives a comparison with respect to the unification of movers. He says that if there are two movers, each of which in itself moves a certain mobile object in a certain time through a certain space, then when the powers of these two movers are joined, they will move that which is composed of these moved weights through an equal space in an equal time. For here also the same proportion is preserved.

962. Next where he says, "**Then does this hold . . .**" [745], he gives the same rules of comparison for other motions.

Concerning this he makes three points. First he explains the divisibility of those things to which the comparison of motions pertains. Secondly, where he says, ". . . **thus in twice as much . . .**" [746], he gives the true comparisons. Thirdly, where he says, "**On the other hand . . .**" [747], he rejects false comparisons.

He says, therefore, first in regard to increase that three things are involved, namely, the increaser, that which is increased, and the time. These three things have quantity. And fourthly there is the quantity in respect to which the increaser increases and in respect to which that which is increased is increased. These four things are also found in alteration, namely, the alterer, that which is altered, the quantity of passion in respect to which alteration occurs (which passion is present according to more and less), and the quantity of time in which the alteration takes place. These four are likewise found in local motion.

963. Next where he says, ". . . **thus in twice as much . . .**" [746], he gives the true comparisons.

He says that if a power with respect to these motions moves so much in so much time, in twice the time it will move twice as much, and if it moves twice as much, this will occur in twice the time. And similarly the same power will move half in half the time; or if it moves in half the time, half will be moved. Or if the power is double, it will move twice as much in an equal time.

964. Next where he says, **"On the other hand . . ."** [747], he rejects a false comparison.

He says that if in a motion of alteration or increase a power moves so much in so much time, it is not necessary that half of the power move half as much in the same time or the same amount in half the time. For perhaps it would happen that it will increase or alter nothing, just as it was said that a halved power cannot move a whole weight, either through a whole space or some part of it. When he says, ". . . in half as much time half of the object will be altered: or again, in the same amount of time it will be altered twice as much," "half" and "double" (which are in the accusative) must not be understood to mean "half or double of the mobile object" but "half or double of that in which the motion occurs," that is, of quality or quantity, which are found in these two motions in the same way that length of space is found in local motion. Other than this these motions and local motion are not similar. For it was said in regard to local motion that if so much power moves so much of a mobile object, then half of the power will move half of the mobile object. But here it is said that half of the power may move nothing. This must be understood of the whole, complete mobile object, because a halved motive power will not move it either through so much quantity or quality, or through half of it.

BOOK VIII
THE FIRST MOTION AND THE FIRST MOVER
LECTURE 1 [250b11–251a7]
Whether or Not Motion Began or Will End
The Text of Aristotle
Chapter 1

748. *It remains to consider the following question. Was there ever a becoming of motion before which it had no being, and is it perishing again so as to leave nothing in motion? Or are we to say that it never had any becoming and is not perishing, but always was and always will be? Is it in fact an immortal never-failing property of things that are, a sort of life as it were to all naturally constituted things?* 250b11–15

749. *Now the existence of motion is asserted by all who have anything to say about nature, because they all concern themselves with the construction of the world and study the question of becoming and perishing, which processes could not come about without the existence of motion.* 250b15–18

750. *But those who say that there is an infinite number of worlds, some of which are in process of becoming while others are in process of perishing, assert that there is always motion (for these processes of becoming and perishing of the worlds necessarily involve motion), whereas those who hold that there is only one world, whether everlasting or not, make corresponding assumptions in regard to motion.* 250b18–21

751. *If then it is possible that at any time nothing should be in motion, this must come about in one of two ways: either in the manner described by Anaxagoras, who says that all things were together and at rest for an infinite period of time, and that then Mind introduced motion and separated them; or in the manner described by Empedocles, according to whom the universe is alternately in motion and at rest—in motion, when Love is making the one out of many, or Strife is making many out of one, and at rest in the intermediate periods of time—his account being as follows:*

> *"Since One hath learned to spring from Manifold,*
> *And One disjoined makes Manifold arise,*
> *Thus they Become, nor stable is their life:*
> *But since their motion must alternate be,*
> *Thus have they ever Rest upon their round":*

for we must suppose that he means by this that they alternate from the one motion to the other. 250b21–251a5

752. *We must consider, then, how this matter stands; for the discovery of the truth about it is of importance, not only for the study of nature, but also for the investigation of the First Principle.* 251a5–8

COMMENTARY OF ST. THOMAS

965. After the Philosopher has shown in the preceding book that there must be a first mobile object and a first motion and a first mover, in this book he plans to inquire into the nature of the first mover and the first motion and the first mobile object.

This discussion is divided into two

parts. First, he sets forth something which is necessary for the following investigation, namely, the eternity of motion. Secondly, where he says, **"Our enquiry will resolve . . ."** [763], he begins to investigate the problem.

Concerning the first part he makes three points. First he raises the problem. Secondly, where he says, **"Let us take our start . . ."** [753], he explains the truth according to his own opinion. Thirdly, where he says, **"The arguments that may . . ."** [767], he answers objections to the contrary.

Concerning the first part he makes three points. First he raises the problem. Secondly, where he says, **"But those who say . . ."** [750], he gives opinions on both sides. Thirdly, where he says, **"We must consider, then . . ."** [752], he points out the usefulness of this consideration.

Concerning the first part he makes two points. First he raises a problem concerning that which he intends to investigate. Secondly, where he says, **"Now the existence of . . ."** [749], he answers an unasked question.

966. Concerning the first part it must be noted that Averroes says that in this chapter Aristotle does not intend to inquire universally whether motion is eternal but only whether the first motion is eternal.

But if one considers both the words and the procedure of the Philosopher, he will see that this is totally false. For the Philosopher's words are spoken universally of motion, because he says, **"It remains to consider the following question. Was there ever a becoming of motion before which it had no being, and is it perishing again so as to leave nothing in motion?"** [748]. From this it is clearly apparent that he is not asking about any determinate motion. Rather he asks universally whether at

some time there may have been nothing in motion.

From Aristotle's procedure also this clearly is false.

The first reason for this is that it is always his custom to argue to a proposition from proper things. And if one considers the following arguments which he introduces, in none of them does he use as a middle anything which pertains properly to the first motion, but rather to motion in general. From this it is clear enough that he intends to inquire here about the eternity of motion in general.

A second reason is that if it were already proven that one or more motions are eternal, it would be useless for him to ask below whether some things are always moved, since this would already be proven. It is also ridiculous to say that Aristotle repeats his own thought below from the beginning, as if he had omitted something, as the Commentator suggests. For Aristotle had the opportunity of correcting his book and of supplying in the proper place what had been omitted, so that he would not proceed in a disorderly way. If this chapter is explained according to the intention of the Commentator, all that follows will appear to be confused and disordered. Nor is this strange, for from one inconsistent position others follow. The fact that Aristotle intends below to inquire into the eternity of the first motion is even more apparent from the fact that he uses that which he demonstrates here as a principle. This he could in no way do if he has proven here that the first motion is eternal.

Moreover, the argument by which Averroes was moved is perfectly silly. He says that if it is said that Aristotle intends here to ask about the eternity of motion in general, it will follow that the consideration of Aristotle would be weakened here. For it is not apparent from what is determined here how motions can always be continuous to each other.

But this is not so. In this chapter it is sufficient for Aristotle to prove in general that motion is eternal. In the immediate sequel he inquires how the eternity of motion is continued, whether because all things are always moved, or because all things are sometimes moved and sometimes at rest, or because certain things are always moved and other things are at times moved and at times at rest.

Accordingly it should be understood that it is his intention in the present chapter to investigate motion in general.

He asks, therefore, with respect to this whether motion at some time began to be, so that before this there was no motion at all, and whether at some time it will cease so that afterwards nothing is moved: or, on the contrary, whether it never began and never will cease, but always was and always will be.

He gives an example dealing with animals, because some have said that the world is a certain large animal. We see that animals are alive so long as some motion is apparent in them. When every motion ceases, animals are said to be dead. Likewise in the whole universe the motions of natural bodies are thought of as a kind of life. If, then, motion always was and always will be, this life, as it were, of natural bodies will be immortal and without end.

967. Next where he says, **"Now the existence of . . ."** [749], he answers an unasked question.

In the preceding books Aristotle has spoken about motion in general not applying his remarks to things. Now, however, inquiring whether motion always was, he applies the common consideration of motion to the existence which it has in things. Therefore, one might say that in this consideration one must ask whether motion has existence in things before one asks whether motion is eternal, especially since some have denied the existence of motion.

He answers this by saying that all who have spoken of the nature of things affirm that motion exists. This is clear because they say that the world was made, and also because they all admit the generation and corruption of things, which could not occur without motion. It is, therefore, a common supposition in natural science that motion has existence in things. Therefore, no question is asked about this in natural science, just as in any science no question concerning the suppositions of that science is raised.

968. Next where he says, **"But those who say . . ."** [750], he gives opinions on both sides of the question which he has asked.

First he gives the opinions of those who say that motion is eternal. Secondly, where he says, **". . . whereas those who hold . . ."** [751], he gives the opinions of those who say that motion is not eternal.

For a clear understanding of the first part, it should be known that Democritus proposed that the first principles of things are indivisible bodies which are mobile per se and eternally. He said that the world was made by chance from a coming together of these bodies. This applies not only to the world in which we exist but also to infinite other worlds insofar as the coming together of the above mentioned bodies has made worlds in diverse parts of an infinite void. He did not, however, propose that these worlds would endure forever. Rather some of them come to be through the aggregation of atoms, and some are corrupted by the separation of atoms. Therefore, all the philosophers who propose this along with Democritus say that motion is eternal, because they say that the generation and corruptions of some worlds are eternal. And this can occur only with motion.

969. Next where he says, ". . . Whereas those who hold . . ." [751], he gives contrary opinions.

He says that all who hold that there is only one world which is not eternal, hold in regard to motion what follows according to reason, namely, it is not eternal.

If, therefore, it is granted that there was a time in which nothing was moved, this may occur in two ways, just as it can be maintained in two ways that this world has not always existed. The first view is that this world so began that it never was before, as Anaxagoras held. The second view is that the world so began that at some time it was not, but before that time it existed, as Empedocles held.

And accordingly Anaxagoras said of motion that at one time all things were together, one mingled with another, and nothing was separated from any other thing. In this mixture of things it was necessary to hold that everything was at rest. For there is no motion without separation, since everything which is moved withdraws from one thing in order to tend toward another. He held, therefore, that this mixture and state of rest of things pre-existed in an infinite time, so that at no earlier time was there any motion. And intellect, which was the only thing not intermixed, began anew to

cause motion and to separate things from one another.

But Empedocles said that in one part of time something was moved, and again in another part of time all things were at rest. For Empedocles held that friendship and strife are the first movers of things. The proper function of friendship is to make one from many, while strife makes many from one. Since the existence of a mixed body requires that its elements be joined into one, and since the existence of the world requires that the elements be distributed in their proper places in an orderly way, he held that friendship is the cause of the generation of mixed bodies, and strife is the cause of their corruption. But, on the contrary, in the whole world friendship is the cause of corruption and strife is the cause of generation.

Thus he held that the whole world is moved either when friendship makes one from many, or when strife makes many from one. And he held that rest exists in the intermediate times, not indeed so that nothing is moved, but in respect to the general mutation of the world.

Since Aristotle has stated the opinion of Empedocles, he also gives his words, which are difficult because he wrote in verse.

Empedocles expressed his opinion in these words, which are to be understood as follows. "Didicit nasci," that is, a thing is usually generated, "inquantum ex pluribus fit unum" [insofar as one comes to be from many], "iterum," that is, in another way, "ex uno geminato," that is, from the composite, "perficiuntur plurima," that is, many come to be by separation. For some things are generated by composition and some things are generated by separation.

And as we see this in particular generations, "sic fiunt res," that is, the universal generation of things in respect to the whole world must be understood in the same way. "Et nullo modo est ipsius saeculum unum," that is, there is not one state of duration of things. Rather at one time the world is being generated, at another time it is being corrupted, and at another time it is in an intermediate state. For "saeculum" means the measure of the duration of a thing.

Moreover, he expresses the distinction of these durations when he adds, "sic autem permutantur." It is as if he were to say that one duration is that in which a thing is changed by congregation or separation. One might think that the world comes to be in an instant and that the generation of the world does not require a duration, that is, some time. To reject this he adds, "neque simul perficiuntur" [they are not completed at once], but through a long delay of time.

Next in regard to the other duration he says, "sic autem semper sunt immobiles," that is, in the time which is intermediate between generation and corruption things are at rest.

And one might believe that before this there was always change, and afterwards there always will be rest. To reject this he says, "secundum circulum," as if he were to say that there is a circle in which things are changed and then are at rest and then are changed and so forth to infinity.

Next are added the words of Aristotle who explains the words of Empedocles, especially the phrase, "sic autem permutantur."

He says that the words "sic permutantur" must be understood to mean "from here to there," that is, from some beginning up to now. This does not mean that there always was motion, or that afterwards it began. Rather it means that motion is interrupted.

970. Next where he says, **"We must consider, then . . ."** [752], he points out the usefulness of this consideration.

He says that consideration must be given to what the truth is concerning this question. For to know the truth about this question is elementary, that is, very necessary, not only for the consideration of natural science but also for the science of the first principle. For both here in Book VIII and in the Metaphysics he uses the eternity of motion to prove a first principle.

This way of proving that a first principle exists is most effective and cannot be resisted. For if it is necessary to posit one first principle on the assumption that the world and motion are eternal, this is much more necessary if the eternity of these things is denied. For it is clear that every new thing needs some innovating principle. Therefore, only if things exist from eternity can it seem to be unnecessary to posit a first principle. And if it follows even from this assumption that a first principle exists, it is shown that it is absolutely necessary for a first principle to exist.

LECTURE 2 [251a8–252a3]
Arguments for the Eternity of Motion

The Text of Aristotle

753. *Let us take our start from what we have already laid down in our course on Physics. Motion, we say, is the fulfilment of the movable in so far as it is movable. Each kind of motion, therefore, necessarily involves the presence of the things that are capable of that motion.*

In fact, even apart from the definition of motion, every one would admit that in each kind of motion it is that which is capable of that motion that is in motion: thus it is that which is capable of alteration that is altered, and that which is capable of local change that is in locomotion; and so there must be something capable of being burned before there can be a process of being burned, and something capable of burning before there can be a process of burning. **251a8–16**

754. *Moreover, these things also must either have a beginning before which they had no being, or they must be eternal. Now if there was a becoming of every movable thing, it follows that before the motion in question another change or motion must have taken place in which that which was capable of being moved or of causing motion had its becoming. To suppose, on the other hand, that these things were in being throughout all previous time without there being any motion appears unreasonable on a moment's thought, and still more unreasonable, we shall find, on further consideration. For if we are to say that, while there are on the one hand things that are movable, and on the other hand things that are motive, there is a time when there is a first mover and a first moved, and another time when there is no such thing but only something that is at rest, then this thing that is at rest must previously have been in process of change; for there must have been some cause of its rest, rest being the privation of motion. Therefore, before this first change there will be a previous change.* **251a16–28**

755. *For some things cause motion in only one way, while others can produce either of two contrary motions: thus fire causes heating but not cooling, whereas it would seem that knowledge may be directed to two contrary ends while remaining one and the same. Even in the former class, however, there seems to be something similar; for a cold thing in a sense causes heating by turning away and retiring, just as one possessed of knowledge voluntarily makes an error when he uses his knowledge in the reverse way.* **251a28–251b1**

756. *But at any rate all things that are capable respectively of affecting and being affected, or of causing motion and being moved, are capable of it not under all conditions, but only when they are in a particular condition and approach one another: so it is on the approach of one thing to another that the one causes motion and the other is moved, and when they are present under such conditions as rendered the one motive and the other movable. So if the motion was not always in process, it is clear that they must have been in a condition not such as to render them capable respectively of being moved and of causing motion, and one or other of them must have been in process of change; for in what is relative this is a necessary consequence: e.g., if one thing is double another when before it was not so, one or other of them, if not both, must have been in process of change. It follows, then, that there will be a process of change previous to the first.* **251b1–10**

757. *(Further, how can there be any "before" and "after" without the existence of time? Or how can there be any time without the existence of motion?* **251b10–12**

758. *If, then, time is the number of motion or itself a kind of motion, it follows that, if there is always time, motion must also be eternal.* **251b12–13**

759. *But so far as time is concerned we see that all with one exception are in agreement in saying that it is uncreated: in fact, it is just this that enables Democritus to show that all things*

cannot have had a becoming; for time, he says, is uncreated. Plato alone asserts the creation of time, saying that it had a becoming together with the universe, the universe according to him having had a becoming. 251b13–17

760. *Now since time cannot exist and is unthinkable apart from the moment, and the moment is a kind of middle-point, uniting, as it does in itself both a beginning and an end, a beginning of future time and an end of past time, it follows that there must always be time; for the extremity of the last period of time that we take must be found in some moment, since time contains no point of contact for us except the moment. Therefore, since the moment is both a beginning and an end, there must always be time on both sides of it. But if this is true of time, it is evident that it must also be true of motion, time being a kind of affection of motion.)* 251b17–28

761. *The same reasoning will also serve to show the imperishability of motion: just as a becoming of motion would involve, as we saw, the existence of a process of change previous to the first, in the same way a perishing of motion would involve the existence of a process of change subsequent to the last: for when a thing ceases to be moved, it does not therefore at the same time cease to be movable—e.g., the cessation of the process of being burned does not involve the cessation of the capacity of being burned, since a thing may be capable of being burned without being in process of being burned—nor, when a thing ceases to be mover, does it therefore at the same time cease to be motive. Again, the destructive agent will have to be destroyed, after what it destroys has been destroyed, and then that which has the capacity of destroying it will have to be destroyed afterwards; (so that there will be a process of change subsequent to the last) for being destroyed also is a kind of change.* 251b28–252a4

COMMENTARY OF ST. THOMAS

971. After he has raised the question of the eternity of motion, he intends here to show that motion is eternal.

This discussion is divided into two parts. First he proves his position. Secondly, where he says, **"The arguments that may . . ."** [767], he answers possible objections to the contrary.

Concerning the first part he makes two points. First he gives arguments to prove the eternity of motion. Secondly, where he says, **". . . and cannot have existed . . ."** [762], he gives arguments against the opinions of the philosophers who hold the contrary.

Concerning the first part he makes two points. First he shows that there has always been motion. Secondly, where he says, **"The same reasoning . . ."** [761], he shows that there always will be motion.

Concerning the first part he makes two points. First he proves the propo-

sition with an argument taken from motion. Secondly, where he says, **"Further, how can there be . . ."** [757], he uses an argument taken from time.

Concerning the first part he makes three points. First he sets forth a certain thing which is necessary for the following proof. Secondly, where he says, **"Moreover, these things also . . ."** [754], he introduces the proof of the proposition. Thirdly, where he says, **"For some things cause . . ."** [755], he shows the necessity of this proof.

972. He says, therefore, first that to prove the proposition, we ought to begin with those things which have already been determined in the Physics, so that we may use them as principles. By this he wants us to understand that the preceding books, in which he discussed motion in general and which are thus universally called de Naturalibus, are distinct from Book

VIII, in which he begins to apply motion to things.

He assumes, therefore, what is said in Physics, III, namely, that motion is the act of a mobile object insofar as it is mobile. It is apparent from this that in order for there to be motion, there must be things which can be moved by motion. For there cannot be act without a subject of act. Thus from the definition of motion it is clear that there must be a mobile subject in order for there to be motion.

But even apart from the definition of motion this is apparent in itself, as is clear from the common opinion of all men. For everyone admits that a thing is not moved unless it can be moved. This applies to every motion, for a thing is not altered unless it is alterable, and a thing is not changed in place unless it is mutable in respect to place.

And since a subject is naturally prior to that which is in the subject, we can conclude in regard to individual mutations, both from the standpoint of the mobile object and the mover, that a subject is burnable before it is burned, and a subject is a combustive, that is, able to burn, before it burns. I say "before," not always in time, but in nature.

973. From this proof of Aristotle Averroes takes the opportunity of speaking contrary to what we hold about creation according to faith.

To come to be is to be changed in some way. Moreover, every mutation requires a subject, as Aristotle proves here. Hence it is necessary that everything which comes to be, comes to be from some subject. Therefore, it is impossible for a thing to come to be from nothing.

He adds to this a second argument. When it is said that black comes to be from white, this is not said to occur per

se such that the white itself is converted into black. Rather this is said to occur per accidens because black takes the place of the receding white. Whatever is per accidens, however, is reduced to that which is per se. Moreover, that from which a thing comes to be per se is the subject, which enters into the substance of the thing made. Everything, therefore, which is said to come to be from its opposite comes to be from that opposite per accidens, but from the subject per se. It is not possible, therefore, for being to come to be from absolute non-being.

Thirdly, he adds to this the common opinion of all of the ancient physicists who hold that nothing comes to be from nothing.

Moreover, he gives two reasons why he thinks that the position that something comes to be from nothing has arisen.

The first is that the common man thinks that only those things exist which can be perceived by vision. Therefore, since the common man sees that something has been made visible which was not visible before, he thinks that it is possible for something to come to be from nothing.

The second reason is that the common man thinks that an agent needs matter in order to act because its power is diminished. This, however, is not due to the agent's lack of power, but to the very nature [ratio] of motion. Since, therefore, the first agent does not possess a power which is deficient in any way, it follows that this agent may act without a subject.

974. But if one thinks correctly, he would realize that Averroes has been deceived for a similar reason—the same one which is thought to have deceived us, namely, the consideration of particular beings.

For it is clear that the active potency of a particular agent presupposes a matter which a more universal agent makes, for example, an artist uses the matter which nature provides. Therefore, from the fact that every particular agent presupposes a matter which it does not make, it is not necessary to think that the first universal agent, which is the active power of the whole of being, presupposes something which, as it were, is not caused by it.

Moreover, this does not agree with Aristotle's intention. For he proves in Metaphysics, II, that that which is most true and most being is the cause of being for all existing things. Hence it follows that the very being in potency which primary matter has is derived from the first principle of being, which is the most being. Therefore, it is not necessary to presuppose something for its action which has not been produced by it.

And since every motion requires a subject, which Aristotle here proves and which is true, it follows that the universal production of being by God is neither motion nor mutation, but a certain simple emanation. And so "to become" and "to make" are used equivocally in reference to this universal production of things and in reference to other productions.

Therefore, if we were to think that the production of things by God is from eternity, as Aristotle and many Platonists held, it is not necessary, in fact it is impossible, that some non-produced subject be understood for this universal production. Moreover, if we hold according to the judgment of our faith that God did not produce things from eternity, but that He produced them after they were not, it is not necessary to posit some subject for this universal production.

It is clear, therefore, that what Aristotle proves here, namely, that every motion requires a mobile subject, is not contrary to the judgment of our faith. For it was said that the universal production of things, whether from eternity or not, is neither a motion nor a mutation. Motion or mutation requires that a thing be otherwise now than it was before, and so the thing would be previously existing. Consequently we are not now talking about the universal production of things.

975. Similarly, when he says that a thing is said to come to be from its opposite per accidens and from its subject per se, this is true of particular productions, according to which this or that being comes to be, for example, a man or a dog. However, this is not true of the universal production of being.

This is clear from what the Philosopher has said in Physics, I. For he said there that if this animal comes to be insofar as it is this animal, it is not necessary that it comes to be from "non-animal" but from "this non-animal." For example, man comes to be from non-man, or horse from non-horse. But if animal as animal comes to be, it must come to be from non-animal. If, therefore, some particular being comes to be, it does not come to be from absolute non-being. But if the whole of being comes to be, that is, if being as being comes to be, it must come to be from absolute non-being, if it can be said that it "comes to be" (for "comes to be" is used equivocally, as was said).

What he introduces concerning the opinions of the ancient philosophers is not applicable. For the ancient natural philosophers were unable to arrive at the first cause of the whole of being. Rather they considered the causes of particular mutations.

The first of them considered the causes only of accidental mutation, holding that everything which comes to be is altered. The next ones arrived at an understanding of substantial changes. The last ones, as Plato and Aristotle, came to a knowledge of the principle of the whole of being.

Therefore, it is clear that we are not moved to hold that something comes to be from nothing because we think that only visible things exist. Rather, on the contrary, we hold this because we do not consider only particular productions from particular causes, but the universal production of the whole of being from the first principle of being. Neither do we hold that a diminished power needs matter in order to act, as if it were deficient in natural power. Rather we say that this pertains to a particular power which does not have power over the whole of being, but which causes some being.

And so it can be said that a diminished power makes something from something, just as we might say that a particular power is less than a universal power.

976. Next where he says, **"Moreover, these things also . . ."** [754], having shown that motion requires a mobile object and a motive power, he argues as follows.

If motion has not always existed, one must say either that mobile objects and motive powers were made at some time before which they were not, or else they are eternal. Therefore, if it is said that every mobile object has been made, one must say that before the mutation which is taken as the first, there was another mutation and motion, according to which was made the mobile object itself which can be

moved and was moved. This inference depends on what has gone before. If it is granted that motion has not always existed, but rather there is some first mutation before which there was none, then it will follow that that first mutation had some mobile object, and that this mobile object was made, before which it was not. For it was granted that all mobile objects have been made. Everything which comes to be, before which it was not, comes to be through some motion or mutation. Moreover, the motion or mutation by which the mobile object comes to be is prior to the mutation by which the mobile object is moved. Therefore, before the mutation which was said to be first, there is another mutation, and so on to infinity.

If, however, it is said that mobile objects were always pre-existing, even though no motion existed, this seems to be irrational and the words of those who are unlearned. For it is immediately apparent that if there are mobile objects, there must be motion. For natural mobile objects and movers exist together, as is clear from Book III. And when movers and natural mobile objects exist, there must be motion.

But in order to proceed more profoundly in search of the truth, we should say that this same thing must happen even if it is granted that movers and mobile objects always pre-exist before motion. This follows if it is granted that these have been made, that is, if prior to the mutation which is given as first, there was another mutation to infinity. This is clear as follows. Let it be granted that there are mobile objects and movers, and at some time the first mover began to move and something was moved by it, and before this nothing was moved, but there was rest. It is then necessary to say that another mutation occurred earlier in the mover or mobile object which the first mover begins to move. This is clear as follows.

Rest is the privation of motion. Privation, however, is not in that which is receptive of a habit or form except through some cause. There was, therefore, some cause either on the part of the mover or on the part of the mobile object which was the cause of rest. Therefore, while it endured, there was always rest. If, therefore, at some time the mover begins to move, this cause of rest must be removed. But it cannot be removed except through some motion or mutation. Therefore, it follows that before the mutation which was said to be first, there was another earlier mutation by which the cause of rest was removed.

977. Next where he says, **"For some things cause motion . . ."** [755], he proves the necessity of the preceding argument.

One might say that it happens that a thing is at one time at rest and at another time in motion without any pre-existing cause of rest being removed. Hence he wishes to reject this.

Concerning this he makes two points. First he sets forth a certain thing which is necessary for his position. Secondly, where he says, **"But at any rate . . ."** [756], he proves his position.

He says, therefore, first that some movers move singly, that is, in only one way, and others move in respect to contrary motions.

Things which move in only one way are natural. For example, fire always heats and never causes coldness. But

intelligent agents move according to contrary motions, for contraries seem to be treated in one science. For example, medicine is the science of health and sickness. Hence it seems that a doctor by his own knowledge is able to move according to contrary motions.

He makes this distinction of movers because in regard to things which act through intelligence what he has said does not seem to be true, that is, it does not seem to be true that if a thing is moved after it was at rest, then the cause of that rest must first be removed.

For intelligent agents seem to be related to opposites without any mutation occurring in themselves. Hence it seems that they can move and not move without any mutation.

Therefore, lest this destroy his argument, he adds that his argument holds in a similar fashion for things which act through intellect and for things which act through nature.

Things which act through nature always move per se to one thing, but sometimes they move to the contrary per accidens. And for this accident to occur, there must be some mutation. For example, a cold thing always makes cold per se, but per accidens it heats.

It heats per accidens when it is changed in some way, either insofar as it is turned to another site so that it is related in another way to that which it now makes hot and which it previously made cold, or else insofar as it disappears entirely. For we say that the disappearance of cold causes heat just as a helmsman by his absence causes the sinking of a ship. In a similar way cold becomes the per accidens cause of heat either by a greater withdrawal or a greater nearness, just as in winter the inner parts of animals are warmer as the warmth withdraws farther inside because of the encompassing cold.

And the same applies to intelligent agents. For although there is one science of contraries, nevertheless there is not equal science of both. Rather it is principally of one. For example, medicine is ordained per se to produce health. If, therefore, it happens that a doctor uses his knowledge to induce illness, this will not be through his knowledge per se but per accidens, because of something else. And in order for that other to occur which before was not, some mutation is necessary.

978. Next where he says, **"But at any rate . . ."** [756], he introduces the proof of his position.

He says, therefore, that since agents which act through nature and agents which act through intelligence are thus related in a similar way, we can say universally that whatever has the potency to do or to suffer or to move or to be moved cannot move or be moved in every disposition in which it is found. Rather this occurs insofar as such things exist in some determinate state and nearness to each other.

And he concludes this from the foregoing. For it has already been said that in both natural agents and voluntary agents there is not one cause of diverse things unless this cause exists in some other disposition. Therefore, whenever a mover and the moved approach each other with a suitable nearness, and likewise when they are in whatever disposition is required so that one moves and the other is moved, then the one must be moved and the other must move.

If, therefore, there has not always been motion, then it is clear that they did not exist in such a relation that one moves and the other is moved. Rather they existed in such a way that it was not possible for them to move and be moved. Afterwards, however, they do exist in such a relation that one moves and the other is moved. Therefore, one of them must have been changed.

In all things which are called relations we see that a new relation occurs only through a mutation of one or the other. For example, if a thing which before was not double is now made double, then if one of the extremes is not changed, at least the other must be changed. And so, if a new relation should occur so that one thing moves and another is moved, one or the other must be moved first. Hence it follows that there is a certain mutation which is prior to the mutation which was said to be first.

979. Next where he says, **"Further, how can there be . . ."** [757], he proves his position with an argument taken from time.

First he sets forth two things which are necessary for the following proof.

The first is that there cannot be a before and after unless there is time. For time is nothing other than the before and after according to which things are numbered.

The second is that there cannot be time unless there is motion. This is clear from the definition of time which he gave above in Book IV, saying that time is the number of motion in respect to before or after.

980. Secondly, where he says, **"If, then, time . . ."** [758], he comes to a conditional conclusion from what was said in Book IV.

For he stated there, according to his opinion, that time is the number of motion. In the same place he said that other philosophers have held that time is a certain motion.

Whichever of these may be true, it follows that this condition is true: if time is eternal, then motion must be eternal.

981. Thirdly, where he says, **"But so far as time . . ."** [759], he proves the antecedent of the above condition in two ways.

He does this first by means of the opinions of others. He says that all philosophers except one, namely Plato, seem to agree that time is ungenerated, that is, time did not begin to be after it previously was not. Hence even Democritus proves that it is impossible for all things to have been made as if they began anew, because it is impossible for time to have been so made that it began anew.

Only Plato "generates time," that is, only he says that time was made anew. For Plato says that time was made together with the heavens. And he held that the heavens "were made," that is, they have a beginning of duration, as Aristotle here imputes to him, according to which his words seem to sound superficial. The Platonists, however, say that Plato said that the heavens were made in the sense that they have an active principle of their being but not in the sense that they have a beginning of duration. Therefore, Plato alone seems to have understood that there is no time without motion. For he did not hold that time existed before the motion of the heavens.

982. Secondly, where he says, **"Now since time . . ."** [760], he proves the same thing through reason. It is impossible to say or to think that there is time without the "now," just as it is impossible for a line to exist without a point.

Moreover, the "now" is a certain intermediate, having such a nature [ratio] that it is both a beginning and an end, that is, the beginning of the future and the end of the past. From this it seems that time must be eternal. For whatever time is taken, its extreme on either side is a "now." This is clear because no part of time is in act except the "now." For what has passed has already gone, and what is future as yet is not. Moreover, the "now" which is taken as the extremity of time is a beginning and an end, as was said. Therefore, on either side of any given time there must always be time. Otherwise the first "now" would not be an end, and the last "now" would not be a beginning.

From the statement that time is eternal, he concludes that motion must be eternal. And he gives the reason for this conclusion. Time is a certain property of motion, for it is its number, as was said.

983. It seems, however, that Aristotle's argument is not effective. For the "now" is related to time as a point is related to a line, as was explained in Book VI. But the nature [ratio] of a point is not such that it is a middle. Rather there is a point which is only the beginning of a line and another point which is only an end. It would happen, however, that every point is a beginning and an end insofar as it is a part of an infinite line. It cannot be proven, therefore, that a line is infinite because every point is a beginning and an end. Rather, conversely, from the fact that a line is infinite, it can be proven that every point is a beginning and an end. Therefore, if it seems that every "now" is a beginning and an end, this is not true unless it is granted that time is eternal. It seems, therefore, that in assuming this, Aristotle pre-

supposes the eternity of time, which he ought to prove.

Averroes, however, wishing to save Aristotle's argument, says that the "now" is always a beginning and an end insofar as time does not stand still, as does a line, but rather is in flux.

This clearly is not at all pertinent. For from the fact that time is flowing and not standing still, it follows that one "now" cannot be taken twice as one point can be taken twice. But the flux of time has no bearing on the "now" being both a beginning and an end. For the same nature [ratio] is found in the inception and termination of every continuum, whether permanent or in flux, as is clear from Book VI.

984. Therefore, we should re-interpret Aristotle's statement that every "now" is a beginning and an end, which he wishes to derive from what he assumed first, namely, that there is no before and after unless there is time. He uses this assumed principle only to conclude that every "now" is a beginning and an end. Let it be granted that some "now" is the beginning of some time. It is clear, moreover, from the definition of "beginning" that the beginning of time is that before which no time exists. Therefore, there is something "before" or "earlier" than this "now" which was given as the beginning of time. But there is no before without time. Therefore, the "now" which was given as the beginning of time is also an end of time. And in the same way, if a "now" is an end of time, it follows that it is also a beginning, because it is the nature [ratio] of an end that after it there is nothing of it. But there is no after without time. It follows, therefore, that the "now" which is an end is also a beginning of time.

985. Next where he says, **"The same**

reasoning . . ." [761], he shows that there will always be motion.

He proves this from motion. The argument given above which was taken from motion concluded only that motion never began. But the argument taken from time concluded both that motion never began and that it will never cease.

He says, therefore, that the same argument which proves that motion never began can also be used to prove that motion is incorruptible, that is, that motion will never cease. For just as it follows, if there is a beginning of motion, that there was some mutation prior to the mutation given as first, so if it is held that motion at some time ceases, it will follow that there will be some mutation after the mutation which was given as last.

He explains how this follows by abridging what he has said more fully above about the beginning of motion. For he said that if motion begins, mobile objects and movers either began or always were. And a similar distinction can be made here, because if motion ceases, mobile objects and movers will remain or they will not. And since he has shown above that the same thing follows in either case, here he uses only the second way, namely, if it is granted that motion ceases, then mobile objects and movers will cease.

On this supposition he says that the actual motion and the mobile object do not cease at the same time. Rather, just as the generation of the mobile object is prior to its motion, so the corruption of the mobile object will be later than the cessation of its motion. And this is clear because it happens that a burnable object remains after the burning stops.

And the same thing may be said of

the mover as was said of the mobile object. For the moving being in act and the moving being in potency do not stop together. Thus it is clear that if the mobile object itself is corrupted after the cessation of motion, then there must be a corruption of that mobile object.

Moreover, since it was granted that all movers and moved objects cease, then the thing which corrupts will necessarily be corrupted at a later time. And since corruption is a mutation, it follows that there are mutations after the last mutation. Since, therefore, this is impossible, it follows that motion endures forever.

986. These, then, are the arguments by which Aristotle intends to prove that motion always was and never ceases.

One part of his position, namely, that there was always motion, conflicts with our faith. For according to our faith nothing has always existed except God alone, Who is altogether immobile, unless one wishes to say that motion is divine understanding. But this meaning of motion is equivocal. For Aristotle does not here mean motion of this kind, but motion in its proper sense.

But the other part of his position is not altogether contrary to faith. For as was said above, Aristotle is not treating the motion of the heavens, but motion in general. But according to our faith we hold that the substance of the world at some time began to be but it will never cease to be. We hold also that some motions will always be, especially in men, who will always remain, living an uncorruptible life, either damned or blessed.

Indeed some, attempting in vain to show that Aristotle has not spoken contrary to faith, have said that Aristotle does not intend here to prove as a truth that motion is eternal, but to introduce arguments on both sides, as if for a point in doubt. But because of his method of procedure this appears to be nonsense. And besides, he uses the eternity of time and of motion as a principle to prove the existence of a first principle, both here in Book VIII and in Metaphysics, XII. Therefore it is clear that he assumes this as proven.

987. But if one correctly considers the arguments given here, the truth of faith cannot effectively be opposed to such arguments.

For arguments of this kind are effective in proving that motion did not begin by way of nature, as some have held. But it cannot be proven with these arguments that motion did not begin in the sense that things were produced anew by the first principle of things, as our faith holds. This is clear to one who considers the individual inferences which are given here.

For when one asks whether or not movers and mobile objects have always existed if there has not always been motion, one must answer that the first mover has always existed. All other things, whether they be movers or mobile objects, have not always existed but began to be from the universal cause of the whole of being. It was shown above, moreover, that the production of the whole of being by the first cause of being is not a motion, whether or not it is granted that this emanation of things is from eternity.

Thus, therefore, it does not follow that before the first mutation there is another mutation. However, this would follow if movers and mobile objects were newly produced in being by some particular agent which acts on some presupposed subject which is changed from non-being to being, or from privation to form. Aristotle's argument deals with this type of beginning.

988. But since we hold that at least the first mover has always existed, we still need to give an answer to his next deduction, in which he concludes that if motion begins to be anew when movers and mobile objects pre-exist, then movers and mobile objects must not previously have been in that disposition in which they are while there is motion. And thus some mutation must precede the first mutation.

If we speak about motion itself, the answer is easy. Mobile objects were not previously in the disposition in which they now are, because previously they did not exist. Hence they could not be moved. And as was said, existence is not acquired through a mutation or a motion, but through an emanation from the first principle of things. Thus it does not follow that there was a mutation before the first mutation.

But there remains a further question about the first production of things. If the first principle, which is God, is not related differently now than He was before, He does not produce things now rather than before. And if He were related differently, at least a mutation on His part will be prior to the mutation which is first.

Now if He were an agent only through nature, and not through will and intellect, this argument would conclude with necessity. But because He acts through His will, He is able through His eternal will to produce an effect which is not eternal, just as through His eternal intellect He can understand a thing which is not eternal. For a known thing is in a certain

way the principle of action in agents who act through the will, just as a natural form is the principle of action in agents who act through nature.

989. Let us pursue this further. We do not see that the will puts off doing what it wishes unless something is expected in the future which does not yet exist in the present. For example, I do not wish to make a fire now but later in the future when I expect cold, which is the reason why I make the fire; or at least it is expected at the present time. Moreover, since time succeeds time, this cannot occur without motion. Therefore, a will, even if it is immutable, cannot put off doing what it wills except by some intervening motion. And so it is not possible for a new production of things to proceed from an eternal will unless intermediate motions succeed each other to infinity.

But such objectors do not see that this objection proceeds from an agent in time, that is, from an agent who acts in a presupposed time. For in an action of this kind which occurs in time, one must consider some determinate relation to this time or to those things which are in this time, so that it occurs at this time rather than at the other. But this argument has no application to a universal agent which produces even time itself together with the rest of things.

For when we say that things were not eternally produced by God, we do not mean that an infinite time has preceded in which God ceased from acting, and that after a determined time He began to act. Rather we mean that God produced time and things together in being after they were not. And so we need not consider that the divine will willed to make things not then, but afterwards, as if time already existed. Rather we need only consider that He willed that things and the time of their duration should begin to be after they were not.

If, however, one asks why He willed this, without doubt it must be said that He did this for His own sake. For just as He made things for His own sake so that a likeness of His goodness would be manifested in them, so He wills them not always to be so that His sufficiency would be manifested in this, that when all other things do not exist, He has within Himself every sufficiency of beatitude and of power for the production of things.

This indeed may be said insofar as human reason can understand divine things. Nevertheless, the secrets of divine wisdom, which cannot be comprehended by us, are preserved.

990. Since, therefore, the answer to this argument proceeds from the supposition that there has not always been time, it remains to answer the argument through which it seems to be shown that there was always time. Aristotle perhaps gives the argument concerning time after the argument concerning motion because he thought that the preceding argument concerning motion was not effective unless it is granted that time is eternal. Therefore he says that whenever there is time, it must be admitted unhesitatingly that there is a "now." That every "now," however, is a beginning and an end of time cannot be conceded unless it is also granted that there has always been motion such that every indivisible that is taken in motion, which is called an "impulse," is a beginning and an end of motion. For "now" is related to "impulse" as time is related to motion. If, therefore, we hold that there has not always been motion but that there is a first indivisible in motion before which there was no motion,

then there will also be a "now" in time before which there was no time.

We have already shown above, in explaining the text, that what Averroes says in confirmation of this argument is not effective.

And Aristotle's position that there is no before and after without time is also not effective.

For when we say that the beginning of time is that before which none of it is, it cannot be said on account of this that the "now" which is the beginning of time is preceded by a time which is signified by "before." In the same way if in regard to magnitude I say that the beginning of a magnitude is that outside of which none of it is, it cannot be said that "outside of that beginning" signifies a place existing in nature, but only an imaginary place. Otherwise one could posit a place outside the heavens whose magnitude is finite, having a beginning and an end.

In a similar way the first "now" which is the beginning of time is not preceded by a time existing in nature, but only in our imagination. And this is the time which is designated when it is said that the first "now" is a beginning of time "before" which there is no time.

Or it can be said that when the beginning of time is said to be that before which there is no time, the word "before" does not remain affirmative, but becomes negative. Thus it is not necessary to posit a time before the beginning of time. With respect to things which are in time, it happens that some time pre-existed their beginning. For example, when it is said that the beginning of youth is that before which there is no youth, it is possible to understand the "before" affirmatively, because youth is measured by time. Time, however, is not measured by time. Hence time did not pre-exist its beginning. And so the word "before," which is used in the definition of the beginning of time, cannot remain affirmative, but becomes negative.

There is, however, a duration before time, namely, the eternity of God, which has no extension of either before or after, as does time, but is a simultaneous whole. This does not have the same nature [ratio] as time, just as divine magnitude is not the same as corporeal magnitude.

Thus when we say that outside the world nothing exists except God, we do not posit any dimension outside the world. In the same way when we say that before the world nothing was, we do not posit a successive duration before the world.

LECTURE 3 [252a4–b6]
Arguments Against Anaxagoras and Empedocles Who Held That Motion Is Not Eternal

The Text of Aristotle

762. If, then, the view which we are criticizing involves these impossible consequences, it is clear that motion is eternal and cannot have existed at one time and not at another: in fact, such a view can hardly be described as anything else than fantastic.   252a4–5

763. And much the same may be said of the view that such is the ordinance of nature and that this must be regarded as a principle, as would seem to be the view of Empedocles when he says that the constitution of the world is of necessity such that Love and Strife alternately predominate and cause motion, while in the intermediate period of time there is a state of rest. Probably also those who, like Anaxagoras, assert a single principle (of motion) would hold this view.   252a5–11

764. But that which is produced or directed by nature can never be anything disorderly; for nature is everywhere the cause of order. Moreover, there is no ratio in the relation of the infinite to the infinite, whereas order always means ratio. But if we say that there is first a state of rest for an infinite time, and then motion is started at some moment, and that the fact that it is this rather than a previous moment is of no importance, and involves no order, then we can no longer say that it is nature's work; for if anything is of a certain character naturally, it either is so invariably and is not sometimes of this and sometimes of another character (e.g., fire, which travels upwards naturally, does not sometimes do so and sometimes not) or there is a ratio in the variation. It would be better, therefore, to say with Empedocles and any one else who may have maintained such a theory as his that the universe is alternately at rest and in motion: for in a system of this kind we have at once a certain order.   252a11–22

765. But even here the holder of the theory ought not only to assert the fact: he ought also to explain the cause of it; i.e., he should not make any mere assumption or lay down any gratuitous axiom, but should employ either inductive or demonstrative reasoning. The Love and Strife postulated by Empedocles are not in themselves causes of the fact in question, nor is it of the essence of either that it should be so, the essential function of the former being to unite, of the latter to separate. If he is to go on to explain this alternate predominance, he should adduce cases where such a state of things exists, as he points to the fact that among mankind we have something that unites men, namely Love, while on the other hand enemies avoid one another: thus from the observed fact that this occurs in certain cases comes the assumption that it occurs also in the universe. Then, again, some argument is needed to explain why the predominance of each of the two forces lasts for an equal period of time.   252a22–32

766. But it is a wrong assumption to suppose universally that we have an adequate first principle in virtue of the fact that something always is so or always happens so. Thus Democritus reduces the causes that explain nature to the fact that things happened in the past in the same way as they happen now; but he does not think fit to seek for a first principle to explain this "always": so, while his theory is right in so far as it is applied to certain individual cases, he is wrong in making it of universal application. Thus, a triangle always has its angles equal to two right angles, but there is nevertheless an ulterior cause of the eternity of this truth, whereas first principles are eternal and have no ulterior cause. Let this conclude what we have to say in support of our contention that there never was a time when there was not motion, and never will be a time when there will not be motion.   252a32–252b6

COMMENTARY OF ST. THOMAS

991. After the Philosopher has given arguments to show that motion is eternal, he here gives arguments against Anaxagoras and Empedocles who held the contrary.

Concerning this he makes two points. First he gives an argument against their position. Secondly, where he says, **"And much the same . . ."** [763], he argues against the argument which they used.

He says, therefore, first [762] that since it has been shown that motion is eternal, it should not be said that sometimes there is motion and sometimes there is not, as Empedocles and Anaxagoras maintained. For to say what they said is comparable to fiction, because they held this without reason. Everything which is held without reason or without divine authority seems to be fiction. Divine authority, however, prevails over human reason much more than the authority of a philosopher prevails over some feeble argument which is offered by a boy.

What we hold through faith is not to be compared to fiction, even though we believe without reason. For we believe on divine authority, which is attested to by miracles, that is, by those works which only God can perform.

992. Next where he says, **"And much the same . . ."** [763], he objects to the argument which they used.

Concerning this he makes three points. First he states that their argument is inconsistent. Secondly, where he says, **"But that which is produced . . ."** [764], he shows that the argument is more inconsistent in regard to Anaxagoras' position than in regard to Empedocles' position. Thirdly, where he says, **"But even here the**

holder . . ."** [765], he shows that it is not consistent according to the opinion of Empedocles.

He says, therefore, first that there also seems to be a fiction if one were to say that sometimes there is motion and sometimes not because this is natural and must be taken as a principle. Now Empedocles seems to say that things necessarily are such that at one time they have friendship, at another time they have strife and are moved, and in the intermediate time they are at rest. It is as if one were to say that the reason why a warm thing heats is that this must be so, and the fact that a warm thing heats is taken as a principle.

In the same way Empedocles holds as a principle that things necessarily are such that sometimes they are moved by friendship, sometimes by strife, and sometimes they are at rest.

And perhaps in the same way Anaxagoras and all others who posit one active principle would say that it must be taken as a principle that motion began after an infinite time in which it was not.

993. Next where he says, **"But that which is produced . . ."** [764], he shows that Anaxagoras used this argument more inconsistently than Empedocles.

It is clear that when something is given as a principle, it ought to be in accordance with the nature of the thing, that is, the nature of the thing should be such that it is consistent with it. For example, we accept as a principle that every whole is greater than its parts, because the meaning [ratio] and nature of a whole is such that it exceeds the quantity of a part. Now when Empedocles says, ". . . such is the ordinance of nature . . ." , he means "this must be taken as a principle." And Anaxagoras would say the same thing, although he does not express it.

Now it is clear that no natural thing nor anything which naturally agrees with things can exist without order. For nature is the cause of order. For we see that nature in its own operations proceeds in an orderly way from one to another. Therefore, that which has no order and which is not according to nature cannot be taken as a principle.

But two infinites do not have an order to each other. For there is no proportion of infinite to infinite. And every order is a certain proportion. Therefore, it is clear that it is not the work of nature for a thing to be at rest in an infinite time, and later begin to be moved through an infinite time, without any difference between this time and that so that the motion occurs now rather than before; nor is it the work of nature for there to be no order between two things of which when one fails the other begins and motion occurs, as Anaxagoras held. For whatever is in nature is always related in the same way, and is not at one time related in one way and at another time in another way. For example, fire is always borne upward. Or else there is some reason why it is not related in the same way. For example, animals do not always increase. Rather they are sometimes diminished, but there is a reason for this.

Therefore, it does not seem to be in accord with nature that in an infinite time things were at rest and later began to be moved, as Anaxagoras held.

And so it is better to say, as Empedocles said, or as others have thought, that the whole universe is at rest during one period of time and then it is moved during another period of time. For this may have some order, since there is a proportion of finite to finite.

Moreover, it must be realized that the belief of our faith is not similar to the position of Anaxagoras. For we do not hold that before the world there were infinite spaces of time which must have a proportion to the following time. Rather we hold that before the world began there was only the simple eternity of God, as was said, which is totally outside the genus of time.

994. Next where he says, **"But even here the holder . . ."** [765] he shows that the previous argument is not consistent even for Empedocles.

First he explains his position. Secondly, where he says, **"But it is a wrong . . ."** [766], he rejects a certain false opinion.

He says, therefore, first that anyone who asserts what Empedocles said ought not only to affirm what he says, but should also give a reason for his statement. He should add nothing more than the given reason requires, and he should be unwilling to accept something as a principle without proof. And to clarify what he accepts as a principle he should add either an induction, which is given for natural principles which are derived from the experience of sensible things, or a demonstration, which is given for principles which are demonstrated by prior principles. But Empedocles pays no attention to this. Even though he posits friendship and strife as causes, nevertheless, friendship and strife do not have such a nature [ratio] that one of them moves after the other. Nor is the nature [ratio] of friendship such that it is converted into strife, or vice versa. Rather the nature [ratio] of friendship is such that it unites, and the nature [ratio] of strife is such that it separates.

And if it is to be determined further that in one part of time one of these unites and in another part of time the other separates, this must be made clear in particular cases. The fact that friendship unites and strife separates is clear in men because friendship brings men together and strife drives them apart. Therefore, Empedocles assumes this for the whole universe because it seems to be so in some cases. But his point that friendship and strife move successively in equal times needs some clarifying reason, for this does not seem to occur in men.

995. Next where he says, **"But it is a wrong . . ."** [766], he rejects a certain false opinion. One might think that whatever always is does not have a cause because we see that the things among us which are caused begin anew. And therefore in other cases it would seem that whenever a question is reduced to something which always is, it is not necessary to seek a further cause or reason. Therefore, Empedocles could say that friendship and strife always move according to equal times, and hence another reason for this need not be sought. Aristotle rejects this by saying that it is not correct to think that something is a principle because it always is or always occurs. Democritus reduced all natural causes to this by assigning a principle to things which come to be anew, but he did not wish to seek a principle for that which is eternal.

In some cases this is correct, but not in all cases. It is clear that a triangle always has three angles equal to two right angles; but there is a cause of this enduring quality. But there are some perpetual things, for example, principles, which have no cause.

996. What is said here should be noted well. For as is said in Metaphysics, II, the disposition of things in being and in truth is the same. Hence just as some things are always true and yet have a cause of their truth, so Aristotle thought that some beings are eternal, namely, celestial bodies and separated substances, but nevertheless they have a cause of their being.

From this is it clear that, although Aristotle held that the world is eternal, he did not believe that God is the cause only of the motion of the world and not its being, as some have said.

Finally, he concludes to his main point in an epilogue. He says that these things have been said to show that there will be no time in the future, nor was there a time in the past, in which there is no motion.

LECTURE 4 [252b7–253a21]
He Answers Arguments Which Seem to Prove That Motion Is Not Eternal

The Text of Aristotle
Chapter 2

767. *The arguments that may be advanced against this position are not difficult to dispose of. The chief considerations that might be thought to indicate that motion may exist though at one time it had not existed at all are the following:*

First, it may be said that no process of change is eternal; for the nature of all change is such that it proceeds from something to something, so that every process of change must be bounded by the contraries that mark its course, and no motion can go on to infinity. 252b7–12

768. *Secondly, we see that a thing that neither is in motion nor contains any motion within itself can be set in motion; e.g., inanimate things that are (whether the whole or some part is in question) not in motion but at rest, are at some moment set in motion; whereas, if motion cannot have a becoming before which it had no being, these things ought to be either always or never in motion.* 252b12–16

769. *Thirdly, the fact is evident above all in the case of animate beings; for it sometimes happens that there is no motion in us and we are quite still, and that nevertheless we are then at some moment set in motion, that is to say it sometimes happens that we produce a beginning of motion in ourselves spontaneously without anything having set us in motion from without. We see nothing like this in the case of inanimate things, which are always set in motion by something else from without: the animal, on the other hand, we say, moves itself; therefore, if an animal is ever in a state of absolute rest, we have a motionless thing in which motion can be produced from the thing itself and not from without. Now if this can occur in an animal, why should not the same be true also of the universe as a whole? If it can occur in a small world it could also occur in a great one; and if it can occur in the world, it could also occur in the infinite; that is, if the infinite could as a whole possibly be in motion or at rest.* 252b17–28

770. *Of these objections, then, the first-mentioned—that motion to opposites is not always the same and numerically one—is a correct statement; in fact, this may be said to be a necessary conclusion, provided that it is possible for the motion of that which is one and the same to be not always one and the same. (I mean that e.g. we may question whether the note given by a single string is one and the same, or is different each time the string is struck, although the string is in the same condition and is moved in the same way.) But however this may be, there is nothing to prevent there being a motion that is the same in virtue of being continuous and eternal: we shall have something to say later that will make this point clearer.* 252b28–253a2

771. *As regards the second objection, no absurdity is involved in the fact that something not in motion may be set in motion, that which caused the motion from without being at one time present, and at another absent. Nevertheless, how this can be so remains matter for inquiry; how it comes about, I mean, that the same motive force at one time causes a thing to be in motion, and at another does not do; for the difficulty raised by our objector really amounts to this—why is it that some things are not always at rest, and the others always in motion?* 253a2–7

772. *The third objection may be thought to present more difficulty than the others, namely, that which alleges that motion arises in things in which it did not exist before, and adduces in proof the case of animate things: thus an animal is first at rest and afterwards walks, not having been set in motion apparently by anything from without. This, however, is false; for we observe that there is always some part of the animal's organism in motion, and the cause of the motion*

of this part is not the animal itself, but, it may be, its environment. Moreover, we say that the animal itself originates not all of its motions but its locomotion. So it may well be the case—or rather we may perhaps say that it must necessarily be the case—that many motions are produced in the body by its environment, and some of these set in motion the intellect or the appetite, and this again then sets the whole animal in motion: this is what happens when animals are asleep: though there is then no perceptive motion in them, there is some motion that causes them to wake up again. But we will leave this point also to be elucidated at a later stage in our discussion.

253a7–21

COMMENTARY OF ST. THOMAS

997. After the Philosopher has given arguments to prove that motion is eternal, he intends here to answer possible objections to the contrary.

Concerning this he makes two points. First he gives the arguments. Secondly, where he says, **"Of these objections . . ."** [770], he answers them.

Concerning the first part he gives three arguments and states his intention. He says that it is not difficult to answer possible objections to the contrary.

From three arguments it seems indeed to follow that motion began to be at some time before which it did not exist at all. The first of these is that no mutation is infinite, which he proved above in Book VI. With the same argument it can be proven that no mutation is eternal.

No terminated mutation is eternal, just as it is not infinite. But every mutation is terminated. For every mutation is naturally from something to something, and these two are contraries. And so the termini of every mutation must be the contraries between which the change occurs. But since contrariety of the termini is not clear in every local motion, he adds that it is common to all motion that nothing is moved to infinity. For nothing is moved to that which it cannot attain, as was said in Book VI. Therefore, it is clear that no mutation is eternal, just as it is not infi-

nite. Hence, if no mutation is eternal, it seems to be possible to designate a time in which there is no mutation. This first argument deals with motion.

998. The second argument deals with the mobile object and is given where he says, **"Secondly, we see . . ."** [768].

If motion cannot come to be anew before which it was not, it seems consistent to say of anything that it either is always moved or is never moved. For if in regard to one mobile object it is possible that there is sometimes motion and sometimes not, this argument applies equally to the whole universe. But we see that it is possible for a thing to be moved which before was not moved either in respect to the whole or in respect to one of its parts. For example, this is clear in inanimate things in which a mobile object begins to be moved, although before neither the whole nor a part was moved. Rather it was totally at rest. It follows, therefore, that in the whole universe there can be motion which before was not.

999. But although in inanimate things it is clear that motion begins anew in something, with no motion pre-existing in that same being, nevertheless, it is clear that motion pre-exists in some exterior being by which it is moved. The third argument, therefore, deals with animals, which are not moved by an extrinsic being, but by

themselves. He gives this argument where he says, **"Thirdly, the fact . . ."** [769].

That motion begins when before it was not is much more apparent in animate things than in inanimate things. For when we have been at rest for some time, with no motion existing in us, we begin at some time to be moved. The principle of our motion is from ourselves, even if nothing extrinsic should move. In inanimate beings this does not occur. Rather some extrinsic being always moves them, either by generating, or by removing an obstacle, or by imparting violence. It follows from this that if an animal is at some time completely at rest, then in some immobile being motion begins to be when before it was not, and this occurs not by some extrinsic thing which moves, but by the very thing which is moved. And if this can occur in an animal, it seems that there is nothing to prevent the same thing from happening in the universe. For an animal, and especially man, has a certain similarity to the universe. Hence it is said by some that man is a little world. And so, if in a little world motion begins when before it was not, it seems that the same thing can also occur in the large world. And if this happens in the world, it can also happen in an infinite whole, which some posit outside the world, provided that there is an infinite which can be moved and be at rest.

1000. Next where he says, **"Of these objections . . ."** [770], he answers the above arguments in order.

In answering the first argument he says that it is correct to assert that motion between contraries cannot endure as one and the same in number. Perhaps this is necessary, as he will prove below. Since this has not yet been

proven, he leaves it open to question. But someone might say that even motion between contraries can always be one in number because of the identity of a mobile object which is moved back and forth from contrary to contrary. For example, a thing is moved first from white to black, and then from black to white, and so forth. He adds, therefore, that it is impossible for the motion of one and the same mobile object to be always one and the same through repetition. And he explains this with an example. Suppose that a harp string is in a situation of this kind, and the mover who plays the harp is in a similar situation in moving. There is a problem as to whether two strokes on one harp string are one and the same motion and sound, or whether they are always different.

Nevertheless, whatever may be true of other mobile objects, nothing prevents a motion which is not between contraries, such as circular motion, from remaining always the same and continuous and perpetual. This will be more clear from the following. Therefore, although every motion is finite in respect to its termini, nevertheless some motions can be continuous and perpetual through repetition.

1001. Next where he says, **"As regards the second . . ."** [771], he answers the second argument.

He says that there is no inconsistency if an inanimate being begins to be moved when before it was not moved, if this happens because an extrinsic mover is sometimes present and sometimes not. For it is clear that motion must pre-exist in the mover which at some time becomes properly a mover when previously it was not. But this seems to be a difficulty which must be investigated: when the mover exists, is the same thing sometimes moved by the same thing and sometimes not? For he said above that this could not occur except through some previous mutation either on the part of the mobile object or on the part of the mover. And thus motion always pre-exists whether the mover pre-exists or not. Hence it seems that this must be asked because he who introduced this argument seems only to inquire why things which are at rest are not always at rest and why mobile objects are not always being moved.

1002. Next where he says, "The third objection . . ." [772], he answers the third argument.

He says that the third objection especially makes us think that motion can exist when before it was not, as seems to happen in animate things. For it seems that an animal which before was at rest is afterwards moved by a progressive motion, with no motion caused from the exterior. And so it seems that no motion preceded the animal's motion, either in the animal itself or in another, as was said of inanimate things.

But it is false that the motion of the animal did not come to be from something exterior. For in animals we always see some natural motion, that is, something which is not moved by the will. The cause of this natural motion is not the animal itself through its appetite. Rather the cause of this natural mutation is perhaps the air and ultimately a celestial body, as is clearly apparent when an animal body is altered by the warmth or coldness of the air.

He says "perhaps," because in an animal there is also natural motion from an interior principle, as is clear in the mutations in the vegetative soul which are seen in the digestion of food and the subsequent changes. These are

called natural because they do not follow apprehension and appetite. But it seems to be contrary to that which is proper to animals for them to move themselves. Therefore, he adds that when we say that an animal moves itself, we do not refer to every motion but to local motion, according to which an animal moves itself through apprehension and appetite.

Therefore it is possible—in fact it is necessary—that in an animal body there are many changes from the container, that is, the air and a celestial body. Some of these move the intellect or the appetite, and as a further result the whole animal is moved.

1003. Moreover, it must be noted that he here describes the way in which celestial bodies act on us. They do not act directly on our souls, but on our bodies. When our bodies have been moved, motion occurs per accidens in the powers of the soul which are acts of corporeal organs, but not necessarily in the intellect and in the intellective appetite, which do not use corporeal organs. Sometimes, however, the intellect and the will follow some of the above mutations, as when one through reason chooses either to follow, or reject, or do something because of a passion which has arisen either in the body or in the sensitive part. Therefore he does not say that all motions which are caused by the container move the intellect or the appetite. Rather he says "some," in order to completely exclude necessity from the intellective part.

He gives, moreover, examples of the things which he has said. In those who sleep there seems to be the greatest rest in respect to animal motions. Moreover in them there is no sensible motion, that is, no motion which proceeds from sensible apprehension.

Again, awakened animals arise because of some motion existing interiorly, either from the work of the nutritive soul, as when the evaporations which cause sleep disappear when food is digested, and the animal is aroused, or because the body is altered by the container through warmth or coldness.

And so it is apparent to the careful thinker that never does any motion appear anew in us unless it is preceded by some other motion. And he promises that he will make this much clearer in what follows.

Things May Be Moved or at Rest in Five Ways. The First Two Ways Are Dismissed

The Text of Aristotle
Chapter 3

773. Our enquiry will resolve itself at the outset into a consideration of the above-mentioned problem—what can be the reason why some things in the world at one time are in motion and at another are at rest again? Now one of three things must be true: either all things are always at rest, or all things are always in motion, or some things are in motion and others at rest; and in this last case again either the things that are in motion are always in motion and the things that are at rest are always at rest, or they are all constituted so as to be capable alike of motion and of rest; or there is yet a third possibility remaining—it may be that some things in the world are always motionless, others always in motion, while others again admit of both conditions. This last is the account of the matter that we must give; for herein lies the solution of all the difficulties raised and the conclusion of the investigation upon which we are engaged.

253a22–32

774. To maintain that all things are at rest, and to disregard sense-perception in an attempt to show the theory to be reasonable, would be an instance of intellectual weakness: it would call in question a whole system, not a particular detail; moreover, it would be an attack not only on the physicist but on almost all sciences and all received opinions, since motion plays a part in all of them. Further, just as in arguments about mathematics objections that involve first principles do not affect the mathematician—and the other sciences are in similar case—so, too, objections involving the point that we have just raised do not affect the physicist; for it is a fundamental assumption with him that motion is ultimately referable to nature herself.   253a32–253b6

775. The assertion that all things are in motion we may fairly regard as equally false, though it is less subversive of physical science; for though in our course on physics it was laid down that rest no less than motion is ultimately referable to nature herself, nevertheless motion is the characteristic fact of nature;   253b6–9

776. moreover, the view is actually held by some that not merely some things but all things in the world are in motion and always in motion, though we cannot apprehend the fact by sense-perception. Although the supporters of this theory do not state clearly what kind of motion they mean, or whether they   253b9–13

777. mean all kinds, it is no hard matter to reply to them. Thus we may point out that there cannot be a continuous process either of increase or of decrease: that which comes between the two has to be included. The theory resembles that about the stone being worn away by the drop of water or split by plants growing out of it: if so much has been extruded or removed by the drop, it does not follow that half the amount has previously been extruded or removed in half the time; the case of the hauled ship is exactly comparable: here we have so many drops setting so much in motion, but a part of them will not set as much in motion in any period of time. The amount removed is, it is true, divisible into a number of parts, but no one of these was set in motion separately: they were all set in motion together. It is evident, then, that from the fact that the decrease is divisible into an infinite number of parts it does not follow that some part must always be passing away: it all passes away at a particular moment.   253b13–23

778. Similarly, too, in the case of any alteration whatever, if that which suffers alteration is infinitely divisible it does not follow from this that the same is true of the alteration itself, which often occurs all at once, as in freezing.   253b23–26

779. *Again, when any one has fallen ill, there must follow a period of time in which his restoration to health is in the future: the process of change cannot take place in an instant; yet the change cannot be a change to anything else but health. The assertion, therefore, that alteration is continuous is an extravagant calling into question of the obvious; for alteration is a change from one contrary to another.*   **253b26–30**

780. *Moreover, we notice that a stone becomes neither harder nor softer.*   **253b30–31**

781. *Again, in the matter of locomotion, it would be a strange thing if a stone could be falling or resting on the ground without our being able to perceive the fact.*   **253b31–33**

782. *Further, it is a law of nature that earth and all other bodies should remain in their proper places and be moved from them only by violence; from the fact then that some of them are in their proper places it follows that in respect of place also all things cannot be in motion. These and other similar arguments, then, should convince us that it is impossible either that all things are always in motion or that all things are always at rest.*   **253b33–254a3**

COMMENTARY OF ST. THOMAS

1004. The Philosopher has shown in Book VII that movers and mobile objects do not proceed to infinity. Rather there is some first. And he has just shown that motion always was and always will be. Here he proceeds further to investigate the condition of the first motion and the first mover.

This discussion is divided into two parts. First he shows that the first motion is eternal and that the first mover is totally immobile. Secondly, where he says, **"This matter will be ..."** [851], he proceeds from this to explain the nature of the first motion and the first mover.

The first part is divided into three parts. First he sets forth for this problem a fivefold division. Secondly, where he says, **"To maintain that ..."** [774], he dismisses three parts of this division. Thirdly, where he says, **"We have now to take ..."** [785], he asks which of the two remaining alternatives is truer. For the truth which he intends to seek depends on this.

1005. He says, therefore, first that the beginning of the following discussion, in which we intend to investigate the first motion and the first mover, pertains to the above difficulty (which

he introduced in answering the second argument); namely, does it happen that certain things are sometimes moved and sometimes at rest, and are not always moved or at rest, as a result of which motion in general is eternal.

He says that with respect to motion and rest things must be disposed in three ways.

One mode is that all things are always at rest and nothing is moved at any time; the second mode is that all things are always moved and nothing is at rest; the third mode is that some things are moved and some are at rest.

But the third mode is again divided into three modes.

The first of these is that some things are moved and some are at rest in such a way that those which are moved are always moved and those which are at rest are always at rest, and there is nothing which is sometimes moved and sometimes at rest.

The second mode is contrary to this, namely, all things are naturally moved and at rest, and there is nothing which is always moved or always at rest.

The third mode is a division of this second mode; namely, some things are always immobile and are never moved; others are always mobile and are never at rest; and others can be both moved and at rest so that they are sometimes moved and sometimes at rest.

This last alternative must be determined by us as the truth, because in this is found the answers to all of the objections. When we shall have shown this, we shall have reached the end which we intend in this work; namely, we will have arrived at the first eternal motion and the first immobile mover.

Thus the third member of the first division is divided into three parts, and there results a total of five members of this division.

It must be noted, moreover, that in three parts of this division all beings are held to be of one disposition, as is clear in the first part, in which it was said that all things are always at rest; and in the second, in which it was said that all things are always moved; and in the fourth, in which it was said that all things are sometimes at rest and sometimes moved. In the third part beings are divided into two dispositions; namely, certain things are always moved and certain things are always at rest. In the fifth part beings are divided into three dispositions; namely, certain things are always moved, certain things are never moved, and certain things are sometimes moved and sometimes not. It must be noted that in this last part he does not mention rest, but immobility. For the first mover, which is never moved, cannot properly be said to be at rest. For, as was said in Book V, that is properly at rest which is moved naturally but is not being moved.

1006. Next where he says, "To maintain that . . ." [774], he dismisses three parts of the above division.

First he shows that not all things are

always at rest. Secondly, where he says, "The assertion that . . ." [775], he shows that not all things are always moved. Thirdly, where he says, "Nor again can it be . . ." [783], he rejects the third alternative in which it was said that things which are moved are always moved and things which are at rest are always at rest.

Concerning the first part he makes three points.

His first point is that it is due to a certain weakness of the intellect that some say that all things are at rest, reaching this conclusion through a sophistical argument which ignores the senses. This position arises because the intellect is not sufficient to answer sophistical arguments which contradict things which are manifest to the senses. Moreover, it is said in Topics, I, that one should not bother to argue against certain positions or problems in which one questions the need for sensation or suffering. Hence against this position it is not necessary to argue because of the folly of the speaker.

Secondly he says that this problem concerns not some particular being, but the whole of being. And it does not pertain only to natural philosophy, but in a way it pertains to all the demonstrative sciences and to all the arts which make use of opinions, as rhetoric and dialectic. For all the arts and sciences make use of motion. The practical arts, as it were, direct certain motions, and natural philosophy speculates about the nature of motion and mobile objects. Mathematicians make use of imagined motion, saying, for example, that a moved point makes a line. And the metaphysician deliberates about first principles. Therefore, it is clear that the denial of motion is repugnant to all the sciences.

However, an error which pertains

to all beings and to all sciences is not to be disproved by the natural philosopher, but by the metaphysician. Therefore, it is not in the province of the natural philosopher to argue against this error.

Thirdly, he says that it is not in the province of the mathematician to reject irrational and improper difficulties about the principles of mathematical doctrine. And the same is true for the other sciences. Similarly, it is not in the province of the natural philosopher to reject a position of this kind which is repugnant to his own principles. For in every science a definition of its subject is set forth as a principle. Hence in a natural science it is set forth as a principle that nature is a principle of motion. Therefore, for these three reasons it is clear that it is not in the province of natural philosophy to dispute this position.

1007. Next where he says, **"The assertion that . . ."** [775], he dismisses the second alternative in which it was stated by Heraclitus that everything is always moved.

First he compares this opinion to the preceding one which held that everything is always at rest. He says that to maintain that everything is always moved, as Heraclitus does, is also erroneous and contrary to the principles of natural science. But this position is less repugnant to art than the first position.

And it is clear that it is repugnant to this art. For it deprives natural science of the supposition that nature is a principle not only of motion but also of rest. And so it is clear that rest is just as natural as motion. Hence, just as the first opinion, which destroyed motion, was contrary to natural science, so also is this position, which destroys rest.

Moreover, he says that this opinion is less contrary to this art because rest is nothing other than a privation of motion. And the point that there is no privation of motion more readily escapes notice than the point that there is no motion. For there are some slight and feeble motions which are barely sensible. And so it may seem that something is at rest which is not at rest. But large and powerful motions cannot escape notice. Hence it cannot be said that the senses are deceived in perceiving motion as they are in perceiving rest.

Therefore, secondly, where he says, **". . . moreover the view is actually held . . ."** [776], he explains how some have held this second position.

He says that some, namely Heraclitus and his followers, have maintained that whatever exists is always moved, and not just some things, or at some time. But this motion is hidden from our senses. If they were asserting this of some motions they would be correct, for some motions are hidden from us. But since they do not designate the type of motion about which they speak, but rather they speak of all motions, it is not difficult to argue against them. For there are many motions which clearly cannot be eternal.

1008. Thirdly, where he says, **". . . thus we may point out . . ."** [777], he gives arguments against the above opinion. He does this first with respect to the motion of increase; secondly, with respect to the motion of alteration, where he says, **"Similarly, too, in the case . . ."** [778], and thirdly, with respect to local motion, where he says, **"Again, in the matter of locomotion . . ."** [781].

He begins with increase because Heraclitus was especially drawn to his position from a consideration of increase. For he saw that one is increased by a small quantity in one year, and supposing that increase is continuous, he believed that in every part of that time one is increased by some of that quantity. However, this increase is not sensed because it occurs in a small part of time. And he thought that the same is true of other things which seem to be at rest.

Aristotle argues against this by saying that it is not possible for a thing to be increased or decreased continuously such that the increased quantity is so divided with reference to time that at every moment some part of it is being increased. Rather after the increase of one part there is an intermediate time in which nothing is increased and in which there occurs a disposition for the increase of the next part.

He clarifies this with examples. First, we see that many raindrops erode a stone. Secondly, we see that plants growing in stones divide the stones.

If many raindrops wear off or carry away so much of a stone in so much time, we cannot say that earlier in half the time half of the raindrops carried off half of this quantity. For what happens here is the same as that which occurs in dragging a boat. For if a hundred men drag a boat over so much space in so much time, it does not follow that half of them will move the boat through half of the space in the same time, or through the same space in twice the time, as was said in Book VII. Likewise, if many raindrops erode a stone, it does not follow that some part of these raindrops earlier removed half as much in some time.

The reason for this is that that which is removed from the stone by the many raindrops is divisible into many parts. Nevertheless, none of these many parts is removed from the stone separately. Rather all the parts are removed together insofar as they are in potency in the removed whole.

He speaks here about the first part which is removed. The fact that a large quantity was removed from the stone by the raindrops over a long period of time does not prevent some part from being removed earlier by part of the raindrops. Nevertheless one must arrive at some removed quantity which is removed as a whole and not part after part. In the removal of that whole, therefore, none of the preceding raindrops removed anything. Rather they disposed a certain amount for removal. The last raindrop acts in virtue of all when it removes that which the others disposed for removal.

The same is true of decrease. If a thing decreases a certain amount in a certain time, it is not necessary to say that in every part of that time some of that quantity is subtracted, even though that quantity be divided to infinity. Rather at some time a whole will go away at once. And the same is true of increase. Hence it is not necessary that a thing be increased or decreased continuously.

1009. Next where he says, "Similarly, too, in the case . . ." [778], he opposes the above position with respect to alteration. He gives three arguments.

First he says that what was asserted about increase must also be said of any alteration. For although a body which is altered is infinitely divisible, nevertheless because of this it is not necessary that the alteration be divided to infinity such that in every part of time some of the alteration occurs. Frequently alteration occurs swiftly such that many parts of the altered body are altered together, as occurs in the jelling or congealing of water. For some whole of the water is congealed at one time, and not part after part. (If, however, a large amount of water is given, nothing prevents it from congealing part after part.)

It should be noted that what is said here about alteration and increase seems to be contrary to what was said in Book VI, where it was shown that motion is divided according to the division of time and of the mobile object and of the thing with respect to which there is motion.

But it must be understood that in Book VI Aristotle was treating motion in general, and was not applying his remarks to any mobile objects. Therefore, what he treated there about motion concerns the requirements for the continuity of motion. Here, however, he is speaking of the application of motion to determinate mobile objects in which it happens that a motion, which could be continuous according to the common nature [ratio] of motion, is interrupted and is not continuous.

1010. He gives the second argument where he says, "**Again, when anyone has fallen ill . . .**" [779].

He says that if someone who is ill is to be cured, he must be cured in some time and not in an instant. And it is further necessary that the mutation of being cured tend toward a definite terminus, namely, to health and to nothing else. Therefore, every alteration requires a determined time and a determined terminus (because every alteration is to a contrary, as was said in Book V). But no mutation of this kind is always continuous. Hence, to say that something is altered always and continuously is to doubt the obvious.

1011. He gives the third argument where he says, "**Moreover, we notice . . .**" [780]. He says that even over a long period of time a stone does not become harder or softer. Hence it is foolish to say that all things are always altered.

1012. Next where he says, "**Again, in the matter of locomotion . . .**" [781], he opposes in two ways the above opinion in respect to local motion. First he states that some local motions and states of rest are so obvious that they cannot go unnoticed. It would be strange indeed if a stone which is thrown downward or which rests on the ground would go unnoticed. Hence it cannot be said that all things are always moved locally because local motion is unnoticed.

1013. Secondly, where he says, "**Further, it is a law . . .**" [782], he reasons as follows. Earth and every other natural body are at rest from the necessity of nature when they are in their proper places, and they are removed from their proper places only by force. But it is clear that some natural bodies are in their proper places. It must be said, therefore, that some things are at rest with respect to place, and not all things are moved locally.

Finally he concludes that from the foregoing and other similar arguments one can come to know that it is impossible either for all things to be always moved, as Heraclitus maintained, or for all things to be always at rest, as Zeno and Parmenides and Melissus asserted.

LECTURE 6 [254a3–b6]
It Cannot Be Said That Some Things Are Always at Rest and All Other Things Are Always Moved

The Text of Aristotle

783. Nor again can it be that some things are always at rest, others always in motion, and nothing sometimes at rest and sometimes in motion. This theory must be pronounced impossible on the same grounds as those previously mentioned: viz. that ,we see the above-mentioned changes occurring in the case of the same things.

254a3–7

784. We may further point out that the defender of this position is fighting against the obvious, for on this theory there can be no such thing as increase: nor can there be any such thing as compulsory motion, if it is impossible that a thing can be at rest before being set in motion unnaturally. This theory, then, does away with becoming and perishing. Moreover, motion, it would seem, is generally thought to be a sort of becoming and perishing; for that to which a thing changes comes to be, or occupancy of it comes to be; and that from which a thing changes ceases to be, or there ceases to be occupancy of it. It is clear, therefore, that there are cases of occasional motion and occasional rest.

254a8–15

785. We have now to take the assertion that all things are sometimes at rest and sometimes in motion and to confront it with the arguments previously advanced.

254a15–16

786. We must take our start as before from the possibilities that we distinguished just above. Either all things are at rest, or all things are in motion, or some things are at rest and others in motion. And if some things are at rest and others in motion, then it must be that either all things are sometimes at rest and sometimes in motion, or some things are always at rest and the remainder always in motion, or some of the things are always at rest and others always in motion while others again are sometimes at rest and sometimes in motion.

254a16–22

787. Now we have said before that it is impossible that all things should be at rest: nevertheless we may now repeat that assertion. We may point out that, even if it is really the case, as certain persons assert, that the existent is infinite and motionless, it certainly does not appear to be so if we follow sense-perception: many things that exist appear to be in motion. Now if there is such a thing as false opinion at all, there is also motion; and similarly if there is such a thing as imagination, or if it is the case that anything seems to be different at different times; for imagination and opinion are thought to be motions of a kind. But to investigate this question at all—to see a reasoned justification of a belief with regard to which we are too well off to require reasoned justification—implies bad judgment of what is better and what is worse, what commends itself to belief and what does not, what is ultimate and what is not.

254a23–33

788. It is likewise impossible that all things should be in motion or that some things should be always in motion and the remainder always at rest. We have sufficient ground for rejecting all these theories in the single fact that we see some things that are sometimes in motion and sometimes at rest. It is evident, therefore, that it is no less impossible that some things should be always in motion and the remainder always at rest than that all things should be at rest or that all things should be in motion continuously.

254a33–254b4

789. It remains, then, to consider whether all things are so constituted as to be capable both of being in motion and of being at rest, or whether, while some things are so constituted, some are always at rest and some are always in motion; for it is this last view that we have to show to be true.

254b4–6

COMMENTARY OF ST. THOMAS

1014. After rejecting two parts of the above [cf. n.1005] division, he here rejects the third part, namely, that it would be possible to say that beings are divided into only two dispositions such that some things are always at rest and others are always moved, and that there is no third genus of beings which sometimes are moved and sometimes are at rest.

He rejects this in two ways.

First he rejects this, just as he did the two previous positions, because it is repugnant to the senses. For not only do we see by the senses that certain things are moved (by which he destroyed the first position that everything is always at rest), and that certain things are at rest (by which he destroyed the second position that everything is always moved), but we also see that mutations or variations from motion to rest and from rest to motion occur in the same things. From this it is clear that there are some things which are sometimes moved and sometimes at rest.

1015. Secondly, where he says, **"We may further point out . . ."** [784], he disproves the same thing by showing that those who introduce this difficulty are opposing things which are clear in nature.

First he discusses the motion of increase. We see the motion of increase in things which were not always increased. Otherwise, if they were always increased, the increase would not be to a determined quantity, but to infinity.

Secondly, he discusses violent local motion. Motion is not violent unless a thing which previously was at rest according to its nature is moved contrary to its nature. For motion is not violent

unless there is a recession from natural rest. If, then, nothing which is at rest can be moved, it follows that that which is naturally at rest cannot be moved later by violence.

Thirdly, generation and corruption are destroyed by this position. For generation is a mutation from non-being to being, while corruption is from being to non-being. In order for a thing to be corrupted, it must previously have been a being for some time. And in order for a thing to be generated, it must previously have been non-being for some time. However, that which is being or non-being for some time is at rest (we are speaking of rest in the broad sense). If, then, nothing at rest can be moved, it follows that nothing which is not for some time can be generated, and nothing which is for some time can be corrupted.

Fourthly, this position universally destroys every motion. For in every motion there is generation and corruption, either simply or in a qualified sense. For that which is moved to something as to a terminus is generated "this" in respect to the motions of alteration and increase, or it is generated "in this" in respect to local motion. For example, that which is moved from black to white, or from small to large, becomes white or large, and that which is moved to some place comes to exist in that place. But when a thing is changed from something as from a terminus from which, either a "this" is corrupted, as in the motion of alteration and increase, for example, black or small, or else a "from here" is corrupted, as in local motion. Since, then, in every motion there is generation and corruption, then when the above position denies generation and corruption, it consequently denies all motion.

Therefore, since the things which have been said are impossible, it becomes clear that some things are moved, not always, but sometimes, and some things are at rest, not always, but sometimes.

1016. Next where he says, **"We have now to take ..."** [785], he investigates the other two alternatives of the above division.

First he explains his intention. Secondly, he develops this intention, where he says, **"Now of things that cause motion ..."** [790].

Concerning the first part he makes three points. First he shows to what position the fourth alternative pertains. Secondly, where he says, **"We must take our start ..."** [786], he summarizes what was said in this chapter. Thirdly, where he says, **"It remains, then ..."** [789], he shows what remains to be said.

He says, therefore, first that to hold that all things are sometimes at rest and sometimes moved pertains to the ancient arguments which we discussed when we treated the eternity of motion. Especially Empedocles seems to have held that all things are at one time moved under the rule of friendship and strife and in the other intermediate times they are at rest.

1017. Next where he says, **"We must take our start . . ."** [786], he summarizes what was said in this chapter.

First he summarizes the division given above. Secondly, where he says, "Now we have said ..." [787], he summarizes the refutation of the first part in which it was held that all things are always at rest. Thirdly, where he says, "It is likewise impossible . . ." [788],

he summarizes the refutation of the other two alternatives.

He says, therefore, first that in order for his intention to be made more clear in the following, we ought to start with those things which we have just determined, and take the same beginning as before; namely, beings must first of all exist in one of these three dispositions: either all things are at rest, or all are moved, or some are at rest and some are moved.

And this third alternative is again divided into three. For if some of the things which exist are at rest and some are moved, then it must be that either all things are such that they are sometimes at rest and sometimes moved, or certain things are always at rest and certain things always moved, or else a third alternative is added to these two; namely, there are some things which are sometimes at rest, but not always, and other things which are sometimes moved, but not always.

1018. Next where he says, **"Now we have said . . ."** [787], he disproves the first alternative.

He says that it was asserted above that it is not possible for all things to be always at rest. But something must here be added to this. He says two things against this position.

First he says that it is necessary to posit some motion at least in the soul. For someone might wish to say that it is true that nothing is moved. This is what the followers of held, saying that being is infinite and immobile. But this does not seem to be so according to the senses. Rather many beings are moved, as the senses judge.

If, therefore, someone were to say that the opinion which holds that something is moved is false, it follows that motion exists. For if there is false opinion, there is motion. And universally if opinion exists, motion exists. Similarly, if fantasy exists, motion exists.

This is so because a fantasy is a motion of the sensitive part which is made by a sense in act. And opinion is a motion of reason which proceeds from reasoning. And it still more clearly follows that there is motion in opinion or fantasy, if at one time something seems to us to be so and at another time not. This happens when things seem to us to be sometimes at rest and sometimes not. Therefore, it absolutely follows that motion exists.

Secondly, against this opinion he says that to attempt to destroy this opinion and to seek an argument to prove those things which we ought to hold in greater dignity than to say that they need proof (for they are per se obvious) is to judge poorly in distinguishing between better and worse in morals, between the credible and the incredible in logic, and between principles and non-principles in demonstrations.

For he who searches for an argument to prove things which are per se obvious, and thus are principles, does not know that they are principles while he intends to prove them through other principles. Similarly, it seems that he does not know how to recognize what is credible and incredible. For what is credible per se he intends to prove through another as if it were not credible per se. Nor does he seem capable of distinguishing between better and worse, because the more obvious he proves through the less obvious. Now it is obvious per se that some things are moved. Therefore, we should not try to prove this with arguments.

1019. Next where he says, **"It is likewise impossible . . ."** [788], he rejects the two other alternatives of the foregoing division.

He says that just as it is impossible for all things to be always at rest, so too it is impossible for all things to be always moved, or for some things to be always moved and others to be always at rest so that there is nothing which is sometimes moved and sometimes at rest. Against all of these it is sufficient to ground our belief on one thing; namely, we see that certain things are sometimes moved and sometimes at rest. From this it is clear that it is impossible to say that all things are continually at rest, which was the first alternative, or that all things are continually moved, which was the second alternative, or that certain things are always moved and others are always at rest, and there is no intermediary.

1020. Next where he says, **"It remains, then . . ."** [789], he shows what remains to be said. He concludes from the foregoing that since three alternatives of the above division cannot stand, it remains to be considered which of the other two is truer, whether, namely, all things can be moved and be at rest, or whether certain things can be moved and be at rest while there are some things which are always at rest and some which are always moved. This last is what we intend to demonstrate. For thus it will be shown that the first motion is eternal and the first mover is immobile.

Whatever Is Moved Is Moved by Another

The Text of Aristotle
Chapter 4

790. *Now of things that cause motion or suffer motion, to some the motion is accidental, to others essential: thus it is accidental to what merely belongs to or contains as a part a thing that causes motion or suffers motion, essential to a thing that causes motion or suffers motion not merely by belonging to such a thing or containing it as a part.*

Of things to which the motion is essential, some derive their motion from themselves, others from something else: and in some cases their motion is natural, in others violent and unnatural.

254b7–14

791. *Thus in things that derive their motion from themselves, e.g., all animals, the motion is natural (for when an animal is in motion its motion is derived from itself): and whenever the source of the motion of a thing is in the thing itself we say that the motion of that thing is natural. Therefore the animal as a whole moves itself naturally; but the body of the animal may be in motion unnaturally as well as naturally: it depends upon the kind of motion that it may chance to be suffering and the kind of element of which it is composed. And the motion of things that derive their motion from something else is in some cases natural, in others unnatural: e.g., upward motion of earthy things and downward motion of fire are unnatural. Moreover the parts of animals are often in motion in an unnatural way, their positions and the character of the motion being abnormal.* **254b14–24**

792. *The fact that a thing that is in motion derives its motion from something is most evident in things that are in motion unnaturally, because in such cases it is clear that the motion is derived from something other than the thing itself. Next to things that are in motion unnaturally those whose motion while natural is derived from themselves—e.g. animals—make this fact clear; for here the uncertainty is not as to whether the motion is derived from something but as to how we ought to distinguish in the thing between the mover and the moved. It would seem that in animals, just as in ships and things not naturally organized, that which causes motion is separate from that which suffers motion, and that it is only in this sense that the animal as a whole causes its own motion.* **254b24–33**

793. *The greatest difficulty, however, is presented by the remaining case of those that we last distinguished. Where things derive their motion from something else, we distinguished the cases in which the motion is unnatural: we are left with those that are to be contrasted with the others by reason of the fact that the motion is natural. It is in these cases that difficulty would be experienced in deciding whence the motion is derived, e.g., in the case of light and heavy things. When these things are in motion to positions the reverse of those they would properly occupy, their motion is violent: when they are in motion to their proper positions—the light thing up and the heavy thing down—their motion is natural; but in this latter case it is no longer evident, as it is when the motion is unnatural, whence their motion is derived.* **254b33–255a5**

794. *It is impossible to say that their motion is derived from themselves: this is a characteristic of life and peculiar to living things.* **255a5–7**

795. *Further, if it were, it would have been in their power to stop themselves (I mean that if e.g. a thing can cause itself to walk it can also cause itself not to walk),* **255a7–9**

796. *and so, since on this supposition fire itself possesses the power of upward locomotion, it is clear that it should also possess the power of downward locomotion. Moreover if things move themselves, it would be unreasonable to suppose that in only one kind of motion is their motion derived from themselves.* **255a9–13**

797. *Again, how can anything of continuous and naturally connected substance move itself? In so far as a thing is one and continuous not merely in virtue of contact, it is impassive: it is only in so far as a thing is divided that one part of it is by nature active and another passive. Therefore none of the things that we are now considering move themselves (for they are of naturally connected substance), nor does anything else that is continuous: in each case the mover must be separate from the moved, as we see to be the case with inanimate things when an animate thing moves them. It is the fact that these things also always derive their motion from something: what it is would become evident if we were to distinguish the different kinds of cause.* 255a13–18

COMMENTARY OF ST. THOMAS

1021. After the Philosopher has explained his intention, he here begins to develop it; namely, not everything is sometimes moved and sometimes at rest. Rather there is something which is absolutely immobile, and something which is always moved.

This discussion is divided into two parts. First he shows that the first mover is immobile. Secondly, where he says, **"And further, if there is . . ."** [849], he shows that the first mobile object is always moved.

The first part is divided into two parts. First he shows from the order of movers and mobile objects that the first mover is immobile. Secondly, where he says, **". . . but also by considering . . ."** [844], he proves the same thing from the eternity of motion.

The first part is divided into two parts. First he shows that the first mover is immobile. Secondly, where he says, **"Since there must always . . ."** [837], he shows that the first mover is eternal.

Concerning the first part he makes two points. First he explains something that is necessary for the proof of what follows; namely, whatever is moved is moved by another. Secondly, where he says, **"Now this may come about . . ."** [806], he proves his position.

He has shown above at the beginning of Book VII that whatever is moved is moved by another with a common argument taken from motion itself. But since he has begun to apply motion to mobile things, he shows that that which was proven universally above is universally verified in all movers and mobile objects.

Hence the first part is divided into two parts. First he gives a division of movers and mobile objects. Secondly, where he says, **"The fact that a thing . . ."** [792], he explains the proposition in individual cases.

Concerning the first part he makes two points. First he divides movers and mobile objects. Secondly, where he says, **"Thus in things that . . ."** [791], he explains this division.

1022. First, therefore, he gives three divisions of movers and mobile objects.

The first of these is that some movers and mobile objects move or are moved per accidens, and some per se. Here he uses "per accidens" in the broad sense, according to which it includes even that which is "according to a part." Hence, to explain the meaning of "per accidens," he adds that a thing can be said to move or be moved per accidens in two ways. First, those things are said to move per accidens which are said to move because they are in certain movers. For example, it is said that music cures, because he who cures is musical. Similarly, those things are said to be moved per accidens which are in things which are moved, either as located in a place, as when we say that a man is moved because he is in a ship which is moved, or else as an accident in a subject, as when we say that white is moved because a body is moved. Things are said to move or be moved per accidens in another way insofar as they move or are moved according to a part. For example, a man is said to strike or be struck because his hand strikes or is struck. Those things are said to be moved or to move per se which are free of the two preceding modes. For they are not said to move or be moved because they are in other things which move or are moved, nor because some part of them moves or is moved.

Omitting things which move or are moved per accidens, he subdivides those which are moved per se. First, of those things which are moved per se some are moved by themselves, such as animals, and others are moved by others, such as inanimate things.

He gives a third division; namely, some things are moved according to nature, and others are moved outside of nature.

1023. Next where he says, **"Thus in things that . . ."** [791], he explains how motion according to nature and motion outside of nature is found in things which are moved by themselves and in things which are moved by another.

He says first that things which are moved by themselves (as are animals, which move themselves) are moved according to nature. He proves this from the fact that they are moved by an intrinsic principle. We say that those things whose principle of motion is in themselves are moved by nature. Hence it is clear that the motion of an animal by which it moves itself, if com-

pared to the whole animal, is natural, because it is from the soul, which is the nature and form of the animal. But if it is compared to the body, it happens that motion of this kind is both natural and outside of nature. For this must be considered according to the diversity of motions and of elements from which the animal is constituted. If an animal is composed of predominantly heavy elements, as is the human body, and if it is moved upward, then this motion will be violent in respect to the body. But if it is moved downward, this motion will be natural to the body. If, however, there are some animal bodies which are composed of air, as some Platonists held, then the contrary must be said of them.

Secondly, he explains how violent and natural motion are found in things which are moved by another.

He says that some of these are moved according to nature; for example, fire is moved upward and earth downward. But some are moved outside of nature; for example, earth upward and fire downward. This latter is violent motion.

Thirdly, he gives another mode of unnatural motion in animals according to which the parts of animals are often moved outside of nature if one considers the natures [ratio] and modes of natural motion in the parts of animals. For example, a man bends his arms forward and his legs backward; but dogs and horses and such animals bend their front feet to the rear and their rear feet to the front. But if a contrary motion occurs in animals, the motion will be violent and outside of nature.

1024. Next where he says, **"The fact that a thing . . ."** [792], he proves that whatever is moved is moved by another.

He shows this first in cases in which it is obvious. Secondly, where he says, **"The greatest difficulty . . ."** [793], he shows this in cases in which it is open to question.

He omits, however, things which are moved per accidens, because such things are not themselves moved, but are said to be moved because some other things are moved. Among things which are moved per se, it is especially clear that things which are moved violently and outside of nature are moved by another.

For it is clear from the very definition of violence that things which are moved by violence are moved by another. For as is said in Ethics, III, the violent is that whose principle is outside, the patient contributing none of the force.

After he has shown that things which are moved by violence are moved by another, he shows that things which are naturally moved by themselves, as animals are said to move themselves, are also moved by another. For in these cases it is clear that something is moved by another. But there can be a difficulty of how one should designate the mover and the moved in these cases. At first sight it seems (and many think this) that that which moves and that which is moved are distinct in animals, just as they are in ships and in other artificial things which do not exist according to nature. For it seems that the soul which moves is related to the body which is moved as a sailor is related to a ship, as is said in De Anima, II. Thus it seems that a whole animal moves itself insofar as one part of it moves another. Whether the soul is related to the body as a sailor to a ship he leaves for investigation in De Anima. He will explain later how a thing is said to move itself inso-far as one part of it moves and another part is moved.

1025. Next where he says, **"The greatest difficulty . . ."** [793], he explains his position in cases in which there is greater difficulty.

Concerning this he makes three points. First in regard to cases in which there is greater difficulty he states that whatever is moved is moved by another. He is referring to heavy and light things when they are moved according to nature. Secondly, where he says, **"It is impossible . . ."** [794] he shows that such things do not move themselves. Thirdly, where he says, **"It is the fact that . . ."** [798], he explains how they are moved.

He says, therefore, first that it is rather clear that the proposition "whatever is moved is moved by another" applies to things which are moved by violence and to things which move themselves. The main difficulty arises in the remaining alternative of the last division, namely, in things which do not move themselves, but are nevertheless moved naturally.

He says the "last" division; namely, of things which are not moved by themselves but by another, some are moved outside of nature and some on the contrary are moved according to nature. In the latter cases the difficulty is: by what are they moved? For example, heavy and light things are moved to their contrary places by violence and to their proper places by nature, that is, the light is moved upward and the heavy downward. But what moves them is not clear when they are moved by nature as it is when they are moved outside of nature.

1026. Next where he says, **"It is impossible . . ."** [794], he proves with four arguments that such things do not move themselves.

The first of these is that to move one-self pertains to the nature [ratio] of life and is proper to living things. For by motion and sensation we distinguish the animate from the inanimate, as is said in De Anima, I. Now it is clear that these things are not living or animated. Therefore they do not move themselves.

1027. He gives the second argument where he says, **"Further, if it were . . ."** [795]. The argument is as follows.

Things which move themselves can also be the cause of their own rest. For example, we see that by their appetites animals are moved and stopped. Therefore, if heavy and light things move themselves by natural motion, they would be able to stop themselves, just as if a man is the cause of his own walking, he is also the cause of his non-walking. But we see that this is false, because such things are not at rest outside of their proper places unless some extrinsic cause prevents their motion. Therefore they do not move themselves.

But someone might say that even though such things are not the cause of their own rest outside of their proper places, nevertheless, they are the cause of their own rest in their proper places. Hence he adds a third argument where he says, **". . . and so, since on this supposition . . ."** [796]. The argument is as follows.

It is irrational to say that things which move themselves are moved by themselves with respect to only one motion and not a plurality of motions. For that which moves itself does not have its motion determined by another, but determines its own motion. Sometimes it determines for itself this motion, and sometimes another. Hence, that which moves itself has the power to determine for itself either this

or that motion. Therefore, if heavy and light things move themselves, it follows that if fire has the power to be moved upward, it also has the power to be moved downward. But we never see this happen except through an extrinsic cause. Therefore they do not move themselves.

It should be noted, however, that these two arguments are probable with respect to those things which are apparent in things which move themselves among us. Such things are found to be moved sometimes by this motion, sometimes by another motion, and are sometimes at rest. And so he did not say "impossible" but "irrational," which is his custom when speaking of probables. For he will show below that if there is some self-motion in which the mover is altogether immobile, then it is moved always and by one motion. But this cannot be said of heavy and light things in which there is not something which is not moved per se or per accidens, since they are generated and corrupted.

1028. He gives the fourth argument where he says, **"Again, how can anything . . ."** [797]. The argument is as follows.

No continuous thing moves itself. But heavy and light things are continuous. Therefore, none of these moves itself.

He proves as follows that no continuous thing moves itself. The mover is related to the moved as agent to patient. When, however, the agent is contrary to the patient, a distinction is necessary between that which naturally acts and that which is naturally acted upon. Therefore, insofar as some things are not in contact with each other, but are altogether one and continuous both in quantity and form, they cannot be acted upon by each other. Therefore, it follows that no continuous thing moves itself. Rather the mover is separated from that which is moved, as is clear when inanimate things are moved by animate things, as a stone by a hand. Hence in animals which move themselves there is a certain collection of parts rather than a perfect continuity. For one part can be moved by another, but this is not found in heavy and light things.

LECTURE 8 [255a19–256a2]
He Explains How Heavy and Light Things Are Moved

The Text of Aristotle

798. *The above-mentioned distinctions can also be made in the case of things that cause motion: some of them are capable of causing motion unnaturally (e.g., the lever is not naturally capable of moving the weight), others naturally (e.g., what is actually hot is naturally capable of moving what is potentially hot); and similarly in the case of all other things of this kind. In the same way, too, what is potentially of a certain quality or of a certain quantity or in a certain place is naturally movable when it contains the corresponding principle in itself and not accidentally (for the same thing may be both of a certain quality and of a certain quantity, but the one is an accidental, not an essential property of the other). So when fire or earth is moved by something the motion is violent when it is unnatural, and natural when it brings to actuality the proper activities that they potentially possess.*   **255a18–30**

799. *But the fact that the term "potentially" is used in more than one sense is the reason why it is not evident whence such motions as the upward motion of fire and the downward motion of earth are derived.*   **255a30–33**

800. *One who is learning a science potentially knows it in a different sense from one who while already possessing the knowledge is not actually exercising it. Wherever we have something capable of acting and something capable of being correspondingly acted on, in the event of any such pair being in contact what is potential becomes at times actual: e.g., the learner becomes from one potential something another potential something: for one who possesses knowledge of a science but is not actually exercising it knows the science potentially in a sense, though not in the same sense as he knew it potentially before he learnt it. And when he is in this condition, if something does not prevent him, he actively exercises his knowledge: otherwise he would be in the contradictory state of not knowing.*   **255a33–255b5**

801. *In regard to natural bodies also the case is similar. Thus what is cold is potentially hot: then a change takes place and it is fire, and it burns, unless something prevents and hinders it.*   **255b5–7**

802. *So, too, with heavy and light: light is generated from heavy, e.g., air from water (for water is the first thing that is potentially light), and air is actually light, and will at once realize its proper activity as such unless something prevents it. The activity of lightness consists in the light thing being in a certain situation, namely high up: when it is in the contrary situation, it is being prevented from rising. The case is similar also in regard to quantity and quality.*   **255b8–13**

803. *But, be it noted, this is the question we are trying to answer—how can we account for the motion of light things and heavy things to their proper situations? The reason for it is that they have a natural tendency respectively towards a certain position; and this constitutes the essence of lightness and heaviness, the former being determined by an upward, the latter by a downward, tendency.*   **255b13–17**

804. *As we have said, a thing may be potentially light or heavy in more senses than one. Thus not only when a thing is water is it in a sense potentially light, but when it has become air it may be still potentially light; for it may be that through some hindrance it does not occupy an upper position, whereas, if what hinders it is removed, it realizes its activity and continues to rise higher. The process whereby what is of a certain quality changes to a condition of active existence is similar: thus the exercise of knowledge follows at once upon the possession of it unless something prevents it. So, too, what is of a certain quantity extends itself over a certain space unless something prevents it. The thing in a sense is and in a sense is not moved by one*

who moves what is obstructing and preventing its motion (e.g., one who pulls away a pillar from under a roof or one who removes a stone from a wine-skin in the water is the accidental cause of motion); and in the same way the real cause of the motion of a ball rebounding from a wall is not the wall but the thrower. So it is clear that in all these cases the thing does not move itself, but it contains within itself the source of motion—not of moving something or of causing motion, but of suffering it. 255b17–31

805. *If then the motion of all things that are in motion is either natural or unnatural and violent, and all things whose motion is violent and unnatural are moved by something, and something other than themselves, and again all things whose motion is natural are moved by something—both those that are moved by themselves and those that are not moved by themselves (e.g., light things and heavy things, which are moved either by that which brought the thing into existence as such and made it light and heavy, or by that which released what was hindering and preventing it); then all things that are in motion must be moved by something.* 255b31–256a3

COMMENTARY OF ST. THOMAS

1029. After he has shown that heavy and light things do not move themselves, he here explains how they are moved. First he explains how they are moved. Secondly, where he says, "If then the motion . . ." [805], he concludes to his main point.

Concerning the first part he makes two points. First he shows that they are moved naturally by something. Secondly, where he says, "But the fact that . . ." [799], he inquires into that by which they are moved.

He says, therefore, first [798] that, although heavy and light things do not move themselves, nevertheless they are moved by something. This may be made clear by distinguishing between moving causes. For just as things which are moved are moved either according to nature or outside of nature, so also in things which move some move outside of nature, for example, a staff does not naturally move a heavy body like a stone, and some move according to nature, for example, that which is actually hot moves that which according to its nature is potentially hot. And the same is true of other such things. And just as that which is in act naturally moves, so that which is in po-

tency is naturally moved, either with respect to quality, or quantity, or place.

He has said in Book II that those things are moved naturally whose principle of motion is in them per se and not per accidens. From this it may seem that when that which is only potentially hot becomes hot, it is not moved naturally, since it is moved by an active principle existing exterior to it. As if to refute this objection, he adds, ". . . when it contains the corresponding principle in itself and not accidentally . . ." . This is as if he were to say that for motion to be natural, it is sufficient if "the corresponding principle," that is, potency, which he mentioned, be in that which is moved, per se and not per accidens. For example, a bench is potentially combustible, not insofar as it is a bench, but insofar as it is wood.

Explaining what he means when he says, ". . . and not accidentally . . ." , he adds that the same subject may be both quantified and qualified, but one of these is related to the other per accidens and not per se. Therefore, that which is potentially a quality is also potentially a quantity, but per accidens.

Since, therefore, that which is in potency is moved naturally by another which is in act, nothing can be in potency and act with respect to the same thing. It follows that neither fire nor earth nor anything else is moved by itself, but by another. Fire and earth are indeed moved by another, but through violence, when their motion is outside of their natural potency. But they are moved naturally when they are moved to their proper acts to which they are in potency according to their nature.

1030. Next where he says, "But the fact that . . ." [799], he explains that by which they are moved. And since that which is in potency is moved by that which is in act, he first distinguishes potency. Secondly, where he says, "As we have said . . ." [904], he explains that by which such things are moved.

Concerning the first part he makes three points. First he shows that it is necessary to know in how many ways a thing is said to be in potency. Secondly, where he says, "One who is learning . . ." [800], he explains these distinctions. Thirdly, where he says, "But, be it noted . . ." [255b14], he answers a certain question.

He says, therefore, first that since being in potency is predicated in many ways, it is not clear what moves heavy and light things in natural motions, for example, fire upward and earth downward.

1031. Next where he says, "One who is learning . . ." [800], he distinguishes being in potency, first in the intellect, secondly in quality, where he says, "In regard to natural bodies . . ." [801], and thirdly in local motion, where he says, "So, too, with heavy . . ." [802].

He says, therefore, first that the potency for science in one who is learning and does not yet have the habit of science differs from the potency for science in one who already has the habit of science but is not using it.

A thing is reduced from first potency to second when something active is joined to its passivity. And then this passivity, through the presence of that which is active, comes to be in this kind of act, which up to this point was in potency. For example, the learner, through the act of the teacher, is reduced from potency to act, to which act is joined another potency. Thus, a thing existing in first potency comes to be in another potency. For one who has science but who is not contemplating it is in a certain way in potency to the act of science, but not in the same way as he was before he learned. Therefore he was reduced from first potency to act, to which is joined a second potency, through some agent, namely, a teacher.

But when one possesses the habit of science, it is not necessary for him to be reduced to second act by some agent. Rather he does this immediately by his own contemplation unless something else prevents him, for example, business, or sickness, or his will. But if he is not impeded so that he cannot contemplate, then he does not have the habit of science but its contrary, namely, ignorance.

1032. Next where he says, "In regard to natural bodies . . ." [801], he explains the same thing with respect to qualities.

He says that what was said above about the potency for science in the soul also applies to natural bodies. For when a body is actually cold, it is potentially hot, just as one who is in ignorance is in potency for knowing. But when it has been changed so that it has the form of fire, then it is fire in act, having the power of acting. And it operates immediately by burning, unless something prevents it by a contrary action or unless it is in some other way impeded, for example, by a withdrawal of the combustible object, just as it was said that after someone has become a knower by learning, he immediately contemplates, unless something prevents him.

1033. Next where he says, **"So, too, with heavy . . ."** [802], he explains the same thing with reference to the local motion of heavy and light things.

He says that a heavy thing becomes light in a way similar to that in which a cold thing becomes hot. For example, air, which is light, comes from water, which is heavy. The water, therefore, is first in potency to become light, and afterwards it becomes light in act, and then it immediately possesses its operation, unless something prevents it. But the now existing light thing is compared to place as potency to act (for the act of a light thing, as such, is to be in some determined place, namely, up). But it is prevented from being up because it is in the contrary place, namely, down. For it cannot be in two places at once. Hence that which holds the light thing down prevents it from being up. And what is said about local motion must also be said of motion in respect to quantity or quality.

1034. Next where he says, **"But, be it noted . . ."** [803], he answers a certain question about the foregoing.

Granted that the act of a light thing is to be up, nevertheless some ask why heavy and light things are moved in their proper places. The reason for this is that they have a natural aptitude for such places. For to be light is to have an aptitude for that which is up. And the nature [ratio] of the heavy is to have an aptitude for that which is down. Hence, to ask why a heavy thing is moved downward is nothing other than to ask why it is heavy. The same thing which makes it heavy also makes it to be moved downward.

1035. Next where he says, **"As we have said . . ."** [804], he shows from the foregoing what moves heavy and light things.

He says that since that which is in potency is moved by that which is in act, as was asserted, it must be realized that a thing is said to be potentially light or heavy in many ways.

In one way, while it is still water, it is in potency to become light. In another way, when air has already been made from water, it is still in potency to the act of the light, which is to be up, just as one who has the habit of science but is not contemplating it is still said to be in potency. For it happens that what is light may be prevented from being up.

But if that impediment is removed, it rises immediately so that it may be up. As was said with respect to quality, when a quality is in act, it strives immediately toward its own operation, just as he who is a knower immediately contemplates, unless something prevents him. And the same applies to the motion of quantity. For when an addition of quantity has been made to quantity, extension follows immediately in the body which can be increased, unless something prevents it.

Therefore, it is clear that that which removes that which prevents and restrains in a certain sense moves and in another sense does not. For example, if a column supports something heavy, and so prevents it from falling, he who destroys the column in a certain sense is said to move the weight supported by the column. Similarly, one who removes a stone which stops water from flowing out of a vessel in a certain sense is said to move the water. He is said to move per accidens, and not per se. For example, if a sphere, that is, a ball, rebounds from a wall, it is moved by the wall per accidens and not per se. It is moved per se by the initial thrower. For the wall did not give it any impetus toward motion, but the thrower did. It is per accidens because, when the ball was impeded by the wall, it did not receive a second impetus. Rather because of the same remaining impetus it rebounded with an opposite motion. And similarly, one who destroys a column does not give to the supported weight an impetus or inclination downward. For it has this from its first generator which gave to it the form which such an inclination follows. Therefore, the generator is the per se mover of heavy and light things. But that which removes an obstacle is a per accidens mover.

He concludes, therefore, that it is clear from what has been said that no heavy or light thing moves itself. Nevertheless the motion of these things is natural because they have a principle of motion within themselves; not, indeed, a motive or active principle, but a passive principle, which is the potency for such act.

From this it is clearly contrary to the Philosopher's intention to say that there is an active principle in matter, which some maintain is necessary for natural motion. This passive principle, which is the natural potency for act, is sufficient.

1036. Next where he says, **"If, then, the motion . . ."** [805], he arrives at the conclusion principally intended in this whole chapter.

He says that if it is true that everything that is moved is moved according to nature or outside of nature and by violence, then it is clear that all things which are moved by violence are moved not only by some mover but by some other extrinsic mover. And further of things which are moved according to nature, some are moved by themselves, in which it is clear that they are moved by something, not indeed, extrinsic, but intrinsic, and some are moved according to nature but not by themselves, as heavy and light things. These latter are also moved by something, as was shown (because either they are moved per se by the generator which makes them heavy and light, or they are moved per accidens by that which removes what impedes or prevents their natural motion). Therefore, it is clear that whatever is moved is moved by some mover, either intrinsic or extrinsic, which he calls "being moved by another."

It Is Impossible For a Thing To Be Moved by Another to Infinity. It Is Not Necessary That Every Mover Be Moved

The Text of Aristotle
Chapter 5

806. *Now this may come about in either of two ways. Either the mover is not itself responsible for the motion, which is to be referred to something else which moves the mover, or the mover is itself responsible for the motion. Further, in the latter case, either the mover immediately precedes the last thing in the series, or there may be one or more intermediate links: e.g., the stick moves the stone and is moved by the hand, which again is moved by the man: in the man; however, we have reached a mover that is not so in virtue of being moved by something else.*   256a4–8

807. *Now we say that the thing is moved both by the last and by the first mover in the series, but more strictly by the first, since the first mover moves the last, whereas the last does not move the first, and the first will move the thing without the last, but the last will not move it without the first: e.g., the stick will not move anything unless it is itself moved by the man.*   256a8–13

808. *If then everything that is in motion must be moved by something, and the mover must either itself be moved by something else or not, and in the former case there must be some first mover that is not itself moved by anything else, while in the case of the immediate mover being of this kind there is no need of an intermediate mover that is also moved (for it is impossible that there should be an infinite series of movers, each of which is itself moved by something else, since in an infinite series there is no first term)—if then everything that is in motion is moved by something, and the first mover is moved but not by anything else, it must be moved by itself.*   256a13–21

809. *This same argument may also be stated in another way as follows. Every mover moves something and moves it with something, either with itself or with something else: e.g., a man moves a thing either himself or with a stick, and a thing is knocked down either by the wind itself or by a stone propelled by the wind. But it is impossible for that with which a thing is moved to move it without being moved by that which imparts motion by its own agency; on the other hand, if a thing imparts motion by its own agency, it is not necessary that there should be anything else with which it imparts motion, whereas if there is a different thing with which it imparts motion, there must be something that imparts motion not with something else but with itself, or else there will be an infinite series. If, then, anything is a mover while being itself moved, the series must stop somewhere and not be infinite. Thus, if the stick moves something in virtue of being moved by the hand, the hand moves the stick; and if something else moves with the hand, the hand also is moved by something different from itself. So when motion by means of an instrument is at each stage caused by something different from the instrument, this must always be preceded by something else which imparts motion with itself. Therefore, if this last mover is in motion and there is nothing else that moves it, it must move itself. So this reasoning also shows that, when a thing is moved, if it is not moved immediately by something that moves itself, the series brings us at some time or other to a mover of this kind.*   256a21–256b3

810. *And if we consider the matter in yet a third way we shall get this same result as follows: If everything that is in motion is moved by something that is in motion, either this being in motion is an accidental attribute of the movers in question, so that each of them moves*

something while being itself in motion, but not always because it is itself in motion, or it is not an accidental but an essential attribute.   256b3–7

811. *Let us consider the former alternative. If, then, it is an accidental attribute, it is not necessary that that which causes motion should be in motion; and if this is so it is clear that there may be a time when nothing that exists is in motion, since the accidental is not necessary but contingent. Now if we assume the existence of a possibility, any conclusion that we thereby reach will not be an impossibility, though it may be contrary to fact. But the non-existence of motion is an impossibility; for we have shown above that there must always be motion.*

256b7–13

812. *Moreover, the conclusion to which we have been led is a reasonable one. For there must be three things—the moved, the mover, and the instrument of motion. Now the moved must be in motion, but it need not move anything else; the instrument of motion must both move something else and be itself in motion (for it changes together with the moved, with which it is in contact and continuous, as is clear in the case of things that move other things locally, in which case the two things must up to a certain point be in contact); and the mover—that is to say, that which causes motion in such a manner that it is not merely the instrument of motion—must be unmoved. Now we have visual experience of the last term in this series, namely that which has the capacity of being in motion, but does not contain a motive principle, and also of that which is in motion but is moved by itself and not by anything else: it is reasonable, therefore, not to say necessary, to suppose the existence of the third term also, that which causes motion but is itself unmoved.*   256b13–24

813. *So, too, Anaxagoras is right when he says that Mind is impassive and unmixed, since he makes it the principle of motion; for it could cause motion in this sense only by being itself unmoved, and have supreme control only by being unmixed.*   256b24–27

814. *We will now take the second alternative. If the mover is not accidentally but necessarily in motion—so that, if it were not in motion, it would not move anything—then the mover, in so far as it is in motion, must be in motion in one of two ways: it is moved either as that is which is moved with the same kind of motion, or with a different kind—*   256b27–31

815. *either that which is heating, I mean, is itself in process of becoming hot, that which is making healthy in process of becoming healthy, and that which is causing locomotion in process of locomotion, or else that which is making healthy is, let us say, in process of locomotion, and that which is causing locomotion in process of, say, increase.*   256b31–34

816. *But it is evident that this is impossible. For if we adopt the first assumption we have to make it apply within each of the very lowest species into which motion can be divided: e.g., we must say that if someone is teaching some lesson in geometry, he is also in process of being taught that same lesson in geometry, and that if he is throwing he is in process of being thrown in just the same manner. Or if we reject this assumption we must say that one kind of motion is derived from another; e.g., that that which is causing locomotion is in process of increase, that which is causing this increase is in process of being altered by something else, and that which is causing this alteration is in process of suffering some different kind of motion. But the series must stop somewhere, since the kinds of motion are limited; and if we say that the process is reversible, and that that which is causing alteration is in process of locomotion, we do no more than if we had said at the outset that that which is causing locomotion is in process of locomotion, and that one who is teaching is in process of being taught; for it is clear that everything that is moved is moved by the mover that is further back in the series as well as by that which immediately moves it: in fact the earlier mover is that which more strictly moves it. But this is of course impossible; for it involves the consequence that one who is teaching is in*

process of learning what he is teaching, whereas teaching necessarily implies possessing
knowledge, and learning not possessing it. **256b34–257a14**

817. *Still more unreasonable is the consequence involved that, since everything that is*
moved is moved by something that is itself moved by something else, everything that has a
capacity for causing motion has as such a corresponding capacity for being moved: i.e., it will
have a capacity for being moved in the sense in which one might say that everything that has a
capacity for making healthy, and exercises that capacity, has as such a capacity for being made
healthy, and that which has a capacity for building has as such a capacity for being built. It will
have the capacity for being thus moved either immediately or through one or more links (as it
will if, while everything that has a capacity for causing motion has as such a capacity for being
moved by something else, the motion that it has the capacity for suffering is not that with which
it affects what is next to it, but a motion of a different kind; e.g., that which has a capacity for
making healthy might as such have a capacity for learning: the series, however, could be traced
back, as we said before, until at some time or other we arrived at the same kind of motion). Now
the first alternative is impossible, and the second is fantastic: it is absurd that that which has a
capacity for causing alteration should as such necessarily have a capacity, let us say, for
increase. **257a14–27**

818. *It is not necessary, therefore, that that which is moved should always be moved by*
something else that is itself moved by something else: so there will be an end to the series.
Consequently the first thing that is in motion will derive its motion either from something that
is at rest or from itself. But if there were any need to consider which of the two, that which
moves itself or that which is moved by something else, is the cause and principle of motion,
everyone would decide for the former; for that which is itself independently a cause is always
prior as a cause to that which is so only in virtue of being itself dependent upon something else
that makes it so. **257a27–33**

COMMENTARY OF ST. THOMAS

1037. After the Philosopher has shown that whatever is moved is moved by another, he begins here to show that it is necessary to arrive at a first immobile mover.

This discussion is divided into two parts. First he shows that it is necessary to arrive at some first thing which is either immobile or self-moved. Secondly, where he says, **"Now everything that is ..."** [819], he shows that even if one arrives at some first thing which moves itself, it is still necessary to arrive further at a first immobile mover.

Concerning the first part he makes two points. First he shows that it is not possible for a thing to be moved by another to infinity. Secondly, where he says, **"And if we consider ..."** [810], he

shows that it is not necessary that every mover be moved.

Concerning the first part he makes two points. First he proves his position by ascending in the order of movers and mobile objects, and secondly by descending, where he says, **"This same argument ..."** [809].

Concerning the first part he makes two points. First he sets forth certain things which are necessary to prove his position. Secondly, where he says, **"If then everything ..."** [808], he gives an argument to prove his position.

1038. He sets forth two things, the first of which is a division of movers.

Since it was said that whatever is moved is moved by something, a thing can be a mover in two ways. In one way it does not move because of itself, that is, by its proper power, but because it is moved by some other mover, which is a second mover. In another way a thing moves because of itself, that is, by its proper power, and not because it is moved by another.

Now this latter mover may move in two ways. In one way the first mover moves that which is next after the last, that is, it moves that which is next after the second mover. This happens when the first mover moves a mobile object through only one intermediary. In the other way, the mover moves the mobile through many intermediaries, as is clear when a stick moves a stone and is moved by a hand, which is moved by a man, who does not move because he is moved by another. Therefore, the man is the first mover because of himself, and he moves the stone through several intermediaries. If, however, he were to move the stone by his hand, he would move through only one intermediary.

1039. Secondly, where he says, **"Now we say . . ."** [809], he compares the first and second movers. When we say that both the first and the last movers move, we say that the first mover moves rather than the last.

This is clear for two reasons. The first is that the first mover moves the second mover, but not vice versa. The second reason is that the second mover cannot move without the first, but the first can move without the second. For example, a stick cannot move a stone unless it is moved by a man, but a man can move a stone without a stick.

1040. Next where he says, **"If then everything . . ."** [808], he proves his position from the foregoing. It was shown that whatever is moved is moved by something. That by which it is moved either is moved or not moved. And if it is moved, it is moved

either by another or it is not. Moreover, these two, that is, that which is moved by another and that which is not moved by another, are so related that when one has been established, so is the other, but not vice versa. For if there is something which is moved by another, it is necessary to arrive at some first thing which is not moved by another. But if there is some first thing which is not moved by another, it is not necessary for there to be some further thing which is moved by another.

This, indeed, is clear per se. But there may be some doubt that if something is found to be moved by another, then there should be found some first thing which is not moved by another. Consequently, he proves this as follows.

If a thing is moved by another, and that again by another, and we never arrive at something which is not moved by another, it follows that we proceed to infinity with respect to movers and things moved. That this is impossible was proven above in Book VII. But here he proves this in a more certain way, because among infinite things there is no first. Therefore, if movers and the things which are moved proceed to infinity, there will be no first mover. But it was already said that if the first mover does not move, then neither does the last mover move. Therefore, there will not be any mover, which is clearly false. Hence a thing is not moved by another to infinity.

Let it be granted that whatever is moved is moved by something, as was shown, and further, let it be assumed that the first mover is moved. Since it has been proven that it is not moved by another, it must be moved by itself.

However, it should be noted that in this argument it is not proven that the first mover is moved. Rather he assumes this according to the common opinion of the Platonists. With respect to the force of the argument it is not to be concluded that the first mover moves itself rather than that it is immobile. Hence in what follows he draws this same conclusion in a disjunction, as will be clear below.

1041. Next where he says, **"This same argument . . ."** [809], he proves the same thing by descending. This argument is the same as the foregoing with respect to the force of the inference, differing only in the order of procedure. He repeats it for greater clarity.

He says, therefore, that the previous argument can be developed in another way. He sets forth propositions which have the same nature [ratio] of truth as the foregoing, but in another order. He said above that whatever is moved is moved by another, and that that by which it is moved moves either because of itself or because of a prior mover. This is the procedure of ascending.

Here, however, he proceeds conversely by descending. He says that every mover moves something and moves by something, either by itself or by another lower mover. For example, a man moves a stone either by himself or by a stick, and the wind hurls something to the ground either by its own power or by a stone which it moves.

He has also stated above that the last mover does not move without the first, but the opposite may occur. In place of this he says here that it is impossible for that which moves as an instrument to move something without a principal mover. For example, a stick cannot move without a hand. But if a thing moves by itself as a principal mover, it is not necessary for there to be an instrument by which it moves. This is clearer in instruments than in

ordered mobile objects, even though it is the same truth. For no one would doubt that the second mover is the instrument of the first. Just as he said above that if something is moved by another there must be something which is not moved, but not vice versa, so here he says by descending that if there is an instrument by which a mover moves there must be something which moves, not by an instrument, but by itself, or else there is an infinite series of instruments. This is the same as an infinite series of movers, which is impossible, as was shown above.

If, therefore, there is something which moves that which is moved, it is necessary to stop and not proceed to infinity. For if a stick moves because it is moved by a hand, it follows that the hand moves the stick. If, however, something else also moves the hand, it also follows conversely that some mover moves the hand. And so what follows for moved instruments must also follow for the movers which move the instruments. But it was proven above that there is no infinite series of movers. Therefore neither is there an infinite series of instruments. Therefore, since a thing which is moved is always moved by another, and since there is no infinite series, there must be some first mover which moves through itself and not through an instrument.

If, therefore, it is granted that this first thing which moves through itself is moved, but there is no other thing moving it (for thus it would be the instrument), it follows necessarily that it moves itself, supposing, according to the Platonists, that every mover is moved.

And so, also according to this argument, that which is moved will either be moved immediately by a thing which moves itself, or else one will at some time arrive at a mover which moves itself.

1042. Next where he says, **"And if we consider . . ."** [810], he shows that not every mover is moved, which was assumed in the above arguments.

Concerning this he makes two points. First he proves that not every mover is moved. Secondly, where he says, **"It is not necessary . . ."** [818], he concludes to his main point from both this and the above arguments.

He says, therefore, first that the following points can be added to the above to prove our position. Concerning this he makes three points. First he sets forth a certain division. Secondly, where he says, **"Let us consider . . ."** [811], he rejects one alternative. Thirdly, where he says, **"We will now take . . ."** [814], he rejects the other alternative.

He says, therefore, first [810] that if everything which is moved is moved by something which is moved, that is, if every mover is moved, this can be taken in two ways. This might be found in things per accidens such that the mover does not move because of that which is moved (for example, we might say that a musician is a builder, not because he is musical, but per accidens). Or the mover might be moved per se and not per accidens.

1043. Next where he says, **"Let us consider . . ."** [811], he rejects the first alternative in three ways.

First he uses the following argument. Nothing which is per accidens is necessary. For what is in a thing per accidens is not in it of necessity, but might happen to be not in it, as music in the builder. If, then, movers are moved per accidens, it follows that

they might not be moved. But when you grant that every mover is moved, then it follows that if movers are not moved, they do not move. It follows, then, that at some time nothing would be moved. This is impossible, however, since it was shown above that motion must be eternal. This impossibility, however, does not follow because we have assumed that movers are not moved. For if it is per accidens that movers are moved, then it will be possible for movers not to be moved. For no impossibility follows from an assumed possibility. The conclusion, therefore, from this is that it is impossible that every mover be moved.

1044. Secondly where he says, **"Moreover, the conclusion . . ."** [812], he proves the same thing with another probable argument, which is as follows.

Three things are found in motion: one is the mobile object which is moved; another is the mover; and the third is the instrument by which the mover moves. Of these three it is clear that that which is moved must be moved, but it is not necessary that it move. The instrument by which the mover moves must both move and be moved (for it is moved by the principal mover, and it moves the ultimate thing moved). Hence everything which both moves and is moved has the nature [ratio] of an instrument.

Therefore, the instrument by which the mover moves both moves and is moved, because it communicates with both, having a certain identity with that which is moved. This is particularly clear in local motion. For from the first mover up to the ultimate thing moved, everything must be in contact with everything else. And so it is clear that the intermediate instrument is the same through contact with the mobile object, and thus is moved together with it insofar as it communicates with it. But it also communicates with the mover. For it is a mover, in the sense that it is an instrument by which it moves. But it is not immobile.

Therefore, from the foregoing it is clear that the ultimate thing moved is indeed moved, but it does not have within itself a principle of moving either itself or another. It is moved by another, not by itself. Hence it seems to be reasonable, that is, probable (we do not care to say at the present time that it is necessary) that there is some third thing which moves, though it is immobile.

For it is probable that if two things are joined per accidens, and if one is found without the other, then that other will also be found without the first. (It is necessary that it can be found without the other, because things which are joined per accidens can be not joined.) For example, if whiteness and sweetness are joined per accidens in sugar, and if whiteness is found without sweetness, as in snow, it is probable that sweetness will be found in something without whiteness, as in cinnamon. Therefore, if a mover is moved per accidens, and if "being moved" is found in something without a "moving," as in the ultimate thing moved, then it is probable that a "moving" will be found without a "being moved," such that there may be some mover which is not moved.

It is clear from this that such an argument has no force in regard to substance and accident, and matter and form, and in similar things, of which one is found without the other, but not vice versa. For accident is in substance per se, and it is per se agreeable to matter to have existence through form.

1045. Thirdly, where he says, **"So, too, Anaxagoras . . ."** [813], he proves the same thing from the testimony of Anaxagoras.

For since there is a mover which is not moved, Anaxagoras spoke correctly when he said that intellect is impassive and unmixed. He said this because he held that intellect is the first principle of motion. For only if it is unmixed will it be able to move and command without being moved. For that which is mixed with another is moved in some way when the other is moved.

1046. Next where he says, **"We will now take . . ."** [814], he takes up the other part of the division, that is, whatever is moved is moved by something which is moved per se and not per accidens.

He rejects this with two arguments, the first of which is as follows. If the mover is moved, not accidentally, but necessarily, and if it can never move without being moved, this must occur in two ways. One way is that the mover is moved with respect to the same species of motion by which it moves. The other way is that the mover is moved according to one species of motion, and that which is moved is moved according to another species of motion.

He next explains the first way where he says, **". . . either that which is . . ."** [815]. We say that the mover is moved with respect to the same species of motion when, for example, that which heats becomes hot, and when that which cures is cured, and when that which moves in place is moved in place.

He explains the second way where he says, ". . . or else that which is making healthy . . ." This means that a thing moves and is moved according to different species of motion.

Next he shows the impossibility of the first way where he says, **"But it is evident . . ."** [816].

It is clearly impossible for a mover to be moved with respect to the same species of motion. For it is not sufficient to stop at some subalternate species, but one must proceed by division all the way to the most specific species. For example, if someone teaches, not only is he taught, but he teaches and is taught the same thing. If he is teaching geometry, he is taught this same geometry. Or if he moves according to the species of local motion which is called throwing, then he is moved according to the same motion of throwing. And this is clearly false.

Next he rejects the second mode, that is, the mover is not moved according to the same species of motion, but rather it moves by one genus of motion, and is moved by another genus. For example, the mover moves with respect to place and is moved by increase, or else the mover moves by increase and is moved by another through alteration. And that which alters it is moved by some other motion.

It is clear that motions are not infinite, either in genus or in species. For it was shown in Book V that motions differ in genus and in species with respect to the differences of the things in which there are motions. Moreover, the genera and species of things are not infinite, as he has proven elsewhere. And so, neither are the genera and species of motion infinite. If, then, the mover must be moved by another genus or another species of motion, this

will not go on to infinity. Rather there will be some first immobile mover.

1047. But someone might say that when all the species of motion are exhausted, there will be a return to the first, that is, if the first thing moved is moved locally, then when all the genera and species of motions have been distributed through different movers, the mover which remains will be moved by local motion. To reject this he says next that if there is this cycle such that that which alters is moved in place (he says this because above he named local motion first and alteration last), then this cycle is the same as if it were said immediately at the beginning that the mover is moved in place, and not only in genus but also in species, as when he said that the teacher is taught.

And that this is so he proves as follows. Whatever is moved is moved more by a higher mover than by a lower one, and consequently much more by the first mover. Therefore, if that which was given as moved locally is moved by the nearest mover which is increased, and that again is moved by something which is altered, and that again is moved by something which is moved in place, then that which is moved with respect to place will be moved more by the first thing which is moved with respect to place than by the second thing which is altered or by the third thing which is increased.

Therefore, it will be true to say that that which moves with respect to place is moved with respect to place. And the same can be said of each species of motion. However, this is not only erroneous, as can be seen in many instances, but it is also impossible. For it would follow that the teacher is learning while he teaches, which is impossible. This is a contradiction, because a teacher has a science but a learner does not. Hence it is clear that a mover is not necessarily moved.

1048. He gives the second argument where he says, **"Still more unreasonable . . ."** [817]. This argument differs from the preceding one only in that the first argument led to certain particular inconsistencies, for example, that the thrower is thrown, or that the teacher is taught. This argument, however, leads to a general inconsistency.

He says that although it is inconsistent that the teacher is taught, the following is even more unreasonable. For if nothing is moved except by that which is moved, then every motive force is mobile. And thus it will follow that every mover is mobile. For example, it might be said that whatever has the power of curing, or which is actually curing, is curable; and whatever has the power of building is buildable. This is more unreasonable than saying that a teacher is taught, for the teacher was first capable of learning, but the builder was never built.

This follows in two ways. For if it is granted that every mover is moved according to the same species of motion, then it follows immediately that the builder is built, and that the one who cures is cured. And if it is granted that the mover is not moved according to the same species of motion, it follows that it comes to the same thing through many intermediaries.

And he explains this. Let it be granted that every mover is moved by another, although it is not moved immediately by the same motion by which it moves, but by another motion. For example, that which has the power to cure is not immediately

cured but is moved by the motion of learning. Nevertheless, since the species of motion are not infinite, by ascending from mobile object to mover we will arrive at some time at the same species of motion, as was explained above.

One of these two is clearly impossible, that is, that the builder is immediately built. And the other, that is, that it comes to this through many intermediaries, seems to be a fiction. For it is inconsistent to say that that which naturally alters necessarily is naturally increased.

1049. Therefore, from an examination of the foregoing arguments [818] (the first of which concluded that whatever is moved is not moved by another to infinity, and the second of which concluded that not every mover is moved), from all of these arguments we can conclude that it is not necessary that that which is moved be moved by another to infinity such that it is always moved by a mover which is moved. Therefore, it is necessary to stop at some first. This first must be either immobile or a mover of itself.

But if it is asked whether the first cause of motion in the genus of mobile objects is that which moves itself or a mobile object which is moved by another, it is probable among all that the first mover is that which moves itself. For a cause per se is always prior to a cause through another. And it is for this reason that the Platonists held that before things which are moved by another there is something which moves itself.

Therefore, we must consider that which moves itself and make another beginning, that is, we must consider that if something moves itself, how is this possible.

LECTURE 10 [257a35–258a5]
How a Thing Moves Itself

The Text of Aristotle

819. *We must therefore make a fresh start and consider the question: if a thing moves itself, in what sense and in what manner does it do so? Now everything that is in motion must be infinitely divisible; for it has been shown already in our general course on* Physics, *that everything that is essentially in motion is continuous.* 257a33–257b2

820. *Now it is impossible that that which moves itself should in its entirety move itself; for then, while being specifically one and indivisible, it would as a whole both undergo and cause the same locomotion or alteration; thus it would at the same time be both teaching and being taught (the same thing), or both restoring to and being restored to the same health.* 257b2–6

821. *Moreover, we have established the fact that it is the movable that is moved; and this is potentially, not actually, in motion, but the potential is in process to actuality, and motion is an incomplete actuality of the movable. The mover on the other hand is already in activity: e.g., it is that which is hot that produces heat: in fact, that which produces the form is always something that possesses it. Consequently (if a thing can move itself as a whole), the same thing in respect of the same thing may be at the same time both hot and not hot. So, too, in every other case where the mover must be described by the same name in the same sense as the moved.*
257b6–10

822. *Therefore when a thing moves itself it is one part of it that is the mover and another part that is moved.* 257b10–13

823. *But it is not self-moving in the sense that each of the two parts is moved by the other part: the following considerations make this evident.* 257b13–15

824. *In the first place, if each of the two parts is to move the other, there will be no first mover. If a thing is moved by a series of movers, that which is earlier in the series is more the cause of its being moved than that which comes next, and will be more truly the mover; for we found that there are two kinds of mover, that which is itself moved by something else and that which derives its motion from itself; and that which is further from the thing that is moved is nearer to the principle of motion than that which is intermediate.* 257b15–20

825. *In the second place, there is no necessity for the mover to be moved by anything but itself; so it can only be accidentally that the other part moves it in return. I take then the possible case of its not moving it: then there will be a part that is moved and a part that is an unmoved mover.* 257b20–23

826. *In the third place, there is no necessity for the mover to be moved in return: on the contrary the necessity that there should always be motion makes it necessary that there should be some mover that is either unmoved or moved by itself.* 257b23–25

827. *In the fourth place we should then have a thing undergoing the same motion that it is causing—that which is producing heat, therefore, being heated.* 257b25–26

828. *But as a matter of fact that which primarily moves itself cannot contain either a single part that moves itself or a number of parts each of which moves itself.* 257b26–28

829. *For, if the whole is moved by itself, it must be moved either by some part of itself or as a whole by itself as a whole. If, then, it is moved in virtue of some part of it being moved by that part itself, it is this part that will be the primary self-mover, since, if this part is separated from the whole, the part will still move itself, but the whole will do so no longer. If on the other hand the whole is moved by itself as a whole, it must be accidentally that the parts move themselves: and therefore; their self-motion not being necessary, we may take the case of their not being*

moved by themselves. Therefore in the whole of the thing we may distinguish that which imparts motion without itself being moved and that which is moved; for only in this way is it possible for a thing to be self-moved.   257b28–258a2

830. *Further, if the whole moves itself we may distinguish in it that which imparts the motion and that which is moved: so while we say that AB is moved by itself, we may also say that it is moved by A.*   258a3–5

COMMENTARY OF ST. THOMAS

1050. The Philosopher has shown that there is no infinite series of movers and mobile objects. Rather there is a first which is either immobile or which moves itself. He shows here that even if there is a first mover which moves itself, it is still necessary to admit a first mover which is immobile.

This discussion is divided into three parts. First he shows that that which moves itself is divided into two parts, one of which moves and the other of which is moved. Secondly, where he says, **"And since that which . . ."** [831], he shows how such parts are related to each other. Thirdly, where he says, **"From what has been said . . ."** [837], he concludes that there must be a first immobile mover.

Concerning the first part he makes two points. First he shows that in that which moves itself one part moves and the other is moved, because a whole cannot move itself. Secondly, where he says, **"But it is not . . ."** [823], he rejects other ways in which one might think that a thing moves itself.

Concerning the first part he makes three points. First he states that a whole self-mover does not move its whole self. Secondly, where he says, **". . . for then, while being . . ."** [820], he proves his position. Thirdly, where he says, **"Therefore, when a thing . . ."** [822], he concludes to his main point.

1051. Since whole and part are found only in divisible things, he concludes from what was proven in Book VI that whatever is moved must be di-

visible into things which are always divisible. For this is the nature [ratio] of a continuum, and whatever is moved is a continuum, if it is moved per se. (It is not impossible for an indivisible thing to be moved per accidens, for example, a point or whiteness.)

This was explained above in Book VI. Everything which he said before Book VIII he called "universal in nature." But in Book VIII he begins to apply to things what he has said above about motion in general. Therefore, since that which is moved is divisible, a whole and a part can be found in everything which is moved. Hence if there is something which moves itself, whole and part will be found in it. But the whole cannot move the whole itself (that is, it cannot totally move itself).

1052. Next where he says, **". . . for then, while being . . ."** [820], he proves his position with two arguments, the first of which is as follows.

The motion of a thing which moves itself all together and at once is one in number. If, therefore, a thing moves itself such that the whole moves the whole, then it follows that the mover and the thing moved are one and the same in respect to one and the same motion, whether it be local motion or alteration.

But this seems to be inconsistent, because a mover and a thing moved are opposed to each other. But opposites cannot be in the same thing in the same way. Hence it is not possible that the mover and the moved be the same in respect to the same motion. For when a thing both moves and is moved, the motion by which it moves is different from the motion by which it is moved. For example, when a stick which is moved by a hand moves a stone, the motion of the stick and the motion of the stone differ in number. Thus, it would follow further that one will teach and be taught at the same time with respect to one and the same knowable object. Similarly, one will heal and be healed with respect to numerically one and the same health.

1053. Next where he says, **"Moreover, we have established . . ."** [821], he gives the second argument, which is as follows.

It was established in Book III that what is moved is mobile, that is, it exists in potency. For that which is moved is moved insofar as it is in potency and not in act. For a thing is moved because, when it is in potency, it tends toward act. But that which is moved is not in potency in such a way that it is in no way in act, because the motion itself is a certain act of the mobile object insofar as it is moved. But this act is imperfect, because it is its act insofar as it is still in potency.

But that which moves is already in act, for what is in potency is reduced to act only by that which is in act. A mover, for example, heats when it is hot, and that which has a generated species generates, as a man generates that which has a human species, and the same is true of other things. Therefore, if a whole moves itself as a whole, it follows that the same thing in the same respect is both hot and not hot, for insofar as it is a mover it is actually hot, and insofar as it is moved it is potentially hot.

And the same applies to all other cases in which the mover is "univo-cal," that is, the same in name and in nature [ratio] as that which is moved. For example, just as heat causes heat, so man generates man.

He says this because there are some agents which are not univocal in name and in nature [ratio] with their effects. For example, the sun generates a man. Even though the species caused by such agents is not the same in nature [ratio], nevertheless in a certain higher and more universal way it is the same. And so, it is universally true that the mover is in act in a certain way with respect to that to which the mobile object is in potency. Therefore, if a whole moves itself as a whole, it follows that the same thing is simultaneously in act and in potency, which is impossible.

From this he concludes to his main point [822]; namely, in that which moves itself, one part moves and another is moved.

1054. Next where he says, **"But it is not . . ."** [823], he rejects certain ways in which someone might think that a thing moves itself.

First he shows that in a thing which moves itself each part is not moved by another. Secondly, where he says, **"But as a matter . . ."** [828], he shows that in a thing which moves itself no part moves itself.

Concerning the first part he makes two points. First he states his intention. Secondly, where he says, **"In the first place . . ."** [824], he proves his position.

He says, therefore, first that it is clear from what follows that a thing does not move itself in such a way that each part of it is moved by the remaining part. For example, if A B moves itself, then A moves B, and B moves A.

1055. Next where he says, **"In the first place . . ."** [824], he proves his position by four arguments. It should be noted that to reach this conclusion he repeats the arguments given above to show that not every mover is moved by another. Hence from the foregoing he here briefly summarizes four arguments.

The first of these he takes from the first argument above which he gave in a double order to show that a thing is not moved by another to infinity. For otherwise there would not be a first mover. And when the first mover is removed, so are the subsequent movers. Hence here he also sets forth the same inconsistency.

He says that if in the first thing moved (which is given as a mover of itself) each part is reciprocally moved by another, then there is no first mover. This is so because, as was said above, a prior mover is the cause of motion more than a later mover.

He also proved above that a thing moves in two ways. In one way a thing moves because it is moved by another, for example, a stick moves a stone because it is moved by a hand. This is a second mover. In another way a thing moves because it is moved by itself, as a man moves. And this is the disposition of a first mover. Moreover, that which moves, but not because it is moved by another, is further removed from the last thing which is moved, and is closer to the first mover, than an intermediary which moves because it is moved by another.

This argument ought to be developed as follows. If in a whole which moves itself each part moves the other reciprocally, then one part does not move more than another. But a first mover moves more than a second mover. Therefore, neither of them will be a first mover. But this is inconsistent, because then it would follow that that which is moved by itself is not closer to the first principle of motion

(which follows no being) than that which is moved by another. But it was shown above that that which moves itself is first in the genus of mobile objects. Therefore, it is not true that in things which move themselves each part is moved by another.

1056. Next where he says, **"In the second place . . ."** [825], he develops two arguments for the same thing from the first argument which he gave above to show that not every mover is moved such that "being moved" is in the mover per accidens. In the above argument he developed two conclusions; first, a mover need not be moved; and second, motion is not eternal. From these two conclusions he formulates two arguments.

First he says that it is not necessary for a mover to be moved by itself except per accidens. And he observes that unless the first mover is understood to be moved by itself, it will not be necessary for the first mover to be moved per accidens. For some have held that every mover is moved, but this occurs per accidens.

When, therefore, it is held that in a self-mover the part which moves is moved by a contrary and equal motion from another part, this will occur only per accidens. But, as we agreed above, that which is per accidens can not-be. Therefore it happens that that part which moves is not moved. Hence it follows that one part of the self-mover is moved, and the other part moves and is not moved.

1057. Next where he says, **"In the third place . . ."** [826], he gives another argument which corresponds to the second conclusion drawn above, that is, the conclusion that motion is not eternal. Here, however, he argues in the reverse order.

If motion must be eternal, it is not

necessary that a mover be moved in return when it moves. What is necessary is that a mover be either immobile or that it be moved by itself.

The reason for this condition is clear from the argument advanced above. For if a mover does not move unless it is moved, and if there is no "being moved" in it except per accidens, then it follows that it happens to be not moved. Consequently, it does not move, and hence there will be no motion. But it was shown above that motion is eternal. Therefore, it is not necessary for a mover, when it moves, to be moved in return. And so it is not true that each part of a self-mover is moved by another.

1058. Next where he says, **"In the fourth place . . ."** [827], he gives the fourth argument which he takes from the argument given above to show that "being moved" is not present per se in a mover which is moved. For otherwise it would follow that the mover is moved by the same motion by which it moves, as was explained above.

Thus, by abridging this argument here, he says that if each part is moved by another, it follows that it moves and is moved in respect to the same motion. Hence it follows that that which heats becomes hot, which is impossible.

Therefore, if each part of a self-mover is moved by another, it follows that a thing moves and is moved in respect to the same motion. For in a self-mover there is one motion, and the part which moves must be moved in respect to that motion.

1059. Next where he says, **"But as a matter . . ."** [828], he rejects another way of explaining this; namely, in a self-mover a part moves itself.

First he states his position. Secondly, where he says, **"For, if the whole . . ."** [829], he proves his position.

He says, therefore, first that if there is a first self-mover, it cannot be said either that one part of it moves itself, or that each one of many parts moves itself.

1060. Next where he says, **"For, if the whole . . ."** [829], he proves his position with two arguments, the first of which is as follows.

A whole is moved by itself either because one of its parts is moved by itself or because the whole is moved by itself.

If it is moved because of its part, then that part will be the first self-mover, because that part when separated from the whole will move itself. And the whole will not be the first self-mover, as was granted.

If, then, it is said that the whole moves itself by reason of the whole, then it is only per accidens that some parts move themselves. But what is per accidens is not necessary. Therefore, in the first thing which moves itself, it must be admitted that the parts are not moved by themselves. Therefore, of the whole first self-mover one immobile part will move, and the other will be moved. For it is possible for a moving part to be moved only if it is moved by another part which moves, or if it moves itself.

It must be noted that Aristotle, by rejecting these two ways, intends to conclude that a moving part in a self-mover is immobile; not, however, that a self-mover is divided into two parts, of which one moves and the other is moved. For it was sufficiently explained in the beginning that a whole does not move itself as a whole.

And so it is clear that it was not necessary for Aristotle to make a five-fold division, as some have said. One alternative is that the whole moves the whole; the second is that the whole moves a part; the third is that a part moves the whole; the fourth is that two parts alternately move themselves; the fifth is that one part moves and the other is moved. For if the whole does not move the whole, for the same reason it follows that the whole does not move a part, nor a part the whole, because in either case it will follow that a moved part moves itself. Hence the fact that the whole does not move the whole is sufficient to conclude that one part moves and the other is moved. But to conclude that the part which moves is not moved, he proves two other things; namely, the moving part is not moved by something which is moved, and it is not moved by itself.

1061. To prove this second point he introduces a second argument where he says, **"Further, if the whole moves itself..."** [830]. The argument is as follows.

If it is granted that the moving part of a self-mover moves itself as a whole, then from the above proof it will follow further that one part of it moves and the other is moved. For it was shown above that a whole does not move itself in any other way except that one part of it moves and the other is moved. Let the moving part of a self-mover be AB. From the foregoing argument it follows that one part of it will be the mover, namely A, and the other part will be moved, namely B. If, then, the whole AB moves itself, as was granted, it follows that the same thing is moved by two movers, that is, by the whole, which is AB, and by the part, which is A. But this is impossible. Therefore, it follows that the moving part of a self-mover is absolutely immobile.

How the Parts of a Self-Mover Are Related to Each Other, And How the Whole Is Said to Move Itself with Respect to Them

The Text of Aristotle

831. *And since that which imparts motion may be either a thing that is moved by something else or a thing that is unmoved, and that which is moved may be either a thing that imparts motion to something else or a thing that does not, that which moves itself must be composed of something that is unmoved but imparts motion and also of something that is moved but does not necessarily impart motion but may or may not do so.* 258a5–8

832. *Thus let A be something that imparts motion but is unmoved, B something that is moved by A and moves C, C something that is moved by B but moves nothing (granted that we eventually arrive at C we may take it that there is only one intermediate term, though there may be more). Then the whole ABC moves itself. But if I take away C, AB will move itself, A imparting motion and B being moved, whereas C will not move itself or in fact be moved at all. Nor again will BC move itself apart from A; for B imparts motion only through being moved by something else, not through being moved by any part of itself. So only AB moves itself. That which moves itself, therefore, must comprise something that imparts motion but is unmoved and something that is moved but does not necessarily move anything else;* 258a9–20

833. *and each of these two things, or at any rate one of them, must be in contact with the other.* 258a20–21

834. *If, then, that which imparts motion is a continuous substance—that which is moved must of course be so—it is clear that it is not through some part of the whole being of such a nature as to be capable of moving itself that the whole moves itself: it moves itself as a whole, both being moved and imparting motion through containing a part that imparts motion and a part that is moved. It does not impart motion as a whole nor is it moved as a whole: it is A alone that imparts motion and B alone that is moved. It is not true, further, that C is moved by A, which is impossible.* 258a21–27

835. *Here a difficulty arises: if something is taken away from A (supposing that that which imparts motion but is unmoved is a continuous substance), or from B; the part that is moved, will the remainder of A continue to impart motion or the remainder of B continue to be moved? If so, it will not be AB primarily that is moved by itself, since, when something is taken away from AB, the remainder of AB will still continue to move itself.* 258a27–32

836. *Perhaps we may state the case thus: there is nothing to prevent each of the two parts, or at any rate one of them, that which is moved, being divisible though actually undivided, so that if it is divided it will not continue in the possession of the same capacity; and so there is nothing to prevent self-motion residing primarily in things that are potentially divisible.* 258a32–258b4

837. *From what has been said, then, it is evident that that which primarily imparts motion is unmoved; for whether the series is closed at once by that which is in motion but moved by something else deriving its motion directly from the first unmoved, or whether the motion is derived from what is in motion but moves itself and stops its own motion, on both suppositions we have the result that in all cases of things being in motion that which primarily imparts motion is unmoved.* 258b4–9

COMMENTARY OF ST. THOMAS

1062. After the Philosopher has shown that a self-mover is divided into two parts, of which one part moves and is not moved, and the other is moved, here he shows how such parts are related to each other.

Concerning this he makes three points. First he states his intention. Secondly, where he says, **"Thus let A . . ."** [832], he proves his position. Thirdly, where he says, **"From what has been . . ."** [837], he draws his main conclusion from all of the above.

He says, therefore, first that there are two types of movers; namely, a mover which is also moved by another, and a mover which is immobile. And again, there are two types of mobile objects; namely, a mobile object which also moves, and a mobile object which moves nothing. Hence it must be said that a self-mover is composed of two parts, one of which so moves that it is immobile, and the other is so moved that it does not move.

The term "necessarily," which he adds, can be understood in two ways. If it is understood that the moved part of a self-mover does not move something which is part of the self-mover, then the text should be read such that "necessarily" remains affirmative and modifies "does not . . . impart motion." For he proves immediately the impossibility of there being, in that which primarily moves itself, a third part which is moved by the moved part. But if it is understood that the moved part does not move something extrinsic, then the term "necessarily" becomes negated. For the moved part of a self-mover does not necessarily move something extrinsic. However this is not impossible.

1063. He next shows how this occurs where he says, **"Thus let A . . ."** [832].

Concerning this he makes two points. First he proves his position. Secondly, where he says, **"Here a difficulty . . ."** [835], he answers a difficulty.

Concerning the first part he makes two points. First he shows how the parts of a self-mover are related to each other. Secondly, where he says, **"If, then, that which . . ."** [834], he explains how a whole is said to move in respect to these parts.

Concerning the first part he makes two points. First he shows that in a self-mover there are only two parts, one of which moves and is not moved, and the other of which is moved and does not move. Secondly, where he says, **". . . and each of these two . . ."** [833], he explains how these two parts are joined to each other.

He explains the first part [832] as follows. Let it be granted that the moved part of a self-mover moves something else which is part of the same self-mover. Let the first part of the self-mover be A, which is an immobile mover. Let the second part be B, which is moved by A, and which moves a third part, C, which is so moved by B that nothing else moves which is part of the self-mover. Now it cannot be said that there is a descent to infinity with respect to the parts of a self-mover, that is, that a moved part in turn moves another. For thus it would move itself to infinity, which is impossible, as was shown above. There will be some part of the self-mover which is moved but does not move. This we call C. And although there may be many intermediaries which move and are moved, there must be a last thing moved, which is C. In the place of all the intermediaries let there be one, namely, B. Therefore this whole, which is ABC, moves itself. If the part C is removed from the whole, AB will still move itself. For one part of it is the mover, that is, A, and the other is moved, that is, B, and that is what is required for a thing to move itself, as was explained above. But C will not move itself or any other part, according to what was assumed.

Likewise, BC does not move itself without A. For B does not move except insofar as it is moved by another, namely, A, which is not part of it. Hence it follows that only AB moves itself primarily and per se.

And so it is necessary that a self-mover has two parts, one of which is an immobile mover, and the other of which is a moved part which cannot move anything which is a part of the self-mover. This conclusion follows from the previous argument.

And he adds that the moved part "does not necessarily move anything else" [258a19]. For the moved part of a self-mover does not necessarily move some other extrinsic thing.

1064. Next where he says, ". . . and each of these two . . .", he shows how these two parts are related to each other.

It must be noted that Aristotle has not yet proven that the first mover does not have any magnitude. He will prove this below. For certain of the ancient philosophers held that there is no substance without magnitude. Hence Aristotle, leaving this open to question before he proves it, as is his custom, says that the two parts of the self-mover, one of which is the mover and the other of which is moved, must be joined in some way because they are parts of one whole. But this is not a union by continuity. For he has said above that a self-mover and that which is moved cannot be continuous, but must be separated. Hence it follows that these two parts must be joined by contact, either in such a way that both parts touch each other, if both parts have magnitude, or such that only one part is touched by the other,

and not vice versa, which is the case if the mover has no magnitude. For that which is incorporeal can touch a body by its own power of moving it, but it is not touched by the body. Two bodies, however, touch each other.

1065. Next where he says, **"If, then, that which . . ."** [834], he explains why a whole is said to move itself when one part moves and the other is moved.

Let us suppose for the present that each part is continuous, that is, each has magnitude. For it was proven in Book VI that whatever is moved is continuous. And let us now assume the same thing in regard to the mover, before the truth is established.

Granting this assumption, three things, namely, to be moved, to move, and to move itself, are attributed to the whole which is composed of two things. Now "to move itself" is attributed to it, not because some part moves itself, but because the whole moves itself. And "to move" and "to be moved" are attributed to the whole by reason of its parts. For the whole neither moves nor is moved. Rather the part A moves, and the part B is moved. For it was already shown that there is no third part, C, which is moved by B. This is impossible if we take that which moves itself primarily, as was explained above.

1066. Next where he says, **"Here a difficulty . . ."** [835], he raises a certain question about the foregoing. First he raises the question, and secondly he answers it, where he says, **"Perhaps we may state . . ."** [836].

This question arises from what was proven above; namely, in that which moves itself primarily there are only two parts, of which one moves and the other is moved. If there were a third, then when it is removed, that which is composed of the first two parts moves itself. And thus this latter is the first self-mover.

From this arises the following difficulty. Let us assume that the part of the self-mover which is an immobile mover, namely, A, is a continuum. From what was said before, it is clear that the part which is moved, namely, B, is a continuum. Every continuum, however, is divisible. The problem, then, is as follows: if some part is subtracted by division from A or from B, does the remaining part move or be moved? If this remaining part moves or is moved, then a part of AB moves itself. Hence, AB does not move itself primarily. And it follows further that nothing moves itself primarily.

1067. Next where he says, **"Perhaps we may state . . ."** [836], he answers this difficulty.

It must be noted that Aristotle has proven in Book VI that in motion there is no first either in respect to the mobile object or in respect to the time or in respect to that in which motion occurs, especially in increase and in local motion. This is so because he was then speaking about motion in general and about mobile objects insofar as they are continuous, not yet applying his remarks to determinate natures. And according to this it would follow that there is not something which is moved primarily, and consequently there is not something which moves primarily, if the mover is a continuum. Thus there would also not be something which moves itself primarily. But now Aristotle is speaking about motion by applying it to determined natures. Therefore, he holds that there is something which moves itself primarily.

He answers the foregoing difficulty as follows. Nothing prevents a continuum from being divisible in potency. Now the mover and the moved are either each continuous or at least one of them is, namely, that which is moved, which must be a continuum. Nevertheless it is possible that a continuum, whether it be the mover or the moved, have such a nature that it cannot be actually divided, as is clear in regard to the body of the sun. And if it happens that a continuum is divided, it will not retain the same potency to move or be moved which it had before. For such a potency follows from some form. A natural form, however, requires a determined quantity. Hence, if a body is incorruptible, it cannot be divided in act. If, however, it is corruptible, and if it is divided in act, it will not retain the same potency, as is clear in regard to the heart. Hence, there is nothing to prevent a first among things which are divisible in potency.

1068. Next where he says, **"From what has been said . . ."** [837], he draws his main conclusion from all of the foregoing.

He says that it is clear from the above that there must be a first immobile mover. For since movers and things moved by another do not go on to infinity, it is necessary to stop at some first which is either immobile or a self-mover. It makes no difference whether movers and things moved stop at a first immobile mover or at some first thing which moves itself. In either case there is a first immobile mover, for in a self-mover one part is an immobile mover, as has now been shown.

LECTURE 12 [258b10–259a21]
The First Mover Is Immobile and One

The Text of Aristotle
Chapter 6

838. Since there must always be motion without intermission, there must necessarily be something, one thing or it may be a plurality, that first imparts motion, and this first mover must be unmoved. 258b10–12

839. Now the question whether each of the things that are unmoved but impart motion is eternal is irrelevant to our present argument; 258b12–13

840. but the following considerations will make it clear that there must necessarily be some such thing, which, while it has the capacity of moving something else, is itself unmoved and exempt from all change, which can affect it neither in an unqualified nor in an accidental sense. 258b13–16

841. Let us suppose, if any one likes, that in the case of certain things it is possible for them at different times to be and not to be, without any process of becoming and perishing (in fact it would seem to be necessary, if a thing that has not parts at one time is and at another time is not, that any such thing should without undergoing any process of change at one time be and at another time not be). And let us further suppose it possible that some principles that are unmoved but capable of imparting motion at one time are and at another time are not. 258b16–22

842. Even so, this cannot be true of all such principles, since there must clearly be something that causes things that move themselves at one time to be and at another not to be. For, since nothing that has not parts can be in motion, that which moves itself must as a whole have magnitude, though nothing that we have said makes this necessarily true of every mover. So, the fact that some things become and others perish, and that this is so continuously, cannot be caused by any one of those things that, though they are unmoved, do not always exist; nor again can it be caused by any of those which move certain particular things, while others move other things. The eternity and continuity of the process cannot be caused either by any one of them singly or by the sum of them, because this causal relation must be eternal and necessary, whereas the sum of these movers is infinite and they do not all exist together. It is clear, then, that though there may be countless instances of the perishing of some principles that are unmoved but impart motion, and though many things that move themselves perish and are succeeded by others that come into being, and though one thing that is unmoved moves one thing while another moves another, nevertheless there is something that comprehends them all, and that as something apart from each one of them, and this it is that is the cause of the fact that some things are and others are not and of the continuous process of change; and this causes the motion of the other movers, while they are the causes of the motion of other things. Motion, then, being eternal, the first mover, if there is but one, will be eternal also; if there are more than one, there will be a plurality of such eternal movers. 258b22–259a8

843. We ought, however, to suppose that there is one rather than many, and a finite rather than an infinite number. When the consequences of either assumption are the same, we should always assume that things are finite rather than infinite in number, since in things constituted by nature that which is finite and that which is better ought, if possible, to be present rather than the reverse; and here it is sufficient to assume only one mover, the first of unmoved things, which being eternal will be the principle of motion to everything else. 259a8–13

844. The following argument also makes it evident that the first mover must be something

that is one and eternal. We have shown that there must always be motion. That being so, motion must also be continuous, because what is always is continuous, whereas what is merely in succession is not continuous. But further, if motion is continuous, it is one; and it is one only if the mover and the moved that constitute it are each of them one, since in the event of a thing's being moved now by one thing and now by another the whole motion will not be continuous but successive.
259a13–21

COMMENTARY OF ST. THOMAS

1069. The Philosopher has shown that there is no infinite series of things which are moved by another, but that there is some first thing which is either immobile or a self-mover. And he has shown further that one part of a self-mover is an immobile mover. Hence in either case the first mover is immobile. Since in the self-movers among us, that is, in corruptible animals, the moving part of the self-mover, that is, the soul, is corruptible and is moved per accidens, he wishes to show here that the first mover is incorruptible, and that it is not moved per se or per accidens.

Concerning this he makes two points. First he states his position. Secondly, where he says, **"Let us suppose..."** [841], he proves his position.

Concerning the first part he makes three points. First he summarizes what was proven above. Secondly, where he says, **"Now the question..."** [839], he omits something which might seem to pertain to his position. Thirdly, where he says, **"...but the following..."** [840], he explains his position.

He says, therefore, first [838] that it has been proven above that motion is eternal and never ceases; and since every motion is from some mover, and since movers do not proceed to infinity, there must be a first mover. But since it has not yet been proven that the first mover is one, there still remains the question of whether it is one or many. And it has been shown further that the first mover is immobile, either

by ascending from things moved to movers immediately to a first immobile mover or else by ascending to a first self-mover, one part of which is an immobile mover.

1070. However, some have held that all moving principles in things which move themselves are eternal. For Plato held that all animal souls are eternal. And if this opinion were true, Aristotle would have already established the proposition that the first mover is eternal. But Aristotle's opinion is that only the intellective part of the soul is incorruptible, even though other parts of the soul are movers.

Consequently, he omits this where he says, **"Now the question..."** [839]. He says that it is irrelevant to the argument at hand whether all principles which move and are immobile are eternal, although some have held this, saying that all souls are incorruptible. He says that this is not pertinent to the present argument, because he will prove his position without this assumption.

1071. Next where he says, **"...but the following..."** [840], he explains what he intends to prove.

He says that from a consideration of what follows it can be made clear that even if not every immobile mover is eternal, nevertheless there must be some immobile being which is in no way moved by anything extrinsic, either simply or per accidens, and yet is that which moves another.

However when he says, "...exempt

from all change . . .", he does not intend to exclude that motion or operation which is in that which acts insofar as understanding is called a motion and insofar as the appetite is moved by that which is desirable. For such motion is not excluded from the first mover which he intends.

1072. Next where he says, "**Let us suppose...**" [841], he proves his assertion that there is a first mover which is eternal and absolutely immobile.

He proves this first by means of self-movers which sometimes are and sometimes are not. Secondly, where he says, "**... but also by considering...**" [845], he proves the same thing by means of moving principles which sometimes move and sometimes do not.

Concerning the first part he makes three points. First he shows that there must be an eternal first mover. Secondly, where he says, "**We ought, however...**" [843], he shows that such a mover ought to be one rather than many. Thirdly, where he says, "**The following argument . . .**"[844]. he proves both points, namely, the first mover is both one and eternal.

Concerning the first part he makes two points. First he rejects a certain argument which someone might use to prove the proposition. Secondly, where he says, "**. . . since there must clearly...**" [842], he proves the proposition.

1073. Someone might argue as follows. Anything which cannot at one time exist and at another not exist is eternal. But since the first mover is immobile, as was shown, it cannot at one time exist and at another not exist. For that which sometimes exists and sometimes does not exist is generated and corrupted. And that which is gener-

ated and corrupted is moved. Therefore, the first mover is eternal.

Aristotle is not impressed with this argument. For someone might say, if he wishes, that certain things sometimes exist and sometimes do not, and yet are not generated and corrupted per se. Consequently, they are not moved per se. For if a thing which has no parts, that is, a thing which is not a composite of matter and form, sometimes is and sometimes is not, it is necessary that this occur without any mutation in it, as can be said of a point and whiteness and any such thing. For it was proven in Book VI that whatever is moved is divisible, and in Metaphysics, VII, it is proven that whatever is generated is composed of matter and form. Therefore, such indivisible things are not generated or changed per se, but per accidens, when other things were generated or changed.

From this it is clear that if a thing is not moved either per se or per accidens, it is eternal. And if it is eternal, it is not moved per se or per accidens, because it is eternal. If we admit the possibility that a thing may sometimes be and sometimes not be without being generated or corrupted, we must also admit the possibility that certain immobile moving principles can be moved per accidens, since at one time they are and at another they are not. But it is in no way possible that all immobile moving principles be such that sometimes they are and sometimes they are not.

1074. Next where he says, "**... since there must clearly...**" [842], he proves his position.

He says that if certain self-movers at one time are and at another are not, there must be some cause of their generation and corruption, by which at one time they are and at another are not. For whatever is moved has a cause of its motion. Moreover, if that which at one time is and at another is not is a composite, it is generated and corrupted. Furthermore, a self-mover must have magnitude. For it is moved, and it was shown in Book VI that nothing indivisible is moved.

But from what has been said, it cannot be concluded that a mover must have magnitude. Hence it is not moved per se, if at one time it is, and at another it is not. If, however, there is a cause of the generation and corruption of self-movers, it must be the cause of their generation and corruption being continued eternally.

But it cannot be said that the cause of this continuation is one of those immobile things which are not eternal. Nor can it be said that the causes of the eternal generation and corruption of some self-movers are certain immobile movers which are not eternal, and that there are other causes of the others. He explains this by adding that the cause of this continuous and eternal generation cannot be one of them nor all of them.

He shows that one of them cannot be the cause. For that which is not eternal cannot be the cause of that which is necessarily eternal.

He shows that all of them cannot be the cause. For if generation is eternal, all such corruptible principles are infinite and do not exist together. It is impossible, however, for one effect to depend on infinite causes.

Moreover things which do not exist together cannot be the cause of something. However, it is possible that of those things which do not exist together, certain ones dispose, and oth-

ers cause, as is clear in the case of successively falling drops which erode a stone. But if many things are the direct cause of something, they must exist together.

Therefore, it is clear that if there are a thousand thousand immobile moving principles, and if there are also many self-movers of which some are generated and some corrupted, and if among these latter some are mobile objects and others are movers, there still must be something over all of these which contains in its power everything which is generated and corrupted in the above way. This is the cause of their continuous mutation, as a result of which at one time they are and at another are not; and as a result of which some are the cause of the generation and motion of certain ones, and others are the cause of generation and motion of others. For every generator is the cause of generation in that which is generated. But corruptible generators receive their power of generation from some first incorruptible being. Therefore, if the motion as a result of which certain things at one time are and at another are not is eternal, as was shown above, and if an effect is eternal only if the cause is eternal, then the first mover must be eternal, if it is one. And if there are many first movers, they also are eternal.

1075. Next where he says, "We ought, however, . . ." [843], he shows that one ought to posit one eternal principle rather than many.

He says that just as one must hold that principles are finite rather than infinite, so one must hold that the first principle is one rather than many. For if the same things happen or result from the assumption of finite principles as from the assumption of infinite principles, it is better to hold that the principles are finite rather than infinite. For in things which exist according to nature, one should always take that which is better, if it is possible. For things which exist according to nature are ordered in the best way. But finite principles are better than infinite, and one is better than many. One first immobile principle is a sufficient cause of the eternity of motion, if it is eternal. It is not necessary, therefore, to posit many first principles.

1076. Next where he says, **"The following argument . . ."** [844], he concludes from the foregoing that there must be a first mover which is one and eternal.

Although it seems that this has been sufficiently proven by the above arguments, someone might maliciously say that the cause of this continual generation is a first eternal self-mover whose mover is not eternal and one. Rather its mover is moved by diverse movers, some of which are corrupted and some generated.

But he intends to reject this. For if motion is eternal, as he has proven above, the motion of the first self-mover which is given as the cause of the whole eternity of motion must be eternal and continuous. For if it were not continuous, it would not be eternal. And that which is consecutive is not continuous. In order for motion to be continuous it must be one, and in order for it to be one it must be the motion of one mobile object and must be from one mover. If, then, there are different movers, the whole motion will not be continuous, but consecutive.

It is absolutely necessary, therefore, that the first mover is one and eternal. But an immobile mover which is moved per accidens is not eternal, as was explained above. Hence it follows that the first mover is absolutely immobile, both per se and per accidens.

LECTURE 13 [259a22–260a19]
The First Mover Is Eternal and Immobile. The First Motion Is Eternal

The Text of Aristotle

845. *Moreover a conviction that there is a first unmoved something may be reached not only from the foregoing arguments, but also by considering again the principles operative in movers. Now it is evident that among existing things there are some that are sometimes in motion and sometimes at rest. This fact has served above to make it clear that it is not true either that all things are in motion or that all things are at rest or that some things are always at rest and the remainder always in motion: on this matter proof is supplied by things that fluctuate between the two and have the capacity of being sometimes in motion and sometimes at rest.* **259a21–27**

846. *The existence of things of this kind is clear to all; but we wish to explain also the nature of each of the other two kinds and show that there are some things that are always unmoved and some things that are always in motion. In the course of our argument directed to this end we established the fact that everything that is in motion is moved by something, and that the mover is either unmoved or in motion, and that, if it is in motion, it is moved either by itself or by something else and so on throughout the series; and so we proceeded to the position that the first principle that directly causes things that are in motion to be moved is that which moves itself, and the first principle of the whole series is the unmoved. Further it is evident from actual observation that there are things that have the characteristic of moving themselves, e.g., the animal kingdom and the whole class of living things.* **259a27–259b3**

847. *This being so, then, the view was suggested that perhaps it may be possible for motion to come to be in a thing without having been in existence at all before, because we see this actually occurring in animals: they are unmoved at one time and then again they are in motion, as it seems. We must grasp the fact, therefore, that animals move themselves only with one kind of motion, and that this is not strictly originated by them. The cause of it is not derived from the animal itself: it is connected with other natural motions in animals, which they do not experience through their own instrumentality, e.g., increase, decrease, and respiration: these are experienced by every animal while it is at rest and not in motion in respect of the motion set up by its own agency; here the motion is caused by the atmosphere and by many things that enter into the animal: thus in some cases the cause is nourishment: when it is being digested animals sleep, and when it is being distributed through the system they awake and move themselves, the first principle of this motion being thus originally derived from outside. Therefore animals are not always in continuous motion by their own agency: it is something else that moves them, itself being in motion and changing as it comes into relation with each several thing that moves itself. (Moreover in all these self-moving things the first mover and cause of their self-motion is itself moved by itself, though in an accidental sense: that is to say, the body changes its place, so that that which is in the body changes its place also and is a self-mover through its exercise of leverage.)* **259b3–20**

848. *Hence we may confidently conclude that if a thing belongs to the class of unmoved movers that are also themselves moved accidentally, it is impossible that it should cause continuous motion. So the necessity that there should be motion continuously requires that there should be a first mover that is unmoved even accidentally, if, as we have said, there is to be in the world of things an unceasing and undying motion, and the world is to remain permanently self-contained and within the same limits; for if the first principle is permanent, the universe must also be permanent, since it is continuous with the first principle.* **259b20–28**

849. *(We must distinguish, however, between accidental motion of a thing by itself and*

such motion by something else, the former being confined to perishable things, whereas the latter belongs also to certain first principles of heavenly bodies, of all those, that is to say, that experience more than one locomotion.)   **259b28–31**

850. *And further, if there is always something of this nature, a mover that is itself unmoved and eternal, then that which is first moved by it must be eternal.*   **259b32–260a1**

851. *Indeed this is clear also from the consideration that there would otherwise be no becoming and perishing and no change of any kind in other things which require something that is in motion to move them; for the motion imparted by the unmoved will always be imparted in the same way and be one and the same, since the unmoved does not itself change in relation to that which is moved by it. But that which is moved by something that, though it is in motion, is moved directly by the unmoved stands in varying relations to the things that it moves, so that the motion that it causes will not be always the same: by reason of the fact that it occupies contrary positions or assumes contrary forms at different times it will produce contrary motions in each several thing that it moves and will cause it to be at one time at rest and at another time in motion.*   **260a1–10**

852. *The foregoing argument, then, has served to clear up the point about which we raised a difficulty at the outset—why is it that instead of all things being either in motion or at rest, or some things being always in motion and the remainder always at rest, there are things that are sometimes in motion and sometimes not? The cause of this is now plain: it is because, while some things are moved by an eternal unmoved mover and are therefore always in motion, other things are moved by a mover that is in motion and changing, so that they too must change. But the unmoved mover, as has been said, since it remains permanently simple and unvarying and in the same state, will cause motion that is one and simple.*   **260a11–19**

COMMENTARY OF ST. THOMAS

1077. After the Philosopher has shown that the first mover is eternal and totally immobile by means of an argument derived from the eternity of the generation and corruption of animals which move themselves, he here intends to prove the same thing by means of an argument derived from moving principles.

Concerning this he makes three points. First he summarizes what has been said at the beginning of this treatise. Secondly, where he says, **"Hence we may confidently . . ."** [848], he develops from the above a proof of his position. Thirdly, where he says, **"The foregoing argument . . ."** [852], he answers a difficulty which was raised above.

1078. He summarizes three points, the first of which is a rejection of certain improbable positions.

He says that not only from the fore-going but also from a consideration of the principles of motion one can conclude that there is a first immobile mover. As was said above, it is clear to the senses that some natural things are found to be sometimes moved and sometimes at rest.

From this it was shown above that none of these three positions is true: all things are always moved; all things are always at rest; all things which are at rest are always at rest and all things which are moved are always moved. For things which are found in both states, that is, in motion and at rest, demonstrate the truth in this matter, for they have the potency to be sometimes moved and sometimes at rest.

1079. Secondly, where he says, **"The existence of . . ."** [846], he recalls the procedure used above to investigate the first immobile mover.

He says that things which are sometimes moved and sometimes at rest are obvious to all. But someone might develop a fourth position by saying that all beings are such that they are sometimes moved and sometimes at rest. Hence we wish to demonstrate a double diversity in nature by showing that there are certain things which are always immobile and other things which are always moved.

In doing this we held first that whatever is moved is moved by something. And that by which a thing is moved must be either immobile or moved. If it is moved, it is moved either by itself or by another. And since there is not an infinite series of movers, it is necessary to arrive at some first principle of motion. Hence, in the genus of things which are moved there is a first principle which moves itself. Furthermore, among all things the first principle is that which is immobile. And it should not be thought to be inconsistent that a thing moves itself, for we clearly see many such beings in the genus of living things and of animals.

1080. Thirdly, where he says, **"This being so, . . ."** [847], he recalls a difficulty which he raised and answered above.

When he proved the eternity of motion, he raised an objection to the contrary dealing with living beings which, although they were previously at rest, at some time begin to be moved. He says that living beings which move themselves seem to indicate that in the whole universe motion comes to be when previously it was not. For in living things we see that at some time they begin to be moved when previously they were not moved.

To answer this difficulty it must be understood that animals move themselves with respect to one motion, namely local motion. For only this motion is found to be subject to appetite in animals. Nevertheless, animals do not properly move themselves with respect to this motion such that no other cause of this motion pre-exists. For the first cause is not in animal itself which is moved locally. Rather other natural, nonvoluntary motions precede, either from within or from without, with respect to which animals do not move themselves. This is clear in regard to the motions of increase and decrease and breathing with respect to which animals are moved, even though they are at rest with respect to local motion, by which they are moved by themselves.

Moreover, the cause of these natural motions is either the extrinsic container, namely, the heavens and the air, by which animal bodies are altered from the exterior, or else it is something which enters animal bodies, as air enters in breathing, and as nourishment enters through eating and drinking. From transmutations of this kind, whether they result from interior or exterior causes, animals which previously were at rest at some time begin to be moved. This is clear in regard to the transmutation resulting from nourishment. For while nourishment is being digested, animals sleep because of the vapors which are released. But when nourishment has been digested and assimilated and the vapors have settled, animals awaken, and rise, and move themselves locally. Nevertheless, the first principle of the motion is something extrinsic to the nature of the animal which moves itself.

Hence animals are not always moved by themselves. For in respect to any animal which moves itself, there will be found some other prior mover which is moved and moves. For if this mover were totally immobile, it would always be related to moving in the same way, and thus animal motion would be eternal. But since this external mover which moves animals is itself moved, it does not always move in the same way.

Hence animals do not always move themselves in the same way. For in all animals the first mover which is the cause of the animal's self-motion, that is, the soul, so moves that it is moved, not indeed per se, but per accidens. For when the body is changed with respect to place, then that which exists in the body, that is, the soul, is changed per accidens. Hence, the whole self-mover is necessarily changed so that it is not in the same disposition for moving.

1081. Next where he says, **"Hence we may confidently . . ."** [848], he proves his position from the foregoing.

First he shows that the first mover is immobile. Secondly, where he says, **"And further, if there . . ."** [850], he shows that the first mover is eternal.

Concerning the first part he makes two points. First he proves his position. Secondly, where he says, **"We must distinguish . . ."** [849], he rejects an objection.

He says, therefore, first that from the foregoing we can show that an immobile moving principle which is moved per accidens cannot cause continuous and eternal motion. The reason why the souls of animals do not always move is that they are moved per accidens. But it was shown above that the motion of the universe must be continuous and eternal. Therefore, the first moving cause in the whole universe must be immobile, such that it is not even moved per accidens.

Just as there ought to be an imperishable and unceasing motion in natural things, as was said above, so also the whole of being, that is, the disposition of this universe, remains in its own disposition and in the same state. For from the immobility of the principle which is given as remaining immobile, it follows that the whole universe has an eternal permanence insofar as it is continuous with the first immobile principle by receiving influence from it.

1082. Next where he says, **"We must distinguish . . ."** [849], he rejects an objection.

He has said that if a mover is moved per accidens, it does not move with an eternal motion. But there seems to be an exception to this. For according to his position the motions of the lower orbs, for example, the sun and the moon and the other planets, are eternal. Nevertheless their movers seem to be moved per accidens, if we follow what he said earlier. For in this latter argument he said that the animal soul is moved per accidens because the animal body is moved as a result of some other motion from an external principle, which motion is not from the soul. Similarly, it appears that the sun is moved by some other motion, as if transferred from the motion of the first orb, with respect to which it is revolved from east to west. However, by that motion it is not moved by its proper mover, but conversely from west to east.

He rejects this objection by saying that to be moved per accidens can be attributed to a thing either with respect to itself or with respect to another, and these are not the same. Therefore, to be moved per accidens can be attributed to the movers of the planets, not such that they themselves are moved per accidens, but such that the orbs moved by them are moved per accidens, which motion is transferred from the motion of the higher orbs. He says that to be moved per accidens by another, that is by reason of another, is present in certain principles of celestial motions insofar as the movers of the orbs are moved by many motions, namely by their proper motion and by the motion of a higher orb. But the other, namely, to be moved per accidens with respect to itself, is found only in corruptible things, that is, in besouled animals.

The reason for this diversity is that the movers of the higher orbs are not constituted in their being by a union to bodies, and their connection is invariable. Therefore, although the bodies of the orbs are moved, their movers are not moved per accidens. But the souls which move animals are constituted in their being by a union to bodies, and they are connected with them in various ways. Therefore, with respect to mutations of bodies, these souls are also said to be changed per accidens.

1083. Next where he says, "And further, if there . . ." [850], he proves that the first motion is eternal. He does this with two arguments, the first of which depends on the foregoing, and is as follows.

Motion which is not eternal is due to a mover which is moved per se or per accidens, as is clear from the above. Since, then, the first mover is immobile and eternal such that it is not moved either per se or per accidens, the first mobile object that is moved by this totally immobile mover must be moved eternally.

It must be noted, however, that above he proved the immobility of the first mover through the eternity of the motion designated above. Here, however, he conversely proves the eternity of motion through the immobility of the first mover. He would be arguing in a circle if he were referring to the same motion.

Hence, it must be said that above he proved the immobility of the first mover from the eternity of motion in general. Therefore, he said that in things which exist there is a certain unceasing and imperishable motion. Here, however, he proves the eternity of the first motion through the immobility of the first mover. From this it is clear that the Commentator is incorrect when he says that above in the beginning of Book VIII Aristotle proved that the first motion is eternal.

1084. He gives the second proof where he says, "Indeed this is clear also . . ." [851]. This argument deals with the eternity of generation.

He says that it is clear that the first motion is eternal because there cannot be generation and corruption and non-temporal mutations unless there is something which moves and is moved. For every mutation results from some mover, as he has already proved above. Therefore, generation and corruption and such mutations must result from some mover.

However, these cannot result immediately from an immobile mover. For an immobile mover will always move the same moved object in the same way since it will not change its disposition and relation to the mobile object. And when the relation of the mover to the mobile object remains the same, the motion will always remain the same. But generation and corruption do not always occur in the same way. Rather at one time a thing is generated, and at another it is corrupted. Hence these do not proceed immediately from an immobile mover, but from a mobile mover. That which is moved by a moved mover, which in turn is moved by an immobile mover, can have a perpetual succession of diverse motions. For since a mobile mover is related in different ways to moved things, it will not always cause the same motion. Rather, because it is in diverse places (if it is moved by local motion) or in diverse species (if it is moved by the motion of alteration), it will cause contrary motions in others, and it will cause a thing to be sometimes moved and sometimes at rest.

He says that it ". . . occupies contrary positions or assumes contrary forms . . ." because he has not yet proven by what species of motion the first mobile object is moved. He will investigate this below.

Therefore, insofar as it is moved, it is the cause of the diversity of motions. But insofar as it is moved by an immobile mover, it is the cause of eternity in this diversity of mutations. Therefore, the eternity of generation shows that the first motion is eternal and is moved by an immobile mover.

It should be understood, however, that these arguments, with which Aristotle strives to prove that the first motion is eternal, do not come to a necessary conclusion. For it may happen, without any mutation of the first mover, that it does not always move, as was shown above at the beginning of Book VIII.

1085. Next where he says, "The foregoing argument . . ." [852], he introduces a conclusion for that which he left unanswered above, namely, why are certain things always moved, while others are not always moved.

He says that the cause of this is clear from the foregoing. For things which are moved by an immobile and eternal mover are always moved. But things which are moved by a moved mover are not always moved. For as was said above, since an immobile mover remains simply and similarly in the same disposition, it will cause a motion that is one and simple.

Local Motion Is the First Motion

The Text of Aristotle
Chapter 7

853. *This matter will be made clearer, however, if we start afresh from another point. We must consider whether it is or is not possible that there should be a continuous motion, and, if it is possible, which motion this is, and which is the primary motion; for it is plain that if there must always be motion, and a particular motion is primary and continuous, then it is this motion that is imparted by the first mover, and so it is necessarily one and the same and continuous and primary.*   **260a20–26**

854. *Now of the three kinds of motion that there are—motion in respect of magnitude, motion in respect of affection, and motion in respect of place—it is this last, which we call locomotion, that must be primary. This may be shown as follows. It is impossible that there should be increase without the previous occurrence of alteration; for that which is increased, although in a sense it is increased by what is like itself, is in a sense increased by what is unlike itself: thus it is said that contrary is nourishment to contrary; but growth is effected only by things becoming like to like. There must be alteration, then, in that there is this change from contrary to contrary. But the fact that a thing is altered requires that there should be something that alters it, something that makes the potentially hot into the actually hot: so it is plain that the mover does not maintain a uniform relation to it but is at one time nearer to and at another farther from that which is altered; and we cannot have this without locomotion. If, therefore, there must always be motion, there must also always be locomotion as the primary motion, and, if there is a primary as distinguished from a secondary form of locomotion, it must be the primary form.*   **260a26–260b7**

855. *Again, all affections have their origin in condensation and rarefaction: thus heavy and light, soft and hard, hot and cold, are considered to be forms of density and rarity. But condensation and rarefaction are nothing more than combination and separation, processes in accordance with which substances are said to become and perish; and in being combined and separated things must change in respect of place. And further, when a thing is increased or decreased its magnitude changes in respect of place.*   **260b7–15**

856. *Again, there is another point of view from which it will be clearly seen that locomotion is primary. As in the case of other things so too in the case of motion the word "primary" may be used in several senses. A thing is said to be prior to other things when, if it does not exist, the others will not exist, whereas it can exist without the others; and there is also priority in time and priority in perfection of existence. Let us begin, then, with the first sense.*   **260b15–19**

857. *Now there must be motion continuously, and there may be continuously either continuous motion or successive motion, the former, however, in a higher degree than the latter; moreover it is better that it should be continuous rather than successive motion, and we always assume the presence in nature of the better, if it be possible: since, then, continuous motion is possible (this will be proved later: for the present let us take it for granted), and no other motion can be continuous except locomotion, locomotion must be primary. For there is no necessity for the subject of locomotion to be the subject either of increase or of alteration, nor need it become or perish; on the other hand there cannot be any one of these processes without the existence of the continuous motion imparted by the first mover.*   **260b19–29**

858. *Secondly, locomotion must be primary in time; for this is the only motion possible for eternal things.*   **260b29–30**

859. *It is true indeed that, in the case of any individual thing that has a becoming,*

locomotion must be the last of its motions; for after its becoming it first experiences alteration and increase, and locomotion is a motion that belongs to such things only when they are perfected. But there must previously be something else that is in process of locomotion to be the cause even of the becoming of things that become, without itself being in process of becoming, as e.g., the begotten is preceded by what begot it; otherwise becoming might be thought to be the primary motion on the ground that the thing must first become. But though this is so in the case of any individual thing that becomes, nevertheless before anything becomes, something else must be in motion, not itself becoming but being, and before this there must again be something else. And since becoming cannot be primary—for, if it were, everything that is in motion would be perishable—it is plain that no one of the motions next in order can be prior to locomotion. By the motions next in order I mean increase and then alteration, decrease, and perishing. All these are posterior to becoming; consequently, if not even becoming is prior to locomotion, then no one of the other processes of change is so either.	260b30–261a12

860. *Thirdly, that which is in process of becoming appears universally as something imperfect and proceeding to a first principle; and so what is posterior in the order of becoming is prior in the order of nature. Now all things that go through the process of becoming acquire locomotion last. It is this that accounts for the fact that some living things, e.g., plants and many kinds of animals, owing to lack of the requisite organ, are entirely without motion, whereas others acquire it in the course of their being perfected. Therefore, if the degree in which things possess locomotion corresponds to the degree in which they have realized their natural development, then this motion must be prior to all others in respect of perfection of existence;*	261a12–19

861. *and not only for this reason but also because a thing that is in motion loses its essential character less in the process of locomotion than in any other kind of motion: it is the only motion that does not involve a change of being in the sense in which there is a change in quality when a thing is altered and a change in quantity when a thing is increased or decreased.*	261a19–23

862. *Above all it is plain that this motion, motion in respect of place, is what is in the strictest sense produced by that which moves itself; but it is the self-mover that we declare to be the first principle of things that are moved and impart motion and the primary source to which things that are in motion are to be referred.*

It is clear, then, from the foregoing arguments that locomotion is the primary motion.	261a23–28

COMMENTARY OF ST. THOMAS

1086. After the Philosopher has shown that the first mover is immobile and the first motion is eternal, he begins here to show what the first motion is and what the nature of the first mover is.

This discussion is divided into two parts. First he shows what the first motion is. Secondly, where he says, "We have now to assert..." [901], he shows what the nature of the first mover is.

Concerning the first part he makes two points. First he states his intention. Secondly, where he says, "Now of the three..." [854], he develops his position.

He says, therefore, first that in order that the foregoing may be more certain it is necessary to make a new beginning and to consider whether there is some motion which happens to be infinitely continuous, and if there is such a motion, what is it and is it the first motion.

But someone might think that the first motion is not a motion which is continuous. To reject this he adds that since motion must be eternal, and since the first motion is eternally continuous because it is caused by a first immobile mover, it is clearly necessary that that motion which is eternally continuous must be the same as the first motion.

1087. Next where he says, **"Now of the three..."** [854], he proves his position, first by means of arguments, and secondly by means of the statements of the ancients, where he says, **"As to locomotion being the primary..."** [899].

Concerning the first part he makes two points. First he shows that local motion is first. Secondly, where he says, **"We have now to show..."** [863], he shows which local motion is first.

He establishes the first point in three ways; first by means of the properties of motions; secondly, by means of the distinction of prior and posterior, where he says, **"Again, there is another . . ."** [856], and thirdly, by means of the order of mobile objects, where he says, **"Above all it is plain..."** [862].

1088. In regard to the first part he gives two proofs, the first of which proceeds as follows.

First he states his intention. He says that there are three species of motion; one with respect to quantity, which is called the motion of increase and decrease; another with respect to passive quality, which is called alteration; and the third with respect to place, which is called local motion. Of these three local motion must be first.

Secondly he proves this as follows. It is impossible for increase to be the first motion.

For increase cannot exist unless alteration pre-exists. For that by which a thing is increased is in a way similar and in a way dissimilar. It is clear that it is dissimilar, for that by which a thing is increased is nourishment, which in the beginning is contrary to that which is nourished because of its different disposition. But when it is added such that it causes an increase, it must be similar. Only through alteration does a thing pass from dissimilarity to similarity. Therefore, before an increase there must exist an alteration through which nourishment is changed from one contrary disposition to another.

Thirdly he shows that local motion precedes every alteration. For if a thing is altered, there must be an alterer which makes that which is potentially hot to be actually hot. If, however, this alterer were always at the same distance from that which is altered, it would not make it hot now rather than before. It is clear, therefore, that in alteration the mover does not remain at the same distance from that which is altered. Rather at one time it is nearer, and at another it is further away. This cannot occur without local motion. Therefore, if motion must be eternal, then local motion must be eternal since it is the first of motions. And if among local motions one is prior to the others, and if the foregoing is true, then the first local motion must be eternal.

1089. He gives the second argument where he says, **"Again, all affections..."** [855]. The argument is as follows.

As was established in Book VII, alterations occur with respect to passions or passive qualities. According to the opinion of the ancients, the first of these seems to be density and rarity, since both heavy and light, and soft and hard, and warm and cold seem to follow from rarity and density and to be distinguished with respect to them (for among the elements, heavy and cold are found to be dense, and warm and light are found to be rare). And this is in a way true, if the order of the passions is based on their nearness to the material principle. For the rare and the dense especially seem to pertain to matter, as is clear from what was said in Book IV. Moreover, density and rarity seem to be a kind of union and separation. And it was precisely in virtue of this union and separation that the ancient philosophers held that the generation and corruption of substances occur. He now uses this opinion as probable before he establishes the truth about generation and corruption in De Generatione. Things which are united and separated seem from this very fact to be changed with respect to place. Hence, local motion is the principle of alteration.

It should be noted that the union and separation of actually existing bodies pertains to local motion. But the union and separation with respect to which the same matter is contained under large or small dimensions does not pertain to local motion, but to the motion of alteration. And it is in respect to this that in Book IV Aristotle established the nature [ratio] of the rare and the dense. But here he is speaking of what is probable according to the opinion of other philosophers.

Moreover, just as local motion is required for alteration, so also is it required for increase. The magnitude of that which is increased or decreased must be changed with respect to place. For that which is increased expands into a larger place, and that which is decreased is contracted into a smaller one. Therefore, it is clear that local mo-

tion is naturally prior to both alteration and increase.

1090. Next where he says, **"Again there is another . . ."** [856], he proves the same thing by distinguishing the modes of the prior and the posterior.

He says that it will be clear from this consideration that local motion is the first among motions. For just as in other cases a thing is said to be prior to another in many ways, this is also true of motion.

In one way a thing is said to be prior such that if it does not exist, the others will not exist, yet it can exist without the others. For example, one is prior to two, since two cannot be unless one is, but one can be if two do not exist. Secondly, a thing is said to be prior in time, for example, that which is further removed in the past from the present now, or nearer in the future, as was said in Book IV. Thirdly, a thing is said to be prior with respect to substance, that is, with respect to the completion of substance, as act is prior to potency and the perfect to the imperfect.

1091. Secondly, where he says, **"Now there must be motion . . ."** [857], he proves that local motion is first in the three ways mentioned above. First he discusses the first way; secondly, the second way, where he says, **"Secondly, locomotion . . ."** [858], and thirdly, the third way, where he says, **"Thirdly, that which is . . ."** [860].

He says, therefore, first that since motion must be eternal, as was proven above, this may be understood in two ways. First there may be some continuous motion; secondly, it may be that motions are consecutively related such that between them there is no intermediate. The eternity of motion is better preserved, however, if motion is continuous. Furthermore, it is more fitting for it to be continuous rather than consecutive because it would then have more of the nature [ratio] of unity and eternity. We ought always to accept what is more fitting in nature, if it is possible. It is possible, moreover, for motion to be infinitely continuous, but this is true only of local motion. This at present we assume; it will be proven later. From this it appears to be necessary to admit that local motion is first.

For the other motions are not required for local motion. It is not necessary that what is changed with respect to place be either increased or altered, for it is not necessary that a body which is moved with respect to place be generated or corrupted. But increase and alteration have place only in those things which are generated and corrupted. But none of these motions occurs unless there is that eternal motion which the first mover moves, and which we said could only be local motion. Therefore, local motion can occur without the others, but not vice versa. Hence local motion is first according to the first mode of priority.

1092. Next where he says, **"Secondly, locomotion . . ."** [858], he proves that it is prior in time.

Concerning this he makes two points. First he shows that, simply speaking, it is prior in time. For that which is eternal, simply speaking, is prior in time to that which is not eternal. Only local motion, however, happens to be eternal, as has been said. Hence, simply speaking, it is first in time.

1093. Secondly, where he says, **"It is true indeed that . . ."** [859], he rejects a certain objection which seems to contradict this. If we consider a new-ly-generated body, local motion is the last in time among all its motions. For it is first generated, afterwards it is altered and increased, and finally it has motion with respect to place when it has been perfected, as is clear in man and in many animals.

But this does not disprove that local motion is absolutely first in time. For before all the motions which occur in that which is generated, some local motion must have preceded in some prior mobile object which is the cause of generation in things which are generated, just as the generator is the cause of that which is generated even though it itself is not generated.

And he shows that the motion preceding generation is local motion and that it is absolutely the first of motions. He says that generation seems to be the first motion in things which are generated because a thing must come to be before it is moved. And this is true of whatever is generated. Nevertheless there must be some moved thing prior to things which are generated, which itself has not been generated. Or, if it has been generated, there must be another prior to it. Hence, either there must be an infinite series, which is impossible, as was shown above, or there must be a first.

But it is impossible for generation to be first. For then it would follow that all things which are moved are corruptible, for whatever is generable is corruptible. Hence, if the first mobile object is generated, it follows that it is corruptible, and consequently so are all other mobile objects. And if generation is not absolutely first, it is clear that none of the consequent motions can be absolutely first. By "consequent motions" I mean increase, alteration, decrease, and finally, corruption, all of which motions follow generation in time. Hence, if generation is not prior to local motion, it follows that none of the other mutations can be absolutely prior to local motion. And so, since there must be something which is absolutely first, it follows that local motion is first.

1094. Next where he says, **"Thirdly, that which is . . ."** [860], he proves that local motion is first in perfection. He proves this in two ways.

The first is as follows. Everything which comes to be, while it is becoming, is imperfect and tends toward its principle, that is, it tends to become like the principle of its own origin, which is naturally first. From this it is clear that that which is posterior in generation is prior with respect to nature. But in the process of generation in all generable things local motion is found to be last, not only in the same thing, but also in the total progress of the nature of generable things. Among these, certain living things are totally immobile with respect to place because they lack organs, for example, plants, which do not have the organs of progressive motion, and likewise many genera of animals. But local motion is present in perfect animals. Therefore, if local motion is present in things which better embrace nature, that is, which achieve a more perfect nature, it follows that local motion is

first of all motions with respect to the perfection of substance.

1095. Secondly, where he says, **". . . but also because a thing . . ."** [861], he shows the same thing as follows.

Insofar as a motion removes less from a mobile object, its subject is to that extent more perfect, and even the motion itself is in a way more perfect. But only in local motion is there nothing removed from the mobile object. For in alteration there is a mutation with respect to quality, and in increase and decrease there is a mutation with respect to quantity, which are in the subject. The mutation of generation and corruption occurs with respect to the form which determines the substance of the object. Local motion occurs only with respect to place, which it contains externally. Hence it follows that local motion is the most perfect.

1096. Next where he says, **"Above all it is plain . . ."** [862], he proves by means of the mobile object that local motion is first.

It is clear that a self-mover most properly moves itself with respect to local motion. Since, therefore, a self-mover is the principle of other movers and mobile objects, and consequently is first among all things which are moved, it follows that local motion, which is proper to it, is first among all motions.

Therefore, he concludes from the foregoing that local motion is the first among all motions.

LECTURE 15 [261a28–b26]
Only Local Motion Can be Continuous and Eternal

The Text of Aristotle

863. *We have now to show which kind of locomotion is primary. The same process of reasoning will also make clear at the same time the truth of the assumption we have made both now and at a previous stage that it is possible that there should be a motion that is continuous and eternal. Now it is clear from the following considerations that no other than locomotion can be continuous.* 261a28–32

864. *Every other motion and change is from an opposite to an opposite: thus for the processes of becoming and perishing the limits are the existent and the non-existent, for alteration the various pairs of contrary affections, and for increase and decrease either greatness and smallness or perfection and imperfection of magnitude; and changes to the respective contraries are contrary changes. Now a thing that is undergoing any particular kind of motion, but though previously existent has not always undergone it, must previously have been at rest so far as that motion is concerned. It is clear, then, that for the changing thing the contraries will be states of rest.* 261a32–261b3

865. *And we have a similar result in the case of changes that are not motions; for becoming and perishing, whether regarded simply as such without qualification or as affecting something in particular, are opposites: therefore provided it is impossible for a thing to undergo opposite changes at the same time, the change will not be continuous, but a period of time will intervene between the opposite processes.* 261b3–7

866. *The question whether these contradictory changes are contraries or not makes no difference, provided only it is impossible for them both to be present to the same thing at the same time: the point is of no importance to the argument.* 261b7–10

867. *Nor does it matter if the thing need not rest in the contradictory state, or if there is no state of rest as a contrary to the process of change: it may be true that the non-existent is not at rest, and that perishing is a process to the non-existent. All that matters is the intervention of a time: it is this that prevents the change from being continuous; so, too, in our previous instances the important thing was not the relation of contrariety but the impossibility of the two processes being present to a thing at the same time.* 261b10–15

868. *And there is no need to be disturbed by the fact that on this showing there may be more than one contrary to the same thing, that a particular motion will be contrary both to rest and to motion in the contrary direction. We have only to grasp the fact that a particular motion is in a sense the opposite both of a state of rest and of the contrary motion, in the same way as that which is of equal or standard measure is the opposite both of that which surpasses it and of that which it surpasses, and that it is impossible for the opposite motions or changes to be present to a thing at the same time.* 261b15–22

869. *Furthermore, in the case of becoming and perishing it would seem to be an utterly absurd thing if as soon as anything has become it must necessarily perish and cannot continue to exist for any time; and, if this is true of becoming and perishing, we have fair grounds for inferring the same to be true of the other kinds of change, since it would be in the natural order of things that they should be uniform in this respect.* 261b22–26

COMMENTARY OF ST. THOMAS

1097. After the Philosopher has shown that local motion is the first among all motions, he shows here which local motion is first.

And since, as was said above, the first motion must be continuous, this discussion is divided into two parts. First he shows which motion can be always continuous. Secondly, where he says, **"It can now be shown . . ."** [894], he shows that that motion is first.

The first part is divided into three parts. First he shows that only local motion can be continuous. Secondly, where he says, **"Let us now proceed . . ."** [870], he shows that no local motion other than circular motion can be continuous. Thirdly, where he says, **"On the other hand . . ."** [890], he shows that circular motion is continuous.

Concerning the first part he makes two points. First he states his intention. Secondly, where he says, **"Every other motion . . ."** [864], he proves his position.

He says, therefore, first [863] that since it has been shown that local motion is the first among all the species of motion, it must now be shown which local motion is first. For, as was explained in Book VII, there are many species of local motion.

And the same method, that is, the same consideration, will also clarify what we have just said and what we have previously assumed at the beginning of Book VIII; namely, there is a motion which is continuous and eternal. For the first motion and continuous motion must be the same, as was shown above. Therefore, both of them fall within the same consideration. Hence, from what will be said it is clear that no species of motion other than local motion can be continuous and eternal.

1098. Next where he says, **"Every other motion . . ."** [864], he proves his position.

Concerning this he makes two points. First he shows that no species of motion other than local motion can be continuous and perpetual, existing as one and the same. Secondly, where he says, **"Furthermore, in the case . . ."** [869], he shows that no two opposed mutations can succeed each other without an intervening state of rest.

Concerning the first part he makes two points. First he proves his position. Secondly, where he says, **"The question whether . . ."** [866], he refutes objections.

Concerning the first part he makes two points. He proves his position first in regard to motions, and secondly in regard to mutations, where he says, **"And we have a similar . . ."** [865].

He proposes, therefore, first a proposition which is commonly true of both motion and mutation; namely, every motion and mutation is from an opposite to an opposite. But local motion is in a certain way excluded from this general truth, as was said at the end of Book VI. For generation and corruption, which are mutations, have as their termini being and non-being. The opposed termini of alteration are contrary passions, that is, passive qualities, like hot and cold, white and black. The opposed termini of increase and decrease are the great and the small, or the perfect and the imperfect in magnitude or quantity.

It is clear, moreover, from what was said in Book V, that motions to contraries are contraries. Therefore, the contrary of a motion to white is a motion to black. But contraries cannot exist together. Hence, while a thing is being moved to white, it is not at the same time being moved to black. What begins to be moved from white to black by a motion of blackening, even though it was moved by a whitening motion while it was becoming white, clearly cannot be moved at the same time by a blackening motion. However, that which existed previously, but was not always moved by some determined motion, must be said to have been previously at rest with a rest opposed to this motion. For everything which can be moved naturally is either at rest or in motion. It is clear, then, that that which is moved to a contrary was at one time at rest with a rest opposed to such a motion. Therefore, no motion which is to a contrary can be continuous and eternal.

If to this conclusion is added what was stated at the beginning, namely, every motion of alteration or of increase or of decrease is to some contrary, it will follow that no such motion can be continuous and eternal.

1099. Next where he says, **"And we have a similar..."** [865], he shows that the same is true of mutations, that is, of generation and corruption. For generation and corruption are opposed both universally in respect to the common opposition of being and non-being and singularly, for example, the generation of fire is opposed to the corruption of fire in respect to the opposition of its being and non-being.

Hence, if it is impossible for opposed mutations to exist together, it follows that no mutation can be continuous and eternal, just as was said above about motions. It is necessary, therefore, for an intermediate time in which there is corruption to be interposed between two generations of the same thing. And likewise between corruptions there is a time of generation.

1100. Next where he says, **"The question whether..."** [866], he refutes three objections. The first is that someone might say that mutations are opposed according to the opposition of their termini. But the termini of gener-

ation and corruption are not contraries, but contradictories. Hence, it seems to follow that generation and corruption are not contraries. And thus the same argument cannot be applied to them and to motions which are contraries.

He answers this objection by saying that it makes no difference whether or not mutations which differ according to contradictory termini are contraries. It must only be true that it is impossible for them both to be in the same thing at the same time. Whether or not they are contraries is irrelevant to the argument.

1101. He refutes the second objection where he says, **"Nor does it matter..."** [867].

Someone may say that what is not always moved must be previously at rest, because motion is opposed to rest. But this does not apply to the mutations of generation and corruption to which, properly speaking, rest is not opposed, as was said in Book V.

He answers this objection by saying that it makes no difference in the argument if it is not necessary for there to be rest in one of the contradictory termini. Nor does it make any difference if mutation is not opposed to rest (for, perhaps, that which does not exist cannot be at rest: corruption, however, is to non-being: and so it seems that there cannot be rest in the terminus of corruption). It is sufficient for the proof if it is true that there is an intermediate time between two generations or between two corruptions. For then it follows that neither of these mutations is continuous.

After this he returns to the first objection and says that it does not matter with respect to contradictory mutations whether they be contraries or not. For not even in the earlier discussion about motions did it matter whether there is contrariety in them but only that they do not exist together. This is not peculiar to contraries, but it is common to all opposites.

1102. He refutes the third objection where he says, "**And there is no need . . .**" [868].

He has said above that motions to contraries are contraries. Since, then, motion is contrary to rest, it seems to follow that one thing has two contraries, which is impossible, as was proven in Metaphysics, X.

In rejecting this he says that there is no need to be disturbed because it seems to follow that the same thing is contrary to many, namely, motion is contrary to both rest and to the contrary motion. But we need to realize that one contrary motion is in a way opposed both to its contrary motion and to rest—to the contrary motion according to direct contrariety, but to rest according to the opposition of privation. This latter shares in contrariety insofar as the opposed rest is the end and the completion of the contrary motion. For example, the equal and the commensurable is in a way opposed both to that which excels and to that which is excelled, or to the great and the small, to which it is opposed in respect to the privation, as is clear in Metaphysics, X. And again it is necessary to realize that opposite motions and opposite mutations do not occur together.

1103. Next where he says, "**Furthermore, in the case . . .**" [869], he shows that not only between two motions or mutations of the same species must there be an intermediate time, and that no one mutation which is to an opposite can be eternal and continuous, but also it is impossible for opposed motions or mutations to so succeed themselves that there is no intervening time. For it seems to be completely inconsistent with generation and corruption to say that when a thing has come to be and the generation has been completed, then corruption must begin at once and that what has been generated does not remain for any period of time. For a thing would be generated in vain unless that which is generated remains in existence.

From these mutations conclusions about the others can be drawn. For since nature always operates in the same way, it is natural for the other cases to be the same. And just as it seems to be inconsistent that what is generated immediately is corrupted as soon as it is generated, so it seems to be inconsistent that as soon as a white thing has been made white, it begins to become black, and what is increased immediately begins to decrease. For in all these cases the purpose of nature would be frustrated.

No Local Motion Other Than Circular Motion Can Be Continuous and Eternal

The Text of Aristotle
Chapter 8

870. *Let us now proceed to maintain that it is possible that there should be an infinite motion that is single and continuous, and that this motion is rotatory motion.*   **261b27–28**

871. *The motion of everything that is in process of locomotion is either rotatory or rectilinear or a compound of the two: consequently, if one of the former two is not continuous, that which is composed of them both cannot be continuous either.*   **261b28–31**

872. *Now it is plain that if the locomotion of a thing is rectilinear and finite it is not continuous locomotion; for the thing must turn back, and that which turns back in a straight line undergoes two contrary locomotions, since, so far as motion in respect of place is concerned, upward motion is the contrary of downward motion, forward motion of backward motion, and motion to the left of motion to the right, these being the pairs of contraries in the sphere of place. But we have already defined single and continuous motion to be motion of a single thing in a single period of time and operating within a sphere admitting of no further specific differentiation (for we have three things to consider, first that which is in motion, e.g., a man or a god, secondly the "when" of the motion, that is to say, the time, and thirdly the sphere within which it operates, which may be either place or affection or essential form or magnitude): and contraries are specifically not one and the same but distinct; and within the sphere of place we have the above-mentioned distinctions. Moreover we have an indication that motion from A to B is the contrary of motion from B to A in the fact that, if they occur at the same time, they arrest and stop each other. And the same is true in the case of a circle: the motion from A towards B is the contrary of the motion from A towards C; for even if they are continuous and there is no turning back they arrest each other, because contraries annihilate or obstruct one another. On the other hand lateral motion is not the contrary of upward motion.*

          261b31–262a12

873. *But what shows most clearly that rectilinear motion cannot be continuous is the fact that turning back necessarily implies coming to a stand, not only when it is a straight line that is traversed, but also in the case of locomotion in a circle (which is not the same thing as rotatory locomotion; for, when a thing merely traverses a circle, it may either proceed on its course without a break or turn back again when it has reached the same point from which it started). We may assure ourselves of the necessity of this coming to a stand not only on the strength of observation, but also on theoretical grounds. We may start as follows: we have three points, starting-point, middle-point, and finishing-point, of which the middle-point in virtue of the relations in which it stands severally to the other two is both a starting-point and a finishing-point, and though numerically one is theoretically two. We have further the distinction between the potential and the actual. So in the straight line in question any one of the points lying between the two extremes is potentially a middle-point; but it is not actually so unless that which is in motion divides the line by coming to a stand at that point and beginning its motion again: thus the middle-point becomes both a starting-point and a goal, the starting-point of the latter part and the finishing-point of the first part of the motion. This is the case e.g. when A in the course of its locomotion comes to a stand at B and starts again towards C; but when its motion is continuous A cannot either have come to be or have ceased to be at the point B: it can only have been there at the moment of passing, its passage not being contained within any period of time except the whole of which the particular moment is a dividing-point.*

To maintain that it has come to be and ceased to be there will involve the consequence that A in the course of its locomotion will always be coming to a stand; for it is impossible that A should simultaneously have come to be at B and ceased to be there, so that the two things must have happened at different points of time, and therefore there will be the intervening period of time: consequently A will be in a state of rest at B, and similarly at all other points, since the same reasoning holds good in every case. When to A, that which is in process of locomotion, B, the middle-point, serves both as a finishing-point and as a starting-point for its motion, A must come to a stand at B, because it makes it two just as one might do in thought. However, the point A is the real starting-point at which the moving body has ceased to be, and it is at C that it has really come to be when its course is finished and it comes to a stand.   **262a12–262b8**

COMMENTARY OF ST. THOMAS

1104. After the Philosopher has shown that no mutation can be continuous and eternal except local motion, he shows here that no local motion can be continuous and eternal except circular motion.

Concerning this he makes two points. First he proves his position demonstratively, and secondly, he proves it logically, where he says, **"If we look . . ."** [884].

Concerning the first part he makes two points. First he proves his position. Secondly, where he says, **"So this is how . . ."** [874], he answers certain objections by means of the truth he has demonstrated.

Concerning the first part he makes three points. First he states his principal intention. He intends to show that it is possible for a certain motion, existing as one, to be infinitely continuous, and this motion is circular motion. He proves the latter point first.

1105. Second, where he says, **"The motion of everything . . ."** [871], he explains what procedure must be used.

Everything which is moved locally is moved either by a circular motion, or by a straight motion, or by a motion composed of both, as when something is moved through a chord and an arc. It is clear that if one of the two simple motions, namely, either circular or straight motion, cannot be infinitely continuous, then much less will that which is composed of both be infinitely continuous. Hence it is permissible to omit composite motions and discuss simple ones.

1106. Thirdly, where he says, **"Now it is plain . . ."** [872], he shows that straight motion through a straight and finite magnitude cannot be infinitely continuous. And thus no straight, continuous motion can be infinite unless an actually infinite magnitude is granted. But this was rejected above in Book III.

He proves this with two arguments, the first of which is as follows.

If there is an infinite motion over a straight and finite magnitude, this must be a reflex motion. For it was shown in Book VI that a thing passes over a finite magnitude in a finite time. Therefore, when it arrives at the end of the finite magnitude, the motion will cease unless the mobile object is returned by a reflex motion to the beginning of the magnitude from which its motion began. But that which is reflected in a straight motion is moved by contrary motions. He proves this as follows.

Contrary motions are those which have contrary termini, as was proven in Book V. But the contrarieties of place are up and down, before and behind, right and left. Everything which is reflected must be reflected in respect to one of these contrarieties. Hence whatever is reflected is moved by contrary motions.

Moreover, it was shown above in Book V which motion is one and continuous, namely, that which is of one subject, and in one time, and in the same thing which does not differ in species. For three things are involved in every motion: the first is the time; the second is the subject which is moved, for example, a man or a god, according to those who call celestial bodies gods; and the third is that in which the motion occurs, which, of course, in local motion is place; in alteration, passion, that is, passive quality; in generation and corruption, species; in increase and decrease, magnitude.

It is also clear that contraries differ according to species. Hence, contrary motions cannot be one and continuous. Moreover, as was said, there are six differentiae of place. Hence, they must be contraries, because the differentiae of any genus are contraries. Therefore it follows that it is impossible for that which is reflected to be moved by one, continuous motion.

1107. But someone might question whether that which is reflected is moved by contrary motions. For contrariety in place does not appear to be as clear and determined as in the other genera in which there is motion, as was said above in Book V. Hence, over and above the argument just given which deals with the contrariety of the termini, he adds an example to prove the same thing.

He says that an example of this is that motion from A to B is contrary to

motion from B to A, as occurs in reflex motion. For if such motions occur at the same time, they arrest and stop each other, that is, one impedes the other and causes it to stop.

This occurs in both reflex straight motion and reflex circular motion. Let A B C be three signs on a circle. It is clear that if a motion starting from A toward B later becomes a motion from A to C in the other direction, this will be a reflex motion. And these two motions impede each other, and the one arrests the other, that is, it causes it to stop. But there will not be reflex motion if a thing is moved continuously from A to B and through B to C.

Therefore, both circular and straight reflex motions impede each other. For contraries naturally impede and destroy each other.

But motions which are diverse and are not contraries do not impede each other. For example, upward motion and lateral motion, either to the right or to the left, do not impede each other. Rather a thing can be moved upward and to the right at the same time.

1108. Next where he says, **"But what shows..."** [873], he gives the second argument to show that reflex motion cannot be infinitely continuous. This argument deals with the state of rest which must intervene.

He says that it is particularly clear that straight motion cannot be infinitely continuous because of the fact that whatever is reflected must be at rest between the two motions. And this is true not only if it is moved through a straight line, but also if it is moved through a circle.

But someone might think that "being moved through a circle" means the same thing as "being moved circularly." To reject this he adds that "being moved circularly," that is, in respect to the property of a circle, is not the same as "being moved through a circle," that is, going through a circle by one's own motion.

For it sometimes happens that the motion of that which is moved is continuous while it goes through part after part according to the order of the parts of a circle. This is "being moved circularly."

But sometimes, when that which goes through a circle comes to the starting-point of its motion, it does not continue on according to the order of the parts of a circle, but goes back in the other direction. This is reflex motion.

And so, whether the reflex motion is in a straight line or in a circular line, an intermediate state of rest must intervene.

1109. The truth of this point may be established not only from sensation, since it is apparent to the senses, but also from reason.

A principle that must be granted for this argument is that there are three things in the magnitude which is crossed; namely, the beginning, the middle, and the end. Now the middle is both a beginning and an end. For with respect to the end, it is a beginning, and with respect to the beginning, it is an end. Thus, although it is one in subject, it is two in reason [ratio]. Another principle that must be granted is the distinction between that which is in potency and that which is in act.

Granting these points, it should be realized from what has been said that any sign, that is, any designated point between the termini of a line over which something is moved, is potentially a middle. It is not actually a middle unless the motion divides the line such that that which is moved stops at

that point and then begins to be moved from that point. Then this middle becomes actually a beginning and an end. It is the beginning of the subsequent motion insofar as the motion begins again; and it is the end of the first motion insofar as the first motion was terminated by rest. Take a line the beginning of which is A, the midpoint B, and the end C. Let a motion from A to B stop at B. And then let the motion begin again from B up to C. It is obvious that B is actually the end of the prior motion and the beginning of the subsequent motion.

But if a thing is moved continuously from A to C without any intervening rest, it is not possible to say that this mobile object has either arrived at or left from the point which is A or the point which is B. It can only be said that it is at A or at B in some "now." (It cannot be said to be there in some time, unless perhaps a thing is said to be somewhere in time because it is there in a "now" of time. Hence, that which is moved continuously in some time from A to C will be at B in a "now," which is a division of that time. And thus it is said to be at B in that whole time according to that manner of speaking in which a thing is said to be moved in a day because it is moved in a part of that day.)

But there seems to be difficulty in saying that that which is moved is not present in or absent from any point in a designated magnitude which is crossed by a continuous motion. Hence to explain this, he says that if one were to concede that a mobile object is present in and absent from some point in a designated magnitude, it follows that it is at rest there. For it is impossible for the mobile object to be present in and absent from B at the same instant. For to be present and to be absent somewhere are contraries, and these cannot exist at the same instant.

Therefore, the mobile object must be present in and absent from a point in the magnitude in different "nows" of time. But between any two "nows" there is an intermediary time. It follows, therefore, that the mobile object A is at rest at B. For everything which is somewhere during some time is in the same place before and after. And the same thing may be said of all other signs or points, for the same argument applies to all.

Hence it is clear that that which is moved continuously through a magnitude is not present and absent, that is, it does not arrive and leave, at any intermediate point of the magnitude. For when it is said that a mobile object is present at some point, or comes to be there, or arrives there, all such expressions signify that that point is the terminus of the motion.

And to say that it is absent from or leaving is to signify the beginning of a motion. The middle point of a magnitude is not actually either the beginning or the end of a motion, since the motion does not begin or end there except potentially (for the motion can begin or end there). Hence, the mobile object is neither present nor absent at a middle point, but is simply said to be there at a "now." For the existence of a mobile object at some point of a magnitude is related to the total motion as the "now" is related to time.

1110. But when the mobile object A uses B as a mid-point and as actually a beginning and an end, it must stop there. For by moving and stopping, it makes the one point two, namely, beginning and end, as occurs also in understanding. For at the same time we can understand one point as one in a subject. But if we understand it separately as a beginning and separately as an end, this does not occur at the same time. In the same way when that which is moved uses a sign as one, it will not be there except in one "now." But if it uses it as two, that is, as an actual beginning and end, it will necessarily be there in two "nows," and consequently in an intermediate time. Therefore, it is at rest.

It is clear, then, that what is moved continuously from A to C was never present or absent, that is, it never arrived at or left, at the midpoint B. Rather it left or departed from the first point A, as if from an actual beginning. And at the last point C it arrived or is present, for the motion is completed there and the mobile object is at rest.

It should be noted that in the foregoing "A" is sometimes assumed to be the mobile object and sometimes the beginning of the magnitude.

1111. From this it is clear that reflex motion, either in a circular or in a straight magnitude, cannot be continuous. Rather a state of rest intervenes. For the same point is actually the end of the first motion and the beginning of the reflex motion. But in circular motion the mobile object does not use any point as an actual beginning or end, but uses every point of the magnitude as a mid-point. Therefore, circular motion can be continuous, but reflex motion cannot.

LECTURE 17 [262b10–264a7]
From the Foregoing Certain Difficulties Are Answered

The Text of Aristotle

874. *So this is how we must meet the difficulty that then arises, which is as follows. Suppose the line E is equal to the line F, that A proceeds in continuous locomotion from the extreme point of E to C, and that, at the moment when A is at the point B, D is proceeding in uniform locomotion and with the same velocity as A from the extremity of F to G: then, says the argument, D will have reached G before A has reached C; for that which makes an earlier start and departure must make an earlier arrival: the reason, then, for the late arrival of A is that it has not simultaneously come to be and ceased to be at B: otherwise it will not arrive later: for this to happen it will be necessary that it should come to a stand there.* 262b8–15

875. *Therefore we must not hold that there was a moment when A came to be at B and that at the same moment D was in motion from the extremity of F; for the fact of A's having come to be at B will involve the fact of its also ceasing to be there and the two events will not be simultaneous, whereas the truth is that A is at B at a sectional point of time and does not occupy time there. In this case, therefore, where the motion of a thing is continuous, it is impossible to use this form of expression. On the other hand in the case of a thing that turns back in its course we must do so. For suppose G in the course of its locomotion proceeds to D and then turns back and proceeds downwards again: then the extreme point D has served as finishing-point and as starting-point for it, one point thus serving as two: therefore G must have come to a stand here; it cannot have come to be at D and departed from D simultaneously, for in that case it would simultaneously be there and not be there at the same moment. And here we cannot apply the argument used to solve the difficulty stated above: we cannot argue that G is at D at a sectional point of time and has not come to be or ceased to be there. For here the goal that is reached is necessarily one that is actually, not potentially, existent. Now the point in the middle is potential; but this one is actual, and regarded from below it is a finishing-point, while regarded from above it is a starting-point, so that it stands in these same two respective relations to the two motions. Therefore that which turns back in traversing a rectilinear course must in so doing come to a stand. Consequently there cannot be a continuous rectilinear motion that is eternal.* 262b15–263a3

876. *The same method should also be adopted in replying to those who ask, in the terms of Zeno's argument, whether we admit that before any distance can be traversed half the distance must be traversed, that these half-distances are infinite in number, and that it is impossible to traverse distances infinite in number—or some on the lines of this same argument put the questions in another form, and would have us grant that in the time during which a motion is in progress it should be possible to reckon a half-motion before the whole for every half-distance that we get, so that we have the result that when the whole distance is traversed we have reckoned an infinite number, which is admittedly impossible.* 263a3–11

877. *Now when we first discussed the question of motion we put forward a solution of this difficulty turning on the fact that the period of time occupied in traversing the distance contains within itself an infinite number of units: there is no absurdity, we said, in supposing the traversing of infinite distances in infinite time, and the element of infinity is present in the time no less than in the distance.* 263a11–15

878. *But, although this solution is adequate as a reply to the questioner (the question asked being whether it is possible in a finite time to traverse or reckon an infinite number of units), nevertheless as an account of the fact and explanation of its true nature it is inadequate. For suppose the distance to be left out of account and the question asked to be no longer whether it is*

*possible in a finite time to traverse an infinite number of distances, and suppose that the inquiry
is made to refer to the time taken by itself (for the time contains an infinite number of divisions):
then this solution will no longer be adequate,* **263a15–22**

879. *and we must apply the truth that we enunciated in our recent discussion, stating it in
the following way. In the act of dividing the continuous distance into two halves one point is
treated as two, since we make it a starting-point and a finishing-point; and this same result is
also produced by the act of reckoning halves as well as by the act of dividing into halves. But if
divisions are made in this way, neither the distance nor the motion will be continuous; for
motion if it is to be continuous must relate to what is continuous; and though what is
continuous contains an infinite number of halves, they are not actual but potential halves. If the
halves are made actual, we shall get not a continuous but an intermittent motion. In the case of
reckoning the halves, it is clear that this result follows; for then one point must be reckoned as
two: it will be the finishing-point of the one half and the starting-point of the other, if we reckon
not the one continuous whole but the two halves. Therefore to the question whether it is possible
to pass through an infinite number of units either of time or of distance we must reply that in a
sense it is and in a sense it is not. If the units are actual, it is not possible; if they are potential,
it is possible. For in the course of a continuous motion the traveler has traversed an infinite
number of units in an accidental sense but not in an unqualified sense; for though it is an
accidental characteristic of the distance to be an infinite number of half-distances, this is not its
real and essential character.* **263a22–263b9**

880. *It is also plain that unless we hold that the point of time that divides earlier from later
always belongs only to the later so far as the thing is concerned, we shall be involved in the
consequence that the same thing is at the same moment existent and not existent, and that a
thing is not existent at the moment when it has become. It is true that the point is common to
both times, the earlier as well as the later, and that, while numerically one and the same, it is
theoretically not so, being the finishing-point of the one and the starting-point of the other; but
so far as the thing is concerned it belongs to the later stage of what happens to it.* **263b9–15**

881. *Let us suppose a time ABC and a thing D, D being white in the time A and not-white
in the time B. Then D is at the moment C white and not-white; for if we were right in saying
that it is white during the whole time A, it is true to call it white at any moment of A, and
not-white in B, and C is in both A and B.* **263b15–19**

882. *We must not allow, therefore, that it is white in the whole of A, but must say that it is
so in all of it except the last moment C. C belongs already to the later period, and if in the whole
of A not-white was in process of becoming and white of perishing, at C the process is complete.
And so C is the first moment at which it is true to call the thing white or not-white respectively.
Otherwise a thing may be non-existent at the moment when it has become and existent at the
moment when it has perished; or else it must be possible for a thing at the same time to be white
and not white and in fact to be existent and non-existent.* **263b20–26**

883. *Further, if anything that exists after having been previously non-existent must become
existent and does not exist when it is becoming, time cannot be divisible into time-atoms. For
suppose that D was becoming white in the time A and that at another time B, a time-atom
consecutive with the last atom of A, D has already become white and so is white at that
moment: then inasmuch as in the time A it was becoming white and so was not white and at the
moment B it is white, there must have been a becoming between A and B and therefore also a
time in which the becoming took place. On the other hand, those who deny atoms of time (as we
do) are not affected by this argument: according to them D has become and so is white at the last
point of the actual time in which it was becoming white; and this point has no other point*

consecutive with or in succession to it, whereas time-atoms are conceived as successive.

Moreover it is clear that if D was becoming white in the whole time A, the time occupied by it in having become white in addition to having been in process of becoming white is no more than all that it occupied in the mere process of becoming white.

These and such-like, then, are the arguments for our conclusion that derive cogency from the fact that they have a special bearing on the point at issue.   **263b26–264a8**

COMMENTARY OF ST. THOMAS

1112. After the Philosopher has shown that reflex motion cannot be continuous and one, he here uses the foregoing to answer certain difficulties.

This discussion is divided into three parts corresponding to the three difficulties which he answers from the foregoing. The second part begins where he says, **"The same method..."** [876]. The third part begins where he says, **"It is also plain..."** [880].

Concerning the first part he makes two points. First he states the difficulty. Secondly, where he says, **"Therefore we must not hold . . ."** [875], he answers the difficulty.

1113. He says, therefore, first that the same argument which he used to prove that reflex motion is not continuous may also be used to answer a certain difficulty.

For the first difficulty is as follows. Let there be two equal magnitudes, one of which is E and the other F. Assume also two mobile objects of equal velocity, one of which is A and the other D. Let A be moved continuously from the extremity, that is, from the beginning of the magnitude, toward C, and let D be moved toward G. And in the magnitude E let us designate an intermediate point B which is the same distance from C as F is from G in the magnitude F. And let us grant that while A by its own continuous motion approaches point B, the mobile object D by its own continuous motion withdraws from F and approaches G. Since

the motions of each mobile object are regular and of equal velocity, it follows that D reaches G before A reaches C. For that which departs first arrives first at the end of an equal magnitude. D, however, departed from F before A departed from B, for D departed when A reached B. Therefore, since A does not arrive at B and depart from it at the same time, it follows that it departs later than it arrives. For if it were to arrive and depart at the same time, it would not begin to be moved afterwards. And so it must be that although A is moved continuously, it rests at B. And thus a continuous motion will be composed of states of rest, just as Zeno held, as was explained above in Book VI.

1114. Next where he says, **"Therefore we must not hold..."** [875], he answers this difficulty by using the foregoing. The above objection supposed that while A is being moved continuously, it arrives at the point B in the middle of the magnitude, and at the same time that A arrives at B, D withdraws from some other point, namely, from F. But this is contrary to what has gone before. For it was said above that when a thing is moved continuously, it can neither be present nor absent, that is, it cannot arrive at or depart from some mid-point.

Therefore we cannot hold what this objection proposes, namely, that when A arrives at B, D simultaneously departs from F. For if it is granted that A arrives at B, for the same reason it is granted that it departs from B. And this will not occur at the same time, but in two instants, so that it will be at rest in the intermediate time.

But as was said earlier, when a thing is moved continuously, it is not present or absent at some mid-point. Rather it was there simply, not indeed through some time, for then it would be at rest, but in a division of time, that is, in some "now," which divides time.

Hence, what the objection proposes, namely, that A would be present at and D absent from some mid-point, cannot be said of continuous motion.

But this must be said of reflex motion.

For if the mobile object G is moved to point D and then is reflected, it is clear that the mobile object uses the terminus D as a beginning and an end, that is, one point as two. Hence it must be said that it rests there.

Nor can it be said that it arrives at and departs from D simultaneously. For then it would follow that simultaneously in the same instant it would be and not be there. For whatever has been moved is in the terminus to which it was moved. And whatever begins to be moved is not in the terminus from which it begins to be moved. For when we say "present at" or "arrives at," we mean that the motion is terminated at that point. When, however, we say "absent from" or "departs from," we mean that motion begins. Hence whatever arrives at or is present at some point must be in that point. And whatever departs from or is absent from some point is not in it. Therefore, since it is impossible for a thing to be and not to be in some point at the same time, consequently it is impossible for it to be simultaneously present in and absent from the same thing, as was proposed many times above.

It should be noted that here he is using the letters in a different way than he did before, using G for the mobile object and D for the terminus—just the opposite of the above.

Moreover, the explanation given above for continuous motion must not be applied to reflex motion. For it cannot be said that the mobile object G is in the terminus D, from which its reflex motion begins, only in a division of time, that is, in a "now," and that the mobile object does not arrive at and depart from the same thing, as was said of continuous motion. For a reflex motion must come to an end which is an end in act and not just in potency, while in continuous motion a mid-point was only potentially a beginning and an end. For a mid-point in a continuous motion is only potentially a beginning and an end, but that from which a reflex motion begins is actually a beginning and an end. The end of a downward motion, for example, of a stone, is the beginning in act of a reflex upward motion, when the stone falling to the earth rebounds upward.

Hence in a magnitude in which motion occurs, the point of reflection is actually a beginning and an end. Thus in these motions there is an actual end of one motion and a beginning of the other. This could not occur unless an intermediate state of rest intervenes. Therefore that which is reflected in a straight line must be at rest. And so it follows that motion in a straight magnitude cannot be continuous and eternal. For a straight magnitude is not infinite, and thus a straight continuous motion cannot be eternal unless it is reflected.

1115. Next where he says, "**The same method . . .**" [876], he states the second difficulty.

Concerning this he makes three points. First he raises the difficulty. Secondly, where he says, **"Now when we first . . ."** [877], he rejects a certain answer given above in Book VI. Thirdly, where he says, **". . . and we must apply . . ."** [879], he gives the true answer.

He says, therefore, first, that using the same method employed above, we can reply to those who advance Zeno's objection and who wish to argue as follows.

Before a thing which is moved reaches its terminus, it must cross half the distance to it. But between any two termini there is an infinity of half-distances, because magnitude is divisible to infinity. And so it is impossible to cross these half-distances, since an infinity cannot be crossed. Therefore, nothing can reach any terminus by moving.

The same objection may be formulated differently, as some have proposed.

Whatever passes through a whole first passes through half of it. And since the half-distance is itself divided in half, the mobile object must first cross half of the half-distance. Hence, whatever is moved numbers each half-distance by arriving at it. But these half-distances can be taken to infinity. And so it follows that if a thing traverses a whole magnitude, it has numbered an infinite number, which is obviously impossible.

1116. Next where he says, **"Now when we first . . ."** [877], he rejects an answer to this objection which he gave above in Book VI.

First he repeats this answer, and secondly he rejects it, where he says, **"But, although this solution . . ."** [878].

He says, therefore, first that the above objection was answered in Book VI when, speaking of motion in general, he said that time is infinitely divisible, just as is magnitude. Hence in the same way both time and magnitude have infinities in themselves. And so there is no inconsistency if the infinities which are in magnitude are crossed in the infinities which are in time. For it is not inconsistent for an infinite magnitude to be crossed in an infinite time. And as was shown in Book VI, the infinite is found in time and in magnitude in the same way.

1117. Next where he says, **"But, although this solution . . ."** [878], he rejects this explanation.

He says that this solution provides a satisfactory answer to one who asks the question in this way: Is it possible to number and pass through the infinite in a finite time? This question was answered by the statement that a finite time has infinities in which the infinities which are in magnitude can be crossed. But this answer is not sufficient for the truth of the thing. For if one neglects to make an inquiry about the magnitude, and if one neglects to ask if infinities can be crossed in a finite time, one might raise the same question about time itself, asking if the infinities which are in time could be passed through since time is infinitely divisible. The above solution is not a satisfactory answer to this question, and so another answer should be sought.

1118. Next where he says, **". . . and we must apply . . ."** [879], he gives the true solution according to what he has established above.

He says that in order to answer this difficulty according to the truth we must say what we proposed in the arguments given above; namely, if one divides a continuum into two halves and then uses the one point at which the continuum is divided as if it were two points, then one makes that point both the beginning of one part and the end of the other. Moreover one does this by numbering and by dividing into two halves.

When a continuum has been so divided, however, it will not be a continuum, whether a magnitude, for example, a line, is divided or whether motion is divided. For no motion can be continuous unless there be continuity in the subject and in the time and in the magnitude which the motion crosses. Therefore, by dividing, one numbers, and by numbering, one breaks up the continuum.

But as long as the continuity of a continuum endures, there is an infinity of halves, not actually, but potentially. For if one causes a half to exist in act, this occurs by division, as was said, insofar as the division is taken as the beginning of one part and the end of the other. Thus the continuum will not remain, but it will cease, that is, the actual halves will not be infinite but will come to an end. This is especially clear if one wishes to number the halves. For he must number one point as two, insofar as it is the end of one half and the beginning of the other. This occurs when the whole continuum is not numbered as one, but rather the two halves are numbered in themselves. For if the whole continuum is taken as one, then, as was said, the mid-point is not taken as a beginning and an end in act but only in potency.

As a result, he who asks whether it is possible to pass through an infinity of time or of magnitude must receive the answer that in a certain sense this is possible and in a certain sense this is not possible. For it is not possible to pass through an actual infinity; but it is possible to pass through a potential in-

finity. And so, since in a continuum the mid-points are only potentially infinite, it is possible to pass through this infinity. For that which is moved continuously passes accidentally through a potential infinity. Per se it crosses a finite line which happens to have in it an infinity of mid-points in potency. But the line itself, with respect to its substance and nature [ratio], is different from these infinite mid-points. For a line is not composed of points. Rather points can be designated in a line insofar as it is divided.

1119. Next where he says, "It is also plain . . ." [880], he answers the third difficulty.

Concerning this he makes three points. First he sets forth the problem and its solution. Secondly, where he says, "Let us suppose . . ." [881], he clarifies each with an example. Thirdly, where he says, "Further, if anything . . ." [883], he introduces a corollary from what he has said.

First he sets forth a problem which is usually raised in regard to generation and corruption. That which is generated ceases to not-be and begins to be. Some time must be assigned, therefore, to the existence of that which is generated or corrupted, and a different time to its nonexistence. For example, if fire is generated from air, in the whole time AB it was not fire but air. But in the whole time BC it is fire. Since, then, this point of time B is common to both times, it seems that in that common instant the same thing simultaneously is and is not fire.

In solving this problem, the Philosopher says that it is clear that unless the point of time which divides the earlier and the later always refers to the later thing, that is, at this moment the thing exists in the same way as it does in the following time, it follows that the same thing is a being and is not a being at the same time, and it also follows that when a thing has been made it is non-being. For it was made when the generation ended, namely, in that "now" which divides the earlier time from the later time. And so, if it did not exist in the whole earlier time, in this "now" when it has been generated, it still does not exist. For this "now" is the end of the earlier time.

He shows how this inconsistency does not follow, however, by adding that the point which is one and the same in number, namely, the "now," is common to each time, namely, the earlier and the later. But although it is one in subject, in reason [ratio] it is not one, but two. For it is the end of the earlier time and the beginning of the later time. But if the "now" which is the thing is taken in itself, that is, if it is taken insofar as it is one in the thing, it is always referred to the later passion.

Or to put it another way: Although this "now" is the end of the earlier time and the beginning of the later time, and thus is common to both, nevertheless, with respect to the thing, that is, insofar as it is compared to the thing which is moved, it always pertains to the later passion. For the thing which is moved is in that "now" the subject of the passion of the later time.

1120. Having set forth the problem and its solution, he clarifies each with examples. First he clarifies the problem where he says, **"Let us suppose . . ."** [881].

He asks us to assume a time ACB and an object D which is moved. In the time A, D is white, and in B it is not white. It seems to follow that in C it is both white and not white. He explains how this follows by adding that if it is white in the whole time A, it follows that it is white in any part of A. Simi-

larly, if it is not white in the whole of time B, it follows that it is not white in any part of B. Since, then, C is found in both times, because it is the end of one and the beginning of the other, it seems to follow that in C the thing is white and not white.

1121. Secondly, where he says, **"We must not allow . . ."** [882], he explains the answer given above.

He says that it must not be conceded that the object is white in every part of A. Rather we must exclude the ultimate "now" C, which is the ultimate terminus of the mutation. For example, if a white thing either was coming to be or was being corrupted in the whole of A, in C it is neither being corrupted nor is it becoming white. Rather it has already been made or corrupted. Moreover, that which has been made, is; and that which has been corrupted, is not. And so it is clear that it is primarily true to say that it is white in C, if the generation of whiteness ends there; or that it is not white, if the corruption of whiteness ends there. And if this is not said, the inconsistencies set forth above will follow, namely, when a thing has been generated, at that point it is non-being, and when it has been corrupted, at that point it is being. And it will also follow that a thing is white and not white at the same time, and universally it is being and non-being.

1122. Next where he says, **"Further, if anything . . ."** [883], he introduces a corollary from the foregoing, namely, time is not divided into indivisible times. For the previous problem could not be answered if this were not granted.

He says, then, that whatever first is not a being and afterwards is a being must at some time become a being. Furthermore, it is necessary that when a thing is coming to be, it is not. If, however, these two suppositions are true, it is impossible for time to be divided into indivisible times.

For let time be divided into indivisible times, and let the first indivisible time be A. Let the second one, which is consecutive to A, be B. And let D, which was not white earlier, and afterwards is white, become white in A, when it was not white. We must grant that this is done in some indivisible and consecutive time, namely, B, in which it already is. If, however, it was becoming white in A, it follows that it was not white in A. In B, however, it is white. Therefore, since between being and nonbeing there is an intervening generation because nothing passes from non-being to being except by a generation, it follows that a generation intervened between A and B. Hence there will be some time intervening between A and B in which it became white. (For it was granted that in the time B, D has been generated.)

And similarly, when it becomes white in that intermediate, indivisible time, it is not white; and so, for the same reason we ought to posit another intermediate time, and so on to infinity. And so it cannot be held that it comes to be and has come to be in the same time.

But the same reasoning does not apply if it is denied that time is divisible into indivisible times. For in this case we say that the time in which it was coming to be and is made is one and the same. It was coming to be and was non-being in the whole preceding time. It has been made, however, and is being in the ultimate "now" of time which is not related to the preceding time as consecutive to it, but as its terminus. But if indivisible times are posited, they must be related as consecutive.

It is clear, moreover, from the foregoing that if indivisible times are not posited, and if a thing becomes white in the whole time A, the time in which it was made and came to be is not greater than that in which it only came to be. For it came to be in the whole time, but it was made in the ultimate terminus of the time. The time, however, and the terminus of the time are not greater than the time alone, just as a point adds nothing to the magnitude of a line. But if indivisible times are posited, it is clear from the foregoing that the time in which it comes to be and is made is greater than the time in which it only comes to be.

Finally he summarizes and concludes to his main point. He says that the above and similar arguments serve as proper proofs that reflex motion is not continuous.

He Shows with Logical Arguments That Reflex Motion Is Not Continuous

The Text of Aristotle

884. If we look at the question from the point of view of general theory, the same result would also appear to be indicated by the following arguments. **264a8–9**

885. Everything whose motion is continuous must, on arriving at any point in the course of its locomotion, have been previously also in process of locomotion to that point, if it is not forced out of its path by anything: e.g., on arriving at B a thing must also have been in process of locomotion to B, and that not merely when it was near to B, but from the moment of its starting on its course, since there can be no reason for its being so at any particular stage rather than at an earlier one. So, too, in the case of the other kinds of motion. Now we are to suppose that a thing proceeds in locomotion from A to C and that at the moment of its arrival at C the continuity of its motion is unbroken and will remain so until it has arrived back at A. Then when it is undergoing locomotion from A to C it is at the same time undergoing also its locomotion to A from C: consequently it is simultaneously undergoing two contrary motions, since the two motions that follow the same straight line are contrary to each other. **264a9–18**

886. With this consequence there also follows another: we have a thing that is in process of change from a position in which it has not yet been: so, inasmuch as this is impossible, the thing must come to a stand at C. Therefore the motion is not a single motion, since motion that is interrupted by stationariness is not single. **264a18–21**

887. Further, the following argument will serve better to make this point clear universally in respect of every kind of motion. If the motion undergone by that which is in motion is always one of those already enumerated, and the state of rest that it undergoes is one of those that are the opposites of the motions (for we found that there could be no other besides these), and moreover that which is undergoing but does not always undergo a particular motion (by this I mean one of the various specifically distinct motions, not some particular part of the whole motion) must have been previously undergoing the state of rest that is the opposite of the motion, the state of rest being privation of motion; then, inasmuch as the two motions that follow the same straight line are contrary motions, and it is impossible for a thing to undergo simultaneously two contrary motions, that which is undergoing locomotion from A to C cannot also simultaneously be undergoing locomotion from C to A; and since the latter locomotion is not simultaneous with the former but is still to be undergone, before it is undergone there must occur a state of rest at C; for this, as we found, is the state of rest that is the opposite of the motion from C. The foregoing argument, then, makes it plain that the motion in question is not continuous. **264a21–264b1**

888. Our next argument has a more special bearing than the foregoing on the point at issue. We will suppose that there has occurred in something simultaneously a perishing of not-white and a becoming of white. Then if the alteration to white and from white is a continuous process and the white does not remain any time, there must have occurred simultaneously a perishing of not-white, a becoming of white, and a becoming of not-white; for the time of the three will be the same. **264b1–6**

889. Again, from the continuity of the time in which the motion takes place we cannot infer continuity in the motion, but only successiveness: in fact, how could contraries, e.g., whiteness and blackness, meet in the same extreme point? **264b6–9**

COMMENTARY OF ST. THOMAS

1123. After the Philosopher has   shown with proper arguments that reflex motion is not continuous, he here shows the same thing by means of common and logical arguments.

Concerning this he makes two points. First he states his intention. Secondly, where he says, **"Everything whose motion . . ."** [885], he proves his position.

He says, therefore, first [884] that if one wishes to approach the demonstration of the proposition rationally, that is, logically, it will be seen from the arguments which will be given that the same conclusion follows; namely, reflex motion is not continuous.

1124. Next where he says, **"Everything whose motion . . ."** [885], he proves his position. He does this first with respect to just reflex local motion, and secondly, with respect to all motion in general, where he says, **"Further, the following . . ."** [887].

The first argument is as follows. Whatever is moved continuously is moved from the beginning of its motion to that which, as an end, it arrives at through local motion. This occurs if there is no obstacle (for it could be deflected in another direction by an obstacle). He gives an example of this proposition by saying that if something arrives at B through local motion, it was moved toward B not just when it was nearby, but immediately when it began to be moved. For there is no reason why it should be moved more toward B now rather than before. And the same is true of other motions.

If, however, it is true that reflex motion is continuous, it will be true to say that what is moved from A to C, and then is reflected to A, is moved continuously. Therefore, in the first part of the motion, from A to C, it was being moved toward the terminus of the last part, which is A. Hence, while it is being moved from A, it is being moved

toward A. It follows, therefore, that it is moved simultaneously by contrary motions. For in straight motions, being moved from the same thing and to the same thing are contraries, although in circular motions these are not contraries. It is impossible, however, for a thing to be moved by contrary, simultaneous motions. Therefore, it is impossible for reflex motion to be continuous.

1125. Next where he says, **"With this consequence . . ."** [886], he brings out another inconsistency from the same thing.

That which is being moved to A while it is being moved from A, can be moved to A only from some opposite position, C, which the mobile object had not yet reached when it began to be moved from A. It follows that it is being moved from a terminus in which it is not, and this is impossible. For a thing cannot leave a place in which it is not. Therefore, it is impossible for reflex motion to be continuous. And if this is impossible, the mobile object must rest at the turning point, namely, at C. From this it is clear that the motion is not one, for a motion which is interrupted by an intervening rest is not one.

1126. Next where he says, **"Further, the following . . ."** [887], he gives three arguments to prove the same thing universally of all motions.

The first of these is as follows. Whatever is moved is moved by one of the species of motion designated above. Similarly, whatever is at rest must have one of the states of rest which are opposed to the above motions. For it was shown in Book V that there cannot be any motion other than those designated.

Let us take a motion which differs from other motions in species, as whitening differs from blackening. The motion under consideration is not distinguished from other motions as one part of a motion is distinguished from the other parts of the same motion, for example, as one part of a whitening is distinct from the other parts of the same whitening. Taking one such motion as was said, it is true to say that that which is not always being moved by this motion, necessarily was previously at rest with an opposed rest. For example, that which is not always being whitened at some time was at rest with a rest opposed to whitening. But this proposition would not be true if some determinate part of the motion were taken. For it is not necessary that that which was not always being moved by this part of whitening was previously at rest with an opposed rest. For it was being whitened previously by another part of the whitening. Because of this he explicitly says, ". . . not some particular part of the whole motion . . ."

He proves the proposition in this way. When one of two privative opposites is not present, the other is present in that which is receptive of them. Now rest is a privative opposite of motion. Therefore, when motion is not present in a mobile object, it necessarily follows that rest is then present in it.

After proving this proposition with the argument set forth above, he assumes the minor by saying that if the straight motions from A to C and from C to A are contraries, and if contrary motions cannot be simultaneous, it is clear that when the mobile object was being moved from A to C, it was not then being moved from C to A. Hence it was not always being moved by the motion from C to A. And so, according to the foregoing proposition, the mobile object must previously have been

at rest with an opposed rest. For it was shown in Book V that rest in C is opposed to motion from C. Therefore it was at rest at C. Reflex motion, then, is not one and continuous, since it is interrupted by an intervening rest.

1127. He gives the second argument where he says, **"Our next argument . . ."** [888]. The argument is as follows.

Not-white is corrupted and white is generated simultaneously; and, contrarily, white is corrupted and not-white comes to be simultaneously. But if reflex motion of any genus is continuous, it will follow that continuous alteration is terminated at white, and begins to withdraw from white, and it does not rest there for any time. For otherwise, if rest intervened, it would not be continuous alteration. But, as was said, when white comes to be, not-white is corrupted, and when there is a withdrawal from white, not-white comes to be. It will follow, then, that not-white is corrupted, and not-white comes to be simultaneously. For these three occur at the same time, namely, becoming white, the corruption of not-white, and becoming not-white again, if reflex motion is continuous without an intervening rest. However it is impossible for not-white to simultaneously come to be and be corrupted. Therefore, it is impossible for reflex motion to be continuous.

This argument, however, seems to pertain to generation and corruption. Hence he says that this argument is more proper than the previous ones, for it is more apparent that contradictories cannot be simultaneously true. Nevertheless, what is said of generation and corruption applies to all motions, since in any motion there is some kind of generation and corruption.

Thus in alteration white or not-white is generated or corrupted. And the same applies to every other motion.

1128. He gives the third argument where he says, **"Again, from the continuity ..."** [889]. The argument is as follows.

As was established in Book V, motion is not necessarily continuous because the time is continuous. For even if they succeed themselves in a continuous time, motions of different species are not continuous, but consecutive. For there must be one, common terminus of the continuous. But there cannot be one, common terminus of contraries and of things which differ in species of white and black, for example. Since, therefore, motion from A to C is contrary to motion from C to A in any genus of motion, as was shown above in Book V, it is impossible for these two motions to be continuous to each other, even if their time be continuous, with no rest intervening. It follows, therefore, that reflex motion can in no way be continuous.

It should be noted that the arguments set forth above are called logical because they proceed from certain common principles, namely, from the property of contraries.

He Shows with Proper Proofs That Circular Motion Can be Continuous and That Circular Motion Is the First Motion

The Text of Aristotle

890. On the other hand, in motion on a circular line we shall find singleness and continuity; for here we are met by no impossible consequence: that which is in motion from A will in virtue of the same direction of energy be simultaneously in motion to A (since it is in motion to the point at which it will finally arrive), and yet will not be undergoing two contrary or opposite motions; for a motion to a point and a motion from that point are not always contraries or opposites: they are contraries only if they are on the same straight line (for then they are contrary to one another in respect of place, as e.g., the two motions along the diameter of the circle, since the ends of this are at the greatest possible distance from one another), and they are opposites only if they are along the same line. Therefore in the case we are now considering there is nothing to prevent the motion being continuous and free from all intermission; for rotatory motion is motion of a thing from its place to its place, whereas rectilinear motion is motion from its place to another place. **264b9–18**

891. Moreover the progress of rotatory motion is never localized within certain fixed limits, whereas that of rectilinear motion repeatedly is so. Now a motion that is always shifting its ground from moment to moment can be continuous; but a motion that is repeatedly localized within certain fixed limits cannot be so, since then the same thing would have to undergo simultaneously two opposite motions. So, too, there cannot be continuous motion in a semicircle or in any other arc of a circle, since here also the same ground must be traversed repeatedly and two contrary processes of change must occur. The reason is that in these motions the starting-point and the termination do not coincide, whereas in motion over a circle they do coincide, and so this is the only perfect motion. **264b18–28**

892. This differentiation also provides another means of showing that the other kinds of motion cannot be continuous either; for in all of them we find that there is the same ground to be traversed repeatedly: thus in alteration there are the intermediate stages of the process, and in quantitative change there are the intervening degrees of magnitude; and in becoming and perishing the same thing is true. It makes no difference whether we take the intermediate stages of the process to be few or many, or whether we add or subtract one; for in either case we find that there is still the same ground to be traversed repeatedly. **264b28–265a2**

893. Moreover it is plain from what has been said that those physicists who assert that all sensible things are always in motion are wrong; for their motion must be one or other of the motions just mentioned: in fact they mostly conceive it as alteration (things are always in flux and decay, they say), and they go so far as to speak even of becoming and perishing as a process of alteration. On the other hand, our argument has enabled us to assert the fact, applying universally to all motions, that no motion admits of continuity except rotatory motion: consequently neither alteration nor increase admits of continuity. We need now say no more in support of the position that there is no process of change that admits of infinity or continuity except rotatory locomotion. **265a2–12**

Chapter 9

894. It can now be shown plainly that rotation is the primary locomotion. Every locomotion, as we said before, is either rotatory or rectilinear or a compound of the two; and the two former must be prior to the last, since they are the elements of which the latter consists. Moreover rotatory locomotion is prior to rectilinear locomotion, because it is more simple and complete, which may be shown as follows. The straight line traversed in rectilinear motion cannot be infinite; for there is no such thing as an infinite straight line; and even if there were, it would not be traversed by anything in motion; for the impossible does not happen and it is impossible to traverse an infinite distance. On the other hand rectilinear motion on a finite straight line is, if it turns back a composite motion, in fact two motions, while if it does not turn back it is incomplete and perishable; and in the order of nature, of definition, and of time alike the complete is prior to the incomplete and the imperishable to the perishable. **265a13–24**

895. *Again, a motion that admits of being eternal is prior to one that does not. Now rotatory motion can be eternal; but no other motion, whether locomotion or motion of any other kind, can be so, since in all of them rest must occur, and with the occurrence of rest the motion has perished.* **265a24–27**

COMMENTARY OF ST. THOMAS

1129. After the Philosopher has shown that no local motion other than circular motion can be continuous, he shows here that circular motion can be continuous and that it is the first motion.

He proves this first with proper arguments, and secondly, with common and logical arguments, where he says, **"Moreover the result . . ."** [896].

Concerning the first part he makes two points. First he shows that circular motion is continuous. Secondly, where he says, **"It can now be shown . . ."** [894], he shows that circular motion is the first motion.

Concerning the first part he makes two points. First he gives two arguments to show that circular motion can be continuous. Secondly, where he says, **"This differentiation . . ."** [892], he concludes from these same arguments that no other motion can be continuous.

1130. His first proof [890] that circular motion is continuous and one is as follows.

That is said to be possible which involves no impossible consequence. And there is no impossible consequence if we say that circular motion is eternally continuous.

This is clear from the fact that in cir-

cular motion that which is moved from some point, for example, A, is simultaneously being moved toward that same point with respect to the same position, that is, with respect to the same course of the mobile object, and the same order of parts is preserved. This does not happen in reflex motion. For when something is reflected, it is disposed to motion with a contrary order of parts, for either the part of the mobile object which was prior in the first motion becomes posterior in the reflex motion, or else that part of the mobile object which faced one direction of place in the first motion, for example, right or up, faces the contrary direction in the reflex motion. But when a thing moves toward that from which it withdrew with circular motion, the same position is preserved. So it can be said that from the beginning of its motion, while it was withdrawing from A, it was being moved toward where it will arrive, namely, A.

And the impossibility of being simultaneously moved by contrary or opposed motions does not follow here as it did with straight motion. For not every motion to a terminus is contrary or opposed to motion from that same terminus. Rather such contrariety is found in a straight line, with respect to which contrariety of place is present. For there is no contrariety between two termini of a circular line, each part of which belongs to the circumference. Rather there is contrariety only with respect to the diameter. For contraries are at the greatest distance from each other. But the greatest distance between two termini is not measured by a circular line, but by a straight line. For infinite curved lines may be described between two points, but only one straight line. Moreover, that which is one is the measure in any genus.

Therefore, it is clear that if a circle is divided in half, and its diameter is AB, motion through the diameter from A to B is contrary to motion through the same diameter from B to A. But semi-circular motion from A to B is not contrary to the other semi-circular motion from B to A. Contrariety, however, was that hindrance which made it impossible for reflex motion to be continuous, as is clear from the earlier arguments. Therefore, there is no hindrance, contrariety is removed, and circular motion is continuous and never ceases.

The reason for this is that a circular motion has its own complement since it is from the same thing to the same thing. Therefore there is no hindrance to its continuity. But straight motion has its complement insofar as it is from the same thing to another. Hence if it is returned from that other to the same thing from which it began to be moved, it will not be one continuous motion, but two.

1131. Next where he says, "**Moreover the progress . . .**" [891], he gives the second argument. He says that circular motion is not in the same things, but straight motion is repeatedly in the same things. This is to be understood as follows.

If something is moved through a diameter from A to B, and again from B to A through the same diameter, it must return through the same mid-points which it passed through earlier; and so it is repeatedly moved through the same things. But if something is moved from A to B through a semicircle, and again from B to A through the other semicircle, that is, if it is moved circularly, it is clear that it does not return to the same place through the same mid-points.

But opposites by their nature [ratio] are concerned with the same thing. Hence it is clear that to be moved from the same thing to the same thing involves no opposition with respect to circular motion, but to be moved from the same thing to the same thing with reflex motion does involve opposition.

Therefore, it is clear that circular motion, which does not return to the same point through the same mid-points, but always passes through different points, can be one and continuous because it has no opposition. But that motion, namely, reflex motion, which while returning to the same point, does so by passing through the same mid-points many times, cannot be eternally continuous. For it would be necessary for the thing to be moved by simultaneous contrary motions, as was shown above.

From this same argument it can be concluded that neither motion in a semicircle, nor motion in any other portion of a circle can be eternally continuous. For in these motions the same mid-points must be traversed many times, and the objects must be moved by contrary motions if a return to the beginning is to occur. This is so because neither in a straight line, nor in a semicircle, nor in any portion of a circle, is the end joined to the beginning.

Rather they are at a distance from each other. Only in circular motion is the end joined to the beginning.

Therefore, only circular motion is perfect, for a thing is perfect if it comes in contact with its beginning.

1132. Next where he says, **"This differentiation . . ."** [892], he uses the same argument to show that no motion in any other genus can be continuous.

First he proves his position. Secondly, where he says, **"Moreover it is plain . . ."** [893], he infers a corollary from what has been said.

He says, therefore, first that from the distinction established between circular motion and other local motions it is clear that no motion in the other genera of motion is infinitely continuous. For in all the other genera of motion, if a thing is to be moved from the same thing to the same thing, it follows that it passes through the same things many times. For example, in alteration it is necessary to pass through intermediate qualities. The object passes from hot to cold through warmness, and if it is to be returned from cold to hot, it must pass through warmness. The same thing is apparent in quantitative motion. If what is moved from large to small is again returned to large, it must twice have been the half-quantity. The same is true of generation and corruption. If air comes to be from fire, and again fire comes to be from air, it must twice pass through the middle dispositions (for a middle can be posited in generation and corruption insofar as one considers the transmutation of dispositions.

And since in the various kinds of mutation the object passes through intermediaries, he adds that it makes no difference whether there are few or many intermediaries through which a

thing is moved from one extremity to the other. Nor does it make any difference if the intermediary is positive, as pale between white and black, or if it is remote, as that which is neither good nor evil between the good and the evil. For no matter how the intermediaries are related, it always happens that the same things are passed through repeatedly.

1133. Next where he says, **"Moreover it is plain . . ."** [893], he concludes from the foregoing that the ancient natural philosophers did not speak correctly when they said that all sensible things are always moved. For these objects would necessarily have to be moved by one of the motions mentioned above, concerning which we have shown that eternal continuity is impossible. This is especially so because they said that alteration is an eternally continuous motion.

For they said that everything is constantly decaying and being corrupted. And they add to this that generation and corruption is nothing other than alteration. Hence when they say that all things are constantly being corrupted, they say that all things are constantly being altered.

In the argument introduced above, however, it was established that no motion is eternal except circular motion. Hence it follows that neither in respect to alteration nor in respect to increase can all things be always moved, as they said.

Finally he summarizes and concludes to his main point; namely, no mutation other than circular motion can be infinite and continuous.

1134. Next where he says, **"It can now be shown . . ."** [894], he proves with two arguments that circular motion is the first of motions. The first argument is as follows.

As we said before, every local motion is either circular, straight, or a mixture of the two. Circular and straight motions are prior to mixed motion, since the latter is composed of them. Of these two, circular motion is prior to straight motion, for circular motion is more simple and perfect than straight motion.

He proves this as follows. Straight motion cannot proceed to infinity, for this would have to occur in one of two ways. First there might be an infinite magnitude through which straight motion passes. But this is impossible. And even if there were some infinite magnitude, nothing would be moved to infinity. That which cannot be never occurs or is generated. It is impossible, however, to pass through infinity. Therefore, nothing is moved in such a way that it passes through infinity. Therefore, there cannot be infinite straight motion over an infinite magnitude.

Secondly, infinite straight motion could be understood to occur over a finite magnitude by reflection. But reflex motion is not one, as was proven above, but is composed of two motions.

If, however, reflection does not occur over a finite straight line, the motion will be imperfect and corrupt: imperfect, because it is possible to add to it; corrupt, because when it has reached the terminus of the magnitude, the motion will cease.

Therefore, it is clear that circular motion, which is not composed of two motions, and which is not corrupted when it reaches the terminus (since its beginning and end are the same), is more simple and more perfect than straight motion. The perfect, moreover, is prior to the imperfect, and similarly, the incorruptible to the corruptible, in nature, and in reason [ratio], and in time, as was proven above when it was shown that local motion is prior to the other motions. Circular motion, therefore, must be prior to straight motion.

1135. Next where he says, **"Again, a motion . . ."** [895], he gives the second argument, which is as follows.

Motion which can be eternal is prior to motion which cannot be eternal, for the eternal is prior to the non-eternal both in time and in nature. Circular motion, however, can be eternal. But no other motions can be eternal because rest must succeed them. And when rest intervenes the motion is corrupted. It follows, therefore, that circular motion is prior to all other motions. The things which he supposes in this argument are clear from the earlier arguments.

He Shows with Common and Logical Arguments That Circular Motion Is Continuous and First. According to the Opinions of the Ancient Philosophers Local Motion Is the First Motion

The Text of Aristotle

896. *Moreover the result at which we have arrived, that rotatory motion is single and continuous, and rectilinear motion is not, is a reasonable one. In rectilinear motion we have a definite starting-point, finishing-point, and middle-point, which all have their place in it in such a way that there is a point from which that which is in motion can be said to start and a point at which it can be said to finish its course (for when anything is at the limits of its course, whether at the starting-point or at the finishing-point, it must be in a state of rest). On the other hand in circular motion there are no such definite points; for why should any one point on the line be a limit rather than any other? Any one point as much as any other is alike starting-point, middle-point, and finishing-point, so that we can say of certain things both that they are always and that they never are at a starting-point and at a finishing-point (so that a revolving sphere, while it is in motion, is also in a sense at rest, for it continues to occupy the same place). The reason of this is that in this case all these characteristics belong to the center: that is to say, the center is alike starting-point, middle-point, and finishing-point of the space traversed; consequently since this point is not a point on the circular line, there is no point at which that which is in process of locomotion can be in a state of rest as having traversed its course, because in its locomotion it is proceeding always about a central point and not to an extreme point; therefore it remains still, and the whole is in a sense always at rest as well as continuously in motion.* 265a27–265b8

897. *Our next point gives a convertible result: on the one hand, because rotation is the measure of motions it must be the primary motion (for all things are measured by what is primary); on the other hand, because rotation is the primary motion it is the measure of all other motions.* 265b8–11

898. *Again, rotatory motion is also the only motion that admits of being regular. In rectilinear locomotion the motion of things in leaving the starting-point is not uniform with their motion in approaching the finishing-point, since the velocity of a thing always increases proportionately as it removes itself farther from its position of rest; on the other hand rotatory motion is the only motion whose course is naturally such that it has no starting-point or finishing-point in itself but is determined from elsewhere.* 265b11–16

899. *As to locomotion being the primary motion, this is a truth that is attested by all who have ever made mention of motion in their theories: they all assign their first principles of motion to things that impart motion of this kind. Thus "separation" and "combination" are motions in respect of place, and the motion imparted by "Love" and "Strife" takes these forms, the latter "separating" and the former "combining." Anaxagoras, too, says that "Mind," his first mover, "separates." Similarly those who assert no cause of this kind but say that "void" accounts for motion—they also hold that the motion of natural substance is motion in respect of place; for their motion that is accounted for by "void" is locomotion, and its sphere of operation may be said to be place. Moreover they are of opinion that the primary substances are not subject to any of the other motions, though the things that are compounds of these substances are so subject: the processes of increase and decrease and alteration, they say, are effects of the "combination" and "separation" of "atoms." It is the same, too, with those who make out that the becoming or perishing of a thing is accounted for by "density" or "rarity"; for it is by*

"combination" and "separation" that the place of these things in their systems is determined.
Moreover to these we may add those who make soul the cause of motion; for they say that things
that undergo motion have as their first principle "that which moves itself"; and when animals
and all living things move themselves, the motion is motion in respect of place. Finally it is to be
noted that we say that a thing "is in motion" in the strictest sense of the term only when its
motion is motion in respect of place: if a thing is in process of increase or decrease or is
undergoing some alteration while remaining at rest in the same place, we say that it is in
motion in some particular respect: we do not say that it "is in motion" without qualification.

265b16–266a5

900. *Our present position, then, is this: We have argued that there always was motion and*
always will be motion throughout all time, and we have explained what is the first principle of
this eternal motion; we have explained further which is the primary motion and which is the
only motion that can be eternal; and we have pronounced the first mover to be unmoved.

266a5–9

COMMENTARY OF ST. THOMAS

1136. After the Philosopher has shown with proper arguments that circular motion is continuous and first, he here proves the same thing with logical and common arguments.

He gives three arguments. In the first argument he says that it is reasonable that circular motion is one and eternally continuous, but straight motion is not. For in straight motion the beginning, mid-point, and end are determined, and all three of these are designated in the same straight line. Therefore, it is in this very line that motion begins and ends. For every motion rests at its termini, namely, either the terminus from which or the terminus to which (these two states of rest he distinguished above in Book V. But in a circular line the termini are not distinct. For there is no reason why one designated point of a circular line should be a terminus rather than another. For each one is similarly a beginning, a mid-point, and an end. And thus, in a certain sense whatever is moved in a circle is always at the beginning and at the end, insofar as any point of a circle can be taken as a beginning or an end. And in a certain sense it

is never at a beginning or an end, insofar as no point of a circle is actually a beginning or an end.

From this it follows that a sphere is in a certain sense in motion and in a certain sense at rest. For as was said in Book VI, while a sphere is in motion, it always remains in the same place with respect to the subject, and to this extent it is at rest. But it is always different with respect to reason [ratio], and to this extent it is moved.

In a circular line itself, then, beginning, mid-point, and end are not distinguished since these three pertain to the center. From the center as from a beginning lines proceed to the circumference. And at the center are terminated the lines which are projected from the circumference. The center is also the mid-point of the whole magnitude, insofar as it is equidistant from every point of the circumference.

Therefore, the beginning and the end of a circular magnitude are at the center which is not touched by that which is moved in a circle. Therefore in circular motion there is no point where that which is moved rests when it arrives there. For that which is moved in a circle is always moved around the mid-point, and does not reach an end, since it is not moved to the mid-point which is the beginning and the end.

Because of this, a whole which is moved spherically in a sense is at rest and in a sense is in continuous motion, as was said.

From what has been said the argument can be formulated as follows. Every motion which is never at its beginning or end is continuous. But circular motion is a motion of this kind. Therefore, etc. And through the same middle it is proven that straight motion cannot be continuous.

1137. Next where he says, **"Our next point . . ."** [897], he gives the second argument. He says that the following two points follow each other conversely, namely, circular motion is the measure of all motions, and it is the first of all motions. For, as is shown in Metaphysics, X, all things are measured by the first ones in their genera. And so, this proposition is convertible: everything which is a measure is first in its genus; and everything which is first is a measure. But circular motion is the measure of all other motions, as is clear from what was said at the end of Book IV. Therefore, circular motion is the first of all motions. Or if it is granted that circular motion is the first of all motions because of the arguments set forth above, the conclusion is that it is the measure of other motions.

1138. He gives the third argument where he says, **"Again, rotatory motion . . ."** [898]. He says that only circular motion can be regular since things which are moved in a straight line are moved irregularly from the beginning to the end.

As was said in Book V, that motion is irregular which does not maintain

equal velocity throughout the whole. This must occur in every straight motion. For in natural motion the greater the distance of the mobile object from the initial rest from which motion begins, the greater the velocity. And in violent motion the greater the distance from the final rest where the motion ends, the greater the velocity. For natural motion tends toward an end, and violent motion toward a beginning.

But this does not take place in circular motion. The beginning and the end of a circle are not found inside the circulation, which forms the circumference, but outside of it, that is, at the center, as was said. Hence there is no reason why a circular motion should be increased or diminished as if approaching a beginning or an end. For it is always at an equal distance from the center which is the beginning and the end.

From what was said in Book V, moreover, it is clear that regular motion is more one than irregular motion. Hence circular motion is naturally prior to straight motion. For to the extent that a thing is more one, it is to that degree naturally prior.

1139. Next where he says, **"As to locomotion . . ."** [899], he proves by means of the opinions of the ancient philosophers that local motion is the first of motions.

He says that the sayings of all the ancient philosophers who made mention of motion attest to this truth. For they held that their principles move by local motion.

First he explains the opinion of Empedocles who held that friendship and strife are the first moving principles: friendship unifies and strife separates. Unification and separation, however, are local motions.

Secondly, he shows the same thing from the opinion of Anaxagoras, who posited intellect as the first moving cause whose work, according to him, is to separate what is mixed.

Thirdly, he shows the same thing from the opinion of Democritus, who did not posit a moving cause, but said that all things are moved because of the nature of the void. But motion which is the result of the void is local motion, or something similar to local motion, for void and place differ only in reason [ratio], as was explained in Book IV. And thus, while they hold that things are first moved because of the void, they hold that local motion and no other is naturally first. They thought that other motions are consequent upon local motion. Following Democritus, they say that increase and corruption and alteration are the result of a certain unification and separation of indivisible bodies.

Fourthly, he shows the same thing from the opinions of the ancient natural philosophers who posited only one material cause, either water, or air, or fire, or some intermediate. From that one material principle they derived the generation and corruption of things through condensation and rarefaction, which are the result of unification and separation.

Fifthly, he shows the same thing from the opinion of Plato, who held that the soul is the first cause of motion. For Plato held that a self-mover, which is the soul, is the principle of all things which are moved. According to him, the proper function of animals and all living things is to move themselves with respect to place autokinesim, that is, with respect to per se local motion.

Sixthly, he shows the same thing from what people say who speak in general and in common. For that alone is properly said to be moved which is moved in place. And if a thing which is at rest in a place undergoes increase or decrease or alteration, it is said to be moved in some way, but not simply.

1140. Next where he says, **"Our present position . . ."** [900], he summarizes what he has said, namely, there has always been motion and there always will be motion, and there is some first principle of eternal motion. We have shown which motion is first and which motion is eternal. We have shown that the first mover is immobile. For all of these points were explained in the preceding discussions.

A Finite Mover Cannot Move in an Infinite Time. An Infinite Power Cannot Reside in a Finite Magnitude. A Finite Power Cannot Reside in an Infinite Magnitude

The Text of Aristotle
Chapter 10

901. *We have now to assert that the first mover must be without parts and without magnitude, beginning with the establishment of the premises on which this conclusion depends.*
                                                                        266a10–12

902. *One of these premises is that nothing finite can cause motion during an infinite time. We have three things, the mover, the moved, and thirdly that in which the motion takes place, namely the time; and these are either all infinite or all finite or partly—that is to say two of them or one of them—finite and partly infinite. Let A be the mover, B the moved, and C the infinite time. Now let us suppose that D moves E, a part of B. Then the time occupied by this motion cannot be equal to C; for the greater the amount moved, the longer the time occupied. It follows that the time F is not infinite. Now we see that by continuing to add to D, I shall use up A, and by continuing to add to E, I shall use up B; but I shall not use up the time by continually subtracting a corresponding amount from it, because it is infinite. Consequently the duration of the part of C which is occupied by all A in moving the whole of B, will be finite. Therefore a finite thing cannot impart to anything an infinite motion. It is clear, then, that it is impossible for the finite to cause motion during an infinite time.*   **266a12–23**

903. *It has now to be shown that in no case is it possible for an infinite force to reside in a finite magnitude. This can be shown as follows: we take it for granted that the greater force is always that which in less time than another does an equal amount of work when engaged in any activity—in heating, for example, or sweetening or throwing; in fact, in causing any kind of motion. Then that on which the forces act must be affected to some extent by our supposed finite magnitude possessing an infinite force as well as by anything else, in fact to a greater extent than by anything else, since the infinite force is greater than any other. But then there cannot be any time in which its action could take place. Suppose that A is the time occupied by the infinite power in the performance of an act of heating or pushing, and that AB is the time occupied by a finite power in the performance of the same act: then by adding to the latter another finite power and continually increasing the magnitude of the power so added I shall at some time or other reach a point at which the finite power has completed the motive act in the time A; for by continual addition to a finite magnitude I must arrive at a magnitude that exceeds any assigned limit, and in the same way by continual subtraction I must arrive at one that falls short of any assigned limit. So we get the result that the finite force will occupy the same amount of time in performing the motive act as the infinite force. But this is impossible.*   **266a23–266b5**

904. *Therefore nothing finite can possess an infinite force. So it is also impossible for a finite force to reside in an infinite magnitude.*   **266b5–7**

905. *It is true that a greater force can reside in a lesser magnitude; but the superiority of any such greater force can be still greater if the magnitude in which it resides is greater.*
                                                                        266b7–8

906. *Now let AB be an infinite magnitude. Then BC possesses a certain force that occupies a certain time, let us say the time EF in moving D. Now if I take a magnitude twice as great as BC, the time occupied by this magnitude in moving D will be half of EF (assuming this to be the proportion): so we may call this time FG. That being so, by continually taking a greater magnitude in this way I shall never arrive at the full AB, whereas I shall always be getting a*

lesser fraction of the time originally given. Therefore the force must be infinite; since it exceeds any finite force. Moreover the time occupied by the action of any finite force must also be finite: for if a given force moves something in a certain time, a greater force will do so in a lesser time, but still a definite time, in inverse proportion. But a force must always be infinite—just as a number or a magnitude is—if it exceeds all definite limits.   266b8–20

907. *This point may also be proved in another way—by taking a finite magnitude in which there resides a force the same in kind as that which resides in the infinite magnitude, so that this force will be a measure of the finite force residing in the infinite magnitude. It is plain, then, from the foregoing arguments that it is impossible for an infinite force to reside in a finite magnitude or for a finite force to reside in an infinite magnitude.*   266b20–27

COMMENTARY OF ST. THOMAS

1141. After the Philosopher has explained the nature of the first motion, he here explains the nature of the first mover.

This discussion is divided into two parts. First he states his intention. Secondly, where he says, **"One of these premises . . ."** [902], he develops his position.

He says, then, first that since it was shown above that the first mover is immobile, it must now be shown that the first mover is indivisible and has no magnitude, that is, it is completely incorporeal.

But before we prove this, we ought to determine first the things which are required to prove this.

1142. Next where he says, **"One of these premises . . ."** [902], he develops his position. First he sets forth certain things which are necessary to prove his main point. Secondly, where he says, **"Now that these points . . ."** [918], he proves his main point.

Concerning the first part he makes three points. First he shows that infinite power is required for infinite motion. Secondly, where he says, **"It has now to be shown . . ."** [903], he shows that there cannot be infinite power in a finite magnitude. Thirdly, where he says, **"But before proceeding . . ."** [908], he shows that the first mover,

which causes eternal and continuous motion, must be one.

He says, therefore, first that one of the things which must be determined prior to the main point is that it is impossible for that which is finite in power to move through an infinite time. He proves this as follows.

In any motion there are three things. One is that which is moved; another is the mover itself; the third is time in which the motion occurs.

Now all of these must be infinite, or else all must be finite, or else certain ones are finite and certain ones infinite, either only one or two.

Let it be granted that A is a mover, B is a mobile object, and C is an infinite time. And assume that some part of A, which is D, moves some part of B, which is E. Granting these assumptions, we can conclude that D moves E in a time which is not only equal to C, in which A moved B, but in a shorter time.

For it was proven in Book VI that a whole mobile object crosses through a designated distance in a greater time than does part of it. Since time C is infinite, it follows that the time in which D moves E will not be infinite, but finite. Let that time be F. Thus just as A moves B in the infinite time C, so D moves E in the finite time F. Since, however, D is part of A, then if one subtracts from A and adds to D, A will be completely removed or exhausted, since it is finite. For if the same quantity is always taken, any finite thing is exhausted by subtraction, as was explained in Book III.

Similarly, B will be exhausted if something is continually subtracted from it and added to E. For B was given as finite. But no matter what is subtracted from time C, even if I subtract the same quantity, the whole of C is not exhausted, because it was given as infinite.

From this he concludes that the whole of A moves the whole of B in some finite time which is a part of C. This follows from the foregoing because an addition to a mobile object and to a mover requires a proportional addition to the time of the motion. But by subtracting from the whole mobile object and the mover, and by adding to their parts, at some time the whole mobile object and the whole mover will be exhausted such that the whole which was in the whole is added to the part. Therefore it follows that, by proportionally adding to the time, a finite time will result in which the whole mover will move the whole mobile object. Hence, if the mover is finite, and the mobile object is finite, the time must be finite.

Thus a finite mover cannot move something with an infinite motion in an infinite time. And thus, what was proposed at the beginning is clear, namely, a finite mover does not move in an infinite time.

1143. Avicenna, however, raises an objection to this proof from Aristotle. The proof does not appear to be universal. For there is a finite mover and mobile object from which it is impossi-

ble to subtract or remove anything, namely, a celestial body, which is not excluded from this proof. And so it seems either that the proof is particular, or else it proceeds from a false supposition.

Averroes answers this objection in his Commentary by saying that although nothing can be subtracted from a celestial body, nevertheless this conditional statement is true: if some part were removed from a celestial body, that part will move, or be moved, in less time than the whole. For a conditional proposition is not prevented from being true if its antecedent is impossible, as is clear in this conditional statement: if a man flies, he has wings. Rather, whatever destroys the truth of a true condition is false, even though the antecedent of the condition be false. Now the truth of the above condition is not consistent with the statement that a finite thing moves in an infinite time, as is clear from Aristotle's deduction. Therefore, from the truth of the above condition, Aristotle concludes that it is impossible for a finite thing to move in an infinite time.

It can be said more briefly, however, that when Aristotle uses removal or subtraction in his proofs, the dissolution of a continuum by subtraction must not always be inferred, for this is impossible in a celestial body. Rather subtraction may be understood according to a designation. For example, in wood which remains continuous, it is possible to designate some point either by touch or by thought, as if dividing the whole, and in this way to remove some part from the whole and to say that there is less whiteness in the part than in the whole. And in this way, too, it can be said that there is less power to move in a part of a celestial body which is removed by designation than in the whole.

1144. Another problem is more difficult. It does not appear to be contrary to the nature [ratio] of a finite mover to move in an infinite time. For if a finite thing is incorruptible or impassive in its nature and it does not withdraw from its nature, it will always be related to motion in the same way. And that which is related in the same way always does the same thing. Hence there is no reason why it cannot move afterwards rather than before. And this is apparent to the senses. For we see that the sun can move lower bodies in an infinite time.

To answer this problem the procedure of the above demonstration must be investigated. For just what conclusion follows from the premises should be clearly understood.

It should be noted that the time of a motion can be understood in two ways, especially in regard to local motion: first with respect to the parts of the mobile object, and secondly with respect to the parts of the magnitude over which the motion passes. For it is clear that one part of the mobile object passes through some point of the magnitude before the whole mobile object does. Similarly, the whole mobile object passes through one part of the magnitude before it passes through the whole. It is clearly apparent from Aristotle's procedure that he is speaking here of the time of the motion insofar as the time of the motion is taken with respect to the parts of the mobile object and not with respect to the parts of the magnitude. For he says in his proof that a part of the mover moves a part of the mobile object in less time than the whole moves the whole. This would not be true if we took the time of the motion with respect to the parts of

the magnitude which is crossed by the motion. For the proportion of the parts of the mover to the parts of the mobile object is the same as the proportion of the whole mover to the whole mobile object. And so a part will always move a part with a velocity equal to that by which the whole moves the whole. Hence, a part of the mobile object, which is moved by a part of the mover, will pass through a magnitude in a time equal to that in which the whole mobile object is moved by the whole mover.

Or perhaps the whole will be moved in less time than a part. For a unified power is greater than a divided power, and the greater the power of the mover, the swifter the motion and the shorter the time. This must be understood insofar as the time of the motion is considered with respect to the parts of the mobile object. For one part of the mobile object passes through a designated distance in less time than does the whole mobile object. And accordingly it is impossible for it to be moved in an infinite time, unless it is an infinite mobile object. It is impossible, moreover, for an infinite mobile object to be moved by a finite mover, for the power of the mover is always greater than the power of the mobile object. Hence an infinite mobile object must be moved by an infinite mover. From this it follows that it is impossible to hold that a finite mover moves a finite mobile object with a motion which is infinite with respect to the parts of the mobile object. Thus when this inconsistency is removed, one must conclude further that infinite motion is given to an infinite mobile object by an infinite mover.

1145. But someone may object to this by saying that Aristotle did not prove above that motion is infinite with respect to the parts of the mobile object such that the motion of an infinite body is called infinite. For the whole corporeal universe is finite, as was proven in Book III and as will be proven in De Caelo, I. Hence it does seem that Aristotle's proof is valid for the conclusion of this proposition; namely, the first mover which causes an infinite motion is infinite.

But it must be said that that which is the first cause of infinite motion must be a per se cause of infinite motion. For a cause which is per se is always prior to one which is through another, as was explained above. The power of a per se cause is directed to a per se effect and not to a per accidens effect. For it was thus that Aristotle taught us in Book II to compare causes to effects. Now a motion may be infinite in two ways, as was said, namely with respect to the parts of the mobile object and with respect to the parts of the magnitude over which the motion passes. Motion is infinite per se from the parts of the mobile object, and infinite per accidens with respect to the parts of the magnitude. For the quantity of motion which is taken with respect to the parts of the mobile object belongs to the motion with respect to its proper subject, and thus is present in it per se. But the quantity of motion which is taken with respect to the parts of the magnitude is taken with respect to the repetition of the motion of the mobile object, such that the whole mobile object which completes its motion over one part of the magnitude crosses another part by repetition. Therefore, that which is the first cause of the infinity of motion has a per se power over the infinity of motion such that it could move an infinite mobile object if there were such an object. Therefore it must be infinite. And even though the first mobile object is finite, it still has a certain similarity to an infinite one, as was explained in Book III. But in order for something to be the cause of a motion which is infinite due to the repetition of a motion (which is per accidens), it is not necessary for it to have infinite power. Rather it is sufficient if it has an immobile finite power. For always remaining the same in power, it could repeat the same effect. For example, the sun has a finite power, and yet it could move the lower elements in an infinite time, if motion were eternal, as Aristotle says. For there is no first cause of the infinity of motion, but it is as if things have been moved to move by another for an infinite time, according to the foregoing position.

1146. Next where he says, **"It has now to be shown . . ."** [903], he shows that the power in a magnitude must be proportional to the magnitude in which it resides. First he shows that an infinite power cannot reside in a finite magnitude, which is his main point. Secondly, where he says, **"Therefore nothing finite . . ."** [904], he shows that a finite power cannot reside in an infinite magnitude.

He proves that an infinite power cannot reside in a finite magnitude by setting forth two suppositions. The first is that a greater power produces an equal effect in a shorter time than a lesser power. For example, a greater power of heating produces in less time an equal heat in that on which it acts. And the same is true of the power of sweetening or throwing or of any kind of motion.

From this supposition he concludes that since an infinite power is greater than a finite one, then if a finite magnitude has an infinite power, it follows that in the same time either one or many patients undergo a greater mutation from such an agent than from another agent of finite power. Or conversely, that which undergoes an equal mutation would be changed by such an agent in less time. Either of these may be understood from his words ". . . in fact to a greater extent than by anything else . . ."

The second supposition is that since everything which is moved is moved in time, as was proven in Book VI, it is impossible for a patient to be changed by an infinitely powerful agent in no time. Therefore, it is changed in time.

From this he proceeds as follows. Let A be the time in which an infinite power heats or drives away. And let the time in which some finite power moves be AB, which is greater than A. Now another greater finite power can be taken. Therefore, if we take another finite power which is greater than the first one, which moves in time AB, it follows that this second power will move in less time. And again, a third still greater finite power will move in still less time. And thus, by always taking a finite power, I shall come to some finite power which moves in time A. For when addition is endlessly made to the finite power, every determinate proportion is exceeded. And at the same time an addition is made to the moving power, there is a subtraction from the time of the motion. For a greater power can move in a shorter time.

Therefore, it will follow that a finite power completes a motion in a time equal to that of the infinite power which moves in time A. This, however, is impossible. Therefore, no finite magnitude has an infinite power.

1147. There are numerous difficulties with this argument.

First, it seems that this argument comes to no conclusion at all. For what per se belongs to a thing cannot be removed from it by any power, however great it may be. For it is not because of a lack of power, or because it is repugnant to an infinite power, that it cannot be said that a man is not an animal. Now to be in time belongs per se to motion. For motion is included in the definition of time, as was shown above in Book IV. Hence, if an infinitely powerful mover is granted, it does not follow that motion does not take place in time, as Aristotle concludes here.

Further, if the Philosopher's procedure is considered, it seems that he concludes that motion does not take place in time because the moving power is infinite. But an infinite moving power cannot exist in a body. For the same reason, therefore, it follows that if such a power is infinite, it will move in no time. Therefore, from the fact that it is impossible for a thing to be moved in no time, it cannot be concluded that no infinite power resides in a magnitude but only that no moving power is infinite.

Further, two things seem to pertain to the magnitude of the power, namely, the velocity of the motion, and its duration. And we see that an excess of power produces an excess in both of these. But with regard to the excess of an infinite power, he has shown above that eternal motion results from an infinite power, but not that an infinite power does not reside in a magnitude. Hence also here, with respect to the excess of velocity, one ought not to conclude that no infinite power resides in a magnitude, but that a power which moves in an infinite time also moves in no time because of its infinity.

Further, the conclusion seems to be false. For the greater the power of a body, the longer can it be preserved in existence. Therefore, if no body has infinite power, no body can endure infinitely. This seems to be false both according to Aristotle's opinion and according to the judgment of the Christian faith which holds that the substance of the world will endure forever.

An objection could also be raised regarding the division and addition which he uses, since they do not agree with the nature of things. But since this was discussed sufficiently earlier, it is omitted at the present time.

1148. In answering these difficulties in order, one must reply to the first objection that the Philosopher does not intend here to give a direct demonstration but rather a demonstration which leads to impossibility. In such a proof one concludes that what is initially given is impossible because from it follows an impossibility. Moreover, it is not true that what is initially given together with the conclusion could possibly exist. For example, if it were granted that there is a power which could remove a genus from a species, it would follow that that power could make a man who is not an animal. But since this is impossible, the first statement is also impossible. But it cannot be concluded from this that it is possible for there to be a power which can make a man who is not an animal. And so, from the statement that there is an infinite power in a magnitude, of necessity it follows that motion occurs in no time. But because this is impossible, it is impossible for there to be an infinite power in a magnitude. But it cannot be concluded from this that it is possible for an infinite power to move in no time.

1149. Averroes answers the second difficulty in his Commentary on this text by saying that Aristotle's argument here deals with the infinity of

power. Now the finite and the infinite pertain to quantity, as was shown above in Book I. Hence neither the finite nor the infinite properly pertain to a power which does not reside in magnitude.

But this answer is contrary both to Aristotle's intention and to the truth.

It is contrary to Aristotle's intention because in the preceding argument Aristotle proved that a power which moves in an infinite time is infinite. And from this he concludes below that the power which moves the heavens is not a power which resides in a magnitude.

It is also contrary to the truth. For since every power is active with respect to some form, it follows that magnitude, and consequently the finite and the infinite, pertain to power in the same way as they pertain to form. Now magnitude pertains to form both per se and per accidens: per se with respect to the perfection of the form itself, as when a small amount of snow is said to have much whiteness according to the perfection of its proper nature [ratio]; and per accidens insofar as a form has extension in a subject, as when a thing is said to have much whiteness because of the magnitude of its surface.

This second magnitude cannot belong to a power which does not reside in a magnitude. But the first magnitude is especially proper to it. For immaterial powers are more perfect and more universal to the extent that they are less contracted by application to matter.

The velocity of motion, however, is not due to that magnitude of power which is per accidens because of the extension of the magnitude of a subject, but rather is due to that magnitude of power which is per se according to its proper perfection. For to the extent that a being is more perfectly in act, it is to that degree more vigorously active. Hence, although a power which does not reside in a magnitude is not infinite with the infinity of magnitude, which is due to the magnitude of the subject, it cannot be said that for this reason it does not cause an infinite increase of velocity, which is to move in no time.

Hence this same Commentator answers this difficulty in another way in Metaphysics, XII, where he says that a celestial body is moved by a double mover, namely, by a mover united to it, which is the soul of the heavens, and by a separated mover, which is not moved either per se or per accidens. And since that separated mover has infinite power, the motion of heavens receives eternal duration from it. And since the mover joined to it has finite power, the motion of heavens receives a determinate velocity from it.

But this answer is not sufficient. For that which moves in an infinite time seems to require infinite power, as the preceding proof concluded, and also that which moves in no time seems to require infinite power, as this proof seems to conclude. Therefore there still remains the difficulty of why the soul of the heavens, which moves in virtue of the infinite separated mover, is caused by that separated mover to move in an infinite time rather than with infinite velocity, that is in no time.

1150. To answer this difficulty it must be said that every power which is not in a magnitude moves through an intellect. For thus the Philosopher proves in Metaphysics, XII, that the heavens are moved by their own mover. Moreover, no power which is in a magnitude moves as if it has intelligence. For it was proven in De Anima, III, that the intellect is not the power of a body.

For this is the difference between an intellectual agent and a material agent. The action of a material agent is proportionate to the nature of the agent. For a thing produces heat to the extent that it is itself hot. But the action of an intellectual agent is not proportionate to its nature, but to the apprehended form. For a builder does not build as much as he can, but as much as the intelligibility [ratio] of the conceived form requires.

Therefore, if there were some infinite power in a magnitude, it would follow that the motion proceeding from it would be according to its proportion, and thus the present proof proceeds. If, however, there is an infinite power which is not in a magnitude, motion would not proceed from it according to the proportion of power, but according to the intelligibility [ratio] of the apprehended form, that is, according to that which is proper to the end and nature of the subject.

There is another thing to be noted. As was proven in Book VI, nothing is moved unless it has magnitude. And so the velocity of motion is an effect received from a thing which moves in something having magnitude. It is clear, moreover, that nothing which has magnitude can receive an effect equally proportioned to a power which is not in a magnitude. For every corporeal nature is compared to incorporeal nature as something particular to the absolute and the universal. Hence, if there is an infinite power which is not in a magnitude, it cannot be concluded that it produces in some body an infinite velocity as an effect proportioned to such a power, as was said.

But nothing prevents the reception in a magnitude of an effect of a power which is in a magnitude, since a cause is proportioned to its effect. Hence, if it were granted that some infinite power exists in a magnitude, it would follow that there is a corresponding effect in the magnitude, namely, an infinite velocity. But this is impossible. Therefore, so is the first statement.

1151. From these remarks the answer to the third difficulty is clear. To be moved in an infinite time is not repugnant to the nature [ratio] of a moved magnitude. Rather this is proper to a circular magnitude, as was shown above. But to be moved with infinite velocity, that is, in no time, is contrary to the nature [ratio] of magnitude, as was proven in Book VI. Hence, according to Aristotle, a motion of infinite duration is caused by a first mover of infinite power. But a motion of infinite velocity is not.

1152. As Averroes remarks at this point in his Commentary, Alexander answers the fourth difficulty by saying that a celestial body receives its eternity and its eternal motion from a separated mover of infinite power. Hence, it is not moved eternally because of the infinity of the celestial body just as it does not endure eternally because of the infinity of the celestial body. Rather both of these are due to the infinity of a separated mover.

Averroes tries to disprove this answer both here in his Commentary and in Metaphysics, XII. He says that is impossible for a thing to receive eternity of being from another for it would follow that what is corruptible in itself would become eternal. But a being can acquire eternity of motion from another because motion is the act of a mobile object from the mover. He says, therefore, that a celestial body in itself

has no potency for non-being because its substance has no contrary. But there is a potency for rest in a celestial body because rest is contrary to its motion. Hence it does not need to acquire eternity of being from another, but it does need to acquire eternity of motion from another.

He says that a celestial body has no potency for non-being because he also says that a celestial body is not composed of matter and form, as if composed of potency and act. Rather he says that it is matter existing in act, and its form he calls its soul. However, it is not constituted in being, but only in motion, by its form. And thus he says that there is in it no potency for being, but only potency for place, as the philosopher says in Metaphysics, XII.

1153. But this answer is contrary to the truth and to Aristotle's intention.

It is contrary to the truth in many ways, first, because he says that a celestial body is not composed of matter and form. For this is absolutely impossible.

It is clear that a celestial body is something in act, otherwise it would not be moved. For what is in potency only is not a subject of motion, as was explained in Book VI. And everything which is in act must be either a subsisting form, as are the separated substances, or must have a form in another which is related to form as matter and as potency to act.

Now it cannot be said that a celestial body is a subsisting form, for then it· would be an intellect in act, and would be neither sensible nor quantified. Hence it follows that it is composed of matter and form and of potency and act. And thus potency for non-being is in it in some way.

But even if it is granted that a celestial body is not composed of matter and form, it still must be admitted that potency for non-being is in it in some way. For it is necessary that each simple subsisting substance either is its own existence or participates in existence. A simple substance which is its own subsisting existence cannot exist except as one, just as whiteness, if it were subsisting, could not exist except as one. Therefore, every substance which is after the first simple substance participates in existence. Moreover, everything that participates is composed of the participant and the participated, and the participant is in potency to the participated. Therefore, in every simple substance after the first simple substance there is potency for being.

He was deceived, moreover, by the equivocal meaning of potency. For potency is sometimes predicated in relation to an opposite. But this is excluded from celestial bodies and from separated simple substances. For according to Aristotle's intention, there is no potency in them for non-being because of the fact that simple substances are forms only, and existence belongs to form per se. Moreover, the matter of a celestial body is not in potency to another form. For just as a celestial body is related to its own figure, of which it is the subject, as potency to act, and yet it cannot not have such a figure, so likewise the matter of a celestial body is related to such a form as potency to act, and yet it is not in potency to a privation of this form, or to non-being. For not every potency is of opposites, otherwise the possible would not be a consequence of the necessary, as is said in De Interpretatione.

His position is also contrary to the intention of Aristotle who, in De Caelo, I, uses in a proof the proposition that a celestial body has the potency or power to always exist. Hence it is not possible to avoid inconsistency when he says that there is no potency for being in a celestial body. For this is clearly false and contrary to Aristotle's intention.

1154. Let us see whether Averroes adequately refutes the answer of Alexander, who says that a celestial body acquires eternity from another. His refutation would indeed be adequate if Alexander had held that a celestial body of itself has potency for being and non-being, and acquires eternal existence from another. And I say this on the supposition that his intention is not to exclude the omnipotence of God through which a corruptible thing can assume incorruptibility. The discussion of this latter point is not pertinent to the proposition. Even granting his intention, Averroes still cannot reach a conclusion contrary to Alexander, who did not hold that a celestial body acquires eternity from another in the sense that it has in itself potency for being and nonbeing, but in the sense that it does not have existence from itself. For everything which is not its own existence, participates in existence from the first cause, which is its own existence. Hence even Averroes admits in De Substantia Orbis that God causes the heavens not only in respect to its motion, but also in respect to its substance. This could not be unless it has its existence from Him. But it has only eternal existence from Him. Therefore, it has its eternity from another. And Aristotle's words are also in agreement with this when he says in Metaphysics, V, and above at the beginning of Book VIII that there are certain necessary things which have a cause of their necessity. Granting this, the solution according to Alexander's intention is clear, namely, just as a celestial body has its motion from another, so also it has its existence from another. Hence, just as eternal motion demonstrates the infinite power of the mover, but not of the mobile object, likewise its eternal duration demonstrates the infinite power of the cause from which it has its existence.

1155. Nevertheless the potency of a celestial body is not related in exactly the same way to being and to being moved eternally.

They do not differ as he says, namely, that with respect to being moved there is in a celestial body a potency for the opposites of motion and rest. Rather there is a potency for opposites which are diverse places.

They differ with respect to something else. Motion in itself occurs in time. But existence in itself does not occur in time, but only insofar as it is subject to motion. Therefore, if there is some existence which is not subject to motion, that existence would in no way occur in time. Hence the potency to be moved in infinite time is related to the infinity of time directly and per se. But the potency to exist in an infinite time, if indeed that existence is mutable, is related to the quantity of time. Therefore a greater power or potency is required for a thing to endure in mutable existence for a greater time. But a potency which is immutable with respect to existence in no way is related to the quantity of time. Hence the magnitude or infinity of time has nothing to do with the magnitude or infinity of the potency for such existence. Therefore, if one grants the impossibility that a celestial body does not have its existence from another, one still could not conclude from its eternity that there is an infinite power in it.

1156. Next where he says, **"Therefore nothing finite . . ."** [904], he

proves that a finite power cannot reside in an infinite magnitude.

He proves this with two arguments. In the first argument he makes three points.

First he states his conclusion. He says that just as an infinite power cannot reside in a finite magnitude, likewise a power which is finite with respect to the whole (for if a part of the infinite is finite, it will have finite power) cannot reside in an infinite quantity.

He introduces this, however, not as though it were essential for the proof of the main proposition, but as closely connected to the conclusion demonstrated above.

1157. Secondly, where he says, **"It is true that a greater . . ."** [905], he indicates a reason why someone may think it is possible for a finite power to reside in an infinite magnitude. We see that a smaller magnitude has a greater power than a larger magnitude, for example, a small fire has a greater active power than much air. But from this it cannot be held that an infinite quantity has a finite power. For if a still greater magnitude is taken, it will have greater power. For example, air which is greater in respect to quantity has less power than a small fire. But if the quantity of the air is greatly increased, it will have a greater power than the small fire.

1158. Thirdly, where he says, **"Now let AB . . ."** [906], he gives his proof, which is as follows. Let AB be an infinite quantity; and let BC be a finite magnitude of a different genus which has a certain finite power; and let D be a mobile object which is moved by the magnitude BC in a time which is EF. Now since BC is a finite magnitude, a larger magnitude can be taken. Let a magnitude twice its size be taken. Now the greater the power of the mover, the smaller the time in which it moves, as was explained in Book VII. Therefore, twice BC will move the same mobile object, D, in half the time, which is FG. The time EF is understood to be divided in half at point G. By thus continually adding to BC, the time of the motion is lessened. But no matter how much is added, BC can never equal AB, which exceeds BC without proportion as the infinite exceeds the finite. And since AB has finite power, it moves D in a finite time. Hence by continually diminishing the time in which BC moves, we come to a time which is less than the time in which AB moves. For whatever is finite is crossed by division. It will follow, therefore, that a smaller power moves in less time, which is impossible. It follows, therefore, that there was an infinite power in the infinite magnitude, because the power of an infinite magnitude exceeds every finite power.

And this was proven by the subtraction of time because it is necessary to hold that every finite power moves in a determinate time. This is clear from the following. If so much power moves in so much time, a greater power will move in a smaller, yet finite and determinate, time according to an inverse proportion, that is, the time is decreased as much as the power is increased. And thus, whatever is added to a finite power, as long as it remains a finite power, will always have a finite time. For there will be a time which is as much less than the earlier time as the power which is increasing by addition is greater than the initially given power.

But an infinite power of motion surpasses every determinate time, as happens with all infinites. For every infinite, for example, in multitude or finite, for example, in multitude or magnitude, exceeds every determinate thing of its genus. And thus it is clear that an infinite power exceeds every finite power in which the increase of power over power is similar to the lessening of time from time, as was said. Hence it is clear that the above conclusion, namely, there is infinite power in the infinite magnitude, follows of necessity from the premises.

1159. Next where he says, "This point may also . . ." [907], he gives another proof of the same thing. This proof differs from the first only in that the first one concluded by taking a finite power existing in a finite magnitude of another genus, whereas the second proof proceeds by taking another finite power existing in another finite magnitude of the same genus, the magnitude of which is infinite. For example, if air is infinite in magnitude and has a finite power, we shall take a finite power existing in some finite magnitude of other air.

Granting this position, it is clear that when the finite power of the finite magnitude is multiplied many times, it will measure the finite power which is in the infinite magnitude. For whatever is finite is measured or exceeded by a smaller finite thing taken many times. Now in a magnitude of the same genus, a greater magnitude must have a greater power, as more air has greater power than less air. Therefore, that finite magnitude which will have the same proportion to the first finite magnitude as the finite power of the infinite magnitude has to the power of the first finite magnitude must have a power equal to the power of the infinite magnitude. For example, if the finite power of the infinite magnitude is one hundred times the finite power of the given finite magnitude, then a magnitude which is one hundred times the finite magnitude must have a power equal to the infinite magnitude. For in a thing of the same genus, magnitude and power are increased proportionately. The conclusion, however, is impossible, for it would necessarily follow either that a finite magnitude would be equal to an infinite magnitude, or else a smaller magnitude of the same genus would have a power equal to a larger one. Since this is impossible, so is the premise from which it follows, namely, an infinite magnitude has a finite power.

Therefore, in summarizing, he draws two demonstrative conclusions, namely, there cannot be infinite power in a finite magnitude, and there cannot be finite power in an infinite magnitude.

LECTURE 22 [266b27-267a21]
The Problem of Projectile Motion

The Text of Aristotle

908. But before proceeding to our conclusion it will be well to discuss a difficulty that arises in connection with locomotion. If everything that is in motion with the exception of things that move themselves is moved by something else, how is it that some things, e.g., things thrown, continue to be in motion when their mover is no longer in contact with them?   **266b27-30**

909. If we say that the mover in such cases moves something else at the same time, that the thrower e.g. also moves the air, and that this in being moved is also a mover, then it would be no more possible for this second thing than for the original thing to be in motion when the original mover is not in contact with it or moving it: all the things moved would have to be in motion simultaneously and also to have ceased simultaneously to be in motion when the original mover ceases to move them, even if, like the magnet, it makes that which it has moved capable of being a mover.   **266b30-267a2**

910. Therefore, while we must accept this explanation to the extent of saying that the original mover gives the power of being a mover either to air or to water or to something else of the kind, naturally adapted for imparting and undergoing motion, we must say further that this thing does not cease simultaneously to impart motion and to undergo motion: it ceases to be in motion at the moment when its mover ceases to move it, but it still remains a mover, and so it causes something else consecutive with it to be in motion, and of this again the same may be said. The motion begins to cease when the motive force produced in one member of the consecutive series is at each stage less than that possessed by the preceding member, and it finally ceases when one member no longer causes the next member to be a mover but only causes it to be in motion. The motion of these last two—of the one as mover and of the other as moved—must cease simultaneously, and with this the whole motion ceases.   **267a2-12**

911. Now the things in which this motion is produced are things that admit of being sometimes in motion and sometimes at rest, and the motion is not continuous but only appears so; for it is motion of things that are either successive or in contact, there being not one mover but a number of movers consecutive with one another: and so motion of this kind takes place in air and water. Some say that it is "mutual replacement"; but we must recognize that the difficulty raised cannot be solved otherwise than in the way we have described. So far as they are affected by "mutual replacement," all the members of the series are moved and impart motion simultaneously, so that their motions also cease simultaneously; but our present problem concerns the appearance of continuous motion in a single thing, and therefore, since it cannot be moved throughout its motion by the same mover, the question is, what moves it?   **267a12-20**

COMMENTARY OF ST. THOMAS

1160. After the Philosopher has proven two things which are necessary for the proof of his main point, namely, that a finite power cannot move in an infinite time, and that an infinite power cannot reside in a finite magnitude, he now proceeds to prove a third point, namely, the unity of the first mover.

Concerning this he does two things.

First he shows that because of a diversity of movers the continuity or unity of motion fails in certain mobile objects which seem to be moved continuously. Secondly, where he says, **"Resuming our main argument..."** [912], he shows that the first mover must be one.

Concerning the first part he makes three points. First he raises an objection concerning things which are thrown. Secondly, where he says, **"Therefore, while we must..."** [910], he answers the objection. Thirdly, where he says, **"Now the things in which..."** [911], he shows that the motion of a thrown body is not continuous.

Concerning the first part he makes two points. First he raises the objection. Secondly, where he says, **"If we say that..."** [909], he rejects a certain solution.

Therefore he first states a difficulty concerning things which are thrown. The difficulty is as follows.

It was shown above, at the beginning of Book VIII, that whatever is moved is moved by another, excluding self-movers, such as animals. A thrown stone is not included in this latter group. Moreover, a body moves as a result of contact. There is a difficulty, therefore, concerning the way in which a thrown thing continues to be moved even after it is no longer in contact with the mover. For it seems that it is then being moved without having a mover.

1161. Next where he says, **"If we say that..."** [909], he rejects a certain solution, said to have been Plato's, which holds that the thrower which first moves the stone moves something else together with the stone, namely the air, and the moved air moves the stone subsequent to the contact of the thrower.

But he rejects this solution because it seems to be just as impossible for the air to be moved without contact with the first mover, that is, the thrower, as it was for the stone. Rather it seems to be necessary that while the first mover moves, everything is moved, and while the first mover rests, that is, ceases from moving, everything rests,

even though that which was moved by the first mover, for example, the stone, causes something to be moved, just as that which moved first, moved.

1162. Next where he says, **"Therefore, while we must..."** [910], he gives his own solution.

He says that if the second mover moves what has been moved by the first mover, it must be said that the first mover, that is, the thrower, gives to the second mover, that is, air or water or any such body which can naturally move a thrown body, the power to move and to be moved. For the air or water receives from the thrower both the power to move and to be moved. But to move and to be moved are not necessarily in the same being, for we have found that there is a mover which is not moved. Therefore, the mover and that which is moved do not stop simultaneously, that is, the air moved by the thrower does not simultaneously cease to move and to be moved. Rather as soon as the first mover, that is, the thrower, ceases to move, the air ceases to be moved, but it is still a mover.

And this is clear to the senses. For when a mobile object has reached the terminus of its motion, at that ultimate point it can move. It is not then being moved but rather has already been moved. Moreover, while the second mover moves, it moves that which is related consecutively to it. And the same principle [ratio] holds for this third being, for it remains a mover even when it is no longer moved. And because the second mover has less power of moving than the first, and the third less than the second, the motion of throwing must cease because there is less power of moving in the consecutive mover than there was in the first mover.

And finally, because of the decrease

in the power of the motive force, we reach a point where that which will be prior to the next object will not cause that next object to have the power of moving but will only cause it to be moved. When this last mover stops moving, that which is moved by it must simultaneously stop from being moved. And consequently, the whole motion will cease, since the last thing moved cannot move something else.

1163. Next where he says, **"Now the things in which . . ."** [911], he concludes from the above that the motion of throwing is not continuous.

He says, therefore, that this motion of throwing occurs in bodies which are sometimes moved and sometimes at rest. This is clear from what has been said, for the motion of throwing ceases due to the decrease of the motive power, as was said.

It is also clear from the above that that motion is not continuous, though it may seem to be. It appears to be continuous because of the unity of the mobile object. It is not continuous, however, because there are many movers, as was said. For that motion results either from many movers which are consecutive or from many movers which are in contact. (It was explained above in Book V and in Book VI how consecutiveness differs from contact.)

And it is apparent to the senses that, in whichever way the diverse movers are related, they are able to move one mobile object insofar as they themselves are moved by some first mover. For in things which are moved by the motion of throwing, there is not just one mover, but many, which are related to each other both consecutively and by contact. And since diversity involves division, the motion of throwing mentioned above occurs through a medium which is readily divisible, namely, through air or water, in which there are a diversity of movers because they are easily divided.

Some say, however, that this motion of throwing is "mutual replacement," that is, contrary-resistance, such that the surrounding air which is moved in some way moves the thrown body, as was said above in Book IV. But the above problem can be solved only in the way set down. For if the "mutual replacement" of the air is said to be the cause of the throwing, it follows that everything moves and is moved simultaneously, that is, the whole of the air moves and is moved simultaneously, and consequently, everything rests simultaneously. But this is clearly false. For we see that there is one thing which is moved continuously no matter what moves it. I say this because it does not have one and the same determinate mover, but many movers.

LECTURE 23 [267a22–b26]
The First Mover Cannot Have Magnitude

The Text of Aristotle

912. *Resuming our main argument, we proceed from the positions that there must be continuous motion in the world of things, that this is a single motion, that a single motion must be a motion of a magnitude (for that which is without magnitude cannot be in motion), and that the magnitude must be a single magnitude moved by a single mover (for otherwise there will not be continuous motion but a consecutive series of separate motions), and that if the mover is a single thing, it is either itself in motion or itself unmoved:*   267a21–25

913. *if, then, it is in motion, it will have to be subject to the same conditions as that which it moves, that is to say it will itself be in process of change and in being, and so will also have to be moved by something: so we have a series that must come to an end, and a point will be reached at which motion is imparted by something that is unmoved. Thus we have a mover that has no need to change along with that which it moves but will be able to cause motion always (for the causing of motion under these conditions involves no effort);*   267a25–267b3

914. *and this motion alone is regular, or at least it is so in a higher degree than any other, since the mover is never subject to any change. So, too, in order that the motion may continue to be of the same character, the moved must not be subject to change in respect of its relation to the mover.*   267b3–6

915. *Moreover the mover must occupy either the center or the circumference, since these are the first principles from which a sphere is derived. But the things nearest the mover are those whose motion is quickest, and in this case it is the motion of the circumference that is the quickest: therefore the mover occupies the circumference.*   267b6–9

916. *There is a further difficulty in supposing it to be possible for anything that is in motion to cause motion continuously and not merely in the way in which it is caused by something repeatedly pushing (in which case the continuity amounts to no more than successiveness).*   267b9–11

917. *Such a mover must either itself continue to push or pull or perform both these actions, or else the action must be taken up by something else and be passed on from one mover to another (the process that we described before as occurring in the case of things thrown, since the air or the water, being divisible, is a mover only in virtue of the fact that different parts of the air are moved one after another); and in either case the motion cannot be a single motion, but only a consecutive series of motions. The only continuous motion, then, is that which is caused by the unmoved mover; and this motion is continuous because the mover remains always invariable, so that its relation to that which it moves remains also invariable and continuous.*   267b11–17

918. *Now that these points are settled, it is clear that the first unmoved mover cannot have any magnitude. For if it has magnitude, this must be either a finite or an infinite magnitude. Now we have already proved in our course on* Physics *that there cannot be an infinite magnitude; and we have now proved that it is impossible for a finite magnitude to have an infinite force, and also that it is impossible for a thing to be moved by a finite magnitude during an infinite time. But the first mover causes a motion that is eternal and does cause it during an infinite time. It is clear, therefore, that the first mover is indivisible and is without parts and without magnitude.*   267b17–26

COMMENTARY OF ST. THOMAS

1164. From the solution of the difficulty which he raised concerning the motion of throwing, he has concluded that a motion caused by many movers is not one and continuous. Here he proceeds to his main point, namely, he proves the unity of the first mover.

Concerning this he makes two points. First he proves his position. Secondly, where he says, **"There is a further difficulty..."** [916], he raises a difficulty and answers it.

Concerning the first part he makes three points. First he proves the unity of the first mover from the continuity of motion. Secondly, where he says, **"...if, then, it is in motion..."** [913], he explains how continuous motion proceeds from one mover. Thirdly, where he says, **"Moreover the mover..."** [915], he shows where the source of continuous motion is.

1165. He proves from the continuity of motion that there must be one mover by beginning with what he has proven above, namely, there must be a motion which is eternally continuous. Continuous motion, moreover, is one, as was established in Book V. Therefore, some one motion must always exist. But in order for this motion to be one, it must be the motion of one moved magnitude (for it was established in Book VI that what is indivisible cannot be moved). Furthermore, this motion must be caused by one mover. For if there are diverse mobile objects or diverse movers, there will not be one motion, and consequently, not a continuous motion. Rather one motion will be divided from another because of a division of the mobile object or the mover, and these motions will be related consecutively. Therefore, there must be one mover, which

either moves and is moved or which moves and is immobile.

1166. Next where he says, **"...if, then, it is in motion..."** [913], he shows how there can be continuous motion from one mover.

Concerning this he makes two points. First he shows how there can be eternally continuous motion from one mover. Secondly, where he says, **"...and this motion alone..."** [914], he shows how this motion is regular.

He says, therefore, first that one motion which is from one mover is from either a moved or an unmoved mover, as was said. If it is a moved mover, it follows that it is moved by another, according to what has been proven above. But this cannot proceed to infinity, as was established above, for this order of movers and mobile objects will end and will arrive at some first mobile object which is moved by an immobile mover, which has no necessity to move because it is not moved by another. For that which is moved by another must move insofar as necessity is placed in it by its mover. And since it is changed from its disposition, it cannot always move uniformly because its disposition varies.

But no necessity is imparted by another to an unmoved mover, and its disposition does not change. Hence it does not move from necessity but rather can always move. For that which moves without being changed itself, moves without fatigue. Some movers become fatigued in moving because they are also simultaneously moved. And because of this fatigue they cannot move forever. Hence it follows that an unmoved mover can move with an eternally continuous motion.

1167. And since, as was said in Book V, regularity and uniformity are required for the perfect continuity and unity of motion, as a result, where he says, ". . . and this motion alone . . ." [914], he shows that motion from an immobile mover is regular.

He says that either only the motion from an immobile mover is regular, or, if other motions are regular, this is the most regular. He makes this distinction because the disposition of a moved mover sometimes remains the same and does not vary for some period of time, at least with respect to sensation. And accordingly it seems to move for some time with a regular motion. But that which is always unmoved causes the most regular motion, for such a mover undergoes no change at all. He says this in order to show that there are certain movers which are not moved by the motion by which they move. For example, a celestial body is not moved by the motion of alteration, but by another motion, namely, local motion. But the first, absolutely immobile mover is moved in no way.

In order for motion to be regular and uniform, not only is it necessary that the mover be absolutely immobile, but the motion must also be uniform such that that which is moved does not have another change joined to that by which it is moved by the immobile mover, just as the local motion of a celestial body is caused by an immobile mover, and no other change is joined to it. For, if it were altered, the same disposition for motion would not always remain in it, and thus the motion would not be uniform.

1168. Next where he says, "Moreover the mover . . ." [915], he shows where the source of the first continuous motion is. Since it has been shown

that the first motion is circular, which motion pertains to a circular magnitude, the first source of this motion must be in the middle, that is, in the center, or in the circumference, for these are the sources of a circular magnitude. For in a circular magnitude, lines are drawn from the center to the circumference, and so one of these must be taken as the source and the other as the terminus.

He proves as follows that the source of the first motion is in the circumference. The closer any motion is to the source of its motion, the faster is its velocity because it receives a greater impression from the mover. But in the motion of the entire firmament, which is due to the first immobile mover, we see that the closer a mobile object is to the outermost circumference, the faster is its motion. Therefore, the mover is in the circumference, and not in the center.

The major premise of this argument is clear. But to clarify the minor premise, we must realize that a double motion is found in celestial bodies. One is the motion of the whole firmament by which the whole firmament is rotated from east to west in daily motion. This is the first motion. The other motion is the one by which the stars are moved conversely from west to east.

In this second motion, the closer that each celestial body is to the center, the faster is its motion, as is clear from the computations of the astronomers, who compute the time of the Moon's motion as one month; that of the Sun, Mercury, and Venus as one year; that of Mars, two years; Jupiter, 10; Saturn, 30; and of the fixed stars 36 thousand years.

But the motion of the whole firmament is just the opposite. For the further a celestial body is from the earth, the faster is its motion, since it traverses a greater magnitude in the same time. For the circumference of circles are greater the more distant they are from the center. And all celestial bodies are rotated in the same time with respect to the motion of the whole. And so the higher body must be the faster. Hence it follows that the source of the first motion is not in the center but in the circumference.

1169. But a problem arises concerning this conclusion. For the first mover, as he concludes below, is indivisible and has no magnitude and its power is not a power which resides in a magnitude. But such a being does not seem to have a determined location in a body. Therefore, it is not proper for the first mover to be in one part of the first mobile object rather than another.

But it must be stated that the first mover is not said to be in some part of its mobile object through a determination of its own substance, but through its power of motion. For it begins to move from some part of its mobile object, and therefore it is said to be in the heavens rather than in earth, and preferably in the east where it begins to move. This cannot be understood in the sense that the first mover is fixed to some determinate part of its mobile object. For no determinate part of the mobile object is always in the east. Rather that part which is now in the east is later in the west. And so it is clear that its motive power is said to be in the east because of the influence of its motion, and not because of a determination of its substance.

With respect to the motion of the spheres it must be realized that they have a certain immobility as well as motion. For the parts are moved by changing place both in the subject and in reason [ratio]. But the whole is moved by changing place only in reason [ratio] and not in subject, as was established in Book VI. And these two are attributed to the two principles of spherical magnitude which were mentioned here. For the source of motion is in the circumference; but the source of immobility is in the fixed center.

1170. Next where he says, **"There is a further difficulty . . ."** [916], he raises a difficulty about the foregoing. First he raises the difficulty and secondly he answers it, where he says, **"Such a movement must . . ."** [917].

He has said above that an immobile mover can cause continuous motion, and so here he asks whether a moved mover can cause continuous motion—really continuous motion, that is, without any such interruption as occurs when someone pushes a body, which is pushed again by another. It is clear that this motion, which is continued in respect to the mobile object, is not really continuous, because the motions are not continuous. Rather one motion is consecutive to the other. For this is not a continuous pushing, rather there is an interruption such that a pushing follows a pushing.

1171. Next where he says, **"Such a mover must . . ."** [917], he answers the above difficulty and shows that no moved mover can cause continuous motion.

It must be said that a mobile object which seems to be moved continuously either is moved immediately through the whole motion by that moved mover itself, or else by many intermediaries, one of which is contacted by another, as was said of the motion of throwing. This distinction applies whether the moved mover moves by pushing or by pulling or by both motions, as occurs in the motion of spinning, as was shown above in Book VII. Nor are there many ways in which a thing is moved locally by a moved mover per se and not per accidens (for what is carried is moved per accidens).

And he has said in reference to things which are thrown that there are different movers. But this seems to be false, because a thrown body seems to be moved continuously by one existing air. In order to reject this, he adds that since air or water is readily divisible, different movers move the object. And they always move as long as the motion of the thrown body endures. And although the air seems to be one, nevertheless, it is many by division.

In both cases, however, that is, whether the moved mover moves by pushing or by pulling, there cannot be one motion. Rather there are consecutive motions because of the explanation given above for the motion of throwing, namely, there are many movers.

It follows, therefore, that only motion from an immobile mover can be eternally continuous. For this mover is always related in the same way with respect to the same disposition in itself. And therefore it can always and continuously be related in the same way to the mobile object so that it always moves it with uniformity.

It should be noted, moreover, that the Philosopher here attributes the eternity of continuous motion to the immobility of the mover, but above to its infinite power. For if the eternity of continuous motion is taken with respect to the repetition of motion, it is due to the immobility of the mover. For if the mover always maintains the same relation, it can always repeat the

same motion. But the infinite power of the mover is related to the entire eternity or per se infinity of the motion, as was said above.

And it is also to be noted that since no moved mover can cause eternally continuous motion, in Metaphysics, XII, he intends to prove a multitude of immobile movers corresponding to the multitude of celestial motions, as if that consideration follows from this one.

1172. Next where he says, **"Now that these points . . ."** [918], he concludes to his main point from what was demonstrated above.

He says that from the above it is clear that it is impossible for the first immobile mover to have any magnitude, either in the sense that it is a body or in the sense that it is a power in a body. For if it has magnitude, that magnitude is either finite or infinite. But it was shown above in Book III in discussing the common properties of nature that an infinite magnitude is impossible. It follows, then, that if it has magnitude, that magnitude is finite. But it can be proven that it does not have a finite magnitude because it is impossible for a finite magnitude to have infinite power. The first immobile mover, however, must have infinite power. Therefore it cannot have a finite magnitude.

He proves that the first immobile mover must have infinite power from what was demonstrated above, namely, it is impossible for some thing to be moved in an infinite time by a finite power. But the first mover causes eternal and continuous motion and exists as one and the same in infinite time. Otherwise, that motion would not be continuous. Therefore, it has infinite power. And thus it does not have finite magnitude. And an infinite magnitude cannot exist. It is clear, therefore, that the first mover is indivisible, both because it has no parts (as is also true of an indivisible point) and because it has absolutely no magnitude, existing, as it were, outside of the genus of magnitude.

And thus the Philosopher ends his general discussion of natural things with the first principle of the whole of nature, who is over all things, God, blessed forever, Amen.

APPENDIX A

BOOK VII, CHAPTER 2

682 (Lecture 3, 682–692). The first mover, not as the cause for the sake of which but as the principle of motion, is together with that which is moved. I say 'together' because there is no intermediate between them. And this is found universally in everything which moves and which is moved.

683. Since there are three motions, i.e., in respect to place, in respect to quality, and in respect to quantity, there must be three things which are moved. Motion in respect to place is local motion; motion in respect to quality is alteration; motion in respect to quantity is increase or decrease. We should speak first of local motion. For this is the *first of* motions.

684. Whatever is moved is moved either by itself or by another. If by itself, then since the mover is in it, it is clear that the mover and that which is moved will be together and there will be no intermediary between them.

685. That which is moved by another is moved in one of four ways. The motions which are from another are four: pushing, pulling, carrying, and twirling. For all the others are reduced to these.

686. Pushing is either pushing on or pushing off. Pushing on occurs when the mover does not leave that which is moved. Pushing off occurs when the pusher leaves.

687. Carrying will be in the three other motions. For that which is carried is not moved in itself but accidentally. For in this that which is moved is either in that which is moved or is on that which is moved. The carrier is moved either by a pushing or a pulling or else it is led on by a twirling. Therefore it is clear that carrying will be in these three motions.

688. Pulling occurs when there is a faster motion of the puller either to itself or to another, not separated from that which is pulled. For pulling occurs both to itself and to another. Other pullings which are the same in species are reduced to these, for example, inhaling and exhaling, and spitting, and whatever bodies are emitted or received, and striking, and combing. Gathering of things is one thing and separating is another. Therefore all motion in respect to place is a gathering or a separating.

689. Twirling is composed of pushing and pulling. For the mover pushes this and pulls that.

690. Therefore it is clear that if the pusher and the puller are together with that which is pushed and pulled, there is no intermediate between that which is moved and the mover.

691. This is clear from what was said. Pushing is motion either from itself or from another to another. But pulling is from another to itself or to another. Thus far there is coming together and going apart.

692. There is throwing when there occurs a faster motion than that which is borne according to nature, a stronger pushing having been made. This being done, it is borne as long as the motion of that which is borne is stronger. Therefore it is clear that the mover and that which is moved are together and there is no intermediary between them.

693 (Lecture 4, 693–696). Neither is there an intermediary between the altered and the alterer. This is clear from induction. For in all cases the ultimate alterer and the first thing which is altered are together.

694. Quality is altered by that which is sensible. There are sensible things by which bodies differ from each other: as heaviness and lightness, hardness and softness, sound and no sound, whiteness and blackness, sweetness and bitterness, wetness and dryness, density and rarity, and their intermediaries. Likewise there are other things which are under the senses. These include hot and cold, smoothness and roughness. For these are passions of the subject of quality. In these the sensibilities of bodies differ insofar as one of these is more and less and in undergoing one of these: becoming hot or becoming cold, or becoming sweet or becoming bitter, or in respect to same other of the things mentioned. The same applies to both animate and inanimate bodies. And certain parts of animate bodies are inanimate. And the senses themselves are altered because they suffer. Their action is motion through the body, the sense suffering something. Animate bodies are altered in respect to all the things by which inanimate bodies are altered. But inanimate bodies are not altered in respect to the things by which animate bodies are altered. For they are not altered in respect to sense, and when inanimate bodies are altered it is concealed from them. Moreover nothing prevents animate bodies also from being unaware when they are altered. For alteration not in respect to sense occurs to them. Therefore if there are sensible passions, every alteration occurs through them. From this, therefore, it is clear that the passion and the patient are together and there is no intermediary between them.

695. Moreover air is continuous with this, and the body is contained by the air. And the surface is terminated at light, and light at sight. Hearing and smelling are similarly related to that which first moves them. In the same way taste and flavour are together. And it is the same in both inanimate and insensible things.

696. And that which is increased and the increaser are together. For increase is a certain addition. For this reason that which is increased and the increaser are together. And decrease: the cause of decrease is a certain subtraction. It is clear, therefore, that there is no intermediary between the ultimate mover and the first thing moved.

BOOK VII, CHAPTER 3

697 (Lecture 5, 697–701). All things which are altered are altered by sensible things. And there is alteration only of those things which in themselves are said to suffer from these. We will consider these.

698. Of the other things one will especially think that there is alteration in figures and forms and habits in regard to both their removal and their reception. For

this seems to be alteration. But this is not so in these things. Rather these things came to be when certain things are altered. For the matter becomes dense or rarefied, or becomes hat or cold. But there is no alteration.

699. That from which the form of statue is we do not call form, nor that from which the figure of pyramid or bed is. Rather we denominate this 'bronzen,' and that 'waxen' and another 'wooden.' But that which is altered we call form. For we say that bronze is wet or strong or hot. And not only thus, but we say the wet and hot is bronze, predicating the matter equally with the passion. Hence, since that from which the form and figure is and which was made is not equally predicated with the figures which are from it; and since things which are altered are predicated equally with the passions; it is clear that there is alteration only in sensible things.

700. Further there is another inconsistency. To say that a man or a house is altered, by taking the end, is ridiculous. If we say that the perfection of a house, either the roofing or the bricking, is an alteration, then when the house has been closed or bricked, it is being altered. However it is clear that that which pertains to alteration is not in things which are becoming.

701. Nor is there alteration in habits. For habits are virtues and vices. And all virtues and vices are relations. Thus health is a certain proportion of cold and hot things, either of these which are within or to the container. Likewise beauty and barrenness are relations. For certain dispositions of the perfect are to the optimum. I call that perfect which is healthy and is disposed concerning nature. Therefore, since virtues and vices are in relation; and since these are not generations, nor is there generation of them or any alteration; it is clear that there is altogether no alteration of habit.

702 (Lecture 6, 702–8). Nor is there alteration of the virtues and vices of the soul. For virtue is a certain perfection. Each thing is most perfect when it attains its proper virtue, and then it is best in respect to nature. Thus a circle is best in respect to nature when it is most circular. And vice is the corruption and removal of these things.

703. Both the reception of virtue and the removal of vice occur when something is altered. Nevertheless, there is alteration of neither of these.

704. It is clear that something is altered. For virtue either is a certain impassiveness or thus passive. But vice is passivity or the passion contrary to virtue.

705. All moral virtue occurs in pleasant and sad things. The pleasure is either in respect to act or through memory or hope. If it is in respect to act, the sense is the cause. If it is through memory or through hope, it is from one's self. The qualities which we have suffered are in those who remember pleasure, or the qualities which we will suffer are in those who hope.

706. Nor is there alteration in the intellective part of the soul. For knowing is best called a relation. This is clear: knowledge does not occur in us in respect to any potency for motions, but when something appears. For we take universal knowledge from experience in respect to the part.

707. Neither, therefore, is there generation of act unless one says that sight and touch are generations. For such things are acts.

708. Since the reception of knowledge is from a principle, there is neither generation nor alteration. For in rest and quiet the soul becomes knowing and pru-

dent. Thus when a sleeping man awakens, or when a drunken man ceases, or when a sick man is ordered, he is not made a knower, although before he could not use and act in accordance with knowledge. When disturbance is changed and the mind returns to its state, the potency for the suitability of knowledge was there. Therefore in this way a thing comes in the beginning to things which exist of knowledge: there is a certain quiet and rest from disturbance. Hence children cannot learn from and judge sensibles, as do elders. For there is much disturbance and motion about them. Moreover disturbance ceases and is driven away sometimes by nature, sometimes by other things. In both cases something is altered, as when one arises and becomes awake to act. It is clear, therefore, that there is alteration in sensible things and in the sensible part of the soul, but not in any other thing, except accidentally.